discover Liverpool

Published by:

Trinity Mirror Media

Trinity Mirror Media
PO Box 48
Old Hall Street
Liverpool L69 3EB

Design / Production:
Vicky Andrews, Zoe Bevan, Daisy Dutton, Jonathan Low, Emma Smart

Business Development Director: Mark Dickinson
Executive Editor: Ken Rogers
Senior Editor: Steve Hanrahan, Editor: Paul Dove, Senior Art Editor: Rick Cooke
Trinity Mirror Media Marketing Executive: Claire Brown
Sales and Marketing Manager: Elizabeth Morgan
Sales and Marketing Assistant: Karen Cadman

Discover Liverpool Special Edition 2011
© Pictures and text, unless otherwise stated:
Ken Pye / Trinity Mirror / Liverpool Daily Post & Echo.
Printed in Slovenia by arrangement with KINT Ljubljana

ISBN 978-1-906802-90-5

Introduction

By Ken Pye

This book is not an academic tome – it is simply a celebration of a city that I love, and one that I wish to share with you through a series of eight, detailed chapters; each one themed to cover a different aspect of the history, heritage, and current life of Liverpool and its suburbs.

As well as being a history, each chapter can be read as a tour, complete with a map and route directions. In this way, you will be able to visit for yourselves, many of the places I tell you about.

The chapters are not chronological journeys through the timelines of Liverpool's history. Rather, they are a practical opportunity to discover the reality and excitement of modern Liverpool, at the same time unravelling the complexities and delights of its past.

Each chapter begins with a list of the main topics, people, and places you will be reading about. This is followed by information on how you can take the tour, with the map. Then there is a detailed introduction, setting the scene.

However, I suggest that you also take an up-to-date edition of the Liverpool A-Z with you as you travel on the tours, to give you more precise location and travel details.

Precise route directions are given in these Information Boxes, which appear at appropriate places in the text. These not only tell you where to drive or walk, and when and in which directions you should be travelling, but they also explain where to make turnings, and when and where to park.

To make navigation easier, they also give street names and other location references; they also identify specific landmarks.

The chapters are presented as a series of short, separate, descriptive articles – in sequence to match my suggested tour route. This also means that you can either use the book as a tour-guide, or as a wealth of historical information, curious facts, fascinating tales, and entertaining anecdotes, which you can simply dip into. Or, you can read it cover-to-cover and the complete history of our wonderful city will unfold for you.

Although the directions to various places of interest are clearly explained in the text, do ask people for help or for their local knowledge, and you will find just how friendly, welcoming, and knowledgeable Liverpudlians can be.

Important Note: Whilst most of the places that you will visit on the Tours are either freely and easily accessible, or generally open to the public, some places are not. Some locations, of course, remain private property and can only be viewed from the outside.

I therefore recommend that you read through each Chapter before setting off. In this way you can check whether or not buildings are open; what the opening times are; establish if there is an entrance fee; and whether or not pre-booking is required.

Specific information about places you can visit is given in the appropriate sections of the text, together with telephone numbers and website addresses, where available. These appear at the end of each article, listed 'To Find Out More'.

Whilst most public buildings do have disabled access, and all the walking elements of my routes are easily managed by people in wheelchairs, it is advisable to check beforehand if you have any particular access requirements. In this way, you will hopefully be able to avoid inconvenience or disappointment. There is so much to see and do in the City, and this book can only really give you a flavour of this. Nevertheless, I hope that what you are about to discover as you read my articles and follow my routes, will prove to be interesting, exciting, dramatic, and surprising.

Bon Voyage.
Enjoy your adventure discovering Liverpool!

NB: The tours contained in 'Discover Liverpool' were thoroughly researched and verified before going to print. However, no responsibility can be accepted for any inaccuracies in any of the information given in this book; particularly location details, availability of access, opening times, availability of toilets, phone numbers, web addresses etc; as changes to these are entirely beyond the control of the author.

Likewise, I cannot be held liable for disruptions to the Tours by road works, traffic diversions, or any other incidents of force majeure: Liverpool continues to be a City undergoing remarkable environmental as well as economic change so, expect the unexpected!

Contents

Alphabetical Subject Contents

Pool of Life & Culture : Part 1

Including:

Crown Street Station and Liverpool's Railways

The Williamson Tunnels

The Wellington Column and The Steble Fountain

Lime Street

The World Museum Liverpool

The Central Libraries

The Walker Art Gallery

St. George's Hall

St John's Gardens

The Metropolitan Cathedral of Christ the King

The Medical Institution

The Everyman Theatre

The Willis Organ and stunning Minton tiled floor inside St George's Hall.
The floor is only uncovered on special occasions

Pool of Life & Culture 1: The Tour

The total distance covered by parts 1 and 2 of this Tour is 5 miles.

This is a circular tour, so you can pick it up at any point on the route. However do always travel in the recommended direction, in this case ANTI-CLOCKWISE, as the route has been designed to get you efficiently around Liverpool's sometimes confusing one-way systems.

To complete both parts, and simply look at everything from the outside, would only take around 2 hours.

However, to really explore and enjoy everything on this Tour – to visit all the museums, galleries and attractions, and to take time out to rest, eat, and refresh yourselves – could take around 11 hours!

And so, I have split it into two distinct parts and, I would suggest, that you take a relaxed day to complete each of them separately. In this way you will explore things at a comfortable pace, have more time to enjoy what you are seeing, and also take time to chat and get to know the Liverpudlians you meet along the way.

NB The Central Libraries and Galleries on William Brown Street, at the time of writing, are undergoing major rebuilding and refurbishment, and may not be open. Please check directly with each venue to avoid disappointment.

Contents

Route Map

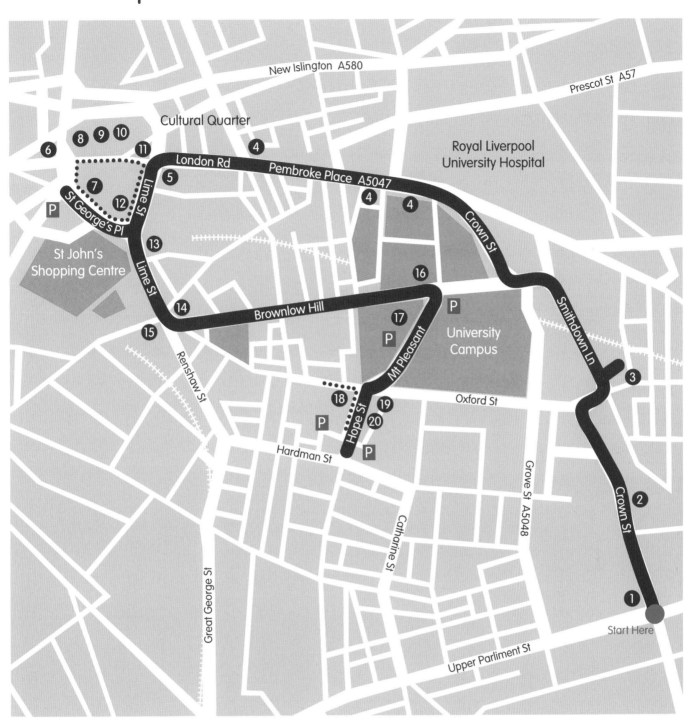

New Islington A580

Prescot St A57

Cultural Quarter

Royal Liverpool
University Hospital

⑥ ⑧ ⑨ ⑩ ⑪

London Rd

Pembroke Place A5047

④

⑦ ⑤

Lime St

🅿 St George's Pl ⑫

④ ④

Crown St

St John's
Shopping Centre

⑬

Lime St

⑯

Smithdown Ln

⑭

Brownlow Hill

🅿

University
Campus

⑮

⑰

🅿

③

Mt Pleasant

Renshaw St

Oxford St

⑱

🅿 Hope St ⑲ ⑳

②

Crown St

Hardman St 🅿

Grove St A5048

Catharine St

Great George St

Upper Parliment St

①

Start Here

Key

Start Here Starting Point

 **1** Map Reference

 Driving Route

⋯ Walking Route

🅿 Parking Points

▨ Railway

The Pool of Life and Culture: Introduction

In 1923, the Swiss psychologist Carl Gustav Jung had a dream. In it, he saw Liverpool as a dark and sooty city but at its heart was a large magnolia tree. This tree radiated light and a feeling of energy. and well-being. Afterwards, Jung described Liverpool as "the Pool of Life" – and so it is.

There is an ancient saying; "All roads lead to Rome". Well, during our 800-year history, all roads led to Liverpool and, from here, to the rest of the world. Those roads were on the high seas.

And the world came here too, sometimes as a crossroads to other places, but hundreds of thousands came here to stay and so created this 'world-class city'. They brought with them their languages, ideas, customs, faiths and their culture.But culture means different things to different people:

To some it is art and literature; to others it is dance and drama, museums, universities, or libraries. Culture can also mean community, language, faith, or tradition. Some people see culture as history and heritage, or architecture and the environment. I believe that culture is how we – as a community of individuals – express, share, develop, and sustain our humanity and our society.

Therefore it is all of these things, and more. In Liverpool we have 'culture' throughout our diverse communities; in every form and to all degrees.

In this chapter I have selected sights, sounds, and stories that will not only demonstrate and illustrate our cultural range and complexity, but that will enable you to experience this variety at first hand. From man-made tunnels to sculpture; from books to theatre; from music to food; from art to architecture; from people to gardens; and from graveyards to cathedrals.

The World in One City was the strap-line that the City of Liverpool used to underscore its bid to become the **European Capital of Culture for 2008**. In that year a British City would be awarded the prestigious title and so benefit from the significant boost in tourism, regeneration, and economic growth that this would generate.

Liverpool desperately needed such an injection of capacity because, in the late 1980s, the European Union (EU) recognised the extreme poverty of Merseyside in general, and of Liverpool in particular. In fact, at that time we were poorer than Sicily.

Following requests for help by the British Government, in the early 1990s, the EU granted Objective 1 Status to Merseyside. This made available vast amounts of grant money for social and economic regeneration projects. However, this simply confirmed in the minds of Liverpudlians that we were 'on our uppers', and that we were all living in a failed City. Nevertheless, we may have been down, but we were far from out.

As Liverpool entered the 21st century, an application form for a fascinating competition landed on the desk of then Chief Executive of Liverpool City Council, now Sir David Henshaw. This was inviting bids from British cities that wanted to win the title of 'European Capital of Culture' for 2008. David, and the then Leader of the City Council, now Lord Mike Storey, decided to 'go for it'. Why not? We had nothing to lose and such a great deal to gain.

Apart from this, if there was one thing that Liverpool had in spades, it was 'culture', in all its forms!

Eventually, at 08.11am on the 4th June 2003, Tessa Jowell MP – at the time Secretary of State for Culture, Media, and Sport – announced the decision in London: Liverpool had been chosen as the nominated British City for the title. The jubilation throughout the City at the declaration was complete, and passionately expressed.

Our successful bid demonstrated that, not only would the build-up to the main 2008 celebration year be well planned and delivered, but that we had a strategy that would take us up to 2010, and on into the future.

2004	The Year of Faith Celebrating our diverse city's many faiths and religions.
2005	The Year of the Sea Showcasing Liverpool's maritime heritage and legacy.
2006	The Year of Performance Celebrating the arts and performance in all its forms; from stage to community.
2007	The Year of Heritage The 800th anniversary of the City receiving its charter as a Town and a Borough, from King John in 1207.
2008	European Capital of Culture The main celebration year when Liverpool really became 'The World in One City'.
2009	The Year of Environment The year that the city celebrated its beauty, elegance, cityscape, parks, waterfront and natural heritage.
2010	The Year of Health and Wellbeing From leading businesses to individuals within our communities, thousands of people took part in events designed to improve our physical and mental wellness. Indeed, this has now grown into the 'Decade of Health and Wellbeing'.
2011	Liverpool – City of Radicals Celebrating a century of radicalism in Liverpool. The year provides a context for investigation into the city's history - culturally, socially and politically - as a place of radical change and progress.

The world-famous Mersey Ferry and Liverpool waterfront

The European adjudicators, who had to give final approval to Britain's nominated City, unreservedly did so, and I recall that I had a full programme of business meetings on the day of the announcement. As I travelled throughout Merseyside, the excitement, joy, optimism, and emotion that had been generated, was so powerful as to be almost overwhelming.

It was a very emotional day. Liverpool is a City that had been vilified and mocked for years: One that was accustomed to negative and stereotypical portrayals in the media, of itself and of its people.

"We are a City that has known true desperation through War and recession, and shared powerful grief following the Hillsborough Disaster and other tragedies, but our winning the title had the effect of restoring our self-confidence and our 'will to win through'"

Originally known as 'European Cities of Culture', the first city to win the title was Athens, in 1985. Florence won in 1986, followed by Amsterdam in 1987, Berlin in 1988, and Paris in 1989. Glasgow won the award in 1990 – the only other British City to do so prior to Liverpool. Other award winning cities include Dublin, Madrid, Copenhagen, and Stockholm. In 1999, the award was re-named as the European Capital of Culture, winners of which include Avignon, Helsinki, Prague, Rotterdam, and Bruges.

As a remarkable added bonus, which further boosted the faith of Liverpudlians in their own future, in 2004 the City was awarded **World Heritage Site Status**. This has now firmly placed Liverpool on the international heritage map, drawing favourable world-wide attention to the City once more, and ensuring that we will now become a major tourist destination. Indeed, the benefits to Merseyside as a whole will be extensive, because of the City's new status.

There are natural World Heritage Sites all over the world, such as the Grand Canyon and the Great Barrier Reef. There are also cultural sites, which include the Great Wall of China, the Taj Mahal, and the Pyramids. Whilst it may seem a little over-ambitious to consider Liverpool in the same light as these places, it is now recognised that ancient civilisations are not the only sites that have had a powerful impact on world events. Indeed, we already have a number of World Heritage Sites in Britain. These include Stonehenge, Blenheim Palace, Ironbridge Gorge, and the cities of Bath and Edinburgh. Seen in this light, it seems much more reasonable that Liverpool should have been awarded such a highly appropriate accolade. Liverpool has 2,500 listed buildings; 26 of these are Grade 1 listed and 85 are Grade II*. Our dock system is unique in the world and, in fact, it was Liverpool that pioneered such facilities and found the engineering skills necessary to develop them. Liverpool therefore, was a major driver of the industrial, commercial, and social revolutions in 18th and 19th century Britain.

Our World Heritage Site status now confirms our credibility as a World Class City, and one that has already taken its first, bold steps into the 21st century – a time of golden potential for Liverpool and Merseyside.

I hope that you enjoy what you are about to discover about the enriching life of our City and, through this, join us as we celebrate who and what we are; our culture; our community; and life itself! Liverpool – the Pool of Life and Culture.

The Superlambanana sculpture has had many homes around the city

The starting point for Part 1 of this Tour is Crown Street, at its junction with Upper Parliament Street.
As you turn into Crown Street you will see the Liverpool Women's Hospital on your left.
Naturally, this is not open to the public, unless you are pregnant of course – in which case, help yourself!
Otherwise, we shall keep on driving!

The Liverpool Women's Hospital

1

The site of the Liverpool Women's Hospital, after the destruction of the area following the Toxteth Riots in 1981, was once earmarked to be a shopping mall. How much better it is then, that the regeneration-site was used to create a place where new life would literally be brought into Liverpool – true regeneration: also, so appropriate after the catastrophe of the Riots. And, what better way is there to celebrate Liverpool's culture than by beginning this Chapter here, at this very special place?

There is a remarkable piece of sculpture in front of the building, named 'Mother and Child'. I have reproduced a photo of this so that we won't block the entrance to the hospital by driving down to look at it!

Opened in 1995, this 230-bed Maternity and Gynaecological Hospital is a single site for women's services, and the facility is state-of-the-art.

The first specialist women's hospital in Liverpool was a combined facility, called the Lying-in Hospital and Dispensary for the Diseases of Women and Children. This was opened in 1841, in Scotland Road in Vauxhall to the north of the City-centre. However, this was too small to cope with the rapidly increasing population at that time, so a new hospital was created, in 1845, in Pembroke Place. This was near the present site of the Liverpool School of Tropical Medicine, which we shall pass later in this Tour. In 1862, the hospital moved once more, this time to another new building erected in Myrtle Street.

At the same time, a Ladies' Charity in Liverpool that had been established in 1796, to care for women in childbirth, was active in the town. This charity would provide a midwife and, if necessary, a doctor to visit the home of women in labour. In the 1860s, it was agreed that this charity and the Lying-in Hospital should merge. This took place in 1869, after which time the hospital in Myrtle Street became known as the Ladies' Charity and Lying-in Hospital.

From this time, other maternity and gynaecological hospitals were established including the Special Hospital for Women in Shaw Street – opened in 1883; a new Lying-in Hospital on Brownlow Hill – opened in 1885; the Oxford Street Maternity Hospital – opened in 1926 (where I was born; though many years later!); The Women's Hospital in Catharine Street – opened in 1932; and the Mill Road Infirmary Maternity Unit – opened in 1947. This was restored following wartime bomb damage, from the original Mill Road Infirmary, which had been built on this site in 1891.

In 1985, the Women's Hospital joined with the Liverpool Maternity Hospital, and with Mill Road Maternity Hospital, under the management of the Liverpool Obstetric and Gynaecology Unit. Becoming an NHS Trust in 1992, it later changed its name to the Liverpool Women's Hospital NHS Trust, in 1994. In 1995, the existing three specialist maternity hospitals' services were merged, and the entire operation moved to the brand new building in Crown Street.

The new, £30million, Liverpool Women's Hospital for Women and Babies, was officially opened by H.R.H. Diana, The Princess of Wales. This hospital is special to my wife and me because this is where, in 1996, Daniel, our last child was born. This was in a deep, warm-water

Mother and Child; outside the Women's Hospital

birthing pool; with me in the pool with my wife, as I assisted in the labour and the delivery. Indeed, the baby was born into my hands; under the water; and I cut his cord.

This was an exceptionally moving and extraordinary privilege for me; both as a father, and as a man.

> **To Find Out More:**
> The Liverpool Women's Hospital
> Phone: 0151 708 9988
> http://www.lwh.me.uk

The entrance to the Women's Hospital

Cross over the mini-roundabout and, past the factory on the right, you will see the open parkland that was once the site of Britain's first passenger railway terminus. The student accommodation, just a little further along on the same side, also sits on the site and has been named 'Stephenson Court' in tribute to the great railway pioneer, George Stephenson. I suggest that you park on the road here, anywhere that is safe and convenient to do so; just to take 5 minutes or so to wander around the site – it is of considerable historical importance, because this is where passenger railways began!

As one drives into Crown Street from Upper Parliament Street, and passes the Liverpool Women's Hospital, one comes to a most significant – and historically and culturally relevant area of the City: Although there is very little evidence of it now, this was once where Liverpool – and the world's – first passenger railway station was situated.

Just a little way along on the right, is a large expanse of open, undulating parkland, with a fat, tall, brick chimney sticking up out of the middle. This is the site of Crown Street Railway Station, and the chimney is in fact, a ventilation shaft; carrying fresh air into the railway tunnel that runs from here. The only other evidence of the importance of this site is in the name of the blocks of Student Flats on the right – Stephenson Court, and the images of ancient steam engines mounted onto the metal gates to this residential compound.

There were a number railway lines in Britain in the early decades of the 19th century, but these were mostly for industrial purposes, such as hauling coal and other goods. However, this all changed when George Stephenson (1781-1848) persuaded the promoters of the Stockton and Darlington Goods Railway in north east England to award him the construction contract. In 1821, with the assistance of his son Robert (1803-59), he began building the line and used his own steam locomotives to provide the motive power.

However, large sections of this line used cables to haul the goods wagons and only the coal trains were drawn by locomotives. Horse-drawn traffic could also use the railway but their owners had to pay a special toll to do so. Nevertheless, the project was a triumph and, when the line was opened in front of jubilant crowds in 1825, the reputation of the Stephensons was assured. This achievement drew the attention of certain wealthy and prominent businessmen from Liverpool and Manchester, who had formed the Liverpool and Manchester Railway Company. They proposed to build a railway that was intended to provide faster transport of raw materials and finished goods, as well as passengers (although this was an afterthought), between the port of Liverpool and the cotton mills of Manchester. Until this time, goods were usually transported by barge and narrow boat, along the Mersey and Irwell Navigation and the Bridgewater Canal, both of which had been built in the previous century. Also, it was felt that a railway would be cheaper to run, and more profitable for its owners and backers. This new link between the two great Northern cities would be the very first, true passenger steam locomotive to run anywhere in the world, and so the Directors of the L&MR hired George Stephenson for the project, in 1826, and he set to work immediately.

The line would consist of two parallel tracks, covering a distance of 35 miles, which would have to be laid over some very difficult terrain, including across the treacherous and very broad Chat Moss. This 12 miles-square expanse of soggy bog, lies 5 miles west of Manchester, directly on the route between the two cities.

This was not the only significant problem that Stephenson had to overcome however, because the line began at Wapping Dock in Liverpool, with the 2250-yard Wapping Tunnel beneath Liverpool, to Crown Street Station here at Edge Hill. This was lit by gas, and its walls were whitewashed. Even when trains were running through it, local people would dress in their best clothes to promenade through the tunnel, and it became a popular attraction. The names of the streets, under which people were walking, were painted on the tunnel walls so that everyone knew where they were. From the station at this point, the line then had to travel through a two mile-long-cutting, at one point up to 70 feet deep, through solid sandstone bedrock at Olive Mount in Wavertree. Then, a viaduct had to be built over the Sankey Brook Valley, supported by nine, 50ft wide arches, each around 70 feet high.

"In 1828, the Railway Directors could not agree on how to power their new transportation system, and so they decided to hold competitive railway trials to choose the most effective locomotive"

These had to take place quickly as work on the tracks was now well underway. And so, beginning on 8th October 1829, at Rainhill just outside Liverpool, a number of steam locomotives were to compete against each other, not just for the contract, but for a prize of five hundred pounds.

George Stephenson had every intention of winning the competition and of using his locomotive on his railway tracks. Consequently, his son Robert, who was then only 24 years of age, concentrated on developing the locomotive and, his entry for the competition, the 'Rocket', went up against five others.

Competitors had to run their locomotives ten times in each direction over a 1½ mile course. After a break to take on water and fuel, another ten runs had to be completed, all of which were timed.

The Rocket met all the requirements easily, and George and Robert Stephenson won the rigorous trials in grand style, having attached a coach to their engine containing 30 passengers. They impressed the judges,

The site of the former Crown Street station

the spectators, and no doubt their passengers, by travelling at speeds of between 24 and 30 miles an hour!

Not only was The Rocket the most scientifically advanced engine at that time, but it also looked good; with its tall smokestack and brightly painted bodywork. Following the contest the fame and popularity of the locomotive was almost universal, and the impact on Britain and the world, of the Rainhill Trials and of George and Robert Stephenson, cannot be underestimated.

A year later the rail link had been completed, and September 15th 1830 was the date of the inaugural run between Liverpool and Manchester. This saw the Rocket drawing a series of passenger carriages laden with dignitaries and officials, including the Duke of Wellington – who was Prime Minister, and the Liverpool MP William Huskisson (1770-1830). Sadly though, the day was marred by a tragedy that took place halfway en-route to Manchester.

This is described later, in the section on St James's Cemetery. Nevertheless, this trip, of a steam-driven locomotive drawing a train of passenger carriages, was the first such journey in the world, and this now fully established Liverpool as one of the greatest centres of industrial and commercial growth. It also guaranteed the future success of George and Robert Stephenson, and the Rocket; perhaps their greatest achievement. This wonderful engine is now on permanent display in the Science Museum in London.

The Liverpool and Manchester Railway was the first railway to carry passengers and goods on a regular basis, and to a timetable. The passenger service proved immensely popular and was soon transporting over 2,000 passengers each day. In the first year of operation the railway also carried over 40,000 tons of goods and, by 1835, this had increased more than five times.

In the same period the amount of coal that was carried increased from 11,000 tons to 116,000 tons.

Seven years after the Liverpool to Manchester Railway opened, Liverpool was linked to Birmingham and then to London, by the Grand Junction Railway. Soon, there was a link from Birkenhead to the Midlands, on the Birkenhead and Chester Railway, which eventually became part of The Great Western Railway. By the mid-19th century, The Lancashire and Yorkshire Railway and the Cheshire Lines Railway had added to the network serving Liverpool, and this expansion drove forward the dramatic industrialisation of Britain and the world.

As a footnote: The district where the M62 Motorway enters the City – to the east of Liverpool at the Queens Drive Flyover, is known locally as 'The Rocket'. This takes its name from the local pub, which itself takes the name of Stephenson's locomotive. The modern railway still runs past here en route to Manchester, through the original deep and dramatic railway cuttings in the sandstone rocks, carved by Stephenson's 'Navvies'. These railway workers would drink their ale and eat their cold meat, bread, and cheese in the small thatched pub that had been built a century before, in 1738. This pub became known as 'The Rocket Pub' from this time, and a modern Rocket pub now stands on the site of the original inn. This is now the 3rd pub of that name on this site. It is from this point that Edge Lane Drive becomes the main trunk road into the City-centre.

To Find Out More:
The Liverpool and Manchester Railway
http://www.spartacus.schoolnet.co.uk/RAliverpool.htm

George Stephenson
http://www.cottontimes.co.uk/stephensono.htm

Railways in the 19th Century
http://www.spartacus.schoolnet.co.uk/railways.htm

Continue on Crown Street to the T-junction at Oxford Street. Turn right and take your first left, into Smithdown Lane. The Williamson Tunnels Heritage Centre is on the right. There is a small car park on site but, if this is full, find somewhere safe and convenient to park on the road outside. I suggest a stop of about 1 hour here.

The Williamson Tunnels and The Mole of Edge Hill

In many ways, there is no better place to begin an exploration of what makes Liverpool a 'Capital of Culture', than in Edge Hill: Here, at the 'Williamson Tunnels Heritage Centre', many of the characteristics that are the essential elements of 'culture' are embodied in the person of one unusual 19th century man. At the Centre you will find history, heritage, entrepreneurship, creativity, eccentricity, philanthropy, ingenuity, design, art, and community-spirit; all in the person of Joseph Williamson, the 'Mole of Edge Hill'.

Underground Liverpool is a labyrinth of tunnels; most are natural but many are man-made, such as those constructed by this remarkable individual.

Joseph was born on 10th March 1769, where is uncertain, but it is known that he moved to Liverpool from Warrington in 1780. He was a very poor young man, but he entered the tobacco and snuff business of Richard Tate, and was to go on to make his fortune. Joseph was diligent and industrious, and he rose rapidly through the business, continuing to work for Thomas Tate, the son of Richard, after his original employer had died, in 1787. At the same time, Joseph became a merchant in his own right, operating his own business just a few doors down the street from Thomas Tate. In 1802, he married the boss's daughter, Elizabeth Tate. This was a shrewd move, as he went on to buy out the firm of Richard Tate a year later and to merge it with his own, soon becoming an extremely wealthy tobacco merchant.

It is likely that to have become so affluent during that period of the Town's economic development, Joseph would have been involved in the Slave Trade, but there is no evidence either one way or the other.

Always an eccentric, on his wedding day and as soon as the vicar had made the pronouncement of marriage, he told his wife to go home and get his dinner ready, leapt onto his horse, and galloped off to join the Liverpool Hunt in his wedding outfit. His appearance was described as being 'uncommonly grand', and it elicited much encouraging comment from his fellow Hunt members. However, he was not usually a smart dresser, and Williamson's preferred outfit was a battered beaver hat, an old patched brown coat, corduroy breeches, and hobnailed boots. Nevertheless, he was known throughout the Town as being a kindly, but nonetheless 'odd' character.

A story, which further demonstrates Williamson's individuality, tells of a party of local gentry that were invited to dine with him. When they arrived, instead of being shown into his dining salon, they were ushered into a plain, unadorned room. Here, he had placed a bare trestle table with forms for seats, and to eat, each

An image that some people believe is of Joseph Williamson

visitor was presented with a bowl of thick porridge and a plate of hard ship's biscuits. They were all invited to 'eat heartily' but many, feeling highly insulted, left the house and so Williamson graciously bowed them out. Once they had left, he turned to those people who had stayed behind, and said to them, 'Now that I know who really are my friends, pray follow me upstairs'.

He then led them to an upper room and flung open a door at the end, to reveal a much greater room, over 70 feet long and 30 feet high, that was gloriously lit by chandeliers. This great Banqueting Hall had been set out for a sumptuous meal, with only the very best food and wines, and this was how Williamson rewarded his true friends for their loyalty. But then, from about 1806, Williamson's renowned eccentricity took a very specific turn.

Edge Hill at that time, was 'out in the country' and largely uninhabited and, from Williamson's house he would have had clear views of the River Mersey. However, Joseph did not look outwards; he began to look down instead and, starting from the cellar of his house in Mason Street, he began to excavate a series of subterranean passages and huge underground halls. These were to become his underground 'kingdom'.

Over the next 35 years, until 1840, Williamson spent £100,000 paying local unemployed men and soldiers returning from the Napoleonic wars, to extend what he had already begun, by excavating a vast network of useless tunnels and rooms in the sandstone under the district. And so, at various depths between ten and fifty feet below the surface, the tunnels began to riddle the area, in all directions from Mason Street and Smithdown Lane. However, these appear never to have been completely mapped, even by Williamson, nor by his vast army of burrowers. Indeed, to date no documentary records of his excavations, their routes, design, or purpose have ever been discovered.

As well as the tunnels and passageways, there are also vast vaults – thirty to forty feet in width – and some are over fifty feet in height. There are also traps, pits, and chasms, all built for unknown purposes. Many tunnels are simply blank-walled or circular passages that lead to nothing more than a dead-end, or which bring you back on yourself in a meaningless journey. In 1925, an investigation of the tunnels was undertaken by the Lancashire and Cheshire Historical Society. Their report provided much of the initial contemporary knowledge about the layout of the labyrinth, and about the construction of the tunnels, including reports that their members had been able to walk along one tunnel for a distance of over mile, without any sign of a boundary!

One question frequently asked and never satisfactorily answered, is what happened to the tons of sandstone rock and rubble, excavated from the tunnels? These Williamson called his 'tumps', and it is believed that most of the fine red stone was given for the building of the nearby church of St. Jude. A lot of it also appears to have been used to erect odd archways, structures, and follies, all around his extensive property, but we will never know for certain where it all went. Perhaps however, the most important questions are 'why did he build tunnels in the first place? Why not some surface construction-work?' He was particularly secretive about his tunnels, and only let certain people have access to them, and even then never to his complete labyrinth; he kept secret the locations of many of his subterranean passageways and rooms. As with so many aspects of this remarkable character's life and history, there is no real evidence, just more speculation. However, new research suggests that many of the early tunnels, particularly along the western side of Mason Street, were constructed in existing quarry workings using the 'cut-and-cover' method. There is also some evidence that much of the quarrying in the area was carried out before Williamson purchased the land, and that the tunnels were constructed to create platforms at the rear of his property, to lay out the then fashionable ornate gardens that formed part of his grounds.

Maybe though, Joseph was simply a genuine philanthropist; a 'good man'? He certainly provided gainful, if somewhat pointless employment to hundreds of local men, and so supported their families who otherwise might have starved. And his men worked willingly and happily for him, even in what must have been exceptionally difficult and uncomfortable physical circumstances. However, ever the caring employer, Williamson would often ply his workers with free barrels of ale or porter, and he gained the soubriquet, 'King of Edge Hill', from a grateful local community.

"When one considers that his entire workforce's labour was manual; with only picks, shovels, and barrows, and that their digging was carried out only by the light of candles and tallow lamps, then this really puts the mammoth nature of the task into a very human perspective"

On one occasion, during manual excavations for Liverpool's new railway, the ground suddenly gave way beneath Stephenson's men. Digging below them was Williamson with a gang of his men – driving forward their own tunnel below the 'official' one. The railway navvies thought that they had fallen into Hell, and that they had met with Satan's Demons when they were unexpectedly confronted by The Mole's naked and semi-naked men; sweating and filthy from their own labours. I imagine that both gangs of workers needed more than just a few flagons of ale after that experience! Indeed, Stephenson's men required a lot of persuading before returning to work.

Williamson's comment to the great railway engineer at the time was typical of a Scouser, and he simply told the Tynesider that he, "had no idea how to build tunnels" but that he, the King of Edge Hill, "could give you lessons in that polite art".

There were a number of entrances into Williamson's underground world, but Joseph had his own private entrance, via a heavy wooden door in the cellar of his house, through his kitchen. Today however, the tunnels can be accessed from the old council stable yard in Smithdown Lane. A number of years ago the Heritage Centre tunnels were inspected by civil engineers, commissioned by the Joseph Williamson Society, and were then checked by the City Council's Building Control and Health & Safety officers. They declared them to be 'structurally sound and perfectly safe'. Indeed, for decades, the Council used the long-abandoned underground network and caverns as a dumping ground for household waste and ash, from all over the City.

Deep in the Williamson Tunnels

Pool of Life & Culture : Part 1

In due course, and after much hard work by the Joseph Williamson Society; the Friends of the Williamson Tunnels; and Liverpool City Council, the dream of making the tunnels publicly accessible and of creating a Heritage Centre, came to fruition. Now a new entrance to the tunnel network has been built, together with a Visitor's Centre and a Museum dedicated to this remarkable Liverpudlian. The Joseph Williamson Society has raised money from various grants and other sources, which has been spent on opening up some of the tunnels to the public, with more to be opened in due course.

This ambitious scheme also saw the renovation and the rebuilding of the stable-block in Smithdown Lane.
The stables are one of the focal points of the tunnels system and themselves have a significant history, as for many years they housed the City's horses. Amongst other duties these animals would have drawn the Lord Mayor's Coach and, in 1954, the stables provided accommodation for Roy Rogers' horse 'Trigger' when the 'Singing Cowboy' and film and TV star visited the City.

From the Visitors Centre in the stable complex there is access to some of the tunnels, and here there is also a bar, a souvenir counter, and facilities for small meetings. Also, if you fancy the idea of doing some digging yourself – helping to reveal and excavate more of the tunnels complex (and providing you are fit and healthy enough!), then you may do so. Just contact the Heritage Centre for more information.

Even if you are not up to digging, a visit to the Heritage Centre and the tunnels is well worthwhile, as is the opportunity to discover more about one of Liverpool's most remarkable, and curious characters.

Joseph's wife Elizabeth died in 1822 and, as a reaction to this, Joseph threw himself into his tunnelling with greater vigour, and some say that he very rarely came above ground after this time. Williamson himself died in 1840, aged 70. He was buried with his wife and her family, in the Tate family vault in St. Thomas's church, where they had married 38 years earlier. This stood at the corner of Paradise Street and Park Lane. In 1905, the church was demolished and, to accommodate the changing road layout, some of the graves were removed, but not all. One of those that remain is the Tate vault and so Joseph Williamson lies there still, in the ground in which he spent so much time in life.

This lost graveyard has now been transformed into a delightful memorial garden. Here, not only are Joseph and his family commemorated, but so are the other people who were once buried on this site.

This garden is now just across the road from the remarkable retail and leisure complex of Liverpool ONE, which has brought a new commercial and social vigour to the city centre.

Whether Joseph will be able to continue to rest easy in his tomb remains to be seen; so perhaps the hotel guests and shoppers in the new retail complex may yet hear from the 'Mole of Edge Hill', from time-to-time!

London Road ④

London Road was the 'old road' to Prescot and Warrington, and later, from these towns on to London.

Nevertheless, it was only a narrow track until, in 1725, a local Act of Parliament was passed for the improvement of the Liverpool to Prescot road, via Old Swan, Broad Green, and Roby. This made the track usable for coaches carrying mail. However, this was only the first of a number of Acts affecting this road and, a further Act, in 1760, enabled the widening and turnpiking of the road so that passengers could now be carried, on the much extended route, via the Midlands and on to the Capital. A 'turnpike' is a toll road with toll-booths, toll-houses, or turnpike gates at one or more points along its route, so-called because the gate would turn or pivot at one end, on an iron stake or 'pike, set into the ground.

The first regular, direct coach-service to Manchester and on to London began, in 1761. This route became very important, and

St Thomas' memorial garden on the corner of Paradise Street and Park Lane

To Find Out More:
Friends of the Williamson Tunnels
Phone: 0151 475 9833
www.williamsontunnels.com
Williamson Tunnels Heritage Centre

The Old Stable Yard
Smithdown Lane
Liverpool
L7 3EE
Phone: 0151 709 6868
www.williamsontunnels.co.uk

On leaving the Williamson Tunnels Heritage Centre, continue along Smithdown Lane until the next road junction, at the traffic lights. Turn right and get into the left-hand lane. At the next set of lights turn left, into West Derby Street, which becomes Pembroke Place.
About 300 yards along on the left, past the roadway into the University Campus and also across the traffic lights at Daulby Street, on the left you will see the neo-gothic, red-brick splendour of Waterhouse's Liverpool Royal Infirmary. Next to this is the Liverpool School of Tropical Medicine.
Cross over the traffic lights at Anson Street, and you will now pass Monument Place on the right, with its statue of George III on horseback.
Cross over the next set of traffic lights at Norton Street, and continue down London Road in the left hand lane. Turn left at the traffic-lights into Lime Street. The Empire Theatre will be on the left-hand corner as you turn, and the magnificent St George's Hall will be on the right.

lucrative, and one of the busiest coaching inns in Liverpool was the 'Saracen's Head'. This stood, between 1810 and 1853, on the site currently occupied by the City Council Headquarters at Municipal Buildings, in Dale Street. Coaches would leave this inn, travel down Dale Street, past Townsend Mill, up what is now William Brown Street and onto 'the London road'. This traffic increased the fortunes of the area, and encouraged the establishment of coaching inns, taverns, and travellers' suppliers all along London Road and beyond. This area then became one of the most densely populated parts of the Town.

Liverpool Royal Infirmary

In 1859, the local businessman and philanthropist William Rathbone (1819-1902), established the first district nursing service in Britain and, in 1862, he set up a School of Nursing to provide trained staff for the existing Royal Infirmary Hospital and for the District Nursing Service.

Rathbone had previously met Florence Nightingale (1829-1910), and they established a professional relationship, working together to change and develop the nursing and healthcare system in the town. (See Chapter: 'Green and Pleasant Liverpool'.)

Through her long experience, Nightingale had made the connection between poor hospital design and the prevalence of hospital diseases, like fever and sepsis. In 1882, the hospital trustees, influenced by Rathbone and others, decided that the existing building was inappropriate to 'a modern service', and agreed to completely rebuild the Infirmary.

In 1895 Alfred Waterhouse (1830-1905) – Liverpool-born architect and founder of the Victorian 'Gothic Revival' in English building design – was brought in to create the new hospital.

He submitted five provisional designs within nine days, and then spent the remainder of 1885 consulting with Nightingale and others to refine his plans. As a result of correspondence with the famous nurse, Waterhouse significantly revised his designs, most notably the basic ward layout – Nightingale favoured pavilion-style wards, with high ceilings and plenty of space between the beds. Waterhouse also incorporated circular wards in his design, but the rectangular, pavilion wards were and still are referred to as the 'Nightingale Wards'.

The Victorian Royal Infirmary closed as a hospital when the current Royal Infirmary was opened, in 1978, on Prescot Street. The current building is now used as a GP Practice; as part of the University Campus – including the Nightingale Wards; and as a Conference Centre, named 'The Foresight Centre'.

As one drives past the building, the vision and foresight of Rathbone, Nightingale, Waterhouse, and of the Victorian Hospital Trustees, is very plain to see – hence the name chosen for the Conference Centre in their building.

To Find Out More:
The Liverpool Royal Infirmary
http://www.priory.com/homol/livpsy/Royal.htm

The Foresight Centre
http://www.foresightcentre.co.uk/

The Royal Infirmary

Liverpool School of Tropical Medicine

In 1898, Sir Alfred Lewis Jones, who was a Liverpool ship-owner, together with other ship-owners such as the Holts and the Bibbys, and with members of the business community, founded the Liverpool School of Tropical Medicine, which was the first of its kind in the world. However, even though as a result of their efforts, millions of people the world over were to benefit from subsequent research and treatment of tropical diseases, the founders' initial motivations were as much economic as they were altruistic.

The shipping lines of Jones and his fellow traders were plying the waters of the Far East, the Indian subcontinent, Africa, and the Tropics, and the crews of their vessels were regularly being struck down by, and were frequently dying of, strange, untreatable illnesses. It is difficult to meet the tides; or to load, sail, and unload your ships with less than a full compliment of able-bodied crew aboard! Also, their sick crew members were bringing these dreadful infections back to Liverpool with them, and so the risk was great, of them spreading the likes of Beri-Beri, Tropical Anaemia, Dysentery, Yellow Fever, and other exotic communicable diseases amongst the population.

"Nevertheless, whatever the reasons for founding the School may have initially been, its outstanding impact on the world and its people – particularly those in the developing world – has been incalculable"

When the School opened, its establishment was recognised by the British medical profession as being of such significance, that it was inaugurated, on the 22nd April 1899, by Lord Joseph Lister, the inventor of antiseptic and aseptic surgery. Before long, the Liverpool School of Tropical Medicine was to become internationally renowned and respected for being at the forefront in its field, and it so remains today.

"As part of its strategy to continue the fight against the world's most dreadful diseases, using the latest technology and the very best scientific knowledge, The School has extended into a £26m research centre for the study of tropical and infectious diseases"

This has doubled the size of the school. Also, in the autumn of 2005, it was announced that the founder of Microsoft, the billionaire Bill Gates, had donated an additional £27.8m from the 'Bill and Miranda Gates Charitable Foundation'. This was used to fund a five-year research project into the causes and cures of some of the world's most deadly illnesses, such as Malaria, Sars, HIV, and AIDS.

The School of Tropical Medicine is a jewel in the crown of our many excellent, and significant, educational establishments in Liverpool.

To Find Out More:
Liverpool School of Tropical Medicine
Phone: 0151 708 9393
www.liv.ac.uk/lstm

Monument Place and King George III

In front of the T J Hughes department store, is Monument Place. This is named after the bronze equestrian statue of King George III that still stands there.

"The king is dressed in a Roman toga, stretching forth his paternal hand over his people"

The composition, sculpted by Sir Richard Westmacott RA, was modelled on the equestrian statue of the Emperor Marcus Aurelius on the Capitoline Hill in Rome. This is why the horse has no stirrups, as they did not have them in the time of the Roman Emperor.

The Liverpool equestrian monument to the King was begun while George III was still alive, but whilst he was too ill too reign and was locked away in Windsor Castle.

However, after completion the statue was put into store and only brought out and finally erected on London Road in 1822, two years after the old King had died.

No-one is quite sure why it was eventually erected, or why Liverpool should decide to honour the late King in this way; he was in fact, a deeply unpopular monarch.

Perhaps its commission had been out of sympathy for his illness, and for the way that he was being treated by his son, the Prince Regent: who was even more unpopular.

Monument Place was so named not long after the statue finally appeared, and this added grandeur to what, by now, had become one of the most significant thoroughfares into the burgeoning town.

It is interesting to note that it is said that Liverpool now has more equestrian statues than any City outside London, and others are to be found on the plateau in front of St George's Hall and at the Pier Head.

Also noteworthy is the fact that, past Monument Place and near the corner of Norton Street, which intersects with London Road at the traffic-lights, once stood Gallows Mill. It was near here, in 1716, that four Jacobite rebels were hanged, drawn, and quartered; their remains being hung in chains. A further 640 supporters of the failed attempt to restore a Stuart monarch to the English throne, were transported to penal-colony plantations.

It was also near here, in 1805, that the last duel in Liverpool was fought.

To Find Out More:
Liverpool Monuments
http://www.liverpoolmonuments.co.uk/

King George III
http://www.spartacus.schoolnet.co.uk/PRgeorgeIII.htm

The Empire Theatre

On the corner of London Road and Lime Street stands the Empire Theatre, which is the second theatre by that name to occupy this site. The first theatre, which opened on the 15th October 1866, was originally named the 'New Prince of Wales Theatre and Opera House'.

At that time this was Liverpool's largest theatre, but it was only about three-quarters of the size of the present building and, on July 29th 1867, its name was changed to the 'Royal Alexandra Theatre and Opera House' to honour the Princess of Wales but, in 1896, it was re-named as 'The Empire'.

All the greatest entertainers of the day performed here, including some of Britain's greatest Music Hall artistes, such as George Formby Senior; Harry Tate; Dane Leno; Florrie Ford; The Two Bobs; and Wilson, Keppel and Betty.

This building closed on Saturday 16th February 1924, and was subsequently demolished, to be replaced by the present building. This opened on the 9th March 1925, with a production of 'Better Days', starring Stanley Lupino, Maisie Gay, and Ruth French.

Since that time, the world's greatest actors and performers have appeared here, including many international stars.

Indeed, Frank Sinatra, Judy Garland, and Bing Crosby all gave concerts here. In 1947, Mae West starred in her own play, Diamond Lill, at the theatre. Laurel and Hardy made a guest appearance here, and the range of other entertainers has been so broad as to include Roy Rogers – The Singing Cowboy, with his horse Trigger, and Charlton Heston!

Although they were not on the same bill! (I have already mentioned Roy and Trigger in the article on the Williamson Tunnels, and they shall appear again shortly.)

The Empire has always staged great opera and ballet performances, with the greatest exponents of both art forms taking centre stage. Indeed, Dame Margot Fontane and Rudolph Nureyev danced here.

All the great modern performers have appeared at the Empire, from Johnny Mathis and The Carpenters, to Neil Sedaka and The Osmonds. Our home-grown British talent has always drawn great crowds too; from Tommy Steel and Adam Faith, to Bruce Forsyth and Victoria Wood; from Morecombe and Wise to Ken Dodd; and from Shirley Bassey to Cilla Black.

"On 9th June 1957, the local pop group, 'The Quarrymen', appeared here in a competition"

The Quarrymen wanted to gain a place on Carroll Levis's popular TV talent show, but they were unsuccessful. The group returned in October 1959, but now with their name changed to 'Johnny and the Moondogs' – once again competing in heats of a talent show.

This time they reached the finals, but could not afford to stay overnight in Manchester where these were to be held, and so they could go no further in the competition.

However, the group came back to the Empire again, on 28th October 1962, but now under their new name of 'The Beatles'.

The group took the City by storm and, over the next two years they appeared at the theatre a further six times; and the rest is history.

In 1999, this Grade II Listed Building underwent a major refurbishment, which included significantly increasing the stage and overall performance facilities.

Also, the backstage areas were extended and state-of-the-art technical equipment was installed.

This means that now, the largest, most dramatic, and most technically sophisticated productions can be staged here, in front of audiences of up to 2,350 people – all seated in the largest two-tier auditorium of any British theatre.

No theatre can be said to be a true theatre unless it is haunted, and the Liverpool Empire certainly has its fair share of spectral residents.

Like the shade of 'Les', who was a painter at the theatre, and whose ghost appears from time-to-time, in the wings – paint pot and brush in hand.

Then there is the much sadder spectre of a young girl, aged about 9 or 10 years old, and wearing a Victorian smock dress and a long overcoat.

She manifests herself, occasionally, in the Stalls Bar, and those that have seen her report that she appears to have tears streaming down her delicate cheeks.

The sound of soft weeping seems to surround her apparition without actually emanating from it, and the effect is said to be exceptionally melancholic.

For more than 40 years she has been haunting the theatre, usually late at night, and just as the building is about to be locked up for the day.

Sometimes, she has been seen being dragged away by a dark-eyed man but, as soon as anyone tries to approach her, she promptly vanishes.

Above, the Royal Alexandra Theatre and Opera House, and right The Empire Theatre as it is today

Some theatre historians believe that she is the ghost of a child who tragically fell to her death, from the balcony to the stalls below, in the original theatre building.

However, spooks notwithstanding, as well as providing a venue for top-rank entertainers and comedians; and for the highest quality plays, dramatic productions, ballet and opera performances; the Empire always has, and continues to stage the greatest shows and musicals.

Here, you can regularly see full-scale productions of musicals such as Guys and Dolls, Oklahoma!, Showboat, Grease, and The Rocky Horror Picture Show. Recent spectaculars have included Cats, Starlight Express, Doctor Doolittle, Beauty and the Beast, The Phantom of the Opera, Evita, and Chitty-Chitty Bang-Bang – complete with all the most staggering special effects.

Liverpool theatre venues can guarantee a fabulous night out, no matter what your tastes are in artist or music but, for the largest spectaculars, in true grand theatre-style, then the Empire Theatre in Lime Street is second to none.

As you enter Lime Street and pass the Empire Theatre, take the right-hand lane in front of St George's Hall.

At the traffic lights at Lime Street Station, turn right into St John's Lane, taking the right-hand lane once again. You will pass the Central Bus Station and the Marriott Hotel on the left, and then the road narrows and bends to the left.

Immediately after the bend, on the left, is a slip road into the Queens Square Multi-Storey car park. Pull in here and park for the next two or three hours or so; as we now explore the Cultural Quarter and Lime Street on foot.

To Find Out More:
The Empire Theatre – Show Listing, Bookings, and Ticket Information
Phone: 0151 702 7320 / 0844 847 2525
http://www.liverpoolempire.org.uk

Empire Theatre History
http://www.bbc.co.uk/liverpool/localhistory/journey/lime_street/
empire_theatre/theatre.shtml

Opposite the Empire Theatre is the area known as the 'St. George's Cultural Quarter'.

This contains, what is universally considered to be, one of the finest groups of 19th century public buildings and civic spaces to be found anywhere in Europe. However, to visit all of these fully, and to view the other sights in and around Lime Street, will take some time.

So you will need to safely and securely park your car in one of the nearby official car parks as we walk through the next parts of this Tour.

The building of the Kingsway Tunnel

> From the Car Park, walk back along Old Haymarket, towards William Brown Street: You will see the entrance to the Mersey Tunnel on the left, and St John's Gardens on the right. We shall now visit the next series of locations in sequence.

At the bottom of William Brown Street, facing St. John's Gardens at Old Haymarket, is the entrance to the Mersey Tunnel to Birkenhead.

Above its Art-Deco entrance and portals are the flanking bronze statues, by Sir W. Goscombe John, of King George V and Queen Mary. The retaining walls on either side of the entrance appear to sweep the traffic in and out, and the striped classical reliefs add to this effect.

Above the entrance is a carved relief showing two winged bulls set on either side of a winged wheel, and this symbolises the swift and heavy traffic that uses this remarkable example of civil engineering. One of the original toll booths still stands on an island near the entrance, and nearby is a tiled mosaic in the pavement, commemorating the opening of the tunnel. The ceremony inaugurating the first Mersey Road Tunnel was performed by King George V in July 1934 and, at that time, and at 2.13 miles, this was the longest underwater road tunnel in the world.

Named 'Queensway', it connects Liverpool with the Town of Birkenhead on the Wirral, and it cost £7,723,000 to build. The Mersey Tunnel, which was begun in 1925 and is now a Grade II Listed Building, was designed by Sir Basil Mott and John Alexander Brodie (1858-1934), who was the Liverpool City Engineer.

Brodie was a remarkable man who made many significant contributions to the environment, infrastructure, and quality-of-life of the people of late 19th and early 20th century Liverpool. These included the City tram network; dual carriageways; tree-lined boulevards with central reservations, down which the trams ran; the Otterspool Promenade land-reclamation project; household and commercial waste recycling projects; and the City Ring Road – Queens Drive. He also invented the nets for football goals! You can discover more about John Brodie in my Tour 'Green and Pleasant Liverpool'.

The magnificent portals at either end of the Mersey Tunnel – at Liverpool and at Birkenhead – were designed by the Liverpool Architect, Herbert J Rowse (1887-1963), and they are perfect examples of his Art-Deco and Stripped-Classical design style. Rowse also designed the Tunnel ventilation-shaft buildings, which include the George's Dock Building at the Pier Head; and he also designed India Buildings, the Philharmonic Hall, and many other significant Liverpool Buildings, all constructed between the Wars.

A second Mersey Tunnel, running from Liverpool to Wallasey, was started in 1967. This comprises two parallel tunnels, each carrying traffic in opposite directions, and each with two lanes.

The drilling for this was carried out using a revolutionary boring machine known as 'The Mangla Mole'. This device was 45 feet long, weighed 350 tons, and ploughed its way relentlessly through the bedrock in record time. The breakthrough between the Wallasey and Liverpool sides took place in 1970, and this tunnel was opened on 24th June 1971, by Her Majesty the Queen, and is called 'Kingsway'.

As we now have one tunnel named Queensway, which was opened by a King, and another named Kingsway, opened by a Queen, to avoid confusion most Scousers call them simply the 'Old' and the 'New' tunnels. However, despite the fame of the road tunnels, a railway tunnel under the river precedes them both.

This was opened, in 1886, by the Prince of Wales and, although it was not the first or longest of its kind in the world, in May 1903 it became the first under-water electrified locomotive system in the world. Originally, of course, this railway operated with steam engines. This meant that it must have been extremely uncomfortable for the passengers as they breathed in the smoke, ash, and steam, and whilst the locomotives rattled through the confined, pitch darkness under the River Mersey. Now however, the much more attractive and comfortable trains of the Merseyrail Underground network use this tunnel.

A drive through the Mersey Tunnels is not included in my Tours, but I suggest that you do make the journeys at some time: Drive to the Wirral through the Birkenhead 'Queensway' Tunnel; drive across the Four Bridges, which connect Birkenhead Docks with Wallasey Docks, and then return through the Wallasey 'Kingsway Tunnel'. There are tolls, but you can make the return trip for around £3.

> **To Find Out More:**
> Mersey Tunnels Users Association
> www.tunnelusers.org.uk/history
> Mersey Tunnels Official Website
> http://www.merseytunnels.co.uk/

> Once you have had a look at the Mersey Tunnel, from the safe vantage point of the opposite side of the road of course (!), make your way into St John's Gardens.

St John's Gardens; The French Prison, and Dr James Currie

Opposite the buildings on William Brown Street, and behind St. George's Hall, are St. John's Gardens. This whole area has a fascinating history because what is now Lime Street was once the edge of The Great Heath.

This vast expanse of open grass, gorse, heather, and isolated rural farms and village communities, stretched from this point through Edge Hill and Wavertree. From these districts it reached the edges of far away Childwall and the ancient Manor of Allerton, which were then considered to be 'out in the country'! The Heath existed right up until the mid-18th century, when parts of it began to be built over. It only completely vanished towards the end of the 19th century, as outlying communities were gradually absorbed within the ever-expanding boundaries of the developing Victorian City (see Chapter 'Liverpool Lost and Found'). However, before this, and until the beginning of the 1800s, what is now Lime Street was the ridge of the Heath, overlooking the Town boundary. The edge of old Liverpool was roughly where the mouth of the Mersey Tunnel now sits, at the Old Haymarket and the end of Dale Street. There was indeed a dale here, where a regular hay market was held.

There were two or three streams behind Liverpool that ran down to this point, flowing from Everton Brow and from Moss Lake (Moss Lake was a large marshy area that stood roughly where Abercromby and Falkner Squares now stand.) These streams combined to feed into the end of a tidal creek that broadened back out from the dale, along what are now Whitechapel and Paradise Street. From halfway down Paradise Street, the creek became the large inlet from the River Mersey; this was the original 'Pool' of Liverpool.

Although there was a bridge across the creek at the dale, no settlements existed beyond it until the early 1700s. Indeed, the bridge was known as Townsend Bridge. At the top of the slope from this point, on what is now the site of the Steble Fountain in front of the Walker Art Gallery, stood a long-established mill known as Townsend Mill.

From the end of the Town, and as it does now, the land sloped upwards towards the ridge at the edge of the Heath. The sea winds from the Mersey blew through Liverpool, to be channelled up this slope, making the hill and its ridge a perfect place to dry washing and operate windmills! And so, probably from the early 1500s, long public washing lines upon which local people could hang out their laundry, had been standing here; as had windmills for grinding corn. This was also the site of the Fall Well, which for very many years had been one of, if not the only source of fresh water for the Town. This was located in open countryside, near the front of the Royal Court Theatre.

The old Town of Liverpool now began to expand across the Pool and its creek and, in the early years of the 18th century, houses, chapels and other buildings began to appear all around the windmills and the Fall Well, and on the Great Heath. The track between Townsend Bridge and Townsend Mill became Shaw's Brow, and almshouses were built here from the 1720s.

By 1749, most of the windmills and the washing lines had all gone, to be replaced by Liverpools first General Infirmary, which had been erected in that year. This had been provided by local, philanthropic individuals who, together with the Town leaders, had become very concerned about the degeneration of public health and hygiene in the growing, and ever more densely-populated community. This was followed by the building of the Seaman's Hospital, which opened in 1752 as two extra wings to the Infirmary.

Also, a local dispensary was opened, in 1778, to supply medicines to the poor and, in 1789, a Lunatic Asylum was erected in the grounds of the Infirmary. These were all located where St. George's Hall now stands.

At this time too, industry came to the district and, as well as the remaining windmills, a rope-works was established alongside the Infirmary; potteries opened up along Shaw's Brow; and a marble yard stood where Lime Street Station now stands. Also, directly opposite the Infirmary complex, where the North Western Hotel now stands, a Mr William Harvey opened the row of limekilns that were eventually to give Lime Street its name. However, in 1804, Harvey reluctantly had to close and dismantle his kilns, and move them to the north shore of the River Mersey. This was because the doctors in the Infirmary were complaining that the acrid smells and fumes were poisoning their patients.

One of the founders of the Lunatic Asylum was Dr. James Currie (1756-1805), who came to Liverpool from Edinburgh in 1780. Almost as soon as he arrived, he established the Institute for the Recovery of Drowned People, and he became a much loved and respected man in the Town. Currie was the first doctor in Britain to use a thermometer and, during a smallpox epidemic, he persuaded many people to be inoculated.

A powerful anti-slavery campaigner, Currie was successful in getting a surgeon appointed to every slave-ship that sailed out of Liverpool, and he examined each candidate personally to ensure that they were suitably qualified.

This was no mean achievement in the Liverpool of the time, and its significance cannot be underestimated: slavery was making Liverpool and its businessmen, extremely wealthy. Consequently, any opposition to the 'Triangular Trade' was not welcomed by these powerful and vested interests. (See Chapter: 'The Liverpool Waterfront'.)

Before the construction of the Infirmary and Asylum, the land below the ridge became the Town cemetery, in 1767, and a small mortuary chapel was erected amongst the new graves.

However, Liverpool's now increasingly rapid urban expansion also necessitated a place of worship being built here, and so the church of St John the Baptist was completed, in 1784, in the heart of the Cemetery. Even though this was a large area of land, by 1854 it had already become so full that it had to be closed, and burials then had to take place elsewhere. The church was eventually demolished, in 1898, by which time the graveyard was home to 27,000 bodies!

Some of the burials had been of French sailors, who had been held in Liverpool as prisoners-of-war from the Napoleonic Wars (1799-1815). Some of these unfortunate men died in the damp, dark, and disgusting dungeons of the Tower of Liverpool, which once stood on the site of modern Tower Buildings, opposite the Royal Liver Building. (See Chapter: 'The Heart of the City'.)

Most however, died of starvation and typhoid in the apalling conditions of what was Europe's first, purpose-built prison. This was erected in 1786, in Great Howard Street where, at its peak during the wars with France, around 4,000 prisoners-of-war were held captive. As a consequence, for a time, the gaol became known as 'The French Prison'.

The French Government was expected to send regular payments towards the prisoners' upkeep but when these stopped the prisoners began to starve to death. However, James Currie was appalled by

St John's Gardens are a great place for a picnic

the conditions in the prison, and by the treatment of the Frenchmen. He saved many of these prisoners from starvation by his personal intervention and he worked tirelessly to improve their living conditions.

Despite Currie's best efforts however, 230 men died, and their bodies were laid to rest in the graveyard of St. John's Church. The French sailors' bones were never removed and they lie here still, interred behind the wall below the plateau of St George's Hall, and surrounded by the flowers and lawns of today's St. John's Gardens. A memorial plaque was erected in the Gardens, on Armistice Day 1924, to commemorate that England and France had fought together as Allies during the Great War of 1914-18, and it reads,

"To her sons who died in captivity in Liverpool 1772-1803
and whose bodies lie here in the old cemetery of St. John the Baptist.
France ever grateful."

Although, I find it difficult to see for what, exactly, the French were expressing their gratitude.

Doctor Currie is also recognised for his literary accomplishments; the most notable of which being that he was the first biographer of the Scots poet, Robert Burns (1759-1796). An ex-patriat Scot, Currie edited the first edition of Burns' works, and published them in Liverpool in 1800. This was specifically to raise funds to support Burns' widow and children, who were living in difficult circumstances in Ayrshire, and also to strengthen the poet's reputation.

As well as all his other many activities and achievements, Currie worked closely with the prominent local historian, author, artist, and banker, William Roscoe, as a religious dissenter and political radical. With Roscoe, in 1795, he was one of the founders of the Liverpool Athenaeum Club. This still continues as a private members' Club for the 'intelligentsia', 'illuminati', and 'glitterati' of the City so, naturally, I am a member! For more information on the remarkable Renaissance Man who was William Roscoe, and about the Athenaeum Club, see Chapters: 'Liverpool Lost and Found' and 'Heart of The City'.

Although crippled by tuberculosis for most of his life, James Currie continued to work long hours and, eventually, the disease took its toll and he died in 1805.

By 1780, the Townsend Mill had been demolished, followed by the Infirmary and Seaman's Hospital, in 1826. These were replaced by newer, larger buildings elsewhere in the Town. In 1835, the Lunatic Asylum was also pulled down and the foundation stone was laid for St. George's Hall.

In 1898, St John's Church was also demolished, and the site was considered by some to be an ideal location for the new Liverpool Cathedral, which was being planned at the time. However, after much debate, this idea was dropped in favour of

St James's Mount as the preferred location. By this time though, the Infirmary and Asylum had gone, and had been replaced on Lime Street by the splendid St George's Hall. This had opened in 1854, and it was now felt that some form of impressive entranceway to the magnificent Concert Hall and Law Courts was needed. This was until – so some people say – it was pointed out that the Hall had been built the wrong way round! Whether or not this is true, it was decided to landscape the old graveyard anyway. And so, with the exception of the bodies of the French Sailors, all of the burials were removed and re-interred elsewhere in the Town, and the Cemetery was then completely redeveloped. The new 'St John's Ornamental and Memorial Gardens' were opened to the public, in 1904, as the delightful gardens that we see now.

As well as now comprising beautifully landscaped and lovingly tended gardens and flower beds, the Gardens are the location for a significant collection of Victorian and Edwardian commemorative statuary and memorials, including a magnificent edifice dedicated to the King's Liverpool Regiment.

This includes the figure of a fearful young drummer-boy who is beating out a tattoo on his drum whilst anxiously waiting for battle to commence. There are also a number of statues erected as tributes to great Liverpudlian philanthropists, such as William Ewart Gladstone (1809-1898) – who was born in the City and who became Prime Minister four times; the local philanthropist ship-owner, Alexander Balfour (1824-1886); William Rathbone (1819-1902) who, amongst other things, was the founder of District Nursing in the City, with Florence Nightingale; Monsignor James Nugent (1822-1905), who founded Ragged Schools and Orphanages in Liverpool; as did Canon T Major Lester, who died in 1903, and whose statue is also in the Gardens.

Many of these statues are Grade II Listed, and the gardens have been a Green Flag site since 2003.

After exploring the cultural and intellectual delights along William Brown Street, you may find this an ideal opportunity for a picnic; and St John's Gardens is no better venue, especially on a warm summer afternoon.

This will then set you up, as we continue to discover how Liverpool will always be a Capital of Culture.

To Find Out More:

St Johns Gardens
Phone: 0151 233 3000
http://www.liverpool.gov.uk/leisure-parks-and-events/
Dr James Currie
http://www.electricscotland.com/history/other/currie_james.htm

From St John's Gardens, cross over William Brown Street and make your way up the road from left to right. The first building that we come to is The World Museum Liverpool.

The World Museum Liverpool

The 'World Museum Liverpool' is the oldest of the National Museums Liverpool (NML) group of galleries and museums, and it is now a Grade II Listed Building.

The founding of the museum began in 1851, with the bequest of the 13th Earl of Derby's magnificent natural history collection to the Town. This included the owl of 'The Owl and the Pussycat' fame, which once resided in Knowsley Hall just outside Liverpool. This is the stately home of the Earl's family (see Chapter: 'A Lordly Heritage').

Edward Lear (1838-1903), the author of the famous poem and of much popular nonsense verse, was also a very talented artist of flora and fauna. He had been commissioned by the Earl to sketch the animals in his extensive private menagerie, and he wrote the poem to amuse the Earl's children. The owl, which was on display in one of the many large rooms of Knowsley Hall, was a particular favourite of the youngsters, "and seemed", said Lear, "to have a story to tell"! And tell it he did!

The Owl and the Pussy-cat went to sea
In a beautiful pea green boat,
They took some honey,
and plenty of money;
Wrapped up in a five pound note.
The Owl looked up to the stars above,
And sang to a small guitar,
'O lovely Pussy! O Pussy my love,
What a beautiful Pussy you are,
You are, You are!
What a beautiful Pussy you are!'

During the mid-19th century it was clear that, in keeping with Liverpool's status as the 'Second City of the Empire', a purpose-built museum would need to be constructed to house the Earle's extensive and comprehensive bequest. And, in due course, the foundation stone for the Free Public Library and Museum was laid in 1857, by William Brown MP after whom the street had been named, and who had donated the princely sum of £6000 towards the building's construction. By the end of the 19th century, the City Museum's collections had grown considerably, and the Corporation of Liverpool decided to combine the urgent need for additional storage and display space with a new technical school. A competition to design the building was announced and, in 1896, this was won by renowned London architect William Mountford.

The building he created, on the corner of William Brown Street and Byrom Street, was opened in 1901, and it blended well into the existing structures; being an imposing, Victorian-Imperial edifice. It has deep but classical windows – some in attractive, recessed bays with their own pediments and sculptures.

There is a bow-front on the corner, with a stepped approach up to a pedimented entranceway, which itself is decorated with a variety of detailed sculpture. Inside, the plaster work, mosaics, beaten copper, and panelled walls, are all fine examples of the artistic design style of the early 20th century, and these are worth studying, and enjoying, in their own right. This is now a Grade II Listed Building.

During the Second World War, enemy bombing in the May Blitz of 1941 destroyed much of the Museum building but, fortunately, the magnificent façade and many of the rarer items in the collections survived. Consequently, the Museum had to remain closed for fifteen years after the War, until the money could be found to restore it. Once all the funds had been secured work began and, as the Museum underwent a complete rebuilding and renovation, it began to re-open in stages. In due course however, it was formally opened, in 1966, by Harold Wilson, then the MP for Huyton and the serving Prime Minister.

During the period of closure and renovation, the size of the collection did not remain static; indeed, this was a time when many new items were added to the Museum's already wide-ranging exhibits. These had been stored in a variety of locations throughout the City, but the largest store was at the former stately home of Carnatic Hall, in Mossley Hill to the south of the City. When the Museum finally opened once again to the public, it presented a spectacular range of artefacts, displays, exhibitions, and experiences, to the continuing delight of the citizens of Liverpool and beyond, including myself. I was an eager young teenager, visiting the partially refurbished Museum, and I took part in a special children's competition. I had to answer questions based on the items in the collection, and I won! I was awarded a £1 Gift Voucher – a princely prize in early 1965 – and I got my name published in the Liverpool Echo. I was 'chuffed'!

One of the features in The World Museum

The World Museum Liverpool

Refurbished and redesigned in 2005, the building re-opened as the World Museum Liverpool. This was all part of a £45m capital development programme across three NML venues – Museum of Liverpool Life, The Walker Art Gallery, and Liverpool Museum; and the exhibition space has now been more than doubled in size. This was because the Technical College building, which from the 1960s had been part of Liverpool Polytechnic College, and later Liverpool John Moores University, was completely taken over and re-integrated into the new museum complex.

Both the Polytechnic and existing Museum buildings were completely and imaginatively re-designed and restored, in a project that took almost 4 years.

This has enabled the World Museum, which is truly worldwide in scope, to create a spacious, welcoming, informative, and entertaining experience for all its visitors, covering archaeology, ethnology, and many of the natural and physical sciences.

Always popular, the Museum attracts visitors from all over Merseyside, the North West, and beyond. Indeed, during the first year of its new incarnation, 582,143 people came to the World Museum. The expansion of the building, its displays and attractions, and the attendant improvements to the provision of research and educational facilities, have enhanced and confirmed the World Museum Liverpool's reputation as one of the finest multi-disciplinary museums in Britain. They can expect continuing high numbers of eager visitors in the years to come.

To Find Out More:
World Museum Liverpool
Phone: 0151 478 4393
http://www.liverpoolmuseums.org.uk/wml/

Edward Lear Homepage
http://www.nonsenselit.org/Lear/

World Heritage Bid – William Brown Street
www.liverpoolworldheritage.com

From the Museum, continue up William Brown Street, and the next building that you come to is home to Liverpool Central Libraries.

The Central Libraries were donated to the City by Sir William Brown, but the inauguration of the Public Library Service in Liverpool was due largely to the work of Sir James Picton (1805-1889).

He was an architect, historian, a Town Councillor, and he was also a member of the local Board that governed his home village of Wavertree.

Until 20 years or so after Picton's death this was an isolated, but ancient community, located well outside the then boundary of Liverpool.

Picton had a particular love for this district, and he did much to research into and preserve its heritage. He chose to live there and, upon the death of his much loved wife, he erected a large clock tower to her memory, in the centre of the village. (See Chapter: 'Liverpool Lost and Found'.)

As chairman of the Liverpool Libraries, Museums, and Arts Committee, from 1851 until his death, Picton's impact on the quality and range of these public resources was profound. He was passionate about providing access to knowledge and ideas to the greatest number of people, and he wanted to ensure that Liverpool's collection of books, pamphlets, articles, private publications, and archives was the best that it could be, and this is why the Central Libraries now comprise many separate collections.

These include the Picton, Hornby, Central, International, and Music libraries.

There are also a variety of other special collections and facilities, such as the Religion and Philosophy Library, the Art Library, and the Science and Technology Library.

The Liverpool City Archive is held at the Central Libraries and, for students of local history such as me, this is a resource that is unsurpassed in the region. The staff at the City Archives are also second-to-none in their professional knowledge and willingness to support genuine researchers. All-in-all, the Libraries offer a wealth of resources for student, business-person, and citizen alike. The Picton Reading Room in the Libraries, which was opened in 1879, houses a major reference collection, and this itself remains one of the architectural gems of the City, and an appropriate tribute to a remarkable man.

The Central Libraries will re-open to the public in Winter 2012 after complete refurbishment.

To Find Out More:

Liverpool City Libraries Information Website
Phone: 0151 233 5829
http://www.liverpool.gov.uk/Leisure_and_culture/Libraries/index.asp

World Heritage
– William Brown Street
www.liverpoolworldheritage.com

Beyond the Central Libraries, and almost at the top of the hill, is The Walker Art Gallery. Next to this is the County Sessions House.

The Rotunda of the Central Libraries, before refurbishment

At the top of William Brown Street – named after a successful 19th century Liverpool Merchant – is the Walker Art Gallery.

This was built, and donated to the City, by Alderman Andrew Barclay Walker (1824-1893), who was a Warrington brewery company owner and the Lord Mayor of Liverpool at the time.

Prior to this, the only other buildings that he had erected, all over Liverpool, had been particularly ornate pubs in which to sell his ales, so the Gallery was a special project for him and was to commemorate his term as Mayor. The Gallery was opened in 1877, by the 15th Earl of Derby, and it received 324,117 visitors in the first four months.

The Walker houses an extensive collection of paintings from all eras and of all styles. There are many priceless works of art on view, including a significant number of famous masterpieces, and it is also home to a fascinating and attractively laid out sculpture gallery.

The building itself is impressive, with its classical stepped approach, which is flanked by the – albeit badly weathered – statues of Raphael and Michelangelo. The exterior walls support friezes that show scenes from the City's history.

On the roof over the entrance sits the 'Allegorical Statue of Liverpool'. All of these external sculptures were executed by John Warrington Wood.

The Walker is internationally renowned; is one of the finest galleries in Europe; and is home to a special exhibition suite of international standards.

The gallery's incomparable and world-renowned collection of Medieval, Renaissance, and 17th & 18th century works, stands alongside the magnificent Victorian and 20th Century displays.

This provides families and connoisseurs alike, with wonderful opportunities to enjoy works of art from all periods, and from all over the world.

To Find Out More:

The Walker Art Gallery
Phone: 0151 478 4199
www.thewalker.org.uk

Directly opposite the entrance to the Art Gallery, stand the Steble Fountain and the Wellington Memorial Column.

The memorial column in the centre of the St. George's Cultural Quarter, stands at the top of William Brown Street and supports a statue of the Duke of Wellington. This had its foundation stone laid in 1861, and it was formally presented to the City on May 16th 1863, accompanied by the firing of a salvo from 19 cannon.

Standing 132ft high, and carved from Darleydale stone, the Wellington Column was designed by George Anderson Lawton from Glasgow. The Duke's figure stands 14ft high, and is cast from the bronze of melted-down cannon, captured from the French at the Battle of Waterloo. The carved panel at the base of the column shows the grand charge from the battle, and the Duke can be seen mounted on his horse, telescope in hand.

The pre-metric, standard Board of Trade measurements of length – at 62 degrees Fahrenheit – are also to be found on and around the column. The shorter ones are embossed onto a bronze panel, which is mounted on the side of one of the plinths. From this plinth, set into the pavement and running parallel with the Steble Fountain, is a long, brass strip. This shows the larger measures of a hundred feet, and of a chain of a hundred links.

Next to the column is the Steble Fountain, which was built in 1879, and it is made entirely of cast iron. It is named after Lt. Colonel Richard Fell Steble, who was the Mayor of Liverpool from 1845 to 1847, and who gave the fountain to the City.

The casting is of an original statue that was designed by Lienard, for the Paris Exposition of 1867. This was transported to America where it now stands in front of the Massachusetts State House, Boston Common, in Boston. Here it is known as the Brewer Fountain.

A steam-driven water pump was constructed, at the cost of £400, to drive the water flow of the Liverpool fountain. This was housed in the basement of St. George's Hall and the sound of its engine often disrupted the proceedings in the courtrooms above. There is now a modern pump driving the fountain.

On hot summer days the fountain provides local children, as it always has, with endless fun when they cuddle up to the naked torsos of the figures of Neptune, Amphitrite, Acis, and Galatea, whilst the water splashes all around them! I speak from happy experience!

The Column and the Fountain stand on a triangular plot of land that was once known as the 'Folly Fair'. For many years a windmill stood here, but this was taken down in 1780.

Also demolished was an eight-story tower, which had been built some years before by a Mister Gibson, who was the manager of the Theatre Royal elsewhere in the City.

The Steble Fountain in front of the Walker Art Gallery

The tower stood adjacent to his teahouse and strawberry garden, in what is now Islington, and local people called it 'Gibson's Folly'. This gave the Folly Fair its name.

Once the site had been cleared, and the land levelled and paved, it was here that the Fair was held, each Easter Monday and Tuesday.

As well as traders and entertainers, the Folly Fair was famous for the 'lifting' competitions: On Easter Monday, the men would attempt to lift up any local women who were in the vicinity, and on Easter Tuesday the women would attempt to do the same with the men. This led to the Fair becoming infamous for 'drunkenness, debauchery and fighting' and, after a number of failed attempts by the local Police to close it down, the Fair died out around 1820.

This was after it had moved to a new location, in what is now Stafford Street, off Islington.

The other building, which now occupies the old site of the Folly Fair, is the County Sessions House.

This elegant structure, at the head of William Brown Street, was designed by the architects F & G Holme, and opened in 1884. It functioned as a local, county courthouse; with three courtrooms; Barristers' and Judges' chambers; administrative facilities and cells.

The exterior of the building blends in well with the other structures in the Cultural Quarter, and the coat of arms in the pediment

To Find Out More:

World Heritage
William Brown Street
www.liverpoolworldheritage.com

The Wellington Memorial

of the portico, which is that of the County of Lancaster, gives the building an authoritative dignity.

The interior is richly decorated, panelled throughout in walnut and oak, and the high ceilings are surrounded by ornate plaster work and, in the entrance hall and vestibules, they are supported by smooth marble columns.

Unfortunately though, the Sessions House is not open to the public, as the building is now used for other purposes.

From the Wellington Column, walk across onto the plateau in front of St George's Hall; here you will find the Cenotaph and the Stone Lions. Take the opportunity too, to study the great, bronze statues on the plateau, and the carved relief panels on the side of the building. The visitors' entrance to the Hall is at the far end in St John's Lane, opposite the Central Bus Station.

Pool of Life & Culture : Part 1

Many buildings and locations throughout Liverpool are used by film and television makers for their productions (see Chapter: 'Liverpool Lost and Found'), and St. George's Hall interior, and the exterior and plateau, are regularly in demand. Indeed, the Hall is now formally recognised as being the first public building ever to feature as a location for a film. This was in a short sequence, produced and featuring the pioneers of moving pictures – the Lumiere brothers. In fact, the area between the Cenotaph and the front of the Hall is frequently the backdrop for films.

At the foot of the steps leading up to the grand entrance of St George's Hall stands the City's Cenotaph. This was originally erected in response to the losses during the First World War; and was designed by Lionel Budden and sculpted by George Tyson-Smith. It was unveiled by the 17th Earl of Derby, on Armistice Day 1930, and it has been the centre of Liverpool's Remembrance Day commemorations ever since.

The Cenotaph is flanked by 4 magnificent stone lions, which are reminiscent of the Landseer lions in Trafalgar Square, London. These however were designed by Charles Cockrell; sculpted in sandstone by William Nicholl; and erected in 1858.

> **To Find Out More:**
> Liverpool Cenotaph
> http://www.lmu.livjm.ac.uk/lhol/
> content.aspx?itemid=125

Of all the buildings in the Cultural Quarter, without doubt the most magnificent is St. George's Hall, which stands at the top of the hill, facing along Lime Street. This is now the largest example of Victorian, classical-revival architecture in the world.

This remarkable building was designed and built by an equally remarkable young man. This was Harvey Lonsdale Elmes (1813-1847) , who was only 23 years old when he won the design competition for a new Assize Court and a Ceremonial Hall.

These were originally conceived as two separate buildings, but a shortage of funds meant that they had to be combined in one structure, and Elmes drew up the plans. By this time, the young architect had already designed the Liverpool Collegiate School in Shaw Street and, in 1841, he now dedicated himself completely to this new project. He wore himself out in the process and, after five years of supervising the Hall's construction, his health began to rapidly deteriorate. He retired to Jamaica to recuperate but unfortunately died there, still a young man. His father described him as being, "a martyr to architecture".

St. George's Hall was completed by

Professor Charles Cockerell, and opened on the 18th September 1854, as Law Courts and for banqueting and concerts, more than 10 years after being commissioned.

With its grand, stepped approach on Lime Street, that stretches the full length of the plateau upon which the building stands, the Hall dominates the whole area. Its huge columns, broad plazas, grand entrances, and richly ornamented stonework, combine to create a structure that is both powerful and beautiful.

"The leaders of Liverpool in the mid-19th century, regarded themselves almost as being the equivalent of Roman Senators, and St George's Hall was, in many respects, their Forum"

This association with Ancient Rome pervaded much of the architecture of the City at that time, and it was reflected in the way the City was led and organised. St George's Hall reflects this association with the Classical World in so many of its design features. Indeed, at the south end of the Hall, overlooking St John's Lane, is a massive portico supported by a double row of columns. Above this, inscribed in Latin, are the words,

> *Artibus Legibus Consiliis*
> *Locum Municipes Constituerunt*
> *Anno Domini MLCCCXLI*

Which translates as,

> *For Arts, Law and Counsel*
> *the townspeople built this place in 1841*

Around the exterior walls of the Hall are a series of carved panels that were added to the building in 1894. Those at the William Brown Street end of the building tell the story of the transformation of Liverpool from a tiny fishing village to a great City. At the St. Johns Lane end, the panels tell the story of Justice. These were sculpted by Thomas Stirling Lee, who won a competition to do so that had been organised by the Town Council.

Lee was a student of the French school of sculpture, and his resulting works caused quite a stir at the time, as some of the panels clearly showed naked girls and young women! Scandal stalked the Town, and it was expected that the sales of pornography would be encouraged by such a salacious public display of lewd nudeness! Lee's contract was initially terminated, but he was reinstated after agreeing to suitably drape the figures in the panels that remained to be completed.

The panels are worth a browse – purely from an artistic perspective of course, as

are the rest of the exterior and the plateau.

Inside, the building is even more impressive, and around the walls of the main concert hall itself, in which there is an outstanding concert organ, are 12 statues of prominent Victorians of the time; each of whom had a significant connection with Liverpool.

The larger than life-size figures reflect the larger-than-life personalities of these men, who are Rev. Hugh McNeil; William Roscoe; Sir William Brown; Samuel Robert Graves; Edward Whitley; Sir Robert Peel; Frederick Stanley; Edward Stanley; Rev. Jonathan Brooks; George Stephenson; Joseph Mayer; and William Ewart Gladstone. Soon, and long overdue, we shall see some of the empty plinths in the Hall, filled with statues of some of the many women who have played their part in the history and life of Liverpool.

St George's Hall is a masterpiece with its great, rectangular, tunnel-vaulted main hall, which was inspired by the Baths of Caracalla in Rome. This Great Hall is lavishly decorated throughout, and the panels in the vast ceiling show images of the Coat of Arms of Liverpool; Greek and Roman symbols of commerce and authority (the caduceus and fasces); mermaids; and tridents. A splendid and richly coloured stained-glass window showing St George slaying the dragon overlooks the space. On the bronze doors, light fittings, and in other pieces of stained-glass throughout the building, the monogram 'SPQL' can be seen. In keeping with the Town's Roman self-image, this represents the phrase 'The Senate and People of Liverpool'.

At both ends of the Great Hall are the Courtrooms, and these are linked by corridors running along the Hall's long sides. Both Courts survive intact and, in each one, the panelled walls still surround the Judges Bench, Jury Box, Witness Box, Barristers' Tables, spectator and court reporter benches and, of course, The Dock – with its steps leading up from, and sometimes back down again, to the cells in the basement beneath.

These cells also survive intact, as do all the other rooms and amenities necessary to oil the wheels of the Victorian criminal justice system, and to service a magnificent civic space.

Not only is the Hall a fine example of art and architecture, but it is also one of scientific achievement. This is demonstrated by the remarkable heating and ventilation system that was designed and installed by Dr. Boswell Reid.

Fresh air was drawn down into the basement, via apertures in the walls, but mainly through shafts at the East Portico end of the building, facing Lime Street.

However, there were no such openings overlooking the Cemetery, which at the time of the Hall's construction, still

St George's Hall by night

occupied the land that is now covered by St John's Gardens. This was in case 'a miasma of death should be drawn' into the building.

Depending on the weather, the air could then be passed over hot water pipes or jets of steam to be heated, or cooled by cold water pipes. The air was then circulated throughout the building by four great fans, each 10 feet in diameter, powered by a steam engine under the Concert Hall. The flow was controlled by a series of canvas flaps, which were manipulated mechanically, and controlled by an army of staff. The whole air-conditioning system was zoned, so that different parts of the Hall could be heated or cooled at different times.

Much evidence of this fascinating and innovative system still remains, and can be seen on the complete guided tours of St George's Hall, which are operated throughout the tourist season.

Perhaps though, the most remarkable feature of the Great Hall is the sunken, Minton Hollins encaustic tile floor. This vast expanse is opulently decorated with images of the Liver Bird; Neptune; sea nymphs; dolphins; and tridents. This also forms part of the ventilation system, as grilles are set into the rim of its large central sunken section, to facilitate the circulation of the air.

The mosaic masterpiece, which takes pride of place in the Great Hall, consists of 30,000 hand crafted tiles and is an immaculately preserved surface. Needing

to be preserved, the tiles are only ever opened up for display a few times a year, and they are usually completely covered by a removable, wooden, ballroom floor.

St. George's Hall has always had a strong place in the hearts of the citizens of Liverpool. No more so than when it was bombed and severely damaged during the May Blitz of 1941.

Crowds of people stood on Lime Street, many in tears as the building burned, whilst hundreds of fire-fighters and volunteers succeeded eventually in quelling the blaze. Temporary repairs were made and, after the War, some restoration was carried out to get the building back into working life. However, money was not available to do all the work that was really necessary, and so, age and increasing atmospheric pollution began to take their toll. Fortunately, this degeneration has been halted, and a £23m award-winning refurbishment project was completed a few years ago. This completely weatherproofed the Hall, and also restored the Small Concert Room to its original white and gold-leafed splendour, and to public use. The exquisite Minton tile floor was re-opened by HRH Prince Charles on St George's Day in April 2007.

St George's Hall is now a focal point for cultural, community, civic, corporate and performing arts activities. In excess of 65,000 witnessed the spectacular Capital of Culture People's Opening in 2008 which was hosted by the Hall.

The Heritage Centre provides visitors with an exciting introduction to St George's Hall and its place in Liverpool's history.

Key features include opportunities to visit the cells used by prisoners awaiting trial; the Criminal Court and Judge's Robing Room; glimpses of the unique ventilation system designed by Dr David Boswell Reid; a Community Room entitled 'World Heritage-Your Heritage' where local groups can exhibit work; and an accessible viewing gallery for the Great Hall.

Throughout the Heritage Centre, imaginative exhibitions, reconstructions and hands-on activities bring the story of St George's Hall alive. Visitors can follow in the steps of the unfortunate prisoners, from prison cell to the dock.

Regular tours are available, so that visitors can discover for themselves the history and beauty that makes up St George's Hall. I hope that you will join one of these tours; you will not be disappointed.

To Find Out More:

St George's Hall
Phone: 0151 225 6911 / 225 6909
http://www.stgeorgesliverpool.co.uk

From St George's Hall plateau you can get a marvellous view of the North Western Hotel and Lime Street Station, which I will tell you about shortly, but to continue the Tour you now have a choice: Either continue walking along Lime Street, across the traffic lights at Skelhorne Street, and all the way along up to the Adelphi Hotel on the left, and the former Lewis's Department Store on the right: Or, you can return to the car park and collect your vehicle, and drive along the rest of Lime Street. Directions from the car park are given after the next article.

Lime Street takes its name from the limekilns that stood, throughout the latter part of the 18th and early years of the 19th centuries, on the site now occupied by the North Western Hotel and Lime Street Station.

Nowadays, Lime Street is the main street through this part of town, and first-time British visitors to Liverpool are often surprised that the City is not in fact a mass of decaying housing estates, failed shipping, and declining industrialisation: In our own country our reputation is sometimes tarnished and stereotypical. However, visitors from overseas do not come to the City with such prejudices, as Liverpool has a very positive image abroad.

"But wherever they are from, our visitors – and they are coming here in their thousands – discover that Liverpool is a green, spacious, vigorous, and exciting City, with a dynamic economy and a contemporary culture second-to-none in the country"

Its community is more positive and energised now than for decades, and the social life, architecture, and regeneration of the city-centre is testament to that.

Now, the true and wonderful character of Liverpool and its people, are becoming much more widely recognised and respected throughout the United Kingdom and the world.

To Find Out More:
Lime Street History
http://www.bbc.co.uk/liverpool/localhistory/journey/
lime_street/binns_lime_street_journey/history.shtml

Opposite St. George's Hall, and between the Empire Theatre and Lime Street Railway Station, stands the massive Victorian elegance of what was once the North Western Hotel. Behind this stands Lime Street Station, the main railway station into the City.

This former 330-room grand hotel was built in 1871, to service passengers on the new railway, as well as those bound for ocean crossings aboard the great transatlantic liners.

It was designed by Alfred Waterhouse (1830-1905), the Victorian architect who built so many of the City's most significant buildings, and about whom we have already heard. Over the main entrance to this huge, neo-Gothic place, is a bust of Minerva - the ancient Roman Goddess of wisdom and the arts. She also sits on top of Liverpool Town Hall, overlooking the City. On the left of Minerva is a full figure, which is in all likelihood a representation of Athena - the Greek version of Minerva. On the right is the figure of the Greek goddess Artemis - the virgin huntress.

This splendid hotel closed in 1933 and, perhaps surprisingly, it remained empty for over sixty years. However, in 1994, it was bought by Liverpool John Moores University. They spent £6 million to completely restore and refurbish the building as halls of residence for students studying in the City. Re-named as North Western Hall, it re-opened on 2nd September 1996.

To Find Out More:
North Western Hall
http://www.travelstay.com/pages/NorthWesternHall.htm

Lime Street Station

With the advent of commercial railways for public transport, in the early 19th century, the first railway station in Liverpool opened, as we have seen, in 1829 at Crown Street in Edge Hill, just outside the Town centre.

"This was ready for the inaugural run, in 1830, of the Liverpool and Manchester Railway, between these two great cities"

It was at this station that the line, at least for passengers, initially terminated. This was because, at the time the Town Council would not permit steam engines to come any nearer to the town centre, because of fears about noise, smoke, and ash. However, goods for the City could get to the town – at least to the docks, and they would be carried down the Wapping Tunnel, from Crown Street to Wapping Dock. This tunnel, now disused and closed off, still survives. However, as the track into the Town had a relatively steep incline, engineers at the time found that the railway locomotives were not powerful enough, nor could they achieve sufficient grip on the rails, to haul trains of goods wagons up to Crown Street Station. Consequently, the full wagons were lowered down the tracks by gravity – the rate of descent being controlled by brakemen, and were pulled back up again on ropes that were driven by a steam turbine and winches!

The engine house for the steam turbines that drove the cables was housed in richly carved, sandstone Moorish Arch, which spanned the railway cutting at Edge Hill. This was a great triumphal edifice, designed to act as a 'gateway' into Liverpool. Sadly, by the 1860s, the main arch span had been demolished to allow for the widening of the track layout. Nevertheless, remnants of it, and of the cable system and engines, still survive in the cutting walls at Edge Hill.

However, this still left the problem of the disgruntled passengers having to make their way into the town centre from Edge Hill, by other means. But, bowing to the inevitable, permission was granted and a new main station at Lime Street was opened, in 1836. To reach this station a new tunnel was cut from Edge Hill, by George Stephenson, with his teams of 'Navvies'. These were workers, many of whom had previously worked as excavators, digging out the network of Britain's canals – or 'navigations': hence the labourers' nickname. As we read in the section on 'The Mole of Edge Hill', it was during the construction of the Edge Hill tunnel that these diggers had their 'Hellish' encounter with their counterparts, who were undermining Edge Hill for the eccentric Joseph Williamson, at the same time.

This new line to the town also required the construction of a new passenger station, at a different location at Edge Hill; this is still the current terminus on the line. The new station and tunnel were opened in the same year, and named as Lime Street Station. Crown Street station then became a coal yard, and the old passenger platforms were used for goods purposes. Nevertheless, once again the carriages with their passengers had to descend to Lime Street by gravity, controlled by a brakeman, and were then rope-hauled by the winding engine back up to Edge Hill.

By 1870, a new class of steam locomotive had become powerful enough to handle the track gradients, and so the cable systems became redundant and the great winches fell into disuse. Remnants of the pulley, the ducts, and the pumping station, which archaeologists believe were in use until 1870, still survive at Lime Street; the Victorians seem to have simply buried the system when it was abandoned.

The station building that we now see on Lime Street is, in fact, the third station to stand on the site, and each subsequent station had to be bigger than its predecessor to cope with increasing traffic and passenger demand. Fifteen years after the first station had been built, this was replaced by a very grand edifice, appropriate for how the proprietors of the Liverpool and Manchester railway saw themselves and their company. Designed by the Town Surveyor, John Foster, this was a long wall facing onto Lime Street, and built in a neo-classical style in keeping with St. George's Hall across the road. It had half-columns incorporated into its design, and its entrances and exits were great porticoed arches. Nevertheless, even this was not considered grand enough and, in 1879, it was replaced by the current building.

"The modern Lime Street Station was the first in the world to have iron arcades and a glass roof covering all the tracks and, a few years ago, this roof was completely restored as part of a major redevelopment"

Lime Street Gateway

Lime Street Station has always been busy, and has always received main line trains from all over the country. During my childhood I experienced the last great days of steam: I remember well the noise and thrill of the great engines as they trundled in and out of the station; belching forth great, eerie clouds of smoke and steam, and filling the air with a singular smell that was at once potent and yet heartening. The last steam locomotive left Lime Street in August 1968; when the 'Stanier Black Five 45110' set off on a special farewell excursion.

A world-class city certainly needs a world-class railway station and, in 2010, Lime Street's multi-million pound new plaza officially opened. Re-named the 'Lime Street Gateway', the radical facelift has managed to recapture the station's glory, with a restoration of the façade and main entrance. The arched gable end of the listed Victorian station building has been revealed, creating a new area of public realm, greatly improved pedestrian access to and from the station, and better links to the city's Cultural Quarter.

The Crown Hotel on Lime Street

Inside the station, the ticket offices and travel centre have also been revamped and all platforms and surrounding areas restored and upgraded.

Now crossover Skelhorne Street and you will come to The Crown pub. Just pop inside and be amazed by this palace of mahogany and intricate plasterwork. The building has deep, cut-glass windows, is awash with beaten copper panels, and would seem more suited to Fin-de-Siecle Paris than Lime Street, Liverpool.

You will then pass The American Bar, which is in the middle of the block. This opened in 1830, and this was once the haunt of Maggie May and her ilk: Yes, she did exist! These 'ladies of ill fame' came in to bring comfort and companionship to the sailors who once frequented it.

During the Second World War, when the GIs were stationed in Liverpool, they discovered the bar and, because of its name, they made it their home-from-home. Once again, the later generations of 'ladies of the night' frequented the bar, this time attracted to soldiers and airmen, as well as the sailors!

Now known as McHale's Irish & American Bar, it is easily identifiable by the large replica Statue of Liberty over the front door.

At the end of the road stands The Vines Pub. This is named after a Mr. Vines, one of the pub's first owners, but it is known locally as 'The Big House'.

An old tavern stood on this site for many years, but this was demolished, and the building that we now see was erected in 1907, in a bold, Baroque style of lavishly decorated carved stone.

On the roof is a completely useless tower, which simply contains a very thin room! The interior is also a masterpiece of

period design and, like the Crown, it is richly adorned with beaten copper and polished brass: But, this is very much more solidly Victorian than its counterpart on the other corner. The lounge and bar walls are panelled, and inside you will also find carved mahogany caryatids and decorated columns, and great mirrors are mounted on the walls.

The fireplace is huge and very impressive, and the plasterwork friezes on the ceilings really provide luxurious and fascinating surroundings.

Behind the walls of the cellars in The Vines, still survive old smugglers' tunnels, which once connected the river with the original tavern.

The Crown, The Vines, and the American Bar are remarkable places to meet Scousers and to have a pie, a pint, and a natter.

To Find Out More:
The Crown
Phone: 0151 707 6027
http://www.bbc.co.uk/liverpool/local history/journey/lime_street/pubs/ crown.shtml
The Vines
Phone: 0151 709 3977
http://www.bbc.co.uk/liverpool/local history/journey/lime_street/pubs/ vines.shtml
McHale's Irish & American Bar
Phone: 0151 709 1538
http://www.bbc.co.uk/liverpool/local history/journey/lime_street/pubs/ american_bar.shtml
Merseyside Campaign for Real Ale
www.merseycamra.org.uk

Pool of Life & Culture : Part 1

The Adelphi Hotel

Walking across Copperas Hill, and on the opposite corner to the 'Big House', you will see the impressive Adelphi Hotel.

Once one of the most luxurious hotels in Britain, the current building was opened in 1914. It was built on the site of a previous Adelphi Hotel, which had been built in 1876. This itself was erected on the site of the Ranelagh Pleasure Gardens. This was a large area of privately created parkland that ran up Copperas Hill, and which contained landscaped gardens and wooded walks, alongside a lake and meandering watercourses. It was here that exhibitions, balls, theatrical performances, and concerts, provided the 18th and 19th century 'glitterati' of Liverpool with 'entertainment and diversions'. As with the North Western Hotel opposite St. George's Hall, The Adelphi serviced rail and ocean-going liner passengers, and it accommodated them in opulent surroundings.

Some of the world's most famous people have stayed in the Adelphi over the years, including the US President Franklin Roosevelt, and his wife Eleanor; and also Winston Churchill and other international political figures. Throughout the 20th century, many of the Crowned Heads of Europe, and beyond, have made the Adelphi their temporary home. Likewise, Laurel & Hardy, Frank Sinatra, Judy Garland, and many other stars of stage and screen have stayed here, whilst playing at the Empire and other Liverpool theatres. Indeed, in 1954, the famous Roy Rogers once rode his equally famous horse, Trigger, up the steps of the hotel and along the corridors, to appear at an upper-front balcony, where they both received the applause and cheers of the crowds standing in the street below.

All grand hotels are the scene of scandals, curious incidents, and significant events, and it was whilst he was a guest at the Adelphi in the early 1970s, that the Russian classical musician Vladimir Ashkenazy announced his defection to the West.

To Find Out More:
The Britannia Adelphi Hotel
Phone: 0151 709 7200
www.adelphi-hotel.co.uk

The Adelphi Hotel in the 1930s

Former Lewis's Department Store and 'Dickie'

Directly facing the Adelphi Hotel, at the corner of Ranelagh Street, is what was built as Lewis's Department Store.

This was originally founded as a clothing store, in 1856, by David Lewis the Jewish businessman and philanthropist and, by 1885, it was the largest store in the North of England. Business was so good that it was completely rebuilt, around 1910.

However, in the Second World War, during the May Blitz in 1941, Liverpool was subjected to six nights of continuous bombardment by the German Luftwaffe; the store was one of many architectural casualties of the Nazi bombs. Nevertheless, the store was completely re-built after the War and the sculptor Jacob Epstein (1880-1959) commissioned to create a special statue. It took him 2½ years to complete and, when the tarpaulins were removed at the official unveiling, on 20th November 1956, the gasps from the crowds signified either shocked surprise or exuberant delight!

The naked man towering over the building's entrance and the street, in all his – relative – glory, generated many complaints and letters to the local newspaper – the Liverpool Echo.

After a fortnight the reaction died down although, it was said that for weeks after the unveiling, the front rooms of the Adelphi Hotel were all booked up, and mostly – though not exclusively – by women!

The male figure dominating the entrance to Lewis's is cast in bronze. He is shown piloting the great vessel that is Liverpool, boldly into the future.

The ship's prow weighs 2½ tons and the figure itself weighs a further 2½ tons. He stands at 18ft 6ins high overall, but I have no information about any other dimensions associated with the figure!

Whilst the official name of the Lewis's statue is 'Liverpool Resurgent', it is known locally, and for obvious reasons, as 'Dickie Lewis'. Scousers will sometimes warn visitors not to stand under the statue on cold and frosty mornings, just in case a large icicle should fall on them with phallic fatality!

Dickie Lewis

If you have walked to this point in the Tour, now is the time to return to the car-park and collect you car.
On leaving the multi-storey car park, turn right into St John's Lane, and get into the right-hand lane.
At the top of the road, turn right at the traffic lights into Lime Street. Continue along here, passing the Crown; the Miniature Statue of Liberty outside the American Bar; and the Vines Hotel.
At the traffic lights just after the Adelphi Hotel, and opposite Lewis's, turn sharp left up Brownlow Hill, and continue up the road. Cross over the traffic lights at Russell Street and Clarence Street, and you will see the tower of the Roman Catholic Cathedral, beyond the buildings on the right. The ornate, red-brick clock tower of the Victoria Building of the University of Liverpool, now comes into view on the left.

The University of Liverpool

The oldest universities in Europe were at Bologna and Paris, and it was English students from Paris who, some time in the mid-1100s and according to tradition, established the first British university at Oxford, in disused convent buildings.

Cambridge University is said to have been founded about a hundred years later, by students who left Oxford after disagreements with the townspeople.

The next British universities to be established were in Scotland in the 1400s; at Glasgow, Aberdeen, and St. Andrews; with Edinburgh University, and Trinity College in Dublin, being established in the 1500s. These remained the only British universities until 1881, when the University College Liverpool was established as one of the first new Civic Universities.

The University College received its Royal Charter, and so became a full university, in 1903, consequently celebrating its centenary in October 2003. In 1949, the University was set to expand and plans for creating a full campus were put in place.

This included the refurbishment and inclusion, in the new precincts, of many fine buildings that already stood in and around the existing Victorian University College buildings.

Some other buildings were demolished, slum and bomb-sites cleared, and new faculty buildings were erected, over subsequent decades.

"The University of Liverpool, which now has a very large campus, was the first 'red-brick' University in the country"

This term was first coined by Professor E Allison Peers – writing as 'Bruce Truscott' in his 1943 book, 'Redbrick University' – and who was one of the University of Liverpool dons.

The phrase was inspired by the red brickwork of the first university building on Brownlow Hill – the Victoria Building, with its glorious clock tower.

This had been built in 1892, and Peers used the term to describe all British universities except Oxford, Cambridge, and London.

The red bricks were the trademark of architect Alfred Waterhouse who designed the building.

Because of his passion for this colour of stonework, his architectural colleagues gave him the nickname of 'Slaughterhouse Waterhouse'!

To Find Out More:
The University of Liverpool
Phone: 0151 794 2000/708 6502
www.liv.ac.uk

Turn right at the traffic lights into Mount Pleasant. There is no parking on the road, but you can park in the underground car park directly beneath the Cathedral itself. The entrance to this is a little further along on the right, and is clearly visible: You will need coins for the parking machines, and it costs about £1 per hour.

Whatever you do, don't think that you can safely park in the University car park opposite the Cathedral – this is for permit-holders only and you are likely to get wheel-clamped.

If, for any reason, the underground car park is closed, there are Pay-and-Display parking bays if you turn right at the end of the road. This road is, in fact, the continuation of Mount Pleasant. As another alternative, cross over at the traffic lights onto Hope Street, and find one of the Pay-and-Display bays on the roadsides. I suggest a stop of about 1 hour to visit the Cathedral.

Pool of Life & Culture : Part 1

The Victoria Tower of the University of Liverpool

The Metropolitan Cathedral of Christ the King

In 1771, although still surrounded by fields, a poor house opened near the summit of what was then known as Brownlow Hill Lane, which was some distance from the town. In 1842, this became the Parish Workhouse, and adjoining it was a House of Correction. Built to house 1800 destitute people this was the largest workhouse in Europe, soon expanding and becoming desperately overcrowded with, by 1900, more than 4000 inmates. Over half of these people were Catholics; many Irish people driven from their own country by famine and poverty, and preferring life in the Workhouse to starvation on the streets. Even by the standards of the time the building was not a very pleasant place and, in 1928, the revision of the Poor Laws closed the Workhouse and brought the property onto the market.

In 1930, the Roman Catholic Archdiocese bought the nine-acre site at the corner of Brownlow Hill and Mount Pleasant, for £100,000, and Sir Edwin Lutyens (1869-1944) was commissioned as the architect for a new cathedral. By this time, Lutyens had already established an excellent and international reputation, having worked on the building of New Delhi from 1912-31 and, in 1919, on the Cenotaph in London.

The site of the old workhouse and prison was cleared and, on Whit Monday 5th June 1933, the foundation stone was laid.

"At the recommendation of the then Pope, Pius XI, the cathedral was dedicated to Christ the King, and Lutyens' original design was for a huge Byzantine-style edifice. This was deliberately in direct contrast to the Gothic style of the Anglican Cathedral, which was then being built half a mile away by Giles Gilbert Scott, and which had been under construction since 1904"

Construction of the Catholic Cathedral began with the crypt, which was completed by 1937, but the War and the expense of the project stopped building once this had been roofed over. Nothing then happened on the site until 1953, when Archbishop Heenan commissioned Adrian Gilbert Scott, the son of the architect of the Anglican Cathedral, to redesign the project on a much reduced scale, whilst retaining Lutyens' original plan for a huge domed building. However, there was still not enough money for this plan to be realised and so, once again, ambitions were scaled down to match the available funds. In 1960 a competition was held to find a new design and, from over 300 entries, Sir Frederick Gibberd's (1908-1984) plan was chosen. This was for a radical and contemporary building designed 'to reflect 1960s energy and creativity'. Work began over the existing crypt, in October 1962, and only five years later, in 1967, the new Cathedral was consecrated.

Sometimes locally referred to as either the Mersey Funnel or Paddy's Wigwam, the building remains controversial, but one only has to stand inside this magnificent place of worship and look around to feel the power of the design. The blending of the colours of the stained glass in the Lantern Tower, which is the largest stained glass window in the world and which represents the Holy Trinity, is particularly stirring.

Below this, the altar and central space; almost completely surrounded by the pews, is the focal point of the worship space and, surrounding this around the nave, are several side chapels. These are dedicated to different devotions and special uses, including the Chapel of the Blessed Sacrament; the Baptistry; the Lady Chapel; the Chapel of Unity; Chapel of Reconciliation; and the Chapel of the Holy Oils. My personal favourite is the chapel dedicated to Saint Joseph, the earthly father of Jesus. The plain wooden panels around the three walls, carved with softly-coloured reliefs showing scenes from the Saint's life, give this chapel a homely warmth.

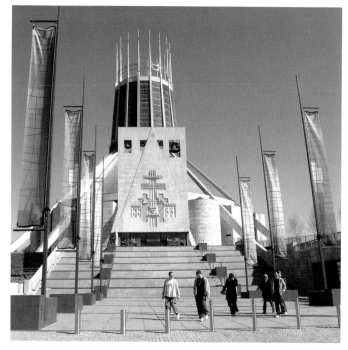

The Metropolitan Cathedral of Christ the King

This is why the tomb of the late Archbishop Derek Worlock has been sited here: A simple surrounding for a man who aspired to simplicity, but who nonetheless achieved great things for the people of Liverpool.

Outside, the front aspect of the building is perhaps its most inspiring: Standing, as it does, on top of a high plateau and at the head of a magnificent stepped approach, the bell tower dominates the entrance. The four bells represent the four Gospel Saints – Matthew, Mark, Luke, and John. Above this, the vast, coned roof of the building narrows towards the tall Coronet Tower.

This is surmounted by the Crown of Thorns, which can be seen from miles around.

At the time of its construction, the design may have been revolutionary and controversial but so were some of the construction techniques and building materials – not all resulting in a satisfactory outcome. Indeed, it has been necessary to spend many millions of pounds simply making essential repairs to the roof, as the concrete was perishing and major fissures were allowing rainwater to create large leaks, further damaging the structure. These problems have now been fully addressed and new funding was secured to construct the stepped approach to the building, together with a purpose-built visitors' centre and restaurant, known as 'The Piazza'. This is at street level, to the right of the new steps. It provides information about the Cathedral, a gift shop, and a restaurant providing high quality food and light refreshments in a very pleasant environment. I heartily recommend it.

This, together with the challenging and contemporary architecture of the Cathedral, makes it a building well worth visiting and it is an excellent place to take a break.

To Find Out More:

The Metropolitan Cathedral of Christ the King
Phone: 0151 709 9222
E-Mail: enquiries@metcathedral.org.uk
http://www.liverpoolmetrocathedral.org.uk/

For those of you with an astrological or Pagan bent, it is said that a ley-line runs the length of Hope Street, and that this is the reason why the two cathedrals ended up being built here, and why also the area has such a particular energy and cultural vibrancy.

Ley lines, or Leys, are alignments of ancient sites that allegedly stretch across the landscape. Such locations or holy places may be situated in a straight line covering distances of anything from one or two, to nine or ten miles.

Leys can be identified from the alignment of religious sites or structures, or indeed, by remnants of ancient tracks and roadways. Ley Lines were 're-discovered' on 30 June 1921 by Alfred Watkins (1855-1935), a locally well-known and respected Herefordshire businessman who, whilst looking at a map for features of interest, noticed that a straight line passed over hill tops through various points of interest, all of which were ancient.

The ley line that connects the Cathedrals of Liverpool also runs directly through the sites of St Francis Xavier Church in Everton, and St Mary's Church at Walton-on-the-Hill; I checked it with a ruler on a map! Whether the lines run through any other current or previous religious/spiritual sites I cannot say. Neither can I say if there is any truth to the existence of such lines, or if this is simply a matter of coincidence.

> **To Find Out More:**
> **Ley Lines**
> http://skepdic.com/leylines.html

The street that leads from the Metropolitan Cathedral of Christ the King, and which leads towards the Anglican Cathedral on St James's Mount, is appropriately named Hope Street – although it is not so named for this reason. Indeed, the road had already been in existence for 150 years before building work began on the Anglican Cathedral.

It was named after William Hope, a local merchant, who built the first house in the street, on the site of the present Philharmonic Hotel.

The street is particularly notable as it is a hub of arts, music, dance, and drama, and it contains some very fine restaurants. I shall refer to these later. Also, on the right-hand corner, is part of the very dispersed campus of Liverpool John Moores University.

Liverpool John Moores University

We are now in the heart of the City's University Quarter; not just of the University of Liverpool, but of the second university to be established in the City. This is the Liverpool John Moores University (LJMU).

LJMU was originally founded as a small mechanics institution (Liverpool Mechanics' School of Arts) in 1825, and the institution grew over the centuries by converging and amalgamating with different colleges, eventually becoming the Liverpool Polytechnic.

In 1992, the Polytechnic became one of the UK's new generation of universities, and it assumed the name 'Liverpool John Moores University', when the Conservative Government of Margaret Thatcher made it possible for such institutions to apply for a charter to deliver degree courses.

The University takes its name from Sir John Moores (1896-1993), the founder of the Littlewoods stores, mail order, and

John Moores

football pools empire, who was a major benefactor of the fledgling university. He was the first Chancellor of the University, eventually succeeded by Cherie Blair. At the time of writing, the current Chancellor of the University is Dr Brian May, lead guitarist of the rock band Queen.

Unlike the University of Liverpool, which is principally located on a central campus around Brownlow Hill and Mount Pleasant, LJMU has commissioned many purpose-built faculty and halls of residence buildings all over the City. However, one of the University's most significant contributions to Liverpool, is that it continues to acquire and restore many of our most misused or neglected historic buildings. These include Georgian terraced properties; a disused convent (history repeating itself perhaps – see previous section on the University of Liverpool); and many pre-existing colleges and educational buildings. The University converts these into administrative, teaching, research, and study centres, or into halls of residence. This not only provides a variety of exciting and interesting environments for University staff and students, and for the community, but this policy preserves and guarantees the future of our architectural heritage.

Apart from fees, LJMU sources significant income from exploiting its commercial as well as scientific, cultural, and educational expertise.

The Aldham Robarts Learning Resource Centre on Maryland Street

Pool of Life & Culture : Part 1

John Moores

John Moores, the founder of the University, was a member of a family that was just one of a long and illustrious list of benefactor families who, throughout Liverpool's history, have contributed so much to the development, progress, and well-being of the City and its people: Enterprising and entrepreneurial families such as the Roscoes, Rathbones, Gladstones, Holts, and the Bibbys – amongst many others.

After an elementary education, John Moores began his working life in the City as a messenger boy, and then as a cable-telegraph operator. In the early 1920s, the laws affecting small-stake gambling were liberalised and, in 1923, John took advantage of the opportunity to establish the Liverpool-based Littlewoods Football Pool company.

Within 10 years he was a millionaire and, by 1939, he had also founded the Littlewoods Mail Order and Retail Store chain. By 1990, Littlewoods had become Britain's richest family-owned business, worth around £1.6 billion.

"Sir John established the John Moores Charitable Trust soon after his initial financial success, and he began to plough millions of pounds back into the City and its communities"

He did this through charitable donations and foundations, and by supporting education and the arts, also new business ventures and entrepreneurs.

Many projects that I have personally been involved in over the years, have benefited from the financial support of the Sir John Moores Charitable Trust, which continues to make a valuable contribution to Merseyside in so many ways, now known as the John Moores Foundation.

John Moores retired in 1977, but divisions within the Moores family soon surfaced and profits fell as a result. He returned to the company as Chairman, from 1980-82, and then as Life President. After his death, in 1993, the old family disagreements resurfaced and parts of the Littlewoods Empire were sold off.

A large bronze statue, commemorating Sir John Moores and his brother and business partner, Cecil, once stood outside the former family store in Church Street. However, in 2006, this was relocated to stand outside their former headquarters building in Old Hall Street. (See Chapter: 'The Liverpool Waterfront'.)

To Find Out More:
Liverpool John Moores University
Phone: 0151 231 2121
www.livjm.ac.uk

Liverpool in fact has three universities; our latest addition being Liverpool Hope University. This was originally Hope University College, which itself grew from an amalgamation of the Roman Catholic Christ's Teacher Training College, and St Katharine's C of E Teacher Training College – both situated on opposite sides of Taggart Avenue in Childwall; and also with the Catholic Notre Dame (Mount Pleasant) College. The combined campus site at Childwall has now been renamed Hope Park, in recognition of this remarkable union into what is now a completely ecumenical, liberal-arts university and the only such institution of its kind in Europe.

Hope University College was founded largely at the instigation of the Roman Catholic Archbishop Derek Worlock (1920-1996) and the Anglican Bishop David Sheppard (1929-2005). Both men, through their genuinely ecumenical spirit and tireless efforts, throughout the 1970s and 1980s, broke down the sectarian divide that for so many generations had been an unpleasant characteristic of parts of Liverpool.

"They built bridges between the faiths and, despite inevitable minority ignorance, the sectarian divide across Merseyside is a thing of the past"

This ecumenical partnership led to the founding of Liverpool Hope University College, which takes its name from Hope Street in the City-centre that connects our two cathedrals. Together with its other campus in Everton – Hope at Everton (See Chapter: 'Fortunes, Fables, and Football'), as well as its many projects throughout the community, Liverpool Hope University adds further excellence to our remarkable range of higher educational establishments and facilities.

After leaving the Metropolitan Cathedral it is worth crossing over the road directly ahead and walking into the end of Hope Street.
On the left hand corner here you will see the curved and columned entrance to the Medical Institution and, beyond this, the Everyman Theatre.

The Medical Institution

As we enter Hope Street, on the left hand corner stands the Medical Institution, with its attractive curved and colonnaded frontage.

This was once the site of an inn and bowling green, which was the birthplace of William Roscoe (1753-1831). Roscoe was a true 'Renaissance Man' and a successful local businessman, abolitionist, Unitarian, author, botanist, and amateur scientist. He was also one of the original founders of the Liverpool Athenaeum. Roscoe features often in this book, as he was so significant to the life and development of Liverpool in the 18th and 19th centuries, and you will have the opportunity to visit his home at Allerton Hall, in the Chapter: 'Liverpool Lost and Found'.

"In 1799, a group of enlightened Liverpool doctors formed the Liverpool Medical Library and later, in 1833, the Liverpool Medical Society"

Both organisations merged and, in 1836, the architect Clark Rampling was commissioned to design and build a home for the new Medical Institution. The site was triangular, which meant that Rampling had to be particularly skillful. He succeeded in creating an attractive and perfectly functional building that contains a lecture theatre on two floors, a central hall, a library, a museum, and committee rooms. All of these spaces are cleverly lit by the use of glazed domes.

Costing £4,000 to build, and opening in 1837, the classical frontage and portico of this Grade II* Listed Building provides a perfect gateway to the Liverpool terraces of Hope Street. The Medical Institution now forms part of the University of Liverpool campus, but still with medical associations.

Indeed, the Doctor Duncan Society holds regular meetings and lectures here, to discuss contemporary medical and health-related issues, and its library remains world-renowned. We shall discover more about Duncan shortly, who was a remarkable and farsighted man who served the people of Liverpool very well indeed.

It is possible to visit the Medical Institution, but only by prior special arrangement, or by attending a lecture.

To Find Out More:
The Medical Institution
Phone: 0151 709 9125
www.lmi.org.uk

The Everyman Theatre

The first building that we see on the left as we enter Hope Street is the Everyman Theatre.

This grew out of the original building on the site, which was Hope Hall – originally a dissenters' chapel that had been built in 1837. This was where 'Love Feasts' were once held by the eccentric community who first worshipped here. But, in 1841, it became the Church of St. John the Baptist and then, in 1853, it was converted into a public concert hall.

The building subsequently became the Hope Hall Cinema in 1912 and, in 1929, it was one of the first cinemas in Liverpool to be equipped for sound. The cinema closed in January 1963, with a showing of 'Sons and Lovers' starring Dean Stockwell and Wendy Hiller.

From this time, the 'Hall' had become a meeting place for local poets like Adrian Henry and Roger McGough; folk musicians; painters; and sculptors, like Arthur Dooley.

The venue developed into the focal point of what became known locally and nationally as 'The Liverpool Scene'. Interestingly, the 'bohemian' and culturally-radical nature of the new community who then used the 'Hall', harked back to the original uses to which the building had been put, as the age of 'make love not war' began to evolve amongst many young people of 1960s Liverpool: Not least of all myself: I threw myself into the 'Free Love: Tune-In, Turn-On, Drop-Out Hippie Culture' with true commitment; but that is another story, for another book!

As more and more people began to frequent the building, it became clear to the artistic community that the Hall had much more potential. And so, in September 1964, Martin Jenkins, Pete James, and Terry Hands – who went on to direct the Royal Shakespeare Company, opened the building as the 'Everyman Theatre', with ambitions of bringing together many elements of the City's artistic and musical culture. However, early productions were 'safe' and included 'Richard III', 'Look Back in Anger', and 'The Importance of Being Ernest'.

Eventually, and as the confidence of the fledgling Theatre Company grew, they became more radical in terms of exploring innovative production styles, and by experimenting with new, home grown writing and performance talent.

Soon, the Everyman was to become very much part of Liverpool's radical sub-culture, during the heady and hedonistic days of the late 1960s and early 1970s.

In 1975, the Everyman Theatre Company left their building and took to the road, whilst their home was completely refurbished and largely rebuilt.

It re-opened, to great public acclaim and a warm welcome, in September 1977.

Crowds gather outside the original Everyman Theatre to watch the fireworks over the Metropolitan Cathedral

As the production company matured, from the 1970s and 1980s, a new breed of contemporary playwright appeared on the scene.

Willy Russell and Alan Bleasdale were among the writers who 'cut their teeth' at the Everyman, with productions such as 'Shirley Valentine', 'Educating Rita', 'Blood Brothers', 'Once A Catholic', and 'John, Paul, George, Ringo and Bert' all debuting here.

Today, the theatre remains a source of encouragement and opportunity to young talent from Liverpool and across the UK.

It is a vibrant and popular venue that stages plays, musicals, concerts, and artistic festivals of all kinds. Indeed, the traditional Christmas Show each year, which is so much more than just a Pantomime and always has a Liverpool theme, regularly plays to packed houses.

Because of its age, the theatre is quite naturally also a place of spooks and spectres, and its back rooms, corridors, passageways, and stairways, are often the scene of disembodied footsteps and strange unexplained shadows. Indeed, there is a male ghost who seems to haunt the rear of the auditorium and the Gents' lavatories. He can be quite scary, but worse than this, is the fact that he leaves behind him an overpoweringly strong smell of wee!

However, the ghost may soon vanish forever, as the old building is replaced by a completely re-built and redesigned Everyman Theatre.

Early in 2011, £28m of redevelopment funding was raised for this major project. July 2011 saw the final performance in the old building, and the new theatre is scheduled to open in 2013.

Despite the temporary loss of this cultural icon, there are many other theatrical centres of excellence in the city. Not least of all being the partner of The Everyman, the Liverpool Playhouse – see Chapter: 'The Heart of the City'.

To Find Out More:
The Everyman Theatre
Phone:
0151 706 9115
www.everyman playhouse.com

After visiting all these buildings and locations, Part 1 of 'Pool of Life & Culture' is over.
If you have taken the suggested time to visit all of the Galleries and Museums etc, then you will have already spent a number of hours on the Tour, and you should be happily worn out!
Unless you have endless stamina; and another 5 or 6 hours available, I suggest that you return to your car and drive home: Complete Part 2 on another day!

Pool of Life & Culture : Part 1

Chinese dancers perform in Liverpool's Lord Mayor's Parade

Pool of Life & Culture : Part 2

Including:

The Philharmonic Hotel

The Philharmonic Hall
and Liverpool's Musical Heritage

Edward Chambré Hardman Heritage Centre

St. Andrew's Church and The Pyramid Tomb

LIPA: The Fame School

Chinatown

St. James's Cemetery

The Anglican Cathedral

Gambier Terrace

Georgian Liverpool

Pool of Life & Culture 2 : The Tour

This is now Part 2 of the Pool of Life & Culture Tour and it picks up where we left off, at the end of Part 1, on Mount Pleasant by the Metropolitan Cathedral of Christ the King.

From here, cross over the traffic lights into Hope Street. As you drive along here you will see many restaurants and bars that now meet the gastronomic needs of Liverpudlians.

First though, as you approach the traffic lights at Myrtle Street and Hardman Street, you will see the Philharmonic Hotel on the right-hand corner. We shall visit this shortly.

Across the junction and on the left, you will see The Philharmonic Hall.

On the other corner you will see the building that was once the School for the Blind. Cross the traffic lights, and park anywhere on Hope Street that it is safe to do so.

There are plenty of pay-and-display places on Hope Street and the surrounding roads, however, you are going to be here for the full two hours – at least, so feed the meter!

I recommend ¾ hour to explore this part of Hope Street and Rodney Street on foot, but add on an additional hour if you intend to visit the exhibition and home of Edward Chambré Hardman.

There is a two-hour limit on the parking machines, so you may have to return to your car to buy extra time, especially if you decide to sample the delights of one of Hope Street's many restaurants or hostelries.

Contents

Route Map

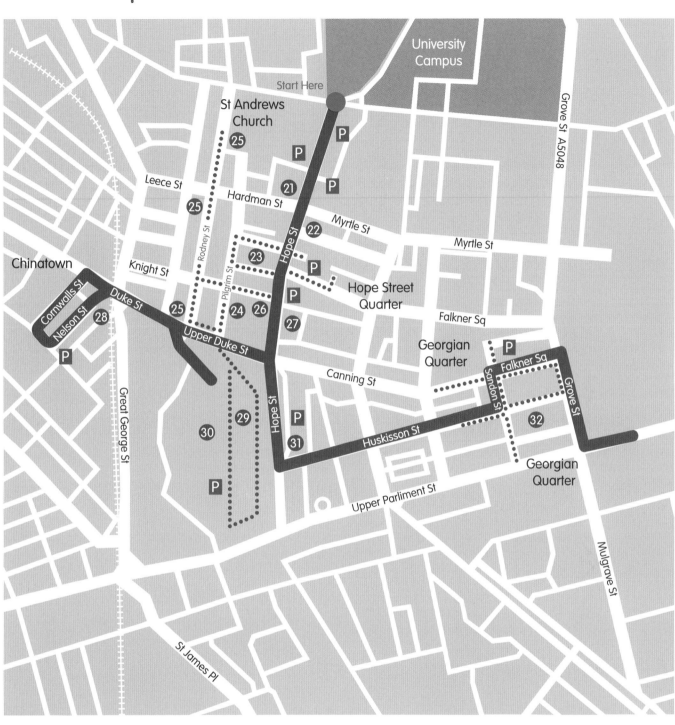

University Campus

Start Here

St Andrews Church

25

Leece St

21

Hardman St

25

P

P

22

Myrtle St

Myrtle St

Rodney St

23

Hope St

P

Chinatown

Knight St

Pilgrim St

P

Hope Street Quarter

Cornwalls St

Duke St

25

24 26

P

Falkner Sq

Nelson St

28

Upper Duke St

27

Georgian Quarter

P

Falkner Sq

P

Great George St

29

Hope St

Sandon St

Grove St

30

P

31

Huskisson St

32

Georgian Quarter

P

Upper Parliment St

Mulgrave St

St James Pl

Grove St A5048

Canning St

Key

Start Here — Starting Point

1 — Map Reference

Driving Route

Walking Route

P — Parking Points

Railway

Pool of Life & Culture : Part 2

Towards the end of the Tour we shall be driving through parts of the Georgian Quarter of Liverpool, and I will talk a little about the history and architecture of that area later. However, we are coming into Georgian Liverpool now, which is why I recommend that you park your car, and spend the next part of the Tour on foot.
I shall begin by telling you something about the fascinating people and places of this half of Hope Street, and the adjacent streets; beginning with the fabulous Philharmonic Pub (make sure to go into the Gent's Urinals), and our renowned Philharmonic Concert Hall.

The Philharmonic Hotel

The fabulous Philharmonic Hotel and Dining Rooms – locally known just as the 'Phil' Pub, not only serves a fine pint with good humour and happy fellowship, but the building itself is another of the City's architectural gems. It was designed and built, between 1898 and 1900, by Walter Thomas and School of Art craftsmen, and it is a main feature on all the guided tour trails – not just mine.

This is because of some very attractive carved copper panels; and fine, intricate plaster ceilings, which are illuminated by crystal chandeliers. Carved woodwork and delicate mosaics adorn the walls, and these add to the impression that one is in some sort of theatrical set rather than in a pub.

Visitors always pay special attention to the remarkable gent's urinals, which are made from a particularly attractive roseate marble, and are a must for any tourist – but do check that they are unoccupied first, as it could prove problematic to be closely scrutinising the facilities, especially whilst they are in use – regardless of your gender! Because of this risk, one woman visitor was too embarrassed to look at the urinals herself, even though assured that they were empty. She asked a couple of young men if they would be so kind as to take her camera and photograph these architectural wonders on her behalf. Like all Scousers, they were very willing to oblige and to be given the opportunity to be helpful to a stranger. However, as these lads were indeed typical Scousers, their sense of humour took over, and when the woman had her photos developed and printed, ready to show her friends and family, full frontal images of the urinals were not her only souvenir.

Who knows, perhaps this woman was to be inspired by these urinals; rather like an aspiring pop-star who used them during the 1970s. The manufacturer's name on the urinals, which is inscribed on them, is 'Adamant' and, as this young man was standing in a urinal with his future in his hands, he was inspired to rename himself 'Adam Ant'!

Two small snugs in the pub are decoratively named Brahms and Liszt, typical of the Scouse sense of humour, and the Dining Rooms on the first floor are also sumptuously decorated in carved wood, stained glass, and intricate mosaic work. Former US President Bill Clinton, whilst a student at Oxford, had a girlfriend from Liverpool. On his visits with her to her home town, their favourite pub was 'The Phil', and it retains that same popularity with the student community.

The exterior of the pub is also noteworthy for its fine stonework, but especially for the ornamental gates made from wrought iron and gilded copper, in a very elaborate Art-Nouveau style. I heartily recommend a visit to, and a drink in 'The Phil', and don't miss the urinals – in more senses than one!

Inside the Philharmonic Pub

Those famous urinals!

To Find Out More:
Merseyside Campaign for Real Ale
www.merseycamra.org.uk

The Philharmonic Dining Rooms
Phone: 0151 707 2837
http://www.visitbritain.com/

The Philharmonic Hall and Liverpool's Musical Heritage

The Philharmonic Hall

The stunning Philharmonic Hall is reputed to have the finest acoustics of any classical concert hall in the world, and it is the home of the Liverpool Philharmonic Symphony Orchestra. This is an orchestra of the highest international standing and it was also the first in the world to have its own concert hall. However, this was not to be built until some years after the Orchestra had been established.

The original 'Philharmonic Society', now the 'Royal Liverpool Philharmonic Society' (RLPS), gave its first performance on the 19th March 1840, in 'Mr Lassell's Saloon', which was a dancing academy in Great Richmond Street. However, these were cramped quarters and, in 1843, the increasing public support and larger audiences necessitated a move. This was to the hall of the recently built Collegiate School in Shaw Street, Everton – then known as Liverpool College. However, the school hall was not ideal, either acoustically or in terms of other amenities and, in 1844, the committee of the Philharmonic Society instructed the architect John Cunningham to prepare plans for a new concert hall. This was to be built on the newly developed and highly fashionable Hope Street. Cunningham's first plan was rejected as being too small, but his second was accepted, as this was for a hall designed to seat 2,100 people, and with 250 orchestra and chorus seats. The foundation stone of the new building was laid in 1846, and construction began the following year.

The new concert hall was opened in 1849, and the Liverpool Philharmonic Orchestra went on to establish itself as one of the finest orchestras and choruses in Britain.

Throughout the latter half of the 19th century the reputation of the Orchestra was growing in stature, and they were now performing in concert venues all over Britain. This recognition grew internationally, especially during the early decades of the 20th century. Also, back home in Liverpool, the Philharmonic Hall was attracting large crowds of concert-goers for each performance. However, on July 5th 1933, a loose spark in the organ loft started a fire that swept rapidly through the building. Despite the best efforts of the Fire Brigade, the Philharmonic Hall was completely destroyed. Nevertheless, the RLPS and the people of Liverpool were not daunted and, by 1939, sufficient funds had been raised to see the present Philharmonic Hall erected in its place, on the same site.

The new Hall was designed and built by Herbert J Rowse, who designed many of Liverpool's most famous buildings during the 1930s, as well as, and as we have already seen, the entrance portals to the Mersey Tunnel. Rowse decorated his new concert hall with Egyptian motifs, because his design concept was influenced by the

recent discovery of the tomb of the Pharaoh Tutankhamen. Indeed, Egyptian ornamentation forms one of the main design elements of Art-Deco for the same reason.

The auditorium of the Hall is adorned with very appealing panels, each showing Greco-Roman female figures performing various dances, and in equally various states of undress. These were, and no doubt still are, of great interest to young schoolboys who visit the hall for concerts and 'music-appreciation lectures'. In the grand foyer are two large sculpted panel scenes, showing 'Apollo being instructed by Pan', and 'Apollo enchanting the world by his art'. All of these were sculpted by Edmund C Thompson, and they enhance the overall aesthetic appeal of the building.

> "In the entrance foyer of the Concert Hall is a memorial plaque that is dedicated to the musicians in the ship's band, aboard the ill-fated transatlantic liner, RMS Titanic"

On the night of April 14th 1912, these gallant men in an attempt to keep up morale amongst the desperate and panicking passengers, continued to play as the vessel was sinking. They were heard by some of the few passengers who had managed to get into the lifeboats, to be playing the hymn 'Nearer My God To Me', as the stricken vessel broke up and slipped beneath the freezing waters of the North Atlantic Ocean. All the musicians perished, and their names are recorded on the plaque in tribute to their own courage and sacrifice. When the wreck of the Titanic was discovered in 1985, subsequent salvage expeditions recovered many items from the surrounding

debris field. Amongst these was the cornet owned by one of the musicians. You will learn more about the Liverpool-registered Titanic, in the Chapter on 'The Liverpool Waterfront'.

Film also has a place at the 'Phil': The Concert Hall houses a large, magnificently ornate, and full-size cinema screen that rises up through the floor of the concert stage, and on which are shown seasons of classic films. This is now the only fully functioning such elevating cinema screen surviving in Europe.

Always imaginative, in 1994, the Royal Liverpool Philharmonic Orchestra was the first in the world to play underwater: During the special 60th Anniversary Celebration of the opening of the Mersey Tunnel between Liverpool and Birkenhead, the underwater roadway had been closed to vehicles for a day, to allow people to walk through it. The orchestra played at the centre of the tunnel, directly on the boundary between Liverpool and the Wirral, entertaining the thousands of pedestrians who passed through it with a high quality performance, conducted by Carl Davis.

Everyone knows about Liverpool's connection with the world of rock and pop music, because of The Beatles and other home-grown 'popular' musicians and singers; and an illustrious association it is too. Indeed, I was very much part of that scene during my teenage years; being the lead singer in a couple of pop groups throughout the 1960s.

Nevertheless, one thing that the existence of the 'Phil' demonstrates is that our association with classical and more 'serious' music is just as distinguished.
In 1901, the first performance of Elgar's 'Pomp and Circumstance March No 1' was given at the original Philharmonic Hall. The composer dedicated it to Alfred

A carol concert at the Philharmonic Hall

Rodewald who, at the turn of the century, was a great patron of the 'Phil'. Also, the first performance of Benjamin Britten's 'Young Person's Guide to the Orchestra' was given at the modern 'Phil', in 1946.

The list of Principal Conductors of the Royal Liverpool Philharmonic Orchestra reads like a 'Who's Who' of 20th century classical music. This includes Zeebrugge, Bruch, Richter, Boult, Halle, Sir Henry Wood – who established the Prom Concerts at the Royal Albert Hall – Sir Malcolm Sargent, Sir Charles Groves, Libor Pesek, and Sir Simon Rattle.

Likewise, the roll-call of world-renowned artists who have conducted, performed, or worked in the City is amazing, and includes Franz Liszt, Felix Mendelssohn, Nicollo Paganini, Sergei Rachmaninov, Johann Strauss Snr., Pablo Casals, and Yehudi Menhuin. Also, Jenny Lind – The Swedish Nightingale – sang here; John Philip Sousa was here, in 1905; Giacomo Puccini, in 1911; and George Gershwin, in 1929.

Vasily Petrenko joined The RLPO as Chief Conductor in 2006 and is recognised as one of the exceptional musicians of his generation. And so, for more than 150 years the Royal Liverpool Philharmonic Society, its orchestra, and its choir, have been at the heart and soul of Liverpool and Merseyside's cultural life. Long may they continue to be so!

To Find Out More:
Royal Liverpool Philharmonic Society
Phone: Reception: 0151 210 2895
Box Office: 0151 709 3789
www.liverpoolphil.com

On Hope Street stands the building that was once the School for the Blind, hence the carvings of dextrous hands around the building. (You can find out more concerning the Liverpool Blind School, in the Chapter 'Liverpool Lost and Found'.)
Off Hope Street on the right, just across from the Philharmonic Hall, is Rice Street; walk down here and you will come to Ye Cracke Inn, on the right.

Ye Cracke

Ye Cracke Inn has been at the heart of the artistic and musical subcultures of the City for generations.

It was in this pub that John Lennon would skive off from his studies, at the nearby Art College, and he is said to have met his future wife Cynthia at a dance there, and then taken her to the Cracke for a drink afterwards. After closing-time, John took her to Stuart Sutcliffe's flat in Gambier Terrace, to 'cement' their relationship. There has been a pub on this site for over 150 years, and Ye Cracke was once called the Ruthin Castle, but only a small part of the pub is actually a listed building.

The most significant part of this popular watering hole is the 1900s 'War Room' (or 'War Office'), which is a small snug, in which drinkers would discuss Britain's overseas military operations during the Second World War. A gloriously complicated and colourful painting adorns one wall of the main room and, on the opposite wall, is an artist's impression of what the Battle of Waterloo looked like – although what the Beatles' Yellow Submarine is doing there is anybody's guess!

I have very happy memories of the Cracke when, as a young man of 18 or 19 during the 1960s, I would regularly spend Friday nights here with my mates. We would sing along to the songs of Bob Dylan and others, accompanied by anyone who could play an acoustic guitar. We would swig vast quantities of Newcastle Brown Ale straight out of the bottles – before that became fashionable, and bang out the rhythm of the music on the large, wooden tables. Halcyon days! Do call in to the Cracke to sample its atmosphere, perhaps have a pint and something to eat, and get to know some of the locals or the students who frequent the pub. You will have fun!

To Find Out More:
Ye Old Cracke
Phone: 0151 709 4171
http://www.beerintheevening.com/pubs/s/44/4454/Ye_Olde_Cracke/Liverpool

Merseyside Campaign for Real Ale
www.merseycamra.org.uk

Walk down Rice Street to Pilgrim Street, and turn left here. You will immediately see the Pilgrim Pub, with its swinging sign, on the right. This old and narrow road will then take you past No 38 Pilgrim Street – the old Tuck Shop of the Institute Boys School, and then to the ticket office for the Edward Chambré Hardman House.

Ye Cracke Inn

Across Pilgrim Street, at the bottom of Rice Street, is the curious Pilgrim Pub.

A passageway leads you from the street, through the yard of the pub, and into the main lounge and bar areas. Even the yard is an attractive place to sit and drink – covered over with trellis as it is, and with comfortable seating. The food here is pretty good, as is the range of beers and wines. However, what make the place special are its atmosphere and the friendliness of the clientele. Do give it a try sometime.

> **To Find Out More:**
> The Pilgrim Pub
> Phone: 0151 709 2302
> http://www.beerintheevening.com/
> pubs/s/83/8395/Pilgrim/Liverpool

On Pilgrim Street, at its corner with Mount Street, stands number 38. Clearly this was once a shop and it is now a private home. However, in the days when the nearby Liverpool Institute for Performing Arts was a boys' grammar school, this was the local Tuck Shop.

I would visit here sometimes as I had a number of friends who attended the Institute. I was fascinated by the fact that, not only was this tiny, dimly-lit shop run by a very old, grey, and wrinkled woman, with sharp features and even sharper personality, but the walls were lined with shelves.

Most of these were laden with glass jars containing sweets and toffees of all sorts; including such exotic delights as Uncle Joe's Mint Balls; Pear Drops; Aniseed Balls – a particular favourite of mine; Cinder Toffee; Pineapple Chunks – another favourite; and of course, Everton Toffee.

However, the top shelf was different, as this contained about 15 to 20 ornately-shaped containers, some plain and some decorated, and these were all spaced out evenly. It was rumoured amongst the boys, that these contained the cremated ashes of the shopkeeper's relatives and, taking advantage of the poor woman's slight deafness, it was a standard game to ask her for "2 ounces of Uncle Fred" or "a quarter of Great Granny, please", at the same time as ordering portions of Mint Imperials, or bars of Crunchie!

After passing the 'Tuck Shop of Cremated Delights' and by strolling along Pilgrim Street, you will be going down one of the oldest streets in this part of Georgian Liverpool. This is clear from the houses, back gardens, and unusual buildings that line both sides of this narrow road.

On the right, at the rear of No. 59 Rodney Street, is the entrance to the exhibition that is dedicated to the life and work of the remarkable photographer Edward Chambré Hardman.

His home and studio, which are now maintained by the National Trust, are located on Rodney Street – the next road down – but you can only access the exhibition from Pilgrim Street. Here is his story.

The long career of Edward Chambré Hardman ran from 1923, until his retirement in 1966, and he lived in Rodney Street from 1948, until his death in 1988.

Chambré Hardman spent his working life taking portraits of Lancashire and Cheshire society, which was a lucrative profession. This financial security enabled him to indulge his private passion for recording images of, and the passing of time in and around Liverpool, Chester, and the North West.

"These photographs, together with his landscapes from around Britain, and his portraits of the leading 20th century entertainers who visited Liverpool, form a record of the most significant 20th century incidents and individuals in the region"

Hardman was born in County Dublin in Ireland, in 1898, and he was the son of a keen amateur photographer.
Following in his father's footsteps, by the age of fourteen young Edward had entered and won a number of photographic competitions, in a variety of local and national magazines. However, in 1917, he took a commission in the Ghurkha Rifles in India, where he stayed until 1922, and this was then his full time career. Nevertheless, whilst stationed in the sub-continent, his interest in photography not only continued but his skills developed, and it was in that country that he experimented with taking some remarkable soft-focus images.

Whilst in India he met a fellow officer, Kenneth Burrell, and they decided to become partners and to establish a professional photography business together. In 1922, they left the British Army, travelled to Liverpool, and launched the photography company of 'Burrell and Hardman Ltd', at 51a Bold Street.

In 1926, the now successful company took on a young graduate from Liverpool Institute High School for Girls (now Blackburne House) in Hope Street. This was Margaret Hamilton, and she became a skilled photographer in her own right, and an integral part of the business. Edward and Margaret fell in love and, in 1932, they married, and their love was deep and sustained. However, by 1929, Burrell had decided to leave Liverpool and, from that time onwards, Hardman ran the business with his staff and later with Margaret, retaining the original name of the partnership. He and Burrell remained close friends until the latter's death, some years later.

In 1948, the business moved to 59 Rodney Street, and 'Burrell and Hardman' became the fashionable choice for portrait photography. Hardman's reputation resulted in him being commissioned by the Liverpool Playhouse Theatre to photograph the up-and-coming stars of the time. These included Ivor Novello, Michael Redgrave, Robert Donat, and Patricia Routledge. He also photographed many of the most prominent individuals, families, locations, and events of the 20th century, and his collected works are now a priceless record of the times.

Although he officially retired in 1966, Hardman continued to take photographs, and exhibit his pictures. However, in 1970 his wife Margaret died, his world collapsed, and he became a despondent and frail old man, fading from public view.

Edward Chambre Hardman

Hardman's house

Fortunately however, in 1979, he came to the attention of the local Social Services Department who saw to his care and well-being. As the Social Workers looked after him, and tidied up around him, they realised that there was an important collection in his home and they contacted Peter Hagerty, the Exhibitions Director of the Open Eye Art Gallery in Liverpool.

In 1980, Peter persuaded Hardman to set up a trust to protect his work and legacy and, upon the photographer's death in 1988, the Edward Chambré Hardman Trust took control of his house and his collection. By the 1990s however, the Trust acknowledged that they could no longer continue to maintain and preserve this unique collection, and they asked for help.

A partnership was then formed between Liverpool City Council, the National Trust, and The National Museum of Photography Film and Television in Bradford. Together, these organisations successfully bid for a grant from the Heritage Lottery Fund, to restore the house and its contents with a view to opening it to the public. This was done in September 2004, and now the National Trust manages the property, which is open to the public all year round.

"Inside, visitors will find exhibitions on Hardman's life, times, and works, and also astounding displays of prints, negatives, glass plates, cameras, wartime ration books, letters, and other memorabilia"

As well as viewing the house, and selections from the photographic archive, there is a computer presentation detailing the history of Rodney Street and the story of Edward Chambré Hardman himself. However, this is not a free-flow exhibition, tours can only be taken at pre-set times during the day. These are frequent, but are often half-an-hour apart. Consequently, it is as well to telephone first to check on times and availability, although tours can be booked just by turning up. For reference, the fully-guided tours are well-worthwhile, and take a little over an hour to complete.

By doing it this way, you can wander around Rodney Street and its fascinating environs, whilst waiting for your tour time to come around. However, do please remember that the entrance to the House is actually in Pilgrim Street, directly at the rear, not on Rodney Street.

It will be time well spent, as you shall discover.

To Find Out More:

The Edward Chambré Hardman Collection
http://www.mersey-gateway.org/chambrehardman/

The National Trust: The Hardmans' House
59 Rodney Street, Liverpool L1 9EX
Bookings: 0151 709 6261
www.nationaltrust.org.uk
email: thehardmanshouse@nationaltrust.org.uk

At the end of Hope Street, we turn right onto Upper Duke Street, with the Anglican Cathedral on our left. We are now walking in front of Mornington Terrace, which is a group of beautiful Georgian Houses. This was once the site of a bowling green, adjacent to the windmill that once stood where the Oratory now stands, in front of the Cathedral.
We now turn right into Rodney Street.
We shall walk down Rodney Street on the odd-numbered side first, and come back again, on the even-numbered side, as far as Mount Street. As you walk, do take the time to look at the architecture, which is very fine, and also look out for plaques on the house fronts. These indicate the former residences or birthplaces of a number of significant Liverpudlians, who achieved either national or local fame.

Rodney Street – Part One

Rodney Street is named after Admiral George Brydges, who was awarded the title of 1st Baron Rodney after his victory at the Battle of Les Saintes against the French, in the West Indies, in 1782. Building of large, terraced houses began in 1783, and continued for some decades. Originally, wealthy merchants set up home here but, increasingly during the 19th century and later, it became the place where doctors and consultants established their practices and their homes. Indeed, the street is often locally referred to as 'Liverpool's Harley Street' because of the large number of private medical practices that are situated here. Now, almost every sort of medical practitioner represented here, from standard – though expensive – GPs to various specialists; from dentists to fertility clinics; and from practitioners of the Alexander Technique to Homoeopathists. All human life is here!
Rodney Street is however, more that its occupants; it is an example of the best of Georgian City architecture, and to stroll down the pavement is to be presented with a terrace of different yet harmonious period doorways and frontages.

The first house of any significance on the street is number 59, the home of **Edward Chambré Hardman**, about whom we have already heard.

Rodney Street

Over the road, at number 80, is the home of the author and biographer, **Lytton Strachey**.

Strachey (1880-1932) was born in London, but came to Liverpool to read history at the University of Liverpool. He then studied at Cambridge, where he made friends with such eminent people as John Maynard Keynes, Leonard and Virginia Woolf, and Clive Bell. He became, with them, a member of the intellectual and sexually-nonconformist Bloomsbury Group and his first great success, and his most famous achievement, was 'Eminent Victorians', which he wrote in 1918. This is a collection of four short biographies of Victorian heroes, written in a frank and uncompromising style, and which exposes the hypocrisy of the Victorian social milieu.

Continuing down the odd-numbered side of Rodney Street, we come to number 35. This was the first house to be built in the street, was erected in 1783, and leased by the banker **William Roscoe**. This important 18th century character was a significant founding-father of the City, and there are many references to him throughout this book, as you have already seen.

Further along, at number 11, lived **Nicholas Monserrat** (1910-1979), who was the author of many seafaring tales, including 'The Cruel Sea'. As a boy of around 16, I was privileged enough to be invited to have tea with the author, whom I found to be charming and exceptionally bright. He was fun to talk to and, because of his own background as a Naval Officer, he told me many thrilling tales of his exploits.

Number 9 was the home of **Arthur Clough** (1819-1861) who was a well-known Victorian poet. He had studied at Rugby public school, under the headmastership of Dr Thomas Arnold (of Tom Brown's Schooldays fame), and who made many important reforms to the English Public School system.

Arthur was a prodigy, and he became a favourite of Arnold who acted as a surrogate father to him, encouraging the boy's remarkable intellect and literary gifts. Clough had a fascinating life, including going over to join the French Revolution on the side of the insurgents, and later, working with his wife's cousin, Florence Nightingale, on her hospital reforms. Clough died at the early age of 42.

Anne Clough (1820-1892) was Arthur's sister, and she too went on to great things. She was great campaigner for women's suffrage and education, and went on to establish a number of schools and colleges for women. She also became the first woman principal of Newnham College, founded in 1871, which was initially a residence for women who were attending lectures at Cambridge University. Anne was invited to take charge and, by 1879, the College was fully established with its own tutorial staff.

Now we come to St Andrew's Church.

St. Andrew's Church

Towards the end of Rodney Street, as it nears Mount Pleasant, you will find yourself on the corner of Maryland Street. Here stand the ruins of Saint Andrew's Church. This was opened in 1815, to serve a sizeable Scots settlement in the district, and was once described as 'an ornament to the Town'. However, having been unused for many years, and following a severe fire in 1983, it has been left neglected and derelict ever since. Indeed, one of the towers had to be demolished for safety, before it fell down.

The church and its adjoining Sunday School building, both of which are Grade II Listed Buildings – for all the good this status did them – together with the Cemetery, were bought privately in 1988. The buyer was a doctor from Wolverhampton, who announced plans to restore the buildings and to re-open them as office accommodation and medical consulting rooms, and planning permission for these proposals was granted in 1992. However, nothing whatever was done to repair or redevelop the church, despite Liverpool City Council issuing the owner with 'Repairs Notices', in 2001.

Fortunately however, the future of the church now appears to have been secured, because it was acquired by Liverpool City Council. They committed £250,000 for emergency repairs to the building and to improve the site.

This put a halt to the degeneration of the building, but its long-term future is still being discussed. But the popular English Heritage Open Days – where hidden treasures across the UK open their doors to the public – have seen St Andrew's Church welcoming visitors to learn about conservation work, including stonemasons using 200-year-old skills to carry out repairs.

> "The churchyard of St. Andrew's is interesting, because of the fascinating pyramid-shaped tomb belonging to a man called William McKenzie"

He was an early promoter of the railways and an avid poker player, who died in 1868. To guarantee his success at cards, legend has it that he sold his soul to the Devil. According to the strict terms of his will, and in an attempt to thwart the Devil from claiming his due, McKenzie's reasoned that if his body was not buried within the ground then the Devil could not claim his soul.

Consequently, or so the story goes, his corpse remains under the pyramid, seated at a card table, and holding a winning hand of cards. A ghostly figure, wearing a frock coat and top hat, is frequently sighted around Rodney Street and its side streets and alleys.

This is believed to be the restless spectre of William McKenzie; perhaps the Devil is extracting his due after all!

McKenzie's tomb at St Andrew's Church

To Find Out More:
Edward J Kelly
Haunted St Andrews Church
http://www.edwardjkelly.com/standrewsgraveyard.htm

Rodney Street – Part Two

Crossing over the road, we now look at the houses on the even-numbered side of the street, beginning with numbers 2-10 Rodney Street, which are where the administrative headquarters of Liverpool John Moores University are located.

The City's links to America have always been of vital economic and social significance and, because of the cotton trade, Liverpool supplied, funded, and supported the Confederate cause during the American Civil War. Number 4 Rodney Street was the home of **James Maury** (1774-1840) who, appointed to the post by George Washington, was the United States Consul to Liverpool from 1790 to 1829. In the 20th century, the building became a private nursing home, and it was here, on 19th September 1934, that **Brian Samuel Epstein** was born.

In adult life, Epstein ran his family's music stores – NEMS (North of England Music Stores), in Great Charlotte Street and Whitechapel in Liverpool.

"On 28th October 1961, a youth called into the Whitechapel branch asking for a copy of a record called 'My Bonnie' by then unknown group The Beatles"

Brian Epstein did not stock the recording and, priding himself on being able to meet his customer's needs, he decided to search it out. When he got the copy and played it, he wanted to hear the group for himself. So, on 9th November 1961, he tracked them to a seedy, basement warehouse club called 'The Cavern', in Mathew Street, where the group were playing to local office workers during the lunch-hour. It was here that he heard The Beatles for the first time and in due course he became their manager. The rest, as they say, is history.

In 1967, whilst The Beatles were in India learning Transcendental Meditation from the Maharishi Mahesh Yogi, they received some tragic news.

On 27th August, Brian Epstein had died in his London flat, from an overdose of the drug 'Carbital'.
He was only 32 years of age. The man who set the Beatles on their road to fame and fortune now lies at rest in the Jewish Cemetery, Long Lane, Aintree, to the north of the City.

At number 34 lived **Henry Booth**, who was a founder and director of Liverpool and Manchester Railway, about which we have already heard.

Number 54 was the home of the remarkable **Dr William Henry Duncan** (1805-1863). He was born in Liverpool, at 108 Seel Street, which in the 1950s and 60s became the

Blue Angel Night Club. Duncan's father was a merchant, whilst his mother was sister to Dr James Currie. (See the article on St. Johns Gardens and Dr Currie.) Graduating as an MD from Edinburgh University in 1829, Duncan began practising in his home City. Soon he became an outspoken critic against the appalling standards of public health and hygiene in Liverpool, and he complained about the evils of "the black spot on the Mersey", and of the high rates of mortality to be found here.

These were caused by the squalid living conditions, and by a lack of clean water and sanitation, particularly but not exclusively to be found amongst the poor. This situation reached disaster proportions when, in 1845, famine flooded the Town with thousands of destitute Irish immigrants, fleeing from the Irish Potato Famine.

As a direct consequence of this massive and sudden increase in the population of Liverpool, the City acquired statutory powers and, when the Liverpool Sanitary Act of 1846 was enacted on 1st January 1847, Dr. Duncan was appointed as Liverpool's – and the world's – first Medical Officer of Public Health: This in a year when 300,000 people came to Liverpool from Ireland.

Duncan created a Public Health Service and staffed this without any model to guide him. He also began to address social conditions, and to fight the now regular outbreaks of typhus and cholera that were rife across Liverpool. Another battler against the disease was the amazing Kitty Wilkinson, who is referred to elsewhere.

Duncan's appointment pre-dated a national Act by several months and his unceasing work in the poor and overcrowded parts of the City, plus his overall Public Health schemes, had a profound impact on Liverpool. These led to substantial and dramatic reductions in mortality rates, and Dr Duncan's methods were soon being emulated in towns and cities across the country, and the British Empire.

At number 62, **William Ewart Gladstone** (1809-1898) was born. He was Prime Minister four times; 1868-74, 1880-05, 1886, and 1892-4; and although Queen Victoria found him boring, he and his successive Liberal Governments were responsible for some significant 19th century social reforms.

We will continue along Rodney Street, but only as far as Mount Street, because we shall now turn left here and walk back up to Hope Street; passing the Liverpool Institute for the Performing Arts, and the former Art College, as we do so.

A Case History, by sculptor John King, stands outside LIPA

LIPA – The 'Fame' School

Halfway along Mount Street, which runs between Hope Street and Rodney Street, you will find the 'Liverpool Institute for Performing Arts', sometimes known as 'The Fame School' or simply as 'LIPA'.

The building was originally opened, in 1837, as the Mechanics Institute, but in due course it became The Liverpool Institute Boys' Grammar School. Paul McCartney became a pupil here in 1953, and was joined a year later by George Harrison. However, the birth of LIPA came about when, in May 1989, Sir George Martin – the Beatles former producer – introduced now Sir Paul to an enthusiastic man named Mark Featherstone-Witty.

Just before this meeting, Paul had made a home movie about his time as a pupil at the Institute, and this had meant him wandering around the then derelict and empty Institute building. He was struck by the idea of trying to save his old school, if only he could find some way of turning it to a practical use – a necessity if public sector funding was going to be involved. The idea of a 'music school' was mentioned to him by a Toxteth resident, but needed the right person to help realise this vision, and Mark was just that man! Paul told Mark about his movie and his hopes for his old school building; and Mark told Paul about his own ideas for

a Fame School: Serendipity struck, and the dream of LIPA was about to become reality! The challenges were big, and involved devising a new performing arts curriculum; renovating a Grade II Listed derelict building; and gaining bureaucratic, industry, and professional support. Whilst Paul McCartney donated £3 million to the project, it took the support of many major partners to raise the £20m finally needed but, in due course, the money was raised and Liverpool Institute for Performing Arts was founded in 1996.

"LIPA is now one of the most significant learning centres for the performing arts locally, regionally, nationally, and internationally; indeed, a third of the student body comes from overseas"

Some 22 people apply for each available place, and 75% of traceable graduates (it is easy to lose track of international graduates) after three years, still work in arts and entertainment. LIPA graduates appear on TV, on stage in the West End, and they perform in international and regional shows. They have hit singles and albums, and they are working for companies such as Sony Music, MTV, the Discovery Channel, Lucas Arts, and on the Harry Potter films. They also engineer for Britney Spears, and produce for the Artic Monkeys.

Adjacent to LIPA, facing onto Hope Street, stands the former Liverpool Art College building. John Lennon was accepted here as a student in 1957. It was here that he met and made a close friendship with Stu Sutcliffe, about whom we shall hear more shortly. John also met his first wife Cynthia here and, in the college basement, the three friends would regularly be joined by Paul McCartney and George Harrison, who would come in from the grammar school next door to share lunch, talk about music, and to practice playing their guitars. The Art College Building is no longer a place for study, the Art Faculties have moved out to other locations within the Liverpool JMU campus. The building has been converted into apartments.

Outside LIPA, on the pavement at the top of Mount Street, stands a fascinating piece of public sculpture – with which Liverpool is increasingly well-supplied. This work is called 'A Case History' and is by the Canadian artist John King, who was assisted in the work by local artist Ken Reid. It is a pile of around 30 pieces of different types and sizes of travelling bags and suitcases, which are cast in silica-based concrete. Unveiled in 1998, and costing £45,000 of National Lottery money, the luggage replicates bags and luggage carried by passengers and porters, who have used Liverpool as a ship passenger terminal. However, the bags are worth a closer look, as many of them have tags with the names of people who made a significant local impact. See if you can find tags for Arthur Askey, the Beatles, the late Cllr Lady Margaret Simey, and Sir Giles Gilbert Scott – the architect of Liverpool Cathedral. A number of the suitcases are also cast from their owners' original cases, including one of Sir Paul McCartney's guitar cases, and the briefcase in which Mark carried the first £50,000 raised for the LIPA project!

To Find Out More:
Liverpool Institute for Performing Arts
Phone: 0151 330 3000
www.lipa.ac.uk

Diagonally across Hope Street, from LIPA and the Art College, you will see Blackburne House.

Set slightly back from Hope Street, and commanding the whole block between Falkner Street and Blackburne Place, stands Blackburne House. This was built in 1788, as a detached mansion 'out in the country' by John Blackburne, who originally came from Warrington, where the family seat was at Orford Hall.

Prior to building his grand mansion on the outskirts of Liverpool Town, Blackburne established himself as a salt refiner, for which he was renowned (see Chapter: 'Ancient and Modern'). He became exceptionally wealthy, hence his being able to afford such a splendid home, and he became the Lord Mayor of Liverpool, in 1760.

However, he also generated significant income through his active participation in, and encouragement of the Slave Trade.

Blackburne became a member of the Liverpool 'establishment' and, as such, he came into conflict with the rising tide of more radical local businessmen and politicians, such as William Huskisson MP, Dr James Currie, and William Roscoe.

These men, amongst many others, were promoters of Catholic Emancipation; benefactors and encouragers of the working classes; and particularly, advocates for the abolition of Slavery.

(For more on Slavery, see Chapter: 'The Liverpool Waterfront'.)

As the movement to bring an end to the 'Triangular Trade' gained momentum in the Town, Blackburne was one of the most vocal advocates for its retention. Meanwhile, in 1807, an eager young man named George Holt, moved to Liverpool from Rochdale in Lancashire.

He intended to make his fortune, and indeed he did – becoming a very successful and extremely wealthy cotton broker and merchant. He soon established a family home and estate at Sudley House in Mossley Hill, to the south of the City near Sefton Park. George had a large and equally successful family, and two of his sons, Philip and Alfred, went on to found the Ocean Steamship Company and the Blue Funnel Shipping Line – both based in Liverpool.

Despite the fact that he made most of his money from cotton, Holt was also an abolitionist, so it was a nice irony when, in 1844, he bought Blackburne House from John Blackburne.

George became a great benefactor to the Town, particularly in the field of education, and he had acquired Blackburne House not as a home for himself, but as a place to develop his ideas for the education of women.

This was because he was also an ardent advocate of Women's Rights and, as such, and in common with so many other leading Liverpudlians at that time, he was an enlightened man. Holt immediately offered the large building to the directors of the

Blackburne House

Mechanic's Institute across the road, which in due course became Liverpool Institute Boys' School, and is currently the Liverpool Institute for the Performing Arts (LIPA). Holt wished to see Blackburne House established as a girls' school, in memory of his daughter Emma Jane, who had recently died. At this time, there were no other girls' schools in Liverpool, and so Blackburne House officially opened as the first such school in the Town, on 5th August 1844.

With over 300 pupils in its first year, it offered lessons in English, reading, spelling, grammar, arithmetic, drawing, vocal music, natural philosophy, natural history, chemistry, needlework, and callisthenics. The curriculum was impressive even by our modern standards, but particularly so for girls and young women in Victorian England. Such was the school's success, that courses were established at Blackburne House for the training of women as teachers, 'for the benefit of the country at large'.

Blackburne House Girls' School prospered, with George Holt as Director and President, until his death in 1861. The Holt family then handed the entire estate to the Mechanic's Institute in his memory, and a memorial tablet recording this was erected, and can still be seen, above the main staircase inside Blackburne House. The school was taken over by Liverpool City Council in 1905, together with the other schools that were managed by the Mechanic's Institute.

In 1975, Blackburne House was named as a Grade II Listed Building, and it continued as a successful school until 1986, when it was closed. This was because of falling attendance figures due to the overall population decline in Liverpool at that time.

Then, unfortunately, this significant and very attractive building was left derelict until 1992. However, supported by a major fund-raising campaign, the Women's Technology

and Education Centre – then based in Hardman Street – commissioned two women architects to convert the building into a high-quality training and resource centre for women. This opened in 1994, and it has a mission statement, which reads:

"To provide education for women who are disadvantaged, to encourage and enable them to develop their full potential, through the provision of high quality learning and facilities"

Blackburne House is a place where much creative and capacity-building work is delivered by an imaginative and professional team of staff. The courses being offered, and the opportunities being created, are innovative and relevant; particularly in the BME communities. Consequently, I am sure that John Blackburne is rotating in his grave at a rate of knots, whilst George Holt will be 'sleeping the sleep of the just'!

As a footnote; you might like to know that, on certain nights, the sounds of hooves and wooden wheels can be heard clattering over cobblestones in Blackburne Place.

Suddenly, you will see, travelling at a stately pace along the old, Georgian street, a Victorian handsome cab complete with cloaked and hatted driver. However, as this heads towards Hope Street it begins to fade, and it disappears completely by the time that it reaches LIPA.

To Find Out More:
Blackburne House
Phone: 0151 709 4356
http://www.blackburnehouse.co.uk/

Hope Street Restaurants & their Historic Homes

Hope Street is a place to come back to and to indulge yourself in, when you have more time: At the theatres or the Concert Hall; in the excellent pubs; on a romantic night or two at the Hope Street Hotel; or to enjoy an excellent meal in one of the many outstanding restaurants on the Street.

Time was, even as recently as ten years ago, one could count the really good restaurants of Liverpool on the fingers of one hand. These days we are spoilt for choice; and how wonderful that is, especially to a bon-vivant such as me!

Throughout the City there are the broadest range of restaurants; serving food of the highest quality; prepared with skill and passion; and served with warmth and professionalism. These establishments represent every conceivable nationality of cooking; every style; all sorts of ingredients; many techniques of preparation; and available to all budgets. Some of the best chefs now work in Liverpool, in some of the most attractive and inspired establishments. Hope Street is particularly well served with superb places to eat and whilst taste is very much a personal thing, I am confident that you will not be disappointed by visiting any of the restaurants on Hope Street.

Whilst serving food of excellent quality, a number of these eating-houses are in buildings that have interesting histories.

The London Carriage Works at No. 40 Hope Street is part of the **Hope Street Hotel**, a five-star, Conde Nast rated, bistro hotel, which – like the restaurant – just keeps on winning awards.

The building was erected in 1867, as 'The London Carriage Works', where high quality horse-drawn coaches and carriages were built to order. From 1889 until 1903. a firm of booksellers had occupancy, and then it reverted to a carriage works, but this time for motor vehicles.

It was also a furniture shop but, by the early 1990s, it was left empty and derelict. Fortunately, in time to stave off likely demolition, the building was bought by two local entrepreneurs who completely rebuilt and refurbished the attractive premises and, in 2004, they re-opened it as a 48-room luxury, bistro-hotel and a four-star restaurant. Over the door of the building is a bust of General Gordon of Khartoum, who was a national hero at the time of the building's construction. There is also the head of Neptune on another wall; probably reflecting the maritime heritage of the City.

The London Carriage Works restaurant is one of Liverpool's premier establishments and, though expensive, you get what you pay for. And what you get here is of the very highest standards; both in food-quality and service. This is all overseen by award-winning Chef Patron, Paul Askew, whose professionalism and imagination is reflected in his delicious dishes.

On the same side of the road as the Carriage Works you will come

The Hope Street Feast festival takes place in September

to **60 Hope Street Restaurant**, on the corner of Rice Street. This is another building with an interesting history. I first remember this address as being a smoke-filled Jazz club, known as 'Jess's Place'. I would frequent this intimate and somewhat exclusive basement venue in the mid-1960s, as I was getting into the swing of my Hippie period.

Here I would lounge on the bean bags, drinking a new and exotic beer known as lager, and smoking cigarettes made up of exotic blends of tobacco. I would listen to pieces being read by a new breed of poet, such as Roger McGough or Adrian Henry. I would immerse myself also, in really excellent jazz and blues music, which was always played live by a range of excellent bands and solo performers.

Later, the attractive Georgian terraced property became a private nightclub called 'Chauffeurs', and then it reverted to what it had been originally built as – a private home.

Then, as the millennium approached, the building was bought by the two Manning brothers, Gary and Colin, who refurbished it and re-opened it as an extremely stylish and popular, top-class restaurant. Gary oversees the kitchen, whilst Colin Manning oversees front-of-house.

The Hope Street Hotel and London Carriageworks restaurant

To Find Out More:
The London Carriage Works
& Hope Street Hotel
Restaurant: 0151 705 2222
Hotel: 0151 709 3000
www.tlcw.co.uk
www.hopestreethotel.co.uk

60 Hope Street
Phone: 0151 707 6060
www.60hopestreet.com

Pool of Life & Culture : Part 2

The Bronze Doors on the Street Called 'Hope'

Liverpool's third university, Liverpool Hope University, received its charter in 2005, and takes its name from Hope Street.

It is the only ecumenical university in Europe and has campuses in the Childwall and Everton districts of the city.

Because Hope Street connects Liverpool's Catholic and Anglican Cathedrals, this was felt to be the most appropriate name for an institution that had been founded by two of the city's most remarkable religious leaders.

The then Roman Catholic Archbishop of Liverpool, Derek Worlock (1920-1996), and his colleague, Anglican Bishop of Liverpool, David Sheppard (1929-2005) had created the university's foundation college as a symbol of Christian unity.

Both men, through their genuinely ecumenical spirit and tireless efforts, throughout the 1970s and 1980s, broke down the sectarian divide that for so many generations had been an unpleasant characteristic of parts of Liverpool.

In tribute to these genuinely Christian men, a sculpture, by Stephen Broadbent, was unveiled in 2008. This takes the form of two, 15ft high bronze 'doors', each one

The Sheppard-Worlock Statue on Hope Street, designed by Stephen Broadbent

depicting one of the religious leaders, and the symbols of their lives, characters and achievements. The sculpture stands outside the London Carriage Works restaurant.

> You should now return to your car, drive off along Hope Street, passing Blackburne House and the Art College, and turn right at the crossroads, into Upper Duke Street. On the left, you will pass the entrance road into the grounds of the Anglican Cathedral; we shall return here shortly. Halfway down the hill, at the traffic lights, you will see the Blackie and the Chinese Arch to your left. Turn left at the traffic lights, and then immediately right, into Nelson Street, under the Chinese Arch. Park anywhere here that it is safe and convenient to do so. Unless you are dining in Chinatown, I suggest a 15-minute stop here.

Derek Worlock and David Sheppard pictured on Hope Street in the 1980s

At the top of Nelson Street, to the left of the **Chinatown Arch**, stands **'The Blackie'**. This former church, with its curved entrance on a stepped plinth and surmounted by a large dome, is now a popular and successful community arts centre.

Inside, the building is cavernous, with a large central space, a basement chapel area, and also many separate rooms and offices. It acquired its local nickname as a result of the colour of the external stonework, which became progressively dirtier and blacker as pollution levels increased over the decades.

This was prior to the introduction of the Clean Air Act, in the 1960s. In 1987, the filthy, black-stained exterior of the building was thoroughly cleaned, but 'The Blackie' it remains.

> **To Find Out More:**
> **The Blackie**
> Phone: 0151 709 5109
> http://www.theblackie.org.uk/

Liverpool once had the largest and oldest Chinese community outside mainland China, and many Chinese people still live in **Chinatown** and throughout Merseyside.

They are now well-established and well-integrated into the community, whilst retaining their own identity and rich cultural heritage. Liverpool was officially twinned with Shanghai in 2000 and, in so doing, we cemented our links with China.

This partnership has already brought new business developments to both cities.

This can be seen clearly in Chinatown, initially by the magnificent Chinese Arch that constitutes its gateway, and which stands at a height of 44 feet at the top of Nelson Street. This is the largest such arch outside China, and it was designed by Mr Zhang, and built in Shanghai by the South Linyi Garden Building Company. It was then dismantled and shipped to Liverpool, where it was reconstructed by eight Shanghai craftsmen, who worked every day for three months, only taking three days off during that time. The site for the arch was carefully selected by Feng Shui Masters, to ensure good fortune to the local community, and it was unveiled in September 2000. There are 200 dragons carved into the arch, 12 of which are pregnant as this is considered a sign of very good fortune indeed. The five colours relate to the five Chinese elements of earth (yellow), wood (green), metal (white), water (black), and fire (red).

I once observed a European man talking knowledgeably to a small crowd of people who were gathered around him at the foot of the arch. They were listening raptly to his every word, as he explained the mystical,

Liverpool's Chinese Arch on Nelson Street

convoluted, and complex meaning of the Chinese characters that appear in the panel in the centre of the main span of the arch. This really amused me, because he was very wrong, and most certainly NOT one of the official Liverpool Blue Badge City Guides who all really do know their stuff! The characters simply translate as – reading from right to left naturally – 'Middle Kingdom', which was the ancient name for China.

In the heart of Chinatown is the Pagoda – which it is not! However, this otherwise fairly ordinary building is the local Community Centre. Its full name is the 'Community and Cultural Centre of a Hundred Harmonies', and here Chinese culture is enjoyed, preserved, and warmly shared with the rest of the community. Chinese New Year is celebrated with tremendous enthusiasm every year throughout Chinatown, centred on Nelson Street. The Dancing Dragons, the Lion Dance, the fire-crackers, fairground rides, food-stalls, and Bazaar-like atmosphere always attract hundreds of people to join in the fun.

There are many Chinese restaurants here, offering a wide range of gastronomic experiences, some of which require a very adventurous spirit. The local pub is **The Nook** where a former landlady, Mrs Eileen Jones who was renowned for her amazing range of exotic hats, began the tradition that still continues to this day, of shouting 'drinking-up time' and 'last orders' in Chinese. In the immediate vicinity can be found a selection of shops selling Chinese books, videotapes, and art and craft materials. A number of grocery shops and wholesalers supply the widest range of fruit, vegetables, herbs, spices and other ingredients, which enable even the most demanding of chefs to prepare authentic, oriental cuisine.

In 1958, most of the population of Liverpool's Chinatown became extras in a major feature film, playing villagers of war-torn Wang Chang in the film, The Inn of the Sixth Happiness. Filming did not take place in California however but in North Wales, near the village

of Nantmor in the hills above Beddgelert, and fleets of taxis and coaches transported whole families of people to where the walled, Chinese-town had been recreated.

Over 120 local children were part of the team of extras, and Ingrid Bergman, who was the star of the film, treated them to the entire stock of a local ice-cream seller.

She was playing the lead role as Gladys Aylward, the Liverpool Missionary upon whose life-story the film was based.
I was 7 years of age at the time, and on holiday in Wales with my family. From our Butlin's Holiday Camp in Pwllhelli we went on a coach trip to visit the film set. I remember being amazed by the vast number of Chinese people all in one place at one time, and all of them speaking with broad Scouse accents. Ingrid Bergman never brought me an ice cream, though.

Gladys Aylward was born in 1902 and was the daughter of Nonconformist parents. She had a strong Christian faith and was determined to become a missionary. As a young woman, Gladys came to Liverpool where she worked as a parlour maid, whilst she applied in person to the Missionary Society, which was based in the City. But they rejected her. She persisted, but they still refused her, on the grounds that she was too short, young, and inexperienced.

Nothing Gladys could say persuaded the Society that she was up to the job. Nevertheless, she was convinced that God had other plans for her and, in 1930, at her own expense, and unaccompanied, she travelled to China. Here, she joined an elderly Scottish missionary in the remote outpost of Yangzheng in Shanxi province. Together, they established a Christian Mission; a school; and an orphanage, in order to convert the population to Christianity, and which the two women named the 'Inn of the Sixth Happiness'. This was based on the Chinese proverb, which says that there are five happinesses; Christianity was to be the sixth.

To give herself credibility with the Chinese authorities, Gladys became a Chinese citizen in 1931, and managed to gain an appointment as the official 'Foot Inspector'. In this role, she was responsible for enforcing the recently introduced law, which outlawed the ancient custom of female foot-binding. In 1940, during the Second World War, she led 100 children to safety, on foot from Shanxi – then occupied by the Japanese – across mountainous and war-torn territory. The story of this remarkable act of faith and courage was eventually to be told in the film, 'The Inn of the Sixth Happiness'. Gladys stayed in China until 1949 when she returned to Britain, where she died in 1970. However, there is a postscript to this story.

I met Gladys Aylward, although I did not realise this at the time. She visited the Sunday School where I was now an 8 year-old pupil. I remember that the Superintendent told us that we all had to sit up 'straight' with our arms folded, as she introduced a 'very special visitor'. I then remember a small woman walking around us children to speak to one or two of us.

She came over to me and, with a very precise and 'posh' manner of speech, patted me on the head, and told me that 'Jesus was filling me with his sunshine'. The Vicar of my church told me, some years later, who this impressive and – to a small Liverpool boy – slightly scary woman had actually been.

She had apparently returned to Liverpool to coincide with the opening of the film about her adventures in China.

My own relationship with the Chinese Community in Liverpool became much more intimate when, in 1981, I married a local Chinese girl, and we have three, wonderful children.

To Find Out More:
History of Liverpool Chinatown
Liverpool Chinatown Business Association
Phone: 0151 709 3221
http://web.ukonline.co.uk/lcba/ba/history.html

Chinatown
http://www.liverpoolcityportal.co.uk/attractions/china_town.html

Pagoda Chinese Community Centre
Phone: 0151 233 8833
http://www.ljmu.ac.uk/International/60078.htm

Nelson Street is a One-Way street, so continue to the crossroads, and turn right into Granville Street South. You will pass the Granville Young Persons' Centre on the left. Take the next road on the right, which is Cornwallis Street, and follow this to the T-Junction. Turn right here into Duke Street.
As you do so, look across the road, through the iron gates into the private residential estate.
There you will see a large, bronze statue of a man in a Roman toga. This is William Huskisson MP, whose tragic claim to fame you will learn about on our visit to St James's Cemetery. At the traffic lights, continue across up to the next set of lights, at Rodney Street. Turn right here, into the Cathedral grounds, and follow the road around to the left, into the car park. There is a fee, payable as you exit, so have coins ready for the machine.
The route around the Cathedral is One-Way, so drive around and take your first available parking space.
From here, we shall take a look at the Oratory; take a stroll through the sunken Cemetery; and explore the Anglican Cathedral. I suggest a stopping time of 1½ hours.

St. James's Burial Ground and the Oratory

㉙

The Oratory

Halfway up Upper Duke Street from the Chinese Arch, heading towards Hope Street and directly opposite the end of Rodney Street, is the entrance road into the Anglican Cathedral.

By following this approach road the first building that one sees, standing alone on the left behind the railings, is a mortuary chapel known as 'The Oratory'. Designed in the form of a miniature Greek Doric Temple, the Oratory is a fine example of the 'Greek Revival' in 19th century architecture. It stands on its own miniature acropolis on a pediment, overlooking what once was the original tunnelled entrance to the old quarry that is now St. James's Cemetery.

"This delightful little building was erected on the site of an ancient windmill and it is one of the City's many listed buildings"

It was designed as a chapel to service the cemetery and built, in 1829, by John Foster Jnr. (1786-1846). Funeral services would be held in the Oratory before burials took place, but it was also used as a place for memorials and monuments to the deceased. When the cemetery eventually closed, the Oratory fell into disuse, however, in 1986 the building became the responsibility of the newly formed National Museums Liverpool (NML), and it now houses many fine pieces of sculpture and statuary, executed by significant 19th century artists. To view the interior of the Oratory and its treasures, appointments can be made by contacting the NML.

The Oratory

To Find Out More:
The Oratory – St James's Cemetery
Information on access to the Oratory, from National Museums Liverpool – Phone: 0151 478 4178
http://www.stjamescemetery.co.uk/

Huskisson's mausoleum in St James' Burial Ground

The Burial Ground

A gateway in the railings, alongside the Oratory, leads you to a tunnelled passageway carved in the sandstone of St. James's Mount.

This descends to the sunken St. James's Cemetery, which is laid out in the shadow of the Anglican Cathedral. This cemetery was once a quarry, and records referring to this go back as far as 1572. Stone from here was used to build many of Liverpool's famous older buildings, such as the Town Hall, and was also used to construct our outstanding Dock Walls. These now form part of Liverpool's World Heritage Site.

Originally overlooking the quarry and well before the cathedral was built, the top of the mount was once the site of Liverpool's first public park. In 1767, Thomas Johnson the then Mayor of Liverpool, was concerned about rising bread prices and so, to provide extra employment for local, poor, working men, he paid them to clear the top of the mount. What had previously been known as Quarry Hill was levelled, landscaped, terraced, and planted with trees and shrubs. In 1768, this was re-named Mount Sion and opened as a public pleasure ground.

Seven years later, the site was re-named as St James's Mount after a nearby church, the name that it retains. A coffee house and tavern were soon built, serving people of 'superior class', and windmills appeared at either end of the terrace. One of these was

located at the opposite end of the mount, along an old pathway, and it survived until 1800. The other, as we have seen, was replaced by the Oratory in 1829. By 1825, the quarry was exhausted, and it was decided to convert it into an Anglican cemetery. The rapidly expanding population of the City was causing major sanitary problems; one of the most pressing being the lack of public burial space. The only other public cemeteries at this time were the burial ground at what is now St John's Gardens, behind St George's Hall, which was opened in 1767; and a Necropolis at Low Hill, which was opened in 1825.

These were inadequate and, in a fine example of forward planning, the architect of the Oratory was also commissioned to convert the quarry into a cemetery. This was opened as a 'City of the Dead' in the same year as the Oratory. With great ramps and terraces – designed to take full funeral carriages and processions, it contains over 100 rock-hewn catacombs, and was modelled on the Père-Lachaise cemetery in Paris.

However, by the early decades of the 20th century, and after 57,774 burials, it was found that every time a new grave was being dug, old bones from previous burials were being disturbed, and it was clear that the cemetery was becoming overcrowded.

And so, it was decided to close it and, in 1936, the burial ground was developed as a park. Many of the gravestones were re-sited, with some of them lining the walls facing the ranks of catacombs. A number of these burial chambers were never used and they remain open. Sadly, during the 1980s and 90s, the Cemetery was neglected and often vandalised. The graves became overgrown or damaged and it became a civic disgrace.

A conference of bishops that took place at the Cathedral in 2001, drew attention to this fact and so the joint owners of the land – Liverpool City Council, National Museums Liverpool, and the Liverpool Diocese, were forced to take action. Funding was found, and the 'Friends of St. James's Cemetery' group was formed.

Thanks to the sterling work that has been carried out by these remarkable volunteers, and after 457 hours of work, the Cemetery was re-landscaped to make it more accessible and attractive as a public place. Their work included the planting of 371 wild roses, adding beauty and fragrance to what can be a fascinating stroll through some remarkable, moving, and noteworthy gravestones and memorials.

These include, in the centre of the Cemetery, the distinctive – and now completely restored – mausoleum of **William Huskisson MP** (1770-1830), also designed by John Foster.

The circumstances surrounding this man's death are significant, and I have taken the details of the incident from a contemporaneous report in the Guardian Newspaper, and from the local Gore's Liverpool Advertiser, which both reported the tragedy at the time.

The incident occurred on September 18th 1830, which was expected to be a momentous day for the future commerce of Liverpool and Manchester, as well as for Britain. This was the day of the inaugural run of the world's first passenger railway between the two great commercial cities of the North West. In the early hours of the afternoon the bunting was out, the bands played, and the crowds thronged the railway tracks at Edge Hill, as the convoy pulled out of the station.

The Duke of Wellington (1769-1852), who was Prime Minister at the time, was in his own carriage on the southern track. This was being pulled by the locomotive, 'Northumbrian'.

"On the parallel northern track was a procession of six trains, each pulled by different locomotives. These were Phoenix, North Star, Dart, Comet, Arrow, and the Meteor"

The other train was, of course, the Rocket. This had been designed and built by George Stephenson and his son Robert, who had won a competition to find the most successful design for a new steam engine, held the previous year at the Rainhill Steam Trials.

The train carrying all the distinguished guests, had stopped to take on water halfway along the route, at the Parkfield Watering-Station.

Amongst the important people in the Prime Minister's train were William Huskisson, the local MP, and his wife. During the 1820s, Huskisson had been one of the primary backers of the Liverpool and Manchester Railway and, in 1826, had helped to secure the legislation that would allow construction to begin. As the dignitaries' train had stopped, this provided an opportunity for the carriages full of people on the northern track, to pass by and get a good look at the 'great and the good'.

At this point, the VIPs got out to stretch their legs and to socialise, and Huskisson thought that this might be a good time to heal a long-standing breach between himself and the Duke of Wellington.

After shaking the Duke's hand, and still standing on the step of the carriage, the Liverpool MP realised that another train, headed by George Stephensons 'Rocket', was advancing towards him on the parallel tracks, only five feet away from those of his own train.

All the people who had been walking around very quickly began to scramble back aboard their own carriages, leaving Huskisson as the last person standing on the ground, with his hand on the open carriage door. It was clear to observers that he was too close to the approaching locomotive, and the engineer shouted out to him from the Rocket. At the same time, people called to him from his carriage, and this confused him. As he struggled to pull himself back into the VIP's carriage, his strength failed and, already weakened by a recent illness, he fell backwards in front of the Rocket.

The unfortunate MP was struck by the engine and he fell to the ground. As he did so, his left knee was thrown across the southern track in a bent position, and the wheels of the succeeding carriages crushed his thigh and leg.

The reporter for Gore's Liverpool Advertiser takes up the story;

'Though we distinctly heard Mr. Huskisson shriek as the carriage passed, we had no idea that any serious mischief had happened... Several of the Directors and of the distinguished visitors from the Duke of Wellington's carriage immediately crowded around to offer their services...

Inside the Oratory

Mr Huskisson said: "Where is Mrs Huskisson? I have met my death. God forgive me."'

'The Northumbrian engine, and the carriage which contained the band, were detached from the state carriage; and Mr Huskisson, having been carefully placed on a board, was carried upon men's shoulders, and deposited in the carriage of the band...

Mr Stephenson taking charge of the engine, set out towards Manchester at a most terrific rate, travelling from the place where the accident happened to Eccles Bridge, at the rate of 34 miles an hour...'

At Eccles, the mortally injured man was taken to the local vicarage, whilst George Stephenson continued with the Northumbrian, to find medical assistance at the Manchester station. By this time, it was about four o'clock in the afternoon. Meanwhile, Huskisson was losing massive amounts of blood, and was failing fast. When the surgeons eventually arrived at the vicarage, it was decided not to amputate as this was bound to kill him, so he was given massive doses of laudanum, which did little to relive his agony. Huskisson took hold of the arm of one of the surgeons, a Mr Whatton, and spoke to him. Here the reporter takes up the narrative once more,

'"I wish you to tell me candidly what you think of my case."

Mr Whatton replied, "It is a very bad one, and I fear, sir, that you cannot survive." Mr Huskisson rejoined, "No, that I have fully made up my mind to, from the first; but how long do you think I have to live?"

The answer was, "It is impossible to say exactly; but probably not more than four, five, or at most six hours."

"Thankyou," said Mr Huskisson, and terminated the conversation.'

William Huskisson dictated his last will and, with his wife, he took the sacrament, although his breathing was by now very laboured. Shortly after this, the dying man said,

"I hope I have lived the life of a Christian," and then thanked the surgeons for, 'their kind attentions to him'.

As the newspaper then reports;

'Mr Huskisson took an affectionate leave of the sorrowing friends who surrounded his bedside, and a most tender farewell of his devoted wife, and precisely at nine o'clock, expired.'

Every day, without realising it, hundreds of passengers on modem trains pass the site of Huskisson's accident at Parkside. A memorial was placed here at the time and it still stands bearing an inscription, part of which reads,

"The accident changed a moment of the noblest exultation and triumph that science and genius had ever achieved into one of desolation and mourning..."

William Huskisson was a much respected man in Liverpool and throughout Britain, even though his campaigns for radical new policies, such as Catholic emancipation, made him the target of much vitriol; hence this original conflict with the Prime Minister. Huskisson's death, and the manner in which it occurred on such an otherwise illustrious day, shocked the nation. The public subscription that was rapidly taken up was sufficient to erect his magnificent tomb and mausoleum, which now stands in the centre of St. James's Cemetery. This marks his life, and commemorates him as the world's first railway fatality.

Interestingly, late at night in the immediate vicinity of the mausoleum, ghostly footsteps can be heard, so take care that you don't meet the ghost of St. James's Cemetery; whoever he or she might be!

Immediately behind the temple mausoleum is the grave of **John Foster Jnr** (1787-1846), the architect of the Oratory and of the Cemetery. Here also is the grave of **Edward Rushton** (1756-1814).

He was blind, and had been a sailor, a journalist, a poet, and a human rights campaigner. He is best remembered as being the founder of the Liverpool School for the Blind – the first such school in the world. (See Chapter: 'Liverpool Lost and Found'.)

"A number of other significant local characters are buried here, including William Lynn, who founded the Grand National; Captain Harrison, who was the master of the Great Eastern; and two of Admiral Horatio Nelson's officers, each of whom lived to be over 100 years old"

Here also is the grave of the miniature-painter **Sarah Biffin** (1784-1850), who was miniature herself. She painted exquisite tiny portraits using only her mouth, as she had been born without arms or hands. She had only limited use of her legs and feet, and was only 37 inches in height. Born in Somerset in 1784, as a young girl Sarah's dexterity came to the attention of a travelling artist called Dukes. He agreed to teach her to paint and, in return, she travelled with him on a sixteen-year contract, exhibiting her skills in a Freak Show. She had her own booth alongside the Fat Woman, the Human Skeleton, and the Pig-Faced Lady, where she signed autographs and painted fine miniature landscapes.

Despite earning vast amounts of money for Dukes, she was never paid more that £5 a year by him. However, when her contract expired she escaped from Duke's clutches, and rapidly improved both her skills and her fortunes. She received a medal from the Society of Arts in 1821, and became a fashionable celebrity; being patronised by George III, George IV, William IV, Queen Victoria, and many other illustrious patrons, including the King of Holland.

As well as 'crowned heads', Sarah painted portraits of many famous people, including the virtuoso violinist Paganini on one of his many visits to Liverpool, and Charles Dickens refers to Sarah in his novels, 'Nicholas Nickleby' and 'Martin Chuzzlewit'.

Fashions changed and, unfortunately, Sarah's fortunes waned. She took lodgings in Duke Street in Liverpool, in 1842, where, at the age of 63, she was dependent on a pension of £12 a year that had been granted to her by William IV. Her eyesight began to fail, and she became infirm.

The wealthy Rathbone family, who were local philanthropists, then arranged a public subscription. This raised enough money to buy her an annuity but, in 1850, she died at the age of 66. If you find her grave in the cemetery – which I confess I have never been able to do – then I understand that the inscription on her tomb is moving and sincere. Please, do tell me where it is if you do find it.

In the centre of the Cemetery, near the pathway to the chalybeate spring (see below), lies the wonderful **Kitty Wilkinson** (1786-1860). She was born in Londonderry and, as a child and towards the end of the 18th century, Kitty and her family moved to Liverpool. She came, along with thousands of other immigrants from Ireland, who were trying to escape from grinding poverty at home, only to be forced to continue to live in hunger and squalor in the Town's slums.

Kitty Wilkinson

As a young woman, Kitty voluntarily nursed local people, especially during the many outbreaks of cholera and typhoid that ravaged the poor areas of the Town. Day and night this courageous woman visited the homes of the sick and dying, and every morning she made enough porridge to feed sixty people. Kitty also gave up her own bedroom so that twenty children, whose parents had the fever, might themselves be washed and tended there; she also adopted various orphaned children. Kitty would care for families who were living not only in back-to-back houses and grim courts but also in cellars. These were often flooded, infested with rats and parasites, and epidemics were rife.

In 1832, Kitty opened her cellar kitchen, which had a large water boiler, as a washhouse for the clothes and bed-linen of cholera victims. She also encouraged local people to bathe and wash themselves there. The result of this was that the incidence of cholera in her community began to decrease, also, people began to recover. It became clear to Kitty, and to the Corporation of the Town, that there was a clear link between hygiene and health. This inspired them, in 1842 - fourteen years after the cholera outbreak, to open a public baths and wash-house. This was established in Frederick Street, and Kitty and her husband became its first superintendents. Later, and as I have already mentioned, Dr. William Henry Duncan was appointed as Liverpool's - and the world's - first Medical Officer of Public Health. He went on to improve water cleanliness, and he also instigated many other developments in health and hygiene-management.

Herman Melville, the American author, commented on how impressed he was when he first saw Liverpool's' docks, he was equally impressed, but differently, by other things he witnessed.

"…..the cellars, sinks, and hovels of the wretched lanes and courts near the river…. In some parts of the town, inhabited by labourers, and poor people generally, I used to crowd my way through masses of squalid men, women and children who at this evening hour, in those quarters of Liverpool, seem to empty themselves into the Street, and live there for the time ….. Poverty, poverty, poverty."

In fact, by the latter half of the 19th century, Liverpool became known throughout England as 'the black spot on the Mersey'. In particular, the Vauxhall area to the north end of the Town, there were 142,000 people living per square mile; mostly Irish immigrants. On average, their life expectancy was 17 years. These desperate people congregated in this district, and in neighbouring Everton, hoping to find support and community with their own countrymen but finding only more poverty and pestilence.

Kitty Wilkinson died in 1860 at the age of 73, a heroine of the ordinary people of Liverpool, and she is commemorated in a window in the Lady Chapel in the Anglican Cathedral.

Standing against the cliff wall, directly below the great Cathedral, you will find pitiful ranks of tombstones that mark the burial places of children from the old **Bluecoat School** orphanage – now the Bluecoat Arts Centre, in School Lane, in the City-centre.

The stones list the children's names, and there are dozens and dozens of them. Here also can be found graves belonging to members of three families, each of whom were related to victims of Jack the Ripper!

At the bottom of the lowest ramp, which leads up to the terraces of catacombs that are cut into the wall below Hope Street, is the classical monument to Liverpool entrepreneur and philanthropist, **William Brown**, who died in 1863.

As we have seen, the street in the city-centre on which can be found the Walker Art Gallery, the Central Libraries, and the World Museum Liverpool, is named after him.

Another, very lavishly-carved monument is dedicated to, **'Captain Elisha Lindsey Halsey**, from Charleston, South Carolina'. He was the Captain of the 'Thomas Bennett', sailing from Liverpool, and he was well known to be a martinet and bully. In 1844, whilst at sea, he got into an argument with the ship's cook and threatened to shoot him! The cook retaliated by fatally stabbing Captain Halsey.

The cook was brought back to Liverpool to stand trial for murder, but he pleaded self-defence, and the very sympathetic Liverpool jury were happy to acquit him.

One of Liverpool's many underground rivers emerges as a **chalybeate spring**, in the centre of the wall of the Cemetery, just below all the catacombs opposite the cathedral. This was discovered in 1773, by Dr. Thomas Houlston. 'Chalybeate' means 'containing iron salts', and Houlston believed that the water had curative properties – particularly for eye problems, nervous disorders, and rheumatism. Its use by local doctors in the 18th century enhanced Liverpool's reputation as a Spa Town.

The spring, the source of which is unknown, flows into a stone basin and, inscribed on a plaque on the wall above it are the words:

"Christian readers view in me,
An emblem of pure charity,
Who freely what I have bestow,
Though neither seen nor heard to flow,
And I have full returns from Heaven,
For every cup of water given"

And so, what was for so many years a neglected and vandalised lost garden of remembrance, has now become a pleasant landscaped park, and a place where people can stroll, sit and think in quiet, if somewhat macabre, surroundings.

A 19th century image of St James' Burial Ground

To Find Out More:
St James's Cemetery
http://www.stjamescemetery.co.uk/
William Huskisson MP
http://www.spartacus.schoolnet.co.uk/PRhuskisson.htm
Kitty Wilkinson
http://www.mersey-gateway.org/server.php?show=ConNarrative.171
Dr William Henry Duncan
http://www.mersey-gateway.org/server.php-show=ConWebDoc.145

The Anglican Cathedral

Above the Cemetery, on St. James's Mount, stands one of the world's most atmospheric and impressive Neo-Gothic buildings – the Liverpool Anglican Cathedral. This was designed by the 22 year-old Giles Gilbert Scott (1880-1960), who was a Roman Catholic, and it took over 74 years to complete. Over the West Porch of the Cathedral, as one approaches from the Oratory, a colossal statue can be seen. This is by Elizabeth Frink, and is entitled 'The Welcoming Christ'. This was Frink's final work before she died in 1993, and the sculpture indeed welcomes you to this truly wonderful place.

Towards the end of the 19th century, the Anglican Church Authorities wished to build a great cathedral for the recently formed Diocese of Liverpool. After much debate about an appropriate site, St James's Mount was selected and, in 1901, the top of the Mount was cleared, and work on the new building began.

The foundation stone was laid by King Edward VII in 1904, and the first part of the building to be completed was the Lady Chapel, which was later consecrated, and immediately used for worship in 1910. This became the central church of the Diocese until 1924, by which time the choir and north transept had been constructed, which meant that the building could then be fully consecrated as the Cathedral. This was the first time that a new cathedral had been consecrated in England since the 13th Century, and not only were King George V and Queen Mary present at this event, but also 8 Archbishops and 45 Bishops from all around the world.

During the bombing of the City in World War Two, the south wall and the stained glass windows of the Lady Chapel were destroyed. This part of the Cathedral was then out of commission for 15 years. However, it was also during the War that the last stone on the highest point of the tower was laid, in very cold weather, and by the architect himself on the 20th February 1942. This was a real triumph of faith, in the face of the Nazi assault on Liverpool and Britain and, throughout the War, construction work was never halted.

Between 1950 and 1960, the first bay of the nave was built and, by the summer of 1967, the second bay was almost complete. On 25th October 1978, Queen Elizabeth II came to share in a great service of thanksgiving and dedication to mark the completion of the building. Unfortunately, Giles Gilbert Scott did not live to share this very special moment, as he died in 1960. He is buried just outside the West Door, and his memorial is set in the floor at the centre of the Cathedral, directly below the tower. However, rather like Sir Christopher Wren's memorial in St. Paul's Cathedral in London, if you want to see Scott's true monument, then stand in the transept of the building and just look around you.

Amongst his other claims to fame, Scott also designed the old red telephone box, one of which stands inside the Cathedral, thus celebrating his greatest and his smallest achievements. The building has many remarkable statistics associated with it, including that

- It has the tallest stained glass windows in England, at 53ft high;
- It has the highest vaulting in the world, at 175ft;
- It has the highest and heaviest peal of bells in the world; the largest bell being named, like the clock in the Liver Buildings, 'Great George', no doubt also in tribute to King George V.
- It is the largest Anglican, and the 4th largest cathedral in the world.

The carvings and sculptures throughout the building – especially the figures representing Art, Culture, the Vices, and the Virtues – are truly magnificent and, completed as they were in the mid-1930s, they are a fine example of Art-Deco composition. As well as these figures; the reredos behind the altar; the delightful Lady Chapel - with its window dedicated to famous women of Liverpool and a 15th Century Madonna by Della Robbia; and the staggering central vaulting and awe-inspiring tower, all combine to leave the visitor truly moved by their visit. Do take time to study and enjoy all these wonderful examples of true art and craftsmanship.

The visitor facilities and information services here are outstanding and include **'The Great Space'**. This is a fascinating audio-visual tour, including an impressive CGI fly-through of the building. However, for a very special addition to your visit, lifts carry you up to the base of the main tower. From this point, a flight of 108 steps (be warned) takes you to the roof, from where the panoramic view is unexcelled on Merseyside, and is equally inspiring.

"Inside the Cathedral can be found two curiosities: 'the whispering arch' over the tomb of Lord Derby, and a tiny bronze mouse"

This tiny figure is crouching, partially hidden somewhere around the memorial figure of Lord Derby on his tomb – I challenge you to find it! The mouse's nose is brightly polished, as rubbing it is supposed to bring good luck.

To experience the unusual feature of the arch that spans the roof above Lord Derby's tomb, one person should stand at the base of one of the recesses in the wall, at one end of the monument. Someone else should then stand in the same position at the other side of the arch, and then whisper softly into the wall. Even the softest sound will be clearly heard at the other side, as the voice is carried overhead, through the channel in the stonework.

The atmosphere inside the Cathedral is one of calm; and the 20th century carvings, paintings, and tapestries provide a great deal of interest as you stroll beneath the warm sandstone of the vaulted roof. The cathedral is a perfect place for a break, for some tranquil reflection and, if you are so inclined, perhaps for a prayer.

To Find Out More:
The Anglican Cathedral
Phone: 0151 709 6271
E-mail:
info@liverpoolcathedral.org.uk
www.liverpoolcathedral.org.uk

On leaving the Cathedral grounds, turn right at the traffic lights, back into Upper Duke Street, and take the next right, into Hope Street. Park anywhere you can on the left of the road, just to take a quick look at Gambier Terrace. This runs parallel to Hope Street, behind the high hedge.
This is also an opportunity to see the magnificent side-view of the Cathedral, in all its neo-gothic, sandstone grandeur.

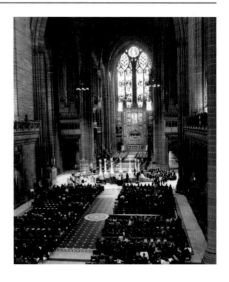

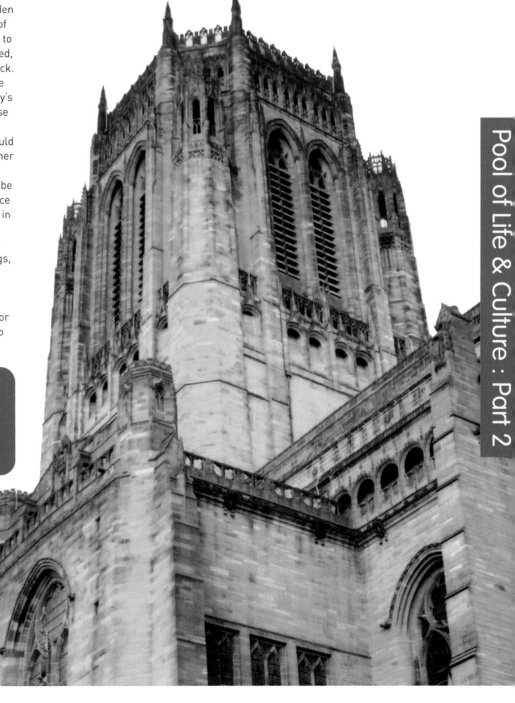

The Anglican Cathedral

Pool of Life & Culture : Part 2

Directly opposite the Cathedral, on the left of Hope Street and standing behind a wall and high hedges, is Gambier Terrace. This is named after Admiral James Gambier (1756-1833), who was involved in the bombardment of Copenhagen in 1807, during the Napoleonic Wars. He performed so well that he was given command of the Channel Fleet, from 1808 to 1811, and was subsequently made the Governor of Newfoundland, in Canada. The terrace was built around 1836, and it remains a very desireable address to have.

Many famous people have lived, and some still live in this impressive row of apartments and, for a while, John Lennon shared a flat at No 3 with Stuart Sutcliffe, his friend from Art College. By this time, John had met and started to go out with a girl called Cynthia Powell, and she would often stay overnight here with him after telling her mother that she was staying with a girlfriend.

John and Stuart were very close friends, and Stuart was recognised as having genuine artistic ability, far surpassing John's. But this never caused friction, as John really appreciated his friend's talent, and was proud of, and encouraged him. When, in 1959, Stu sold a painting for £65 – an unheard-of sum for a student's painting in those days, John convinced him to buy a bass guitar and join the band that John was a member of; known as 'The Quarrymen'. This too was real friendship, because Stu had no musical talent whatsoever, and could not really play the guitar at all. He would mostly stand on stage, with his back to the audience, so that no one could spot that he was not really playing. Before their first big break, which was a two-week tour to Scotland backing Johnny Gentle, Stu is partially credited with coming up with the name Beatles, by jokingly suggesting 'Beetles' as a play on Buddy Holly's Crickets. John however, would later like to say that the name came to him as part of a vision that he had experienced, of a man floating on a flaming pie who said 'you will be known as the Beatles'!

When the group's first manager, Alan Williams, fixed up a club tour for the group in the Reeperbahn, the 'Red-Light' district of Hamburg, Stuart went with them. Here he met and fell in love with Astrid Kirchherr, a German photographer. Astrid changed Stu's clothes and gave him a new, distinctive hairstyle, which all the Beatles later copied. Whilst on their second trip to Hamburg, Stu decided to continue his art studies at the Hamburg State Art College, where Astrid had studied. When the tour ended and the rest of the Beatles went back to Liverpool, Stu stayed in Hamburg with Astrid, having decided to give up any thoughts of a future in pop music. This was not an easy parting, because they were all close friends.

It was a great tragedy when, a year later on 10th April 1962, and following a series of violent headaches, Stuart Sutcliffe (often referred to as 'the Fifth Beatle') died in Astrid's arms of a cerebral haemorrhage, just as he was being carried to hospital in an ambulance. Ironically, the Beatles arrived the next day, to start another Hamburg tour.

On Thursday 23rd August 1962, John Lennon and Cynthia Powell married at the registry office in Mount Pleasant. Present as witnesses and guests were Paul McCartney, George Harrison, Brian Epstein, and Cynthia's brother and his wife. Ringo had only just joined the group so was not invited. Brian owned a flat around the corner, at 36 Falkner Street, and he allowed John and Cynthia to honeymoon here for a short while. But, they soon moved to John's childhood home, at 'Mendips', on Menlove Avenue.

On 8th April 1963, John and Cynthia Lennon had a son, Julian, but sadly, their marriage was not to last. This was because, in 1966, at a private preview of her 'new-wave' art exhibition at the Indica Gallery in London, John met the Japanese artist Yoko Ono. They became close friends and, as this relationship grew, John's feelings for Cynthia faded. In November 1968, 6 years after their wedding, John divorced Cynthia, and he left her and Julian to set up a new home in New York, with Yoko.

Gambier Terrace, overlooking St. James's Cemetery

To Find Out More:
Gambier Terrace
http://canning.merseyworld.com/gterrace.htm
Stu Sutcliffe Portfolio
http://www.beatlesagain.com/bstu.html
Yoko Ono
http://www.yoko-ono.com/
Cynthia Lennon
http://www.jibboo.com/beatles/wives/cynthia.htm

From Hope Street, take the next turning on the left, into Huskisson Street – as we now re-enter The Georgian Quarter. Cross over the junction at Percy Street, passing St Bride's Church on the left, and then cross over the next junction, at Catharine Street.
Follow the road all the way down until you come to the 'No Through Road' signs at Falkner Square. Turn left here and then first right. Park anywhere here that it is safe, convenient, and legal to do so. I suggest a 30-minute stop here, to explore the surrounding roads and to take a stroll around the gardens in the centre of the Square.

The last sections of this Chapter have taken us through The Georgian Quarter of Liverpool, and we continue through this district as we now conclude our journey through the cultural heart of our City.

The Georgian Quarter is bounded to the south by Upper Parliament Street; to the east by Grove Street; to the north by Myrtle Street; and to the west by Pilgrim Street and Hope Street.

This whole area not only adds to the architectural and cultural charm of Liverpool but also to its historical and social significance.

'Georgian' is the term used to identify the classic architectural styles that were current in Britain between about 1720 and 1840. It is named after the four British Kings, all named George, who reigned during the Hanoverian period. This style followed on from the English Baroque styles of architects such as Sir Christopher Wren, Sir John Vanbrugh, and Nicholas Hawksmoor.

It is best described as being Palladian or Neo-Classical, but in a much more understated way than was to be the case later, under the Victorians, who also used Ancient Greece and Rome as a basis for their design concepts. During the Hanoverian period, Georgian architecture was much more well-proportioned and 'clean'; with symmetry, balance, and simplicity being

the key elements. Indeed, mathematics and a 'scientific approach' to design – in keeping with the times – became an important part of the constructional integrity of buildings; the dimensions of most structures being composed of multiple cubes. This was the time of the English Enlightenment (1650-1800), when alchemy developed into true science, and when ideas became philosophy. These informed politics, commerce, entrepreneurship, art and, of course, architecture.

That is not to say that decoration and adornment did not form part of the overall Georgian aesthetic; it certainly did. However, a certain 'tasteful discretion' was employed so as not to overwhelm the observer with the ornamentation. This was because the straightforward, classical lines of the buildings themselves were considered, by the architects of the day, to be of much greater importance.

"In the early decades of the period, designers such as Colen Campbell, Lord Burlington, William Kent, and Thomas Archer led the transition from Baroque to Early-Georgian"

But, from the mid-1760s, the Neo-Classical styles became more pronounced, as is seen in the work of Robert Adam, Sir William Chambers, and James Wyatt. From around 1800, the Greek-Revival style began to be more emphasised. This was until the emerging Victorian tastes dictated a major change – from the clean and minimalist to the embellished, the flamboyant and, some might say, the overwhelming. This is clearly seen in Liverpool's many Gothic-Revival buildings, built after around 1840, by the likes of the Liverpool architect Alfred Waterhouse. But this is as much a matter of taste today, as it was when all the buildings of pre-20th century Liverpool were built. Much of the Georgian Liverpool that we now see was built towards the end of the period when, in 1800, the then Liverpool Corporation Surveyor, John Foster, Sr. (1758-1827), prepared a gridiron plan for streets of new houses, covering an area of peat bog known as Mosslake Fields. This was to the east of Rodney Street. His son, also named John, and as we have seen, was to become the architect of the Oratory and St James's Cemetery, and also of St Andrew's Church in Rodney Street.

Whilst Rodney Street, Hope Street, and the magnificent terraces along Upper Parliament Street, are all excellent examples of Liverpool's Georgian architecture,

Pool of Life & Culture : Part 2

Falkner Square

Falkner Street, Falkner Square, and Canning Street are particularly fine.

Falkner Square was one of the earliest public open spaces within the Town boundary, being acquired by the Corporation in 1835. The Square remains almost as it was when it was first designed and built, by the family of Edward Falkner, from the Fairfield district of Liverpool – near Kensington.

Edward Falkner was born in 1760, and he grew up to become a vigorous young man who intended to have a life filled with excitement and experience. He joined the military and was a dedicated and enthusiastic soldier, progressing rapidly up the ranks. After leaving the army, Edward settled to home life in his home town and, in 1788, and at the very young age of 28, he became Sheriff of Lancashire. He was effective and well-respected in this role, but he always remained ready for adventure.

Such an opportunity presented itself when, in 1797, news came that the French were mustering to invade England. Edward sprung into action and, within a day, he had recruited 1000 fighting men – equipped and ready not only to defend Britain, but to immediately embark for France and to overwhelm any invasion force that they found there.

When the French government heard what Falkner had done, and in how short a space of time, they took this as a clear indication of British determination and military strength, and instantly cancelled their invasion plans. Falkner became a local and national celebrity, which helped his business interests.

A wealthy man, Edward and his family decided to invest in land and property. This was the time when the new properties were being built all around what was to become the Georgian Quarter, and this presented a speculative opportunity. Falkner commissioned an architect and he designed and built Falkner Square, which Edward originally intended to name 'Wellington Square'. However, the townspeople of Liverpool dubbed it 'Falkner's Folly', because, for some years, many of the well-appointed new houses remained empty. This was because this whole area was considered to be too far out of town, and so impractical to live in, or to conduct business from. Nevertheless, Falkner was undaunted and, in due course the whole area became much more fashionable and desirable. The Square was particularly so because of its enclosed garden.

This was a 'key garden', which was only available to residents of the Square. They each had a key to the gates that excluded the general public from the delightful trees and garden that Falkner had planted there. However, as mentioned above, this was soon taken over by the Town, and made available to the general public.

Huskisson Street and the Anglican Cathedral

"Falkner Square remained a comfortable community until the Second World War, when the Square was commandeered as a location for public air-raid shelters"

After the War, in common with much of inner-City Liverpool, and particularly this area of Toxteth, Falkner Square fell into decline. The once luxurious houses became neglected, and those families that could afford to, sold up and moved away to less depressed areas of Liverpool, or out of the economically failing City altogether. Most of the properties in and around Falkner Square, and the nearby roads, were bought by private landlords who converted them into flats. These soon became overcrowded, poorly maintained, neglected and much less desirable. Falkner Square became a place to avoid. Not so now though. In recent decades, and mostly thanks to local Housing Associations and the City Council, this whole area is once again one of the most attractive places to live in Liverpool. Many more professionals, families, and students have moved back into the area, and the delightful gardens of Falkner Square have been beautifully restored. Still fully open to the public, they are well maintained by the Council and are a perfect and shaded oasis in the heart of this busting, residential, inner-City area. Indeed, the Gardens are used for numerous community events and have been a Green Flag site since 2003.

Huskisson Street, Falkner Street and Falkner Square, and Canning Street are deliberately and carefully maintained. Especially Canning Street and Falkner Street, where the City Council has restored the cobbles, the lamp-posts and other street furniture, and encouraged local property owners to do the same to their buildings. This is why these streets, and so many in this area, are now regularly used as locations for film and television productions. Indeed, Liverpool is the most filmed British City outside London, and is considered by film producers to be the second most film-friendly City in the world, outside New York.

This is because of the work of the Liverpool Film Office, in partnership with Merseyside Police and Liverpool City Council, who work to make it as easy and practical as possible to film here. It is rare indeed not to see a film or TV crew at work somewhere in the City, especially in the Georgian Quarter of Liverpool (See Chapter: 'Liverpool Lost & Found').

To complete this Tour, you need to leave Falkner Square by driving onto Grove Street and turning right.
At the traffic lights, turn left into Upper Parliament Street.
This will then bring you back to where we began Part 1 of this Tour, at Crown Street.

Dancers at Liverpool's Brouhaha Festival

Pool of Life & Culture : Conclusion

And so, there you have it: Liverpool became the European Capital of Culture for 2008 and, as far as I am concerned at least, it remains so. Hopefully, you will now understand and recognise why the City, and its people, won the accolade in the first place; and I trust that you have enjoyed discovering the cultural richness – in all its forms – that this Chapter will have shown you.

  However, all I have really been able to do is scratch the surface – there is so much more to discover and enjoy, in and around Liverpool. My remaining Chapters will help, but do use them as only a starting point, so that you can take the time necessary to really get to know the wonderful people and places that make up my remarkable home City.

The
Soul Supply

Magic

Amon Din

Four Clefs

l Wire

p

The Blue
Mountain Boys

Pete King

Eric Allanda
New Orleans K

Amoeba

The
Flyaways

Samantha
Krisp

Carol &
The Memories

Com

&
owns

The
Demon Fizz

Chas McDevitt Four
& Shirley Douglas

Charlie Galbr
Jazz Band

Doug Richford
Jazz Band

The Addicts

Cartridge

Bob

own

South California
Purple

The
Four Blues

Eddie Storm
The Clubmer

Business

The Bobby Mickleburgh
Jazz Band

Arnold Greenyard

The Cheetahs

Cac
The P

s

The
Ivan Meads

Flying Hat
Band

Tapestry

ris &
lassics

Bill Lesage

The
Cock-a-Hoops

The
Delar

The
Expressions

The
Perfumed Garden

Black Cats

The
Black Cats

The Angel

eats

Denny Seyton
& The Sabres

Four
Quarters

Pete Hartigans
Jazz Band

Alan H
Bler

Pandoras
Box

Factotums

Max Cannon

Beckets Kin

rs

The

The Denny Mitchell
Soundstation

S

TON REED

The Heart of the City

Including:

The City Squares, the Theatres, and the Markets

Radio City Beacon

The Bluecoat Arts Centre

Church Street and Lord Street

Liverpool ONE

Derby Square

Castle Street

Liverpool Town Hall and The High Street

Exchange Flags and The Nelson Memorial

Water Street

Tower Buildings and The Tower of Liverpool

Chapel Street

Liverpool Parish Church of Our Lady and St. Nicholas

Top Secret: The Western Approaches Museum

Old Hall Street and Commercial District

Tithebarn Street and St Patrick's Cross

Dale Street and its Alleys

Stanley Street and The Gay Village

Mathew Street and The Cavern Quarter

The Conservation Centre

The Cavern Wall of Fame on Mathew Street, with the names of artists who have played at The Cavern

The Heart of the City : The Tour

This is a circular walking tour that covers a distance of about 4 miles.
It begins at Ref No 1 on the Map, which is The Queen Square Multi-Storey Car Park, off Whitechapel in the City Centre.
The suggested time for the completion if this Tour is around 4½ hours in total, but add an extra couple of hours if you intend to visit all of the attractions and galleries etc, that are referred to in the text.

NB Please remember to check all opening times and admission charges before setting off, to avoid disappointment should any venues be closed

Contents

Route Map

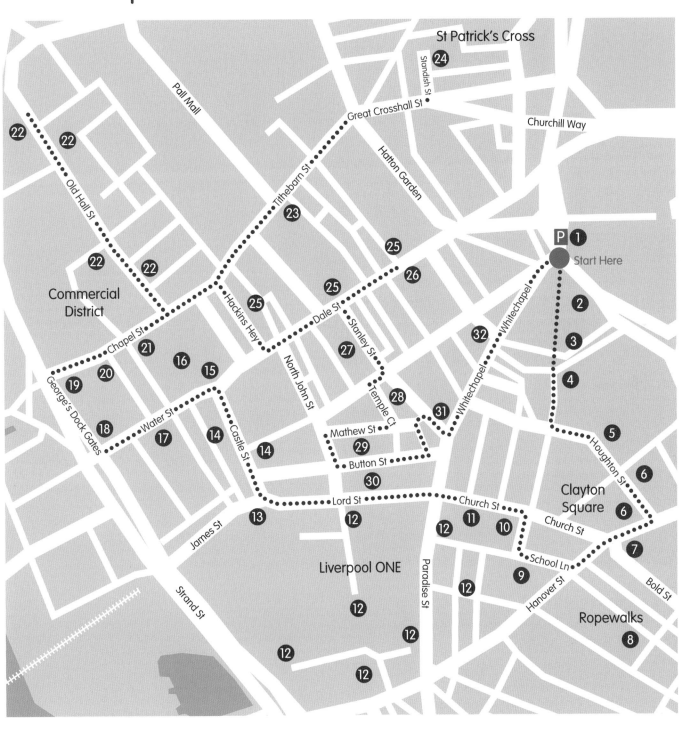

St Patrick's Cross

Commercial District

Clayton Square

Liverpool ONE

Ropewalks

The Heart of the City

Key

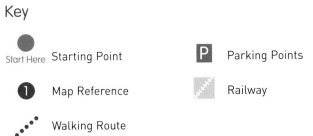

Start Here Starting Point

1 Map Reference

••• Walking Route

P Parking Points

▨ Railway

The Heart of the City
Introduction

In this chapter we are going to explore the centre of the bustling modern City of Liverpool but, as we do so, we shall be rediscovering the roots of the town and its people, and we shall be able to trace the growth of its built environment.
Much, inevitably, has changed over the centuries, but nevertheless, so much of Liverpool's historical past remains, and we see this as we walk around the City.

Liverpool (or 'Leverpul' as it was then known) began as an obscure, tiny, early-Medieval fishing village.

After King John (1167-1216) came here, in 1207, and created a new Town and Borough, he instructed that seven streets be laid out in an 'H' formation with an extended central cross. All of these have survived to modern times – although they are much widened and altered now of course.

They are, Whiteacre Street (which became Old Hall Street); Moore Street (which became Tithebarn Street); Juggler Street (which became High Street, and on which the Town Hall stands); Bank Street (which became Water Street); and Chapel Street, Dale Street, and Castle Street, which retain their original names. In this chapter we shall be able to rediscover each of these.

"As we shall also learn, it was the building of the world's first enclosed wet dock in the Town, in 1715, which began the transition of Liverpool from a quiet fishing and sailing port into a modern City."

However, it was during the 19th century that the character of Liverpool really began to alter; from being, at the end of the 18th century, a small yet bustling Hanoverian town surrounded by a collection of rural villages; to having become, by the turn of the 20th century, a rapidly expanding, densely-populated, industrial and commercial conurbation, which was steadily absorbing its outlying communities.

It was also the 19th century that saw the economic and social divisions within the population that began to affect the geographical and environmental nature of the town.

In 1790, only those who could afford to, were building houses in the new and very desirable districts just outside the town centre – in Everton, on the high ridge and its flanks; in the developing district of Hope Street, Abercromby and Falkner Squares, and around Canning Street; and further afield in Woolton, Wavertree, and Childwall. Those who could not afford to move, remained trapped in the Town-centre and, as the population steadily increased, these people found themselves living in equally increasing degrees of overcrowded squalor.

Indeed, in 1790, a survey of the Town reported that people were living in the cellars of buildings, because there was not enough existing housing to meet demand. The same report stated that

7,000 people had been discovered living in 2,000 cellars; many in streets and alleys within the Town centre, off Dale Street, Old Hall Street, and Tithebarn Street; and also in and around Park Lane in Toxteth. There was little or no light in these damp, disease-ridden basements, and even less – if any at all – sanitary provision or water supply.

Many poorer people were also living in courts. These dwellings surrounded a central yard on three or four sides, where all the tenants would often share a single lavatory.

As the population grew so did the number of these courts, and the census results for 1841 reveal that in the Town (and also in the now heavily populated districts of the Dingle and south Toxteth) 56,000 people lived in courts, with a further 20,000 living in cellars.

It was in the middle decades of the 19th century, and especially after the massive influx of people into Liverpool as a result of the Irish Potato Famine, that the great 'Middle-Class Exodus' from Liverpool town centre began.

Those with the means to do so, now decamped to new properties being built in and around Princes and Sefton Park, in Aigburth and Mossley Hill, and to the north of the Town, in Crosby. Even Everton was no longer a desirable place to live, because the slums, courts, and terraces of tenements were beginning to spread north and east. Soon, this district, together with Vauxhall, Scotland Road, Kirkdale, Anfield, and Walton; as well as the Dingle and Garston to the south, were becoming overcrowded, working-class communities.

In 1864, 18,000 dwellings, including 3,000 courts, were declared unsanitary by the Corporation and, over the next 30 years these were demolished (although it must be said that many courts survived up to the late 1930s). In 1869, the Corporation built Britain's first municipal housing – St Martin's Cottages in Silvester Street, off Scotland Road.

These replaced the old courts and the Victorian tenements and cellars, with terraces of '2-up 2-down' houses; many of which survive in the districts surrounding the heart of modern Liverpool. Such housing estates were also created in places like Garston, Wavertree, Edge Hill, and Old Swan. These dwellings each had their own water supply, and a back yard with an outside lavatory that was connected to the sewer system.

As time passed, many homes were connected to the gas supply and, eventually, to an electricity supply. However, a significant number of these properties, whilst better than the cellars and the courts, were themselves eventually to become the slums of the early 20th century. Consequently, many of these were demolished after World War One,

Liverpool people gather around a bomb crater in 1940

The Squares, the Theatres, and the Markets

As we begin this exploration of the many beating hearts that together make up the centre of our thriving City, I have brought you to where three squares converge. It is in these places that we can trace back to the time of the some of Liverpool's earliest markets and theatres; places full of the hustle and bustle of human life and leisure.

Queen Square and The Royal Court Theatre

The Royal Court Theatre on Roe Street

to be replaced during the 1920s and 30s by more modern Council houses and estates. But then came the Second World War and Liverpool's near devastation by German bombs – particularly in the City-centre. Indeed, Liverpool was the most heavily bombed City outside London.

Whilst this devastated the economic and social infrastructure, it also strengthened the particular human bond and sense of community-identity that so distinguishes the people of Liverpool and Merseyside.

"We are justly proud of who and what we were, and of what we are now, as a community; and of what we are achieving as a regenerating City: As you are about to discover for yourself"

I am beginning this Tour from a centrally located car park; at Queen Square, in the heart of the City-centre.

From the main exit of the Car Park, walk into Queen Square. You will see the rear entrance of the City-centre Marriott Hotel in front of you. Against this wall are a small shrubbery and a large stone slab. This is a memorial to HRH Diana the Princess of Wales. The towering Radio City Beacon will be ahead of you too; and this is difficult to miss!

Turn right into the square, and then immediately left, along the walkway at the right-hand end of the hotel. There is a rank of bus stops along the pavement at this point.

Take the pedestrian crossing, across the busy bus-lanes, towards Williamson Square. You will see the Royal Court Theatre on your left – up the road from the Shopping Precinct. Follow the walkway between the Shopping Centre and the Travel Centre into Roe Street, this then leads into Williamson Square. The Playhouse Theatre will be on your left and the fountain on your right.

Where the modern bus station, the City-centre Marriott Hotel, the multi-story car park, and a range of new bars and restaurants now stand, Queen Square was once the heart of the market area of 19th century Liverpool.

"In fact, the square was often called the 'Covent Garden of the North' because of the vast quantities of fresh flowers, fruit, and vegetables that were bought and sold here."

Business here was mostly wholesale, and took place every day of the week, except Sundays; beginning around three or four o'clock in the morning. But, by the early afternoon, Queen Square would be deserted except for odd bits of crushed fruit on the cobbles, empty wooden boxes, and old wrapping papers blowing around the gutters.

Most of the commerce carried out here was conducted by independent traders, and so the buying and selling was brisk, highly noisy, and intensely competitive. I can just about remember this market and, as I describe it, I can still smell the aroma of apples and oranges stacked in piles in their crates; combined with the warm and earthy smell of the horses that drew the carts; and the heady fragrance of the vast array of multi-coloured flowers that gave the square a unique vibrancy.

From Queen Square we cross over the bus lanes and enter Williamson Square. As we do so you can see the magnificent, brick-built Royal Court Theatre, facing towards Queen Square and opposite the Bus Station.

This area of Liverpool was certainly the 'theatre-land' of the 19th century and remains so, to some extent today. The Royal Court Theatre stands not far from the Empire Theatre on Lime Street, near 'The Fall Well', which was once the main water supply for the Medieval town of Liverpool, and this was rediscovered in 1965 during local excavations.

The present Royal Court was built in 1938, replacing a previous Victorian theatre that stood on the site, and it has played host to some of the greatest actors and actresses in some classic productions. It has also played host to spectacular concerts and, for a generation, it was the home of a very popular Christmas Pantomime. In modern times, the Royal Court has staged performances by stand-up comics, solo performers, and by rock and pop bands. These have included David Bowie, REM, Marillion, Elvis Costello, George Michael, U2, Oasis, and Blur. Indeed, in the mid-1980s, I produced a rock-concert at the theatre, to raise funds for the charity, Dr Barnardos, and the theatre still hosts many charity and fund-raising 'specials'.

In 1990, the building was listed as Grade II, which helped to secure its future survival. The theatre has now received a major grant from the Heritage Lottery Fund towards refurbishment and redevelopment. This gurantees that the theatre will remain a significant part of Liverpool's theatrical heritage.

To Find Out More:
The Royal Court Theatre
Phone: 0870 787 1866
http://www.royalcourtliverpool.co.uk/

The Playhouse Theatre

Williamson Square ③

As we pass into Williamson Square, we are entering an area that, from the late 1740s, was developed as an exclusive, residential neighbourhood and part of it was laid out by the family of shoemakers who gave the Square its name. Williamson Square is now one of the busiest areas in the City-centre. The focal point of this popular public space is the fountain, which comprises 20 jets of water that produce a double arch, rising out of the pavement up to a height of four metres.

A computer controls the fountain, which produces two different displays every hour, and which also varies the height of the water throughout the day. Throughout the evenings, the fountain is illuminated by coloured lights, which produce a continuously changing pattern and, at 10.30 every night, the fountain is turned off to be replaced by a dramatic misting effect.

"A specially written poem, given to the City by the local poet, Roger McGough, is inscribed in the granite pavements surrounding the fountain."

Celebrating the theme of 'water', the poem can be read from any position around the fountain.

As we entered Williamson Square, and where the Sports Shops are now sited, once stood the Theatre Royal. When it opened, in 1772, the Theatre Royal was the largest theatre outside London.

Always popular with local people, the theatre only employed the services and talents of actors from the London theatres, until 1778, when provincial players were used for the first time. The Theatre Royal had a particularly grim association, because Junius Brutus Booth (1796-1852), a very popular local actor who was a regular player at the theatre, sailed from Liverpool to America, in 1821, to begin a new life. It was his son, John Wilkes Booth (1838-1865) – also an actor – who, in 1865, assassinated Abraham Lincoln whilst the President was watching a performance at Ford's Theatre in Washington. The Theatre Royal building was demolished in 1965, when the whole area was being redeveloped.

Williamson Square Fountain

The Playhouse Theatre ④

The theatre that now stands at the head of Williamson Square is the Playhouse Theatre.

"This occupies the site of a concert hall that was opened in the early decades of the 1800s, as the 'Star Music Hall'."

In 1911, the Star was sold, eventually becoming the 'Liverpool Playhouse Theatre', and home to 'The Liverpool Repertory Company. From its very beginnings, the Playhouse attracted some of the best actors including, as child performers, Gertrude Lawrence and Noel Coward. Later company members included Robert Donat, Lillian Braithewaite, Cecil Parker, John Gregson, Clive Brook, C Aubrey Smith, Richard Burton, Michael Redgrave, Diana Wynyard, Rex Harrison, Patricia Routledge, Anthony Hopkins, and Richard Briers; so it is clear that the Liverpool Playhouse launched a wealth of talent onto the national and international acting scene.

The Liverpool Playhouse, which is now the oldest repertory theatre in the country, together with the Everyman Theatre in Hope Street (see my chapter: 'The Capital of Culture'), is now jointly managed by Liverpool City Council, and it remains a thriving venue.

To Find Out More:
The Playhouse Theatre
Phone: 0151 709 4776
http://www.everymanplayhouse.com/

As a footnote, it is worth noting that for many years the Codman Family performed first on Lime Street, and then regularly here in Williamson Square. They are a long line of Punch and Judy showmen, descending from Richard Codman (1832-1909) who arrived in Liverpool in 1860. Their puppet shows have delighted Liverpool's children and adults alike since that time and, currently, the sixth generation of 'Professor' Codman continues to give public performance throughout the City, and at private parties and events.

To Find Out More:
The Codman Family
Phone: 0151 220 7819 or Mobile 0467 700359
http://members.lycos.co.uk/codmanspunchandjudy/

Punch and Judy on the Web
http://www.punchandjudy.com/

From Williamson Square, take the pedestrianised street up the right-hand side of the Playhouse Theatre – this is Houghton Street. Just past the Stage Door of the theatre, on the left, is a set of steps that lead up to the base of the Radio City Beacon and the entrance to the Studios.

Radio City Beacon

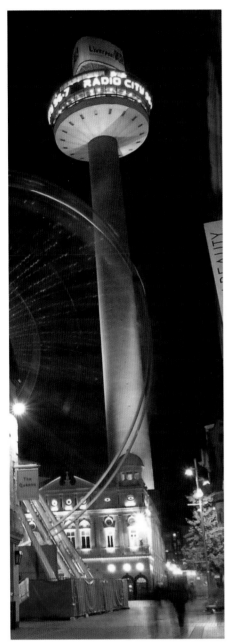

The Radio City Beacon

The St. John's Beacon, towering 450 feet over the heart of the City and above Williamson Square, St. John's Retail Market, and Clayton Square, was once a restaurant built on top of a chimney!

When the modern St John's Market was opened, in 1965, the smoke from the incinerators that burned the waste from the two floors of small traders' stalls and shops would be carried away through this colossal pipe, high above the City.

"However, within a few months of the beacon-chimney coming into action, so did the Clean Air Act!"

This made such rubbish burning illegal, and so the chimney part of the Beacon became redundant. Nevertheless, a high-speed lift, which had been installed as part of the design of the tower, would take intrepid members of the public right up to its summit. Here, they could stroll around the open observation platform behind a windswept grill on the roof, and have a snack in the Cafeteria. Or, if they had plenty of money, they could dine in the plush restaurant located on the floor below this, which used to revolve on a giant turntable once every 30 minutes!

Long since closed, the restaurant and observation platform were replaced, in 2000, by the studios and offices of commercial radio station Radio City. It is possible to go up to the top of the Radio City Beacon and have a guided tour of the Studios complex, complete with spectacular 360° views across the region, and these are bookable in advance. The studios can also be booked as a small conference venue.

> **To Find Out More:**
> **Radio City Tower**
> Phone: 0151 472 6800
> http://www.radiocity.co.uk/

From the steps at the entrance to the Radio City Beacon, continue past the entrance to St John's Market on the left and you will enter Clayton Square. You will see the entrance to the Clayton Square Shopping Centre directly ahead of you, so go inside and have a wander around, but leave through the directly opposite entrance, which leads you out into Ranelagh Street, in front of Central Station.

NB: If you are doing this Tour on a Sunday, the Shopping Centre is only open between 11.00am and 4.40pm so, if it is closed, make your way around the outside of the building, to the right, until you reach the junction with Church Street. Turn left and, across the pedestrian crossing, you will see Bold Street, leading up the hill to St Luke's Church. The old Lyceum Club will be on the left-hand corner.

St John's Market and Clayton Square

St John's Market

Not only was Liverpool the centre of world trade – in fact at one time, more than a third of all the country's imported foodstuffs passed through the Port of Liverpool – but it was also the heart of regional trade. Queen Square and Williamson Square, together with nearby Clayton Square and Great Charlotte Street, were the sites of most of the local markets; although there were many more throughout the City.

By 1890, there were six main markets in town-centre Liverpool and, as well as the fruit and veg market, fish were on sale at Great Charlotte Street Market, whilst St John's Market also sold fish, as well as poultry, meat, and more fruit and vegetables.

Exotic fruits from all around the world were also on sale here, and nearby were two open markets – one that sold live animals and birds, and another for the sale of ironmongery, crockery, and household goods.

St John's Market was completely rebuilt in 1965, but a trading hall for small, family-owned stalls – selling a variety of products and commodities – was retained on the upper floor: Thus maintaining a long tradition of independent commerce, which is so much a part of Liverpool life. However, the current owners are hoping to completely re-build and refurbish the retail complex once again, to compete with Liverpool ONE.

The Heart of the City

Crowds watching the World Cup in Clayton Square

Clayton Square

Across the way from St John's Market stands the modern Tops Plaza Retail Centre at Clayton Square, however, before 1750 this was an area of open countryside. The leaseholder of the land at that time was Sarah Clayton (1712-79), who was the daughter of a colliery owner and tobacco merchant, William Clayton. William was a MP for Liverpool from 1698 to 1714, and had been Mayor of the Town in 1689, and he was a wealthy and influential man. His daughter inherited not just his wealth, but his enterprise and strong character, and it was Sarah Clayton who built the square between 1745 and 1750. She not only laid out the square, but also the surrounding streets, which she named after her relatives by marriage; Cases, Elliot, Dawson, Richmond, Tyrer, Houghton, and Parker.

Clayton Square was one of the bustling hearts of the City, right up to the 1980s when, as part of the Council's vision for economic growth in the City centre, the square was torn down, as were most of the surrounding streets. This once attractive Georgian square, with its fine buildings and attractive narrow streets, was replaced by the current, 285,000 square feet, glass, brick, and steel shopping mall.

> **To Find Out More:**
> St John's Market
> http://www.stjohns-shopping.co.uk
>
> Clayton Square Shopping Centre
> Phone: 0151 709 4560
> http://www.claytonsquare.co.uk

Walking down the hill, make your way to the foot of Bold Street, at its junction with Ranelagh Street and Hanover Street going off to the right.

I will now tell you something of the Lyceum Club, which stands facing you on the left-hand corner of Bold Street, and of this shopping street itself. Then, our Tour will take us into Hanover Street.

The RopeWalks Area and New Clubland

The Lyceum Club

The Lyceum Club was formed in 1759, when a group of like-minded 18th century merchants and men of letters, decided to meet together to share their business opportunities and to exchange political and ideological views. They were also men who made use of the large library of books that had been acquired by William Everard May. However, some years later, the members of the Lyceum Club, which included such luminaries as William Roscoe, Doctor James Currie, and William Rathbone, agreed that the books needed a new home. These men were also free-thinkers and very much against the slave trade, and so they also needed somewhere to meet in privacy and security. This had to be away from the many Coffee Houses and other private clubs that thrived in Liverpool during the 18th century, and which were rowdy and unwelcoming to these abolitionists. This was in a town that was thriving from 'The Triangular Trade' of Slavery. (See my Chapter: 'The Liverpool Waterfront'.)

And so, in 1801, Thomas Harrison (1744-1829) was commissioned to design a permanent library, with reading rooms and a private Coffee House. When the new building was completed at the corner of fashionable Bold Street, the premises and the library of books – which May had by then donated to the Club – were only accessible to members and their guests.

For over 170 years the Lyceum Club thrived but, in the 1970s, and because membership numbers had fallen, it became uneconomic for the Club members to continue to occupy this grand building. Consequently, they moved into smaller premises in Paradise Street but, sadly, the Lyceum Club was dissolved some years later.

> "The Lyceum building itself has since been a Post Office, and a succession of Wine Bars and Restaurants."

Fortunately however, not only the exterior of the Club has survived, but also its magnificent interior, although this has been much altered over the years.

The RopeWalks Area

Alongside the Lyceum you can see the long, straight road that is Bold Street, leading up the hill off Hanover Street. This road, together with its parallel roads of Wood Street, Fleet Street, Seel Street, Gradwell and Parr Streets, and Duke Street, are part of an area that has been lately re-named as 'The RopeWalks area'. This is because these streets were all originally laid out, as far back as the mid-17th century, as the centre of the old Town's rope-making industry.

Rope-making for sailing ships was once the dominant trade around this district, and Town records first refer to it as far back as 1650.

> "As the numbers of sailing vessels using the port increased, by 1790 there were 23 rope-makers in this area of the Town."

The process required a narrow and straight stretch of open ground, longer than the length of rope being made, so that long strands of hemp could be spun into rope by a rope-maker. He would first attach one end of a bundle of fibres, packed in a bag at his waist, to sets of rotating hooks that were fixed to a spinning wheel at one end of the ropewalk. He would then slowly walk backwards, paying out the fibres and twisting them together as he walked, and as the wheel entwined them into thin yarns. Bundles of these yarns would next be attached to the rotating hooks, and also to a single, swivelling hook at the far end of the ropery. The same mechanism would then be used to plait together increasing numbers of these yarns, until ropes of the required thickness were produced. Because of the paying out process of the original fibres, these manufacturing grounds became known as 'ropewalks', and long narrow pathways were originally laid out for this purpose.

In due course, rope-making moved to other parts of Liverpool and, towards the end of the 18th century, the ropewalks streets and those that connect them developed into an area of warehouses and businesses. This was one of the districts where merchants of the time lived 'over the shop'; before the idea of building out-of-town houses and family estates became fashionable. During the 1941 Blitz the area suffered significant bomb-damage and, in common with the rest of the City-centre industrial and business districts, the streets fell into decline, decay, and dereliction after World War Two.

However, RopeWalks has now established itself as part of the 'City-Centre Living' community, and many historic warehouse buildings have been refurbished as apartments and new businesses, following major inward investment. Also, this area has become one of Liverpool's main districts for nightclubs, bars, restaurants, and of creative industries, which means that life and the economy are now thriving in this very old part of the City.

As we now walk right, into modern Hanover Street, and from here further into the retail heart of Liverpool, we shall see how the City-centre is continuing to develop. Even so, hidden within its streets are some real gems that continue to connect us to our past.
One of these is 'The Bluecoat', which is found in School Lane, the second road on the right, off Hanover Street.

The Bluecoat Arts Centre

9

Walking down what is a very old lane, past the modern Friends Meeting House on the left, we come to the magnificent Bluecoat Arts Centre, which is the oldest building in the centre of the City.

Towards the end of the 17th century, Bryan Blundell, who was a master mariner; together with the Reverend Robert Styth, who was Rector of Liverpool, purchased an old schoolhouse that had stood in School Lane for many years. They had become aware of the large number of poor and orphaned children – mostly boys – who were wandering the streets of the Town, destitute and abandoned. These remarkable men developed the school so that these boys could now be clothed, fed, and educated; financially supported by charitable donations and by Blundell's own resources.

Nevertheless, it soon became obvious that the building was inadequate for the numbers of children who were now knocking on the door of the school, begging for food. Also, Blundell wanted to give these boys a permanent home, and a chance of a better future. And so, the old school was demolished, and the building that we now see was opened in 1718, as the Liverpool Blue Coat School (also referred to as the Blue Coat Hospital). A Latin text, set high in the wall above the main entrance, when translated tells us that the school was 'dedicated to the promotion of Christian charity and the training of poor boys in the principles of the Anglican Church'; although girls too were eventually accommodated here. Other reminders of the Bluecoat's original purpose are the medallions, showing the heads of children, which appear on the two wings on either side of the front courtyard.

There were later extensions and alterations to the School, especially to the rear, making this a very large building for the period and, by the time of Blundell's death in 1756, the Bluecoat School was home to over 100 boys and girls.

By the beginning of the 20th century, and after nearly 200 years of occupancy, the School had outgrown its original home. And so, in 1906, the children and staff moved to a new, larger, and very grand school building in the Liverpool suburb of Wavertree. The Bluecoat School changed and developed over the years and soon became one of the City's most successful and prestigious secondary schools. (See my Chapter: 'Liverpool Lost and Found'.)

Once the children left, the building in School Lane became known as Bluecoat Chambers, and was a popular venue for art exhibitions, debates, discussions, poetry readings, musical concerts, recitals, cultural lectures, and study programmes. It also became a centre for working artists and craftspeople, who ran their small businesses from the Centre.

"As the oldest Arts Centre in the country, the Bluecoat has always been at the forefront of the arts."

The Bluecoat Arts Centre

Indeed, in 1911, a truly significant Post Impressionist exhibition took place at the Bluecoat, exhibiting works by Picasso, Matisse, Cezanne, and Van Gogh; this was the first exhibition by these artists outside London. However, on the night of the 3rd May 1941, and like so many ancient City buildings during the Second World War, the Luftwaffe dropped incendiary bombs on the Bluecoat, gutting the concert hall and the adjoining rooms. The following night, the rear wing was destroyed by a nearby bomb-blast, and the damage totalled over £32,000 – at 1940s prices.

Restored in the 1950s, the Bluecoat Arts Centre has, for over half a century, been host to a wonderful range of facilities, including many cultural and arts-associated shops and small businesses, bookshops, a gallery for displays of contemporary art, a design and display gallery, a concert room, small music rooms and studios, workshops, and a café. The building is now owned and operated by the Bluecoat Arts Centre, a registered Charity and, a couple of years ago, the Trustees commissioned a complete restoration and refurbishment of this wonderful building. The Bluecoat now houses art galleries, a purpose-built performance space, artist's studios, a café, restaurant, retail outlets, and rented units for creative businesses. Its courtyard garden is a good place for a quiet coffee or a conversation with friends.

This beautiful Queen Anne structure draws people from the bustling shopping-centre of town, into the quiet tranquillity yet intellectually-stimulating surroundings of this treasured building.

To Find Out More:
Bluecoat Arts Centre
Phone: 0151 709 5297
E-mail: admin@bluecoatartscentre.com
http://www.bluecoatartscentre.com/

The Heart of the City

The Athenaeum

The Retail Heart of Liverpool

With its unassuming entrance, next to a jewellery store in Church Alley, off School Lane, stands the remarkable institution that is The Athenaeum.

With the closure of the Lyceum Club, this left only two of the original private members' institutions in Liverpool – the Athenaeum, and also the Artist's Club in Eberle Street off Dale Street. However, the Athenaeum was one of the original 'gentlemen's clubs' in the Town, being founded in 1797, initially as a private newsroom. Like the Lyceum, it too was established by entrepreneurs, slavery-abolitionists, free-thinkers, and political radicals, who regarded themselves as the commercial and intellectual champions of Liverpool, and also as the drivers of its expansion, prosperity, and social growth.

This particular group of men though, needed news, and this could only come from parliamentary reports, political pamphlets, broadsheets, and from the early newspapers that were now being published in London. Unfortunately, this was at a time when there were few reliable news or mail services between the Capital and Liverpool, and when the few roads that existed were still only primitive thoroughfares. And so, the founding members of the Liverpool Athenaeum commissioned express-riders and messengers, and special regular coaches, to bring all the latest news, information, and ideas back to the Town, on a regular basis.

They therefore required a commodious and private establishment in which to make all of this information more accessible, and so they paid for the construction of the Athenaeum News Room and Library in Church Street, facing the end of Parker Street. The building opened in 1799, preceded its London namesake by 27 years and, over the following decades, the Institution was to amass an excellent collection of navigation charts, maps, globes, and reference works.

In the rooms on the upper floor, even from the earliest years of the Athenaeum's existence, was an extensive, valuable, and comprehensive collection of books; many of which were from the private library of one of the Athenaeum's founding members, William Roscoe (1753-1831). In later years, this library grew into one of the world's most highly-regarded private literary collections.

In the 1920s, the Corporation of Liverpool needed to widen Church Street, to accommodate a new tram system through the City, and so, in 1928, The Athenaeum moved to its current premises in Church Alley. Although the building is clearly early

20th century from the outside, inside, you could believe that you were visiting the private apartments, ballrooms, and studies of an 18th century stately home.

For over 210 years, The Athenaeum and its library have provided outstanding facilities and resources to some of the most significant individuals in Liverpool's and the Nations' history. People such as Dr William Duncan, Sir James Picton, Thomas Brocklebank, Bishop Chavasse, Sir Ronald Ross, and very many others, too numerous to mention here. The Athenaeum remains a place to meet and engage with senior professionals from all walks of life, whilst also being somewhere to research, relax, and retreat to, in what the Institution accurately describes as:

"... a haven in the heart of Liverpool that offers a distinguished setting and an atmosphere unrivalled in the City of Liverpool"

However, because this is a private members' building, the Athenaeum is not generally open to the public, although it can be hired for conferences and meetings, and it is also licensed for weddings and other private celebrations and functions. My obvious passion for the Athenaeum is a giveaway of the fact that I too am an enthusiastic Proprietor of the Institution. As such, I urge you to take the opportunity to book a visit to our premises if you can: Ask if I am there when you come in and, if I am, I will generously allow you to buy me lunch in the Dining Room!

To Find Out More:
The Athenaeum
Phone: 0151 709 7770
www.theathenaeum.org.uk

Passing the Athenaeum, at the end of Church Alley turn left into Church Street.
We are now going to take a look at this street and then cross over Whitechapel onto Lord Street.
We shall then continue up to Derby Square.

As well as the market area around Williamson and Clayton Squares, and the shopping streets around Bold Street, the main shopping area of Liverpool also extends along **Church Street** and up **Lord Street**.

From these streets, roads lead off to the left into what is now one of Britain's premier retail and leisure complexes – Liverpool ONE. I shall talk more about this shortly, but first, a little about these two streets, before they became full of shops.

Until the late 17th and early 18th centuries, Church Street and Lord Street did not exist.

"In fact, where Church Street now stands was part of the Great Heath, and an area known locally as the Great Waste"

Where Lord Street now stands was once the site of the Castle Orchard and then of no more than a few isolated houses and smallholdings. These had been built on the fringes of the original Seven Streets of the old Medieval town and overshadowed by Liverpool Castle, which then stood at the top of the hill.

During this time also, the existing southern boundary of the Town was marked by a broad, tidal creek that ran from just beyond the end of modern Dale Street. This was fed by streams and brooks from the hills above Liverpool, and it flowed past where the entrance of the Mersey Tunnel now sits, through Old Haymarket, and along the line of what are now Whitechapel and Paradise Street. It then broadened out dramatically, into a wide inlet of the River Mersey, which was then known as the 'Pool' of Liverpool, and which had given the Town its name.

The Pool covered the area upon which the Bus Station, Canning Place, and Police Headquarters now stand. This meant that the ancient town of Liverpool was entirely contained between the creek and the river, mostly located around a bluff of land that pushed out into the Mersey. The only roads out of the Town were Whiteacre Street to the north, and Tithebarn Street and Dale Street to the east; each of these then being no more than large cart-tracks.

This all changed in 1688, when Lord Molyneux, who was Constable of Liverpool Castle, cut a track through the castle orchard, laid out what is now Lord Street (named after him), and bridged the creek. This opened up new areas beyond the Pool and the creek and, by 1705, houses and businesses had begun to appear on new streets. As we shall see in 'The Liverpool Waterfront' chapter, in 1715 the

Pool of Liverpool was filled in and the land around this reclaimed, creating Liverpool's first dock, which eventually became known as the Old Dock. The creek was culverted, and this still flows under our modern streets, into the Mersey. The path of the creek was later renamed as Paradise Street and Frogg Lane. This part of the road was so named because the little creatures were bred here – for what purpose I hate to speculate – but then the road became known as Whitechapel.

Over the next 200 years Liverpool steadily expanded. The original Seven Streets were widened and surfaced, and were eventually surrounded and criss-crossed by the thoroughfares, streets, and alleys that now constitute the modern City.

St Peter's Church

The entire block of buildings, of which The Athenaeum is only one part, was once the site of one of the most significant churches in the City. In the final decades of the 17th century, there was a huge rise in the population of Liverpool, and business opportunities began to rapidly increase as a result. It was this that had persuaded Lord Molyneux to build his new street, and the Corporation soon began to follow suit. Also, in 1699, and to meet the spiritual needs of the larger numbers of people now moving into the Town, the ecclesiastical authorities created Liverpool as a parish in its own right and, in 1700, construction began on a new church on a continuation of Lord Street.

Until that time, the Town had only been a small part of the much larger and very ancient parish of St. Mary's at Walton-on-the-Hill, to the north of the City. This was originally the parish church for the whole Hundred of West Derby. (See Chapter: 'Fortunes, Fables, and Football'.) Costing £4,000 to build and dedicated to St. Peter, the new Town church, pictured below, was consecrated in 1704 and, at that time, it still stood amongst open fields. Historians now believe that this was the first church to be built in Britain after the Reformation.

During the next two centuries, Liverpool's expansion was exponential and, in 1880, Queen Victoria granted Liverpool a Royal Charter to become a city, and it also now became a diocese in its own right. St Peter's was adopted as Liverpool's first Cathedral, but it was soon felt that the new city deserved a much grander and significant building. In 1904, the foundation stone of a great, neo-Gothic structure was laid by King Edward VI, on top of St James's Mount, and soon the Anglican Cathedral began to rise above the City. (See Chapter: 'Pool of Life & Culture'.)

This rendered St Peter's Church obsolete and, in 1922 and as part of the great widening of Church Street, the 200 year-old building was demolished. Only three things remain to indicate that the church ever stood here; one is in the name of the street, and the second is the pair of crossed keys of St Peter, carved high up into the Church Street frontage of the building. The third relic is a brass Maltese cross, which was set in a granite slab and placed in the pavement outside the building. This can still be clearly seen, outside the entrance to Keys Court, which leads into Liverpool ONE, and it marks the location of the original door to the church.

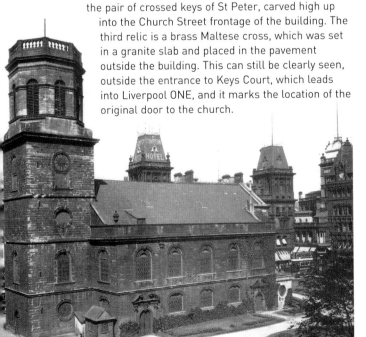

Liverpool ONE

For Liverpudlians, at least for the last 100 years, the heart of the City of Liverpool has always been in and around the Church Street and Lord Street areas. For most people, this is where they mean when they say that they are "going into town to do some shopping", and this is where most of the City's principal department stores and retail outlets are located. However, since the year 2000, the heart of the city has changed out of all recognition. This has particularly been the case in the large area bounded by Church Street and Lord Street, Derby Square, Strand Street, Wapping, Liver Street, Hanover Street, and Paradise Street. This central zone was taken over by Grosvenor – part of the vast holdings of the Duke of Westminster – to become 'Liverpool ONE'. This is 42 acres of shops, leisure, and residential facilities, composed of six distinct districts; 30 individually designed buildings; 1.6 million square feet of retail space; a 14-screen cinema; 230,000 square feet of restaurants, cafés, and bars; together with more than 450 new apartments, hotels, offices, a revitalised five-acre park, and the new public transport interchange.

This has been created whilst retaining many of the historically and architecturally valuable buildings that give the City-centre its character and significance. This includes part of the Old Dock, which was discovered during the excavations for Liverpool ONE.

This can now be visited on pre-booked tours, enabling you to see for yourselves, where Liverpool – the crossroads of the seven seas – really began.

Find Out More:
Tours of Liverpool's Old Dock
Phone: 0151 478 4788
www.liverpoolmuseums.org.uk/maritime

Liverpool ONE
Phone: 0151 232 3100
http://www.liverpool-one.com

The whole area behind the shops on the left of Church Street and Lord Street is the 'Liverpool ONE complex'. An information centre is located at 5 Wall Street where you can find leaflets and booklets and purchase merchandise such as mugs, pens, key rings and Liverpool ONE Superlambananas.

At the top of Lord Street you will come to the statue of Queen Victoria that dominates Derby Square. The Queen Elizabeth II Law Courts stand on the left; James Street leads down to the river, directly ahead; and Castle Street leads to Liverpool Town Hall, on the right.

Shopping at Liverpool ONE

The Heart of the City

Queen Victoria Memorial

Three significant structures have stood on the summit of what was once a rocky headland overlooking the River Mersey, and on which Derby Square is now located. The first of these existed centuries before the Square did, and this was **Liverpool Castle**.

The Town's great bastion, probably completed between 1232 and 1237, was an impressive and important stone structure, erected on the highest point between the River Mersey and the original tidal 'Pool' of Liverpool, precisely where Queen Victoria's statue now stands. This afforded excellent views, not just of the surrounding land but of the river, and so was an excellent strategic position. The Castle was built by William de Ferrers (1193-1254), who was the Sheriff of Lancaster, and was constructed of great sandstone blocks surrounded by a moat, which in places had to be hewn out of the solid rock.

The records describing the castle are good, and the building was rectangular in design, with tall, broad, circular towers at three of its corners, and a large gatehouse, barbican, and portcullis at its fourth. This main entrance was also guarded by a drawbridge, on a causeway across the broad, deep moat. The Castle towers and barbican were connected by high, curtain walls topped by battlements, and these strong walls enclosed a large courtyard.

This building was designed to be self-sufficient in times of siege, consequently, the Castle had its own bakehouse, brewhouse, and well. There was also an apple orchard on the west side of the Castle, overlooking the river, and a stone-built dovecot on the south.

The Castle soon developed into a residence, with accommodations for the De Ferrers family, their servants, and their soldiers. They occupied the Castle until 1266, when it was taken over by other nobles. By 1347, the Castle's facilities had developed, and there were now a large hall and a chapel in the main courtyard. The hall was big enough to be a dining space for all the occupants, and this also provided full stabling for the horses and other livestock:

"People and animals tended to occupy the same space in those days – imagine the smell!"

In 1445, the Molyneux family were made Constables of the Castle, and were granted title to it. This family remained in possession of the building for the next 200 years, eventually becoming the Earls of Sefton. (See Chapter: 'A Lordly Heritage'.) The Castle was besieged on a number of occasions, during various wars, rebellions, and baronial differences of opinion and, in 1559, was described as being in a state of disrepair. As the building was still deemed to be of strategic local importance, money for re-roofing it was allocated to the Molyneux family by the King.

During the English Civil War, Liverpool and its Castle were besieged and taken by Prince Rupert of the Rhine, on behalf of King Charles I. (See Chapter: 'Fortunes, Fables, and Football'.) However, after being occupied by Royalist Cavaliers, the Roundheads under Cromwell retook the Castle and, throughout this turbulent time, the ancient building suffered much damage and dilapidation.

After the Civil War, Liverpool Castle was largely demolished and, with the Restoration of King Charles II, the ruins then became Crown Property for about another 70 years.

In 1700, the Town Council of Liverpool obtained an annual lease on the old Castle and, by 1710, they had ordered that its moat should be filled in.

When this was completed, the site around the building was cleared to be made into a marketplace: this opened in 1721. In gratitude to the then Earl of Derby, who was a great benefactor to the Town, the area around the Castle was named **Derby Square**; the name that it retains today. The very last remnants of the Castle were finally removed in 1726.

In its place, the grand **St. George's Church** was built, but this too was eventually demolished, in 1899, and the site was cleared. However, it did not remain vacant for long because, within a few years, it became the chosen location for **Liverpool's memorial to Queen Victoria**. This was unveiled in 1906, to commemorate the Monarch, who had died in 1901. As is now becoming clear, during the Second World War the German Luftwaffe severely damaged the City, and completely devastated the area surrounding the monument.

It was considered an omen that, despite the appalling bombing that the City suffered, the Old Queen remained standing, completely unscathed by the worst that Hitler could deal out, and so the monument deserves a closer inspection as you walk around this area.

Nothing now survives of St. George's Church to show that it ever existed, and all that remains of Liverpool Castle is a commemorative plaque on the side of the Queen's memorial.

However, in Derby Square, in the cellar under Castle Moat House, a large section of the old castle moat survives. In the middle of what is now a surfaced and brick-lined cellar, stand the massive columns that support the current building. Also, in the middle of the floor, and under a wooden trap-door, is a short access shaft to a very ancient tunnel. This once led from the moat to the bottom of James Street, which was once the original shoreline of the river. Indeed, when I recently inspected this shaft there was a very deep layer of very wet and sticky river-silt covering its base, indicating that this tunnel still probably reaches the Mersey: so not all the evidence of our ancient history has vanished!

From Derby Square, walk along Castle Street towards the Town Hall. However, in terms of architecture, this road is one of the most spectacular in the City, so do make sure that you really take a close look at all the buildings as you pass by, and pay particular attention to the carvings and ornamentation on their facades, and on their roofs and gables.

Don't simply look around in the City – look up too!

The Seven Streets of Liverpool

As I mentioned in my introduction to this chapter, since the earliest Medieval times, the original fishing village consisted of no more than a few cart tracks. But then, the tiny community of Liverpool rose to prominence when, in 1207, King John (1167-1216) was attracted here. This was because its Pool provided him with a sheltered, deep water inlet and port, from which he could launch his invasion fleets of Ireland. To increase the population of the village and so generate income, trades, and crafts, and to initialise a strong economy, he granted Liverpool a Charter, creating it a Town and a Borough. This gave exemption from certain tolls and taxes, ownership rights to those who could afford to buy and farm strips of land in the area, and permission to erect a home and conduct certain trades. These new opportunities attracted ambitious entrepreneurs and the Town of Liverpool embarked on a new destiny. Then, in 1328, King Edward III ordered that all Liverpool streets should be paved. Gradually, when expansion really did get underway, the number of streets, roads, alleys, and passageways increased rapidly and exponentially.

I am now going to guide you along each of the original seven Medieval streets in turn; beginning with the street that connected the Castle with the Town Hall.

Castle Street (14)

Castle Street is the location for some truly wonderful, mostly 19th century, buildings. These are constructed in a range of architectural styles, and I always tell visitors to the City not only to look around them, but also to look up, and this should certainly be the case whilst you are walking along Castle Street. The gargoyles, mounted statues, intricate carvings, colourful mosaics, finely detailed traceries, and ornate gables that adorn these buildings, are a real feast for the eyes, whatever one's taste in building design happens to be.

"Most of these buildings were erected as banks, insurance offices, shipping offices, and company headquarters; so they were designed to impress – which they still do."

Some of the best buildings are as follows:
On the left-hand corner of the street, at the Derby Square end, at No 62 Castle Street stands the former **North and South Wales Bank**; later **The Midland Bank**; and then **Trials Hotel and Bar**. Now it is a boutique hotel and restaurant known simply as **62 Castle Street**.

The exterior of the building is everything that could be expected from a solid, 19th century bank, but do go inside and see how the original bank interior has been preserved, whilst accommodating a modern conversion.

Further along on the left, at No 48, is a building that sports four plain columns, and four carved busts set as medallions; then, on the corner of Brunswick Street is the former **Adelphi Bank**, with its pink and grey façade and green onion dome. 'Adelphi' means 'brotherly love' and the building is decorated with panel reliefs and statuettes on this theme; notably on the magnificent bronze doors. On these, you can see scenes depicting the relationships between David and Jonathan, Castor and Pollux, Patroclus and Achilles, and Roland and Oliver; some of whose relationships were perhaps a little more than simply brotherly! Crossing over the end of Brunswick Street, on the opposite corner at **44 Castle Street**, stands a building with a distinctive and attractive Dutch gable.

Over the road at No 31 Castle Street, on the corner of Cook Street, stands the former **Bank of England Building**. Again, this structure is everything one might expect of Liverpool's local office of the Nation's Bank. In the mid-19th century, the Bank of England built

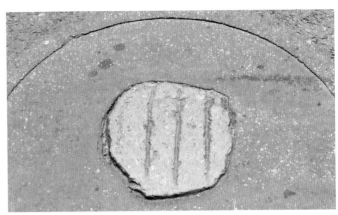

The Sanctuary Stone, in front of the Natwest Bank on Castle Street

three branch banks – in Manchester, Liverpool, and Bristol – and all of them were designed by C.R. Cockerell, but Liverpool's is the largest and grandest.

The next building along is the Grade II Listed **Norwich Union Building**, which was built between 1846 and 1847. Although not as striking as its next-door neighbour, the temple front, the four Corinthian columns, and a pediment that is set above the tall ground floor, all combine to present a very imposing façade.

Further along on the same side of Castle Street is **Queens Avenue Arcade**, and it is worth a stroll inside here to look at the buildings, but also to perhaps have a snack or a drink in one of its small cafés. Return back to Castle Street and, continuing towards the Town Hall you will come to the former **British and Foreign Marine Insurance Company Building**, which was built in 1889, and is Grade II Listed. With its attractive bays, detailed gable ends, and ornamented stonework, this is a very engaging structure. However, of special interest are the highly-detailed, coloured mosaic friezes of shipping scenes, which decorate the building halfway up its face.

Opposite the Queens Arcade, and back on the other side of Castle Street once more, stands the Grade II* Listed **NatWest Bank**. This is another very solid, fiscal building, which was originally built as the headquarters of Parr's Bank. Designed by Richard Norman Shaw, who had just completed Albion House on the corner of James Street and The Strand, for the White Star Line, this building was opened in 1902. It is worth having a look inside, just to get a feeling of the overwhelming space of the interior beneath a large dome, giving one the impression of being in the grand lounge of an early transatlantic liner. (Perhaps this had been Shaw's intention.)

Outside this bank can be found the oldest relic in Castle Street – the **Sanctuary Stone**. This is a greenish-coloured stone, about 18 inches in diameter, with four parallel lines scored across it. It was first referred to in 1292, and the area between this and another such stone, which once stood in Dale Street near the end of Stanley Street, marked the area covered by the Town Fair.

From Medieval times, fairs were held here on 25th July and 11th November. For ten days before and after these events, protection from arrest was secured within the precincts of the fair, mainly for debtors who would otherwise have been thrown into prison.

The Sanctuary Stone on Dale Street has long since disappeared, but this one can still be clearly seen set into the roadway, about seven or eight metres in front of the Bank, and about four or five metres to the right of its main entrance.

> **To Find Out More:**
> Castle Street
> http://www.liverpoolworldheritage.com

Now make your way to the Town Hall – have a look at the magnificent frontage and then go inside. The foyer is well worth a look, but the main rooms are only open on special occasions. However, if you have a friendly word with the charming concierges on the door, they may very well be prepared to allow you to wander around a little; unless there is a function or a main Council Meeting taking place of course.

Liverpool Town Hall and Juggler Street

15

Dominating the vista at the head of Castle Street stands Liverpool Town Hall. This faces onto Dale Street but it officially stands on High Street, which was originally named 'Juggler Street', and this is the second of our Seven Streets.

This ancient street got its first name because of the itinerant minstrels, mummers, entertainers, and peddlers who used to ply their trades here, and this ancient track connected Dale Street with Old Hall Street – originally known as Whiteacre Street.

The present Town Hall is the third such building on this site, but the first civic building here is referred to, in records dating back to 1511, as a 'Gilde House'. This is likely to have been the property of the local landowner, Reverend John Crosse who, in 1515, bequeathed the building to 'the Mayor, Aldermen, and Burgesses' of the Town. About this time, records refer to the town stocks and pillory being sited opposite the Town Hall. Court records of the time report that a 'naughtie person' was fined 2s. 6d. and sentenced to a period in the stocks for 'being sire of a bastard'; and that a 12d. fine was imposed on someone else for 'urination upon the Town Hall steppes'. There was also a town ducking stool, which was located near the 'Watering Place', on the site of the corner of today's Vauxhall Road and Marybone, at the end of Tithebarn Street.

"This was used to punish wives and daughters who 'misbehaved', particularly those 'whose nagging became intolerable to their men folk'!"

Civic Records refer to the ducking stool needing refurbishment in 1578, because 'it was sorely in good use and being in much want of repair', and to a completely new one being built in 1637. This was replaced again in 1657, and repaired in 1695. It was then replaced again, in 1712, so it was obviously getting a lot of use!

In 1674, the Corporation ordered the demolition of the old building and the construction of a new Town Hall. This was set back from where the original Town Hall had stood and, when it was completed, the new building became known as 'The Exchange'. This was because the ground floor had an open colonnade, inside which local traders and merchants could

conduct business. On the upper floor there were meetings rooms, and the whole building was surmounted by a large turret.

However, this building eventually became dangerously unstable and it began to subside! And so, in 1748, the Town Council commissioned John Wood (1704-1754), a prominent architect from Bath, to design and build a much grander building, and the foundation stone was laid that same year.

The new Town Hall was opened, in 1754, amid great celebrations. But, fifty years later in January 1795, a disastrous fire damaged the Town Hall. It proved impossible to extinguish the blaze owing to a severe frost, which had frozen the water pipes, and it was purely by chance that a great part of the building survived. The architect, James Wyatt (1746-1813) was given the responsibility of restoring and reconstructing the Town Hall, which is the building that stands today. On the top of the dome, which has four clock faces flanked by lions and unicorns, sits the statue of Minerva, who is the Goddess of Wisdom. Carved in terracotta, and covered in 87,000 square inches of gold leaf, she watches over the building and the City.

Above the porticoed main entrance to the Town Hall, and overlooking Castle Street, is the South Balcony. It is from here that the Lord Mayor, visiting Royalty, stars of stage and screen, and those individuals receiving the Freedom of the City, all acknowledge the cheers of crowds below. The interior of the

Town Hall is magnificently decorated throughout, and it has been fully restored to its original late-Georgian design. The two ballrooms and fine suites of civic rooms on the upper level make this one of the most significant such buildings in the country. Indeed, on a visit to the Town Hall in the early years of the 20th Century, King Edward VII compared the rooms to those of the Tsar's Winter Palace in St. Petersburg, remarking that they were,

'the best-proportioned in all Europe'

Because of its beauty, the Town Hall is a very popular venue not only for civic functions but also for private celebrations, with an average of 800 events being held here each year. In 2002, the building was voted the best Town Hall in the country, by the National Association of Civic Officers, and it is opened annually to visitors when all the rooms and treasures are put on display. However, it is unlikely that the building will be open when you visit, although do check first. Nevertheless, you will be allowed into the foyer and entrance hall, where a number of treasures are on display inside large glass cabinets.

> **To Find Out More:**
> Liverpool Town Hall
> Phone: 0151 225 5530
> http://www.civichalls.liverpool.gov.uk

Liverpool Town Hall

Leaving the Town Hall, it is well worth making a complete exterior circuit of the building, just to take in its architecture and styling, but then go back to the rear, onto Exchange Flags. In the centre of this grand plaza stands the magnificent memorial statue group, dedicated to Admiral Horatio Nelson.

Exchange Flags and The Nelson Memorial

Directly behind the Town Hall is Exchange Flags and, as you walk along High Street to enter this large plaza, you will be travelling along old Juggler Street.

Exchange Flags and The Nelson Memorial

Trading in all kinds of commodities – but particularly in cotton – had taken place in the Town Hall and the Exchange for centuries. However, the merchants of 19th century Liverpool had long needed a larger area to conduct business than that provided by these buildings and so, in 1808, an area behind the Town Hall was enclosed on three sides by intricately-carved colonnaded archways, supporting a large office-block complex. The plaza that this enclosure then created was paved with large flagstones, thus giving the area its name.

In 1906, traders left Exchange Flags for a brand new Cotton Exchange in Old Hall Street, which we shall see later in this Tour. Old Exchange Flags and its magnificent colonnades were demolished in 1939, to be replaced by the current buildings that still surround the large piazza.

Fortunately, if narrowly, these buildings and the Town Hall escaped the destruction during the German bombing raids, and this vast complex of offices has recently been completely refurbished. Some are being let as offices once again, but many have been converted into luxury apartments.

In the centre of this open square stands a magnificent monument that commemorates the victory of the British Fleet, over the French and Spanish Fleets, at the Battle of Trafalgar on October 21st 1805. The large sculptured group is specifically dedicated to one of Britain's greatest naval heroes, Admiral Horatio Nelson (1758-1805), who was the Commander of the British Fleet during this conflict. (This was the first piece of public sculpture ever erected in Liverpool.)

However, Nelson was already a great favourite of Liverpudlians well before Trafalgar, because he kept the seaways open for the City's shipping trade, thus allowing commerce to flourish and profits to be made. In fact, in 1798, the Town conferred the Freedom of the Borough upon Nelson whilst he was at sea aboard his flagship HMS Victory.

As another mark of their appreciation for the English Admiral, the merchants and Corporation of Liverpool commissioned the forging of a ceremonial sword, which they invited Nelson to receive at a formal presentation in Liverpool. However, he was unable to accept the invitation because he was killed before this event could take place. This tragedy occurred just at the moment of his greatest triumph, at Trafalgar, when he was shot and fatally wounded by a sniper, who was positioned high in the rigging of a French ship as it engaged HMS Victory. Nevertheless, in theory the sword is still Nelson's, because once the decision had been taken to award him the weapon it became his property. However, because it was never formally claimed, the sword remains in Liverpool, taking pride of place in a display cabinet of City Treasures, in Liverpool Town Hall.

The monument in Exchange Flags was sculpted by James Wyatt who, as we have seen, re-built the Town Hall. It comprises a large bronze group showing Nelson's apotheosis at the top, and this is surrounded by bronze plaques showing scenes from some of his engagements. Perhaps most powerful of all the monument's images however, are the four, chained captives – racked by anguish. These are not slaves, but symbols of Nelson's four great victories at Cape St. Vincent, the Nile, Copenhagen and, of course, at Trafalgar.

To Find Out More:

Exchange Flags
http://www.exchangeflags.co.uk

The Nelson Monument
http://www.liverpoolmuseums.org.uk/maritime/exhibitions/nelsonmonument/

From Exchange Flags return to Dale Street in front of the Town Hall, and turn right into Water Street. This is full of remarkable buildings so, once again, look up as well as looking all around as you walk down the hill in the direction of the river.

Water Street (17)

Turning right in front of the Town Hall takes us from the end of Dale Street – which we shall explore more fully later – onto Water Street. This is now the third of the Seven Streets on our journey, and it was first known as 'Bonk Street'. This was because the original road ended roughly where the modern street does today, at its junction with The Strand. In Medieval times though, this was actually the bank of the river, and the word 'bonk' was Lancashire dialect for 'bank'. It was at this point that the Monk's Ferry from Birkenhead would land, and passengers would walk up Bonk Street into the Town. (See Chapter: 'The Liverpool Waterfront'.)

As Liverpool and the river became more important, this was also the point of embarkation for all kinds of vessels, before the building of the Liverpool's first dock in 1715. A significant number of these were troop ships belonging to the powerful Stanley family, who played a significant role in British History from the early 15th century. We shall learn more about the Stanley's in the next article.

From around 1540 the street had been renamed as Water Street, and it was to become one of the best residential streets in the Town because, at that time there were no suburbs. As we have already seen, wealthy merchants and their families first lived in the heart of the Town, in suites of rooms directly over their shops, manufactories, warehouses, and counting houses. As well as these being located in the Ropewalks district of the Town many were also located in and around Water Street. It was only towards the latter decades of the 18th century that these people began to leave the expanding town centre. They moved to new terraces of large houses then being built in what is now called 'The Georgian Quarter' of Liverpool. (See Chapter: 'Pool of Life & Culture'.) Those that could afford to, bought large estates well outside the Town in places like Crosby, to the north; and in Allerton, Childwall, and Woolton in the south. (See Chapters on 'Liverpool, Lost and Found', and 'Green and Pleasant Liverpool'.)

Most of the buildings and warehouses that remained on Water Street were replaced, in the late 19th and early 20th centuries, by the buildings that stand on the Street today, and many of these are well worth closer

The Heart of the City

inspection. The first building of significance is on the left, at No 7 Water Street, standing between Lower Castle Street and Fenwick Street. This was the **Bank of Liverpool Building**, and it was built in 1895, in the style of an Italian Palazzo, and was subsequently refurbished in 1930. In later years it became the **General Accident Insurance Building**. Now reopened as **Il Palazzo** serviced offices, this imposing, Italianate structure is a fine building. Of particular note are the two magnificent panther's heads that adorn the great bronze doors. The animals' teeth have been polished over the years, to a high shine, by the thousands of African sailors who have rubbed them to bring themselves strength, fortitude, and success: very important when you are 'a stranger in a strange land'. Why not give them a rub yourself as you go past? You never know ...!

On the other side of Water Street, at No 4, is what was once **Martins Bank**, which merged with **Barclays Bank** in 1969. Standing on the site of on old coaching inn, called the Golden Talbot Inn, this Grade II* Listed building is one of the many magnificently distinctive buildings in Liverpool, which were designed by the Liverpool architect, Herbert J Rowse (1887-1963). The was constructed between 1927 and 1932, and it is a beautiful structure. Inside, beyond the massive bronze doors, the original stylish and capacious interior was once described as being 'Jazz Age Parisian with fine Egyptian motifs'. The smaller doorway, to the left of the main entrance, has some fine reliefs set into the portals. These depict large figures of Neptune and, at his feet, stand naked African boys carrying money bags. Intentional or not, these carvings starkly reveal Liverpool's association with the Slave Trade. (See Chapter: 'The Liverpool Waterfront'.)

The vaults here, held Britain's entire gold reserve for safe-keeping, during World War Two but, no longer a bank, the building's owners are redeveloping it for other commercial uses

Back across the road once more, standing between Fenwick Street and Drury Lane, is the magnificent Grade II Listed **India Buildings**. This extremely large office complex – it covers an entire block – was also designed by Herbert J Rowse and was constructed between 1924 and 1931, at a cost of £1,250,000. Built as the new head offices of the Blue Funnel Shipping Line, which was owned by the Holt family, this outstanding structure was the architect's first significant commission and it launched his career.

One of its most dramatic features is the fine, barrel vaulted arcade of shops, which runs through the building between Water Street and Brunswick Street. This was actually a stipulation made by Liverpool Corporation before they would approve Rowse's design, as his new building was to be erected directly over Chorley Street, so India Buildings is the only building in Liverpool that has a street running right through it! It is worth going inside to look at the overpowering size and space of the arcade, and to enjoy the fine Art-Deco interior, which style was typical of the work of Rowse.

Opposite India Buildings is Covent Garden and, between this and Tower Gardens – which leads through to the gardens of Liverpool Parish Church – stands the unique **Oriel Chambers**, which is Grade I Listed. Built in 1864 by the relatively unknown Liverpool architect, Peter Ellis, this was certainly ahead of its time in terms both of its design and in its construction methods. It was one of the first office buildings to be clad in glazed curtain-walling, and its magnificent oriel windows protrude 2ft 6ins out from the frame of the building, thus filling the interior with light, and making the working environment airy and spacious. However, Ellis's design was so radical for the time – flying as it did, in the face of popular, post-renaissance styling – that the reaction from his fellow architects was completely hostile. Consequently, Ellis really suffered for his art, because he was forced out of practice by the public and by his professional colleagues. After this, Ellis's only other architectural commission was 16 Cook Street, off Castle Street, which is also a remarkable building of equally significant architectural merit.

As we come to the end of Water Street, on the right-hand corner and guarding what was one the point of embarkation for Lord Stanley's troops, once stood Liverpool Tower: On this site now stands modern Tower Buildings.

Tower Buildings and The Tower of Liverpool

Tower Buildings

There is little that now survives from Liverpool's Medieval past, however, many names and buildings still have significant associations with our distant history, and one of these is Tower Buildings.

This fascinating architectural confection gleams in the sun, and sits like an ornate wedding cake, facing the Royal Liver Buildings across the main road. In fact, both buildings were designed by the same architect – Walter Aubrey Thomas (1859-1934). In his design for Tower Buildings, which was completed in 1908, Thomas partially castellated its roof, and incorporated small turrets at each corner; these are meant to recall the original building that once stood here.

Erected in 1256, and facing the sometimes turbulent waters of the river Mersey and directly on the shoreline, a large mansion-house once occupied the site. This had been constructed of red sandstone but who its builder was is unknown. However, by the year 1360, records show that the house had become the property of Sir Robert Lathom. Then, in the reign of King Henry IV, it passed into the hands of Sir John Stanley (c1350-1414), a gentleman who owned estates throughout Lancashire and Cheshire and who, in 1405, had been granted the Lordship of the Isle of Man by the King.

In 1406, he made an application to the Monarch to be allowed to fortify the building, which the King granted. Sir John then expanded and redesigned the house, renaming it the 'Tower of Liverpool' in due course, challenging his neighbours the Molyneux family who, in 1445, became established in nearby Liverpool Castle.

In gratitude for his support at the Battle of Bosworth in 1485, and at which he defeated Richard III, Henry Tudor – now King Henry VII – awarded Sir Thomas Stanley the hereditary title of 'Earl of Derby'. There had been previous nobles with this title, but now its award to the Stanley family consolidated their power throughout England, as well as at home in Liverpool. (See Chapter: 'A Lordly Heritage'.)

"After the Civil War, Oliver Cromwell executed the 7th Earl of Derby for supporting Charles I and consequently, the Stanley family lost most of their land and holdings."

Nevertheless, after the Restoration of the Monarchy, by 1665 the 8th Lord Derby had recovered all the family estates, including the Tower. But, by 1737, Liverpool Corporation was leasing the Tower from the then Earl and, in 1745, part of the building was converted into a prison. The dungeons here were airless, tiny, overcrowded and "foul beyond belief". (See Chapter: 'Pool of Life & Culture'.)

The upper rooms of Liverpool Tower were used for civic functions, until the new Town Hall was completed in 1754, and the Corporation eventually bought the Tower outright, in 1774. By July 1811, the prison was closed following the completion of the new Liverpool Prison in Great Howard Street. After its long and colourful history, in October 1819 the Tower was demolished, to accommodate the widening of Water Street, and its materials were sold for £200. Initially replaced by a row of warehouses, in 1846 the first 'Tower Buildings' was designed and built on the site by Sir James Picton. In 1906, this was replaced by the present Grade II Listed building. As well as offices, the current magnificent structure contains shops, flats and apartments, and a luxurious penthouse suite.

To Find Out More:
Modern Tower Buildings
www.tower-building.co.uk

Chapel Street and Liverpool Parish Church

Turn right at the bottom of Water Street, and walk along the road in front of Tower Building, this is George's Dock Gates. You will soon pass a little passageway known as Prison Weint, and beyond this is the attractive sandstone gateway into the gardens of Liverpool Parish Church. However, we shall enter these grounds from another point, so keep walking until you come to the corner of Chapel Street. Here you will see the Simpson Water Fountain.

At the corner of Chapel Street, set into the wall of Liverpool Parish Church, stands the **Simpson Fountain**. This stands precisely where the original chapel of St. Mary del Quay once stood, in early Medieval times, and we shall hear about this ancient chapel shortly.
The fountain is a memorial to William Simpson who was a much respected 19th century local philanthropist.

Liverpool Parish Church

Turn right into Chapel Street and follow the line of the wall until you come to the front of the church. Here, up a slight incline and some steps, is
Old Churchyard and the gardens of Liverpool Parish Church.
I suggest a stop of around 30 minutes here to walk around the gardens and the church.

In the attractive gardens at the corner of Chapel Street stands Liverpool Parish Church. This is dedicated to Our Lady and St. Nicholas, and is known as **The Sailors' Church**.

Chapel Street retains its original name and is the fourth of the Seven Streets on our Tour. It takes its name from the earliest place of Christian worship in the Medieval village of Liverpool, which stood very close to the site of the present church. This was then right on the water's edge, where the Simpson Fountain now stands, and was the **Chapel of St. Mary del Key, or Quay**, which was a place of pilgrimage. Records dating from 1206 refer to this as being originally an Anglo-Saxon chapel made of wattle and daub and, between 1355 and 1361, a new church dedicated to **St. Mary and St. Nicholas** was built next to the old chapel.

The new church consisted of a chancel, a nave, a western tower, and a large aisle, but Liverpool at this time was only a small part of the greater parish of Walton, administered by St. Mary's Church, at Walton-on-the-Hill. (See Chapter:'Fortunes, Fables, and Football'.) This meant that Our Lady and St. Nicholas remained as only a local place of worship until the Reformation and, in 1673, it was described as 'a place of great antiquity'. Around this time, the original waterside chapel of St. Mary del Quay was bought by the Liverpool Corporation, for the sum of 20 shillings. The ancient building was then variously used as a town warehouse, a school, a private house, a boathouse, and eventually a tavern; but it was finally demolished in 1814.

In 1699, when the population of the Town had risen to about 5,000 people, Liverpool was created an independent parish with two churches: Our Lady and St. Nicholas – by then often called the 'Old Church' or simply 'St. Nicholas' – and a new parish church of St. Peter, which stood in Church Street. 'St. Nick's', as the church later also became affectionately known, was the church that the seafarers used to pray in, and to worship at before setting sail on perilous sea voyages.

"It was also the place of worship and prayer for the families and friends of sailors at sea, whilst separated from their loved ones"

And it was here too. that seafarers and their families would come to give thanks, following a safe return from a long voyage. In 1774, Our Lady and St. Nicholas Church was almost entirely rebuilt, with a new tower being added in 1746.

The role of the church in the life of the waterfront and of the Town continued but, despite the many new churches then being built in Liverpool, no opportunity was taken to replace the 'Old Church' with a more up-to-date building. There had been repeated warnings that the spire was unsafe and, on 11th February 1810, as people were assembling for Sunday morning service, the bells were being rung very vigorously. This caused the church steeple to suddenly collapse, and it crashed into the nave killing 25 people and injuring many others. Of the dead, 21 were aged under 15, most of whom were girls from the nearby Moorfields Charity School.

Because of this tragedy, the architect Thomas Harrison was brought in to redesign and rebuild the tower. In 1815 the work was completed, and the new 120ft high tower with its spectacular flying buttresses was surmounted by a beautiful – but much more lightweight – lantern spire, which is a further 60ft high.

Since 1916, Our Lady and St. Nicholas has been the Parish Church of Liverpool and, whilst the nave of the church was destroyed by enemy bombing in 1940, the tower and spire survived. A new nave was built and this was consecrated in 1952. There are many references in this book, to the catastrophic bombing of Liverpool during World War Two, and it is in the churchyard here that one can find the **Blitz Memorial**. This very powerful piece of sculpture was created by Tom Murphy, and unveiled by HRH the Duke of Edinburgh, in July 2000. It takes the form of a spiral staircase with a young boy playing with his toy plane on the top step. His mother, clutching her baby, pleads with her son to stop his play and to come and shelter from the bombs that are falling all around.

The church has a charm and simplicity that provides a pleasant haven from the bustle of the Dock Road and the stresses of City-life. The church garden is surprisingly tranquil, despite being so close to a major thoroughfare. Indeed, in 2003 the Civic Trust awarded this garden, together with Calderstones and Reynolds parks in the City suburb of Woolton, with Green Flag status. Many more of our parks have now achieved this accolade.

The bells of the church have a special significance to local residents in that, whilst everyone born within the City boundaries can claim to be a genuine Scouser, only those who are born within the sound of the church bells of Liverpool Parish Church can be truly called **Dicky Sams!** This is an old Lancashire term for a Liverpool man and it predates 'Scouser'. It derives from the woollen muffler that Liverpudlian men, especially those working on the docks, traditionally used to wear around their necks.

Do make time to go inside the church, and perhaps to spend a few moments here in quiet prayer or contemplation, regardless of your faith. You will find the atmosphere peaceful and welcoming, and the church has warmth in its design and layout.

To Find Out More:
Liverpool Parish Church
Phone: 0151 236 5287
http://www.livpc.co.uk

From the church return to Chapel Street and turn right.
Continue up the road and, on the right, you will pass the
Hargreaves Building – now the ZIBA Restaurant and Raquet Club.

The Racquet Club

The Liverpool Racquet Club was founded in 1874, to provide an
opportunity for 'sporting gentlemen' to play games of Real Tennis
and other racquet games. A site was chosen in Upper Parliament
Street in Toxteth, which was then one of the most exclusive
residential areas in Liverpool. In 1877, the Club was opened with
two racquet courts and an American bowling alley, the latter being
converted, in 1894, into two 'fives courts' – one Eton and one Rugby.

Then, after 100 quiet years of Club life, during the early morning
of the 6th July 1981, the Racquet Club and all its furnishings and
records, were totally destroyed by fire during the Toxteth Riots.

"A new home had to be found for the Club
and its members and, in November 1982,
the Hargreaves Building on Chapel Street
was purchased."

This was converted from offices to a private club, enabling the
members – amongst whose ranks I was in due course to number –
to enjoy excellent facilities, when the Racquet Club re-opened in its
new home, on the 20th May 1985. These included private rooms for
overnight accommodation; a private dining room and bar; a member's
lounge; a billiards room; two squash courts; a miniature swimming
pool; gymnasium equipment; and full changing facilities.

For the next ten years or so, the Racquet Club was a popular
watering hole for local business people and professionals but, by the
end of the 1990s, there were not enough paying-members to keep the
Club on a viable financial basis. Sadly therefore, the building had to
be sold, and the Racquet Club ceased to exist in the early 2000s, at
least in its original form. Nevertheless, in 2003 and after a complete
restyling and refurbishment, the building re-opened as a bistro hotel,
still named the Racquet Club and with private membership, but now
owned by a husband and wife team who operate it as a purely
commercial operation. With the ZIBA Brasserie and Bar on the
premises, which are open to the public, the Club is once again at the
centre of business and professional social life in this part of the City.

To Find Out More:
The Racquet Club & ZIBA Restaurant
Phone: 0151 236 6676
http://www.racquetclub.org.uk/

The first road on the right, past the old Pig and Whistle
pub, is Rumford Street. A plaque on the corner of
the building at the end, which is in fact the rear of
Exchange Flags, commemorates this as the location
of the Wartime Headquarters of the Western
Approaches Naval Command. The Museum is on the
left of Rumford Street, but this has seasonal opening
times, so do phone up beforehand to make sure that
it is not closed.
If it is open, then it is very well worth a visit, and I
suggest a stopping time of around 30-40 minutes.

The Racquet Club

Top Secret:
The Western Approaches Museum

Liverpool's role throughout the Second World War, particularly
during The Battle of the Atlantic, cannot be underestimated.
A visit to the Underground War Rooms, in Derby House in Exchange
Flags, makes this clear giving a fascinating insight into wartime
conditions and military strategies in Britain at that time.

When War was declared, the operational headquarters for Atlantic
defence and conflict was being constructed in the basement of
Derby House, under Exchange Flags. Upon completion in 1941,
this became the home of the **Western Approaches Command**,
known as **The Citadel**. It was from here that the Battle of the
Atlantic was fought, from 50,000 square feet of gas-proof and
bomb-proof bunkers, beneath Liverpool.

Our City has played a significant role in many of the conflicts that
have affected Britain throughout history, not least of all during the
English Civil War. However, most vital of all was our role from 1939
to 1945, and few cities contributed more to the War-effort, or
suffered more as a result, than did Liverpool.

After the fall of France in 1940, and before America came into the
War in December 1941, Britain stood completely alone against the
Nazi juggernaut that had rolled out across Europe. Liverpool was
vital to the nation's survival, because it was through the Port that
the convoys of ships to and from America, and from the Empire,
and – in due course – Russia, brought food and other supplies to
beleaguered Britain.

Hitler was perfectly aware of our strategic position, and so he
wanted to completely obliterate Liverpool. He ordered Hermann
Goering's Luftwaffe to 'bomb them into oblivion', and the first
air-raids took place in the autumn of 1940. These continued
intermittently until, just before Christmas of that year, there came
three nights of mass raids. The results of these attacks left great
gaps in the streets of Liverpool and much loss of life.

Nevertheless, the most violent aerial assault – the real Blitz, was launched against the City during the nights of 1st to 8th May 1941. It was the worst week of sustained raids on any part of Britain, including the Capital, and was an all-or-nothing attempt by the Germans to wreck the port from which the Western Approaches were being defended. After this, the Nazis continued to bomb Liverpool, almost every night during the remainder of May and through the first two weeks of June. Altogether, there were 79 separate air-raids during the Blitz, and it was estimated that, out of the almost 300,000 homes in Liverpool at that time, around 200,000 were damaged – 11,000 of those being destroyed. Indeed, throughout the City and its suburbs, there were 15,000 Blitzed sites.

Many important buildings were struck by either incendiary or high-explosive bombs, including the Customs House, India Buildings, the Corn Exchange, the Central Library, The Bluecoat Arts Centre, and the Museum. However, the work of the Port had to go on; people had to live their lives, and so they struggled to get to work through bomb-cratered and rubble-strewn streets.

The intermittent raids that followed the Blitz during the remainder of the War, though still bad, were not as terrifying compared with those that the people had already been through. Nevertheless, there was still much damage to property and loss of life and, between July 1940 and January 1942, the Luftwaffe bombing-raids on Liverpool killed over 4000 people, and injured over 10,000 more.

As well as the bombing of the City, from the very first days of the War, Hitler launched concerted U-Boat attacks on the Allied Convoys that were coming in and out of Liverpool, and so the **Battle of the Atlantic** began. This was the longest running campaign of the War as it lasted for the entire duration of the conflict.

From the first days of the War, operations to protect the Allied Convoys and to direct combined operations against the enemy, were commanded from under Exchange Flags. Here, deep underground in over 100 rooms, and with the most sophisticated communications and code-breaking equipment available, the Battle of the Atlantic was fought – including the sinking of the German Battleship 'Bismarck', amongst many other enemy vessels.

The first attack on a British ship was the sinking of the 'SS Athenia', which was on its way from Liverpool to Canada, only 24 hours after War was declared in September 1939. The final encounter was the sinking of the British freighter 'Avondale Park', and of a Norwegian minesweeper, in the final days of the War, in May 1945.

Nevertheless, during the conflict more than 1,000 convoys thwarted the Germans and safely entered Liverpool, bringing with them much needed supplies of food, materials, munitions, and men.

From early in 1940, aircraft used in keeping the shipping lanes clear were imported in parts and assembled near Ellesmere Port, in the south of the Wirral Peninsular across the River Mersey. And, from Derby House, **Admiral Max Horton** who was the C-in-C of the Battle of the Atlantic and the Citadel, would direct his 'Scarecrow Patrols' to seek and destroy enemy U-Boats in the North Atlantic Ocean. When Horton died, in 1951, the King instructed that his body be taken to Liverpool for a state funeral.

"It seemed that the entire City turned out to pay their respects, and Naval Ratings from all over Britain lined the procession route to the Anglican Cathedral, where he is buried."

Atlantic convoys were always protected by an escort force, commanded by the well-respected **Captain Frederick John 'Johnnie' Walker** (1896-1944), whose leadership skills were renowned. His force was very successful and, on one patrol in March 1944, they sank six German U-Boats.

During the Battle of the Atlantic the Allied losses were astronomical. Over 12.8 million tons of Allied and neutral shipping was destroyed, but the loss of life was the real catastrophe: Royal Naval losses totalled 73,600; with also 30,000 killed from the Merchant Service; 6,000 from Coastal Command; and 29,000 from the Anti-U-Boat Flotilla. Memorials to these gallant sailors can also be found at the Pier Head, together with memorials to the Merchant Navy, to Norwegian Seamen, to Belgian Merchant Seamen, and to 'All Those Lost At Sea'. It is here too, that an outstanding commemorative statue to 'Johnnie' Walker has been erected.

The underground command centre was preserved intact after the War and remained completely untouched for over 40 years, until the rooms were refurbished and re-opened, but this time to the general public as 'The Western Approaches Museum'. And so, to get some sense of how the Battle of the Atlantic, and other Wartime strategies were run from this secret bunker under our streets, pay a visit to this remarkable museum.

To Find Out More:
The Western Approaches Museum
Phone: 0151 227 2008
www.liverpoolwarmuseum.co.uk/

The Map Room in the Western Approaches Museum

Return to Chapel Street and continue along to the right.
You will pass the rear entrance to Exchange Flags, and opposite this is the end of Old Hall Street.

If you would like to take a look at some of the buildings along this ancient road then walk along the left side of Old Hall Street, cross over at the top opposite the Radisson Hotel, and return along the other side of the road. The descriptions of the buildings, in the article overleaf, are set out in the order in which you will pass them.

Old Hall Street and The Moore Family

Old Hall Street is the fifth street in our 'Seven Streets stroll', and it was originally known as **Whiteacre Street**. It acquired its current name in the early-19th century, when it was still only a narrow cart track, and the name comes from **More Hall**. This was the family seat of one of the earliest and most significant land-owning families in Medieval Liverpool. To set the scene for this important street, I will tell you about the Moore (More) family.

Records are uncertain as to when the Moores built their home here, but it is believed to have been around 1230, and it is thought to have stood on what is now the corner of Old Hall Street and Union Street – where the City Exchange now stands. More Hall contained a hall, a parlour, a great chamber, a buttery, closet, dairy, kitchen, brewhouse, stable, garret, cheese chamber, and a large outhouse with two spare beds: This large complex was clearly just as significant as the family were, and the Moore family were a key dynasty within Liverpool for many centuries.

Records show that, in 1246, Ranulf de Mora (Moore) was Liverpool's first recorded Reeve – although Liverpool had almost certainly had a Reeve since its foundation in 1207. In Anglo-Saxon times, a Reeve was the representative of the Monarch or of the Lord of the Manor, in a shire or district, and he was responsible for managing the administrative affairs of the community. This is where the term 'sheriff' come from, as this derives from 'shire-reeve'. The Moores were also particularly associated with the chapel of St Mary del Quay, which they probably helped to establish, and around 1400 they moved out of More Hall when they acquired the manor of Kirkdale, a mile or two to the north of the Town. Here, they built a much grander mansion named Bank Hall, and it was from this time that More Hall became known as Old Hall.

> "The ancient fortifications of the Town of Liverpool once ran across Old Hall Street, when it was still Whiteacre Street."

These consisted of a mud and brick wall behind which was a deep ditch, and with a number of mud forts positioned along its length – very much in the ancient Roman model. This probably ran close to the path of Tithebarn Street (when it was still known as Moore Street, and which we shall visit shortly), so Old Hall was just outside this protective barrier.

This meant that when Prince Rupert besieged the Town during the Civil War (1642-1651), the building was ransacked by his troops, who also burnt the farm buildings and outhouses that were part of the estate. After the Civil War, Old Hall was restored and re-occupied once more – being used as a Dower House.

Whilst the most influential and wealthy landowners of Liverpool, and of the surrounding countryside, had always been the Stanley and the Molyneux families – respectively the Earls of Derby and of Sefton, the Moores of Bank Hall, and the Crosses of Cross Hall – which stood where the Council Municipal Buildings now stand on Dale Street, were just as influential within the Borough boundaries and the surrounding Manors:

Eventually, because of financial difficulties, the Moore family left Liverpool and sold Old Hall and its surrounding lands to Lord Derby, in 1712. The rest of their estates, including Bank Hall, were subsequently also sold to Lord Derby, in 1724.

Once they left Bank Hall, the Moore family ceased to have any real influence in the Town and, as for Old Hall, this had disappeared 50 years previously when, in the 1840s, Old Hall Street was being widened. The grand old Manor House was completely demolished in this redevelopment, and no trace of it remains.

The area of the City that we are now exploring – around Old Hall, Tithebarn, Chapel, and Dale Streets, is the historic heart of the City and the place where these Lord of the Manor consolidated and demonstrated their wealth. It was here also that they exercised their various degrees of political power; not just as Town Burgesses, but as Bailiffs, Justices of the Peace, Sheriffs, Deputy Lieutenants, Aldermen, Mayors, and the like. As we are discovering, all of these streets are now home to some fine buildings; old and new. Many of these are significant in terms of their history, significance, design, and architecture, and we shall now look at some of these in Old Hall Street; beginning here at the Chapel Street end.

Old Hall Street and The Commercial District

Leading from the heart of Liverpool's original, medieval Seven Streets, Old Hall Street is now a direct link between the 13th and 21st centuries; because we are now walking into our new, economic powerhouse – the 'Commercial District'.

The first building that you see on the left, is No 100 Old Hall Street; the headquarters of the **Liverpool Chamber of Commerce**.

Crossing over Fazakerley Street and then Union Street now brings you to the **City Exchange**. Amongst other things, this is the headquarters of the Liverpool Daily Post and ECHO and of Trinity Mirror Regionals, the publishers of this book. It is likely that this building was the original site of the Old Hall. Behind the City Exchange, but perhaps best seen from the Waterfront, is the massive, sandstone-coloured block-house building that was the former headquarters of the Royal & SunAlliance Insurance Company. Known as 'The Sandcastle', Downing Investments have completely refurbished the 390,000 sq ft office block.

The former cottages at the Radisson Hotel

Re-named '**The Capital**', this unique building is playing a key role in the regeneration of this whole area as Liverpool's burgeoning Commercial District.

Crossing over Brook Street, and passing the **Passport Office**, we next come to the **Liverpool SAS Radisson Hotel**. This is part of the famous Swedish hotel chain, and it is one of the raft of high-profile international hotel chains that have chosen to build new hotels in the City. A particularly interesting feature of the hotel are the two 18th century fishermen's houses, which appear to stand side-by-side yet separate from it, outside its reception area in Old Hall Street.

The exterior of these buildings has been preserved and restored, giving the illusion from the front that they are still occupied, private homes. However, they now constitute part of the lobby bar of the hotel. Alongside the hotel stands the **Beetham Tower**. There are a number of high-rise buildings called Beetham Tower in Britain, each financed and owned by the Beetham Organisation, and this one, at 111 Old Hall Street, is 295ft tall and has 30 floors. At this point we now Cross over Old Hall Street and, almost directly opposite the hotel, is No 100 Old Hall Street, otherwise known as '**The Plaza**'.

Previously, this was the 'JM Centre', the headquarters of the Littlewoods Organisation. Put on the market by the Moores family a few years ago, the JM Centre was bought by Bruntwood, a company that specialises in redeveloping office buildings. However, in tribute to the founder of Littlewoods, Sir John Moores, statues of him and his brother, Cecil, stand proudly in front of the tall office and apartment block.

Landmarks of the Commercial District tower over the city centre

To Find Out More:
The Liverpool Daily Post & Echo
Phone: 0151 227 2000
http://www.liverpoolecho.co.uk
http://www.liverpooldailypost.co.uk
The SAS Radisson Hotel
Phone: 0151 966 1500
www.radissonsas.com
Beetham Tower
Phone: 0151 476 6666
http://www.beetham.eu
http://www.panoramicliverpool.com
The Story of the Cotton Industry
http://www.spinningtheweb.org.uk/

NB: It is important to note that this 'Moores' family have nothing whatsoever to do with the original 'Moore' family of Old Hall.

Immediately past The Plaza, turn left into **St. Paul's Square** – an area of stunning skyscrapers and dynamic office complexes; this is the hub of Liverpool's commercial renaissance. Many major banks, insurance companies, developers, financial services, marketing companies; amongst many others, have their offices here.

This was once the location for 'St. Paul's Church', a replica of St. Paul's Cathedral in London (consecrated in 1769). Demolished in 1901, the site was later the location for **Liverpool Stadium** – opened in 1932. This was a very popular sports stadium; the scene of some spectacular boxing and wrestling tournaments. It was also used as a venue for rock concerts, and for many acrimonious and militant union meetings, during the industrial unrest of the 70s and 80s. The stadium closed in 1985 and was demolished in 1987.

Once you have explored around the 'shining temples of economic energy', return to Old Hall Street and continue back towards Chapel Street.

Perhaps the most significant building on Old Hall Street is the one that we come to after crossing over Virginia, Prussia and Edmund Streets, and this is **The Cotton Exchange**.

The first buying and selling – or 'exchange' – of cotton was done by 'chapmen' (travelling salesmen) who travelled around the towns, farms, and villages, and who had their offices and store rooms in the back rooms of convenient local inns. As the cotton industry rapidly expanded throughout Britain and the world, in the late 18th and 19th centuries, it became necessary to establish central market places, or exchanges, for the buying and selling of cotton. Consequently, Cotton Exchanges were constructed in many major towns.

Liverpool Cotton Exchange, originally around Exchange Flags, acted as a giant clearing house for the international cotton trade, by managing and co-ordinating the importing and exporting cotton and cotton goods, and their distribution. The first recorded cotton auction took place in Liverpool in 1757, and the first cotton exchange building in the Town was opened in 1808. A new and larger Exchange was built here in Old Hall Street in 1906, to meet the need for more offices, and to take advantage of new working methods and technological innovations: Telephones, rather than letters and messenger-boys, became the method of business communication. As can be imagined, this revolutionised the face of commerce, and the Cotton Exchange on Old Hall Street was at the cutting edge of this commercial revolution.

"The Cotton Trade in Liverpool supported, and was supported by, many other trades and professions – not least if all shipping of course."

These included dock-labour; warehousing; inland transportation – by horse-drawn carts, canals, and railways; provision merchants; maintenance companies; insurers; clerking; solicitors; messenger companies, etc. Sadly, a major element of the Cotton Trade was the Slave Trade, and I discuss this in my Chapter: 'The Liverpool Waterfront'.

The economy of Liverpool was built on cotton, and without it the City would have collapsed. Indeed, there is a popular story that cotton bales were used as part of the foundations of the Liver Building. This is probably no more than a myth, but it shows how important cotton is to Liverpool's history, and the Cotton Exchange building – now Grade II Listed – has been at the core of this for 100 years, and is set to continue being so.

The last building of any significance on Old Hall Street, stands between Ormond and George Streets, and is the **Albany Building**. This was erected in 1856, for a wealthy banker named Richard Naylor, and the building's architect was J K Colling, who also designed the National Portrait Gallery in Trafalgar Square in London.

The Albany was originally built as a meeting place for Cotton Brokers, and it is one of the earliest examples of early-Victorian office buildings in Liverpool. It was an important location for international cotton merchants, and The Albany successfully combined office accommodation and meetings facilities with basement warehousing – which was a specific requirement of the flourishing Cotton Trade at that time.

In the centre of the building was an open courtyard (now roofed over), where the cotton brokers would meet to examine cotton samples in the bright daylight. This Grade II Listed building has been transformed into luxury apartments.

At the end of Old Hall Street, cross back over the road so that you are on the Exchange Flags side once more. Turn left, and continue along until you come to Exchange Street East.
Cross over this road, and Chapel Street now becomes Tithebarn Street.
You now have a choice: You can continue along Tithebarn Street or you can turn off towards Dale Street as directed later, and this decision depends largely on your remaining stamina and available time. If you follow Tithebarn Street, you will only pass one or two interesting buildings but, after about a ten-minute walk, you will cross over a junction and come to the site where St Patrick is said to have preached before setting off to convert the Irish to Christianity. You can then return to where we are now and take the road leading to Dale Street.

If St. Patrick is not of interest, then follow the route directions after the article on Tithebarn Street.

At the junction of Chapel Street and Old Hall Street was once the ancient crossroads where the **White Cross** stood. This was a tall cross set upon a base of five stone steps. It is first mentioned in Town records in 1599, but was certainly much older than this. It was such an important location, in the heart of the Seven Streets of the Town, that it was one of only two locations that, from 1653 and during the winter months, were illuminated by candle lanterns at night: Liverpool's first street lights! The other illuminated location was **High Cross**, which stood at the junction of Castle Street and Dale Street, in front of where the Town Hall now stands. It was from this latter cross that Town proclamations were made. However, important markets were regularly held at White Cross; cattle were traded here, and it was the site of the first fish market in Liverpool.

"Vegetables were also sold here, and people would come from miles around to buy potatoes brought in from Formby: These were so valued that they were often given as gifts!"

We are now walking along Tithebarn Street, which is the sixth of our seven original streets of Liverpool. The first name for this was 'Moor', or 'More Street', and it was either named for the Moore family. or perhaps after the moorland that it then ran through.

In 1523, the Mayor of Liverpool gave Sir William Molyneux permission to build a barn on the street, to store the tithes of the Parish of Walton. These tithes were collected as a tax for the benefit of the local clergy and religious houses, at the rate of a tenth of all local produce and livestock. However, after the Dissolution of the Monasteries, by King Henry VIII in 1536, the building was completely taken over by Sir William, who then used it as a barn in which to store his own stocks of corn. This was paid over to Molyneux, by local people, as his fee for the mills that he owned throughout the Town, which were used for grinding and milling the townsfolk's crops. Because the barn was such a focal point in the community, over the years and through common usage, the name Moor Street was dropped in favour of 'Tithebarn Street'; first appearing in Town records under this name, in 1708.

The old Tithebarn during the 1800s

The actual site of the barn was on the corner of Cheapside, on the south side of Tithebarn Street, and there is some confusion about when it was demolished. The original **Tithebarn** is said to have been pulled down by 1674, however, other records say that the main structure and oak roof of this ancient building survived up to the early 19th century.

This street was the original north-south thoroughfare of the Town, and it became more important as Liverpool grew in influence and population. However, it twisted and turned its way through ancient

Town and, in places it was only 15 feet wide, which was very narrow indeed for the main road that it was. By the early 19th century this caused much complaint from the townspeople and so, in 1820, Tithebarn Street was widened and all the remaining Medieval buildings, including the remains of a very ancient barn, were swept away. It is not clear whether or not this was the Tithebarn but, whatever it was, sadly nothing now remains of the barn, except its name.

The Superlambanana sculpture on Tithebarn Street

At the end of Tithebarn Street, on its corner with Vauxhall Road, and outside the JMU Avril Robarts Building, is one of Liverpool's modern icons – **The Superlambanana**. Designed in 1998, by New York artist, Taro Chiezo, this bright yellow comment on the dangers of genetic engineering, stands 17ft tall, and has become a very popular addition to Liverpool's cultural character. In 2008, as part of Liverpool's celebrations as European Capital of Culture, 125 replicas of the sculptures, each a quarter the size and individually designed and themed, were placed around the city; they formed part of a trail which people could follow to see if they could locate and indentify them all.

If you are visiting St Patrick's Cross, after passing the end of Hackins Hey and the next road along, Tempest Hey, you will pass two pubs on this side of the road; The Railway Inn and The Lion Tavern.
The next road along is Moorfields, and opposite the end of this, across on the other side of Tithebarn Street, stands the former hotel building for the now disused Exchange Station, which is now named Mercury Court.
It is best to cross over Tithebarn Street at this point, using the pedestrian crossing in front of Mercury Court. Continue then along Tithebarn Street, on the Mercury Court side, crossing Pall Mall and other roads until you reach some modern buildings at the end of the road; these are part of Liverpool John Moores University.
You will now be facing the four-way road junction of Vauxhall Road, Marybone, Great Crosshall Street, and Hatton Garden. Carefully cross over this very busy junction, taking Great Crosshall Street, down the hill to the right of the Cosmopolitan Housing Association building. About 200 metres further along, turn left into Standish Street.
After visiting St Patrick's Cross, reverse your route and return back along Tithebarn Street. Cross over the road at Mercury Court once again, and return to the end of Hackins Hey. Walk down here to join Dale Street, where we will turn left.

St Patrick's Cross

Standish Street is now a quiet cul-de-sac, in the centre of a new housing development, and tucked away in one of the busiest areas of the outskirts of the City.

The current tranquillity of the street belies is former bustling life, when it was lined with poor-quality housing occupied by mainly Irish immigrants.

Here too was **Holy Cross Church**, demolished only a few years ago in the face of much local opposition, and which had been built in 1860 to serve this large Catholic community. The church had been erected near what had, for centuries, been accepted as a very important religious site and as such a place of pilgrimage for

The Standish Street Pieta

people from all over Britain and Ireland.

Many people still believe that it was on this site that, in AD 432 and on the instructions of Pope Celestine, St Patrick preached his final sermon before setting sail on a

treacherous voyage to Ireland, to convert the people there to Christianity.

In the centre of this quiet close is a well-kept piece of lawn, surrounded by low railings and shaded by trees. Here, as well as some memorial plaques and tablets, is a large sandstone cross that originally stood inside Holy Cross Church. Also, contained within a large, Perspex, vandal-proof box, is a highly-coloured, life-size **Pieta**. The monument also includes part of the foundation stone and stained glass from the church, and two time capsules are buried in the ground, containing other artefacts from this once important parish church.

Dale Street and Its Alleys

As we walk down **Hackins Hey**, even though we are still in the original Medieval heart of ancient Liverpool, we are now in the network of alleyways that began to appear as the Town began to expand slowly, in the 17th century. This street was laid out at Edward Moore's suggestion, along a croft between Dale Street and Tithebarn Street that was occupied by John Hackins, who was a tenant of Moore. This became known as Hackins Hey; 'hey' being a derivation of the French word 'haie', meaning land enclosed by hedges. Indeed, in the late 1600s it was Edward Moore, the then owner of Old Hall, who first began to develop Liverpool beyond the original streets and he now began to build new roads, many of which still exist today.

Halfway down Hackins Hey is a narrow road that runs alongside some currently vacant land. This is **Quakers Alley**, which takes its name from the Town's first, purpose-built Friends Meeting House; although the word 'Quaker' was originally a term of abuse for followers of this Christian sect, which was actually named 'The Society of Friends'. Around the time of the English Civil War, in the 17th century, many people began to regard the established Anglican Church as corrupt. Consequently, a number of 'dissenting' religious doctrines developed, gaining in strength and popularity as the century unfolded. In 1654, Quakerism came to Huyton, just outside Liverpool, and soon began to gain followers in the Town.

The Liverpool Meeting House was erected in Hackins Hey about 1709, and it had its own burial ground. The building was used by the Society of Friends until 1791, after which time they met in Hunter Street, and then in Paradise Street. As for their original home, after the Friends moved out this was used as a school, until 1861, when it was demolished. Whether or not the graves of the 18th century Friends still exist, beneath the modern buildings around Quakers Alley, I cannot say.

At the bottom half of Hackins Hey you will find some very old houses and pubs, the first of which is **Jupiters**, which runs alongside Quakers Alley. This is a somewhat Spartan, Gay-Friendly Bar, with a significant Lesbian clientele, because we are now on the fringes of Liverpool's Gay Quarter. Next door to Jupiters is **Ye Hole in Ye Wall**, which claims to be the oldest pub in Liverpool, and this may well be correct. This quaint little tavern is attractive inside, with brown leather seats, oak panelling, and beaten copper ornamentation. The casks of ale, uniquely, used to be on the upper floor and the beer had to be piped down to the bar.

Next to Ye Hole in Ye Wall, on the corner of Dale Street, is **The Saddle Inn**. This was once an important coaching inn, and is now also a pub of warm welcomes and good ales. Indeed, I would recommend any of these three pubs for a pleasant, and occasionally unorthodox, pint!

At the end of Hackins Hey we now turn left into Dale Street, which is the last of the Seven Streets of old Liverpool that we shall be exploring on this Tour. But our journey of discovery does not end here, because we have yet to stroll through part of the Gay Quarter, and the Cavern Quarter.

However, there is much to see along Dale Street and in the quaint alleys and the odd, narrow streets that branch off it. Before I guide you through these though, let me tell you something of the origins of this important thoroughfare.

"Dale Street existed long before any of the other Seven Streets appeared, and its name is probably a corruption of 'Dele Street', which derives from the Saxon 'Dele' or 'Dale', meaning a valley."

The road was named after a vale that once existed, near where the entrance to the Mersey Tunnel and St John's Gardens now stand.

As the Town developed, Dale Street became the most heavily populated street in Medieval Liverpool, and the first reference to it appears on a document dating from the reign of Edward III. Even so, at this time it would have been no more than a few metres wide, if that, with small, irregular cottages on either side of it. Nevertheless, our definition of 'heavily populated' is not the same as it was even during the time of Elizabeth I. It was during the reign of 'Good Queen Bess' that the following list of 'the Burgesses of Leverpul' then living in the Town was produced:

Dale Street	72	Juggler Street	15
Whiteacre Street	8	Bank Street	13
Castle Street	23	Moore Street	13
Chapel Street	7		

Liverpool was regarded at that time as being a busy town! But the land behind the houses on Dale Street would have been mostly fields or gardens, plus one or two tanneries, weaving sheds, breweries, and pinfolds for livestock.

By 1725, houses had extended as far down Dale Street as the dale itself, but beyond this were still open fields and the Great Heath. However, and after the opening of the wet dock, and as shown on an influential map of the Town from 1765, much of the rest of the Town had already begun to expand, and its population had risen rapidly. Nevertheless, Dale Street remained a narrow track until the end of the 18th century. It was at this time that most of its cottages and their surrounding fields and outbuildings began to be swept

The Heart of the City

away, as the streets of Liverpool began to be considerably widened and new larger houses and commercial properties were erected. It was behind these new facades of the Seven Streets that the warrens of poorer houses, tenements, and courts began to develop throughout the 19th century, and as the population of the Town now increased at a phenomenal and exponential rate.

Dale Street was first improved between 1786 and 1790, after Castle Street had been widened, and it became the principal coaching route out of the Town to Manchester, Birmingham, and London. However, Hackins Hey gives us an idea of how narrow the original Seven Streets of Liverpool actually were, because this has remained largely unaltered since it was first laid out.

Commercial building on Dale Street began at the western end, near the Town Hall, with the construction of the Queen's Insurance Building in 1839, and the Liverpool and London Globe Insurance Building, in 1857, and it is this Victorian and Edwardian Dale Street that we shall now see, as we stroll along the road.

> To explore Dale Street we shall now walk along the front of Rigby's Tavern. Staying on this side of the road you will pass the narrow passageway of Leather Lane. Passing next the end of Eberle Street and crossing over Moorfields, you should continue along Dale Street until you pass Vernon Street, Hockenhall Alley, and finally come to Cheapside.

The first building that we come to, as we turn left into Dale Street from Hackins Hey, is **Rigby's Buildings**. This is Grade II Listed and, although it carries the date of 1726, the present building is probably no older that around 1850. It takes its name from Alderman Thomas Rigby who, though of very humble beginnings, entered the licensed trade and soon made his fortune. He went on to own many pubs and hotels, and he acquired the building that now bears his name around 1852, although it was then known as Atherton Buildings. He wanted this building because of its large yards and warehouse capacity at the rear, and he used this as storage and supply facilities for his rapidly expanding empire of hostelries.

When he took it over, the building had quite a plain frontage so, in 1865, Rigby added the complex plaster façade and the collection of small gargoyles over the doorways. These are in pairs, and are wooden carvings of mock-Medieval grotesques, which are a curious adornment to this otherwise very Victorian building.

The narrow lane that runs under the eaves of Rigby's Tavern, up towards Tithebarn Street, is **Leather Lane**. This was once the pathway that led to Leather Hall, where animal hides where cleaned and traded, near where Mercury Court now stands. Later, a leather market was situated in the Lane itself.

Almost opposite the end of Hackins Hey, on the opposite side of Dale Street, is the Grade II Listed **Queen Insurance Building**. Built in 1839 for the Royal Bank, this was one of the first commercial buildings that were deliberately constructed with more office space than was originally needed by the owners. This was so that they could rent out the rest of the premises, to generate income and off-set some of the building costs, so this was therefore a trend-setting speculative development. A spectacular and very detailed Royal Coat of Arms quite literally crowns the façade, and the central passageway leads to Queen's Avenue Arcade, which we saw on Castle Street.

To the left of the Queen Insurance Building, between the Sayers cake shop and the cold and soul-less modern office block on the corner of North John Street, stands the **State Insurance Building**. This Grade II Listed building is only half of the original structure, which originally extended to the end of North John Street, but it was truncated by Hitler! Built in 1906, by Aubrey Thomas who, as we have seen, also designed the Royal Liver Building and Tower Buildings, this is a marvellous neo-gothic structure with its heavily-ornamented gables, turrets, and window frames.

Across North John Street is the complex and overwhelming construction that is the **Royal Insurance Building**. This Grade II* Listed structure was designed by J. Francis Doyle and opened in 1903. The wrought-iron balustrades; the carved pediments and framing; and the detailed frieze of sculpted panels – by C.J. Allen, and which show characters from the world of commerce, all make the building an outstanding piece of Edwardian baroque architecture. The sundial on the side of the building adds curiosity, whilst its golden dome is very much the icing on this particular confection.

The next road along from the Rigby's side of Dale Street is **Eberle Street**. Here can be found two of the City's most popular Gay Night Clubs – Garlands and the G-Bar, as well as one of the City's two surviving, fully private members' clubs, The Artist's Club: The other being the Athenaeum Club in Church Alley.

Standing between Eberle Street and Moorfields is the **Liverpool and London Globe Insurance Building**. Built between 1855 and 1858, this Grade II* Listed building was designed by C.R. Cockerell, the architect of the Bank of England in Castle Street.

Looking across Dale Street once more, and adjoining the Royal Insurance Building, is **The Temple**. As with the Hargreaves Building that we saw in Chapel Street, this was designed in an Italianate style by Sir James Picton for Sir William Brown, and it was opened in 1865. Above the main entrance to The Temple can be seen four hands clasped together, and the words, 'Harmony Becomes Brothers', and the round, arched entranceway that is set below the large turret in this Grade II Listed building, once opened onto an arcade.

This then led to a complex of Lawyers' and Barristers' Chambers. This building has recently been refurbished and, whilst it is still home to one of Liverpool's major law firms, the rest of The Temple now has mixed commercial and residential use, and it is laid out around one of the new City squares that are appearing throughout Liverpool town centre.

Beyond the Temple stands the magnificent, Grade II Listed, **Prudential Assurance Building**. Built between 1885 and 1886, this was designed by the renowned Liverpool architect, Alfred Waterhouse.

"Over the main entrance stands a life-size female figure in a Greco-Romanesque costume. This is the figure of 'Prudentia' – and she was invented by the company as their symbol"

As we continue along Dale Street, we next cross over the end of **Moorfields**. This road, as its name suggests, was once the site of fields owned by the Moore family, and it was first recorded as a street in 1697. The buildings between modern Moorfields and Vernon Street now stand on the site of what were once two narrow alleys – Batchelors Weint and Glass House Weint. In the latter, Liverpool's Tennis Court was once located: Not 'Lawn Tennis', but the 'Real Tennis' that had been played in England since Tudor times.

Next, we cross over Vernon Street, and then we come to **Hockenhall Alley**. The Hockenhalls were a Cheshire family, originally from Tranmere near Birkenhead. Thomas Hockenhall was a 17th century mayor of Liverpool, and it was his family who laid out and gave their name to this narrow, Medieval street.

Looking back across Dale Street from the end of Hockenhall Alley, we see – between Cumberland Street and Sir Thomas Street, the building that for many years was the **Conservative Club** and then an administrative annexe of Liverpool City Council. This is a Grade II Listed building, which opened in 1883, and the exterior is decorated by many intricate carvings, including 13 naked boys – or 'putti' – representing various trades and professions; such as stonemasonry, architecture, astronomy, and navigation.

The final road that we now come to, off the left side of Dale Street, is Cheapside. Here we shall see two buildings that are literally, and figuratively, opposites: A prison and a pub.

Cheapside, originally called Dig or Duck Lane, is one of the oldest streets in the City, and at one time this was the only route from

Dale Street through to Tithebarn Street. By the beginning of the 18th century there were already cottages on the side of the narrow street on which the pub now stands, whilst the opposite side was mostly occupied by vegetable gardens, by tanners' and skinners' yards, and by a watch factory. The factory and the leather works were demolished in the mid-19th century, and the **Main Bridewell** was built on the site, in 1866, by John Weightman, who was the Corporation Surveyor.

What is now a Grade II* Listed building was a grim place, constructed at a time when crime was rife in Liverpool, becoming the town centre's main lockup for 160 years. The Bridewell was first used to hold petty criminals, in its 47 cells, on four floors. However, for most of the 20th century it was operated by the Police rather than by the Prison Service, and they only used it as a holding facility for people arrested in the City, who were then to appear in the adjoining Magistrates Courts. Even so, the officer in charge was still known as the Governor. The structure of the building is very solid and very thick brick, and it sits in suitably forbidding and Dickensian squatness, behind a tall, austere wall.

"The prison was always busy, and often full, especially on Friday and Saturday nights as the clubs and pubs were 'letting out'!"

The Bridewell closed in 1999, but then the Police, who owned the building, realised that it might come in useful again during the Millennium celebrations, so it was temporarily re-opened! Finally closing again in 2000, the Victorian jail has yet to find a new purpose.

Opposite the Main Bridewell is the **Rose and Crown Pub**, this early 19th century inn is a great place to stop for a pub meal and a pint, in quaint surroundings. This was always popular with the local Police Officers, and with Magistrates from the nearby Courts. For this reason, the pub was also known 'unofficially' as 'The Pig and Whistle'! These guardians of Law and Order would often find themselves rubbing shoulders with members of the criminal fraternity, who had also gone into the pub to either drown their sorrows before a case, or to celebrate after one!

Just past the end of Cheapside and attached to the Prison, is the **City Magistrates Court** building. This too is a now a Grade II Listed building, although it is not at all attractive because of its plain and unimaginative design. Now that a new Law Courts Building has opened on Tithebarn Street, the old Courts are surplus to requirements and so are to be sold. We shall wait to see what becomes of the building.

Ye Hole In Ye Wall Pub

Opposite the Magistrate's Court and Cheapside, between Sir Thomas Street and Crosshall Street, stands Municipal Buildings.

Cross over Dale Street at this point, and have a look inside the foyer of Municipal Buildings where you will find a bust of John Weightman, the building's architect.

The Crosse Family and Municipal Buildings

As we have seen, it was the granting of the Charter to Liverpool, by King John in 1207, that first attracted people here, because of the benefits and incentives that went with the new status. And, over the coming years, families and individuals – with ambition and entrepreneurship – came here to establish themselves and to seek their fortunes. These included families who, as you will discover throughout my tours, were to become very significant in the developing Town. Such families as the Stanleys; the Molyneuxs; the Norrises; the de Waltons; the Gascoignes, and the Moores.

So too came the Crosse family; originally from the Wigan area, and they succeeded to much of William de Liverpool's property, whose family had ceased to be an influence in the area by the 15th century, despite obviously taking their name from the Town. This inheritance made the Crosses as rich as the Moores and, between them, both families had considerable influence in the growing Town. As with the other manorial and land-owning families, the Crosses also needed a local family seat, so they built Crosse Hall. This stood where the Municipal Buildings now stand, at the corner of Crosshall Street and Dale Street. By the beginning of the 16th century, the Crosses had become extremely powerful and were also major landholders.

The family lived in Crosse Hall until 1697, when they moved away from Liverpool, to reside at Shaw Hall in Chorley. However, they kept ownership of the grand mansion and its estates for some years. Then, around 1750, Crosse Hall and its surrounding lands were sold, and the grand mansion was soon pulled down.

"Over the next 60 years or so, a variety of buildings occupied the former Crosse estate and, in 1810, the site of Crosse Hall became the location of The Saracen's Head Inn."

This was a very popular watering hole and, with the improvement of the roads, the inn soon became one of the most important coaching inns in Liverpool: Mail, and later, passenger coaches would leave the inn, travel down Dale Street and up what is now William Brown Street, past Townsend Mill. They would then drive along 'the London road', which was the 'old road' to Prescot and Warrington. From these towns, the coaches continued on to the Midlands, and then via all points onwards to the Capital. (See Chapter: 'A Lordly Heritage'.)

In 1853, the old inn was demolished, and Municipal Buildings, now Grade II* Listed, was built on the site between 1860 and 1866, also by John Weightman. A bust of the architect, and a plaque marking the site of the Saracen's Head Inn, can be found in the entrance foyer to Municipal Buildings.

The new headquarters for the Town Council was, and remains, a remarkable building – inside and out. Designed in the popular post-Renaissance style of the time, the large building – with its tall and unusual clock tower and spire, is bristling with curious ornamentations. When it first opened, Municipal Buildings was home to many of the Corporation's most important departments; such as the Office of Health and Smoke Inspectors; the Superintendent of the Scavenging Department; and the Inspector of Nuisances. Today, and together with Millennium House on Victoria Street, Municipal Buildings remains at the centre of the Local Authority Administration of the City of Liverpool.

To Find Out More:
Liverpool City Council
Phone: 0151 233 3000
http://www.liverpool.gov.uk

> Leaving the main entrance of Municipal Buildings, turn left into Dale Street, and walk back in the direction of the Town Hall. Crossing over the ends of Sir Thomas Street, Cumberland Street, and Davies Street, turn left into the next road, which is Stanley Street. This is the main part of Liverpool's developing Gay Quarter.

Stars and Garters

As well as The Ropewalks Area being a centre of Clubland and Nightlife in the City, so is the area that we are now coming into. In fact, it could be argued that this is where it all began – in the 1950s and the 1960s; especially in the Mathew Street area. But first, let us take a stroll through Liverpool's burgeoning 'Gay Quarter'.

Stanley Street and The Gay Village

The Mayor leads the Liverpool Pride parade in 2010

Stanley Street takes its name from the Stanley family, the Earls of Derby, who are so key in the life and history of Liverpool. This street was originally developed as one of the principal locations for the growing commercial trade in the late 19th century. Indeed, it is home to one of the most striking commercial buildings in the City-centre, the Grade II Listed **Granite Buildings**, standing at No 6 Stanley Street. This was built in 1882, and is so called because of its austere granite façade.

However, this road is becoming better known as the hub of Liverpool's developing 'Gay Village'. The first Gay Bar on this street opened up in the 1970s at **Paco's Bar**, which was always very popular. Then came **Jodi's Club** – just next to the **Lisbon Bar** on the corner of Victoria Street, which is one of the City's longest established Gay pubs. However, the Gay community have been an important part of Liverpool life for generations.

Liverpool's Gay Scene began with the Black Cat Club and the Magic Clock, in the 1950s; through to the Lisbon, Royal Court, and Roebuck pubs, in the 1960s; and then to the Bonaparte, the Bears Paw, The Masquerade, The Pyramid, the Bar Royale, The Archways, and Sadie's Bar, in the heady days of Flower Power, Punk, and the New Romantics. This means that Gay nightlife and culture have been integral to the City for over half a century.

"This reached a popular peak in the 1970s and 80s and we are now seeing an exciting resurgence of 'Queer Culture'."

Liverpool's Gay Quarter is not yet as significant as Canal Street is in Manchester, but it is getting there! Most of the Gay bars, clubs, and restaurants are to be found in and around this part of the City, but now the City Council is unanimously backing a plan to invest seriously in the establishment of an 'official' Gay Village, hopefully to eventually rival Manchester's Gay Quarter. The Council is mapping out the neighbourhood's boundaries and actively attracting Gay businesses to the area. This will be the first time that a LGBT (Lesbian, Gay, Bi-sexual and Transgendered) Village has been specifically created by an act of a city council. Historically, in most cities, Gay neighbourhoods have sprung up on their own, usually as the result of several Gay-focused or owned businesses opening, or following a boom in the real estate market, but in Liverpool this growth will be deliberately encouraged.

Our City has always been innovative and creative, and that such imagination and open-mindedness should be part of Liverpool's development plan is commendable. Indeed, as well as **Gay Pride Events**, the annual **Homotopia Festival** that now takes place in Liverpool celebrates Gay culture, history, and heritage.

As well as providing much-needed support for the cultural and community life of the City's large GLBT community, this is all a shrewd business move on the part of the Council. The 'Pink Pound' is not a myth; indeed, the disposable income of people with little or no family responsibilities can be significant to a local economy, and

a strong and unified GLBT business community will help to develop its regenerating central core.

Apart from this, the Gay Village will add to the wonderful mix that is the diverse City of Liverpool, and this will increase the vibrancy, colour, entertainment, and good-humour of the developing City-centre, and we will hopefully see the **Rainbow Flag** flying from more buildings in the Heart of the City.

> To Find Out More:
> Gay Liverpool
> http://liverpoolgayscene.com/
> Liverpool Pride
> http://www.liverpoolpride.co.uk

> At the road junction, cross over and turn right into Victoria Street. Take the first turning on the left into the pedestrianised Temple Court.
> You are now entering The Cavern Quarter.

Mathew Street and The Cavern Quarter

Naturally, there are many places throughout Liverpool that have associations with the Beatles, and none more so than where we are now, in what has been named the 'Cavern Quarter' of the City-centre. Here you will find many specialist shops and bars, each one dedicated to the memory of the Fab Four; nevertheless, a few are of particular significance.

> At the bottom of Temple Court, if you turn left into Button Street, you will immediately find the Beatles Shop. Turning right from Temple Court however, takes you into Mathew Street, and this is the best route to take to explore the Quarter.

On the left, as you walk into **Mathew Street**, is an Irish theme pub called **Flanagan's Apple**. Set into the wall is a plaster bust of the Swiss psychologist, **Carl Gustav Jung** (1875-1961). He was a contemporary of Freud, but they had differing views about human psychology. In 1927, Jung had a dream about Liverpool. This had a profound effect on him and, in his book 'Memories, Dreams, Reflections', he recounts the dream, and analyses it by saying,

'But I had a vision of unearthly beauty, and that was why I was able to live at all. Liverpool is the 'pool of life'. The 'liver', according to an old view, is the seat of life – that which 'makes to live'.

The next place of special interest is the **Grapes Pub**, on the right of Mathew Street. Although redecorated in the intervening years, this pub remains largely unaltered from the days when the Beatles used to drink here, before playing at the Cavern Club further up the street (they could only get coffee or Coca-Cola at the Club, which did not have an alcohol licence). A plaque marks the place where, in the back lounge, the Beatles used to sit. Above the seat, behind protective glass, is a piece of the original wallpaper that covered the wall at the time. Next to the Grapes is the **Rubber Soul Bar**, lavishly decorated in Fin-de-Siecle style and, beyond this there are a number of other bars, clubs, and shops; most with a Beatles theme, but many without.

Towards the end of Mathew Street, on the right, is the **Cavern Wall of Fame**, which records the name of every artist or group that appeared at the original Cavern Club, since it opened. These include Stevie Wonder, The Who, Gene Vincent, Little Richard, and The Rolling Stones. Standing in the corner of the Wall of Fame, in front of the window of the adjacent **Cavern Pub** (not to be confused with the Cavern Club over the road), is a black, life-size, fibreglass **statue of John Lennon**, as he looked in the early 60s. This was sculpted by David Webster, and unveiled in 1997 by Gerry Marsden, the lead singer of another of the Brian Epstein stable of groups, Gerry and The Pacemakers. The Cavern Pub is worth a visit as it is filled with Beatles memorabilia, and is quite atmospheric.

Throughout this area there are many pieces of artwork and sculpture, including a terracotta piece by John's first wife, Cynthia Lennon (located in the wall just to the right of the doorway into the Cavern Club). This contains the first two stanzas of the Beatles song **'In My Life'**, and the words are a poignant memorial to John –

> There are places I remember all my life,
> Though some have changed
> Some forever, not for better
> Some have gone and some remain.
> All these places have their moments
> Of lovers and friends I still can recall
> Some are dead and some are living
> In my life I loved them all.

Opposite the Cavern Club and set high up in the wall, is another piece of artwork, the Liverpool sculptor Arthur Dooley's 1974 tribute to 'Four Lads Who Shook the World'. Named **'Beatle Street'**, this cost £500, and was a gift to the City from Pete Price, who is a popular, and long-established local club compere, DJ, and radio broadcaster. A range of clubs, wine bars, and restaurants, and the **Cavern Walks Shopping Centre** – with its own life-size group sculpture of the Beatles in the atrium, all add to the facilities here in the Cavern Quarter.

To Find Out More:
Mathew Street Webcam
http://www.mathew.st/webcam.php
Merseyside Campaign for Real Ale
www.merseycamra.org.uk

The Cavern Club

An essential place to visit in the Quarter is the Cavern Club, which is below the Cavern Walks shopping centre. The entrance is opposite the **Liverpool Wall Of Fame**, which commemorates every Number 1 Hit Record, produced by Liverpool groups and singers. The display highlights the fact that more No 1's can be credited to entertainers from Liverpool than to anywhere else in the world and, at the time of writing, this stands at 56! The first woman to top the British charts was Liverpool-born Lita Roza, in 1953, singing the seminal 'How Much Is That Doggie in the Window?' The last No 1 to be currently listed on this wall is 'The Tide Is High', which became a hit for Atomic Kitten, in 2002.

Arguably, the first **Cavern Club**, situated at number 10 Mathew Street, was the most famous beat club in the world, however, it opened first as a jazz club, on 16th January 1957, when it was the haunt of 'Beatniks' and 'Bohemians'! By 1960, Country and Western Music was being performed here alongside the Jazz sessions – there were no Discos or DJs in those days! Around this time too, the 'Skiffle' craze was in full swing, following the example of Lonnie Donegan, and this gave birth to the boom in amateur and semi-professional 'skiffle groups' all over Merseyside. One of these was 'The Quarrymen', of which John Lennon was a member, and they first played at the Cavern in August 1957.

Soon, Skiffle transposed into 'Rhythm and Blues', and then into 'Beat Music' and early British 'Rock 'n' Roll'. The Quarrymen transposed too, into the Silver Beatles, and then into The Beatles. It was on 17th February 1961 that the Beatles first performed at the Cavern, with Pete Best as Drummer, and with Paul McCartney and George Harrison completing the 'Beat Combo'. (See Chapter: 'Green and Pleasant Liverpool'.)

The Cavern then became the breeding ground for many groups and solo performers throughout the 1960s, and the Beatles went on to international stardom after playing the last of 275 performances there in just two years, on 3rd August 1963.

The Original Cavern closed in 1973, and the cellar club was filled in, in 1981, when the warehouse above it was demolished. There was a subsequent incarnation of the Cavern, just across Mathew Street, but the current Cavern Club was re-built on its original site in 1984. In fact, 85% of the reconstructed club is built on the original site, and 15,000 of the bricks used in its creation came from the old venue.

One of the best features of the modern Cavern is the accurate reconstruction of the stage on which The Beatles and so many other famous performers appeared, throughout three decades. It was on this stage that the Cavern Club set the feet of many local young people on the road to a career in Pop Music, and gave birth to 'The Mersey Sound' and to a cultural phenomenon. The new Cavern Club has all the atmosphere of the original venue, and you will find your visit here a fascinating experience.

As a footnote; on North John Street at the end of Mathew Street, is **The Hard Day's Night Hotel**, which is the world's first Beatle-themed hotel. It has been named after the Beatles first feature film, which was directed by Richard Lester and issued in 1964. The refurbished former Victorian office block has been transformed into a 120-bedroom, state-of-the-art hotel, each floor of which is dedicated to a Beatles record album. The rooms are individually decorated with themed murals, a luxurious penthouse sits on the roof, and a basement bar links directly to the Cavern Club.

To Find Out More:
The Cavern Club
Phone: 0151 236 1965
http://www.cavernclub.org
Hard Days Night Hotel
Phone: 0151 236 1964
http://www.harddaysnighthotel.com

The Heart of the City

After visiting the Cavern Club, return to Mathew Street and turn right, and then go into the Cavern Walks retail centre, which stands over the Club. You can have a stroll around the shops here, take a look at the commemorative statue of the Fab-Four in the tall atrium, and then exit the building through the opposite entrance, which leads into Harrington Street.

Cavern Walks

30

This remarkable example of contemporary architecture stands between Mathew Street and Harrington Street, and it has entrances on both roads. Opening in the spring of 1984, it was designed by **David Backhouse** from West Derby, and built by Tyson's.

Inside this stylish shopping centre and office complex is a tall and tapering atrium, with balconies that overlook a number of attractive shops and eating establishments. However, of particular note is the exterior of the building, which towers over the surrounding streets and is highly decorated in attractive, glazed terracotta. On the Mathew Street side of the building are carvings of doves of peace and Lancashire roses. These were created by Cynthia Lennon, who was John Lennon's first wife and is the mother of Julian Lennon.

When David Backhouse was designing the building, he said that he wanted it to be as much a work of art, as of architecture.

The 'Gorilla with a Lipstick' by David Backhouse, designer of Cavern Walks

"A critic of his design said that, 'art is to architecture like lipstick is to a gorilla!'"

David's reply to this ridiculous and short-sighted comment, is given in the small figure, which is of a gorilla holding a powder compact and applying lipstick! To take a look at the **Gorilla**, as you leave the Centre turn right into Harrington Street and, over the large doorway to the centre's underground car-park, you can see the small figure, carved in an oval relief, above the lintel.

As the foundations for the Cavern Walks were being sunk, engineers from Tysons discovered a large lake below the road – possibly an old, man-made waterworks. It was big enough for Tysons builders to sail around on, in a dinghy! The company's professional skills were equal to this new task and, without even attempting to drain the water, they constructed the foundations so that they simply straddle it: So, under Cavern Walks is indeed a cavern, and a small, mysterious, lost 'boating lake'!

Now turn left along Harrington Street, out of Cavern Walks and, just as the road dog-legs past the BHS Store, on the right you with see some 'musical seats' with a Beatles theme. From here, stay on this road as it wends to the right and becomes Button Street. After a hundred metres or so you will come to a junction, walk left here, into Rainford Gardens. You will see the Beatles Shop in front of you at the corner. Continue straight on, passing the shop to the right, and this leads you onto the lower half of Stanley Street. Across the road and to the left, you can see the Eleanor Rigby Statue facing you, set against the wall.

Eleanor Rigby

31

Sitting on a bench in lonely isolation, in a recess against the side wall of the **Met Quarter Shopping Centre**, sits the sad and slightly forlorn bronze sculpture of Eleanor Rigby. She features in the Beatles' song of that name and she actually existed. However, she was never known to the Beatles because she died many years before any of them were born: Lennon and McCartney simply took her name from a gravestone in St. Peter's Church, in Woolton Village, in the south of the City (see my Tour, 'Liverpool Lost and Found').

Eleanor is depicted as a shabbily-dressed woman, sitting alone on the bench, and feeding scraps to a few birds. This evocative and melancholic monument, was sculpted by the actor, and former 1950s Rock Singer, **Tommy Steele**, and he sold it to the City for 'half-a-sixpence'. This sum was the title of a West-End stage musical in which Tommy

was starring at the time. Inside the sculpture he placed a four-leafed clover, representing luck; a page of the Bible, representing spiritual help; a football sock, representing action; copies of the Dandy and the Beano comics, representing entertainment; and four sonnets for lovers. The sculpture is dedicated to 'all the lonely people...' and was unveiled by the sculptor, on 3rd December 1982. At the time, Tommy explained,

"I put them all inside the statue so she would be full of magical properties. I give Eleanor to Liverpool with an open heart and many thanks for my happy times in the City".

From the Eleanor Rigby statue, walk down Stanley Street towards Whitechapel. The entrance to the Met Quarter Shopping Mall is on the left-hand corner. Turn left here, and continue along Whitechapel, crossing Sir Thomas Street and Peter Street. You now come to the Conservation Centre of the National Museums Liverpool.

I suggest that you take a short stroll around the Met Quarter.

On the way to the last stop on this Tour, we pass **The Met Quarter**.

This exciting, ultra-modern, 'designer shopping mall' was opened in 2006, and is a flagship development in the regenerating Whitechapel area. Inside are a full range of top-line retail outlets, plus comfortable places to eat and take a coffee. However, whilst much of the Met is new-build, the rear of the complex was previously the main Post Office in the City. This was built between 1894 and 1899 and designed by Sir Henry Tanner.

Crossing over Sir Thomas Street and narrow Peter Street, we now come to The Conservation Centre, housed in what was formerly the **Midland Railway Goods Warehouse**. This magnificent, Grade II Listed building was built in 1874, by the architects Culshaw and Sumners. The large and solidly-constructed storage depot has won many plaudits from architectural commentators over the years, and what goes on inside it today is just as special.

This is because, between 1995 and 1996, the old building was redesigned by local artist and architect Ken Martin. It was then re-opened as the place where the most amazing and skilled restorations are carried out, of sculpture, art-works, and objects of significant cultural and historic importance. This award winning Conservation Centre is a workshop of wonders.

Conservators based in this unique venue look after National Museums Liverpool's diverse collections. Everything from Egyptian mummies to motorbikes gets preserved and restored here.

Government cuts mean that the National Conservation Centre closed to visitors in December 2010. But the valuable work continues inside.

> **To Find Out More:**
> **The Met Quarter**
> Phone: 0151 224 2390
> http://www.metquarter.com/
> **The Conservation Centre**
> Phone: 0151 478 4999
> http://www.conservationcentre.org.uk

> Leaving the Conservation Centre, cross over Whitechapel and turn left. This then returns you to where we began this Tour, at the car park in Queen Square.

Sir Paul McCartney at The Cavern Club

The Heart of the City: Conclusion

And so, we have now come to the end of our walk around the parts of Liverpool where it all began – through the seven Medieval streets of the old village; and also through the more modern streets of the City.

"The civic motto of Liverpool reads, 'DEUS NOBIS HAEC OTIA FECIT', which translates as, 'God has made this leisure for us'."

This is a quotation from a poem by the classical Roman poet Virgil, which centres on a conversation between two characters – Meliboeus and Tityrus. The latter is explaining his good fortune at being able to take it easy and enjoy the good life; 'God has given me this leisure', he states.

'But tell me of this God of yours, my friend', asks Miliboeus. Tityrus explains that the God to whom he refers is 'the City that men call Rome'.

The City Fathers, who chose our motto, clearly saw Liverpool as a latter-day Rome. This was because, just as the commercial success of ancient Rome had provided a culture for its citizens, the merchants of Liverpool used their own commercial success to become patrons of the arts and music; the creators of parks and civil architecture; and the providers of education, social care, and patronage. They, like a deity, provided leisure for their citizens.

The Latin words for leisure and business are, respectively, 'otium' and 'nec-otium', from which we get 'negotiation'. In other words, the Romans saw business and commerce as something that you did in order to have leisure. In the same way, the City Fathers of Liverpool saw it as their responsibility to provide leisure for its citizens. This sensible philosophy – that one should not work for its own sake, but as a means to provide pleasure in life – is at the core of Liverpool life and attitudes. Nevertheless, business is indeed taken very seriously in the City, and almost as seriously as having fun is!

"The complex 'personality' that is Liverpool makes this a wonderful City, and its people are warm, generous, and welcoming"

I hope that this Chapter has given you the opportunity to truly get a 'feel' for Liverpool and its people; also, that you now regard yourself as being amongst friends; and that you have discovered for yourself, their heart at the Heart of the City.

Liverpool Lost and Found

Including:

Picton Clock and The Smallest House

Wavertree Lock-Up and The Monks' Well

George Harrison's Boyhood Home

Childwall Woods and
All Saints Parish Church

The Childwall Abbey Hotel

Gateacre Village

The Old Schoolhouse,
Woolton Woods and Camphill

John Lennon's Boyhood Home

Allerton Tower, Allerton Hall
and Clarke Gardens

Paul McCartney's Boyhood Home

Calderstones Park

Bishop Eton Monastery

The smallest house (right), now part of the Cock & Bottle Pub on Picton Road

Liverpool Lost and Found: The Tour

The total distance covered by this Tour is 16 miles, and the suggested time for completing it, and for visiting all the sights and buildings, is 3 hours.

However, this does not include time to visit the interiors of either John Lennon's or Paul McCartney's homes; nor does it allow time to visit fully each of the parks. Neither does this estimate include time for lengthy rest and refreshment stops. If you do fully visit all the places suggested on the Tour then it will take between 6 and 8 hours to complete.

This is a circular tour, so you can pick it up at any point on the route. However, do always travel in the recommended direction, in this case CLOCKWISE, as the route has been designed to get you efficiently around Liverpool's sometimes confusing one-way systems.

NB Please remember to check all opening times and admission charges before setting off, to avoid disappointment should any venues be closed

Contents

Route Map

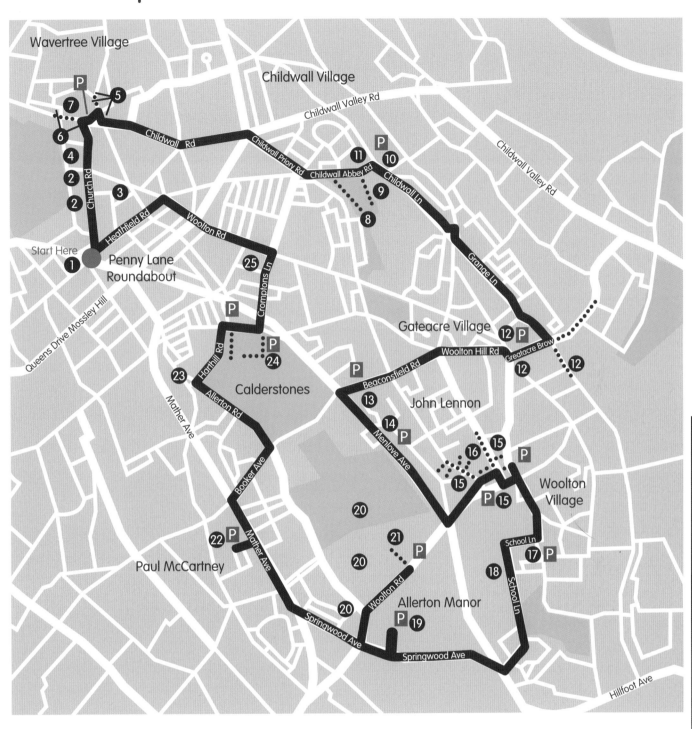

Key

- **Start Here** — Starting Point
- **1** — Map Reference
- Driving Route
- Walking Route
- **P** — Parking Points
- Railway

Liverpool Lost and Found
Introduction

Like Rome, Liverpool is built on seven major hills, but this is not the only association that we have with the 'Eternal City'. The many remarkable public and civic buildings in Liverpool, which were built by the Victorians, are testament to their belief that, as Rome was the capital of that great empire, so Liverpool was the trading capital of the British Empire. However the development of the City began, if only slowly, centuries before the Victorian era.

In the 1st century AD the Romans came to the River Mersey, to the River Dee, and to The Wirral; establishing themselves at 'Deva', which became the modern City of Chester. The Anglo-Saxons came to what is now Merseyside, in the 5th and 6th centuries, when it was part of a vast area of ancient England known as Mercia. And so too, came the Vikings, around 960AD. Although these invaders settled in the area, it is unlikely that the population of what was to become modern Liverpool ever consisted of more than a few families of farmsteaders and fisherfolk: certainly not until the Norman Conquest of 1066. In fact, the first written reference to 'Leverpul' does not appear until 1190.

In 1086, William of Normandy ordered the great national assessment of the value of his newly-conquered territories – The Domesday Book. And, whilst outlying communities such as Wavertree and Childwall are recorded in that great survey, there is no mention of Liverpool.

Clearly, it had no value or significance at that time, although it is believed to have been one of six, un-named berewicks – barley farms – that are recorded as being part of the much more important Manor of West Derby.

As we have seen, it was in the early years of the 13th century that the tiny fishing village, on the banks of an insignificant river in the North West of England, began its transition into a growing and developing town. Indeed, Liverpool continued as a small community until, by the beginning of the 18th century, the township began to develop its docks and its commercial and trading interests.

As a result, the population grew, and so did the need for space. Consequently, the boundaries of the town began to expand. In fact, the growth of Liverpool was dramatic, particularly during the 18th and 19th centuries.

In 1700, the population of the town was 5,715, but within only 40 years this had increased to 18,000 people. Within 30 years this had doubled and, by 1801, it had reached a figure of 78,000, and this growth did not slow down. By 1821 the population figure had reached 119,000; by 1841, 286,000; by 1871, 493,000; and, by 1901, it had risen to 685,000 people. In fact, in 1835, the boundaries of the Town were first extended, amnd half of Toxtath Park, and the communities of Everton, Kirkdale, and a part of West Derby, officilly became part of Liverpool.

By the end of the 19th century, Liverpool was recognised as 'the Second City of The Empire' after London, and the City Fathers considered that it was important that the official status of the Town should be elevated.

The first stage in this process was by the creation of a 'Bishopric of Liverpool', in 1880. Then Liverpool Borough Council petitioned the Government who granted Liverpool the status of 'City', in 1882.

It was from this time, and as the boundaries of the new City expanded even further, that Liverpool almost trebled in size: Particularly when, in 1895, the nearby villages of Walton, Wavertree, the rest of Toxteth, and more of West Derby came within the new boundary.

Over the following decades, the other local villages were also absorbed, including Childwall, Gateacre, Woolton, Allerton, Garston, Fazakeley, Croxteth, Speke, and the remainder of West Derby. Fortunately, these districts retain much of their original identity, and they are all worth exploring in their own right.

Whilst we shall visit, throughout this book, many of the ancient communities that were absorbed by the City, for this chapter in particular I have selected five of these places.

As we explore the City, we discover that these 'lost' villages can easily be found once again, and that they retain much of what made them distinctive.

Originally standing on the edge of Childwall Heath, the ancient village of Wavertree was linked by farm tracks to the neighbouring manor of Allerton and the village of Childwall. These would wind their way across the Great Heath, which once covered this entire district and stretched back to Liverpool, as far as where St George's Hall now stands, on Lime Street.

Wavertree was a township in the parish of Childwall, in the Hundred of West Derby, and is now home to a greater number of listed buildings than almost any other district of Liverpool. It is here that we shall begin our exploration.

The Author, aged seven, sitting on the Salisbury Stone in Wavertree Green

A former bus shelter and café stand at the junction of Smithdown Road and Church Road, opposite the end of Penny Lane and on a large roundabout used as a bus terminus. This is the 'Shelter in the Middle of the Roundabout', which features in the Beatles' song "Penny Lane". Our Tour begins by travelling up Church Road, which is the road that runs up the hill directly behind the 'Shelter'.
Following this brings you into Wavertree Village.

Wavertree Village

The Village is mentioned in the Domesday Book as 'Wauretree', and it was here, in 1867, that large upright stones from a megalithic tomb were discovered. The tomb was sited on Olive Mount just up the hill from the Monks' Well, and shows that this must have been quite a well-established community, with some significance if the local tribes decided to bury their dead here. At the same time, flint arrowheads and scrapers were unearthed alongside Bronze Age burial urns containing human remains, which suggest a pre-1000 BC settlement, making Wavertree one of the City's most historic local districts.

It is likely that the name of this district means 'a settlement near a spring on a wasteland', indicating that this prehistoric community was centred on the local spring that ultimately, in medieval times, became 'The Monks' Well' (see p98). However, 'Wavertree' could also just as easily mean what it says – 'a place of waving trees' – possibly aspen.

The Monks' Well

As you proceed up Church Road you will pass the Bluecoat School on the left, halfway up the hill. 'Dilworth's Folly' is directly opposite this, across the road. Beverley Road, which leads to the site of the old Haunted Mill, is also opposite the main entrance to the school.
Past the Bluecoat, again on the left, is Holy Trinity Church, directly opposite which, and in front of the Parish Hall, are the mounting steps.

To Find Out More:
The Wavertree Society
http://www.liverpool.ndo.co.uk/
wavsoc/page2.html

The Bluecoat School and Holy Trinity Church

The Bluecoat School

The Bluecoat School is the first building of any significance that we see as we make our way into Wavertree Village.

This was opened in 1906, when the pupils were transferred here from the original orphanage building that still stands in Liverpool city-centre, and which is now the Bluecoat Arts Centre (see Chapter: 'Heart of the City'). This was because, by the turn of the 20th century, the old building was not large enough for the needs of the times. The number of pupils was expanding, and improved standards required by new legislation necessitated the construction of the new Bluecoat School, which we now see on Church Road. Nevertheless, even in the new building, the school was still principally an orphanage for boys and girls until the late 1940s and, between the Wars, it was a familiar sight to see the children walking through Wavertree Village, dressed in their old-fashioned blue uniforms and caps.

In 1949, the Bluecoat became a 'secondary bi-lateral' school – day pupils as well as boarders – for boys only. Girls were re-admitted in 1990, but only to the 6th Form, when the dormitories and boarding facilities were closed due to a lack of demand. In 1997, after a number of years operating as a comprehensive school, the Bluecoat changed its status and became a Grant Maintained School. Now, and after a major redesign and refurbishment, the 21st century Bluecoat School remains one of the top secondary schools on Merseyside.

To Find Out More:
Bluecoat School Official Website
Phone: 0151 733 1407
http://www.bluecoatschool.net

Immediately across the road from the school is a magnificent block of three Edwardian gabled houses. Officially named **Dovecourt** but known locally as the 'Tudor House', it was also referred to as 'Dilworth's Folly'.

When the contract for the building of the new school was put out to tender, two local builders, Isaac Dilworth and Charles Berrington (after whom a local road is named), desperately wanted to win the contract. Using materials that were specified for the new school, they designed and built Dovecourt as a 'demonstration model' but, to no avail. The contract went to another local building firm, Morrison & Sons, who also were the main contractors for the Anglican Cathedral, and so Dilworth and Berrington's business failed.

Bluecoat School

②

Holy Trinity Church

Adjacent to the Bluecoat School is Holy Trinity Church, which the poet John Betjeman described as 'Liverpool's best Georgian church'.

Until Holy Trinity was built, the nearest church was All Saints in the village of Childwall, whose parish extended from Wavertree, out as far as Speke and beyond.

However, this was not adequate to meet the demands of the rising number of middle-class merchants who, throughout the late 18th and early 19th centuries, were looking to the villages surrounding Liverpool to establish themselves in their own 'country seats' as the 'new aristocracy'. These people needed a church of their own to match their status and so, in 1794, Holy Trinity was built by John Hope.

It remained a 'Chapel of Ease' – that is a sort of sub-church, used as a place of worship for parishioners who lived some way from the main parish church at Childwall – until 1867, when it became a parish church in its own right.

By 1911, the congregation had grown to such an extent that the church needed to be extended. This was very skilfully carried out by Charles Reilly – who was Professor of Architecture at Liverpool University – but the join still shows!

Holy Trinity Church

On the other side of the road from Holy Trinity, in front of the church hall, can be seen the 'mounting steps'. Originally across the road, this was used by nineteenth century churchgoers to get back in the saddle after services. It is believed however, to pre-date the church and, to judge by its well-worn steps, it may well have first been erected as a field-stile.

> **To Find Out More:**
> Holy Trinity Church History
> http://cam.derringer.co.uk/Liverpool/
> Holy Trinity Church Website
> Phone: 0151 733 2172
> www.holytrinitywavertree.org.uk

The Haunted Mill

③

Opposite the Bluecoat School is **Beverley Road**, and just behind the houses at numbers 35 and 37 is where the mid-15th century **Wavertree Mill** once stood, on land between two quarries.

The mill in fact pre-dated these quarries, which were only excavated from the late 18th century onwards. These produced sandstone that was used to build Holy Trinity Church and also Wavertree Lock-up – which we shall see shortly – as well as many other local buildings.

From the time it was erected, until the 17th century, the mill was owned by the reigning Monarch and all local tenants were obliged to have their corn ground there. From the Crown, it then became part of the rights of the Manor of Childwall, and eventually passed into the hands of the Marquess of Salisbury. In due course the quarries fell into disuse and, by the mid 19th century, they were being used as tips for household waste, mostly ashes. They were gradually filled in to become known locally as the **Bin-Field**.

By 1873, Wavertree Mill had stopped regular work, but it does seem to have been in occasional use. Indeed, in the mid-19th century, the mill was believed by local people to be cursed, following several mysterious accidents there: In 1866, ten-year-old Richard Matthews was killed when he was struck by the sails of the windmill and, some years later, a local girl had her hair caught by the sails, and was reported in the local newspaper as having been 'scalped and was rendered insensible for twelve hours, but happily she recovered'.

As useful as the mill was, local people began to believe that the quarry had become the home of 'a spirit of great wickedness' that

had cursed the neighbourhood. Eventually, following advice from the church minister and as a result of local pressure, each night to keep the spirit at bay, the miller would set the sails of the mill so that they cast the shadow of a cross onto the Bin Field, touching all four corners. No more nasty incidents are recorded after that!

In 1895, a severe storm destroyed the sails of the mill, and damaged the building so much that it was beyond repair; although it had already ceased grinding corn in 1890, when the lease from the Marquess of Salisbury expired. The mill was eventually demolished in 1916.

By the 1930s, the land on which the mill had stood was considered suitable for house-building, and it was from this time that the new local roads and houses began to appear. However, the remnants of the mill remained, on the last patch of open land on the site, until 1986. It was in this year that the City Council gave permission for these to be removed and the modern houses in Beverley Road were then built. Before this was done however, there was a full archaeological survey of the site and now, some of the mill's stonework, together with an old millstone, are to be seen in the front garden of the new houses. A plaque on them records the position of 'The Haunted Mill'.

> **To Find Out More:**
> Wavertree Mill
> http://www.dhwav.btinternet.co.uk/page59.html

Cross over the traffic lights at Fir Lane and, immediately on the left is The Royal School for the Blind; on the site of Wavertree Manor. The third gate along from the left is the original entrance, which once led to the door of the manor house. Opposite this is a playing field that was once part of Wavertree Green. Also on the left, beyond the Blind School, is the Coffee House Pub. Passing Hunters Lane on the left the White Cottage can then be seen, opposite which is the supermarket that was once the Abbey Cinema.

Across Fir Lane, which is the road that runs down the side of the churchyard of Holy Trinity, is the Royal School for the Blind.

Standing on Church Road North, the school is built in the grounds of what was once the Wavertree Hall estate. Also known as **Hamilton Hall** the building no longer exists, but the front wall is original and in it stand replica gates that, quite deliberately, cannot be opened.

In the 18th century, the daughter of the house eloped with the coachman, outraging her father. He ordered that the gates be permanently locked and the path ploughed up so that she 'could never return home'. These instructions were written into the deeds of the property and, although the original gates were replaced in 1955, these still remain locked and there is only grass from the gates to the front of the school!

The Royal School for the Blind was originally built in 1898, after Wavertree Manor – which was considered at the time to be of no historical interest – was completely demolished. The money for the present school building was provided by an anonymous donor, and it was built to replace an older school that stood on the corner of Hardman Street and Hope Street, in the centre of Liverpool.

This school had been built in 1851, and this itself had replaced the first Blind School which, from 1791, had stood in Commutation Row, adjacent to Lime Street. This had been founded as the first such school in Britain, by Edward Rushton (1756-1814), a Liverpool sailor who was blind himself and an indefatigable 18th century campaigner for human rights.

The Blind School building on Hope Street still stands, but is now disused.

However, by 1893, a new building was needed to comply with the 'Elementary Education (Blind and Deaf Children) Act', and so the site in Wavertree was chosen. Throughout the years the school has grown and been altered to keep pace with modern requirements, and it has just undergone a complete refurbishment and extension, to make it one of the most modern facilities of its kind in Europe.

The school was awarded the 'Royal' prefix by Her Majesty the Queen in 1966, in recognition of its tremendous work.

To Find Out More:
The Royal School for the Blind
www.rsblind.org.uk

Edward Rushton
http://www.btinternet.com/
~m.royden/mrlhp/local/rushton
/rushtondnb.htm

The permanently locked gates that once led to Wavertree Hall

Beyond the Royal School for the Blind, still on the left-hand side of Church Road North, we pass a number of fine period buildings, each of which has their own architectural merit.

One of these is the **Coffee House pub**, which is probably Wavertree's oldest surviving pub, and it was certainly standing on this site in 1777. It was also the meeting place for the Liverpool Hunt, and it was here that the stirrup cup would be taken before the hunt would set off across Childwall Heath and the surrounding countryside: 'The unspeakable in pursuit of the uneatable'!

Beyond The Coffee House, on the same side of Church Road North, is a range of buildings that can still be recognised on 150-year-old maps of Wavertree. Jenkins' Funeral Directors business occupies **White Cottage**, which is still believed to be the oldest building in Wavertree. In fact, if you walk down Waterloo Street, which is the road to the left of the White Cottage, you will see the cottage wall. This has some blocked up windows in it, and it is unclear what it originally enclosed. However, it is generally regarded as being the oldest wall in the village.

My 11-year-old son Danny, photographed in 2007, on the Mounting Steps

At the roundabout, upon which stands Picton Clock, turn right. Approximately 100 yards further along, The Village Lock-Up can be seen. Take the road that forks to the left of this building. This is Lake Road, park here alongside the children's playground. A 30-minute stop is suggested here.

Liverpool Lost and Found

Leaving your car, I suggest that you first take a walk around the Lock-Up and playground (the site of the lake), and then stroll alongside the railings, up Mill Lane, to the top of the playground where you will find the Monks' Well.

Wavertree Lock Up

In the centre of Wavertree Village is the village green, and upon this stands the Sheriff's Lock-Up.

Apart from the playing fields for the Bluecoat School, on the corner of Church Road and Woolton Road, this small plot is all that now survives of the once extensive **Wavertree Green**. It is also the only surviving piece of common land in the City, so if you have any livestock that you wish to graze, this is the place to do it!

During the late 17th and early 18th centuries, Wavertree was significant enough to warrant its own Sheriff. He carried a whistle and handcuffs, and also a beautifully decorated truncheon. Although crime was rare in the village, in 1768 the Constable had to arrest one Betty Conley for a felony.

As there was no prison at this time in the village, guards had to be paid to watch over her for 8 days and 8 nights, at a cost of 9s. 4d. She was eventually transported to Preston – at a further cost of £1. 12s. 2d. – only to be found not guilty. A citizens' meeting later instructed the Sheriff to be more careful in future!

However, this incident did eventually lead the village to invest in a Lock-Up, which was built in 1796.

"This had also become a necessity, to accommodate the large number of drunks who had made rather too merry in the many village pubs, especially the day-trippers who had over-indulged on their outings to picturesque Wavertree"

The Village Sheriff was now equipped with a handcart that had been built especially for transporting the inebriates from the pubs to the Lock-Up.

He would wheel this up and down Church Road, Mill Lane, and High Street collecting 'customers' for overnight accommodation! However, the building originally had a flat roof, through which friends of the prisoners would frequently knock holes, aiding many

Wavertree Lock Up, on the remaining Village Green

to escape by lowering down ropes or ladders. But that was OK as far as the Sheriff was concerned, because he was paid for each person that he locked up, not for how many of them were still in the Village Gaol the following morning!

In 1832, the Lock-Up served as a temporary mortuary for victims of a local cholera epidemic and, during 1845 and 1846, it housed refugees from the Irish Potato Famine who had no other form of shelter. By 1852, the building had passed its useful life and was subsequently 'beautified' by James Picton in 1869, with a pointed roof and a weather-vane, and maintained as a village 'ornament'.

The Lake

Between the Lock-Up and the children's playground is Lake Road, which joins Mill Lane – so-called because it was once the main road from the nearby village of Old Swan to the Old Mill in Wavertree Village.

Lake Road gets its name from the fact that what is now the children's playground was, until 1929, a small lake surrounded by trees and fed by the Monks' Well spring.

The lake originally covered a larger area than the size of the modern playground would indicate. Indeed, the lake probably gave rise to the ancient settlement of Wavertree in prehistoric times, and it had always been an important local resource, not only as a water supply but also as a 'common pond'.

"By 1861 however, the lake had become overgrown, weed-infested, and very dirty. As a result, the Local Authority decided to clean it up and they began to plant trees around the edge"

By the 1920s, the Local Authority had become concerned that the lake was becoming a danger to local children, particularly as the local population was growing rapidly. They decided to drain the lake and fill in the site, and this was done in 1929.

However, the deciding factor for removing the lake was the need to widen the road for the new tram-tracks that were beginning to criss-cross the City at this time.

The Monks' Well

At the end of the playground railings, on the corner of Mill Lane and North Drive, you will come to the Medieval Monks' Well, which is believed at one time to have served a local monastery in the area.

The well used to stand further back from the road, at a point where the spring bubbled out from the sandstone beneath Olive Mount. It is uncertain when the well was moved to its present location, but it is certainly recorded as being here at least 600 years ago.

This spring not only fed the well, but also the village lake. From the lake, before the area became built-up, a brook ran down behind where Wavertree Manor once stood, across the land now forming Wavertree Playground, to run alongside what is now the Brook House Pub on Smithdown Road.

"Now culverted, the brook still follows this route, and then flows via Greenbank Park Lake to become the 'River Jordan', when it feeds into Sefton Park Lake"

From here, again through culverts, it then runs under Aigburth Vale and Otterspool Park and into the River Mersey.

The spring, and therefore the Monk's Well, appears never to have run dry, and it provided water for the whole area. Indeed, in times of drought, water was sold to neighbouring communities for a penny a can.

In the well, under the archway, a few steps once led down to a stone cistern in which the water collected. This has now been bricked up for safety. However, local legends tell of secret chambers below the well, leading from the old steps and cistern, into hidden tunnels and passageways.

These are said to have connected the Wavertree Monks with those of Childwall Abbey and Childwall Priory, in nearby Childwall Village: But, as neither of these latter buildings were actually religious houses, this seems to be highly unlikely.

Regardless, the Monk's Well is in an excellent state of preservation, and still bears an original Latin text, which reads: 'QUI NON DAT QUIOD HABET DOEMON INFRA RIDET. ANNO 1414'.

This freely translates as, 'He who here does nought bestow, the Devil laughs at him below'.

This inscription does appear to be original, but the old Medieval cross had long been lost and so, in an attempt at restoration, it was replaced in the late 19th century and inscribed, according to tradition, 'DEUS DEDIT, HOMO BEBIT'. This translates as, 'God gives, man drinks'.

Picton Clock and The Smallest House

From the Monks' Well retrace your steps back around the perimeter of the playground again. Continue along High Street, in front of the shops, and you will pass Picton Clock on the left.
You will then pass The Lamb Hotel and the Cock and Bottle pub.

Picton Clock

Known locally as 'Picton Clock', the clock tower that stands in the middle of the roundabout at the heart of the village is actually named **The Sarah Pooley Clock**.

This has been a local landmark for over 120 years. It was built by Sir James Picton, a local architect and historian, and was unveiled in 1884 as a memorial to his wife. She died in 1879 and, after 50 years of very happy marriage, James was heartbroken.

The clock has a number of interesting inscriptions, one of which reads: 'Time wasted is existence; used is life'.

Sir James Allanson Picton (1832-1889), was one of Liverpool's most prominent citizens and benefactors. He was renowned as an architect, antiquarian, and author; writing much on Liverpool's history, particularly 'Liverpool Memorials', which is still a valued reference-work.

In 1847, having deliberately chosen the very highest point in Wavertree, Olive Mount – which is 215 feet above sea level, he built a large, red sandstone house on Mill Lane, called 'Sandy Knowe'. Knighted in 1881 by Queen Victoria, Sir James lived at 'Sandy Knowe' until his death there in 1889. The Picton Library in William Brown Street in the City is Picton's own memorial.

The Smallest House

Opposite the clock tower, standing on High Street, is **The Lamb Hotel**.

This pub dates from the 1850s, and it stands on the site of an older inn that was referred to as early as 1745. The Lamb was built as a coaching inn but coaches never used it. Instead, William Dilworth – of 'Dilworth's Folly' on Church Road fame – ran horse-drawn omnibuses from here to Liverpool City.

He was a direct rival to Joseph Mattinson's horse-trams, which ran from the Coffee House around the corner, and the competition between the two entrepreneurs was fierce.

Wavertree was a very popular day-trip out from the City, because the village's numerous inns and taverns – and open countryside – were very appealing to the citizens of the Town, and so there was a profitable tourist market to be serviced!

The district had been a popular destination since the 18th century, when trippers from Liverpool first descendede on the village, for the fairs held on the green.

Morris dancers, bull and bear-baiting, cock-fighting, boxing, wrestling, and races were just some of the entertainments on offer. The Lamb is a pub of character and you could certainly do worse than stop here for a small libation. However, you could also do so at the next pub down the same road, and a little further on from The Lamb.

This is **The Cock and Bottle**. This too is a very old pub, which is attractive both inside and outside, and which also serves excellent beers. However, of particular significance, is the fact that part of this pub now accommodates what was once the **smallest house** in Britain.

This was built in 1850, in what was a passage alongside the inn, and it was originally 6ft wide and 14ft from front to back.

There are stories of a couple raising eight children and also of another very large resident who had to go upstairs sideways. This was after the staircase had been widened to 16 inches, from its original width of 8 inches!

The last inhabitants of the Smallest House, Mr. and Mrs. Richard Greaves, moved out in 1925. The building then remained empty, until 1952, when one of the side walls was knocked through and it became part of the Cock & Bottle pub.

In 1998, the then owners of the pub restored the external appearance of the house, which can be clearly seen from outside the pub.

The pub recently changed owners again and they detached the 'smallest house' from the pub again. Whilst they have

Picton Clock (The Sarah Pooley Clock Tower)

retained the exterior appearance of the tiny dwelling, behind the miniature facade is now a staircase, leading up to a new apartment in the roof of the building. Because it is no longer a self-contained home, this curiosity can no longer claim the title of 'smallest house', which is now held by a house in Conway, in North Wales.

Walking back from the Cock and Bottle pub you will come to a broad passageway between two buildings.
Walking through here, and turning into the first small road on the right, brings you to Arnold Grove.

Arnold Grove and George Harrison

Arnold Grove, George Harrison's birthplace

Old Childwall Village

The Lodge House for the original Childwall Hall Estate

It was here, at **No. 12 Arnold Grove**, and on 25th February 1943, that the late and much-missed George Harrison (1943-2001) was born.

This was a very cramped house for the Harrison family and, on the 2nd January 1950, they moved to 25 Upton Green, Speke. At the time this was considered a socially-upward move but, on the 1st October 1962 they moved again, this time to 174 Macketts Lane in Hunts Cross; a much posher residence!

George Harrison was the youngest member of the Beatles, and his dad was a bus driver whilst his mother kept house.

As a young boy, George attended Dovedale Primary School, which is in a road off Penny Lane, and he was two years behind John Lennon who was also a pupil there.

As a Grammar School boy, George then went to Liverpool Institute, where he was one year behind Paul McCartney: Liverpool is a relatively small place and such coincidences are common.

To Find Out More:
Official George Harrison Website
www.georgeharrison.com

Returning to your car, from the end of Lake Road turn right and drive into Mill Lane. Turn left at the junction and continue through two sets of traffic lights along Childwall Road, up to the roundabout at Childwall Fiveways. Take the 3rd exit, and drive up the hill along Childwall Priory Road.

At the top of the hill, on the right behind railings, is a delightful copse of trees that forms a traffic island. Keep straight on, but take the next road on the left, which forks down the hill. This is Childwall Abbey Road. Immediately on the right can be seen the original Lodge House and the entrance into Childwall Wood; once the Childwall Hall Estate.
A further 500 yards down the hill, also on the right, is the entrance to Campus Manor, the studios of Lime Pictures. Beyond Campus Manor, at the bottom of the hill, are the Childwall Abbey Hotel and All Saints Parish Church, both standing on opposite sides of Score Lane.
Turn left at the T-Junction, and on the right is the pub car park. Park here. To visit the church and take a quick drink at the pub, allow 30 minutes. If you wish to walk back up to the Lodge House and have a stroll around Childwall Wood, then add a further 30-40 minutes.

From Wavertree, Childwall Road connects with Childwall Fiveways and the southern districts of the City; these have always been the wealthier communities of Liverpool.

The north of the City has always been the poorer area, with the 19th century 'servant and labouring classes' living in Anfield, Everton, Kensington, and Edge Hill. These people would work as daily domestic servants for the middle and upper merchant classes in Childwall, Allerton, Woolton, and Mossley Hill. Before the days of the omnibus, these servants would have to walk across the City to reach their places of work, at very early hours of the morning, and home again very late at night, often for seven days a week.

From Childwall Fiveways, Childwall Priory Road leads up to the 'triangle', with its fascinating stand of holly trees, and from here Childwall Abbey Road leads off past Childwall Wood, into the original ancient Childwall Village.

Childwall gets its name from the old Norse words, 'kelda' meaning a well, and 'wall' meaning field. The district was once known for its clear streams and pure wells, and the local road, Well Lane, is evidence of this. Old Childwall Village is sited on the sides of the hill that was once the high point of Childwall Heath, which stretched from here all the way to Wavertree, on towards Edge Hill, and to what is now Lime Street in the City-centre.

The earliest reference to Childwall is to be found in the Domesday Book of 1086, and the parish – and its manors and communities – became an important and profitable holding throughout the Middle Ages. Indeed, the parish had many owners, including religious houses, monarchs, and great baronial families. However, by the beginning of the 1700s, these significant districts on the outskirts of Liverpool were to have a new landlord. During the 18th century, one of the new breed of Liverpool entrepreneurs, and a member of the new middle-classes, was an attorney called Isaac Greene.

In 1718, he purchased the Manors of Much and Little Woolton, Childwall, and the Manor House of Childwall Hall, having already acquired the Manors of West Derby, Wavertree, and Everton, from the Earl of Derby the previous year.

Today however, Childwall is much more built-up, but there are still many attractive and interesting features of the Village, and we will visit these now.

To Find Out More:
Welcome to Childwall –
www.childwall.moonfruit.com
Domesday Book
www.nationalarchives.gov.uk/domesday

8

Childwall Hall and Woods

At the entrance to Childwall Wood stands the old lodge that once guarded the entrance to the estate of Childwall Hall. This was built in the 18th century by the famous architect, John Nash, and it is all that now remains of the former Manor buildings.

When Isaac Greene died, in 1749, his daughter Mary inherited the estate. She married Bamber Gascoigne, an ancestor of his 'University Challenge' namesake, who then built a new Childwall Hall in 1780, replacing the original house.

Bamber died in 1824, and his daughter Frances Mary inherited his property. She married James Brownlow William Cecil, the 2nd Marquess of Salisbury, which is how this family became owners of much of Liverpool during the 19th century, taking ownership of Isaac Green's vast local land holdings.

Childwall Hall and grounds were subsequently let to a series of tenants until, in 1922, it became a golf club. When the club's lease ran out in 1939, the City Council bought fifty acres of land from Lord Salisbury, who gave a further four-and-a-half acres and the hall as a gift.

After the War, it was planned to use Childwall Hall for a new County College, but it was found to be riddled with dry rot and too expensive to renovate. In 1949, it had to be pulled down and a new college was built on the site, which opened in 1955.

In 1960, the wood, which was once part of the landscaped park that surrounded the Hall, was separated from the rest of the college grounds and opened to local residents. In 1966, the wood and surrounding lands were then taken over by Liverpool City Council and opened to the general public. 'Childwall Wood and Fields' remains public open space, and is one of the City's Local Nature Reserves.

With the 'ravine' – once the coach drive up to the entrance of the Hall, the stands of trees (some of which are quite ancient), the natural plantings and wildlife habitats, the generous ranges of rhododendron bushes, and the meandering pathways, Childwall Wood makes a delightful place to visit.

Childwall Wood

Hollywood Comes to Liverpool

9

Childwall College closed in 1989, when the building and grounds were sold to **The Mersey Television Company**, established in 1982 by Phil Redmond, who renamed the site Campus Manor.

The long-running Channel 4 drama, Brookside, was filmed on the studio sets of Campus Manor, although the main Brookside Housing Estate was actually on the borders of the Croxteth Hall Estate, in West Derby. The very first episode of the soap opera formed part of the Channel's opening night on-air, and production continued uninterrupted for 21 years, with over 2,900 episodes.

Mersey Television was sold to All3Media, in 2005, when it was led by a skilled local management team. In 2006, the company changed its name to **Lime Pictures** with 'LiMe' reflecting the company's roots in 'Liverpool and Merseyside', and it is now one of Liverpool's biggest employers, with over 500 staff. This means that the company is the UK's largest independent producer of film and television drama. Popular television programmes, such as Hollyoaks (Channel 4), and Grange Hill (BBC), have been filmed on the site, and Lime is currently working on a wide range of new and imaginative drama projects.

Many parts of inner-City Liverpool and its suburbs are frequently used as locations for film and television production. Our woods and parks are also favoured filming-sites, and it is now quite usual and normal to see film crews and mobile dressing rooms dotted throughout Liverpool. At this point in this Chapter, it is worthwhile mentioning the role of the **Liverpool Film Office**.

Not only are television programmes made in Liverpool, but many British and international feature films are produced here also. Because of the work of the Liverpool Film Office, this source of

A full-scale location shoot on Water Street

revenue to the City is expanding. The Film Office was set up in 1989, by the City Council, as a direct response to the volume of requests that they were receiving from film-makers wishing to film in the City. Producers regard the imaginative and dynamic work done by the small team at LFO, plus the willingness of the City Council to work in partnership, as positive encouragement. The office advises on suitable locations, and has a database (now available online through a regional film/tv portal) of more than 10,000 sites that are available locally; from Georgian terraces to modern concrete and steel buildings, plus many landscaped and natural settings. They also have a list of over 450 local professionals who can provide skills and services to the industry.

This high level of official co-operation, and our wealth of original, period, and attractive architecture and environment, has now made Merseyside in general, and Liverpool in particular, second only to New York as the world's most popular destination for film producers.

Liverpool has doubled for St. Petersburg, Dublin, Moscow, and Venice, and films shot here include Chariots of Fire, In The Name of the Father, The Hunt for Red October, Titanic, 51st State, Backbeat, Yentl, Yanks, and all of the early Beatles Films.

A lavish production of The Forsyte Saga was filmed in the City, with Rodney Street being used to depict Victorian Britain; Croxteth Hall and grounds being used for the more stately scenes; and a house adjacent to Princes Park was used as the Forsyte family home.

"A production of The Hound of the Baskervilles found Liverpool's Canning Street doubling as Baker Street in London"

The magnificent ballroom in Lord Derby's home at Knowsley Hall was also used for some magnificent set pieces and, in fact, this 1730's mansion features regularly in film and television productions. Since 2002, the City has also been the home of **LA Productions** and **Liverpool Film Studios**. And, despite its Hollywood sounding name, LA Productions is actually an abbreviation for Liverpool Film Academy Productions Limited.

This company is presided over by Colin McKeown, who is an established and respected film and television producer.

Born in Huyton, on the eastern edge of Liverpool, Colin is the creator of such TV series as, Liverpool ONE, Nice Guy Eddie, and of the feature film Liam, and he has a worldwide reputation for professionalism and high quality standards.

The Grange Hill set at Lime Pictures

LA Productions has established itself as a great inward investor, and the Company has set up Liverpool's only film academy, providing training courses for a whole range of film-making skills including editing, sound mixing, DOP, directing, writing, accounting, design, make-up, and wardrobe.

The Academy is therefore contributing to the sustainability of the industry as a whole, and is ensuring that local people can break into the industry with genuine expertise at their fingertips. The facilities side of LA Productions was Liverpool Film Studios, and this became a real asset to the region and to the industry.

Right across Merseyside, we certainly have a wealth of external film locations and remarkable architectural backdrops to offer producers, but what if the weather is bad? What if you need sophisticated special effects; editing suites; sound-recording systems; specialised makeup services; design space; costume design facilities; or conference and administration space?

Liverpool Film Studios is located in a converted warehouse on Boundary Street, to the north of the city-centre and here, a team of talented professionals created a major production complex.

This includes five studios; a sound stage; two large workshops for the construction of film sets; 12 smaller workshops; a makeup room and office space.

Films can be edited, and all post-production work carried out on-site. Initially costing £500,000 to set up, the Studios are the industry's first one-stop-shop for movie-making on Merseyside.

Indeed, this complex housed the production team that shot 51st State.

Liverpool has always been renowned for the famous people who perform in front of the cameras, but now our reputation for technical skill and professional expertise behind the cameras is just as celebrated.

Hollywood has certainly come to Liverpool to such an extent that, perhaps now, Liverpool can show Hollywood a thing or two!

Colin McKeown

To Find Out More:
Lime Pictures
Phone: 0151 722 9122
http://www.limepictures.com

LA Productions
Phone: 0151 933 8282
www.laproductions.co.uk

Liverpool Film Office (North West Vision)
Phone: 0870 609 4481 Ext: 4
www.northwestvision.co.uk

Liverpool Film Studios
Phone: 0800 037 7191
www.liverpoolfilmstudios.co.uk/

All Saints Parish Church ⑩

All Saints Parish Church is the oldest surviving Medieval church in Liverpool. Indeed, Childwall Village itself was much more significant than Liverpool until well after the time of King John, and there is a reference to a priest at 'Cilduuelle' in the Domesday Book. This clearly suggests that, in the 11th century, at least a chapel existed on this site.

Some archaeologists believe that, because of the layout of the graveyard, the Church could be Anglo-Saxon in origin, which would certainly make it over 1,000 years old. However, whilst there are some pieces of Saxon carved stone in the west wall, and some Norman stonework in the north chancel aisle, the main structure of the present church building dates principally from around the mid 1500s. The parish records date from 1557, and are among the earliest in the country.

The church remained virtually untouched throughout the 16th and 17th centuries but, in 1716, 'Plumbe's Chapel' was added to the north wall. In 1739, the 'Isaac Greene Chapel' was built, and this passed to the Gascoigne and then the Salisbury families. This is now used as the choir vestry.

Of the three lych gates in the wall of the graveyard, the oldest one has the date '1728' carved on its central column, and this has been in continuous use since that date. The original tower was replaced in 1810, and the church was extended and re-pewed between 1834 and 1853. The present roof dates from 1892.

Inside the church there are memorial brasses that are considered the best in the North of England. Also of interest are the heraldic hatchments throughout the church, which are original to many of the ancient families of the district, including the Gascoignes, the Walkers of Calderstones, the Ashtons of Woolton Hall, and the Hardmans of Allerton.

The first mention of a graveyard at Childwall is in a document from 1386, but no detailed records exist before 1557 and the oldest gravestones only date from 1620 and 1686.

"The exterior of the church boasts a number of curious features, such as the gargoyles, which include the heads of tigers and boars. However, of special interest is the **Lepers' Squint**"

This survives as a small arched window with a grille, cut in the wall at ground level, to the left of the front entrance to the church. In medieval times, a community of lepers lived down in the valley, behind the

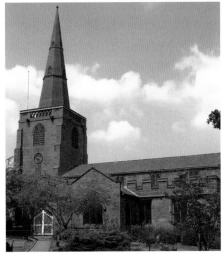

All Saints Parish Church

The Lepers' Squint

church. Leprosy was common in England during this period and, although cut off from the rest of the community, these unfortunate people were still entitled to attend church services and make confession. However, this could only be from the outside of the building, after all the rest of the parishioners were safely inside. The lepers would gather outside at the 'Squint' during the service, and the priest could hear their individual confessions through the grille, and from a position of relative safety. The lepers would then leave, returning to the valley before the congregation emerged.

What we see of the Squint today would formerly have been set in a recessed doorway at shoulder height, inside which the lepers could comfortably stand upright.

This is because the level of the ground was originally much lower. But, as more and more people needed burial, the ground level had to be periodically raised with new earth.

Also, by the late 17th century, the Squint would no longer have been required for its original purpose, and so it was glazed to become just another window. However, viewed from inside the church the original height of the Squint can clearly be seen.

To Find Out More:
All Saints Parish Church
Phone: 0151 737 2169
http://www.allsaints-childwall.org/

The Childwall Abbey Hotel ⑪

The names 'Priory' and 'Abbey', which feature in the road names in the village, as well as in the name of the inn, would seem to refer to religious buildings from times past, but there were neither of these at Childwall.

The 'Priory' was in fact a farmhouse that stood near Childwall Fiveways, but this was demolished in the 1930s, as the new road system was being constructed.

'Abbey' may refer either to the architectural style of old Childwall Hall, or simply to the fact that the land was once part of the territory owned by the Monks of Stanlawe Abbey on the Wirral.

However, the origins of the pub are certainly medieval, and part of the building is said to be the Chapel of St. Thomas the Martyr, dating from 1484. The building once had a door dated 1608, but that came from an Allerton farmhouse.

The main structure of the present pub, though certainly old, probably stands on the site of a much earlier inn.

"As well as offering good food and ales, The Childwall Abbey also, until the mid-20th century, provided accommodation. Indeed, at the end of the 19th and during the early years of the 20th centuries, the Abbey was popular with actors travelling to perform in Liverpool. The renowned thespians Henry Irving and Ellen Terry, and the author of 'Peter Pan' – J M Barrie – have all left their names scratched in the windows of some of the upstairs rooms"

If you can time your visit to Childwall for mid-morning on a Saturday or Sunday, then you could take a stroll through the Woods, perhaps followed by a pint and some lunch at the pub.

After this, a visit to the church would complete your time spent in this charming 'lost village'.

To Find Out More:
Childwall Abbey Hotel
Phone: 0151 722 5293

Merseyside Campaign for Real Ale
www.merseycamra.org.uk

Liverpool Lost and Found

Turn left out of the car park into Score Lane and continue past the church. Follow this as it becomes Childwall Lane. Halfway along on the left, you will see the restored and replaced **Childwall Village Cross**, overlooking what was once part of the Great Heath that, up to the 19th century, stretched from here right into the heart of the old town of Liverpool. At the end of this road, turn left at the T-Junction by the Falstaff Pub, and then turn right at the next T-Junction, onto Gateacre Park Drive.

Next take the road which forks left. This is Grange Lane, which will take you into Gateacre Village. You will pass Gateacre Comprehensive School on the right. Rumour has it that school was built back-to-front! After about 1/2 mile, do note the attractive cottages, and Victorian neo-Tudor buildings on your right, as you enter the village. As you approach the crossroads in The Village, slow down just before the traffic lights, because there is a cobbled driveway on the right. This gives access to the car park of the Black Bull pub: Park here. A suggested stopping time here is between 15 minutes and an hour, depending on how much of the village you wish to explore, and whether or not you wish to sample any of the local ales!

Gateacre Village

Gateacre is a picturesque village, and it comes as a surprise to those who stumble upon it as they travel around the rambling suburbs of Liverpool.

It has an odd, quasi-rural feel about it, which gives the village a feeling of being trapped in time. This is despite the fact that Gateacre is at the intersection of some very busy modern roads.

The name of the village probably means 'road (gata) to the field (acre)' and derives from Middle English, although some historians feel it derives from the Anglo-Saxon 'Gottesacker' or 'God's Acre'. This shows that the village is indeed quite ancient. Gateacre was once known as Little Woolton, as it is so close to the nearby village of Woolton, which itself was originally known as Much Woolton, because of its larger size.

Gateacre itself is now built-up but, at the turn of the last century, it was a very isolated village set amongst the local farms. Nothing in the village is older now than the 17th century although, despite its modern suburban setting, the heart of the village retains an attractive rural charm.

It is still an enchanting place to visit and explore, and it is home to charming pubs and inns, and to delightful cottages and houses – from a whole range historical periods and architectural styles. All of these are scattered around a charming village green, and the general ambience of the village is one of Victorian charm.

The gazebo on the village green

Gateacre Brow and the Village Green ①

Having parked your car at the **Black Bull**, you will see in front of the inn, on the **Village Green**, a sandstone gazebo that houses a water fountain.

This was erected in 1883, and it has some very intricately carved figures on it, including animals, mermaids playing instruments, and a Liver Bird. Also, you will find a very large and gruesome gargoyle, which appears to be jumping out from one side. Also on the green, and standing directly in front of the pub car park, is a **bronze bust of Queen Victoria** mounted on a tall pedestal.

This was placed here in 1887, as a donation from Sir Andrew Barclay Walker, of brewing fame, and who also gave the Walker Art Gallery to the City.

"The bust was restored some years ago and, in what has now become an annual tradition on her birthday, local children ceremoniously wash and wax the 'Old Queen' amid much fun and frolic"

To explore the village we are first going to walk back along Grange Lane, which is the road along which we drove into the village. Immediately on the left you will pass the sandstone walls of some old mews buildings. Walking through the archway here takes you into a cobbled courtyard, which is surrounded by modern restorations of what were once stables and storehouses for an adjacent manor house. Note the roofs of these buildings, as they retain some of the original wooden features of the mews.

Continuing along Grange Lane, and next to the mews, you come to the delightful cottages of **Paradise Row** and, next to these, a large manor house that has been converted into separate dwellings, now called **Soarer Cottages**.

Now, return back along Grange Lane into the village and follow this across the road junction, at the traffic lights, as this now becomes Halewood Road (this is a very busy junction, so do take care as you walk across).

To Find Out More:
A Brief History of Gateacre
http://www.liverpool.ndo.co.uk/
gatsoc/page9.html
The Gateacre Society
http://www.liverpool.ndo.co.uk/
gatsoc/index.html
Merseyside Campaign for Real Ale
www.merseycamra.org.uk

About 100 yards or so along on the right, you will soon pass the **Brown Cow pub**, which was converted from two early-19th century cottages. Just past this stands the **old school house**, which has been converted into apartments, but which nevertheless retains its architectural and 'community' appeal.

If you keep walking along Halewood Road for another 250 yards, on the left and standing on the corner of The Nook, you will come to blocks of new flats behind a railing.

This was, until a couple of years ago, the site of the Gateacre Hall Hotel. This building had been constructed around the original Gateacre Hall, which was thought to have been built in the middle of the 17th century.

Whilst the Hall was discernible in amongst the accretion of buildings that constituted the hotel, the hostelry itself was of absolutely no architectural merit. This was a great shame, as the old Hall had been a significant local building.

However, all this is now academic as the lot has been ploughed into the ground, to be replaced by the modern apartment blocks.

Now the only remnant of the original Hall and its grounds is the **Slave Gate**. This is a white, stone, arched gateway containing a wrought-iron gate.

This had been taken from the old Liverpool Tower that once stood at the foot of Water Street in the city-centre; where Tower Building now stands.

"For generations this has been known as the 'Slave Gate', in the belief that slaves were reputed to have passed through this gate, into the old Tower, where they were then sold"

However, whilst the gate may well be from the Tower, the association with slavery has no basis in fact.

Very few slaves ever passed through the port, and even less were ever sold here, except at very infrequent private sales. Slaves were generally shipped directly from Africa to the Americas and the West Indies, and any slaves who did come to Liverpool would usually have been the servants of wealthy merchants and aristocrats.

Returning back along Halewood Road, and turning right at the traffic lights into what is now Belle Vale Road, will immediately bring you to a row of **18th century cottages**. This delightful terrace is very attractive and shows what the village must have looked like in Georgian times.

If you have the time, you might like to continue walking for a further ½ mile or so to where, on the bend of the road, you will find St. Stephen's Parish church.

Alongside this is a wonderful row of late Victorian, mock-Tudor houses, known as **Church Cottages**.

These are set apart from the road, in one of the last remaining original closes in the village, and they are worth the extra walk.

Back at The Village Green once more, a walk up the hill in front of the Black Bull – along Gateacre Brow, takes you past a delightful set of shops on both sides of the road. However, whilst the ones on the right are particularly attractive, directly opposite these, on the corner of Sandfield Road at **No 28 Gateacre Brow**, is a delightful Victorian-neo-Elizabethan building. Its attractive gables and half-timbered decorations make it look as if it was designed as a mansion house for a wealthy merchant. In fact, it was the local telephone exchange!

Built in 1889, by the National Telephone Company, it was designed by Walter Aubrey Thomas who also built the Royal Liver Building.

The Telephone Exchange was on the first floor and the ground floor has been variously, amongst other businesses, a grocer's, a bank, and an insurance company.

On the outside walls of this engaging building, are a series of plaster panels depicting scenes from the Bible, including Adam and Eve; Moses in the Bullrushes; the Annunciation; the Nativity; the Circumcision; and the Massacre of the Innocents.

Continuing up Gateacre Brow, across Sandfield Road, stands the **Unitarian Chapel**. This delightful building, set in a small churchyard, was built at the end of the 17th century and is one of the oldest churches in Liverpool. In 1700 it was licensed as: 'A meeting place for an assembly of Protestants dissenting from the Church of England for the exercise of their religious worship'.

From this chapel, and its congregation, developed the powerhouse of Unitarian families such as the Roscoes and the Rathbones, who led the City's greatest entrepreneurial and social achievements.

Half way up Gateacre Brow, still on the left, you will see the **Bear and Staff pub**.

This is a good place to get some lunch or a snack, and is an excellent base from which to stroll through the village, if you choose to park here instead of at the Black Bull.

This pub, like the Black Bull, probably dates from the 18th century, and the names of all the pubs in the village reflect the rural origins of this delightful community.

To Find Out More:
Pictures of Gateacre Village
http://www.liverpool.ndo.co.uk/gatsoc/pics/index.html
South Liverpool: Childwall & Gateacre
http://uk.geocities.com/allertonoak@btinternet.com/merseySights/SouthLiverpoolCG.html

The Slave Gate

Leaving the pub car park, turn right, back onto Grange Lane and then turn right at the traffic lights, up Gateacre Brow. You will pass the old Chapel and The Bear and Staff Pub on the left. Turn right at the mini-roundabout, into Rose Brow, and then first left up Woolton Hill Road. You will pass the entrance to the Anglican Bishop's House on the left, and also some very attractive properties; some quite old. Follow the road up the hill to the roundabout, and take your 2nd exit into Beaconsfield Road. The Children's Centre and Convent of St Gabriel's will be on your left. Again, some of the properties on this road are old and attractive. Not unlike myself really! The gates to what was once the Strawberry Field Children's Home are almost at the bottom of the hill, on the left, opposite the entrance gates to the Lower Lee School. This is a narrow and busy road, so park carefully if you intend to look at the gates.

Woolton Village

Woolton Village was originally called 'Wulfa's Tun' or 'Wulfa's Farmstead'; probably after a Teutonic chieftain who settled in the area and cultivated it.

The Village has passed through the hands of the Knights of St. John of Jerusalem, who owned it from 1178 for 300 years; and, after the dissolution of the monasteries, on to Henry VIII; Queen Elizabeth I; and then to King James I. This King was much in need of money and so, in 1609, he sold the manorial rights to William, the 6th Earl of Derby. Woolton, as with Wavertree and Childwall, then passed to Isaac Green and, via his daughter, to Bamber Gascoigne. Finally, Woolton too passed to the Marquess of Salisbury.

From the late eighteenth century, the rural community of Woolton and the surrounding villages took on more local significance, as the rising wealthy and status-conscious merchant classes began to build their estates in the district, and as the new middle-classes built slightly less grand houses in the Village itself.

The population of Woolton increased rapidly during the 19th century: In 1801, 439 people were recorded as living here but, by 1901, the population had risen to 4,750. The quarry, which was opened by James Rose (who was known locally as 'The King of Woolton), became a profitable enterprise and attracted workers from all over the district. Also, many victims of the Irish Potato Famine ended up in Woolton and, by 1851, 24 percent of the local population were from Ireland.
They not only worked at the quarry, but also further afield in the village of Garston, near Speke. Here they were employed at the tannery, a button factory, and on the new docks and railway yards in that riverside community. These workers moved into purpose-built houses, courts, and cottages in new streets all around the quarry in Woolton, but as these were poorly and densely-built, and extremely unsanitary, living conditions were squalid and dangerous.

These streets still exist, though more modern buildings have now replaced many of the original houses, cottages, and courts.

Stone from Woolton built many of Liverpool's buildings including, in due course, the Anglican Cathedral, but the quarry closed in the 1970s. Now, this surrounds a modern housing estate, not so imaginatively named **The Old Quarry**.

Woolton was absorbed into the expanding City of Liverpool in 1913 and, although losing much of its semi-rural character, a number of attractive and historic buildings and cottages remain. Indeed, as one wanders around the village one can see many fine examples of architecture from over three centuries. However, before we come to The Village proper, there are one or two places to visit en route.

> **To Find Out More:**
> **Woolton Village**
> http://wooltonvillageuk.tripod.com/
> **The Marquess of Salisbury**
> http://en.wikipedia.org/wiki/
> Marquess_of_Salisbury

Mendips, John Lennon's boyhood home

Strawberry Field

The one-time Salvation Army Children's Home, 'Strawberry Field', about which the Beatles wrote the song of the same name, stood in grounds off Beaconsfield Road, just behind John Lennon's house.

This was opened in 1936, in what was originally a large Victorian mansion, and John and his friends would often come here to play.

However, the large house was badly damaged by Wartime bombing in the 1940s. Restored after the War, it was eventually demolished in the 1970s, to make way for more modern residential units for the children and staff. For 68 years this had been the place where orphaned and needy children had been brought up and cared for by the Christian charity.

Now however, the red iron gates are all that remain of the Children's' Home, as the organisation closed the facility down

Strawberry Field Gates

forever, in June 2005. The gates, which are now replicas, face the road, directly opposite the entrance to Lower Lees School.

John and his Auntie Mimi would come here regularly, to the fund-raising summer fetes held at the children's home, and later, as a successful Beatle, John made a donation to build a new extension to the care home, and this was named Lennon Court when it was opened in 1979.

> **To Find Out More:**
> **Liverpool: John & Paul –**
> http://www.angelfire.com/stars/
> LennonMcCartney/
> http://www.music.indiana.edu/som
> /courses/rock/penny.html
> **Salvation Army – Strawberry Field**
> www.salvationarmy.org/heritage.nsf/
> 0/51c204d5d4cabc5980256c46002
> eac11?OpenDocument
> **Strawberry Field – Central Park New York**
> http://www.centralparknyc.org
> /virtualpark/southend/
> strawberryfields
> **Yoko Ono Official Website**
> http://www.yoko-ono.com/

Menlove Avenue and 'Mendips'

John Lennon

The magnificent tree-lined avenue that runs through Calderstones and out to Speke is called Menlove Avenue and, on the left at No. 251 - **Mendips**, is John Lennon's childhood home.

He lived here for 18 years, from 1945 to 1963, with his Aunt Mimi and Uncle George Smith, and with their three cats Titch, Sam, and Tim; and the dog, Sally.

John lived here as a child; as an art student; and also, for a short time, with his first wife Cynthia and their baby son Julian.

John, who was born on the 15th July 1940, was brought up by his Aunt and Uncle because his mother, Julia, had found that she could not look after him. Not long after John's birth, Julia was deserted by her husband, Freddie, and then she had a number of other relationships. Towards the end of the War, Julia met and moved in with John Dykins, and had two daughters with him. Julia and John Dykins were very happy, and in fact lived in Blomfield Road in nearby Allerton. It was during this period of calm and security that Julia felt able to re-enter her son's life. John was now a teenager and, as he and his mum shared the same free-and-easy outlook on life, they started to grow very close and began to re-build their relationship.

John had developed his interest in Skiffle and Rock and Roll music by this time and Julia encouraged him. Mimi however, so disliked his guitar playing, finding it such an annoyance, that she banished John to the small front-door porch to practice there, just below his bedroom at the front of the house. Mimi was also fiercely opposed to John's musical ambitions but, nonetheless, she was very loving towards her nephew: Even more so after the sudden death of her husband, in 1955.

John began to be a regular visitor to his mum and stepfather's home, and Julia in turn became a frequent visitor to Mendips, taking a great interest in her teenage, art-student son. It was after one such visit, at 10pm on the night of Wednesday 15th July 1958, that Julia waved goodbye to her sister Mimi at the gate. Julia then crossed over the first half of the dual carriageway to make her way home but, as she stepped into the second roadway of Menlove Avenue, she did not see the grey saloon car, being driven by an off-duty Policeman, that was heading towards her. She was struck at speed by the car and was flung quite some distance away. Julia was critically injured. Neighbours knocked at Mendips, and Mimi ran over to her sister. She travelled with Julia in the ambulance, but John Lennon's Mum was pronounced dead on arrival at Sefton General Hospital, on Smithdown Road.

A month later, at the inquest, a verdict of misadventure was declared and, at a subsequent trial, the Police officer was acquitted of any wrongdoing. The effect of his mother's death on John was profound and, some years later he described the incident as, "the worst night of my life. I lost my mother twice; once as a chiold of five, and then again at seventeen. It made me very bitter inside". On the Beatles White Album, John recorded his feelings about his mother in his song, 'Julia', and he also named his first son, Julian, in commemoration of his Mother.

John left Menlove Avenue in 1963, to live with Stu Sutcliffe; his friend from Liverpool Art College, in a flat in Gambier Terrace. This is an attractive residential parade of flats and apartments that overlooks Liverpool's Anglican Cathedral, on Hope Street. (See Chapter: 'Pool of Life & Culture, Part 2'.) Aunt Mimi however, continued to live at Mendips until 1965, when John bought her an expensive house, overlooking Poole Harbour in Dorset.

With his fellow Beatles, John went on to fame and fortune. However, in due course he was to leave Cynthia and Julian, to live in New York with Yoko Ono. Tragically, John Lennon was shot and killed in front of his apartment building, by Mark Champan, on the 8th December 1980. Mimi died in 1991.

In the summer of 2002, on a visit to the City to rename the airport as 'Liverpool John Lennon Airport', Mendips was bought from its current owners by Lennon's widow, Yoko Ono. She immediately donated it to the National Trust. The house has now been fully restored to be as close as possible to how it would have looked when John lived there, and it is now open to the public on specially organised tours (see the '20 Forthlin Road' article, following).

Woolton Village in the 19th Century

At the bottom of Beaconsfield Road turn left at the traffic lights into Menlove Avenue. Approximately 500 yards further along on the left, just past the bus stop, is Number 251, 'Mendips', John Lennon's old home. Again, this is a busy road so park here safely and carefully.

To Find Out More:	
Mendips www.nationaltrust.org.uk/beatles	John Lennon Official Website http://www.johnlennon.com/

Continue along Menlove Avenue and turn left at the traffic lights into Allerton Road.
Crossing the next set of traffic lights you will immediately pass the entrance to a large supermarket on the left.
The road now forks to the left; this is still Allerton Road, so take this as it leads you into the heart of Woolton Village. Park anywhere that it is safe and legal to do so, as soon as you find an opportunity, and you can begin your walking tour of The Village from this point. Or, you can continue all the way down Allerton Road until you reach a T-Junction at some 'No Entry' signs. Turn right here into Church Road South, and then immediately left into High Street.
Follow this to the traffic lights and turn left into Woolton Street. This leads you to the village cross-roads and there are two parking options here. Either turn into the sunken car park on the left, to the right of the Estate Agents offices, or turn right and park in the car park of The Elephant pub. To stroll through the entire village, and to explore St Peter's Church and Eleanor Rigby's Grave, a $^1/_2$ to 1-Hour visit time is suggested.

Wandering Around Woolton

We now come into the centre of Woolton where there is still a great deal of the old and historic village left to appreciate.

Woolton Village is one of those places where parking and then walking around is an absolute must. And so, if you have parked on Allerton Road, continue to walk along here; exploring all the roads, streets, alleyways, and courts, that branch off from one side of the road, as you go. You will be surprised by just how much of old Woolton remains.

At the end of the road, cross over, and do the same on the other side of the road, now in the opposite direction, until you have completed a full circuit and returned to your car. If you park at **The Elephant**, or in the sunken car park off Woolton Street, a circular stroll up and down Allerton Road will still be your main route through the nooks and crannies of the village.

"Woolton became a conservation area in 1969, and Allerton Road is its heart. This is also an attractive suburban shopping street, parts of which would remind one of a setting for a 'Miss Marple' mystery"

From the village crossroads at Woolton Street you will first pass some appealing little shops, but then look out for the following streets, buildings, and places:

About 100 yards into Allerton Road is the imposing Victorian, **Woolton Village Club**. This was opened, 'for the whole community of Woolton', in September 1885, and was equipped with a bowling green, billiards room, bar, concert area, and many other facilities. The club is still fully used today.

Next, to pass some fascinating homes and chapels, turn down Church Road South; then right into High Street; and then right again, down Quarry Street South; to rejoin Allerton Road. Here, on the corner, but currently under threat, stands **Woolton Swimming Baths**. It was here, at the age of 11, that I learnt to swim.

Now, crossing over to explore the opposite side of Allerton Road, have a look in Chapel Place, and then stroll up Quarry Street, as far as Clay Cross Road on the right. On the left as you walk up, take a look down **Pit Place**, and down Roddick, Rose, and Castle Streets, which will give you a perspective on what working life might have been like in Woolton in the 19th century.

Double back along Quarry Street, and this time branch off into **The Old Quarry**, which is the centre of the quarry; then down **St. Mary's Court**, in which you will find the **Methodist Chapel**, now the public library, and built in 1834; and then stroll down Mount Street.

Old Woolton still remains amongst all the new houses, particularly in the next roads off on the left; St. Mary's Street, where you will find the local Catholic Church of St. Mary's, set back in a secluded area and on its own small mount; Garden Street and Rushton Place.

Eleanor Rigby's grave in St Peter's burial ground

The next road along is Church Road. A short walk up this hill will bring you to **St Peter's Anglican Church** (see right), with **Eleanor Rigby's tombstone** in the front of the graveyard. Across the road from the church is the early-Victorian school. In the playground, behind the railings, is the **St. Peter and St. Paul Centre**. Behind this is the large hall in which, on 6th July 1957, Paul McCartney first met John Lennon, and the story of The Beatles began.

Back at the corner of Church and Allerton Roads once more, and behind some railings, is the sunken car park. This was once The Lodes Pond and therefore a main water supply to the village.

As you have walked around the village you will have passed a number of tea shops, cafes, and small restaurants, any of which would be a good place to rest and refresh yourself, as would any of the local pubs that you will also have passed.

Back on Woolton Street, The Elephant is worth a look, athough an alternative might be the Coffee House Pub, just a little further along to the right, on Speke Road. This is smaller and cosier, having been built in 1641.

If you have the time, why not take in a show in the luxurious, small but perfectly formed, **Woolton Picture House**, in Mason Street? This locally-owned cinema is a glorious gem.

To Find Out More:
Woolton Village
http://wooltonvillageuk.tripod.com

Building began on the original St. Peter's church in July 1827 when the foundation stone was laid by the Earl of Derby.

However, this church became inadequate and so it was demolished and replaced, some 15 yards higher up the road, by the present building, which opened in 1887.

The Lych Gate at St Peter's Church

Although typical of Victorian churches of the time, it is an attractive building with a light and pleasantly decorated interior. Its clock tower, with its ring of eight bells; the war memorial; a Victorian lych gate; and well-kept grounds make for an interesting visit. However, perhaps of particular note is that, in the graveyard near the front wall of the church, stands the tombstone of **Eleanor Rigby** and other members of her family. Nothing else is known about this woman, and it cannot be said that she or her circumstances in any way resembled those of the character from the Lennon and McCartney song that bears her name.

"Stone from Woolton Quarry built St. Peter's Church, and it was here, on 6th July 1957 that Paul McCartney was introduced to John Lennon"

Ivan Vaughan, who was a pupil with Paul at Liverpool Institute Boys School, sometimes played tea-chest bass for a local skiffle group known as 'The Quarrymen'.

One of the other group members was John Lennon, who had named them after his school, Quarry Bank Grammar School, now Calderstones Comprehensive School.

Ivan told Paul that the group was worth seeing and that they were playing that afternoon at a fete being held in the field behind the church. Paul was no stranger to St. Peter's as he was a chorister there and, as there might be a chance for him to meet some girls, he cycled from his home in Allerton to see The Quarrymen. Paul was impressed with what he saw, and he returned that evening to see them play again, as they had also been booked to perform in the church hall for a dance.

During a break in their performance, Paul was showing the members of the group his skills as a guitarist, by playing 'Twenty Flight Rock' and 'Be-Bop-A-Lula'. Paul then remembers that a 'beery old man stumbled over to him and breathed down his neck'. Paul, at 14 years of age, was wondering what the old drunk wanted, but this character then said, "Twenty Flight Rock is one of me favourites".

This was John Lennon and, although only 15 years old himself, he seemed like a 'real big man' to Paul. This was how what was to become one of the world's greatest song-writing teams met for the first time.

John said later, that he had more or less decided to ask Paul to join the group there and then, but it was a week or so after this meeting that a formal invitation was made. Paul accepted and, on 18th October 1957, he made his debut with the group.

'The Quarrymen' eventually became 'Johnny and the Moondogs'; then the 'Silver Beatles'; and then 'The Beatles'. From the church hall in Woolton they went on to completely re-shape rock music and to influence an entire generation.

The stage in the church hall, which has always been on the tourist route for Beatles fans, was due to be demolished as part of a major refurbishment of the building. The loss to posterity would have been significant but it was rescued by National Museums of Liverpool. It can now be seen in the Museum of Liverpool, at Mann Island, near the Pier Head.

To Find Out More:
St Peter's Church Woolton
http://www.stpeters-woolton.org.uk/

If you parked on Allerton Road to explore The Village, drive down to the No Entry signs and turn right into Church Road South.
Turn left into High Street and take the right-hand lane. Turn right into Speke Road.
If you parked in the sunken car park or in the Elephant pub, you will need to retrace your journey and head back to the traffic lights at High Street. Cross straight over these into Speke Road.
As you enter Speke Road, you will see a large, detached, attractive Georgian House facing you. In front of this stands Woolton Village Cross.
As you then drive down Speke Road, you will pass, on the right, the entrance to St Julie's Girls High School, and just beyond this the entrance to the 18th century Woolton Hall. Unfortunately, at the time of writing this is closed off, because the building is due to be converted into a nursing home.
Just after the bend take the next road on the right, into School Lane, and park as soon as it is safe and convenient to do so. The Old Village School is located just a little further up School Lane, on the left, adjacent to a small triangle of enclosed parkland.

The Old School House

The old Woolton Village School House, which stands in its own green on the bend in School Lane, is dated 1610.

However, many historians believe it to be much older and that it is one of the earliest elementary schools in Britain. Indeed, the Gothic windows at either end of the building seem to indicate that it may well have been a pre-reformation chapel.

There are many references to it in documents dating from the early 17th century and, in fact, the Catholic martyr St. John Almond declared at his trial, in 1612, that he was educated at a school in Much Woolton, and it is likely that it was this same establishment.

The school house was unusually well-built, with walls made up of stones 11 inches thick, some of which are 4 feet long. It is this quality of construction that has allowed the building to survive into modern times. The school house has also been a cottage, a barn, and a cowshed but, for much of the 20th century it stood empty and derelict. Fortunately, it has now been completely restored and refurbished whilst retaining its original external structure and charm. Appropriately enough, it has reverted to one of its original functions and is now a pre-school nursery.

To Find Out More:
Woolton Village School et al
http://bdaugherty.tripod.com/liverpool/woolton.html#history

Liverpool Lost and Found

Continue along School Lane, past the Old School House, and follow it around to the left and up the hill. Almost immediately on your right you will see a modern, private and gated housing estate, called Birch Hill Mews. At the far end of this small estate is the open gateway into Woolton Woods and Camp Hill.
Park anywhere along here, where it is safe and convenient to do so. Walk through the gate and follow the path to the right to explore the Woods, and to the left to explore Camp Hill. A 1-Hour visit time is suggested, to have a good look at the Woods, and to drink in the views across the River Mersey Estuary from the top of Camp Hill.

Woolton Woods, on the flanks and summit of Camp Hill

Woolton Woods and Camp Hill

On this high hilltop, overlooking Woolton, Allerton, and Hunts Cross, and with magnificent views across the river, is Woolton Woods. And this is more than simply a stand of trees.

This whole hilltop, which is one of Liverpool's seven hills, once formed part of the estates of Nicholas Ashton of Woolton Hall. His third son by a second marriage, Henry Ashton, is the first recorded owner of Woolton Woods as a separate estate.

Here, on the top of Camp Hill in 1837, he built a large house with stables, outbuildings, and a walled garden. Following the Ashtons, the Woolton Woods estate passed through the ownership of the Shand and Gaskell families.

It was during the ownership of the latter family that, in 1888, the remarkable gardener, Harry Corlett (1866-1946), was employed. He was a skilled and imaginative horticulturalist who was responsible for revitalising the estate and the walled garden in particular.

During World War I, the house was used as a nursing home and hospital for wounded soldiers and, in 1917, it was bought by Colonel J P Reynolds. He kept it in a holding capacity until, after the War, the Council could afford to buy it. From this time it became a public park and, throughout all these transitions, Harry Corlett remained the head gardener. He oversaw the refurbishment of the walled garden, and its re-opening, in 1921, as an Old English Garden. In 1927, he also installed the floral cuckoo clock, which once sounded the quarters and the hours through a speaker in the trees overhead.

When it opened, the clock had 18,670 plants in the design and the 8-feet-long minute hand weighed 72lbs when fully loaded, and it remains a feature of the garden. When Harry Corlett died, his ashes were scattered in his beloved Old English Garden.

Although some of the outbuildings remain now as private homes, Henry Ashton's house was pulled down in 1948. It was during this demolition that remnants of an ancient fortification were found, although the name for this high ridge above Woolton Village – 'Camp Hill' – had been in use for centuries before this: The hill had long been known as having once been the site of an Iron-Age camp or fort.

Since before the Romans came to Britain, and perhaps as early as 150BC, the 250ft-high sandstone ridge of Camp Hill was an ideal place to observe the surrounding land, and to watch out for potential enemies. The native inhabitants, the Brigantes, constructed a defensive outpost that was about 80 yards in diameter, with ramparts between 10 and 15 feet high. Evidence of a Roman settlement have recently been discovered nearby, so it is quite likely that they, and the local tribespeople, fought for control of the Hill. It is also probable that this vantage point was later used by the Anglo Saxons and the Vikings.

Camp Hill is also now a public open space, and it still provides spectacular vistas; not only of the surrounding area, but also down to the river shore and beyond to the Wirral and, on clear days, the Snowdonia National Park in North Wales. Woolton Woods, its gardens and Camp Hill are one of Liverpool's many Green Flag public open spaces.

Leaving Woolton Woods you will continue down the hill along School Lane. About 200 yards on the right, past the entrance to the Woods, you will see the sunken gardens of the Camp Hill Estate. These may be worth a 5-minute stop. The wall on the opposite side of School Lane now encloses what was once the estate deer park. Follow School Lane around the right-hand bend and, at the road junction, turn right onto Hillfoot Road. NB: Traffic moves along this dual-carriageway at high speed, so make your turn carefully. Once on Hillfoot Road, immediately take the left fork into Springwood Avenue. On the right, just beyond the Crematorium and Cemetery, is the driveway into the Allerton Hall estate. A visit time of 15-minutes or so is suggested here.

The Ancient Manor of Allerton

'Allerton' is a common English place-name, which means 'the elder enclosure', and is derived from the Anglo-Saxon 'alr tun'.

The Domesday Book records the 'Manor of Alretune' as being held by three Thanes – a Thane being the Anglo-Saxon equivalent of a Knight – and is described as being 1,586 acres in size.

Between the 12th and 13th centuries, Allerton was part of the Royal Manor of West Derby and was a royal forest, with hunting, chasing, and hawking under the jurisdiction of the Master Forester of West Derby. For many years the Lathom family seem to have been the chief overlords of the district but, in the 13th century, the Manor's territorial rights were held by Richard de Allerton.

When Cromwell seized the Royalist Lathom estates after the English Civil War (1642-51), these included the Manor of Allerton, which passed to the merchant Richard Perceval. The large estates that comprised the Manor were subsequently held by a succession of influential families; including the Hardmans, the Roscoes, the Cleggs, and the Baileys.

Following the Industrial Revolution, this part of the City was also where many of Liverpool's rising merchant families, who regarded themselves as Britain's new aristocracy, spent their considerable wealth creating 'Stately Homes' surrounded by large gardens and landscaped grounds.

Indeed, the district of Allerton became one of the foremost residential areas of Liverpool. Some magnificent mansions were built there in the 18th and 19th centuries, designed by architects such as Thomas Harrison, Harvey Lonsdale Elmes, Alfred Waterhouse, George Gilbert-Scott, and Richard Norman Shaw.

Many people from outside the City picture Liverpool as being a depressed, post-industrial conurbation, and they are very surprised to discover just how much open space exists throughout the suburbs of the City. Allerton is at the heart of this and, indeed, a number of the old estates have been converted into fine parklands and green spaces, many of which are open to the public. (See Chapter: 'Green and Pleasant Liverpool'.)

Allerton Hall

Allerton Hall and Clarke Gardens

(19)

Allerton Hall stands majestically in what remains of the original Allerton Estate.

From the ownership of the merchant, Richard Perceval, in 1736, the Hall was sold to the Hardman family for £7,700. Then, in 1799 the Hall and a considerable area of adjoining land was bought by William Roscoe. He was a significant and influential local businessman, who was one of the leaders of Liverpool's economic and philosophical renaissance during the late 18th and early 19th century.

As we have heard, he was also a famous and highly regarded merchant, artist, society and literary figure, and Allerton Hall became the centre of much of the intellectual and cultural life of Liverpool, during his time here.

When Roscoe left it, in 1816, the Hall was described as 'a capital mansion, with gardens, pleasure grounds, plantations, and demesne lands'. These lands covered 153 acres and the Manor of Allerton.

Passing through a variety of owners, in 1888, Thomas Clarke bought Allerton Hall – he was a Liverpool tobacco merchant. Clarke re-built and extended the house and landscaped the extensive grounds. He died there in 1911 and, in 1923, in memory of their mother, the six children of the family gave the palatial three-storey house and its estate to the City. The park was renamed Clarke Gardens to mark this generosity.

At the entrance to the grounds of Allerton Hall can be seen a gun emplacement block, or 'pillbox'. This is a legacy of the Second World War, and a reminder that during this period both the Army and the National Fire Service used Allerton Hall and park. After the War, the building became the offices of the Electricity Authority until 1965, when the house and grounds were re-opened to the public.

Allerton Hall, a Grade-II Listed Building, is now leased by the Council to a brewery, which operates it as an attractive family pub and restaurant. The grounds are well kept, and are a popular gathering place for Liverpool families wanting a quiet stroll, perhaps before a satisfying pub lunch.

Adjacent to Clarke Gardens is an extensive area of emergent woodland, which is named the Eric Hardy Local Nature Reserve. This was created in the 1980s and was named in honour of the well-known local naturalist.

> **To Find Out More:**
> Allerton Hall – The Pub in the Park
> Phone: 0151 494 2664

Leaving Allerton Hall, turn right into Springwood Avenue, and then right again at the traffic lights onto Woolton Road. Note the World War Two gun emplacement (pillbox) on the corner of the Allerton Hall Estate. On the left of Woolton Road you will pass Allerton Park House, Springwood House (now a nursing home) and Springwood Lodge. Passing the end of Allerton Road, and about 500 yards further along on the left, beyond the entrance to the Leonard Cheshire 'Orchard' Estate, you will find The Lodge House and Entrance to the grounds of Allerton Tower. There is no vehicular access to these, so park on the road as soon as it is safe and convenient to do so. A visit time of 30 minutes is suggested to look at these very attractive gardens.

Springwood Lodge

Springwood House

On the side of Woolton Road that faces Allerton Hall stands Springwood House. This old house was built around 1840, by William Shand, who was a wealthy merchant. He made his fortune in trade with the West Indies and named the house after the estates that he had owned in Antigua. After his brief tenancy, Thomas Brocklebank, another great Liverpool merchant and ship-owner, bought Springwood in 1844. The house remained in his family's ownership until 1914; the year of the outbreak of the Great War. The estate then became a military training ground with officers being quartered in the house. Coincidentally, one of those officers was Captain Geoffrey Brocklebank, Sir Thomas's son.

Liverpool Corporation bought the huge 123-acre Springwood estate in 1921, and built streets of council houses on the surrounding land. However, the house remained, but stood empty until 1928, when the Springwood Tenants' Association took it over as their community centre. Alterations to the house for this Association, in the summer of 1933, revealed a maze of cellars that were intersected with walls three feet thick. These cellars had been used for storing food and wine and for baking bread. There were also large larders, with stone shelves, in which was found a collection of old-fashioned equipment. These included iron hooks for hanging venison; baking troughs; quaint, square cheese-presses; and massive ovens.

During the Second World War, Springwood was once again used for military purposes but, after the conflict, it returned to the Corporation's custody. In June 1948, the British Electricity Authority then took it on lease for office accommodation and, in due course, the building was bought by the Leonard Cheshire Foundation. This charitable organisation converted the building into a home for the disabled and it is now a privately-run nursing home.

Allerton Priory

Driving past the end of Allerton Road, we come to the grounds that were once part of the Allerton Priory Estate.

In 1806, William Roscoe of Allerton Hall sold this 55-acre section of his large estate, to John Moss, a Liverpool merchant. In 1812, Moss sold it to Dr Peter Crompton, of Eton House, and after whom the nearby Crompton's Lane is named. He ran a school on the site where Bishop Eton Monastery now stands, and we shall visit this later.

Crompton eventually sold the estate to William Calton Rutson, another Liverpool Merchant, who erected a fine house on the estate, which he called Allerton Lodge. Rutson died in 1817, and the estate then passed to his son, William Rutson, DL, JP. In 1832, the Allerton Lodge estate was sold once again, this time to Theodore Woolman Rathbone (son of William Rathbone of Greenbank Hall), and it was around this time that the Lodge was being referred to as 'Allerton Priory'.

As shall be seen, in 1849, Rathbone sold half of the estate to Hardman Earle, who there created the Allerton Tower estate, next to the Priory estate. Then, in 1866, Rathbone sold the remaining Allerton Priory estate to John Grant Morris, who was a colliery proprietor and one-time Lord Mayor of Liverpool. Morris immediately demolished Allerton Lodge and commissioned the Liverpool-born architect, Alfred Waterhouse, to build the present house, at a cost of around £18,000. The new mansion was formally named Allerton Priory, and the Morris monogram, 'JGM', and the date, 1867, were inscribed on the inside of the front entrance porch.

Becoming a home for unmarried mothers and their babies in 1897; and then a school for girls with educational special needs, in 1915; Allerton Priory and its grounds are now a private residential estate.

Allerton Manor and Golf Club

In the grounds of Allerton Park Golf Club you will find the remains of Allerton Manor.

This was designed in the early 1800s by Thomas Harrison (who was also the architect of the Lyceum Club in the City-centre), for the wealthy merchant and privateer, Jacob Fletcher and his family. Unfortunately, the house was destroyed by a catastrophic fire soon after completion, and so the house was re-built, in 1815, on the same site.

Jacob's sons, Jacob and Caleb, inherited this house from their father. They were great huntsmen who kennelled their hounds on land near the present All Hallows Church in Calderstones (see below) and, for many years the Allerton Manor was a meeting place for the Liverpool Hunt.

The Fletcher family went on to own Allerton Manor for 104 years but, after they left the district, the house and the surrounding estate were bought, in 1923, by the City Council for the sum of £40,000. They converted the land into a Municipal Golf Course and the Manor House into the Club House.

However, in 1944, Allerton Manor was once again completely gutted by fire because the Fire Brigade could not get across the golf course to put out the blaze.

Although part of the building, and some outbuildings, were restored to provide café and other facilities for the Golf Club, very little of the original structure remains. Now, only part of the colonnaded wall and porticoed entrance survive of this once great house, but even these are only a shell; surrounding a motley collection of huts, large metal containers, and overgrown shrubbery.

Allerton Park Golf Club is a private facility that has a challenging 18 and 9-hole course. This is now set in a beautiful woodland area, and it is an interesting, up and down 5,494-yard, Par 67 course.

If you wish to visit the course or view the estate, the entrance to which is in Allerton Road, you will need to contact the club directly, in advance.

To Find Out More:
Allerton Park Golf Club
Phone: 0151 428 8510

Allerton Tower

21

Woolton Road, which runs between Woolton Village and what was once the village of Garston, now bisects what was the original Allerton Hall Estate.

Beyond Springwood, Allerton Road, the Allerton Priory estate, and the new Leonard Cheshire 'Orchard' residential care community, stands what remains of the Allerton Tower estate.

Sir Hardman Earle purchased half of the Allerton Priory estate in 1849 – his family had been wealthy merchants in Liverpool, since 1700. Earle was an influential and respected businessman, who was also a director of the Liverpool-Manchester Railway. As such, he was a witness to William Huskisson's fatal accident on its opening day, when the Liverpool MP was killed by the Rocket Steam Locomotive; thus becoming the world's first railway fatality (see Chapter: 'Pool of Life & Culture').

Prior to acquiring the estate, Earle had commissioned Harvey Londsdale Elmes, the architect of St. George's Hall and Liverpool Collegiate School, to design a new house for him. By the time Earle actually took ownership of the land, the young architect had died, in 1847. However, the grand house was still built to the original design, on 78 acres of ground. In 1868, Earle acquired more land, so that the

Allerton Tower

view across the fields from his house could remain unspoilt.

In 1924, the Earle family left the estate and sold it to the City Council for £22,000. However, in 1937, and despite a massive public outcry, the house was demolished because the cost of repairing the extensive damage caused by dry rot was considered prohibitive. Today, only the orangery remains of Elmes's design, plus stables, servants' quarters, and outbuildings. These are set in very attractive grounds and gardens that are open to the public.

On leaving Allerton Tower, continue along the dual-carriageway and get into the right-hand lane. You will need to make a U-turn at the traffic lights, to bring you back down Woolton Road again. NB: This is a main junction and it is always busy. Please take great care when executing your manoeuvre, and leave plenty of space for passing vehicles as you make your turn. At the junction of Springwood Avenue again, turn right at the traffic lights and continue along to the next junction. Turn right on this dual carriageway, which is Mather Avenue. Cross over the traffic lights and then, approximately 300 yards further along, take the first road on the left; this is Forthlin Road.

20 Forthlin Road

22

Paul McCartney's childhood home, at No. 20 Forthlin Road in Allerton, stands about a mile away from John Lennon's home at Mendips.

Paul was born in 1942, and the McCartney family had moved here in 1955, from a tough estate in Speke. Sadly, not long after moving homes, and after a short illness, Paul's mum died. Paul's father, professional musician Jim, now had to bring up his children on his own.

As a teenager, Paul would take his guitar into the bathroom to practice, as he liked the acoustics there. He was encouraged in his music by his father, and the home environment was one of warmth and love. After meeting John Lennon at the church fete in Woolton Village, Paul and his new friend would sit in the front room of Forthlin Road, writing songs in exercise books – the beginning of the great Lennon and McCartney song-writing partnership.

In 1964, Jim McCartney moved out of Forthlin Road, to a large house in Heswall on the Wirral, bought for him by a now successful and wealthy Paul. After a number of different owners, the Allerton property was bought by the National Trust for £55,000, in 1995.

They fully restored the McCartney home to its 1950s appearance and furnishings, and opened it to the public in 1998.

Now, a combined tour gives public access to both this house and to 'Mendips'. However, to ensure that local residents are not inconvenienced by tourists or their vehicles, the interiors of both houses may only be visited as part of guided visits, which run from the city-centre and from Speke Hall. Do check with the National Trust first though to confirm departure points and times.

To Find Out More:
The National Trust – 20 Forthlin Road
Contact Phone Numbers: 0870 900 0256 or
0151 427 7231
www.nationaltrust.org.uk/beatles

Paul McCartney Official Website
www.paulmccartney.com

Liverpool Lost and Found

Return back down Forthlin Road, turning left into Mather Avenue.
Take the right-hand lane and, at the traffic lights, turn right into Booker Avenue.
A new block of apartments stands on the right-hand corner. On the opposite corner is a large detached house.
The owner here has a large flagpole in his front garden from which he flies a variety of flags. What is he flying today I wonder? Approximately 500 yards on the left of Booker Avenue, take the third road, which is again, Allerton Road. (This road gets around a bit doesn't it?) We are now coming into the Calderstones District, and the Calderstones Park estate is behind the wall on the right.

Calderstones

Originally part of the Manor of Allerton, this whole area was mostly rural, right up until the late 19th century.

But, what makes this once-isolated community significant was the discovery and excavation of a chambered tomb, which is thought to have dated from the late Neolithic or early Bronze Age.

Local people had known of the tomb's existence for many years, but had largely ignored it, except for stealing some of the larger stones now and again for building! But, in the 19th century, this site attracted the attention of local archaeologists and scientists who began to excavate, investigate, and research it.

Once extensively unearthed, the tomb itself was of great interest, but more so were the large standing stones that encircled the entrance: Even though axes of the late Neolithic period had already been found in Toxteth, West Derby, Woolton, and Wavertree, carved stones from this period are very rare. However, the construction of this site was very similar to other sites found in Anglesey and Ireland.

Nevertheless, the markings on the stones are unique and are of European significance; making the Calder Stones particularly important. Prior to these legitimate excavations, very little was known about the Calder Stones, until the 1800s, when the industrious academics reported that:

"...in digging about them, urns made of the coarsest clay, containing human dust and bones, have been discovered, there is reason to believe that they indicate an ancient burying-place."

Sometime later, the nearby road was being widened, so archaeologists took advantage of the opportunity to dig once more into the burial-mound.

This time they discovered more of the stones, but these were found to have beautifully detailed, and clearly discernible carvings on their surfaces, of spirals and 'cup and ring' marks, and also some hand and footprints; the latter having extra fingers and toes!

Further reports said: "When the stones were dug down to, they seemed rather tumbled about in the mound. They looked as if they had been a little hut or cellar. Below the stones was found a large quantity of burnt bones; white and in small pieces. There must have been a cart-load or two."

"During the mid and later 19th century, certain academics had declared the Calder Stones to have been part of a Druidical circle"

This gave rise to much local speculation and tall tales about that mysterious Pagan cult.

These so caught the public imagination at the time that, when new roads were built in the area, some were given appropriate names: hence, Druids Cross Road, Druidsville Road, Druids Gardens, and Druids Park.

However, by the closing years of the century this view had been revised, when it was established that the stones were most likely once part of a ruined dolmen.

This had initially been mistakenly taken for a circle, because the layout of the Calder Stones seemed to follow the traditionally accepted Druidic pattern. Nothing of the rural Calderstones community remains, as this district is now part of the southern suburbs of Liverpool. Nevertheless, the location is still charming and pleasant.

Likewise, nothing now remains of the Neolithic Tomb, except the Calder Stones, which are on display in Calderstones Park, which is magnificent, and which we'll visit shortly. But first, let's discover a few of the other curiosities that the Calderstones district has to offer.

To Find Out More:
Calderstones
Chambered Tomb
http://myweb.tiscali.co.uk/
celynog/calderstones.htm

About 300 yards along on the right off Allerton Road, almost opposite Ballantrae Road, is the entrance to the Rhododendron Walk of Calderstones Park. When these are in bloom it is worth stopping and taking a stroll along here. However, this will add a further 30-minutes to the Tour time.

You will next come to the junction of Harthill Road, and All Hallows Church will be facing you on the left. The scion of the Glastonbury Thorn used to stand at this end of the church garden.

Jesse Hartley's 'test' stone

The Calder Stones in the Harthill greenhouses, before bein

All Hallows Church was built by John Bibby, who was born in 1810, and who became a successful iron and copper merchant in Liverpool; owning a large foundry at Garston near Speke.

His first wife, Fanny, who bore him eight children, was the daughter of Jesse Hartley, the civil engineer, one of whose greatest works was the Albert Dock (see Chapter: 'The Liverpool Waterfront').

A small granite obelisk – a quarry specimen once sent to Hartley – was brought from Hartley's Bootle residence on his father-in-law's death in 1860, by John Bibby, who erected this in his grounds at Harthill. This obelisk still stands in what is now Calderstones Park. Although marrying a second time, John Bibby was deeply affected by his first wife Fanny's premature death, which occurred in 1852.

And so, in memory of her, between 1872 and 1876 John built All Hallows Church, close to the family home at nearby Harthill House.

Designed in the Gothic style, by G Enoch Gregson, the church is a very fine sandstone building, with an imposing tower.

"Undoubtedly its real 'crowning glory' is the set of 14 stained-glass windows that were designed by Edward Burne-Jones and William Morris"

In the grounds of the church once stood a flowering thorn; this was planted in 1958, and was an offshoot of the **Glastonbury Thorn**. This in turn is said to be the staff of Joseph of Arimathea who, whilst on a visit to England accompanied by the young Jesus of Nazareth, planted his staff in the ground on January 5 (Old Christmas Eve), at what centuries later was to become Glastonbury Abbey. The staff miraculously flowered the following day, and it was from this legend of Jesus' visit to England, that the poet William Blake took the story for his poem 'Jerusalem':

'And did those feet in ancient time, walk upon England's mountains green?
And was the holy Lamb of God in England's pleasant pastures seen…?'

However, the Allerton Thorn does not seem to have survived very long, and it died soon after its initial planting, although the date of its final removal is uncertain. All Hallows is a Grade I Listed Building, and as such is rightly regarded as a precious jewel of the local heritage. As a footnote: Glastonbury Abbey is where St Patrick is buried, and the Saint preached his farewell sermon in Liverpool in AD 432, before setting off to convert the Pagan Irish to Christianity. The site of this still survives, in Standish Street in the City-centre, where a plaque and a pieta statue commemorate the event (see Chapter: 'The Heart Of The City').

> **To Find Out More:**
> **All Hallows Church Allerton**
> Phone: 0151 724 1561
> http://www.allhallowsallerton.org.uk/
> **The Glastonbury Thorn**
> http://www.mystical-www.co.uk/glastonbury/hawth.htm

...ved to their present location, in the vestibule in Calderstones Park

Turn right up Harthill Road and you will pass Calderstones Comprehensive School on the left. This was John Lennon's old school but, more significantly, my children were all students here! The entrance to the old Harthill estate is on the right, at the end of Harthill Road. You will see the Gog and Magog gates with the statues of the Four Seasons on either side of these.

Parking here to have a brief look at the gates is a good idea, and you can also walk to the Calder Stones from this point: Simply follow the broad path from the gates, for about 5 minutes, until you come to a large greenhouse, known as The Vestibule. The stones are inside here. Alternatively, drive to the main car park, on Calderstones Road, and walk to the stones from there.

At the end of Harthill Road, turn right at the Gog and Magog gates into Calderstones Road. Continue along here for approximately 500 yards. The main car park for Calderstones Park is on the right, almost opposite the end of Cromptons Lane, and 100 yards before the road joins Menlove Avenue.

A 1-Hour visit time is suggested to explore the park: Longer if you really want to investigate every nook and cranny of this large and magnificent public open space.

Anyone in the park will tell you where the main sights are, such as the lake, the various special gardens, and the 1,000-year-old Allerton Oak.

Liverpool Lost and Found

The Ha Ha

As you drive up Harthill Road, on the left stands Calderstones Comprehensive School. This was built as 'Quarry Bank House', in 1866, later becoming a school. In the days when John Lennon was a pupil here, it was known as 'Quarrybank High School'.

Adjoining what is now Calderstones Park once stood Harthill House.

This was built in about 1825, by Stanley Orred Perceval, who was a relative of Spencer Perceval MP. He was the only British Prime Minister to have been assassinated, and he was murdered, in 1812, by John Bellingham who lived in Duke Street in Liverpool.

The gates and walls that now stand at the corner of Calderstones and Harthill Roads are all that now remain of Harthill House. These once formed part of one of the entrances to the Harthill Estate, and the figures are two Atlantes, sometimes referred to as **Gog and Magog** after the legendary, ancient-British giant 'Gogmagog'. Also, on the walls, stand the large and badly weathered sculptures of the **Four Seasons**.

Throughout the 18th century, the land on which Calderstones Park now stands was being farmed by the Mercer family who, in 1814, sold it to a Liverpool merchant, Thomas Martin. The estate was subsequently acquired by Joseph Need Walker, a shot manufacturer, who built the original Calderstones House in 1828.

By 1875, the estate had passed into the hands of Charles McIver, who was the joint founder of the Cunard Shipping Line with Samuel Cunard, and he built a new house in the centre of the estate, known as '**The Mansion House**'. McIver owned the very first private telephone to be installed in Liverpool, in 1880. It linked the Mansion House with his other family estate at 'Verdala Tower', which was situated a quarter of a mile away, in what is now the southwest corner of the park.

In 1902, the MacIver family eventually sold the Calderstones estate, for the sum of £43,000, to Liverpool Corporation who opened it as a public park, in 1905. The original Mansion House in the centre of the estate became the home for various departments of the Council, but this is now closed and has an uncertain future. It is not open to the public.

"The grounds directly in front of this building boasts an original 'ha-ha', which is a grassy moat that is walled on the house side, but with a slope up to ground level on the other. This ingenious trench was so designed to prevent grazing livestock from getting too close the house. In this way, the family could have a clear view of their estate, without the obstruction of a wall or fence"

As we have seen, the park takes its name from the **Calder Stones**, which are six irregular sandstone slabs, with their 'cup and ring' marks, that once stood outside the entrance to the park. These originally formed part of the 'Calderstones Chambered Tomb', which was a Neolithic Chief's Tumulus. This had originally been erected around 4,800BC, and it was therefore older even than Stonehenge – which itself is older than the Pyramids of Egypt! Stonehenge was built around 3100BC, and the oldest pyramid in Egypt is the stepped Pyramid of Zoser, which was constructed around 2600BC.

The name 'Calder' is derived from the Celtic word 'Galdar' or 'Wizard' and local – and baseless – legends say that the ancient Druids held mysterious rites and rituals around the Calder Stones. For some years these ancient monoliths were left where they had been found, as they were too large to move but, in 1845, they were re-erected as a stone circle inside the low, circular wall that still

The landscaping is skillful, and there is also a tranquil **Japanese Garden**; a pretty **Rose Garden**; and a charming **Old English Garden** – each separately walled to preserve their individual characters.

"In the centre of the Old English Garden is the grave and memorial to Jet of Iada, a black Alsatian dog who became a hero during the Second World War."

At the age of nine months old, he was trained as a search and rescue dog, and was responsible for locating people trapped in the rubble of bombed buildings.

One such rescue, of people lost beneath a collapsed hotel in Chelsea, earned Jet the 'Dickin Medal', which is the canine equivalent of the Victoria Cross. After the War, Jet raised funds for the PDSA (People's Dispensary for Sick Animals), and helped find people lost in the Whitehaven Mining Disaster of 1947. Jet died only seven years old, much loved by his mistress, and a real hero.

As well as these ornamental gardens, Calderstones Park also offers many other natural attractions, and perhaps one of the most fascinating of these is the **Allerton Oak**. This ancient tree, which stands in the middle of the park, is reputed to be at least 1,000 years old. Iron bars support some of its huge branches, under which the

The Lotty Sleigh blazes in 1864

ancient court used to be held. On 15th January 1864, the vessel the **Lotty Sleigh** caught fire as it lay at anchor on the River Mersey, nearly four miles away.

The Rock Ferry Steamer 'Wasp' went to the rescue of the ship, which was laden with 11 tons of gunpowder. 'Wasp' rescued the crew just before the vessel exploded, breaking every window on the waterfront on both sides of the river. Shrapnel from the blast travelled so far that it also shattered two of the Allerton Oak's fine branches, but the tree still bears an annual crop of acorns!

All of Liverpool's parks are glorious, and each has special points of interest, however, Calderstones and Harthill is one of the most attractive and varied.

stands outside the main entrance to the park. In 1954, the City Council decided to remove the stones for cleaning and preservation. Six of the large standing stones now survive and, in 1964, these were moved to their current location in the glass **'vestibule' conservatory building**. (It is near this building, adjacent to the railings, that the granite obelisk monument to Jesse Hartley may be seen.)

The Calder Stones are a registered ancient monument and, as such, need to be protected. The City Council is currently reviewing options to improve the conservation and display of the Stones with English Heritage, Merseyside Archaeological Service, and World Museum Liverpool. They can be viewed close up, only by prior appointment with the Ranger Service.

However, they can be seen through the windows of the building so, if you have not already visited them from the Harthill Gates entrance, walk into the park and past the Mansion House. Take the path to the right of the children's playground, then turn right again, passing the **Text and Rose Gardens** on the left. The vestibule is then another 100 yards or so on the left.

There is an attractive lake in the park, and some delightful walks, which are bordered by rhododendron bushes that are magnificent when in flower.

To Find Out More:
The Calderstones
http://www.btinternet.com/~m.royden/mrlhp/local/calders/calders.htm
Calderstones Park
Phone: 0151 233 3007

To end this Tour we shall now visit the grounds only of Bishop Eton Monastery.
To do so, leave the car park at Calderstones Park and drive up Cromptons Lane.
Continue along this road across the traffic lights and up the hill.
Turning left at the next set of lights brings you into Woolton Road (this road gets about a bit too, doesn't it?).
The monastery is immediately on the left.
I am sure that the monks will not mind you driving through their gates and parking for a minute or two.
It really is a tranquil setting.

Liverpool Lost and Found

In the mid-19th Century, the Potato Famine that ravaged Ireland from 1845 until 1850 resulted in a massive influx of Irish people into Liverpool, and created a huge rise in the number of Roman Catholics in the Town.

This caused a backlash from the indigenous, Protestant majority, fuelled by the militancy of the Loyal Order of Orangemen (The Orange Lodge) and the Protestant-Tory Town Council (see Chapter: 'The Liverpool Waterfront).

Nevertheless, the Catholics were here to stay and they organised themselves and received some local support, as well as encouragement and funds from outside Liverpool. This, together with their commitment to their own faith and people, was sufficient to create a Roman Catholic infrastructure by the building of churches, schools, missions, and the establishment of welfare organisations for their growing community.

In the mid-19th century, it was recognised that a resident Catholic Bishop was required in the Town, and so Eton House was acquired. This had been built as a school in 1776, by a Unitarian Minister called Hezekiah Kirkpatrick. Ownership then passed to Dr Peter Crompton, who was a former master of Eton College. The road upon which the new school stood at the corner of Woolton Road, was named after him.

Crompton intended that his school should become recognised as 'the Eton College of the North', and in this he was largely successful.

But then, in 1843, the Roman Catholic Archdiocese acquired the building as the first Catholic Bishop's Palace in Liverpool, becoming known as Bishop Eton from this time.

Bishop Eton Monastery

By 1851 however, the building had become the home of members of the Redemptorist Order. This community of monastic priests is a deeply evangelical order, founded in 1732 and otherwise known as the Congregation of the Most Holy Redeemer – hence Redemptorists – who see their prime role as being the securing and strengthening of Catholic Faith.

The monastery chapel became a parish church in 1962, and this is now a vital part of the local community.

The Redemptorist priests at Bishop Eton continue to provide retreats in Woolton for priests and members of the laity, and they also follow their mission throughout the region, and beyond.

To Find Out More:
The Redemptorists
Phone: 0151 722 1108
www.bishopeton.org.uk
www.redemptorists.com

To end this Tour, turn left out of Bishop Eton Monastery and continue along Woolton Road. Cross over the traffic lights at Queens Drive. Next, take the 3rd road on the left, this is Heathfield Road.
This will bring you back to the 'Shelter in the Middle of the Roundabout' at Smithdown Road and Penny Lane, where our Tour began.

Liverpool Lost and Found: Conclusion

We have come to the end of this exploration of some of Liverpool's most attractive districts, but which are perhaps less familiar to outsiders.
I chose the title of this Chapter carefully, because so many people assume that the City of Liverpool is just that – one great conurbation. You will have now discovered that this is far from the case, and that the City is indeed made up of many small communities, which were once completely independent and often quite isolated, separate settlements. These have been all but lost

within the mass of modern Liverpool, but it is easy to find them again if you know where to look, and once you understand what you are seeing. As I mentioned in the introduction to this Chapter, the places that we have just visited are only a few of the fifteen or more lost villages that now comprise modern Liverpool.
Each ancient community has added to the sum total of what makes Liverpool such a fascinating and vibrant place, and I hope that what you have experienced so far will make you want to discover for yourself the remaining 'villages' of Liverpool.

This shop, which stands opposite the Lamb Hotel in Wavertree, is one of the few remaining, original, Georgian bow-front shops in Liverpool

Green and Pleasant Liverpool

Including:

Princes Road Synagogue

The Greek Church

Toxteth Park and King John's Hunting Lodge

Sefton Park

The Palm House

Greenbank Park

Penny Lane, Pete Best's Shop, Dovedale Road

Sudley House Art Gallery

Mossley Hill

The Robin Hood Stone

Liverpool Cricket Club

Otterspool Park and Promenade

The Ancient Chapel of Toxteth

Princes Park

Ringo Starr's Boyhood Homes

The Palm House in Sefton Park

Green and Pleasant Liverpool: The Tour

The total distance covered by this Tour is 20 miles, and the suggested time for its completion is 5 Hours.
Allow extra time for however long you wish to spend strolling through the 4 recommended parks, and the Sudley House Art Gallery.
To visit the Greek Church, the Synagogue, and St Margaret's Church, you will need to make separate arrangements to do so, directly with their administrators. This is also true of the Ancient Chapel of Toxteth.
Contact details are listed in each appropriate article in the Tour.
This is a circular tour, so you can pick it up at any point on the route. However, do always travel in the recommended direction, in this case CLOCKWISE, as the route has been designed to get you efficiently around Liverpool's sometimes confusing one-way systems.
NB Please remember to check all opening times and admission charges before setting off, to avoid disappointment should any venues be closed

Contents

Route Map

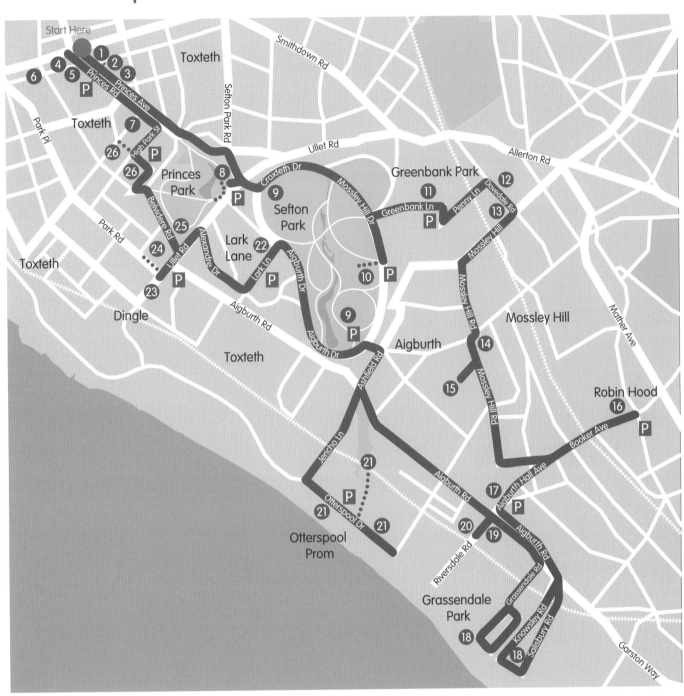

Start Here

Toxteth

Princes Rd
Princes Ave

Toxteth

High Park St

Princes Park

Belvidere Rd

Park Pl

Park Rd

Toxteth

Alexandre Dr

Ullet Rd

Dingle

Aigburth Rd

Toxteth

Lark Lane

Lark Ln

Aigburth Dr

Croxteth Dr

Sefton Park Rd

Ullet Rd

Sefton Park

Mossley Hill Dr

Greenbank Park

Greenbank Ln

Penny Ln

Allerton Rd

Dovedale Rd

Mossley Hill

Mossley Hill Rd

Smithdown Rd

Aigburth

Mossley Hill

Robin Hood

Mather Ave

Booker Ave

Aigburth Hall Ave

Aigburth Rd

Jericho Ln

Ashfield Rd

Otterspool Dr

Otterspool Prom

Riversdale Rd

Grassendale Park

Grassendale Rd

Knowsley Rd

Salisbury Rd

Garston Way

Key

- Start Here — Starting Point
- 1 — Map Reference
- Driving Route
- Walking Route
- P — Parking Points
- Railway

Green and Pleasant Liverpool
Introduction

The first-time visitor to Liverpool could be forgiven for assuming that, because they were coming to a post-industrial City, they would be seeing nothing but docks, offices, shopping centres, and heavily built-up areas of terraced houses that were originally built for Victorian working-class communities. Whilst this is certainly the case in large parts of Liverpool, there is much less of the 'dark, satanic mills' about my home town, and much more of 'the green and pleasant land' than most people expect.

Visitors are also surprised by the open squares and spacious streets in the heart of the City; by the breadth and openness of our waterfront, and by the broad avenues and boulevards that radiate from the City-centre into the extensive suburbs.

They are also amazed by just how many hills the City is built on, even on its immediate outskirts. Indeed, as well as a number of smaller 'heights', Liverpool is built on seven major hills, and these are Walton Hill, Everton Ridge, High Park or Toxteth Ridge, Mossley Hill, Allerton Hill, Olive Mount, and Woolton Ridge. Whilst some of these hills are now built-up residential areas, others are open areas of park or woodland, with pathways, playgrounds, and places to play football or games. In fact, within half a mile of the City-centre one comes to the landscaped flanks of the highest hill within the City boundary, that of Everton Ridge. This once densely populated area now comprises broad stretches of open grassland, landscaped in terraces, with winding pathways and with steps up to the highest church in the City – St. Georges Church, Everton. From here there are magnificent views across the River Mersey, to the Wirral Peninsular, and beyond to North Wales. And this recreation ground is typical of how the City of Liverpool has made the best use of the available open land, to the benefit of the people.

Before receiving its charter as a Town and Borough, from King John in 1207, Liverpool was a tiny community on the banks of the River Mersey. However, the land was open, fertile, and excellent for farming and settlement. It also had two vast forests situated just outside the Town limits. One was to the east, at West Derby, and the other was the very large forest of Toxteth, which features in this Chapter. Indeed, there were so many deer and wild boar roaming in this forest that the King claimed it as a Royal Hunting Park.

It remained as such, until Oliver Cromwell disafforested the land and parcelled it out to local people for them to farm and build homes on, following the English Civil War (1642-51).

Despite this, and the passing of many centuries, parts of both of these historical areas of park and woodland remain and they are open to the public, as is so much land in and around the City. Liverpool, in fact, is a very green City, and the pockets of open space in the town-centre, together with the broad band of the suburbs – with their numerous public parks – that border the City, combine to make it a very pleasant environment in which to live and work.

Credit for this must go to the people of Liverpool themselves for it was they who, in the mid-19th century, and as the City's population and conurbation was rapidly expanding, campaigned for the creation of landscaped space for free public amenity. Indeed, between 1801 and 1865, the population of Liverpool increased from 78,000 to 500,000 and, in 1850, the Corporation Improvement Committee decided to prevent urban spread by creating a green belt of land around the perimeter of the town. Also, urban life at that time was particularly grimy, congested, and unhealthy, and people needed room to breathe, and to escape to from the dirt and oppression of the Town; they needed places in which to freely play, relax, and refresh themselves.

The Committee identified large areas of woodland and arable land, as well as stretches of moss and heathland. They employed the best architects and landscape gardeners to re-shape and reconstruct this land, and to create what they and the people regarded as 'the lungs of the Town'. And so, the period from 1870 to 1904 became the golden age for the building of parks, throughout Liverpool and its neighbouring districts and communities.

However, and as you will discover in this Chapter, the first of Liverpool's parks was a private venture. Named after Prince Albert, the consort of Queen Victoria, it was the idea of a local entrepreneur called Richard Vaughan Yates.

The first of the public parks created by the Corporation of Liverpool was Newsham Park, in 1846; Wavertree Park, in 1856; Sheil Park, in 1862; and Stanley Park in 1870. Then came Sefton Park in 1872; soon to be followed by Calderstones Park – acquired in 1902 and formally opened in 1905; and Walton Hall Park which, although acquired around 1913, did not open to the public until 1934. It is a remarkable fact that Liverpool's parks and open spaces now cover approximately 3,000 acres, or one-ninth of the City's land area.

The method used by the Corporation of Liverpool to fund the creation of many of these very large parks, was quite ingenious, and they stole it from Richard Vaughan Yates!

Following his example at Princes Park, the Corporation set about buying the necessary small parcels of land from local landowners, or larger tracts from the aristocrats who then owned much of the land in and around Liverpool: Such people as Lord Derby, Lord Sefton, and the Marquess of Salisbury. Next, not only were landscape gardeners employed to begin the work on the parks, but also architects and designers.

Swans glide across the lake in Princes Park

Whilst these latter professionals had some role to play in the design and building of the parks and their amenities, principally, they were employed as house-builders.

This was because the third step taken by the City-Fathers, again following Yates's original methodology at Princes Park, was to build large, detached, and individually-designed residential properties – most with stables and carriage houses, and with separate quarters for domestic servants. These were erected in a large perimeter around the designated park area.

Not only did the sale of these expensive and desirable properties pay for the initial purchase, reclamation, and landscaping of the parkland, but they also met the costs of the installation of amenities such as lakes, watercourses, grottoes, boat-houses, pavilions, bandstands, tea-rooms, and lavatories. Profit was generated also – this was a shrewd business idea! Then, developing Yates's initial idea, behind this first residential perimeter the Corporation erected a second, outer ring, of slightly smaller properties. These had only limited or indeed, no separate stabling or servants' accommodation. However, there were staff-quarters in the main house.

Next, and radiating out from the rim of these residential wheels, came the spokes. These were streets of smaller, but still quite grand, terraced houses. These too were architect designed, but they stood in attractive, tree-lined avenues. However, they did not have facilities for live-in servants, but they contained all the facilities necessary for non-residential domestic staff to service the families who would occupy them.

The best surviving example of this innovative form of urban planning is to be seen in and around Sefton Park.

And so, the inner, largest properties were sold to the new 'aristocracy' of the merchant classes; the outer perimeter to the upper-middle classes and to ambitious and aspirational professionals; and the terraced properties were bought by the upwardly mobile middle-classes and trades-people.

"This all fitted in very well with the highly-stratified 19th century way of life, and the Corporation made pots of money!"

This was all highly entrepreneurial, eminently practical, economically creative, and very Victorian. Our energetic forefathers therefore, bequeathed to modern Liverpudlians a considerable legacy of living open land that continues to be one of Liverpool's greatest assets and public resources.

This Chapter begins at the outskirts of the City proper, at Toxteth. I then take you to four of the city's main public parks; through a Victorian private housing estate, filled with glorious homes and with its own exclusive esplanade; and it will also take you past curiosities like the Robin Hood Stone and Stanlawe Grange. You will also visit a delightful art gallery in the southern suburbs; a late medieval chapel; a famous synagogue and an entrancing Greek Church; and also to a glorious, cast iron and glass Palm House.

All-in-all, this Chapter will give you a real flavour of how much the City of Liverpool is blessed with wonderful parklands, in pleasant and fascinating urban settings.

Ancient Toxteth

Our story begins on the edge of the ancient district of 'Toxteth', which derives from the Celtic name of a local farm, called 'Toki's Steading'. This is mentioned in the Domesday Book as 'Stochestede', implying a stockaded area to protect livestock. The Domesday Book was ordered by William the Conqueror in 1086, as a complete survey of his newly subjugated territory. It was so called because it was regarded as a final and irrevocable authority, and so there was no appeal against it, any more than there was to be on the day of the Last Judgement before God; hence 'Domesday'!

In 1207, the King bought this large tract of land from the Molyneux family who owned all of this part of southern Liverpool at that time, all the way down to the river and on to Garston. This wealthy family were descendants of Norman invaders who came to Britain with William, and they were to go on, in due course, to become the Earls of Sefton. (See Chapter: 'A Lordly Heritage'.)

John then stockaded the entire district of Toxteth and created a private hunting forest for himself and his courtiers, and he used this regularly. He employed a Master Huntsman and 49 Wardens to police the park and to prevent local people from poaching the animals.

"To aid them in their game-keeping the Wardens had 10 horses, two packs of dogs, and 52 spaniels"

There were two lodges for these Wardens; one on the edges of what is now Sefton Park, and one at Otterspool.

Toxteth Forest remained a Royal preserve until 1426, when King Henry VI granted it to Thomas Stanley. But, in 1446, the Molyneux family regained their former lands, when the King awarded the Master Forestership of all the Royal Forests and Parks, including Toxteh, to Sir Richard Molyneux.

Losing their estates for a period after the Civil War - by which time Toxteth had been partially disaforested, a later Sir Richard Molyneux, in 1604, took ownership of the district for his family once more.

"In order to cultivate the land, Sir Richard allowed the Puritans to occupy and farm it and, by 1611, there were over twenty families in the district"

Indeed, Toxteth was to remain a rural community until the beginning of the 19th century. The Puritans had been invited here from Bolton, Ormskirk, and the Midlands by Sir Richard. He was a Roman Catholic, and so no stranger to prejudice himself, in those turbulent centuries under the Tudor and Stuart monarchs.

He promised them a safe-haven from persecution but, sadly, he was unable to keep his promise. We shall also hear more about the Puritans and their local centre of worship, here in Toxteth, later in this Chapter.

To Find Out More:
The History of Toxteth
http://www.toxteth.net/places/liverpool/history/early%20days.htm

Domesday Book
www.nationalarchives.gov.uk/domesday

Green and Pleasant Liverpool

To begin this Tour you will need to park in the immediate vicinity of Princes Road, near its junction with Upper Parliament Street. This avenue is too busy to park on directly, so I suggest that you do so in Upper Hampton Street, which runs alongside the former Nursing College, off Princes Road. You can also park in the next road down on the left, alongside the Synagogue; this is Selborne Street.
Unless you have pre-arranged visits to St Margaret's Church, The Synagogue, and The Greek Church, I suggest a visit time of 15 minutes to view the exteriors of the buildings featured in the first section of the Tour.

Florence Nightingale and William Rathbone; Mary Seacole

Florence Nightingale and William Rathbone

Florence Nightingale

At the top of Princes Road, on its left-hand corner with Upper Parliament Street, we can see a large monumental relief, with recessed seats, set into the wall.
This was unveiled in 1913, and it is specifically dedicated to Florence Nightingale (1829-1910), but also to nurses in general. It was built by public subscription and such was the feeling of gratitude to Florence Nightingale, for her contribution to the development and professionalising of nursing and hospital care in the Liverpool, that the fund was five times over-subscribed.
The wall in which the memorial is placed surrounds what was originally a purpose-built nursing training school.
This was established in 1898, by Florence Nightingale and the local philanthropist William Rathbone (1787-1868), to train District Nurses, and to extend the training facilities that Florence and William had previously begun at the Royal Infirmary in the city-centre. Here, they had together designed a revolutionary form of public hospital layout, and the 'Nightingale Wards' are still recognised as being innovative and practical. (See Chapter: 'Pool of Life & Culture'.) Rathbone had been prompted to involve Florence Nightingale in the improvement of local nursing services, after coming to recognise and value the work of Agnes Jones, who led the nursing team at the Brownlow Hill Infirmary.

The professional collaboration of these two intelligent and influential individuals was to benefit not only the people of Liverpool, but of Britain and beyond. William Rathbone was the 6th son to bear the name 'William' – something of a tradition in his family, who were an illustrious breed that had been associated with Liverpool for many years.

"He was dedicated to the care of the poor, often visiting the sick and needy himself, and providing money for their relief and support"

The **Nursing Training College** building at the corner of Princes Road, by the 1970s, had become a private, Christian Bible School, and then became a privately run hotel. However, the building will always be a monument to two great people who contributed so much to the quality of life of Liverpudlians.

To Find Out More:
Florence Nightingale Museum website
http://www.florence-nightingale.co.uk/

The Rathbone Family Website
http://www.rathboneuk.org/who.aspx?ID=4

Mary Seacole

Florence Nightingale, of course, was already a national heroine in Victorian Britain by the time she came to Liverpool. Her establishment and organisation of nurses on the battlefields of the Crimea in particular (during the 1854-56 War between Britain and France on one side, and the Russians on the other), had won her honour and renown. However, one cannot refer to Florence Nightingale without discussing the wonderful work of the less well-known Mary Seacole (1805-1881).

"Mary Seacole was born Mary Jane Grant in 1805, in Jamaica, which was then a British colony"

Her mother was a free, Black, Jamaican, and a doctor, who ran a boarding house for British soldiers and sailors on that Caribbean island. Mary's mother taught her the arts of Creole medicine, and the two women treated and nursed the British and the local people, with equal skill and compassion.
As Mary neared her 50th birthday, she heard from her Army friends in Jamaica about the Crimean War. They described the desperate need for nurses with her skills and experience, and they told her that there was a campaign to recruit 40 nurses, to work with Florence Nightingale at the Scutari Barrack Hospital in Turkey.
Mary travelled to the recruitment offices in England where, despite being armed with excellent references from high-ranking British officers, she was repeatedly rejected. The British could not accept that not only a woman, but a Black woman at that, should be taken

seriously as a nurse, no matter how qualified or experienced she might be.
Refusing to have her dreams dashed Mary had, by 1855, successfully raised sufficient funds to pay for her passage to the Crimea. Here, she established the British Hotel to provide accommodation, food, and nursing care. Mary also braved the battlefields in order to nurse wounded soldiers, regardless of which side they were on, gaining a reputation for professionalism and devotion equal to that of Florence Nightingale.
After the end of the War Mary spent her final days in London, working as masseuse to Princess Alexandra the Princess of Wales, and travelling back and forth between England and Jamaica.
At the age of 76, and following a short illness, she died on the 14th May 1881, and is buried in Kensal Rise Catholic Cemetery in north-west London.
The work done by this remarkable woman is commemorated in the name of 'Mary Seacole House', here in Toxteth. It is also continued in this specialist Care and Advice Centre, which assists people from disadvantaged communities, who suffer from mental health issues. Here, they can find love, understanding, and highly-skilled professional support.

To Find Out More:
Mary Seacole
www.maryseacole.com/maryseacole/pages

The Church of St Margaret of Antioch

Beyond the former nursing college and on the same side of the road, is the church of St. Margaret of Antioch.

This was designed, in 1869, by George Street, who went on to design the London Law Courts in 1871. It was built by Robert Horsfall, a member of the family that built many of Liverpool's churches. The outside of the building is pretty, if somewhat simple and plain, with a small statue of the Saint set in an ornate niche above the front entrance. Inside however, the church is spacious – though a little dark, and is richly decorated with marble and tile.

The walls are painted with stencilled decorations of flowers and the images of saints. Tiled niches and recessed framed panels contain religious scenes in a combination of painting and mosaic. Fluted columns of layered, coloured marble, support broad, intricately-painted arches that support the vaulted, beamed roof. Like many of the images around the walls, the ceiling is painted in a medieval style and in bright colours. The wooden ceiling panels show a magnificent choir of angels, playing a range of musical instruments, all of which are painted in rich golds, reds, and greens.

After many years of neglect and decay, through lack of funds, St Margaret's has recently benefited from a major refurbishment and restoration. This gives me great personal satisfaction, as this is the church where my wife and I were married, in March 1981.

To arrange a visit please contact the Vicar.

To Find Out More:
St Margaret's Church
Phone: 0151 709 1526

The Church of St Margaret of Antioch

The Princes Road Synagogue

The building next to St Margaret's Church, at number 5 Princes Road, is the former **Streatlam Towers**. This was a grand Victorian mansion, and it has a unique, round, staircase tower and a fairy-tale castle roof. This was once the home of James Lord Bowes, who also opened part of the building, in 1894, as **The Museum of Japanese Art**. For 10 years this was extremely popular, but then it closed and the collection was dispersed. The separate entrance to the old museum can still be seen, to the left of the entrance steps, and still with the Japanese Royal Chrysanthemum Emblem carved in the stonework.

Next to this stands the Princes Road Synagogue. This was designed and built, in a Moresque style, by architects W & G Audsley, and it was consecrated on 3rd September 1874.

The costs for the project were met completely by local fund-raising and, at the time, this was the largest synagogue in Britain – accommodating as it does, up to 900 people. It is a richly decorated and impressive building with a high, vaulted ceiling, which is beautifully carved and decorated. At the end of the nave, overlooking the wide central space, is a great rose window. This not only adds light, but also emphasises the magnificence of the interior.

This is certainly one of the most beautiful synagogues in Britain, and perhaps in Europe, and because of this it welcomes visitors from all over the world; whether of the Jewish Faith or not.

The Synagogue features on the English Heritage website, because of its cultural and architectural significance, and the building is often used as a location for films and television programmes.

The Jewish community for many generations has, and continues to be, a vital part of Liverpool life. Many of the City's most famous sons and daughters, and most significant benefactors, are of this faith. Prominent Jewish Liverpudlians include Ian Broudie, the lead singer of the pop group the Lightning Seeds; the late Judge Rose Heilbron QC; Edwina Currie MP; solicitor, E Rex Makin; former Attorney General, Lord Peter Goldsmith; the much missed entertainer and local benefactor, Frankie Vaughan; and the Beatles manager, Brian Epstein.

Founded in the mid-18th century by a handful of immigrant peddlers, probably of German extraction, Liverpool's was the first Jewish community in the north of England and, for over a century, it was the largest outside London. Originally, the Jewish population in Liverpool stood at 100 people in 1789, but this grew to 1000 in 1825, and by 1914, to its largest figure of 11,000. However, by the 1950s, the population had declined to 8,000 and today it stands at approximately 3,000 people with 4 synagogues in Liverpool.

There are a number of Jewish sites of significance throughout the City and these form part of the Liverpool Jewish Heritage Trail. I recommend this as yet another way to discover more about the breadth of our City's community history, and our current ethnic, racial, and religious vitality.

To Find Out More:
Harold House Jewish Youth & Community Centre
Phone: 0151 475 5671
http://www.liverpooljewish.com

Jews in Liverpool
http://www.somethingjewish.co.uk/articles/293_liverpool _jews.htm

Princes Road Synagogue
Phone: 0151 709 3431
www.princesroadsynagogue.org

On the opposite side of Princes Road to the Nightingale Hotel, but with its entrance behind in Berkeley Street, stands **The Greek Orthodox Church of St. Nikolas**.

This splendid Byzantine church, with its red brick, white facings, pink domes, arched windows, and dramatic frontage, is a gem in the heart of Toxteth.

In 1810, a small number of Greeks settled in Liverpool, but they were too widespread to be able to organise themselves into a community. However, by 1846, there were a larger number of Greek merchants and cotton traders operating from the port, and they provided both the funds and the impetus to bring the disparate local Greek community together. One such entrepreneur was George Michael Papayiannis who, in 1855, founded the great shipping company, 'Ellerman Papayiannis'.

He became the first president of the Greek Community in Liverpool and, in 1863, he called a meeting and proposed the setting up of a fund-raising appeal to build a Greek Church in the City. Within an hour more than half the cost of the building had been raised by pledges just from amongst those present.

At the same meeting a committee was elected, who bought the land and commissioned the Greek architect, G Potessaro – who was resident at that time in the City – to design the building. He donated his services free of charge.

The famous builder, Henry Summers, was commissioned to build the church and when it was completed, in 1870, it was only the second Greek Orthodox Church in England. The church was consecrated on 4th January 1871, in full Eastern Rites, by His Grace the Archbishop of Syra and Tinos, Alexandros Lycourgos. At the time, he was making an historic visit to Britain from Constantinople, in an attempt to unite all the churches of the Christian faith. The ceremony was attended by representatives of the Archbishops of Canterbury and York, and by a large congregation of Greek and English people.

By the early 1900s the Greek community in Liverpool had dwindled, due to many people emigrating to Australia, America, Europe, and Alexandria. By 1957, the church had fallen into disrepair due to a lack of funds. Fortunately, Greek ship-owners made significant financial contributions, and many Greek sailors gave their time and muscle-power to rebuilt and renovate the building. By 1963, the Greek community in Liverpool had increased.

This was as a result of the civil war that was then taking place in Cyprus, between the Greeks and the Turks, and many Greek Cypriots had fled their homeland to settle in Liverpool. The local community began to flourish once more, and a priest from

The Greek Church

Cyprus was brought over to service the growing congregation at St. Nikolas.

The building is a remarkable example of traditional Greek church design, with Anglo/Victorian overtones. As such, it makes a fascinating stop on any tour of the City. Four domes surmount octagonal glazed drums on the roof and make the building very distinctive. Some of these windows are glazed with blue glass to give the illusion of blue, Greek skies to the congregation below. Inside this spacious church, the arched ceilings are painted pale blue to complete the effect, and the roof is supported on slender white columns with intricately carved capitals, which connect in sweeping curves with the domes above.

The altar is backed by a tall, broad, carved oak reredos, which is punctuated by panels depicting religious scenes and images of the Saints and Patriarchs.

The glass chandeliers suspended on long chains, the white walls, and the carved stone pulpit – which is reached by a curving wooden stairway, all add to the charm and romance of this lovely building.

Regular services are held here, by the still thriving Greek community from across Merseyside and, although the building is not normally open during the week, a courteous phone call to the Greek Priest will encourage him to open the church to genuine and serious visitors.

> To Find Out More:
> The Greek Church of St Nikolas
> Phone: 0151 724 3500

Money On The Move

Almost at the end of Princes Road, and next to the Greek Church, is the NatWest Bank. The original building on this site was completely gutted during the Toxteth Riots, in July 1981.

This was because local people believed that the Bank was investing in South Africa, and therefore bolstering the racist Apartheid regime in that country, and this made it a particular target during the conflagration. After the Riots, the frontage and main part of the bank were completely rebuilt, using money provided by the Government. This was a truly unprecedented response, but the administration of Prime Minister Margaret Thatcher recognised that an important gesture of economic commitment to the Toxteth Community was necessary. It is only a shame that it had taken the worst civil disturbances on the British mainland, since the Civil War, to drive home that message!

However, the rear of the building was not damaged in the riots, and it is this part of the bank that gives it its particular significance. This is because, even though the main entrance of the bank has always faced Upper Parliament Street, here at the back is an awning and a teller's window, providing a drive-in banking facility. This had been an integral part of the bank's original design when it opened in 1959, and provided motorists with a means of depositing or accessing their cash whilst 'passing through', and without having to get out of their vehicles. The bank first opened as a local branch of The Westminster Bank, and it became the first, purpose-built drive-in bank in Britain.

6

A Dictator Comes to Liverpool

Adolf Hitler

As you will be discovering by now, Liverpool is home to many eccentrics, characters, and curious stories. Perhaps though, one of the most unlikely tales is based on evidence that was discovered in the New York Public Library, in the late 1970s. Although open to doubt, these documents appear to confirm a long-held belief that Toxteth was once the temporary home of the 20th Century's greatest villain.

Running off Princes Road, and directly opposite the Church of St Margaret of Antioch, is **Upper Stanhope Street**. Living, for a short while, at number 120 – long-since demolished, was an impoverished art-student who was visiting Liverpool from Europe. Born in Austria, on April 20th 1889, by his late teens this young man was moody, irritable, anti-social, and permanently dishevelled. Then, following many disagreements with his bullying father, and having failed in his ambition to become a fine artist, he wanted to escape his problems. He also wished to avoid National Service and so, in November 1912, he left his home in Vienna and travelled to England.

At the age of 23, he had come to stay in Liverpool with his half-brother, Alois, and his Irish wife, Bridget Elizabeth Dowling. Alois had met his future bride in London, in 1910, and the couple had moved to Liverpool soon afterwards. By the time their German relative came to stay with them they were running a restaurant in Toxteth.

"The following year, in April 1913, the young man returned to his homeland where, at the outbreak of the First World War, he was conscripted and became a corporal in the German Army. His name was Adolph Hitler"

At the outbreak of World War One, Hitler's half-brother abandoned his wife, and their young son William Patrick Hitler, and returned to Germany. Alois died there, in Hamburg, in 1939. Bridget and William moved to London in 1924, but, as World War Two loomed, they discreetly left England to settle in New York. From there they toured the USA trying to capitalise on their links with Adolph Hitler until, in 1941, America entered the War. Then, Bridget and William changed their name and vanished from public view.

Bridget died in 1969, and her son died in 1987, but William had married and had children, and grandchildren. However, none of these American citizens now go by the name of 'Hitler'!

> **To Find Out More:**
> **Did Hitler Come To Liverpool?**
> http://www.btinternet.com/~m.royden/mrlhp/local/hitlerinliverpool/makinghistory.htm
>
> **Hitler's Irish Relatives**
> http://www.dowlingfamily.info/i1910hit.htm

> Now continue down Princes Road, noting the magnificent houses on either side of the Boulevard. On the left, by the second set of pedestrian crossing lights, is the Beaconsfield Street Methodist Centre. If you can find a safe place to park on the road, then you can stop for a quick look at the 'Flying Jesus Statue'. At the end of the Boulevard you will see the main gates to Princes Park, directly facing you across the roundabout, but we shall visit this Park from a different access point, later in this Tour.

7

The 'Boulevard'

This road, which leads through Toxteth to the south of the City, is named **Princes Avenue** on the left of the central reservation, and on the right as 'Princes Road'. These roads, which were opened in 1846, are known locally and collectively as **Princes Boulevard**, for obvious reasons, because they combine to make one of the City's many tree-lined avenues.

From the late nineteenth century, until the 1950s, the central part of the Boulevard was once the site of the tramway that ran from the City-centre out to the southern suburbs of Liverpool. The city's tramways were one of many imaginative civic projects

carried out in Liverpool, by one of our greatest City Engineers – John Alexander Brodie (1858-1934).

We shall discover more about this remarkable man, later in this chapter.

The Boulevard bisects an area of once-luxurious Victorian and Edwardian mansion houses – complete with accommodation for the family-servants – which faced the prestigious roadway. Behind these were terraces of comfortable family homes, some large enough to require the services of non-residential domestic staff.

At the head of the central reservation is a plinth that originally supported the bronze

statue of William Huskisson MP (1770-1830), who was killed by George Stephenson's Rocket Locomotive. (See Chapter: 'Pool of Life & Culture'.)

However, during the Toxteth Riots, in 1981, his statue was pulled down by rioters in the mistaken belief that he was connected with slavery. This now stands in the heart of the Chinese Quarter of Liverpool, in Coopers Terrace, off Duke Street. This followed a complete restoration at The Conservation Centre, which is one of the outstanding facilities of the National Museums of Liverpool. (See Chapter: 'The Heart of the City'.)

> At the roundabout, in front of Princes Park Gates, take the left fork along Croxteth Road, as it snakes around the left of the Park perimeter; passing Bentley Road on the left. Take the right-hand lane and, at the traffic lights, turn right into Sefton Park Road. At the next set of traffic lights, turn sharp right into Windermere Terrace – almost doubling back on yourself. Park as soon as is convenient and safe to do so. Toxteth Park Higher Lodge is on the corner of Windermere Terrace and Sefton Park Road. You could leave your car to visit Princes Park from this point, because either end of the bow of Windermere Terrace will give you pedestrian access. If you are not visiting the Park at this point, then I suggest a 10-minute stroll to view The Lodge and the houses in the Terrace.

Having travelled down 'The Boulevard' and through part of modern Toxteth, we now approach Sefton Park. As we turn into Sefton Park Road, on the right-hand corner can be seen the magnificent, 19th Century apartment block of Princes Park Mansions. Beyond the gardens and driveway into the Mansions is the glorious, neo-gothic, official residence of the Vice Chancellor of the University of Liverpool.

As mentioned previously, this whole area down to the river was part of King John's private hunting forest, and parts of his Higher Hunting Lodge survive within Park Lodge. This is the house that stands on the corner of Sefton Park Road and Windermere Terrace, just opposite the gates to Sefton Park, but it is not open to the public.

The main building is from the Tudor period and this was refurbished and restored in the 1920s. During this work, two original Elizabethan fireplaces were uncovered, as well as parts of the original Medieval hunting lodge. These included 3ft thick sandstone walls, some wattled walls, secret cupboards, and bricked-up mullioned windows. The current owner has the date 'AD 1207' mounted on the gates to record the origins of his home.

Whilst in the Terrace, it is worthwhile exploring this charming, bow-shaped cul-de-sac, and taking a look at the arresting, detached, Victorian mansion houses, once occupied by wealthy 19th century merchants. If you follow the terrace all the way around to the left, this is a good access point into Princes Park if you wanted to explore here too – although we will be returning to Princes Park later in this Chapter.

One of the grand mansions on Windermere Terrace

Leaving Windermere Terrace, drive straight across the traffic lights, through the large park gates, into Sefton Park. Keep left and, at the roundabout, turn left onto the perimeter road. This is Aigburth Drive, which then becomes Mossley Hill Drive.

Park anywhere along here if you wish to explore the park, although it is best to do so from our next stopping point at the Palm House, which you will soon see ahead of you through the trees on the right, as you follow the perimeter road all the way around, until it ends at The Iron Bridge. Park by the bridge.

Sefton Park is virtually the only public open land that remains from what was once the 2000-acre, Royal Deer Park of King John and, apart from Toxteth Park Lodge, no other evidence survives of the district's royal heritage. Indeed, the park we now see is very much a Victorian creation.

By the 16th century, the need for food for the growing local population took precedence over leisurely hunting ventures, and the Deer Park was formally closed as such in 1592. As we have seen, the land, including what are now modern Sefton Park and the district of Toxteth, was then bought from the King by the Earl of Derby. He then allowed farmers to move in and work the land. In 1604, the land was bought from Lord Derby by Sir Richard Molyneux who invited the Puritan dissidents to settle on his estate, near the river at Otterspool, and which we shall visit later. This whole area, including what is now Sefton Park, remained rural until the latter part of the 19th century.

To enter the park, we drive through some striking granite and sandstone gates and, as we do so, on the right we pass one of two 19th century park lodges. These were built in a half-timbered, neo-Tudor style, in 1870, and the other lodge is situated at the opposite side of the park, by the lake, on Aigburth Drive. Both lodges watch over gateways to what is one of the most beautiful parks in Europe.

In 1867, as part of its major plan to create urban parks throughout the Town, Liverpool Corporation bought 375 acres of land, for £263,687, from the Molyneux family who were by this time the Earls of Sefton. Numerous smaller plots were also acquired from other local landowners. The new park was named after the Earl, and the perimeter road around the park is Croxteth Drive, which was named after his family seat at Croxteth Hall, in West Derby. A competition was held to find a suitable designer for the new park, with a prize of 300 guineas being offered to the winner. The successful submission was a combined proposal from Edouard André – Gardener-in-Chief to the City of Paris and gardener to Napoleon III, and his partner, Lewis Hornblower of Liverpool. André was a protégé of Joseph Paxton – as was Edward Kemp who designed Liverpool's Stanley Park, and by this time André had worked with both men on the creation of Birkenhead Park on The Wirral.

"When the work was completed, Sefton Park was opened, in 1872, by Prince Arthur, and it remains one of the largest urban parks in Britain, outside London"

There was a Grand Bazaar and 'Horse-Leaping' on the opening day, with a special pageant and boating on the lake.

As well as many other permanent amenities in the park, there was a perimeter horse-riding track designed to emulate 'Rotten Row' in Hyde Park, and part of this survives. The local gentry would take their carriages or horses out on Sunday afternoons, and parade around the park, to the general delight and entertainment (mostly) of the promenading visitors to the new public leisure grounds.

Throughout the early decades of the 20th century Sefton Park continued to develop, and new public amenities were added, including an aviary. Also, in 1928, Mr George Audley – a wealthy businessman from Birkdale near Southport, who loved children – donated to 'the children visitors to Sefton Park', a replica of the Peter Pan statue from Kensington Gardens in London. This was unveiled during a special summer pageant, by a niece of Sir James Barrie, the author of 'Peter Pan'. Nearby, stood a model

of Wendy's Hut from Barrie's story; two small cannons – said to be from the Royal Yacht; and the 'Jolly Roger' Pirate Ship. Only the Peter Pan statue now remains and, following a major restoration at the Conservation Centre of the National Museums Liverpool, this has been re-sited in the grounds of Sefton Park Palm House.

In 1932, George Audley also donated to the park, an aluminium replica of the Shaftesbury Memorial Fountain (Eros Statue) from Piccadilly Circus in London but, unfortunately, he died before it was unveiled. This has also been completely restored and stands near the new cafe and former aviary garden at the heart of the park.

Sefton Park is the scene for fairs, circuses, concerts, fireworks displays, sports events, public celebrations, and major civic events, such as The Women's 10K Run and the Africa Oyé Festival. Indeed, I have organised and run a number of major events here over the years, the largest of which was a sponsored walk to raise funds for a national charity in the 1970s. This attracted almost 15,000 people, both as participants and spectators.

It is worth noting, that Sefton Park is included on the English Heritage Register of Parks and Gardens of Special Historic Interest, as a Grade II* park. This is one of ten such sites in the City. The park is also a beautiful place simply to explore and meander through, with its many attractive landscaped features, garden areas, and intricate pathways. It is indeed a great place to play, picnic, share time with family and friends, and just to relax in; so do take time to explore it fully, and I am sure that you will really enjoy your visit.

> **To Find Out More:**
> **Sefton Park**
> Information Line: 0151 225 4877
> http://liverpool.gov.uk/leisure-parks-and-events/

To simply visit the Fairy Glen and the Palm House from our next stopping point, I suggest a visit time of 30 minutes. Add a further hour if you then wish to explore the rest of the Park from this point.

Winter at Sefton Park

Sefton Park Palm House

The **Iron Bridge** is closed to vehicles, and it spans the Upper Brook, which becomes the River Jordan as it passes through the park. From the bridge, the brook can be clearly seen coming from the north of the City through a culvert, into an overgrown and neglected valley, and feeding into a pool in what is private land.

From here, it passes under the bridge and enters **The Fairy Glen**, on the edge of Sefton Park proper. This delightful area is easily accessible through gateways in the railings at either end of the bridge. At the end of a narrow pathway, which leads from the side of the road down a landscaped embankment, you pass through a grove of rhododendron bushes. Then, at the end of this track, you will discover a delightful 'secret' garden of more rhododendrons, and of other plants and flowers. These are set in a landscaped basin, through which the little river gurgles over a miniature waterfall, and through some stepping stones.

Back up at road level, and above The Fairy Glen at the end of the Iron Bridge, is a broad, tree-lined roadway that leads back into the main park. Walk along here for about 200 yards and it will bring you to Sefton Park Palm House, set back slightly on the left.

This magnificent structure is the crowning glory of the park and is a remarkable piece of Victorian art and architecture. It is built of cast and wrought iron, and stands over 80 feet high on a red granite base. Donated to the City by the millionaire, Henry Yates Thompson – the grand nephew of Richard Vaughan Yates, the creator of nearby Princes Park – the Palm House opened in 1896. It cost over £10,000 to build and plant out, and it contains many pieces of sculpture.

Also, the Palm House is surrounded by eight, great, marble and bronze statues of renowned world-explorers, naturalists, and botanists.

In 1939, the glass was painted in camouflage colours to prevent moonlight being reflected from the surface, and so attracting the bombs of the German Luftwaffe. Nevertheless, in 1941, a nearby bomb exploded and completely shattered the glass but, fortunately,

Sefton Park Palm House from the air

left the rest of the structure standing though severely destabilised. It was re-glazed and re-opened in 1956, but the different types of metal in the building contributed to its degeneration. This was because the 1950s renovations included an enhanced heating regime, to develop the 'winter garden' into more of a tropical hothouse, and the different expansion rates of the metals weakened the structure. Maintenance of the glass canopy became increasingly difficult, because of financial cutbacks, vandalism, and storm damage. Indeed, by the 1970s and 80s, the Palm House had become derelict and even more badly vandalised. Fortunately, by this time all of the statuary – both inside and outside – had been removed for safekeeping and restoration. However, the costs of refurbishment were so high that the building was threatened with demolition.

This news shocked local people, including myself and, in 1991, at a public meeting in nearby Lark Lane Community Centre, attended by over 800 people, we launched a campaign to save the great building. With the full support of the Liverpool City Council, this led to a partial refurbishment and re-opening in 1993 and, in 1997, the Heritage Lottery Fund and English Heritage made grants to allow a complete restoration to take place. Work began in 2000, and the magnificent Palm House was re-opened on September 6th 2001, to much joy and celebration, in which I and my family were very happy participants.

It is now possible to enjoy again the tranquil interior of the Palm House, with its collection of exotic plants and moody Victorian sculptures, such as 'The Angel's Whisper', and 'Highland Mary'. Following the restoration, all the statuary and sculpture were returned to their original locations in time for the grand re-opening, and so it is also fun to walk around the outside of the Palm House, and gaze into the life-size faces of Charles Darwin, Christopher Columbus, Henry the Navigator, John Parkinson, André Le Notre, Captain James Cook, Mercator, and Linnaeus.

On the plinth supporting the statue of Columbus is a plaque, which reads,

'The discoverer of America was the maker of Liverpool'

This is certainly true, because our trade with America, especially its Southern States, in commodities such as cotton, tobacco, and sugar, made Liverpool and its 18th and 19th century merchants extremely wealthy. However, the Slave Trade was part of this 'Triangular Trade' between Britain, Africa, and America, which is why Britain took the side of the Confederacy during the American Civil War (1861-65). (See Chapter: 'The Liverpool Waterfront'.)

Even after the abolition of slavery, the commercial links with the USA remained and, for many years, the American Servicemen who were stationed at the Burtonwood Military Base just outside Liverpool, annually on the 12th October – Columbus Day, held a special ceremony outside the Palm House. Here, they would lay a wreath at the base of the statue of the Portuguese explorer, who discovered their land in 1492.

Joining these monuments in the enclosure surrounding the Palm House now stands the statue of Peter Pan. This was re-sited here in December 2005, following a major restoration that was carried out by the Conservation Centre of the National Museums Liverpool, and funded jointly by EU grants and the City Council. Once again, the figure of the 'little boy who never grew up' delights modern children, as it delighted me as a toddler.

"This unique building, which is Grade II* Listed, is open to the public free of charge, and is the setting for concerts, plays, and exhibitions. It is also available for hire, and is a great place for family celebrations as well as for other events"

It is managed by the Palm House Trust and Liverpool City Council, and maintained by City Council gardeners and staff. The mission of the Trust is to promote and develop the Palm House as a beautiful and creative botanical space for the people of Liverpool.

Before leaving Sefton Park do make time to explore as much of it as you can; particularly the perimeter of the boating-lake – remembering to take some bread to feed to the ducks! Although, we shall be returning to the park and the lake later in this Chapter.

To Find Out More:
Sefton Park Palm House
http://www.palmhouse.org.uk/
Information Line: 0151 726 2415
Administration: 0151 726 9304
Fax: 0151 726 2419
info@palmhouse.org.uk

Conservation of Statues from the Palm House
http://www.liverpoolmuseums.org.uk/conservation/
technologies/casestudies/palmhouse.asp

From the Iron Bridge, retrace your route along Mossley Hill Drive, but now take the next road on the right, which is Greenbank Lane. You will pass the Greenbank Sports Academy and the Greenbank College on your right as you do so.
On the left you will pass a set of allotments. Beyond the College, still on the right, are the University Halls of Residence, with Greenbank House behind the wall at the end of this complex. Directly opposite this, almost at the end of the road and on the left, are the gates to Greenbank Park and its lake. I suggest a visit of 30 minutes here, to stroll around the lake shore and to visit the Walled Garden.

Greenbank Park

"Close to the borders of Sefton Park lies Greenbank Park with an elegant and tranquil boating lake at its heart"

The area was the former home of the Rathbone family who were philanthropists in Liverpool through two centuries. William Rathbone IV, the grandfather of the William who worked with Florence Nightingale, first leased the early 18th century Greenbank House and 24 acres of land, in 1788, from the Earl of Sefton. At first, the family used it as a holiday house, but gradually it became their permanent residence and they remained there until the 1940s. Greenbank House was a venue for many distinguished visitors to Liverpool, who 'had some special opinion to propagate or philanthropic scheme to advance'; because the Rathbones were so influential. The original house had been built by the Earl, on part of his Toxteth Park estate, and the Rathbones eventually purchased the property outright in 1809, the year of William Rathbone's death. Following his death, his widow, Hannah Mary, in accordance with his wishes, made many substantial alterations to the building. A large part was rebuilt in the Gothic Style, and a cast iron screen was added to the house to form a veranda and balcony.

Greenbank House still stands within the University Halls of residence precinct, opposite the park across Greenbank Lane, and can be glimpsed behind the wall. However, this is not open to the general public. Indeed, in 1944 the house and many parts of the Rathbone estate were donated to the University – with which the family had strong connections.

"In 1897, Liverpool Corporation entered into an agreement with the Rathbone family, to purchase part of their land for the sum of £13,000, to develop as residential streets"

However, the sale agreement drawn up by the Rathbones required the Corporation to maintain a significant portion of this land as open space or recreation ground for the general public, 'but they shall be at liberty to let off the whole or any part of the said land to cricket or other clubs, and to use the lake for boating, skating or other purposes'. Also, the Rathbones ensured that, if and when new houses and roads were built, there should always be a well-maintained 'roadway or pathway to allow public access to the lake and to prevent as far as possible the destruction of trees'. It must be remembered that at this time all the area was completely rural, and the Rathbones wanted to preserve as much of this character as possible.

"The Corporation did indeed keep their part of the bargain, and so Greenbank Park was created"

The modern Park now provides space for a full range of leisure activities, with an up-to-date children's playground and football pitches. There are also attractive, mature trees; delightful herbaceous borders and shrubberies; and the lake is well stocked with fish. The park is open 24 hours per day, 365 days per year, and the Walled Flower Garden is open 10am to 4pm in winter, and 10am to 5.45pm in summer. Greenbank Park achieved Green Flag status in 2005.

Greenbank Park boating lake

To Find Out More:
Greenbank Park
Park Ranger Phone Line: 0151 233 3007
www.toxteth.net/places/liverpool/parks/greenbank%20park

Greenbank Halls of Residence
http://www.liv.ac.uk/maps/greenbank.htm

At the end of Greenbank Lane, turn right into North Mossley Hill Road, and then immediately left into Penny Lane. Follow this up the hill and over the railway bridge.
The former site of Pete Best's Greengrocer's Shop is on the left at the bottom of the hill, at number 43 Penny Lane, directly opposite the end of Dovedale Road.

12

Penny Lane and Pete Best

Penny Lane, which passes alongside the sports field of Liverpool College has, of course, many associations with the Beatles, because the lads, particularly John and Paul, knew it well. Amongst the row of shops on the left of Penny Lane, just the other side of the railway bridge, was a fruit and vegetable shop. Until he retired from the retail business a few years ago, this was owned by Pete Best, who was sometimes known as the 'Lost Beatle'.

He was the group's original drummer, and was famously sacked by his fellow group members and by Brian Epstein, to be replaced by Ringo Starr. This was because, even though Pete was arguably the better drummer, Ringo already had quite a following of female, teenaged fans. He was a popular member of another local group, 'Rory Storm and The Hurricanes', and Epstein, Paul McCartney, and John Lennon realised that if Ringo joined the Beatles then his fans would come too, and this could give the fledgling pop-stars the popular fan-base that was essential to their success.

In July 1962, George Martin – the Beatles record producer at Parlophone records – told Brian Epstein that he didn't care for Pete, and that he intended to use another drummer on the recording sessions; he didn't know that the Beatles were already thinking the same thing. On August 15th 1962, Brian called Pete in for a private meeting at his office and, during lunch, Pete Best was told that his services were no longer required. The local Pop Music Magazine, 'Mersey Beat', broke the news on August 23rd, and Pete's fans were very angry indeed. Petitions were signed by hundreds of youngsters, and shouts of 'Pete Best Forever – Ringo, never!" were heard at the Cavern Club. However, for the Beatles, the rest is history!

Nevertheless, as soon as he was ignominiously fired from the Beatles, Pete was approached by Rory Storm and The Hurricanes, they wanted him to take Ringo's place in a sort of tit-for-tat

exchange, but Pete refused. Also, as if to rub salt in the wounds, Epstein then contacted Pete to ask him to consider joining another of his groups, The Merseybeats. Brian wanted to recreate this group as another Beatles but, once again, Pete declined. Nevertheless, music was still in his soul, so Pete joined a new band called 'Lee Curtis and The All Stars', who successfully toured all over the UK and Germany, developing a large fan-base in the process.

Eventually, the group were signed by Decca Records, and so they changed their name to 'The Pete Best Four'. They released a number of singles, and appeared on television in Britain's most popular pop music programme, Ready Steady Go. In 1968, after playing professionally for a decade, Pete decided that he wanted to retire from the music business and devote time to his family. And so, he became a greengrocer in Penny Lane.

Beatles' fans, and Pete's own fans from all over the world – especially Japan – would visit the small shop to pay homage to their idols, and at least have a chat and hopefully get their photo taken with one of the original Beatles. They would also hear 'from the horse's mouth' about his early days with the world's most famous pop group.

Pete Best

He would particularly regale his visitors with saucy tales about the time that he and the other Beatles learnt their trade in the early 1960s, in the Reeperbahn – the red-light district of Hamburg. And so, the tourists would leave Penny Lane, happy that they had spoken with a living embodiment of pop-music history.

However, some say that it was not, in fact, Pete Best that the tourists met! For years, apparently, the ex-Beatles drummer employed a manager for his shop, which Pete seldom visited. The manager was happy to fill the role of 'former famous drummer', thus allowing Pete to persue other interests. So, all over Tokyo, and elsewhere, are hundreds of photographs of happy Japanese pilgrims, standing beside a smiling, anonymous Scouser, with a twinkle in his roguish eye!

"In due course Pete actually did get back on the road because, in 1988, he formed the Pete Best Band, which has been successfully touring ever since"

The Beatles wrote the song 'Penny lane' as a sort of homage to the Lane and, at its junction at the far end with Smithdown Road and Allerton Road, many of the references that they make in the song are still to be seen. The most obvious of these is the 'shelter in the middle of a roundabout'; but you can also find the Bank, where the banker 'has a portrait of the Queen'; and the Hairdresser, with a picture 'of every head he's had the pleasure to have known'!

This area remains a Mecca for tourists from all over the world, visiting the famous Beatles sites and, in fact, you will notice that the 'Penny Lane' road name is painted onto the buildings on the street, or on metal road signs, the legs of which are buried deep in concrete. This is because the standard nameplates were always being stolen as much-sought-after collectors' items.

Dovedale Towers

Turn right into Dovedale Road, passing 'Dovedale Towers' on the left, as you do so. Dovedale Primary School is 200 yards along on the left.

Dovedale Road ⓭

As you turn into **Dovedale Road,** on the left you will see the grand building that was formerly known as **Dovedale Towers.** Once a stately home, this later became the church hall for St. Barnabus' Church at the end of Penny Lane and, as such, it hosted many parish activities. One of these regular events, especially during the 1950s and 60s, were the dances. John Lennon's band, the Quarrymen – a precursor to the Beatles, played here in 1957.

"In the late 1960s, the future lead singer of 'Queen', Freddie Mercury, used Dovedale Towers as 'digs'"

Subsequently a function suite and bar during the last 20 years – under various ownerships and of varying and unpredictable quality, the Towers is still a popular puband function suite.

Just along the road is **Dovedale Primary School,** which John Lennon and George Harrison both attended; John between 1945 and 1951, and George between 1948 and 1950. Ringo attended St. Silas Primary School, across the street from his home in the Dingle, and Paul attended Stockton Wood Primary School, in Speke.

Penny Lane roundabout circa 1930s

To Find Out More:
Liverpool College
http://www.liverpoolcollege.org.uk/index.shtml

Penny Lane
http://www.geocities.com/penneylayne

Penny Lane and Beatles City Tours
http://www.beatlestours.co.uk/beatlespages/pennylane.htm

Pete Best Portfolio
http://www.beatlesagain.com/bpete.html

Pete Best Official Website
http://www.petebest.com/index.asp

To Find Out More:
Dovedale Primary School
Website http://www.dovedale-jun.liverpool.sch.uk/

Alma de Santiago
Phone: 0151 709 7097 www.almadesantiago.com/

At the crossroads with the 'Give Way' sign, turn right into Queens Drive. This is the southern end of the Ring Road that skirts the eastern perimeter of Liverpool.
Driving under the railway bridge will bring you to a set of traffic lights, at which you will turn left, into North Mossley Hill Road.
Follow this up to the T-junction and then turn right into Rose Lane. Now turn immediately left, into Mossley Hill Road, and park on the roadside. Or, you could drive into the car park of Mossley Hill Church on the corner of the road, and park there.

Mossley Hill and The Church

14

We are now in the district of Mossley Hill, which is a pleasant suburb on the fringe of Sefton Park, about 3 miles from the city-centre, and the hill itself is one of the seven major hills of Liverpool. Once described in the early 19th century as '... a distant and pathless waste ... a breezy knoll of bracken ...' it commands excellent views of the surrounding countryside and, on a clear day, of the distant hills of Wales.

Like the Rathbones of Greenbank, other 18th and 19th century merchants and wealthy property owners left their businesses in the City, where they had previously 'lived-over-the-shop', to establish themselves as the new landed gentry, buying land in Mossley Hill, Allerton, and Woolton, and creating their own family-seats. They were the new middle-class aristocracy. One of the new estate properties was 'Rosemont', a large house that once stood on the site of Dale Halls of Residence, opposite Mossley Hill Church, across Mossley Hill Road.

> "In 1932, part of this estate was opened as a zoo, where one of the most popular attractions was a large chimpanzee called 'Mickey'"

He used to play games of football with members of the public but he was also prone to escape. On one such occasion, and after throwing a passing coalman across the street, he was chased through the roads of Mossley Hill by a 'posse' consisting of 15 Policemen, a lion-tamer, a zoo-keeper, some police vehicles, and an ambulance. His last escape was in March 1938, when he ran amok in a school playground, chased by a party of keepers – some of whom were armed. He mounted to the rooftops and tried to hide behind chimney stacks but, unfortunately, and like a smaller version of King Kong, he was shot and fatally wounded by an Army marksman.

Mickey was embalmed and, mounted with his football, he was placed on display in the zoo. He became as much of an attraction in death as he was in life, but the zoo closed at the end of 1938 and he went on permanent display in the Lewis's Department Store in the city. Unfortunately, the building, and Mickey, were destroyed during the May Blitz of 1941.

The parish church of St. Matthew and St. James, Mossley Hill, is a magnificent example of the 'Decorated Gothic' style of church architecture. It was originally designed and built, between 1870 and 1875, by Hubert James Austin and Edward Paley. It was funded using the proceeds of a legacy from an 1830s visitor to the district – the wealthy merchant Matthew Glenton, who felt that Mossley Hill was '... a wonderful site for a church'.

This monumental building stands 188 feet above sea-level, dominating the hill, and it can be seen for miles around towering over the landscape. It has a singular claim to fame, in that it is said to have been the first church in the country to have been bombed. This was in August 1940, when the building suffered almost total destruction. Completely and magnificently restored, it was rededicated in 1953, and the church has fully resumed its place at the heart of the district.

Inside, the high, vaulted ceiling is supported by ranks of fluted and octagonal columns, constructed in alternating plain and smooth sandstone. Though minimally decorated, there is a warm and comfortable feel to the inside of the church.

Mickey the chimp is preserved

To Find Out More:
Mossley Hill Church
Phone: 0151 724 6391
http://freespace.virgin.net/
mossleyhill.church/

Continue along Mossley Hill Road, and you will see the playing fields of Mossley Hill Athletic & Social Club on the left. Immediately opposite this you will see the ornate, sandstone Lodge and gateposts of Sudley House Art Gallery. Pull into the driveway, which leads you to the small car park in the grounds.

15

Sudley House Art Gallery

Another of the new family estates and suburban stately homes, that were built by the rising merchant classes of Liverpool, was Sudley House. This stands on what was, in the late 18th century, part of the Aigburth estate of Thomas Tarleton. This estate was broken up in 1809, and the area now occupied by Sudley House was bought by Nicholas Robinson. He was a local corn merchant who became Lord Mayor of Liverpool in 1828.

> "Robinson built Sudley House in 1824, and it remained in his family until 1883"

It was then sold to the Victorian ship owner and merchant, George Holt, who had founded the Lamport and Holt Shipping Line. He also founded my old school, the Holt High Grammar School, which is now known as Childwall School. The Holt family were Unitarians, in common with so many of Liverpool's great 19th

century benefactors, and they did much to improve life and amenity for local people.

George Holt became very wealthy and he was able to indulge his passion for art. As a result, he amassed a large collection of paintings and sculpture. Upon his death, in 1896, his daughter Emma inherited the house and its grounds, together with the art collection. She continued to live in Sudley House until her own death in 1944. In her will, she bequeathed the estate and her father's art collection to the City, and the building was refurbished and opened to the public as an art gallery.

The Sudley House Art Gallery is now part of the National Museums of Liverpool and it is still set in attractive, though considerably reduced grounds. There are permanent displays in period rooms, with many fine examples of 18th and 19th Century paintings, together with paintings and sculptures on periodic loan from the main collection at the Walker Art Gallery. Indeed, Sudley House now

Sudley House

houses Britain's only remaining complete art collection of a Victorian merchant and entrepreneur. Amongst the paintings, some of which are by Millais, Landseer, Romney, Reynolds, Frith, Holman-Hunt, and Turner, is one of my own personal favourites; 'Oh Swallow Swallow' by Strudwick, who was a disciple of Burne-Jones.

On what was once the croquet lawn, but which is now a small rose-garden at the rear of the house, stands the Sudley Sundial. This was unveiled on 29th October 1989, as a local commemoration of the deaths of 96 people, many of them young people and children, who were crushed to death at a football match at the Hillsborough Ground in Sheffield, on 15th April 1989.

On the front of the plain, black, rectangular granite pedestal, beneath a rose, is inscribed,

"Time marches on but we will always remember"

The main Hillsborough Memorial stands outside the Anfield football stadium of Liverpool Football Club, near the Bill Shankly Memorial Gates (See Chapter: 'Fortunes, Fables, and Football'), and there is another memorial – a large inscribed sandstone slab – that is set into the ground outside the west entrance to the Anglican Cathedral, on St. James's Mount.

To Find Out More:
Sudley House Art Gallery
Telephone: 0151 724 3245
http://www.liverpoolmuseums.org.uk/sudley/

From Sudley House, continue down Mossley Hill Road, passing more playing fields on the left and the I M Marsh Campus of Liverpool John Moores University on the right.
At the bottom of the narrow hill, turn left at the T-junction, into Holmefield Road.
Follow this until it joins Booker Avenue, then turn left.
Follow this across the traffic lights at Brodie Avenue, over the railway bridge at West Allerton Station, and past the entrances to Booker Avenue Primary School on the left.
Archerfield Road is just beyond the entrance to the Infants Department, so turn left into it and park as soon as it is safe and convenient to do so. You will see the Robin Hood Stone, standing tall behind its railings, on the corner of Archerfield Road.

On Booker Avenue, at its junction with the appropriately named Archerfield Road, stands one of the City's ancient relics: this is the fenced-in 'Robin Hood Stone'.

This is an 8ft high sandstone monolith, deeply scored from centuries of what is presumed to be arrow-sharpening. Before being re-sited, in August 1928, the stone stood in a nearby field known as Stone Hey, but it was moved when its original location was being built over by the houses that now cover the area. A plaque on the base of the stone records this.

Whilst it is known that local archers lived and worked here in Medieval times, in the service of the local landowner Sir Richard Molyneux, there is no basis to the legend that claims that Robin Hood once stayed in the district and sharpened his arrows on the stone.

However, the stone is of considerable archaeological and historical significance, and is worth a visit.

In Medieval times, especially during the Hundred Years War, all able-bodied Englishmen, no matter in what part of the country they lived, had to be proficient at the longbow. Men would practice, and keep their arrows sharp, in case the Lord of the Manor, or the King, summoned an army to go to Battle – as we did so often against the French during those turbulent times. So, finding stones around England, like the Robin Hood Stone, is not so exceptional.

The reputation for deadly accuracy, and for the fearlessness of the English Archers, was legendary amongst our enemies especially after the Battles of Agincourt and Crecy: A bowman could release 10 arrows a minute; so that by the time the first one had landed another would be in flight. They were not just fast, they were deadly accurate, and the bows were extremely powerful. This meant that a skilled man – and all those called to military service had to be – could put an arrow through an enemy's helmet visor at 200 yards.

And so, if our men were ambushed or captured in battle, and were not slain, the first two fingers of their right hands would be chopped off, so that they could no longer draw their longbows. They would then be sent back to their own lines as a warning to the English. However, this only provoked the Archers to greater ferocity against the French.

Some historians believe that in defiance, the remaining English Archers lined up on the battlefield in front of the opposing force, prior to an attack would brandish their fingers at the enemy to show them that they still had their own archery-fingers, and as a threat and a warning.

"Some people believe that this is how the raising of two fingers, as a gesture of abuse and aggression, passed into the British lexicon of 'non-verbal communication!'"

You will now need to turn around and return back the way you came, along Booker Avenue.
Go back over the railway bridge and the traffic lights, and follow the road all the way down the hill as it now becomes Aigburth Hall Avenue.
As you come to the end of this road, but well before the traffic lights, park anywhere on the left that is safe and convenient.
You will see Stanlawe Grange on the opposite side of the road, to the immediate left of Aigburth Hall Nurseries.

Stanlawe Grange

Stanlawe Grange

In early Medieval times, much of Aigburth and Garston were once owned by the Cistercian monks from Whalley Abbey in Lancashire, and from Stanlawe Abbey on the Wirral side of the Mersey. (At what is now known as Stanlow.) However, the Liverpool side of the river was where they farmed and stored their produce, rather than where the Monastic Orders were actually based.

"The monks had fish farms in Garston, pig farms at Speke, and arable lands on the Grassendale banks of the river"

On Aigburth Hall Avenue, at No 2, stands Stanlawe Grange. This remarkable building was originally erected by the monks, around 1290, as part of a much larger monastery farming complex. Part of the cruck-frame building was used as a granary, and the cavity walls were filled with husks for insulation. Stanlawe Grange takes its name from the abbey on the Wirral and, after the Dissolution of the Monasteries in 1538, by King Henry VIII, it was converted into a cottage. It was further modified in the 15th century, when it first became known as 'The Grange', and was again modified in the 16th and 17th centuries.

Stanlawe Grange is now the oldest, continually-occupied residence in Liverpool but unfortunately, just after World War I it was necessary to widen Aigburth Hall Drive. As a result, parts of the front of the building, including a courtyard, had to be demolished. In 1967, the owner at that time was an architect, and he carefully restored the building and converted it into two houses. Parts of the building can be clearly seen from the pavement outside but, as it is privately occupied, it is not accessible to visitors.

To Find Out More:
Stanlawe Grange & Monastic Lands
http://www.btinternet.com/~m.royden
/mrlhp/local/monastic/mondoc.htm

Cressington Park

At the end of Aigburth Hall Road, turn left at the traffic lights, into Aigburth Road. Continue past the Toby Carvery Restaurant on the left, and then through the pedestrian crossing lights at St Austin's Church. Now take the next turning on the right, crossing the dual-carriageway and driving through the gates into Cressington Park and onto Salisbury Road. St Mary's Church is on the left of the estate as you go in. Once through the gates turn left – this is still Salisbury Road. Then drive over the railway line and past the station on the right. Note the remarkable range of architectural styles within the Park as you drive down the road. At the bottom you will come to the Cressington Esplanade, and you will turn right. I suggest that you park here, to perhaps take a short stroll for about 10 minutes or so.

At the end of the Esplanade, turn right into Knowsley Road, and drive back up through the estate. When it rejoins Salisbury Road, turn right, and leave the Park through the gates once more. Turn left onto St. Mary's Road.

Grassendale Park

Next, take the 4th road on the left, which is Grassendale Road. A 'Shell' petrol station stands on the corner. Follow this down until you come to the gates of Grassendale Park proper. Go through the gates and continue down North Road, until you reach the Grassendale Esplanade where you turn left. Once again, you might like to park here and take a short stroll. The houses facing the Mersey on the Esplanade here are particularly fine – as is the view across the river.

At the end of the Esplanade, turn left into South Road. Follow this back up as it bends to the left and joins North Road. Turn right, and continue back up Grassendale Road.

Aigburth Road, Cressington Park, and Grassendale Park

Aigburth Road and St. Mary's Road, are the main southern route into the City from Runcorn and Widnes, through Halewood and Speke. This thoroughfare passes through many different communities, including Grassendale – originally 'Gresyndale' which means 'grassy valley' – where a pair of large, ornate gates lead into a private housing-estate known as Cressington Park. This is one of four such enclaves that were built in this area in the 1840's, for wealthy Victorian merchants, in what was at the time open country.

The other private estates leading off from this main road are Grassendale Park, Wood End Park, and Fulwood Park. The four estates each contain some very fine Victorian mansions, as well as one or two earlier and previously-isolated Regency dwellings.

The estates also have houses of more contemporary design; all-in-all making them a haven for students of English architecture. The properties are surrounded by mature trees and many are set in their own grounds and gardens. The detachment of the estates from the nearby bustling roads and industrial land emphasises the peace and tranquility of this community.

"Each park has its own entrance, and covers an area from St Mary's Road down to the banks of the River Mersey"

Cressington and Grassendale each have their own riverside promenade, and Cressington has its own railway station and also its own weather station, the web address for which is listed below. The estates are all worth exploring for their sociological interest, as much as for their architectural value.

To Find Out More:
St Mary's Church Grassendale
Phone: 0151 427 0413
http://www.stmarys-grassendale.co.uk/

Liverpool Conservation Areas: Grassendale and Cressington Parks
http://www.walkingbook.co.uk/liverpool/pages/page2.htm

Cressington Park Weather Station
http://www.8thday.co.uk/weather/page.htm

At the end of Grassendale Road, turn left onto Aigburth Road once more.
At the traffic lights at Aigburth Hall Avenue, turn left into Riversdale Road, and park as soon as is convenient.
Liverpool Cricket Club stands on the corner, and Battlecrease House is across the road, almost directly opposite the side entrance to the ground.

Liverpool Cricket Club

Beyond St. Mary's Church and the gates leading into Cressington Park, and on the same side of the road, we find the entrance to Liverpool Cricket Club standing on the corner of Riversdale Road, which leads down to the river. This ground is internationally famous and has seen many significant Test Matches and competitions in its long and illustrious history. Liverpool Cricket Club is much older than even the Lancashire Cricket Club, being founded in 1807.

This somewhat peripatetic Cricket Club first played at the Mersey Bowman's Ground in Cazneau Street, which was, at the time, just outside the city-centre. In 1829, the Club then moved to a site in Wavertree Road, Edge Hill, and then on to a further three sites in the same area. Indeed the local streets Spofforth Road and Bannerman Street in Edge Hill are named after two famous Australian Cricketers of the 1880's, and they also commemorate the location of the old Club in this area. However, the rapid expansion of the railway in and around that district forced yet

another move and, in 1877, Lord Sefton offered the Club the use of a ground on his estate at Croxteth Park in West Derby, where they stayed until they moved to their present site at Aigburth, in 1881. The magnificent grand pavilion, which still stands as the centrepiece of the Club, was built in the same year and it pre-dates those at Lord's (1891) and Old Trafford (1894).

Many famous cricketers of the time competed at Liverpool Cricket Club, including W G Grace (1848-1915) who played at the Edge Hill ground in 1872 and 1876, and also at the Sefton Park Cricket Club, in 1877.

> **To Find Out More:**
> Liverpool Cricket Club
> Phone: 0151 427 2930
> http://www.liverpoolcricketclub.co.uk/

Battlecrease House and Jack The Ripper?

The large mansion, Battlecrease House, which stands in Riversdale Road directly facing the side of the cricket ground, was the home of Florence and James Maybrick during the latter years of the 19th century.

"Florence met her future husband whilst on board the White Star liner Britannic"

They settled in Liverpool and James continued his profession as a successful and wealthy cotton-broker. However, James was a man of eccentric hobbies, in that he had a morbid interest in illnesses, medicines, and potions. He would spend hours in his laboratory in their large house mixing up strange concoctions, and was frequently to be seen walking around the streets of Liverpool and London, where he also had business interests – carrying a small, black, medical bag.

Florence was soon to discover what family friends and neighbours had already known for many years; that her husband had a dark and unpleasant side to his personality, and that he could be aggressive and extremely short-tempered: Theirs was not a happy marriage. Nevertheless, the couple had two children, but this did not improve their relationship.

Then, in the early spring of 1889, James became ill. He could not eat; endured all the worst symptoms of gastric poisoning and, after suffering and lingering for many weeks, he eventually died. The circumstances of his death were soon the subject of much local

Battlecrease House

gossip, so much so that the Police decided to mount an investigation. Before long, this resulted in Florence being charged with the murder of her husband; by allegedly using arsenic that she had scraped from flypapers, to slowly poison the food of her odious spouse.

Later in the same year, Florence appeared at Liverpool Crown Court, which was then in St. George's Hall. The trial became the sensation of the decade, attracting vast crowds of spectators and extensive press coverage. However, as the details of her life with James came out in court, Florence found herself the subject of great public sympathy. Despite this, on 7th August 1889, she was found guilty of murder and sentenced to be hanged.

There was a public outcry and a press campaign was mounted in her favour. Two weeks after the trial had ended Florence's sentence was commuted to life imprisonment, but Queen Victoria refused to endorse a reduction in the allocated prison term, and Florence Maybrick spent the next 14 years in jail. However, once Edward VII had succeeded to the throne, her sentence was commuted, and Florence eventually gained her release, in 1904.

She moved to America and lived there for the remainder of her life, coming back to Liverpool on a number of occasions, one of which was to attend the Grand National Steeplechase. Eventually, in 1941, Florence Maybrick died a recluse in America, aged 81.

Certain commentators and crime enthusiasts now maintain that there is enough evidence to identify James Maybrick as Jack the Ripper. They maintain that the only reason that his identity was never accurately confirmed at the time, is because Mrs Maybrick got to him first! This theory is based on a diary purporting to be James's own, which was discovered in 1992, and in which he himself describes his role in 'The Whitechapel Murders' in London.

No one knows if the diary is a forgery or, if authentic, simply the ravings of a madman or a 'Ripper wannabe'! Whatever the truth, James Maybrick now lies in Anfield Cemetery, just one of the candidates for the name and crimes of 'Jack the Ripper'!

Battlecrease House remains a private residence, now converted into flats, and although worth looking at from the outside, it is not open to the public.

To Find Out More:
Jack the Ripper – The Maybrick Diaries
http://www.crimelibrary.com/
serial_killers/notorious/ripper/
diaries_13.html

The Maybrick Diaries
– Hoax or Authentic
http://www.suite101.com/
lesson.cfm/18593/1949/3

Beyond Riversdale Road, at the main crossroads with the traffic lights, Mersey Road leads off to the left. On this corner, until 1810, stood 'Aigburth Old Hall'. During the late Middle Ages this was once the residence of 'Adam of Garston', who was one of the new rising class of local landowners, and Aigburth Hall Avenue takes its name from this old building.

From Riversdale Road, turn left onto Aigburth Road once again. Follow this through the next set of main traffic lights, at Mersey Road, and continue past St. Margaret's Boys' School on the left. Beyond the school are the grounds of Otterspool Park; part of the land that was once King John's Hunting Forest of Toxteth Park. At the next set of traffic lights, turn left into Jericho Lane. Immediately on the left you will see the sloping entrance path, and the iron gates, leading into Otterspool Park – but I suggest that you keep driving, as there are safer places to park your car.

At the roundabout, at the bottom of Jericho Lane, turn left – this is Otterspool Promenade. There are many place to park here, from which you can walk along the riverside promenade itself, or go and fly your kite! However, to explore the Vale; the site of Otterspool House; the Ravine; and the location of King John's Lower Hunting Lodge, you need to drive past the Otterspool Pub on the left, and through the first set of 'horseshoe' turns in the road. This brings you alongside the Vale, on the left, so park anywhere you wish along here. The Vale will lead you to all my featured locations. If you come to a 2nd 'horseshoe' then you have come too far.

Otterspool Park

The open land at Aigburth Vale, at the left-hand corner of Aigburth Road and Jericho Lane, was once the site of the very first ancient settlement alongside a small river, which still runs through this district, but which is now mostly culverted. This was known as the **Osklebrok** in the days of the Viking invaders and was fed by two sources; one near edge Lane in the Edge Hill district of the City, known as the 'Lower Brook'; and another that rises in the village of Wavertree – three or four miles to the east, known as the 'Upper Brook'. (See Chapter: 'The Lost Villages of Liverpool'.)

Early settlers, taking advantage of Otterspool's resources in the creek of the Osklebrok and in the Mersey below, may well have been Roman. Evidence supporting this was discovered in 1863, when a local gardener dug up a hoard of 12 brass Roman coins, dating from the years 268-324 A.D. Later that same year, a second coin hoard was found nearby, during the construction of the Cheshire Lines Railway through Otterspool Park.

The quality of the fishing along the nearby length of the river was well known, and many local people sought fishing rights from the Lord of the Manor of Garston. In 1264, that owner was Adam of Garston – who, as we have seen, once resided at Aigburth Hall – and he granted permission for the monks from Stanlawe Abbey to construct fisheries on his land, between Garston Mill Dale and Otterspool. The surviving documents that refer to this arrangement are amongst the earliest references to Otterspool, although sadly, there is no mention of the actual site chosen by the monks for their fishery. Nevertheless, salmon were so plentiful that records tell of the surpluses being fed to the local pigs.

As one turns into Jericho Lane, the iron gates immediately on the left lead into Otterspool Park, and the path leading down from them takes you along an attractive valley, through an atmospheric and overgrown ravine, and into a fascinating basin of parkland. This was once the pool into which the Osklebrok fed, and which itself fed into the Mersey at what was then known as 'Ortipul'. The path also takes you past the site of Otterspool House – of which I will speak shortly – and then on to the promenade along the Mersey riverside. The pathway and ravine are the now dry bed of the Osklebrok.

Before the Civil War, Sir Richard Molyneux, who then owned the former Royal Hunting Lodge of Toxteth, began to clear and enclose part of it into smallholdings. On the southern boundary, many of the new tenants were part of a community of Puritans, most of whom came from the Bolton and Ormskirk areas, whilst others had come from the Midlands. This religious minority had come to Aigburth and Toxteth, at the invitation of Sir Richard, to escape from persecution. It is to the great credit of the Catholic Molyneuxs that they, themselves a persecuted people in those turbulent times, should provide a safe haven for people of a different faith. The Puritans established a community at Otterspool and converted the remains of the hunting forest into arable farmland, and many local roads still follow the field boundaries established by the Puritans. They renamed the Osklebrok the **River Jordan** and gave Jericho Lane the name that it still carries today. Indeed, during that time the whole area became known as 'The Holy Land'.

> "The other of King John's two hunting lodges in Toxteth Park, Lower Lodge, once stood against the 'Osklebrok', near the sandstone railway bridge that now spans the ravine footpath"

This lodge was the home of the renowned 17th century astronomer, Jeremiah Horrocks, about whom we shall hear more shortly. However, the ancient building was demolished in 1863, during the construction of the Liverpool and Garston Railway, and it was replaced by Otterspool Station, itself subsequently demolished. Now only a few large sandstone blocks survive, embedded in the embankment by the ravine, near the arch of the railway bridge.

In the late 18th century, the break up of the Manor of Garston began and, in February 1779, Liverpool Corporation purchased the manorial rights for the whole district, including Otterspool. In December of that year the snuff manufacturers, Messrs Tate, Alexander and Wilson, took out a lease enclosing a portion of the riverside at the mouth of the River Jordan. There they erected a Snuff Mill at a cost of £2,439, together with cottages for workmen. The Mill was probably worked by the water of the pool, from which Otterspool eventually took its name and, in 1810, this was converted to a mill for extracting coconut oil. This second mill was owned by John Moss, a local banker and plantation owner who, in 1811, bought what had then become the Otterspool estate. He embanked and improved his river frontage and, by 1812, he had built a fine mansion house for himself and his family, which he named 'Otterspool House'.

Trade between Manchester and Liverpool had grown steadily over the preceding 100 years, and industrial advances required the transportation of ever-increasing amounts of trade goods and commodities. Moss was Chairman of the Railway Joint Committee which,

Otterspool Promenade

in 1822, published its intention to build 'an iron Rail-Way'.
In due course, railway pioneer George Stephenson (1781-1848) was commissioned to undertake the building of the new railway and, in 1827, during its construction, Stephenson stayed with Moss at Otterspool House.

To test his plans, Stephenson made a model of his locomotive, The Rocket, and ran it along a miniature track that he had laid out along the dry bed of the River Jordan, which makes this very pretty piece of parkland even more significant; as this was therefore, the location for Britain's first model railway!

The Rocket was one of five steam locomotives that, in due course, competed for the right to pull the first passenger railway in the world and, at the Rainhill Railway Trials that were held in 1829, Stephenson's engine won. In 1830, the inaugural journey of the Liverpool to Manchester Railway took place; a new link was established between the two great Northern towns; and the world of transportation was revolutionised. (See Chapter: 'Pool of Life & Culture'.)

Otterspool House survived into the 1920s, by which time it had become the headquarters of a small zoo that had been established within the park. The days of the menagerie were numbered however, when Liverpool Corporation, in 1926, purchased 138 acres of land from the Cheshire Railway Lines Committee for £106,813. In 1931, Otterspool House, which had fallen into disrepair, was demolished. Parts of the foundations, a low balustrade, and some crumbling stonework are all that remain of this significant house, which was replaced by a café and bandstand, which at the time of writing are closed.

As I mentioned earlier, the best place to park is on the roadway through Otterspool Park, and from this point you can explore all of the Park and the Promenade. Indeed, by strolling into the park towards the clearly observable bandstand building, the path of the ancient river can be traced back through the ravine pathway, to the left and behind the building. The vale in which this sits was in fact once the mouth of the ancient river, and the Mersey would have lapped against where you are now parked! On the riverbed pathway you will find some very attractive landscaped grounds, together with natural park and woodland areas, as well as the railway bridge and the site of King John's Lower Lodge.

"The park contains a wide variety of plants, flowers, and shrubs, and there are also extensive open areas making it a delightful, and in many places, a secluded spot for a pleasant stroll"

To explore the Promenade (see following article), simply walk towards the river and you will find the riverfront pathway running from Grassendale in the south, towards the Pier Head in the north. There are a number of attractions along here, and on the adjacent parkland, including 'keep fit' equipment and a childrens' playground. You will also be able to see the massive 'Sitting Bull', which is a sculpture that once graced the Indian Garden, in the 1984 International Garden festival in Liverpool. (See Chapter: 'The Liverpool Waterfront'.)

Otterspool Promenade and John Brodie

Otterspool Promenade is a truly significant engineering achievement.

Construction of a sea wall began in 1929, and during the 1930s and 1940s, the area behind this was in-filled with two million tons of domestic waste; reclaiming 43 acres of foreshore. The costs of construction were more than covered by the savings made on incineration or sea-dumping of the waste. The site was topped off, and officially opened to the public in 1950, with the phrase:

"Wealth from waste and beauty from ashes"

In 1955, the Government gave permission for the 'Prom' to be extended, and over the next thirty years a further 4 million tons of domestic waste were used to extend the promenade and parkland.

As one walks along the Promenade, above the sea-wall, one is not only doing so on top of rubbish, but also over the bedrock of the River Mersey! The product of the excavations of Queensway, the first Mersey Tunnel – the rock, rubble, and clay – were dumped here as part of the reclamation of the land to create the Prom, allowing a further 70 acres of land to be created. Consequently, this provided a significant extension to the public walkway and surrounding open space.

Spoil from the second Mersey Tunnel was used as part of the land reclamation for the 1984 International Garden Festival site.

Now Otterspool Promenade runs from the waterfront near Grassendale to connect with the Riverside Walkway. This leads all the way alongside Riverside Drive to link with the roads through Brunswick Dock, and on past Queen's Dock, King's Dock, and to the Albert Dock and the Pier Head. (See Chapter: 'The Liverpool Waterfront'.)

Otterspool Park

Flying kites at Otterspool

The Promenade is a broad and pleasant riverside walkway, along quite a stretch of the Mersey waterfront, and it provides excellent views across to the Wirral Peninsular. Alongside the 'Prom' are gardens, seating areas, and stretches of open grasslands – ideal for games of football, picnicking, or just for sunbathing or dozing.

The Otterspool scheme was one of many innovative and progressive projects delivered by **John Alexander Brodie** (1858-1934), who was the Liverpool City Engineer from 1898 until his death. He originally suggested this scheme in 1919, as a way of providing an amenity to local residential areas. In 1901, he patented the idea of constructing homes from pre-fabricated concrete slabs, and went on to devise many other imaginative City and highway improvement schemes. One of the most significant of these are the 'boulevards' that criss-cross the City, with reserved central areas originally for tramcars. The first of these ran along Edge Lane to Broadgreen, opened in 1914, and another was, as we have already seen, down the central reservation of Princes Boulevard. It was also Brodie's idea to create a 'ring road' around the City, and this now runs from the north of the City, around the eastern edge of Liverpool to Sefton Park in the south, and is called 'Queens Drive'. Indeed, it begins at the mini-roundabout, adjacent to the Iron Bridge in Sefton Park, and ends at Walton-on-the-Hill. (See Chapter: 'Fortunes, Fables, and Football'.)

Whilst he is clearly recognised for having carried out some remarkable work in Liverpool, what is less well known is that, in the early years of the 20th Century, John Brodie worked with the architect Edwin Lutyens in building New Delhi in India. Here, he was specifically responsible for laying out the road network.

"It is worth noting that, in 1891, Brodie invented and patented football goal-nets"

They were first used however, rather than by either of his hometown's teams, but at Bolton Wanderer's ground when they played against Nottingham Forest. (I am afraid that I do not know the result of this match!)

John Brodie was an energetic public servant, and the people of Liverpool owe much to his creativity and foresight.

To Find Out More:
The History of Otterspool
http://www.btinternet.com/~m.royden/mrlhp/local/otterspool/otters.htm

Otterspool Promenade
http://www.mersey-gateway.org/server.php?show=ConGallery.64

John Alexander Brodie
http://www.mersey-gateway.org/server.php?show=ConWebDoc.144

Turn around on Otterspool Prom, and return to the roundabout at the bottom of Jericho Lane. Turn right here and go back along the Lane, until you come to the traffic lights at the main junction. Go straight across these lights into Ashfield Road.

At the next set of traffic lights, turn left into Elmswood Road. The cul-de-sac, which then branches off on the right, is Aigburth Vale – all that now remains of the 'lost village' of Aigburth. Elmswood Road will now bring you back into Sefton Park. Turn left onto the perimeter road, which at this point, is Aigburth Drive.

About 200 yards further along on the right, you will come to Sefton Park Lake, which is another good place to explore the park from - if you have not done so already. Certainly, a stroll completely around the lakeside is a must.

From the lake, the 3rd road on the left is Lark Lane. Take this road, through the Victorian sandstone gateposts, and park anywhere on the Lane that you can find a space: It does get very busy!

To explore Lark Lane, and the three roads featured below, I suggest a time of around 30 minutes – longer if you intend to stop for a drink or a meal at one of the many restaurants, pubs, and wine bars.

Lark Lane

As we travel around the perimeter road of the Park, you will come to a road that branches off to the left. This leads into Lark Lane, which is well worth exploring, as indeed are three of the curious roads and lanes – some original and some renovated – that branch off it on the left-hand side. These are **Pelham Grove**, **Hadassah Grove**, and **Bickerton Street**.

The Lane was a purpose-built shopping street, which was designed to service the new community that was being established, in all the ranks of new mansion houses and attractive terraces around the park perimeter. It was the sale of these properties that funded the creation of Sefton Park. Lark Lane had, and to a large extent it still has, all the essential shops and services to resource a large and diverse community.

"From a barber's shop and hairdressing salons to clothes shops; from cake and sweet shops to fishmongers and greengrocers; from general grocers to iron-mongers; and from a delicatessen to a florists"

There are also a wide range of more eccentric and quaint establishments, such as a New Age Shop, second-hand book shop, furniture upholsterers, funeral parlour, fire-place restorer, and antique shops. However, where Lark Lane excels is as a place in which to eat, drink, and be merry!

From the glorious and original Victorian **Albert Pub** to **Keith's Wine Bar**, there are many places for a convivial tincture! There is a Mexican Restaurant; and an Indian; and a Chinese; and two Greek restaurants. There is **Moranto's**, and a number of imaginative and modern – some very high-tech – establishments, and some very low-tech ones, such as **The Sunshine Café**, and the Fast-Food Burger and Pizza Takeaway. In fact, there are a few takeaways on the Lane, including a Chinese and an Italian, as well as the excellent **Andy's Fish and Chip Shop** – so, sitting down to eat on the Lane is not always necessary! If you are hungry or thirsty then you will definitely find somewhere on Lark Lane to suit you taste and your budget.

As an additional 'Liverpool Outing', I would particularly recommend a gentle stroll through Sefton Park early on an summer or autumn evening, followed by a meal or a drink on the Lane. This is when the Lane really comes to life, and with a particularly 'bohemian' flavour, as this is the favourite watering spot for students and the local 'intelligentsia' who live in the surrounding houses.

As we leave Lark Lane, we pass along Lark Way and onto Alexandra Drive. Here can be seen yet more magnificent Victorian houses, in which live some of the City's prominent residents. These include members of 'The Real Thing' pop group.

To Find Out More:
Eating Out in Lark Lane
http://www.sugarvine.com/Liverpool/
feature_stories/feature_stories.asp?
story=415

Lark Lane Community Association
http://www.larklane.com/

Merseyside Campaign for Real Ale
www.merseycamra.org.uk

At the end of Lark Lane, and just before it becomes a cul-de-sac, turn right at its junction with Hargreaves Road, into Lark Way. There is a restaurant on the left corner as you turn.
At the end of Lark Way, turn right again, this time onto Parkfield Road. Immediately, turn left into Alexandra Drive. There are some magnificent houses along here. At the end of the Drive, turn left into Ullet Road – Princes Park will be facing you across the road. At the top of Ullet Road, cross over two sets of traffic lights, into Dingle Lane; the former Gaumont Cinema will be on the right-hand corner of this road as you enter it. Park anywhere on the road that it is safe to do so and walk back from here to visit the Ancient Chapel of Toxteth. I suggest a visit time of around 15 minutes – longer if you have a pre-arranged visit to go inside the Chapel. We are now in an old district known as 'The Dingle'.

Knott's Hole at The Dingle

The Dingle

Ullet Road leads from Sefton Park to a part of this local district known as 'The Dingle'. The current residential appearance of this area completely belies what this once was – an area of outstanding natural beauty with a delightful stream, rising in the highest part of Toxteth, and wending its way down the hill that is now High Park Street. From here, and through a series of ponds, it came down Park Road, which was then the valley of the stream. Passing through woodland, dells, and grand estates, including what are now the gates and grounds of the **Turner Nursing Home**, the 'Dingle Brook' as it was known, fed into the River Mersey at a sandstone basin, surrounded by cliffs, known as Knott's Hole, just behind the still-existing headland of Dingle Point.

Knott's Hole was a natural basin that provided a safe and secluded pool, scattered throughout with large boulders, and almost completely encircled by sandstone cliffs that were about 15 to 20 feet high. On top of these cliffs were extensive woodlands and areas of lush bushes and shrubs. Boys from the nearby villages, and often from the Town itself, would come here to leap from the cliffs and boulders, to swim naked and to play in the clean and clear waters of the Mersey – in almost Arcadian surroundings.

> "Families would also picnic on the rocky shoreline, and young lovers would tryst, and plight their troth amongst the secluded groves of willow, aspen, and beech"

Dingle Brook dried up a long time ago, as the surrounding area became developed into industrialised docks and estates of houses for the new workers that were moving into the district. The old watercourses of the brook were then used as sites for drains and sewers. However, the graveyard of the Ancient Chapel, which then stood on the bank of the brook, can still be subjected to flooding in bouts of heavy rain.

In due course, the lease of the whole Dingle Estate was bought by the Corporation of Liverpool, who allowed tipping of household rubbish, ash, and industrial waste in and around the shoreline, and the whole area was completely ravaged and destroyed. Today, the stream has completely gone, the land is largely levelled and built over, and nothing of aesthetic value remains of this once beautiful landscape.

In 1919, the whole Dingle Estate was bought from the Corporation by the Mersey Docks and Harbour Board, and they demolished the remaining isolated mansions and cottages, in preparation for the construction of extensive new oil jetties and petroleum stores. Also, the Board built a new river wall that completely obliterated the natural shoreline and cliffs, including Knott's Hole, and a railway was laid through the riverside walk and woodlands. The whole Dingle riverfront area, right up to this new wall, then became one huge rubbish tip – continuing what the Corporation had begun.

> "Throughout the early decades of the 20th century the whole Dingle Estate became filled with industrial, chemical, and household waste, and with ash"

The burial ground at the Ancient Chapel of Toxteth

Opposite the old Gaumont Cinema and standing at the corner of Ullet Road and Park Road, this tiny place of worship is the oldest structure of significance in the district, and it is listed as a Grade I Building. Registered as Toxteth Unitarian Chapel, it is otherwise known as The Ancient Chapel of Toxteth, even though it is sited in the district that is known as **'The Dingle'**. As we have seen, in the days when Park Road was just a track leading to Toxteth Hunting Park, the Dingle Brook ran through the district, passing through a rocky dell giving 'The Dingle' its name. Local tradition has it that during the English Civil War, Cromwell's troops camped in and around the Chapel to get shelter, and to water themselves and their horses from the Dingle Brook.

As we have also seen, in the early years of the 17th century, and during the reign of King James I, the riverside part of the Toxteth Estate owned by Sir Richard Molyneux, became home to Puritans trying to escape persecution. They settled in an area between Otterspool and here at The Dingle and, by 1611, there were over twenty families in the district; all settled into a comfortable and established community.

These religious dissenters were people who felt that the Reformation had not gone far enough, and they wanted to purge the Church of England of what they regarded as the 'Popish idolatry', in the ceremonies and rituals that it had inherited from the Catholic Church. The name 'Puritan' was originally applied to them as a form of contempt but, in due course and because of its association with 'purity', they adopted the name themselves.

This new community wanted to establish a school for their children, so they erected a small schoolhouse and invited **Richard Mather** of Lowton, near Warrington, to be the Schoolmaster. He accepted the appointment and, even though he was only fifteen years old, he was very successful. However, he soon decided to complete his studies at Brasenose College, and left for Oxford. In the meantime, in 1618, a Chapel was built to service the community as a large addition to the existing schoolhouse building, and this combined structure became the 'Ancient Chapel'.

The design of the Chapel reflected the Puritan desire to move further away from the rites and practices of the Church of England, and included plain wooden seating, no adornments on the walls or fittings, and certainly no decorated or ornamented altar. Even though he had only been away for a couple of years, the Toxteth community urged Richard to return, to now become their Minister. He agreed, preaching his first sermon in the newly-built chapel on 30th November 1618. Mather stayed with the Toxteth Puritans for a number of years. Nevertheless, as a fervent supporter of the Puritan Movement he was unable to reconcile his views with the established church, even though the leaders of the Church of

Also, during and immediately after the Second World War, these tips then received the remains of City-centre buildings that had been destroyed in the Blitz, by the catastrophic bombing of the German Luftwaffe.

After the level had been raised, all the surrounding land became an extension of the oil and petrol-chemical site and the area was covered with huge storage tanks. These, in turn, became redundant and yet more tipping took place.

Despite all of this industrialisation, a short stretch of original – if now much more despoiled – shore survived, right up to 1982.

"For decades this had been known as 'The Cast-Iron Shore' or 'The Cazzie', and it is still fondly remembered by many older Liverpudlians"

The name refers to the cast iron produced at the Mersey Foundry that stood near the Dingle waterfront, and which was used for the construction of the nearby St. Michael's Church, and for St George's Church at the top of Everton Ridge. The results of these industrial processes had tainted and coloured the land around, as well as the shore and the rocks. Nevertheless, families would still come to this shore to escape the overcrowded town, and children would continue to swim and play in the, now not so clean and clear waters of one of the world's greatest rivers.

Opinions and memories vary, but the Cazzie seems to have been situated somewhere between Otterspool and the Herculaneum Dock, with Dingle Point being the place best remembered. But then, in 1982, the Cazzie too went the way of the bulldozers, as building began of the new riverside walkway and embankment that were to form part of the International Garden Festival.

This major regeneration project took place in 1984. (See Chapter: 'The Liverpool Waterfront'.) However, the now empty chemical tanks; overfull industrial dumps; long-abandoned oil-jetties; and silted-up docks of the Dingle, were also swept away, as the whole area was reclaimed and recreated as a fabulous collection of international gardens and modern houses. A new road, Riverside Drive, was created through the site, and the location of Knott's Hole is now covered by a small traffic roundabout. However, a section of the cliffs at Dingle Point still survives nearby, and these are a reminder of what the original shoreline must once have looked like.

You can travel through what were the Dingle Estate, Dingle Point, Knott's Hole, and indeed past the site of the International Garden Festival, as part of my 'Liverpool Waterfront' Chapter.

Ancient Chapel of Toxteth

Green and Pleasant Liverpool

England in Liverpool insisted that he do so. Richard refused to conform to their edicts and so the Anglican authorities twice suspended him as Minister of Toxteth. In fact, despite the best efforts of Sir Richard Molyneux and his family, the Puritans became the victims of increasing persecution. To escape from this harassment, Richard Mather travelled from Liverpool to Plymouth from where, in 1635, he set sail to the New World with the 'The Pilgrim Fathers'. His ship was tiny, and named the 'Mary and John'. Once in America, Mather continued to preach as the Minister of a Congregational Church in Dorchester, Massachusetts, until his death in 1669. His son and grandson became presidents of Harvard and Yale Universities respectively.

Though small (26ft by 30ft approx.), the Ancient Chapel has many attractive architectural features, including a slate roof, two storeys, round-headed windows and entrances, bracketed eaves and gables, and a small octagonal cupola with louvered openings. Inside, there is a pulpit against the east wall; also, north and south galleries, overlooking the body of the Chapel; and sets of box pews, dating from 1650 and 1700.

"There is also a clock on the front of one of the galleries, which was a gift from a member of the congregation in the late 18th century"

The chapel is the oldest dissenting place of worship in the UK and, although substantially rebuilt in 1774, parts of the original walls remain. In 1840, the old schoolhouse was demolished, to be replaced by the present Chapel vestibule, porch, vestry, staircase, and organ loft.

There have been a number of significant members of the Toxteth congregation and community over the years. One of these was **Jeremiah Horrox** (1619-1642), the 'father of British astronomy', who was born in Toxteth Park in 1619. He resided, as we have previously seen, at Lower Lodge in Otterspool Park. A follower of Ptolemy, in 1639, Jeremiah produced a model of planetary motion, and he was the first person to predict the transit of Venus across the face of the sun. Also, amongst many other significant achievements, he calculated the distance from the earth to the sun. Jeremiah died in 1641, at the very young age of 23, and is buried at the Chapel. A monumental slab erected in 1891 pays tribute to him, and a mock-up of his telescope, together with his

original notebooks, are on display in The World Museum Liverpool.

There are many funeral and memorial tablets and stones in and around the Chapel, and outside there is a graveyard built on sloping land, which contains burials dating back to 1795. There is a colonnaded construction in the burial ground, known as 'The Colybarium', where the wealthiest members of the congregation were buried, including some members of the Holt and Rathbone families. The last burials in the Chapel graveyard were made around 1960.

Other prominent people buried here include members of the Melly family; ancestors of the late George Melly (1926-2007), the local artist and jazz singer. George's great-uncle, **Charles Melly** (1829-1888), was a great benefactor to the poor of Liverpool, always giving parties for the poor and especially for children. He started sickness funds and savings clubs for his workers and, in the 1860s with William Rathbone, he raised funds for Lancashire cotton workers. In 1852, local Police officers told Charles that poor Irish immigrants were asking them where they could get water, as they had to drink from horse troughs. At his own expense, Melly installed taps at Princes Dock, and then 12 drinking fountains at Liverpool's railway stations, with a further 40 being installed throughout the town.

> **To Find Out More:**
> **The Ancient Chapel of Toxteth**
> **Phone: 0151 263 4899**

The building almost directly opposite the ancient Chapel, and standing on the corner of South Hill Grove, is a garage and car-repair workshop.

This now occupies the site of the booking hall and the underground station for the old Overhead Railway. This once ran from here, to emerge from the cliff face at Herculaneum Dock on an elevated track, which then ran the full length of the Liverpool Docks all the way to Seaforth at the north end of Liverpool. The station platforms still survive, completely intact, in the sandstone bedrock under the garage, and these can sometimes be accessed when permission is granted by the garage owners. But this is very rare. The Overhead Railway closed in 1956, and is fully described in the Chapter: 'The Liverpool Waterfront'.

Princes Park

Turn around in Dingle Lane, but be careful as it can be busy with traffic, and with lots of children crossing the road, or playing in and around the nearby streets.
Retrace your journey back towards Ullet Road. However, as you pass the Ancient Chapel on the left, and go through the traffic lights, take the next road on the left; this is Belvidere Road.
The Lower School of Belvedere High School will be on the right-hand corner as you turn.
Just to the left of this building, still on the right-hand side of the road, you will see a short drive and some large iron gates leading into Princes Park. This is a good point from which to explore the park, if you have not already done so.

Princes Park is named after Prince Albert, the consort of Queen Victoria. This was the first public park to be established in the City and was founded by a local entrepreneur – Richard Vaughan Yates (1785-1856) – who created the park as a private business venture. He had a grand vision for a providing a large landscaped area of gardens and waterways, to be a place of attractive and peaceful recreation for the people of the growing City. His idea was to build it in what was then countryside, just outside the town itself, but near enough for people to visit it easily.

As already described, Yates had an innovative method for raising funds to pay for the purchase of the land, for the landscaping of his new park, and for hopefully generating a personal profit for himself in the process: He would raise the capital from the sale of building plots for large mansion houses, which were to be constructed around the park perimeter. And so, around 1840, Yates brought in Joseph Paxton (1803-1865) to design his new park, as he wanted the best, and because Paxton already had an excellent reputation by this time.

In 1826, Paxton had become head gardener for the 6th Duke of Devonshire, firstly at Chiswick House and later at Chatsworth House in Derbyshire; and he was still head gardener to the Duke when he designed Princes Park. The Duke's name is commemorated in nearby Devonshire Road. Paxton eventually went on to design Birkenhead Park on the Wirral, which in turn inspired the creation and designs for Central Park in New York; Hesketh Park in Southport; and the Crystal Palace in London, for the Great Exhibition of 1851. Incidentally, Birkenhead Park was the first publicly-funded municipal park in Britain.

Yates hoped that the Corporation of Liverpool would partner him in this venture, but they did not, and he had to finance the project himself. Many large and attractive residences were built around the park, most with private access to the new open space, and to a circular carriage drive that connected the park's four entrances. Most of these fine houses still stand today. Unfortunately, whilst the sales of the large houses did fund the park's creation, they did not generate the income that Yates had hoped for. Consequently, he was forced to establish a charitable trust, which ran the park until 1918, at which time the Corporation took over its management. Nevertheless, he did generate a substantial income for himself from other development projects around Liverpool.

The park opened in 1842, although it was not actually finished until 1845 and, as a focal point, a serpentine lake was created at its centre. This was formed by damming a local stream known as Dickinson's Dingle, which, like the Dingle Brook, fed into the Mersey at The Dingle. The valley of this stream still makes a principal feature of the park because Paxton incorporated this into his design. Winding pathways, gardens, areas of extensive shrubbery, rockeries, a Chinese Bridge, and a Swiss Boathouse on the shores of the lake, were also included in the design. And this made the new Princes Park a very desirable place to live and to visit; which had of course been Yates's idea from the start.

Interestingly, initial public access within Princes Park was limited to certain areas, whilst the landscaped gardens – especially those around parts of the lake – were only available to the residents of the new mansions. This changed over the years; largely because the local people – who came to use the park – kept encroaching on the closed-off areas, establishing a kind of 'perambulatory squatters' rights'!

Even though they had not wanted to join Yates in his financial venture, the shrewd leaders of Liverpool liked his concept of raising funds for public amenities, by building and selling off new properties. And so, as I mentioned in the introduction to this Tour, the Corporation stole Yates's idea! This is why Liverpool's largest urban parks, such as Newsham, Stanley, and Sefton, are surrounded by magnificent mansions and miniature stately homes!

In 1918, the City took over Princes Park from the Yates Family Trust, and they have managed it ever since.

"Although now much reduced in size, Princes Park lake remains popular with anglers, and the park is an attractive place for a peaceful stroll. It is also the venue for public events, celebrations, and community festivals, which attract large crowds from all over the City"

A dancer in the Brouhaha parade makes her way through the city to Princes Park

To Find Out More:
Liverpool Park Ranger Service
Phone: 0151 233 3007

Continue along Belvidere Road, passing the Upper School Buildings on the right.
Just as the road begins to bend sharply to the right, take the road on the left, which is Devonshire Road West. Almost as soon as you have made this turn, take the road immediately on your right. This narrow road is South Street, and it leads you into the locality known as 'The Welsh Streets'.
The 3rd road on the left is Madryn Street, and Ringo Starr's first boyhood home was here, at number 9.

Leave your car parked at the top of Madryn Street, and walk across High Park Street. You will see Admiral Grove facing you on the left, running alongside the Empress Pub. Ringo's second home was here, at number 10 Admiral Grove.

Green and Pleasant Liverpool

Madryn Street has two claims to fame; the first being that Richard Starkey (Ringo Starr), who was born on 7th July 1940, lived at No.9. The second is that, in 1992, No. 35 hit the headlines when it was disturbed by a particularly nasty, violent, and well-authenticated ghost! However, we shall concentrate on the pop-star rather than on the poltergeist!

Richard Starkey was the oldest Beatle, being three months older than John Lennon. Paul McCartney was the next youngest, with George Harrison being the 'baby' of the 'Merseyside Mop-Tops'! Richard's father, who's name was also Richard, was originally a Liverpool dock worker who later worked in a bakery, where he met Richard's mother Elsie. Sadly however, the marriage did not last and the couple separated, with young Richard staying with his mum, in Madryn Street. Later, Elsie met and married Harry Groves, who the boy always referred to as his 'step ladder'!

"By the age of 17, Richard had learned to play the drums, and he became part of Liverpool's Skiffle craze in the 1950s"

In 1957, with his friend Eddie Miles, he formed his own Skiffle Group called 'The Eddie Clayton Skiffle Group' and, in 1959, he joined 'The Raving Texans'. This was a quartet that backed the local singer, Rory Storm (Alan Caldwell), and it was whilst with Rory that Richard acquired the nickname Ringo. This was because of the rings that he wore and also because it sounded 'cowboyish'. He adopted the last name Starr so that his drum solos could be billed as 'Starr Time'.

Ringo first met the Beatles in Hamburg, in October 1960, while there performing with what had by then become Rory Storm and The Hurricanes and he became friendly with his fellow Scousers. Ringo joined the Beatles on the 18th August 1962, as we have seen, after being recruited by John Lennon and Paul McCartney, through their manager Brian Epstein, in the coup against their existing drummer, Pete Best.

Although always a happy child, Richard was a sickly boy, who spent a lot of time in hospital; for appendicitis at the age of 6, at which time he went into a coma for two months; and, at the age of 13, for a cold

Ringo's first home, in Madryn Street.

Ringo Starr

which developed into pleurisy: These long periods of debilitating major illness regularly kept Richard away from school and, by the age of 15, he could barely read and write.

His health continued to cause him problems, and he missed three quarters of the 1964 Beatles tour of Scandinavia, Holland, the Far East, and Australia, to have his tonsils removed.

In the mid-1950s, Ringo and his family moved from Madryn Street, but only about 100 yards away to **10 Admiral Grove**, and he continued to live here until 1965, when the attentions of his fans became too much. After buying his family a 'posh' bungalow in Woolton, Ringo, like the other Beatles, then moved out of the City altogether.

The Beatles' first movie, originally to be called 'Beatlemania', was eventually called 'A Hard Day's Night', because this was how Ringo had described a particularly long and exhausting performance. In due course, Ringo married his long-time girlfriend, Maureen

Cox, on February 11, 1965. They had three children; Zak, Jason, and Lee, although the marriage did not survive. And Ringo's childhood home might not survive either!

At the time of writing, all the streets in and around Madryn Street are under threat of demolition, to be replaced by new housing estates. This is not meeting with universal approval in the district known as **The Welsh Streets** of Toxteth. Many local people wonder why the money that is likely to be spent on tearing down their homes could not be better spent restoring, renovating, and modernising them. A fair question! So, get to see Madryn Street soon, before the wrecking ball has its wicked way on the Welsh Streets!
"Peace and Love!"

To Find Out More:
Ringo Starr Official Website
http://www.ringostarr.com/

Alan (Rory Storm) Caldwell
http://www.lps-athletics.co.uk/history/pembroke/1950s/_overlay/alan_caldwell.htm

Drive out of Madryn Street, and turn right onto High Park Street. Follow this all the way down until it joins Princes Road. Turn left here, and follow the Boulevard, until it returns you to where our Tour began.

Green and Pleasant Liverpool : Conclusion

And so, we now return to not only where this Chapter, but to where the public parks and open spaces of Liverpool first began. In the process of exploring just four of our remarkable landscaped open spaces, and other aspects of our environment that give us room to breathe, we have also travelled through more than eight centuries of our City's history – longer if you count the early establishment of the Cistercian Monks' granary at Stanlawe Grange: And we have done so in just one corner of Liverpool but, arguably, one of its most significant areas – that of the ancient estate and hunting reserve of Toxteth Park.

I hope that this glimpse at the wide range of delights and curiosities that are to be found in our extensive and beautiful open spaces, will encourage you to discover the rest of 'green and pleasant' Liverpool.

A summer rain storm at Sefton Park

The Liverpool Waterfront

Including:

Festival Gardens

Herculaneum and Brunswick Docks

The Overhead Railway Tunnel

Liverpool Marina

King's Dock, and the Arena and Convention Centre

The Albert Dock

The Beatles Story Experience

Tate Liverpool

The Merseyside Maritime Museum

International Slavery Museum

George's Dock Building

The Port of Liverpool Building

The Cunard Building

The Royal Liver Building

The Pier Head and The Mersey Ferries

The Titanic Memorial

Princes Dock

The Dock Road

Clarence Dock and The Irish in Liverpool

Stanley Dock and the Leeds-Liverpool Canal

Liverpool's Albert Dock

The Liverpool Waterfront : The Tour

This Tour is a point-to-point journey, which covers a total distance of approximately 9 miles. It begins at the south of Liverpool's Waterfront – at Otterspool Promenade, and takes you to the North Docks and the Leeds-Liverpool Canal.

The suggested time for the completion if this Tour is 5 hours. However, to fully visit the Beatles Experience, The Tate Gallery, The Merseyside Maritime Museum, The International Slavery Museum, and the Customs and Excise Museum, and to take a trip on the Mersey Ferries, would add an extra 3-4 hours.

Because of this, my suggestion would be that you visit the Albert Dock Museums and take the Ferry Trip as a completely separate half-day outing.

NB This Tour is best taken on a Saturday or Sunday, as traffic is considerably reduced on these days.
Also, please remember to check all opening times and admission charges before setting off, to avoid disappointment should any venues be closed

Key

Route Map

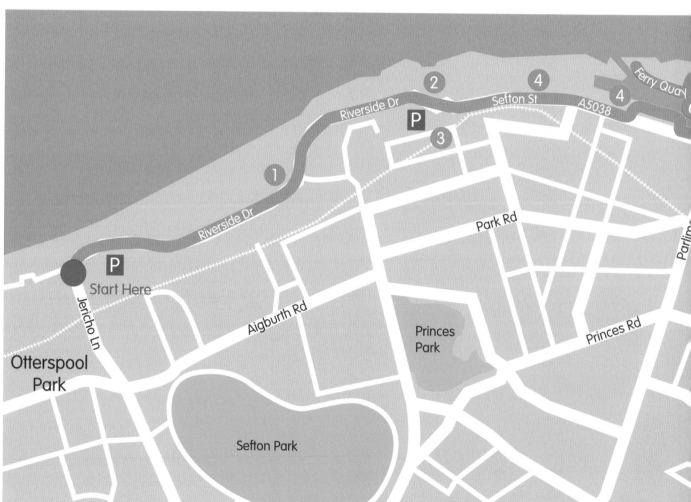

Contents

The Liverpool Waterfront

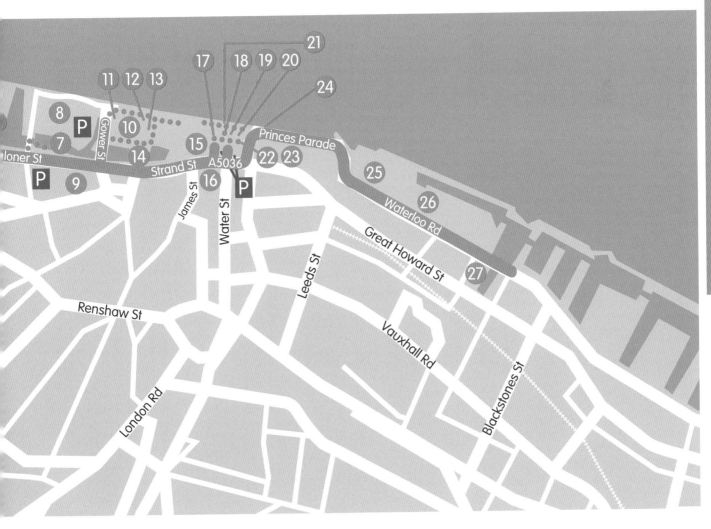

The Liverpool Waterfront Introduction

To travel through the history of Liverpool is to journey along a remarkable timeline. In so doing, we uncover the story of a City that has global significance

Beginning in obscurity, our story soon becomes one of developing strategic significance, and of economic development and population expansion. Then, the saga of Liverpool is one of great worldwide importance and power. However, the tale then unfolds through Wartime destruction; via economic decline, political collapse, and social unrest; to a chronicle of slow recovery leading to a period of major inward investment. Our history then culminates into a narrative of regeneration, economic growth, and of expansion once more.

"However, this fascinating story is far from over, and the future will be just as exciting as the past has been"

And this entire history is traceable along our waterfront: As you follow this Chapter from the South at Otterspool, along the bank of the River Mersey, up to Vauxhall in the North, you will discover our past glories and our failures; our strengths and our weaknesses; our achievements and our remaining challenges. But, above all, you will also be following the story of the people of Liverpool: our diversity, our living heritage, our passion for our City, our pride as Liverpudlians, and our zest for life. And indeed, all human life is here; along the Liverpool Waterfront.

Without the River Mersey Liverpool is unlikely ever to have existed: And it is because of this waterway that the otherwise insignificant little community in the north of England became one of the greatest ports in the world.

As we have seen, this all began with King John in the 13th century, and his need for a deep-water port from which to launch his invasion fleets against Ireland. When, on the 28th August 1207, the King awarded Liverpool its first 'Letters Patent' or 'Charter', this attracted people to the new town and, over subsequent years, business, and the population began to boom. Ship-building began on the Mersey, and not just of invasion fleets, but of trading vessels. These too began to use the port as a base for expanding commerce. All this shipping required maintaining, equipping, and servicing, and so a supply-chain network of enterprise grew up in the Town. Ships also need sailors, so the population grew, as men – often with their families – came to settle here, to 'go down to the sea in ships'.

At the end of the 17th century, the 'Pool' of the Mersey covered an area where Canning Place and the Liverpool ONE retail development now stand. However, by the end of the 1600s, this vital berth and anchorage was silting up and urgent action was required. Also, whilst the 'Pool' was large it was subject to a considerable tidal range. This was a problem for all vessels using the Port, and for the small craft that were by then regularly ferrying across the river.

And so, by the beginning of the 18th century, the leaders of the

The magnificent RMS Titanic sets sail on her ill-fated maiden voyage

Town recognised that the building of a new dock, large enough to accommodate a range of goods vessels, would increase their economic strength.

In 1708, the Corporation appointed Mr Thomas Steers to develop plans, and he proposed the conversion of the Pool into a wet dock. His scheme was to construct floodgates across its mouth to keep vessels afloat during the ebb of the tides. Ships and water would enter the dock at high tide, and then closing the gates would prevent the water running out of the dock, as the tide ebbed. The effect of this was that a ship could unload in 1½ days, as opposed to the 12-14 days that were otherwise needed, especially when unloading was governed by the tidal flow. This was a remarkably innovative idea, and so the world's first, commercial, wet dock was opened, on the 31st August 1715, when the vessels the **Mulbury**, the **Batchlor**, and the **Robert** were the first ships to use it.

Before long, the Dock became inadequate for the dramatic rise in maritime trade, and Liverpool had to create more wet and dry docks. The next dock to open was South Dock, in 1753 and, as its name implies, this was sited just south of the original Dock. It was from this time that Liverpool's first dock began to be known as the **Old Dock**. In due course, and as trade continued to increase, another dock was opened in 1771, and named George's Dock, after King George III. Even so, this dock eventually became too small to cope with the expansion in trade and in ship size and, in 1825, it had to be rebuilt and enlarged. In 1788, the King's Dock opened, followed by Queen's Dock in 1796. In fact, by the beginning of the 19th century, Liverpool had become the second greatest seaport in the kingdom. The number of sailors setting out from the Port had trebled, as had the number of locally owned ships: The tonnage of ships entering the Town now increased ten-fold and this fuelled our continued growth and expansion for the next hundred years.

In 1811, the Old Dock was filled in and replaced by a massive dock to the north, which became Princes Dock, opening in 1821. Clarence Dock was opened in 1830, to take steamers. Consequently, this dock was located some distance northwards, to avoid the risk of fire to the sails and rigging of any adjacent sailing vessels. Indeed, from the Dingle in the South to Seaforth in the North, and covering a distance of some 7½ miles, Liverpool's dock network was to become one of

The scene at Gladstone Dock in October 1967, as dockers return to work following a strike over working conditions

the largest in the world – at its peak totalling 130 individual docks. In fact, the last docks to be opened were the Gladstone Dock system, in 1927, not counting the modern container terminal at Seaforth. The Docks made Liverpool great, because they were a major gateway to Britain, its Empire, and to the rest of the world. Also, they were the service-centres for four forms of trade, each of which had a profound impact on Liverpool's economy and society. These were,

- the international shipping of commodities, and trade with the New World – particularly America
- the slave trade
- the massive influx of immigrants into Britain, and particularly the Irish, as a result of the Irish Potato famines of 1845 and 1846
- the passage through Liverpool of emigrants from the Old World of Continental Europe and beyond, to the New World of the Americas

People not only passed through Liverpool Docks, but very many of them stayed here, making the Town one of the oldest, most culturally rich communities in the country. However, because of our importance as a trading and supply port of men, machinery, and munitions – as well as in commodities – during the Second World War, we became a principal target for German bombers. Also, it was from Liverpool that the Battle of the Atlantic was co-ordinated, and so we became the second most heavily-bombed City in Britain, after London. The docks and the City-centre bore the brunt of this onslaught, especially during the May Blitz of 1941.

"After the War, the fortunes of Liverpool were to alter drastically, because it was at this point in history that the shipping trade began to fail"

By the late 1960s, most of the docks on both sides of the river, were either in rapid decline or already derelict, and these sources of Liverpool's past prosperity were now fuelling its economic collapse. By the end of that decade, Liverpool's time as one of the world's most successful ports was over, at least in its old form.

Nevertheless, what you will also discover as you explore our waterfront is that there are now more trading ships on the River than at any time in Liverpool's history. Also, the international tourist industry is now burgeoning, and the Cruise Liner Facility at Princes Dock is once more seeing the great ocean-going liners of the world transporting people to and from this remarkable City; bringing new life and economic revival.

Liverpool's renaissance is just beginning and, once more, our Waterfront will be at its literal and figurative forefront.

This Tour begins at the extreme southern end of Liverpool's accessible docklands; at Otterspool. The start point is at the end of Jericho Lane, which leads off Aigburth Road. (See Chapter: 'Green and Pleasant Liverpool'.)

This area takes its name from the Puritan Community that lived here after the English Civil War, and from the otters that reputedly had their habitat here, before the area became industrialised.

At the end of Jericho Lane, at Otterspool Promenade, is a roundabout. Take the second exit onto Riverside Drive. Continue along here, across the small roundabout, and on the left we will be passing the site of the former International Garden Festival – now 'Festival Garden'.

Cross over the second roundabout, which was once the location of the idyllically beautiful Dingle Head and Knott's Hole (see Chapter: 'Green And Pleasant Liverpool'). Continue along Riverside Drive, following the signs for the A5036 and Albert Dock.

Liverpool's history has been a chequered one. Sometimes our failures were the result of circumstances beyond our control; such as war or worldwide economic collapse. At other times, however, our problems have been very much of our own making. Indeed, between 1960 and 1985, I would contend that three major factors helped to bring Liverpool to her knees –

- The industrial conflicts and strikes of the late 1960s and early 1970s, resulting in unemployment and economic decline following the closure of many local companies
- The policies of Derek Hatton and the Militant control of Liverpool City Council
- The Toxteth Riots of 1981

Indeed, after the Riots, Michael Heseltine MP was appointed as Minister for Merseyside. He created the Merseyside Development Corporation (MDC) to breathe life back into 865 acres of degenerated dockland.

This area covered all of Liverpool's South Docks, the Central Docks, substantial parcels of land at Bootle in the north, and also dockland at Birkenhead and Wallasey on the Wirral. The MDC also took ownership of a large tract of waterfront land at Otterspool, which comprised old docks, chemical dumps, brownfield sites, and the Cast-Iron Shore or **The Cazzie**, as it was locally known.

That singular name for this stretch of Mersey waterfront dated back to at least 1815, when the architect Thomas Rickman had an iron foundry on this part of the shore, and at a time when the area was an idyllic local beauty spot, known as 'The Dingle'. Local people condensed the name of the shore to the 'Cazzie' and, after the closure of the iron foundry, by the turn of the 20th century this section of the river's edge had become a popular swimming spot for local children.

Adjoining the 'Cazzie' were oil and petro-chemical works, which began on the site in the early years of the 20th Century. This resulted in the construction of storage tanks and jetties, but these had been abandoned in the 1950s, and were largely derelict and dangerous. It was on this site that the MDC decided to construct **The International Garden Festival**, the aims of which were to kick-start environmental and economic regeneration, and bring people back into the City.

The industrial sites were reclaimed, and these, together with the 'Cazzie', were filled in with over 30 million tons of City rubbish and capped with clay and soil. Three million tons of earth were moved to transform the flat, polluted, and neglected site into attractive hills and valleys.

"All over this new landscape, dozens of magnificent gardens were planted, each themed to represent a range of worldwide natural environments, and international horticultural styles."

The **Japanese and Chinese gardens** were particularly outstanding, with temples and pagodas designed and built by craftsmen from those countries. As well as the Orient, amongst the vast selection of nationally-themed gardens were displays from India, Africa, America, Canada, France, and Australia. The gardens also included much artwork and sculpture, including the Blue Peter Ship, on the BBC Garden; a giant, reclining Indian bull; and a full-size Beatles Yellow Submarine. There was also a Sculpture Garden and even a Witches Garden, and a stunning, cigar-shaped building – the Festival Hall – was erected to provide a venue for concerts, exhibitions, and displays during the Garden Festival.

Despite some objections to the concept, as being only 'papering-over-the-cracks', The International Garden Festival was a great success when opened by the Queen, in May 1984. The Festival ran for just a few months, closing in October 1984, after almost

The Festival Garden site after its £3.7m restoration

3½ million visitors had passed through. Part of the land was left as public open space, and the rest was redeveloped as housing estates, whilst the MDC sought for a long-term owner/developer for the site. This was not entirely successful and, essentially, the whole site was left to decay for almost 20 years.

It was particularly sad to see the Festival Hall standing empty for so long, and subsequently vandalised and surrounded by overgrown undergrowth, that was once beautiful, landscaped gardens. Fortunately however, whilst the Festival Hall has been demolished, the Blue Peter Ship, the Sitting Bull, and the Yellow Submarine were saved. The ship is currently in storeage, waiting to be re-sited in the City; the Yellow Submarine stands in front of the Terminal Building at Liverpool John Lennon Airport; and the Sitting Bull has been relocated onto Otterspool Promenade.

But now, Langtree, the current owners of the Garden Festival site, are undertaking a major redevelopment of the parkland and gardens, and of the surrounding land, to build family properties, town houses, and apartments. Many of the original gardens have been restored, together with the Chinese Temple and Japanese Pagoda, giving the whole site a new lease of life: renamed Festival Gardens, these are already open to the public.

To Find Out More:
Liverpool Garden Festival 1984
www.bbc.co.uk/liverpool/capital_culture/2004/04/garden_festival/index.shtml
The Festival Gardens Development
www.festivalgardens.co.uk/

Continue along the A5036, passing the Britannia Inn on the left. There are a number of lay-bys along this stretch of road, and parking embankments on the right; should you wish to stop for a minute or two to take in the views across the river.

Continuing along Riverside Road, you will pass the former Herculaneum Dock behind some new apartments on the right.

Herculaneum Dock

City Quay, on the site of the former Herculaneum Dock

Beyond Festival Gardens, the straight stretch of Riverside Drive from the Britannia Pub, with its unobstructed views across the Mersey to Eastham and Birkenhead on the Wirral, leads us to Herculaneum Dock. This takes its name from the **Herculaneum Pottery** that previously stood on this site, between 1794 and 1841.

At this time, pottery was a major industry in the Town, and it thrived to such an extent that the trade rivalled that of The Potteries in Staffordshire. In fact, the founder of the new factory was a Cheshire man, Samuel Worthington, who brought in a workforce of 50 or 60 experienced potters from Staffordshire, with their families.

He built his pottery on the site of a former copper smelting works, at the South Shore of Toxteth Park, on land then owned by the Molyneux family – the Earls of Sefton. (See Chapter: 'Green and Pleasant Liverpool'.)

"Before long, Liverpool Delft pottery and tiles became, and remain, world famous"

The finished wares were transported from the port, around the coast to all parts of Britain, and also across the Atlantic to the ever-growing markets in America. Almost every type of pottery was produced here, including earthenware, which was decorated in a range of designs, both hand-painted and also using transfers. These included the famous and very popular **Willow Pattern** design.

Around 1820, the Herculaneum Pottery received an important commission for the production of a very large dinner and dessert service, of over 1,000 pieces, for the recently rebuilt Liverpool Town Hall.

This remarkable service survives intact, and is designed in a rich red and gold pattern, with the Coat of Arms of the Corporation of Liverpool on every piece.

"This service was in regular use in the Town Hall until the 1970s, where it is now on show to great effect, in illuminated display cases"

Nevertheless, by 1833, sales were declining as the competition from Staffordshire became increasingly strong and, in due course, the Herculaneum Pottery was forced to close. In 1841, the site was sold and a new dock was constructed in its place.

In modern times, the regeneration of the Herculaneum area gained a new momentum, with the first of two allocations to Merseyside of 'Objective 1 Funding' from the European Union in the mid-1990s. This followed the recognition of the region as one of the poorest and most deprived in Europe.

Consequently, the South Docks of Liverpool were one of the region's first Redevelopment and Regeneration Zones, and much housing, office space, and other amenities – including restaurants, car-

showrooms, and a sports and fitness centre – have been built on the site of the old docks, chemical dumps, and industrial sites. This investment in the area has paid off, now making the Herculaneum Dock area a very desirable location for home, work, and leisure.

The Herculaneum Pottery in the 18th Century

At the next roundabout, take your third exit, into what is labelled 'Private Road' – in front of Greens Health and Fitness Club. Park briefly on the roadside here, at what is the other end of Herculaneum Dock, and you will see the tunnel for the Liverpool Overhead Railway, high in the cliff face above you.

As you come to the roundabout, near the Sports and Fitness Centre at Herculaneum Dock, it is worth remembering that Liverpool has always been the home of much that is unique and revolutionary. A perfect example of this was our own elevated railway, which once ran from here.

By the mid-19th century, the traffic at the docks and the surrounding roads, along the full length of the working riverfront, had reached such a state that terrible congestion occurred on a regular basis. This frequently brought transportation and commerce to a noisy and frustrating halt; the first traffic jams! These were also making it difficult for the thousands of Dockers to get to work, and so some method of relieving the problem was urgently needed.

As ever, the ingenious Liverpudlians rose to the challenge, and here at the Herculaneum Dock, from 1893 to 1956, the Overhead Railway or **Dockers Umbrella** carried specially designed engines and carriages along the full length of the Liverpool Docks system. They ran from here to Seaforth Sands, at the north of the City, where a purpose-built elevated station was constructed. At Herculaneum Dock the station was at ground level, and the tracks and carriages were accessed up a special staircase.

The idea of an overhead railway had been put to the Liverpool Dock Committee as early as 1853, but nothing had come of this. But, by 1878, the level of Dock Road congestion had become so intolerable, along what was then more than six miles of docks, that the plan was revived. The Overhead Railway Company was formed, in 1888, and construction of the transportation system began the following year.

Originally, it had been intended to use steam locomotives – despite the experience of New Yorkers where, from their elevated railway, hot cinders, ash, oil, and water, were regularly dropping onto the heads of the people walking below. Fortunately, this idea was rejected once it was also realised that falling sparks could ignite the timbers of the hundreds of ships moored at the docksides.

Consequently, in 1891, a system of electric traction, supplying power via a third rail, was commissioned from the newly formed Electric Construction Company.

The first overhead train ran in 1892, carrying all the Company Directors and their friends and families. And then, in February 1893, the new railway was officially opened to the public, by Lord Salisbury, as the world's first elevated electric railway.

The 'Overhead' soon covered a distance of 7½ miles and the track ran 16 feet above the Dock Road. The journey took 25 minutes and, with its 17 stations, it was also the first electric elevated railway in the world to use an automatic signalling system. The railway was very popular and commercially successful, and it very soon was carrying over 4 million passengers every year.

Do make a point of stopping near the roundabout at Herculaneum Dock and be sure to look up at the cliff face that towers behind the apartments and the Sports and Fitness Centre. Here, you will see a large, porticoed-archway, set high up in the sandstone wall. Although now bricked up, this shows the point at which a tunnel emerges over the dock, under the houses on the cliff top. This tunnel was for an extension to the Overhead Railway, continuing the line from Herculaneum Dock to an underground station at 'The Dingle'.

Serving all the docks, warehouses, and the light and heavy industry at both ends of the City, this transport system was vital to Dockers and industrial workers alike. The track also passed by the city-centre, at the Pier Head, and so it served the office workers in buildings such as the Cunard and Royal Liver Buildings. This meant that the railway also provided access to the heart of the City itself. As well as this, passengers for the Mersey Ferries could connect with the 'Overhead' at the Pier Head Station, making it in its heyday, a cheap, convenient, and fascinating mode of transport.

"The technology of the railway did not stand still and the Company introduced many innovations"

Liverpool's Overhead Railway, in the early years of the 20th Century

These included, in 1921, Britain's first escalator, which was built at Seaforth Station. This comprised a narrow conveyor belt, with wooden slats, upon which passengers would stand.

However, having been badly bombed during the War, and suffering from severe corrosion, the Railway became very dilapidated and, by the beginning of the 1950s, its condition was giving cause for grave concern. In Post-War Britain, money was not available to adequately repair the Railway, nor to bring it up to the required safety standards. This was despite the fact that it was by this time carrying almost 9 million passengers a year. Consequently, the railway was closed on the 30th December 1956, and subsequently demolished, after 60 years of successful operation.

In its final year, when I was five years old, my mother took me for a trip along the full length of the Railway. She was determined that I should have the opportunity to travel on 'the Overhead' just once, before it disappeared forever. And I am very grateful for the experience. I clearly remember gazing down on the docks as we clattered overhead; looking at what appeared to be hundreds of ships, sailing on the river and berthed in all the docks. I remember crowds and crowds of people, of all shapes and sizes and skin colours, walking the length of the Dock Road. I also remember the smells of the men who crowded the compartment, a reassuring smell to a small boy, of oil, sweat, and Capstan Full Strength cigarettes. I remember too, the sounds of the strange accents of sailors from all over the world, and of the rattling and shaking as the wooden carriages trundled along the clanking and ringing metal track. Even today, the excitement and thrill of it all is a vivid memory.

All that now remains of the Railway are some of the lower track-support girders, set in concrete mounds against some stretches of the dock-road wall. Although the complete underground station at Dingle still exists, with the subway intact, it is now used as a vehicle workshop for a car-repair company up above.

What an asset such a public transport system would have proved to be today, had it survived. However, whilst we may look back on what was once one of our greatest social and economic assets, and breathe a sigh of regret, all may not be lost: as you shall shortly discover!

To Find Out More:
The Liverpool Overhead Railway
http://www.subbrit.org.uk/sb-sites/sites/l/liverpool_overhead_railway/index.shtml

Return to the roundabout at Riverside Drive, and turn right along the A5036. The Jaguar Car Dealership is in front of you as you make the turn and, behind this, is the Chung Ku Chinese Restaurant. You will pass a variety of Car Showrooms on the right; Century Building on the left; Brunswick Station on the right; and a rank of small business premises, behind the railings on the left. At the large roundabout, with the ship's anchor in the centre, continue straight across. Almost immediately on the left, behind the iron railings and the trees, you will now see the Royal Naval Headquarters Merseyside.

We are now on Sefton Street, and from Herculaneum Dock we pass the stylish Chung Ku Chinese Restaurant at Columbus Quay. In front of this is the Jaguar Cars showroom as we now cross over the roundabout, still on Sefton Street, in front of the factory and commercial units that make up the small business quarter of this part of the southern docks.

From this point, we will continue onto Chaloner Street, Wapping, and Strand Street, right up to the Pier Head and, en route, we shall clearly see that the work that was begun by the Merseyside Development Corporation (MDC), in the 1980s, has been continued to great effect. Indeed, a clear example of their successful economic regeneration work is here, at Brunswick Dock.

Brunswick Dock

On the left of Sefton Street, standing on what was once Harrington Dock, is Brunswick Business Park. Established by the MDC, and inside once-derelict and decaying dockside buildings and old railway sheds, there is now a thriving small-business community - with some larger companies - in this successful enterprise centre. Brunswick Dock is at the core of the redevelopment and regeneration of the South Docks area of Liverpool, and all along the rest of Sefton Street you will find more car showrooms, a number of other office and apartment complexes, and developing leisure facilities.

Opened in 1832, Brunswick Dock was designed by the renowned Victorian engineer Jesse Hartley, and it was at the heart of the South Docks – lying as it did between Coburg Dock to the north, and what were Toxteth and Harrington Docks to the south. These latter docks have long since been filled in and built over.

British Waterways took ownership of this and the other docks in the southern system, from English Partnerships, in 2003. The transfer involved a total of 75 acres of dock waterspace that included Canning Half-tide, Canning, Albert, Salthouse, Dukes, Wapping Basin, Wapping Quay, Queens, Queens Branch, Coburg Dock Marina, and Brunswick Dock – all in Liverpool; as well as the Morpeth and Egerton Docks in Birkenhead, across the River Mersey.

The owners are transforming the docks into a year-round area of water-based leisure amenities, including improved moorings, leisure trips, a programme of high-profile maritime events, enhanced water-sports, and extensive heritage interpretation. Also, now owned by British Waterways are some two miles of riverside walkway; a river wall; sections of the Dock Wall; the Water Sports Centre; the 350-berth Liverpool Yacht Marina, as well as several bridges and pontoons.

The cliff-face tunnel at Herculaneum Dock, which once carried the Overhead Railway to the underground station at the Dingle

To Find Out More:
South Docks Toxteth
www.toxteth.net/places/liverpool/docks

British Waterways
www.britishwaterways.co.uk/home/index

Chung Ku Chinese Restaurant
Phone: 0151 726 8191

Royal Naval Headquarters Merseyside

Passing the car showrooms and the railway station, we see a large roundabout in the middle of the road, on which stands – appropriately enough – a huge ship's anchor. Across this roundabout, on the left of Sefton Street and standing behind tall iron railings at East Brunswick Dock, is the Royal Naval Headquarters Merseyside.

This establishment accommodates the Naval Regional Officer Northern England; HMS Eaglet, the Royal Naval Reserve unit in the northwest of England; the Royal Marines Reserve Merseyside; the HQ for the Sea Cadet Corps in the northwest; the Liverpool University Naval Unit; and the naval training craft for Liverpool and Manchester universities.

"Both the Royal Naval Reserve and the Royal Marines Reserve Merseyside support active service units. This means that they can, and do deploy service personnel anywhere in the world where there might be a conflict"

The Liverpool Waterfront

Royal Naval HQ at Brunswick Dock

Locally, HMS Eaglet, and all the Royal Naval services that operate out of the building, support local ceremonies, social projects, and the civic life of Liverpool and the North West, and a well-trained guard turns out several times a year for civic functions. On 2nd May 1993, the 'Freedom of Entry into the City of Liverpool' was conferred upon HMS Eaglet, in recognition of the role that they play in the life and community of Liverpool and of the region. In that same year, the 50th Anniversary Service of the Battle of the Atlantic was organised on behalf of the Royal Navy by Eaglet. More recently, 2003 saw the 60th and final Battle of the Atlantic commemorations: this week-long event was organised by RNHQ Merseyside and included a service at Liverpool's Anglican Cathedral, followed by a parade of thousands of veterans.

To Find Out More:
Royal Naval Headquarters Merseyside
Phone: 0151 707 3344
http://www.royal-navy.mod.uk/server/show/nav.2797

Past RN HQ, take the first road on the left into Navigation Wharf; opposite the Car Showroom.
At the T-junction, turn right and follow this narrow road as it zig-zags between the houses on the right, and the wharf on the left.
This roadway now becomes The Anchorage.

At the end of the road, turn left at the T-junction into Mariners Wharf and, parking briefly on the left just before the security gates, will give you excellent views of Coburg Dock on the left, and of Queen's Dock and the Watersports Centre on the right.

Coburg Dock

Coburg Dock was first developed in 1823, and was completed in a major reconstruction of Liverpool's southern waterfront, between 1857 and 1858. The dock took in general cargo, such as fruit and palm oil, in trade with West Africa and Portugal but, from 1906, much of Liverpool's expanding grain trade was centred on the Coburg Granary, which once stood on the dockside.

Coburg Dock, in common with the northern bank of Brunswick Dock, is now the home of **Liverpool Marina**. This has berths for 325 boats, and access from here to the river is via a dedicated lock. There is a full range of service and maintenance facilities available for yachtsmen and yachtswomen who not only live locally, but who come here, literally, from the four corners of the world. Alongside the dock is the Harbourside Club, which has a bar, restaurant, and Club House facilities for the Liverpool Yacht Club, and the Marina.

Queen's Dock

To the right of Coburg Dock and Liverpool Marina, the next dock in the system is Queen's Dock, which cost £35,000 to build, and was opened on 17th April 1796. The first vessel to enter this very large dock was the American brig 'The Baltimore', although Queen's Dock mainly received Dutch freight vessels, mostly carrying timber; and also whaling vessels of the Baltic Fleet.

The dock is an impressive construction – its gates alone are 42 feet wide and 28 feet deep. The length of the east side is 460 yards, and the west side measures 435 yards long; the north end measures 110 yards long, and the south end 90 yards. Over the entrance is a handsome cast iron swivel bridge, and under this the waterway links directly with Wapping Dock and Wapping Basin, Duke's Dock, the Albert Dock and, through Salthouse Dock, to Canning Dock.

Falling derelict, along with the rest of the Central Docks during the 1960s and 70s, Queen's Dock received a new lease of life when, with the Albert Dock, it was dredged out in the mid 1980s, restored and made the location for a magnificent building that became home to **Her Majesty's Customs & Excise Department**. This five-storey, rectangular and somewhat prison-like structure – perhaps reflecting its function – straddles the old graving dock, and faces the riverfront, overlooking the Riverside Walk. This promenade was constructed by the Merseyside Development Corporation, again in the 1980s, to open up three miles of riverfront between the Pier Head and the Dingle.

"For obvious reasons, the Customs Building is known locally as 'The VATican'!"

Queen's Dock is also the home of the **Liverpool Watersports Centre**, and this well-equipped facility, almost in the heart of Liverpool city-centre, has proved to be a very popular local resource. The centre is the base of operations for **Merseysport**; an organisation that provides quality instruction in all aspects of sailing and watersports. And so, as well as providing a base from which to chase and capture smugglers, Queen's Dock offers opportunities for people to experience directly the skills that made Liverpool great, by taking to the river and the seas themselves.

To Find Out More:
Liverpool Watersports Centre
Phone: 0151 708 9322
www.merseysport.org.uk

Continue along Mariner's Wharf, and follow it as it bends to the left, and as it runs parallel to the river. The road then leads you to Liverpool Marina Bar and Restaurant, where you can park for a break, a snack and a stroll around the Marina. I suggest a 15-minute stop here; longer if you are eating.

Liverpool Watersports Centre with the 'VATican' in the background

Liverpool Marina and Yacht Club

6

Liverpool Yacht Club was founded in 1988, with the establishment of the Marina, and racing is the backbone of the Club's activity. This is a year-round sport, and races take place every weekend – tides permitting. During the summer months there is also an evening series of races, and these cover not only the Mersey Estuary, but also Liverpool Bay, and further afield in the Irish Sea. During the winter, racing is confined to the river.

Races are run under both Channel and LBSA (Liverpool Bay Sailing Association) handicap systems, and they offer competitive sailing for all classes of boats.

The sight of all the yachts at anchor in the Marina is glorious, as this affirms the economic growth of the City. But what is really exciting, is seeing them all sailing out into the river to take part in races, or just for the pleasant experience of sailing on the waters of the Mersey river and its estuary.

Liverpool Marina

To Find Out More:
Liverpool Yacht Club
Commodore John D'Henin
Phone: 0151 677 7305
www.lyc.org.uk

Liverpool Marina
Phone: Office   0151 707 6777
Harbour Club & Bar 0151 707 6888
www.liverpoolmarina.com

Turn left out of the Liverpool Marina car park, onto South Ferry Quay. You will pass the yacht-repair yard on the right, and the slipway on the left, in the heart of this modern residential estate. At the end of the road is a large turning circle, with parking bays. From here you can see the control room for the lock into the Marina; the business premises that cover Brunswick Dock, across the wharf; and more excellent views across the river.

Reverse your route along South Ferry Quay, past the Yacht Club and Marina Bar, returning along Coburg Wharf and Mariner's Wharf to re-join the main road once more at Sefton Street. Turn left here at the traffic lights, and continue across the next set of traffic lights, at Parliament Street, onto Chaloner Street. You will pass the Dolby Hotel and the Leo Casino on the left.

At the next set of traffic lights, turn right into Blundell Street – McDonalds will be on the corner. Park anywhere here that is safe and convenient.

From here you can walk back over the road to take a good look at Wapping Warehouse; the Small Police Station; and the Pump House. You will also get a good view of King's Dock and of the ECHO Arena and BT Convention Centre from this point.

NB: Do make a point of looking at the cast iron stanchions, against the Dock Wall, in front of the Wapping Warehouse Apartments, as these are all that now remains of the Overhead Railway track.

I suggest a 15 minute stroll around Wapping Dock.

7

Jesse Hartley and Wapping Dock

As we cross over the traffic lights at Parliament Street, onto Chaloner Street, we come into the southern end of the City-centre. On the left, we then drive past a couple of budget hotels and a casino that stand overlooking Queen's Dock, but then the next building that we pass on the roadside, is the magnificent Wapping Dock Warehouse, with its adjoining Gate Keeper's Lodge.

The great Victorian engineer, Jesse Hartley, began construction of the dock and its buildings in 1850, and it was opened in 1856.

Jesse Hartley

Jesse Hartley was born in Pontefract in Yorkshire, on 21st December 1780, and he was the son of Bernard Hartley, who was a stonemason, architect, and bridgemaster. The first engineering project that he worked on was the bridge at Ferrybridge, which Jesse assisted his father in building, in 1804. Then father and son built a bridge at Castleford.

Despite having no experience of dock building, Hartley applied for an engineering position at Liverpool Docks. He was successful and, on 24th March 1824, was appointed as a temporary Deputy Dock Surveyor, under the Liverpool architect John Foster Jnr. Then, a few days later and for an unknown reason, Foster resigned his post, Hartley was promoted, and his position made permanent. Whatever the circumstances were that led to this turn of events, Jesse was to remain as Liverpool's Dock Engineer for over 30 years, and he was to become the world's first full-time professional Dock Engineer.

"He had genuine skill, and a style of management that was unique"

First, instead of employing outside contractors, which was the norm at that time, Hartley set up what he called 'The Dock Yard', and employed specialist craftsmen and labourers to carry out all the work 'in-house'. He also devised a new system of monitoring and administrating the ordering and use of work, time, labour, and materials; and he fully understood the concept of cost-effective time-and-motion efficiency.

The Liverpool Waterfront

Hartley's reputation began to spread outside Liverpool, and he accepted a number of private commissions as consultant engineer, including the building of the Grosvenor Bridge in Chester, in 1826, and work on the Liverpool to Manchester Railway, in 1827. Nevertheless, the Docks were his first love and his driving priority and, from 1830, he directed the construction of –

Clarence Dock	– opened 1830
Brunswick Dock	– opened 1832
Waterloo Dock	– opened 1834
Victoria Dock	– opened 1836
Trafalgar Dock	– opened 1836
Albert Dock	– opened by the Prince Consort in 1846
Salisbury Dock	– opened 1848
Collingwood Dock	– opened 1848
Stanley Dock	– opened 1848
Nelson Dock	– opened 1848
Bramley-Moore Dock	– opened 1848
Sandon Dock	– opened 1849
Wapping Dock	– opened 1850
Wellington Dock	– opened 1851
Huskisson Dock	– opened 1852
Canada Dock	– opened 1859

– and also many of the warehouses, slipways, walls, gateways, lodges, dock-master's houses etc etc, that went with them. Hartley also modernised all of the docks that had pre-existed his appointment, except the original Old Dock, which had been filled in by this time.

Hartley's innovations in creating the high Dock Wall (now an integral part of our World Heritage Site); the increased use of locks and internal canals, linking all the docks together; the use of hydraulics to operate cranes, lifting gear, and lock-gate pumping-houses; all clearly demonstrate the energy, ingenuity, and vision of this Victorian leader of the Industrial Revolution.

Jesse Hartley died at his Bootle home, on 24th August 1860, not long after retiring as Dock Engineer. He was buried at St Mary's Church in Bootle, and the City of Liverpool owes him a great deal. Fortunately, so much of his work survives that we can continue to marvel at, respect, and enjoy his buildings today.

Wapping Dock

Wapping Dock was one of Jesse Hartley's later projects, and the Wapping Warehouse was constructed in the same style and form as the Albert Dock. His design incorporated brick vaulting over a cast-iron frame, and the warehouse originally had forty bays, each divided into five, separate, fireproof sections. There is also a row of cast-iron Doric columns supporting great brick arches. This was a state-of-the-art facility for the time and, as at Albert Dock, there were hydraulic lifts to raise and lower goods between the floors. Of real interest though, are the two structures to the right of the

gateway to the dock. The first is a small, round building, with a conical tower, and medieval styling. This was the Gate-Keeper's Lodge, and actually contained what was once the smallest Police Station in Britain, but this is no longer in use – although I am informed that it has never actually been decommissioned!

Behind this, looking like a miniature castle, with another tiny castle on its roof, is the mock-gothic, turreted, pump-house, which controlled the dock gates.

The former Police Station at the entrance to Wapping Quay

One of the most significant features of the Wapping Warehouse itself, was that it was once regularly served – as was the nearby but now demolished LMS Railway Depot – by an underground railway line. This ran from here, back up to the station at Crown Street in the district of Edge Hill, which was the original location of the terminus for the railway coming into Liverpool. (See Chapter: 'Pool of Life & Culture'.)

At first, the early steam locomotives did not have the power to pull wagons laden with heavy goods up the gradient from Wapping to Crown Street, and this was so steep that there was also a risk of the trains running away down the hill to crash at the bottom.

To solve this problem, an ingenious steam-powered pulley system was installed, which carried a rope through ducts in the ground, in a circuit between both stations. Stationary engines were installed at Crown Street, to haul the trains through the tunnel by ropes fed over the pulley wheels. Trains would run down the gradient to Wapping Goods Station by gravity – controlled by a brakeman – and were hauled back up by the powered ropes, which were attached to a heavy geared counterweight.

In due course, locomotives became powerful enough to overcome the gradient problem, and so the winches fell into disuse. Remnants of the pulley, the ducts, and the pumping station, which archaeologists believe were in use until 1870, still survive; the Victorians seem to have simply buried the system when it was abandoned.

"The Wapping Tunnel is 2,250 yards long. It was completed in 1829, and is only one of many mid-to-late 19th century railway tunnels that criss-cross Liverpool City-centre"

These still exist under the bustling and sometimes congested City streets, but only a few are still used. Nevertheless, they have recently been the subject of much discussion, about possible underground road links from Edge Hill into the City centre. This is an interesting idea, and it remains to be seen if a practical use can be found for these remarkable feats of early Victorian civil engineering.

Like so many of Liverpool's docks, Wapping suffered some severe bomb-damage during the Second World War, and part of it was completely demolished. An indication of the fact that the warehouse was originally 232 metres long, are the surviving, free-standing cast-iron columns that stand incongruously on the quayside.

With the post-War decline of the Liverpool Docks, and of the City economy generally, the old warehouse was empty and derelict for decades. However, in the early 1990s, it became part of the initial stages of the regeneration of Liverpool's waterfront. Consequently, Wapping Warehouse was successfully converted into an attractive, modern, residential complex, and renamed as Wapping Quay Apartments. As part of the restoration work, the Hydraulic Tower, which stands on the left of the gates into Wapping Dock, and the Gatekeeper's Lodge on the right, were returned to their former glory: Another tribute to the great Jesse Hartley.

As you drive alongside the Dock Wall, in front of the Wapping Quay Dock Warehouse, you can see some truncated cast-iron girders, about 6 or 7 feet high, mounted against the wall and set in concrete plinths. These are the supporting stanchions of the Overhead Railway track, and are all that remain of this remarkable transportation system.

To Find Out More:
Merseyside Maritime Museum:
http://www.liverpoolmuseums.org.uk/maritime

http://www.timbosliverpool.co.uk/docks/

This is one of the most exciting parts of the City in terms of public amenity and attractions. Apart from the magnificent Albert Dock, which we shall visit shortly, here you will find much new housing; apartment, hotel, and office developments; and a riverside walk. Behind the Wapping Warehouse and next to Queen's Dock, is King's Dock, where a £20 million luxury apartment block has been built overlooking this now filled-in dock site.

It is on King's Dock that Everton Football Club once hoped to build their new stadium, combined with a sports and concert arena with 55,000 seats, at a cost of £300 million. But this proved impractical.

As this was a prestige site, the Liverpool Vision Board decided to try to find other developers for the site, providing that a major conference/events/sports arena formed the principal element of any new scheme.

Eventually, English Partnerships – who own the land; Liverpool Vision; the North West Development Agency; Liverpool City Council; and Government Office North West, all of whom had an interest in the site, agreed a new plan. Work began in October 2005, on a remarkable building that has cost over £140 million and which is named the ECHO Arena and BT Convention Centre Liverpool.

With around 10,600 seats, this is capable of conversion to an exhibition facility of around

ECHO Arena Liverpool

70,000 sq feet. There is also a conference facility, with a 1,350 seat auditorium, and a multi-purpose hall covering 40,000 sq feet.

The success of both the Arena and Convention Centre can only be described as 'outstanding'! The building has gained an international reputation for excellence in terms of facilities, quality, technological excellence and service. Very large Party Political, Union, Professional, and Business conventions take place here, supported by magnificent exhibition facilities. In the Arena, world class performers regularly play to capacity audiences. From animatronic dinosaurs to ice-spectaculars,; from opera stars to international rock stars and bands; from the greatest orchestras in the world to favourite stand-up comedians;

audiences travel here for the very best shows. When the plans for the arena were being drawn up, it was also recognised that the whole area around it could become a major accommodation, parking and catering 'plaza'; not only serving the thousands of people who would be using the new complex, but for Liverpudlians and tourists as well. Now, these plans have been fulfilled, and the space adds another remarkable dimension to the waterfront.

To Find Out More:
Arena and Conference Centre
Phone: 0151 475 8888
www.accliverpool.co.uk

Wapping

9

Chaloner Street now becomes Wapping, and beyond Wapping Dock and opposite Albert Dock are some more budget hotels – the Ibis and The Formula 1 – and also the imposing building which is the **Headquarters of Merseyside Police**.

This tall, rectangular, sandstone block of a building, overlooks Canning Place where the **Central Bus Station** stands. This is also one of the access points into the Liverpool ONE retail and commercial centre (see Chapter: 'Heart of the City'). It was here also that the original **Pool of Liverpool** and later the **Old Dock** once stood.

It is at Canning Place that Wapping now becomes Strand Street, and it is at this point that part of the new commercial area includes **Chavasse Park** – an elevated area of public open space named after a local hero.

"The Rt. Rev Francis James Chavasse (1846-1928), was Anglican Bishop of Liverpool from 1900 to 1923"

He was responsible for inaugurating the building of Liverpool Cathedral, and it is largely because of his efforts that the project actually began and moved ahead at such a rapid pace, considering how mammoth a task it was. He lies buried in the Cathedral, to which he contributed so much of his life.

Chavasse Park commemorates his son Noel (1884-1917), who was posthumously awarded two Victoria Crosses for conspicuous bravery, whilst serving with the Royal Army Medical Corps during The Great War of 1914-18.

Noel Chavasse is only one of Liverpool's many heroes who, over the years, have brought honour to the City.

Deep below Chavasse Park, and the car park for which it is the roof, sits the original Old Dock of Liverpool – or at least what could be saved during the excavations of Liverpool ONE.

As this was being built, archaeologists moved in to rediscover the source of Liverpool's commercial greatness. It was found that a significant section could be saved and preserved; and, if Grosvenor – the developers– were willing to change their construction plans, opened to the public. Thanks to Grosvenor, this was done, and now you can book on a tour to go underground, and see 'where it all began'!

A building of note on this side of Strand Street, is the **Queen Elizabeth II Courts Building**. This imposing granite and sandstone edifice is remarkable only for one particular thing; that it is alleged to have the greatest number of lavatories in any public building in Britain!

Strand Street now becomes The Strand and, at the corner of James Street, which leads up the hill into the City-centre, stands **Albion House**. I will tell of this building, and of its associations with the ill-fated RMS Titanic, in due course.

The Liverpool Waterfront

Turn around in Blundell Street so that you are facing the river again. Turn right at the traffic lights back onto Wapping, now passing the Wapping Warehouse on the left and the Baltic Fleet Pub on the right. You will also pass the casino and a couple of hotels on the left. Take the next road on the left, which is Gower Street into the Albert Dock complex. Follow the signs for the car park, and park in any of the bays as soon as you find one, this gets busy! You will be able to see the Arena and Convention Centre on the left.

From here, we shall visit all the shopping and restaurant areas of Albert Dock, and I suggest a 1-hour stopping time to do this; including time for a drink and a snack, or a light meal.

From here we can also visit the Beatles Story, the Tate Gallery, the International Slavery Museum, the Merseyside Maritime Museum, and the HM Customs & Excise Museum. However, as mentioned at the beginning of this Tour, unless you want a very long day, I suggest that you return to visit these (and take your Ferry Trip – see Mersey Ferries article) as a separate, full day trip.

Nevertheless, there is time in this Tour to visit the Dock itself, one or two of the attractions, and to have a good look at the buildings and shops.

The Albert Dock

The dock in front of the Albert Dock Warehouses, facing Wapping, is Salthouse Dock. This was designed by Thomas Steers, who had previously designed the Old Dock.

Originally named the South Dock, this opened in 1753, but the name was later changed to the Salthouse Dock, because of the salt storage warehouses that once stood on the quayside here.

Before the Albert Dock was built – between 1840 and 1845, the land to the west of Salthouse Dock, fronting the river, contained shipbuilding yards. However, it was decided to create a new, much larger dock, completely surrounded by state-of-the-art warehousing, and so, an Act of Parliament was passed in 1840, and the shipbuilders vacated the site – many moving to the Birkenhead side of the river.

As we have seen, the engineer and architect Jesse Hartley designed this spectacular complex, and it was the world's first fully-enclosed, complete dock and hydraulic cargo-handling system. It was also the first

The Albert Dock

to be built of incombustible materials, using his design for a cast iron, stone, and brick structure, with an innovative, stressed-skin, galvanised iron roof. Hartley also used other, more traditional construction techniques and designs in the complex.

In 1846, the Prince Consort, after whom it was named, officially opened the dock, and it was to become the new heart of the seafaring commerce of the Town. At the opening, Prince Albert said,

"I have heard of the greatness of Liverpool but the reality far surpasses the expectation"

The warehouse buildings around the new dock made the loading and unloading of vessels a very rapid and efficient process, aided by the mechanical lifting and handling devices. The storage facilities were bonded, which meant that import tax became payable only when the goods were ready to leave the warehouse, by which time the owner would have already sold the goods in advance, and so raised the necessary cash to pay the taxes.

Goods handled, stored, and then shipped out again from Albert Dock included plant products like hemp, cotton, sugar, and jute. These were seasonal, so merchants could store them in the warehouses, and then distribute them gradually throughout the year, thus maintaining an income stream and keeping the markets buoyant.

Also, because of the secure nature of the facilities, the Albert Dock warehouses proved ideal for storing very valuable cargoes, such as brandy, tea, cotton, silk, tobacco, and sugar. Nevertheless, as successful as the Albert Dock was, by the 1860s it was losing business. This was due to the fact that Hartley had originally designed it to accommodate sailing ships, not the new breed of large, steam paddle-ships or screw-propelled steamships; the dock basin and entrance were simply too small. Also, these vessels required greater quayside space to handle and move their cargoes, and this is very limited at Albert Dock.

"So the warehouses, which had initially made the Dock popular and profitable, now became its 'Achilles heel'"

Over the next three decades, trade declined at Albert Dock to such an extent that one of the warehouses was then used as a cold store, and for producing ice for packing fish onboard Liverpool's trawler fleet. By 1920, there were almost no commercial ships sailing into the dock, and the warehouses were now only being used for storing goods carried by road, barge, or rail: its glory days had long passed.

Used fully once more, by merchant and military vessels during the Second World War, the Albert Dock complex was very badly damaged as a result of bombing raids carried out by the German Luftwaffe.

But, by the beginning of the 1950s, the use of the dock was again steadily declining, as the whole of the Liverpool Docks system fell into economic degeneration. By 1972, the warehouses had been abandoned and the dock itself completely silted up, becoming a vast tank of grey-brown mud and sludge. The lock gates rusted and the timber infrastructure began to rot. And so, the Albert Dock just sat there, together with so many of Merseyside's docks; in their squalid decay and deterioration – yet another forlorn monument to our once-great City.

In the wake of the Toxteth Riots of 1981, a major triumph of the MDC was the complete restoration, refurbishment, and redevelopment of the entire Albert Dock complex as a major commercial and tourist centre. Significant financial and skills resources were invested in the project, resulting in the successful creation of a very attractive range of shops, bars, restaurants, offices, apartments, and museums.

The new Albert Dock was formally re-opened by The Prince of Wales, in May 1988, and it is now often quoted as being one of the most popular tourist attractions in the UK, outside London.

Two buildings of particular interest at the Dock are the Dock Traffic Office, built in 1847, and the Hydraulic Pumping Station, built in 1870. The former building has four stunning cast iron columns supporting an attractive portico, and on the roof, the chimney stacks have been fashioned to look like vanes. As you will see shortly, this building is now home to The International Slavery Museum.

The Pumping Station, with its tall and ornate chimney stack, was the power source for the swing bridge and the gates at the Canning Half-Tide Dock. Unfortunately, the construction site was ill-chosen and, by the time that restoration was a real possibility in the mid-1980s, serious subsidence had taken place. This necessitated the removal of most of the interior of the building and of all of the old machinery. The shell now contains a very attractive pub and restaurant, and the successful salvage and redesign of the building is a tribute to the modern architects and builders.

In due course, the Albert Dock Company was formed, to take over the management of the Dock, as the Merseyside Development Corporation wound itself up in the late 1980s. The new company succeeded in attracting businesses, enterprises, and tourists to the site; guaranteeing the financial security of the Dock. Building on this success, the Albert Dock Company is currently spending £40 million on redevelopment and further reconstruction, designed to attract larger retailers and business onto what is now the largest group of Grade I Listed buildings in England.

To Find Out More:
The Albert Dock
Phone: 0151 708 7334
www.albertdock.com

To completely explore Albert Dock, I suggest the following walking route:

Once you have parked your car, walk towards the Dock Buildings and you will see the Beatles Museum down a set of steps. Visit this first. Then, go into the Warehouses and turn left. Simply follow the Dock all the way around and you will pass many shops, cafes, sweet shops, restaurants and, most helpfully I am sure – lavatories. You will also come to the Tate Gallery.

After visiting this gallery of contemporary art, follow the perimeter of the Dock, as it now turns right, and walk towards the Maritime Museum. From here you will not only be able to visit all the galleries and exhibits inside the building, but also the dock-buildings and docks that form part of this remarkable museum. The Customs and Excise Museum is in the same building and, from here, you can also visit The International Slavery Museum.

From the Maritime Museum complex, again follow the perimeter buildings around the Dock, to complete a full circle and return you to the car park, near the Beatles Story Experience.

NB: Whilst you are walking around outside the Maritime Museum, do have a look inside the large Pump House Pub, with its tall chimney. This is not only a remarkable piece of reconstruction and salvage work – the building had a massive crack right through it – But it is a good place for a pint and a meal.

The Beatles Story Experience

The Beatles Story Experience was opened in the basement of the Albert Dock, in 1989. Visitors can take a stroll through the cobbled streets of Hamburg, where the Beatles learned their trade as performers at the Star Club. There is also a re-creation of Mathew Street, complete with a replica of the Cavern Club as it appeared in 1962.

The story of the 'Fab Four' then moves forward to the 'flower power' era of the 1960s, when the Beatles became 'Flower Children'.

The final exhibit is the 'White Room'; a poignant re-creation of the room in the home of John Lennon and Yoko Ono, where John composed perhaps his most famous song, 'Imagine'.

The actual Steinway piano, on which he wrote the song, is the centre-piece of the display, and it is on loan to the exhibition from its current owner, George Michael.

The Beatles Story at Albert Dock

> "The song plays softly in the background, as you look at the piano and the otherwise empty room"

As the melody fills the plain and minimalist space, one cannot help but be moved by the tragedy of John's life; being cut short so brutally when, in 1980, he was shot and killed outside his New York apartment, by Mark Chapman. There is now also a tribute to George Harrison in the Museum, whose life was also unfortunately shortened, this time by the lung-cancer.

The museum is one of the highlights of any visit to the City, and a star attraction at the Albert Dock.

To Find Out More:
The Beatles Story Experience
Phone: 0151 709 1963
www.beatlesstory.com

Tate Liverpool ⑫

The Tate Gallery

Tate Liverpool first opened in 1988, as the first branch of the famous London gallery, and it is named after the Liverpool sugar merchant Henry Tate (1890-1955). In a way, the gallery has now 'come home', to establish itself in part of the warehouse complex at the Albert Dock, only a mile or so down the dock road, from where the Tate & Lyle sugar refinery used to stand.

The art gallery is the home of the **National Collection of Modern Art in the North of England**, and was designed by the architect James Stirling, who died in 1992.

The Gallery was subsequently redeveloped, in November 1996, to provide more space for educational activities and events, and improved visitor facilities. Now, Tate Liverpool houses two main types of exhibits; art selected from the Tate Collection, and special exhibitions of contemporary art – bringing together works loaned from other collections, both public and private. The Gallery has always displayed the widest and most provocative variety of objects and images from the field of modern and contemporary art: from the worlds of photography, printmaking, video, performance, and installation, as well as painting and sculpture.

Tate Liverpool has won an international reputation for the range and quality of its displays, collections, and visitor programmes, and makes a particularly fascinating place to visit.

To Find Out More:
Tate Liverpool
Phone: 0151 702 7400
www.tate.org.uk/liverpool

The Merseyside Maritime Museum ⑬

The Maritime Museum is genuinely exciting and fascinating, and exploring it really does begin to unfold the rich history of our seafaring life.

Exhibitions include the history of local shipbuilding; collections of intricately detailed ship-designers' models; and specialist galleries covering such subjects as Emigration and the Titanic.

The collection that was to eventually form the modern Merseyside Maritime Museum began, in 1862, with the donation of a ship model to the Town, initially housed at Liverpool Museum.
In the late 1970s, and thanks to the support of then Merseyside County Council, work began on the creation of a dedicated maritime museum on the Liverpool waterfront.

This opened first, for a trial season in 1980, in old workshop sheds and pilotage buildings that were specially converted for the purpose. These buildings went on to become the Museum of Liverpool Life. However, as we have seen, because of the work of the Merseyside Development Corporation the restoration of the Albert Dock began in 1982. The Maritime Museum then had number of small galleries on the ground floor of the dock warehouse building, just for the Tall Ships Race in 1984, and the **Piermaster's House** was opened to the public in the same year. By 1986, work was completed on the warehouse that currently houses the Museum, and they moved in formally that year. The Museum is housed in the entire Block D of the Albert Dock warehouse complex, and the floors and rooms of the building have been imaginatively redeveloped as galleries, whilst retaining the magnificence of Jesse Hartley's original design. However, this is not all there is to the Maritime Museum, because it also includes all the surrounding dockside buildings, wharves, and docks.

> "You can walk through fully restored dock houses, offices, and workshops, and watch craftsmen performing time-honoured skills in their original surroundings"

Outside, the dry and wet docks house vessels that are also open to visitors, and which are accessed via pathways and bridges, and across dock gates and locks that really add to the experience.

The Maritime Museum also houses Her Majesty's Customs and Excise National Museum, named, **Anything to Declare?** Here, you can find out all about the history of smugglers and how they were, and are – though not always – apprehended by the ever-vigilant forces of The Queen's Excise men and women.

To Find Out More:
Merseyside Maritime Museum
Phone: 0151 478 4499
www.liverpoolmuseums.org.uk/maritime
HM Customs & Excise National Museum
Phone: 0151 478 4499
http://www.liverpoolmuseums.org.uk/customs/

The Maritime Museum

Arguably, the most attractive building in the complex of structures at the Albert Dock is the **Dock Traffic Office**, which was built between 1846 and 1847. This was also designed by Jesse Hartley, in collaboration with Philip Hardwick, and is built of brick, with red sandstone dressings, but its most notable feature is the cast iron Tuscan portico and frieze. This building was the centre of operations for the Dock, and it was from here that its entire use and management was directed.

National Museums Liverpool acquired the building and, following a major, £10 million pound expansion and refurbishment, reopened it in 2007 as The International Slavery Museum.

This Museum is of particular significance in Liverpool, because the City became wealthy and powerful as a result of its trade in tobacco, sugar, and rum, but principally in cotton. The production and transportation of these commodities was dependant on the Slave Trade and, because of this, Liverpool encouraged and invested heavily in this traffic in human life and misery. (This is why Liverpool took the cause of the Confederacy during the American Civil War, sending ships and money to support them.)

Slavery had been a normal and socially acceptable trade throughout Britain since 1553, when the first regular trading took place with Africa. However, the very first slaving ship to set sail from Liverpool was 'The Liverpool Merchant', which sold a cargo of 220 slaves in Barbados, in 1700. Then, in 1737, Liverpool began to invest seriously in the **Triangular Trade**. This was so-called because it consisted of trade goods being shipped from Britain to Africa; slaves then being abducted from Africa and transported to the plantations of America and the West Indies; and sugar, cotton, and tobacco then being shipped to Britain.

"Vast fortunes were made for many Liverpool ship owners and, in 1771 alone, 105 ships sailed from Liverpool to West Africa, and transported 28,200 slaves to the West Indies"

Very few slaves actually set foot in Liverpool, although records show that some people – men, women, and children – were occasionally sold at small, local auctions; and others became house slaves for the more wealthy families in the Town. Nevertheless, you may hear tales of shackles and iron rings, fastened to the walls of dock buildings in the City, but these stories have no basis in fact.

The galleries and exhibits in the Museum are moving and sometimes disturbing, detailing as they do the City's association with this disgraceful traffic in human life. The vivid portrayals of the violent seizure of peaceful and settled people from their homes, and of their subsequent transportation in the bowels of squalid ships, to plantations in America and British Colonies, are powerful indeed.

Most heart-rending though, are the descriptions of the reality of transportation on the **Middle Passage** across the Atlantic, which could take 50-60 days, often in appalling weather conditions.

Packed tightly together on hard, wooden shelves; manacled and chained together naked, with no room to move; given inadequate food; and with no way to relieve themselves other than where they lay; afflicted by sea-sickness, dysentery, and terror, the conditions were foul beyond belief. Many people did not survive the crossing. The personal testimonies of slaves and their descendants serve to clearly illustrate just how Liverpool became wealthy, and Britain became 'Great', through the exploitation of our fellow human beings.

It is estimated that, from the middle of the 15th century to the end of the 19th century, more than 12 million Africans were kidnapped from their homes. In the 18th century alone, 6 million African slaves were transported to the American plantations and, shamefully, Britain had the most powerful of the slave trading fleets.

As the most 'successful' slave trading port Liverpool's record is a real indictment and, during the City's involvement in the trade, 1,360,000 African people were transported in over 5,000 voyages of Liverpool vessels. Indeed, more than half of all slaves sold by English traders were the property of Liverpool merchants and, by the end of the 18th century, the Town had 70% of Britain's Slave Trade.

However, in 1787, a petition for the suppression of the Slave Trade was handed to Parliament from some members of the Society of Friends. Because of this action, in 1788, Liverpool Town Corporation formally declared its opposition to the abolition of the Slave Trade. Nevertheless, and despite years of public meetings, acrimonious debate, protectionism, and downright ignorance, a Bill for the Abolition of Slavery was carried through Parliament in 1807. This outlawed the transportation of slaves by British ships, thus ending the 'Triangular Trade'. The use of slave labour in British colonies, however, did not end until 1836.

Despite this 'loss of revenue' the Port grew at a phenomenal rate, thanks to families like the Rathbones, Holts, Rankins, and Bibbys, who were a new breed of entrepreneurial ship-owners, trading in a variety of goods, other than in human life.

The International Slavery Museum

"They laid the foundation for Liverpool's massive expansion and economic success through the 19th and early 20th centuries"

Liverpool as a City, and as a community of diverse and multi-racial peoples, fully recognises this blight on our history.

However, many other British towns and cities played their part too, and also have the taint of slavery in their histories.

Not least of all being those who provided the goods that were traded for the enslaved people, on the first part of the 'Triangular Trade'.

● Pottery and earthenware – from Stoke and Staffordshire
● Cheap jewellery – from Lancashire towns
● Cotten and linen – from Manchester
● Woollen goods – from Leeds and Bradford
● Glassware – from St Helens
● Knives and axes – from Sheffield

They were all culpable.

The International Slavery Museum in Liverpool not only provides an opportunity for learning and understanding about the Slave Trade, but it is a memorial to the hundreds of thousands of innocent people who suffered and died to make others rich and powerful. Hopefully, it will also go some way towards raising awareness of the joy of diversity, and of the need to combat racism and prejudice, in all its forms and manifestations.

To Find Out More:
The International Slavery Museum
http://www.internationalslavery
museum.org.uk/about.html

The Liverpool Waterfront

From The Albert Dock, return to Wapping and turn left, to continue our journey along the Waterfront.

Passing Salthouse Dock on the left, and the Headquarters of Merseyside Police; Canning Place Bus Station; and the massive new Liverpool ONE retail development on the right, head towards the Liver Building and the other 'Three Graces', that you will see in front of you on the left. From this point the road becomes Strand Street, and you will also pass the north entrance to Albert Dock on the left: You will see the Dock Traffic Office at the end of this road. Cross over all the sets of traffic lights, including those at Mann Island on the left and James Street on the right. On the corner of James Street you will be able to see Albion House. This red-and-white striped building was the home of the White Star Shipping Line.

Once across the junction, take any of the roads on the left, between the Three Graces, and park in the first available pay-and-display bay. There are lots of them in and around this area, but the one-way system can mean that you have to make a couple of circuits to find a parking space. Make sure that you have enough coins for the meters because from here we shall explore the whole Pier Head area.

Wherever you park in this area, begin your gentle stroll by walking back towards Mann Island in the direction of the Albert Dock. Mann Island is a road, but it is also the land between the road and the edge of the docks at the Maritime Museum, which stand three monolithic, black buildings: all part of the new retail, office and apartment development. I suggest 45 minutes just to walk around, but additional time if you have pre-booked a tour of the Royal Liver Building; and an extra hour if you intend to take a trip on the Mersey Ferry. (Do make sure you have checked departure and arrival times beforehand).

Mann Island and The Museum of Liverpool

Mann Island is now a road that leads from The Strand, opposite James Street, down to the river alongside George's Dock Building and the Port of Liverpool Building, and it is also the piece of land between this and the docks of the Maritime Museum. On this now stands a commercial development.

However, at one time, it actually was an island – of sorts – and it has an interesting history.

This part of the waterfront, in the early 18th century, was known as **Nova Scotia**, probably because of the number of seafarers and merchants who either sailed to, or traded with Nova Scotia in the New World. In 1767, work began on constructing George's Dock, and a local merchant, **John Mann** – who was an oil-stone dealer and walking-stick maker – would continuously brag to his friends and neighbours that he would soon be living on an island. Indeed, when the dock opened in 1771, the area where John lived became surrounded by water on three sides, and jokingly became known as 'Mann's Island' as a result.

The name stuck and, in fact, the Town Corporation officially adopted the name 'Mann Island' for the area. John Mann died in 1784, but the name continued even though, in 1900, most of the land was reclaimed so that the new buildings at the Pier Head could be constructed. These were The George's Dock Building and the three structures that, collectively, are often referred to as 'The Three Graces': The Port of Liverpool Building; The Cunard Building; and The Royal Liver Building.

Whilst the island has now been covered by the new office and apartment blocks, at the bottom of the road, overlooking the river, is the stunning new Museum of Liverpool. This replaced The Museum of Liverpool Life, which stood, until June 2006, in converted old pilotage buildings and ship-repair sheds, near the dry docks in the open-air section Maritime Museum.

Now, in a striking, white marble building in the shape of a stylised 'X', and with spectacular views of the Pier Head plaza and the river, the new Museum tells the history of the people and the place.

In four key themes: the Great Port; Global City; People's Republic; and Wondrous Place, and in four large gallery spaces, visitors can encounter, engage with, and be entertained by remarkable items in the collection.

The Museum of Liverpool cost over £65m and is the centrepiece of the combination of buildings at Mann Island, on the waterfront World Heritage Site.

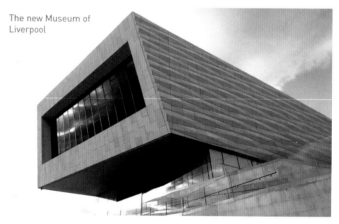

The new Museum of Liverpool

Running along the Pier Head, between the 'Three Graces' and the riverfront, and also passing beneath the Museum, is the newest canal to be cut anywhere in the UK – the extension to the **Leeds-Liverpool Canal**.

In keeping with the designs of the great dock engineers of Liverpool, and using appropriate materials, this new cutting connects the canal from where it originally terminated, at Stanley Dock (which I shall describe later in this chapter), with Princes, Albert, Salthouse and Coburg docks, and on to the South Docks. This means that narrow boats can now sail from the heart of the City of Leeds, directly into the modern and historic waterfront of the City of Liverpool.

Before leaving Mann Island to look at the four remarkable buildings along the roadside here, it is worth just looking back across the central reservation in the middle of the dual-carriageway; this was once the site of the Goree Warehouses. Beyond this, you will see again, Albion House.

To Find Out More:
The Museum of Liverpool
www.liverpoolmuseums.org.uk

Albion House

Opposite Mann Island, Albion House can be seen on the corner of James Street and The Strand and, built in 1898; the 'streaky bacon building' was one of the first of the new commercial buildings to draw inspiration from America.

The architect, Richard Norman Shaw (1831-1912), who had previously built London's New Scotland Yard, reworked that design for Albion House. The building was originally the home office of the White Star Shipping Line, and Thomas Ismay, the proprietor of the shipping company, sent Shaw's collaborator, J Francis Doyle, to America to study American construction techniques.

> "The building of Albion House involved advanced methods of metal fabrication and the most modern electrical and engineering methods"

So, even though the external appearance of the building was not entirely new, its internal design and construction methods were certainly an innovation in Britain.

The White Star Shipping Line were the owners of the **Titanic** and, on the night of the 15th April 1912, frightened and angry people mobbed the building as reports came through of the Titanic's sinking, and as officials shouted news to the crowd from the cast-iron balconies above the street.

We shall discover more about 'Titanic' later in this Chapter.

> **To Find Out More:**
> **The White Star Line**
> www.titanic-titanic.com/white_star_line.shtml

Albion House

So now we shall visit, in turn, the four great buildings at the Pier Head. Do make sure that you complete a full external circuit of each one, to take a really good look at the architecture and adornments on each, before passing on to the next one.
The first is George's Dock Building which is simply outstanding, as you shall see.

17

George's Dock Building

Between James Street and the Royal Liver Building, the 'Three Graces' side of the dual-carriageway is named 'The Goree', whilst the other side is named 'The Strand'. On the corner of Mann Island and The Goree stands the tall, square tower that is George's Dock Building.

This stands on the site of what was once Liverpool's third dock, and which was first named the North Dock. It was subsequently renamed as **George's Dock**, in tribute to the reigning monarch of the time, King George III (1738-1820).

> "Construction work began in 1762 and the dock was opened, nine years later, in 1771"

Initially serving vessels trading with America and the Caribbean, after nearby Princes Dock was opened, in 1821, it lost a lot of its trade. And so, the dock was completely re-built and doubled in size.

However, at the end of the 19th century, it was decided to drain the entire area of George's Dock and use it as building land. In due course, as we shall see, 'The Three Graces' were erected on the site but, whilst The Royal Liver Building sits in the original dock, the others, and The George's Dock Building, actually sit over it. Indeed, the river still washes beneath them, and the lower sections of Water Street and Brunswick Street, between the buildings, are more like causeways. This is because they too run directly over the original dock and above the waters of the Mersey!

George's Dock Building was in fact, the last building on the former dock site, and it is the headquarters for the administration of the Mersey Tunnels. However it is principally the main ventilation shaft for the tunnel that runs between Liverpool and Birkenhead, and which is bored through the bedrock of the river. Built between 1931 and 1934, and designed by the architect, Sir Basil Mott; Liverpool

The obsidian sculpture of 'Night', at George's Dock Building

City Engineer, John Brodie; and the City architect, Herbert J Rowse, the beautiful tower – reminiscent of an Ancient Egyptian Pylon – and which is open to the sky, conceals gigantic fans. These suck down clean air and then pump it into the underground roadway. This is one of 6 such ventilation shafts for the tunnel, 3 on each side of the river, and this building is now Listed Grade II.

There is no doubt that the design and decoration of this tower is very much 'of its time': The carvings, sculptures, plaques, and embellishments, are so Art-Deco and neo-Egyptian that there is a special romance about it. Herbert Rowse contributed to the design of so many of Liverpool's buildings between the Wars, including India Buildings, the Philharmonic Hall, and the entrance portals to the Mersey Tunnel. He was particularly influenced by the opening of the tomb of the Pharaoh Tutankhamen in the mid-1920s and, consequently, Egyptian motifs feature regularly in his work.

"The black basalt figures, representing 'Night and Day' – because the tunnel never closes; the carving of 'Speed-The Modern Mercury' – with his helmet and goggles; and the panels representing engineering and construction, are all superb"

There is also a black marble memorial to the workers who died during the construction of the tunnel. However, the large relief panel entitled 'Ventilation', with its Liver Bird capitals, is like something off a 1930s film set. Just slowly walk around the building and drink in all of its early-20th century artistry.

Tours of the building and of the fans are available. These include a chance to go right down into the Mersey Tunnel refuges; and this is an opportunity not to be missed, although they only take place at particular times.

To Find Out More:
Mersey Tunnel Tours
– George's Dock Building
Phone: 0151 236 8602 etn 206

Liverpool World Heritage Bid
– Pier Head
http://www.liverpoolworldheritage
.com/pierhead.asp

So now we shall look at the structure between George's Dock Building and the River; this is The Port of Liverpool Building. Visitors can go into the atrium of this imposing structure.

The Port of Liverpool Building and The Mersey Docks and Harbour Company

The Port of Liverpool Building

The Port of Liverpool Building

The Port of Liverpool Building is Listed Grade II, and was the first of the three remarkable office buildings to be constructed at the Pier Head, and which are collectively known as **The Three Graces**. This ornate and assertive structure was built as the home of the Mersey Docks and Harbour Board (MDHB), who owned and operated all the docks on both sides of the River Mersey. (See below.)

As George's Dock was being in-filled, the MDHB reserved the southern plot of this new site to build its new headquarters.

Around the same time, the Board invited twelve local architects to design their headquarters, and they offered prizes of £300, £200, and £100 for the winning designs. The contest was won by Briggs & Wolstenholme, but the winning design did not meet all of the MDHB's requirements, and so the architects had to amend their original plans. Indeed, like others of his professional contemporaries, the principal architect of the building, Frank Briggs, was sent to America for inspiration and education.

Suitably motivated, Briggs returned to Liverpool and began work on the new plans. In 1903, and once the new design had been approved, MDHB placed the construction of the headquarters out to tender, and the firm of William Brown & Sons, of Manchester, won the contract.

Work began, and the magnificent, Edwardian, 'cathedral of commerce' was opened 1907. Constructed in Portland stone, the building has a magnificent copper dome, and is decorated with many reliefs, sculptures, niches, pediments, and other features. It is certainly impressive, and its final cost was £350,000. Inside the atrium, which is accessible by the public, are many motifs and symbols to do with international shipping and, in gold lettering around the first floor gallery, are words from the 107th Psalm, which read:

'They that go down to the sea in ships and do business in great waters, there see the works of the Lord and his wonders in the deep'.

The external features of the building include cast iron gates and gate piers, which are decorated with maritime symbols, and lamp holders in the form of naval monuments.

In 1941, the building was struck by a German bomb, which fell through the roof of the building. This burrowed its way to the basement, where it exploded causing considerable damage, and it was not until after the end of the War that the building was completely reconstructed and restored to its original magnificence.

In 1972, the Docks and Harbour Board became the Harbour Company, and the building was also given its current name.

In 1993, the MDHC moved out of the building but retained ownership until, in 2001, they sold it to the development company Downing.

As part of a £20 million investment, the building has undergone a major refurbishment, making it more accessible to the public.

To Find Out More:
Liverpool World Heritage Bid – Pier Head
http://www.liverpoolworldheritage.com/pierhead.asp

18

The Mersey Docks and Harbour Company

The Liverpool Town Corporation was the original port authority of the Liverpool Docks. As we have seen, in 1709 it commissioned the construction of the first enclosed dock on the site of the original 'Pool', and then acted as trustee of the dock estate, until 1858.

As the port expanded, and its management became more complex, between 1845 and 1847, permanent sub-committees were established to manage the finances and day-to-day operation of the rapidly expanding docks system. However, this was cumbersome and inefficient, and the Government, dock users, and competitors from Manchester, all put the Liverpool Corporation under increasing pressure to give up control. Eventually, in 1858, it was decided that a single body was needed to oversee the port, and so the Mersey Docks and Harbour Board (MDHB) was created. This comprised several committees, and it employed senior paid officials, including a harbour master, a marine surveyor, a water bailiff, and an engineer-in-chief; who were all responsible for managing not only Liverpool Docks, but also the developing docks at Birkenhead and Wallasey, across the River Mersey.

In the early 1960s, the MDHB became the first port authority in the UK, and the fourth in the world, to install computer technology. However, in the early 1970s, it was hit by a financial crisis and serious industrial unrest, and the Board almost closed down as a result. With the MDHB unable to meet its mounting debts, in 1972 an Act of Parliament changed the status of the organisation and a private company took its place, to become the Mersey Docks and Harbour Company (MDHC.)

In the same year, the three miles of the south docks, from the Pier Head to Herculaneum Dock, were closed and virtually abandoned by the company. This was because they were too shallow and their narrow quays and dockside sheds were no longer suited to the changing trends in shipping. Nevertheless, by the beginning of the 21st century, the MDHC had built Twelve Quays at Birkenhead, in 2002, creating new and improved ferry and trading links with Ireland.

"This was the Company's biggest investment since 1984, when they opened new docks and the Freeport at Seaforth, at the far north of Liverpool's Docks"

Whilst the new dock developments were taking place on the Wirral, talks were going on behind closed doors, to change the face of the MDHC forever. And, by September 2005, a merger was announced between MDHC and **The Peel Ports Group** – one of the leading property and transport companies in Britain, and with assets valued at over £2bn. This brought together the ownership and management of the Port of Liverpool with Peel's existing operations, creating one of the largest ports groups in Europe.

The Port of Liverpool continues to grow and Peel Holdings have extremely ambitious and visionary plans to revitalise and reconstruct the currently derelict and underused docklands, on both sides of the River Mersey. These schemes are **Liverpool Waters** and **Wirral Waters**. With stunning 21st Century architecture, resources and facilities; and ranks of skyscrapers overlooking new water-based leisure, living and work spaces, these plans have suggested that the Mersey waterfront could become 'The Dubai of Europe'.

To Find Out More:
Peel Holdings
www.liverpoolwaters.co.uk
www.wirralwaters.co.uk

The next Building in the trio that comprise The Three Graces is the Cunard Building. Visitors can also go into the atrium of this building.

The Cunard Building

The Cunard Building

Between the Port of Liverpool Building and the Royal Liver Building stands The Cunard Building, which was built for the world famous shipping line in 1916.

Samuel Cunard (1787-1865) arrived in Britain from Canada in the early years of the 19th century and, with his business partners George Burns and David MacIver, he founded the British and North American Royal Mail Steam Packet Company. Cunard had recognised the massive business potential in the expanding trade between Britain and that continent and, via Britain, and also with Europe. He saw too that the transportation of passengers, as well as goods, was the way of the future. In due course, the small steam packet company would, before long, become the world-famous shipping line that was to bear his name.

In 1840, the company's first steamship, the wooden paddle steamer Britannia, sailed from Liverpool to Boston, Massachusetts, with Cunard and 63 other passengers on board. The crossing took two weeks, was a highly profitable venture, and marked the beginning of regular passenger and cargo services operated by Cunard. Soon, the shipping line was re-named 'The Cunard Line', and its routes, and the size of its fleet, increased rapidly over the succeeding decades. The prosperous company eventually absorbed Canadian Northern Steamships Limited and its principal competition, the White Star Line, owners of the ill-fated Titanic. After that, Cunard dominated the Atlantic passenger trade with some of the world's most famous liners.

By the outbreak of the First World War, the company was internationally renowned, however, it lost 22 ships through enemy action during that conflict, including the 'Lusitania'. The liner was sunk without warning by a German submarine, with a loss of over 1300 lives and, as so many of its passengers were American, the sinking precipitated the entry of the USA into the War. The great Cunard liners 'Mauretania', and the Queens, 'Mary' and 'Elizabeth', were registered in Liverpool, and both proudly bore the City's name on their sterns throughout their periods of service. However, the Cunard Line was only one of a large number of equally renowned and important shipping companies that began their operations from the Port of Liverpool. These included the Holt, Booth, Bibby,

Brocklebank, Harrison, Elder Dempster, Ellerman, Inman, and Ismay Shipping Lines, amongst many others.

The Cunard Building was designed by Willink and Thicknesse, with Arthur Davis as consultant, and it was opened as the final element of 'The Three Graces'. However, this was never an 'official name' for the three buildings at the Pier Head, this was applied to them in later years.

This Grade II Listed office block, which is wider at the back than at the front, has six floors and a basement, and it is based on the design elements of the Farnese Palazzo in Rome. Particularly imposing are the four massive stone eagles on the corners, supporting the Cunard Shield. Symbolising Liverpool's links with North America, the sculptures were carved from a single stone, which weighed 43 tons. These monumental emblems symbolise Liverpool's links with the North American continent, and there are many such architectural features on buildings throughout the City. This is because our links with America have been significant, and vital to Liverpool's economy, since the time when that country was a British Colony. Nevertheless, the Cunard Line also traded around the world and, to represent this, portrait heads of peoples from different races appear around the walls of the building, just above the first floor windows.

This building is not open to the public, apart from the central corridor, as this is very much a working office building. However, it is worthwhile popping in just to get the feel of the place.

To Find Out More:
Liverpool World Heritage Bid – Pier Head
http://www.liverpoolworldheritage.com/pierhead.asp
The Cunard Building
Phone: 0151 236 5407
http://www.cunard-building.co.uk/site/home

The final building in the set is the Royal Liver Building, which is very much a working building with no public access or amenities.
However, if you are getting hungry, there is a café at the Mersey Ferry Terminal, which we shall visit shortly. There are also toilets here.

The Royal Liver Building

The Royal Liver Building was one of the first multi-storey, reinforced concrete, steel-framed buildings in the world; its granite exterior is simply cladding: Once again, the construction methods were following those of the skyscraper builders of New York.

The foundation stone was laid in 1908, and the building was opened in 1911, being the second of the 'Three Graces'. The massive weight of the building is supported on concrete piers, which were sunk into the bed of the old St. George's Dock, to a depth of 40 feet. From the top of the Liver Birds to the base, the building is 322ft high, and if you wanted to get some exercise, you would have to climb 483 stairs to get to the top.

The clock in the tower is known as the **Great George**, and it is bigger than Big Ben at Westminster in London. The clock faces are the biggest in Britain and, to celebrate their manufacture, one of them was first used as a unique dining table, with 40 guests comfortably seated around the 25ft diameter dial.

Once in place in Liverpool, the clock was started at the precise moment that King George V was crowned, hence its name. This was accomplished via a telephone link with an observer at Westminster.

Of all the world-famous icons of Liverpool, the Liver Bird is amongst the top few. Said to derive from the cormorants that once nested in the old Pool of the Town, or from the eagle crest of King John, they carry sprigs of seaweed ('lava' in Welsh) in their beaks. The birds on top of the Royal Liver Building are perhaps the most famous.

They are made from hammered copper plates and are bolted together on armatures of rolled steel. They stand 18

feet high, the head of each bird is 3½ feet long; each leg is 2 feet in circumference; and the wingspan is 12 feet across. The great birds need to be tied down with cables, as the legend says that if they ever fly away, then Liverpool would be doomed! They are of different sexes, and the female stands facing the river: She is waiting for the sailors to come home. The male bird stands facing inland: He is watching to see when the pubs have opened!

The iconic Liver Birds were modelled on a stuffed cormorant that was once kept in the Town Hall, and designed by a German sculptor, named **Carl Bernard Bartels** (1866-1955), who was living in England. However, only three years after the building was opened, World War one broke out, and Bartels was immediately arrested as an 'enemy alien'.

Even though he had been a naturalised Briton for 20 years, Carl was interned on the Isle of Man. The Corporation of Liverpool then removed all reference to his work, and wonderful contribution to the building and to the city. At the end of the war, Carl Bartels was deported to Germany. After some years he was able to return to England, where he died; but still the unacknowledged designer of Liverpool's greatest emblem. I am delighted to be able to right that wrong.

Guided tours around the building are available, and these include a visit to the roof, with a spectacular close-up view of the Liver Birds.

To Find Out More:
The Building Manager
The Royal Liver Building
Phone: 0151 236 2748

A closer look at one of the rooftop Liver Birds

From the Royal Liver Building, now walk back to the open space between the Three Graces and the riverfront. The roadway here is Canada Boulevard, named in tribute to the Canadian Servicemen who fought with Britain in the Second World War; this is why the road is lined with Maple trees. It is through this open space that the extension to the Leeds-Liverpool Canal has been cut, completing the waterway connection between Stanley Dock and the Albert Dock.

Do take some time to look at the excellent equestrian statues, and the other memorials and monuments in the grounds here. And then, take your trip on the Mersey Ferry.

The Pier Head

Between the Three Graces and the river itself is the main public riverside area, which is known as the Pier Head. This takes its name from a stone pier that once acted as a jetty at this point, and which was built in the 1760s. This was originally known as the North Pier, and it jutted out into the river from a site opposite St. Nicholas's Church. Before this however, ferries and sailing vessels would run up on to the Strand (which in those days was literally a 'strand' – a stretch of open sand) at the bottom of Water Street. The Pier was principally built to service people being ferried across the river and, when George's Dock was first built it was pulled down. Ferry passengers then had to get ashore via dangerous, narrow steps that had been cut into the wall of the dock.

However, by the mid-19th century, ferry traffic was increasing substantially, and so an appropriate and safer landing stage was needed to accommodate passengers. Also, there were now greater numbers of travellers embarking and disembarking, to and from the four corners of the world. And so, in 1847, the first floating, wooden landing stage was built at the Pier Head, and this was over 500ft long. Nevertheless, this was soon not long enough and so, in 1873, the new **Princes Landing Stage** was constructed and connected to the existing one at the Pier Head. However, this was totally destroyed by a fire in 1874, but was completely rebuilt two years later, and at a cost of £370,000. The new Pier Head landing stage, floating on the river on 200 huge pontoons, provided docking facilities for the large numbers of Mersey ferry boats; for passenger vessels then regularly visiting the Isle of Man and Llandudno; for other passenger services; and, eventually, for the great transatlantic liners. At the time of its construction, and for many years afterwards, it was the world's longest floating structure; stretching for almost half a mile, from Mann Island to beyond Princes Dock.

Complete with a wonderful range of buildings – all constructed from wood; including shops, covered waiting areas, lavatories, cafés, a post office, administration offices, and shelters for the dock-hands and boatmen; the landing stage was a remarkable complex of services and structures: There were bell towers; sophisticated, adjustable, fingerpost signs, to announce to passengers at which point along the stage the various ferry boats were docking; and, two-tier, drawbridge gangplanks – to enable passengers to, simultaneously, get on and off both the upper and lower decks of the ferries. The landing stage was also wide enough to take cars, lorries, and heavy goods wagons, which would drive onto the stage down an extraordinary floating, iron roadway that formed a fixed link between the stage and the land. This was composed of a series of great metal sections, hinged together horizontally. This construction allowed the roadway to rise and fall with the tides.

Sadly, this wonderful, exciting, entertaining example of Victorian engineering ingenuity was demolished in the early 1970s. It was replaced by a much shorter and staggeringly arid, concrete and steel structure . Fortunately, however, new plans are now in hand to completely redevelop the landing stage.

The open space in front of the Liver Building and its companions is an attractive, if sometimes very breezy place for a stroll. At weekends during the summer, hundreds of people can be found here, sunning themselves on the area that surrounds the equestrian statues of Queen Victoria and King Edward VII. Overlooking the river are cafés and restaurants, and it is from here that the famous Mersey Ferries continue to operate, from the **Ferry Terminal Building**, with its own restaurant, snack bar, lavatories, visitors' centre, and souvenir shop. It is here you will find a Beatles-themed exhibition area and gift shop.

In the Terminal Building you can buy your tickets for the ferries, and no visit here is complete without a sail on the river, so I do urge you to take your own **Ferry 'Cross The Mersey**.

To Find Out More:
The Pier Head
http://www.liverpoolcityportal.co.uk/attractions/pierhead.html
Liverpool World Heritage Bid – Pier Head
http://www.liverpoolworldheritage.com/pierhead.asp

The Mersey Ferries

There have been boats on the Mersey for as long as people have lived here; probably since Neolithic Boat People settled here, about 4,000 years ago. Also, it is likely that the Romans, who came to this part of Britain, may have been the first to use a ferry to cross the river, as remains of Roman roads have been found in Birkenhead on the Wirral, and also at Otterspool and Grassendale in Liverpool. The word 'ferry' comes from an old Norse word, 'feryu', meaning 'passage across the water'. This means that it is just as likely that the invading Vikings – who came to the Mersey too – may also have needed a ferry. Indeed, traces of Norse settlements have been found on both sides of the river.

"However, in recorded history, the first known ferry service was provided by the Medieval monks of Birkenhead Priory, on the shore of the Wirral Peninsula"

This stood on a promontory overlooking both the River Mersey to the east, and a large, broad inlet to the south, known as Tranmere Pool. By 1160, the monks were operating a ferry across the Tranmere Pool, from the Priory to Rock House Ferry, from which the name Rock Ferry derives. During the same time, they also operated a ferry between Woodside – where today's Birkenhead Ferry Terminal stands – across another wide inlet to the north, called Bidston Pool. This landed at the tiny village of 'Seccum', which is mentioned in the Domesday Book, thus giving modern Seacombe its name. So, the first Mersey ferries were actually along the Wirral sides of the river, rather than across it.

However, around 1160, the Tranmere Pool began to silt up, and so the monks then turned their attention to the village across the often-turbulent waters of the River Mersey, and established a ferry to this new destination. This was principally because they had set up granaries at Aigburth and Toxteth, which were then communities to the south of the tiny fishing village of 'Leverpul'. The monks also found that the fishing on the other side of the river was particularly good, and so they established fisheries at Garston, or 'Gaerstun', as it was then known.

As the monks were now crossing the river so frequently, they realised that they could transport other people across too, and so they soon began to provide a ferry service to local travellers, and would row them across for a fee: Farmers, merchants and, perhaps, Medieval tourists! This ferry service became known as the 'Monks Ferry' – a name that lasted for centuries, even after the monks ceased operating it. However, the Monarch always retained overall rights to the ferry services and, once Liverpool received its charter, the ferry service got busier. However, ownership remained in the hands of the reigning Monarch, who would lease rights to various operators.

By 1318, the Priory at Birkenhead was in a very impoverished state, and so the monks petitioned King Edward II for permission to build a hostel in the Priory grounds, and to charge travellers for food and drink. They received his permission and soon business began to grow; so much so that, in 1330, the monks then persuaded King Edward III to grant them a Royal Charter to run the ferry service.

The Liverpool Waterfront

One of the Mersey Ferries

"This gave the monks the exclusive right to ferry travellers, and their goods and chattels, across the River Mersey from Birkenhead to Liverpool, and also to charge a toll for the journey"

This monopoly made the Priory more solvent, and generated sufficient income for the religious community to live quite comfortably, for more than 200 years. This charter has never been revoked and, although the license to operate ferries eventually passed out of the hands of the monks, most of the original terms and conditions still apply. This means that, although a special dispensation was granted through Parliament, to allow modern ferry tickets to be sold on either side of the river, no such dispensation was granted when either of the Mersey Tunnels were opened. This is why tolls are only charged on the Wirral sides of these great, underwater thoroughfares.

By the mid-19th century, the ferry services were either in the hands of private entrepreneurs or companies, but eventually they all passed to the control of the local authorities. The Birkenhead Ferry passed into the hands of the Birkenhead Corporation, whilst the Wallasey Ferries Company, which had landing stages at Seacombe, Egremont, and New Brighton, passed into the control of Wallasey Corporation. The main ferry from Birkenhead to Liverpool, as mentioned previously, became the new Woodside Ferry.

And so, the ferries continued to operate from many points on the Wirral, with all of them docking at the Pier Head floating landing stage at Liverpool, which made the Pier Head a very busy place indeed. This was

particularly so before the building of the Mersey Tunnel, because goods and livestock would need to be ferried across the river, regularly, and in quantity, and so special goods ferries also plied their way to and fro across the Mersey.

However, by the 1950s, goods services were no longer necessary, and only three passenger ferry services operated across the river, providing separate routes to Liverpool from Birkenhead, at Woodside; from Wallasey, at Seacombe; and from the seaside town of New Brighton. Nevertheless, vessels were upgraded, landing stages were modernised, and the facilities for passengers and staff were improved. But then, towards the end of the 1960s, the river began to silt up at New Brighton, resulting in the closure of that ferry service, in 1971. The services from Seacombe and Birkenhead also came under threat of closure. This was because the commuters, who had once been the main users of the services, were now travelling across the river either by the Merseyrail underground rail system, or driving through the Mersey Tunnels. Some urgent thinking was necessary in the face of drastically reduced passenger numbers and increasing deficit, in 1978 the two ferry services were merged under the newly formed Merseyside Passenger Transport Executive, which in due course became 'Merseytravel'. Now, the Mersey Ferries continue to operate as a separate branch of this public transport organisation.

In 1990, following an investment of £5 million, the ferries were 're-launched' principally as a tourist service, but the commuter service was retained during peak hours. Mersey Ferries then established their 'Heritage Cruises', and boats now regularly sail from Liverpool to Seacombe, on to Woodside, and back to Liverpool.

To add to the high-quality tourist experience of the ferry itself, and complementing the Beatles theme of the Pier Head Terminal, both the Seacombe and Woodside terminals have special attractions too. **Spaceport**, at Seacombe, is a fun and exciting science and astronomy based attraction – very popular with children.

At Woodside is the remarkable **U-Boat Story**. Here, visitors can see into the cross-sectioned WWII German submarine, U-534, and enjoy a highly interactive and exciting exhibition.

The Ferries remain very popular, and an integral part of Merseyside's business and cultural life, and so the future of the 'Ferry 'Cross The Mersey' seems assured – almost 850 years after the service first began.

To Find Out More:
The Mersey Ferries
Phone: 0151 639 0609
www.merseyferries.co.uk

Returning to your car from the Three Graces, rejoin the main road and continue north. At the main traffic lights and roundabout, just beyond the Royal Liver Building, take the first left into St Nicholas Place; in front of the Crowne Plaza Hotel. You will see the Titanic memorial obelisk in front of you. Park anywhere here for a few minutes, whilst we take a look at this significant monument.

The Titanic Memorial

The Titanic Memorial

When it was built, at the Harland and Wolff shipyard in Belfast, the RMS Titanic was the largest ship afloat – standing as high as an eleven-storey building.

On 10th April 1912, she set sail with over 2200 passengers and crew, on her maiden voyage from Southampton to New York, via Queenstown in Southern Ireland. But, at 11.40pm on the night of 14th April 1912, she was struck by an iceberg just off Cape Race in the North Atlantic, eventually sinking at 2.20am on the morning of Monday 15th April, with the loss of 1,516 lives. Even today the magnitude of this disaster resonates clearly, particularly as it was so completely avoidable.

There are two memorials to the Titanic disaster in Liverpool, and one of these is at the Pier Head, near the Crowne Plaza Hotel. This is an obelisk, built as a result of the disaster, and erected following a public subscription. It was unveiled in 1916, and was originally intended to be a memorial to the thirty-two engineers who stayed at their posts aboard Titanic on that fateful night. However, World War I broke out before it was completed, and so the dedication was broadened: it is now dedicated as a general memorial to all engineers and stokers who have lost their lives at sea. As such, it is officially called the **Memorial to the Engine Room Heroes**. However, it will always be known locally as 'The Titanic Memorial' and it attracts much attention because of this association. On one side of the obelisk are depicted two stokers standing in front of a furnace door. On the opposite side, two officers holding tools stand in front of a telegraph. On the four corners are the figures of earth, air, fire, and water and, at the top, below a symbolic eternal fame, stand four figures holding lifebelts. An inscription reads,

"The brave do not die,
their deeds live for ever and call upon us
to emulate their courage and devotion to duty"

None of the engineers or engineering officers survived from the Titanic; they stayed at their posts almost until the great ship sank beneath the Atlantic, keeping the boilers stoked and fired, and the ship's lights burning, in the vain hope of attracting rescue ships in time to save everybody aboard. Liverpool's second memorial to the Titanic disaster is dedicated to the ship's band. This sits in the foyer of the Philharmonic Hall on Hope Street, and lists the names of all the musicians, who continued to play as the ship began to sink, and whose last melody was 'Nearer My God To Thee'. (See Chapter: 'Pool of Life & Culture'.)

To Find Out More:
The Titanic Historical Society
www.titanic1.org
The Titanic's Final Resting Place
http://seawifs.gsfc.nasa.gov/OCEAN_PLANET/HTML/titanic.html
The Titanic Story
http://www.titanicstory.com/

Follow St Nicholas Place around to the right as this becomes Princes Parade. The river will be on your left and Princes Dock will be on your right.

Emigration

Throughout the centuries, tens of thousands of people from all over the world came to Liverpool and stayed. They came to escape; to seek relief; and to find new opportunity. However, and particularly throughout the 19th and into the early years of the 20th centuries, literally millions more came to Liverpool to use it as a place of transit and embarkation, and for exactly the same hope-filled reasons.

Emigration to American began almost as soon as the Colonies were founded, in the 17th century, and this grew during the 18th century. However, once America gained her independence, the volume increased rapidly, reaching a peak in the mid-19th century. Indeed, between 1840 and 1914, almost 35 million Europeans left the Old World for the New. During these long decades, 4,750,000 passengers sailed from Liverpool, on ships owned by companies like Cunard and Inman. And, in 1887 alone, 199,441 emigrants sailed from the City: Of these, almost 69,000 were from continental Europe; over 62,000 were British; and over 68,000 were Irish. The numbers of people passing through Liverpool was such, that local transport provision and processing facilities had to expand exponentially to keep pace. In 1895, the Mersey Docks and Harbour Board built Riverside Station at Princes Dock. This was reached by rail through a long tunnel from Edge Hill to Waterloo Station, similar to the tunnel that ran from Edge Hill to Wapping.

Consider what was truly involved for these people in their attempt to improve their lot in life: After leaving behind their loved ones; escaping from poverty and famine, from persecution and pogrom; they faced the uncertainty and confusion of the travel across Britain, where the language and customs were strange. Then, many of them rural peasants, they would be overwhelmed by the size, noise, pace, and pressure of **The Second City of the British Empire**.

They would also have to try to escape the pickpockets, con-men, and others who would try to fleece them as they wandered the streets of Liverpool. After suffering the indignity of personal searches and medical inspections, they would then board their vessels and try to find a secure place to call home, whilst on the ship.

It is easy then, to understand the high emotion that they must have felt as they sailed into New York Harbour and, from 1886, to see the magnificent Statue of Liberty and all that she promised. However, once docked in New York they would have to undergo the rigours of the immigration procedures at Ellis Island. But that is another story for other authors to tell. The inscription on Lady Liberty reads,

"Give me your tired, your poor,
Your huddled masses yearning
to breathe free,
The wretched refuse
of your teeming shore.
Send these, the homeless,
tempest-tost to me;
I lift my lamp beside
the golden door!"

Perhaps this gives a new perspective, on the plight of the hundreds of immigrants and asylum seekers from all over the world, who come to Britain and Liverpool today; all seeking a better life.

To Find Out More:
Leaving from Liverpool
www.diduknow.info/emigrants

Princes Dock 23

Princes Dock

Past the 'Three Graces', standing at the edge of Princes Dock, is the **Crowne Plaza Hotel**. This was the first new building to be erected on the site of what was once one of the busiest docks on the waterfront, serving as it did the transatlantic liners, and latterly as the embarkation point for the Irish Ferries.

However, before the creation of the dock, it was on this site in the 18th century, that Liverpool consolidated its reputation as a popular spa town. As early as 1708 there was a bathing house here, where people would not only swim in the River Mersey, but also drink it. In 1765, where the Crowne Plaza now stands, the **North Pleasure and Salt Water Baths** were opened and Bath Street, which is the start of the Dock Road at this point, takes its name from these popular amenities of the time. In 1794, the Corporation bought the baths, at a cost of £5000, and improved and extended them. By this time, large numbers of wealthy families were coming to the Town each year to use the bathing and spa facilities but, in 1817, the baths were demolished to make way for Princes Dock.

Designed by John Foster and his son, when Princes Dock opened in 1821 it was the first to be enclosed by walls and, for well over a century, more than nine million emigrants were to embark from here bound for the New World: first on large sailing

The Liverpool Waterfront

vessels, then aboard great steam ships and, ultimately, on great ocean-going liners. Also, in the early years of the 20th century, Princes Dock became the centre for the Irish loose-cargo trade.

"It was also from Princes Dock that, during World War Two, tens of thousands of Servicemen and Servicewomen would embark on vessels, carrying them to theatres of war all around the globe"

The emotions of hope, fear, parting, regret, and loss; and also of excitement, anticipation, and joy, which have pervaded the dockside here for almost 200 years, give Princes Dock a tremendous significance and poignancy. I don't know whether it is a good or a bad thing that there is now no evidence at Princes Dock, of this breadth of human experience.

The modern Princes Dock area was part of the vast land holding, on both sides of the Mersey, owned and managed by the Mersey Docks and Harbour Company (MDHC) and now by Peel Holdings. It was the original intention of the MDHC to continue the development of this part of the north docks with more office blocks, but now the strategy has changed: In cultural and social, as well as economic terms, the considerable potential of this site has now been recognised and, consequently, Princes Dock has become an exciting, mixed-use site.

To Find Out More:
Princes Dock
http://www.bwpics.co.uk/gallery/princes.html
Crowne Plaza Hotel Princes Dock
www.cpliverpool.com

The Cruise Liner Facility ㉔

After the Post-War decline of Liverpool as an international port, the City did have occasional one-off visits from cruise vessels like the QE2, but now Liverpool is on all the major tourist itineraries. We shall now see the great cruise liners of the world calling here regularly and, to accommodate these massive vessels, a cruise liner terminal has been built in front of Princes Dock.

We can expect between 30 and 50 such vessels to visit Liverpool every year, and special embarkation and visitor facilities of the highest standards to meet international requirements, are part of the terminal. These include a 250-metre extension and major improvements to the existing Pier Head landing stage, at a cost of £10½ million. Dredging work began on the river early in 2005, ready for the inauguration of the facility, in 2007.

Now, Liverpool ranks alongside the other great tourist ports of the world, such as San Francisco, Venice, and Barcelona and, once again, the Mersey will see international visitors using the waterway and the port.

To Find Out More:
Cruise Liner Terminal
www.merseymaritime.co.uk/press.asp?p=85

At the end of Princes Parade, at the mini-roundabout at Bath Street, turn left into Waterloo Road, passing the Waterloo Grain Warehouse Apartment Block on the left. Park anywhere along here to take a look at this appealing building, and the much less appealing Mersey Tunnel Ventilation Shaft across the road.

Waterloo Dock; The Dock Road and The Dockers ㉕

Waterloo Dock

As we leave all the new development at Princes Dock we turn left onto Waterloo Road. Here, the first prominent building that we see stands on the left, and this is the **Waterloo Grain Warehouse** that overlooks Waterloo Dock.

This dock was one of those designed by Jesse Hartley and it opened in 1834, having initially been dug out by French prisoners-of-war, captured during the Napoleonic Wars. It was named after the great battle that brought an end that conflict, in 1815, and the Dock was originally built for general sailing traffic rather than for goods handling. Indeed, it was from Waterloo Dock, as well as from George's and Princes Docks, that people emigrated to the New World.

However, the uses for the dock changed radically, because of the repeal of the Corn Laws:

At the end of the French Wars the Corn Laws were introduced. They stated that no foreign corn could be imported into Britain until domestic corn cost 80/- per quarter. The high price caused the cost of food to increase and, consequently, this depressed the domestic market for manufactured goods, because people spent the bulk of their earnings on food rather than commodities. The Corn Laws also caused great distress among the working classes in English towns, as these people were unable to grow their own food, and so had to pay the high prices in order to stay alive.

However, in 1844, these hated Laws were removed from the Statute Books, and so it was then legal, and extremely profitable, to import cheaper corn from overseas; principally from North America. As a result, and after the death of Jesse Hartley in 1860, the Mersey Docks and Harbour Board instructed their new Chief Dock Engineer, George Lyster, to design and build three, massive, state-of-the-art grain processing warehouses around the dock basin. These were erected in 1868, at a cost of £559,000 but, because of certain mechanical and design problems, they did not officially become fully operational until 1872.

Nevertheless, when they did come into operation they were the most modern facilities of their day. The whole dock was one hydraulically driven entity, and two great towers, which still exist in the one surviving warehouse building, housed the vertical lifting mechanism, whilst horizontal conveyor belts ran throughout the building to both move and polish the grain. Because of this, the processes were almost entirely mechanical, requiring very little manual input.

Waterloo Dock became significant in another way too, when it became the location of the **Liverpool Observatory**. Indeed, Liverpool has strong associations with astronomy and related discoveries. And, as we have already seen, in the early 17th century Jeremiah Horrocks of Toxteth correctly determined the path of the Moon's orbit around the Earth, and tracked the path of Venus.

"In fact, Sir Isaac Newton said that Horrocks's work was instrumental in his own scientific discoveries."

In 1834, the Royal Navy recommended the establishment of an astronomical observatory in the Port of Liverpool. This was because, at that time, the exact longitude of the Town was unknown, which meant that every ship's chronometer that had been calibrated in the Port would have been inaccurate. Because of this, vessels would not actually be where they thought they where, and might founder, with loss of life and property. Therefore, the purpose of the observatory was to establish Greenwich Time, and to indicate it by dropping the large time ball down a tall vertical shaft. Also, by firing the cannon at the same accurate time each day, the citizens and mariners within earshot could check their timepieces. And so, in 1845, the Liverpool Observatory was opened, and the **Time Ball** and the **One O'clock Gun** were established at Waterloo Dock.

When the grain warehouses were being constructed at Waterloo Dock, a new Observatory was built on the top of Bidston Hill in Wirral and so the original building, and the time ball, were demolished. However, the One O'clock Gun was still fired, but this was now from Morpeth Dock in Birkenhead.

A number of cannons were used for this, including one from the Crimean War, and one of these is now at the Maritime Museum, but the One O'Clock gun was last fired in 1969.

Of the three original warehouse blocks at Waterloo Dock, one was turned into a mill, in 1904 and, in 1925, they were all completely re-equipped for handling oil seeds. During World War Two, the north block was destroyed by enemy bombing in the May Blitz of 1941, and the east block suffered some damage too, although this was from the fall of a bomb that failed to explode, and which was later safely defused.

The west block was demolished, in 1969, to make way for a new 'Coastwise Container Terminal', and grain was kept in the surviving east block, until 1988, when it became empty and neglected. However, in 1990, the attractive building was converted into **Waterloo Apartments**, which involved the removal of all the machinery, but the exterior of this architecturally stunning, and historically significant building, was almost entirely unaltered.

Now, the Grade II Listed Victorian Warehouse retains its barrel ceilings and cast iron trusses, and its open ground-floor arcades.

"Following its conversion, the Warehouse was judged 'Best Urban Renewal' and 'Best Renovation in Britain', by What House Magazine, and it won the 1991 RIBA Design Award"

The One O'Clock Gun

Just opposite Waterloo Warehouse Apartments, on the right of Waterloo Road, is one of the ventilation shafts for 'Kingsway', the Mersey Tunnel that runs from the City to Wallasey, and which was built in 1971.

The Dock Road and The Dockers

Whilst the human cargo of emigrants that passed through the Port was of considerable importance in the wealth-creation of Liverpool, the cargoes of commodities were just as significant.

Thousands of ships 'sailing the seven seas' came to the City from 'the four corners of the world', and they brought with them foodstuffs, spices, tobacco, cotton, livestock, trade-goods, fabrics, minerals, metals, and machinery; the raw materials that were driving forward the Industrial Revolution and the expansion of Britain and its Empire.

All these goods had to be moved and, despite the growth of mechanisation throughout the 19th and 20th centuries, manpower was the cheapest and most effective method of cargo-handling. This is why the Liverpool Dockers were so vital to the life of the Port.

Unfortunately, the supply of labour always exceeded demand, as the population seeking work was ever-increasing. This meant that their jobs were constantly at risk and life was particularly hard for Dockers. This was particularly true before World War Two, when virtually all work on the Docks was casual, with no guarantee of employment. Indeed, up to 1948, Dockers were forced to wait in pens like cattle, to see if they might be picked for a day's work. This was known as working 'On The Lump'.

After the War however, the Labour Government established the 'National Docks Labour Scheme', which was designed to eradicate exploitative management practices. Because of this change, the Docks became heavily unionised, and so insecure and casual labour was replaced by employment stability. This gave Dockers the certainty of regular earnings, which they had been denied for generations.

However, the new system and strong Trade Unions also increased the practice of 'closed-shop' working, and of confrontation with employers. This led to massive industrial unrest on the Docks, resulting in strikes, closures, sackings, redundancies, and economic failures throughout the 1960s, 1970s, and beyond.

At its peak, Liverpool Docks employed 25,000 Dockers, and they were a hive of day and night-time activity; from Seaforth at the north end to Garston at the south.

There were times, in the 1960s, when 100 vessels at a time could be tied up in the Docks, bringing in cargo from all around the globe. Nevertheless, in the 1970s, the Mersey Docks and Harbour Company was hit by a financial crisis; almost being forced into bankruptcy and complete closure.

The management of the organisation had failed to come to terms with the new working practices established after the War, neither had they adapted to technical changes taking place in the maritime

industry. This instability was as obvious to the Dockers and the Unions, as it was to the management, but neither side was prepared to compromise.

This relentless environment of confrontation between dock-workers and employers, coupled with the steady decline in worldwide shipping, tolled the death-knell for the Dockers. The end of the old way of working came when, towards the end of the 1980s, and following a national downturn in the maritime industry, the National Dock Labour Scheme was scrapped, and this provoked a national Dockers' strike. In due course, this was resolved, but only temporarily.

In 1995, another dispute broke out at Liverpool and the Dockers went out on strike once again. As a result, five hundred of them were sacked. This strengthened the determination of the Dockers not to give in, and the strike lasted for months.

However, the ultimate victory of the employers was inevitable, as they were over-manned anyway and so the sacked Dockers never got their jobs back. But it was the introduction of containerisation that truly destroyed the waterfront way of life for those men and their families. Mechanical handling replaced muscle-power, and labour-systems on the Liverpool Docks changed forever.

But time moved on, and the Port of Liverpool is busier now than at any time in its entire history, though far less labour-intensive. The financial turnover of Liverpool's docks is increasing significantly, and the Port handles millions of tons of cargo every year, principally through the **Freeport at Seaforth**.

On a lighter note, the Dockers were a community. They worked in gangs of often highly-skilled men, who developed their own customs, traditions, language, and a unique sense of moral values when it came to handling the goods coming and going through the Port!

They also had a very particular sense of humour, especially when it came to the ironic and typically-Scouse nicknames that they gave each other, such as:

DIESEL	Says, "Diesel do fer our kid, diesel do fer me ma."
SELL THE BED	Always on nights.
SWAN VESTAS	Always on strike.
THE BROKEN BOOMERANG	He never comes back.
THE CLERGYMAN	Never has Sunday off.
THE CORONATION KID	She'll crown me when I get home.
THE MIRROR	Heard saying, "What you do reflects on me."
THE SURGEON	Has everyone in stitches.

THE WEIGHT LIFTER	Waits while you lift.
THROMBOSIS	A bloody clot, always causes problems.
VAN GOGH	Whenever asked for something, shouted, "I've got one 'ere."
WEDDING CAKE	Every time he was asked to do some overtime, he always had a wedding to go to.
WONDERMAN	As he unloaded the crates he always muttered, "I wunder wot's in dis one?"

Continue along Waterloo Road, passing the iron gates at the end of Waterloo Dock. You will then pass the old gates of Trafalgar Dock, and one or two entrances into other Central Docks. However, opposite the end of Cotton Street on the right, you will see the entrance gate-posts to Clarence Dock.

Park anywhere on the left here, to view the small and apparently inconsequential green plaque, fixed to the Dock Wall, just to the right of the gateway. This dock, and the plaque, are far from insignificant however, as you shall now discover.

Clarence Dock;
The Irish Famine and The Irish in Liverpool

26

Clarence Dock

Just beyond Waterloo Dock we pass the sites of what were once Victoria and Trafalgar Docks. All that now remains of these however, are their names carved in plaques and set into the magnificent gate piers in the Dock Road Wall. At one time there were 130 working docks in the full Dock System. All of them were busy but some were more significant than others. Perhaps of greatest importance though, in human terms, is the dock that we now come to.

Opposite the end of Cotton Street, and just before the lifting road-bridge at the massive Stanley Dock Warehouses, are the sites of Clarence Graving Docks and of the main Clarence Dock.

Once, nothing more than a stretch of open sand leading to the river, this part of the Liverpool coast was where the **Wishing Gate** was located. For generations, throughout the 18th and early 19th centuries, this was the site of a small gate at the end of a narrow pier. From here, the families and loved ones of sailors leaving to go to sea, would bid farewell to their menfolk, and make a wish for their safe return.

However, by the end of the 1820s a new dock was necessary, located well away from the main anchorages in the Town. This was to be a base for the newly developing steam ships, the sparks from the smoke-stacks of which might otherwise have posed a threat of fire, to the sailing vessels berthed in adjacent docks. Jesse Hartley was commissioned for the work, which was completed in 1830, and named after William, Duke of Clarence, who was the son of King George III. He was eventually to succeed to the throne as King William IV – the uncle of Queen Victoria.

Nevertheless, within ten years Clarence Dock's role in handling steamships had passed, and it was then used for vessels employed on coastal and Irish Sea routes. As such, the Gates of Clarence Dock were the first sight of Liverpool, for millions of mid-19th century Irish immigrants to Britain and beyond. Ironically, the anguish, emotion, and hope, that had been felt by the men and woman at the ancient Wishing Gate, would now be experienced once more at this place: But this time, by hundreds of thousands of poor people who, escaping from poverty and starvation in Ireland, were coming to Liverpool in the hope of a better life; as we shall see shortly.

Clarence Dock was closed and filled in 1929, and the site was sold for use as a power station. The three large chimneys of the Clarence Dock Power Station were a familiar Mersey landmark, until they were demolished along with the power station, in 1994. The site remains empty and unused now, except for the occasional open air event or temporary concert venue. Although, MDHC and Peel Holdings have dynamic plans for all of the Central and North Docks.

As mentioned previously, 'Liverpool Waters', will be a £5.5 billion complex of towers, offices, retail, leisure, and residential facilities would open in 2025.

The plans also include the creation of a monorail, running from the docks all the way to Liverpool John Lennon Airport at Speke - a 21st century 'Overhead Railway'!

The Irish Famine and The Irish in Liverpool

The exploitation of the Irish by the British goes back to Medieval times, and persisted through to the 18th & 19th centuries. It was then that the British Crown granted vast Irish estates to Protestant absentee landlords.

Ireland is a fertile country, and large quantities of wheat and other crops were being produced. However, the vast bulk of this produce was exported to England, including most of the livestock. This meant that the Irish peasantry never had access to the fruits of their labour, nor could they have found the money to pay for it – even if they had been allowed to buy it. This left only potatoes for the Irish people to live on and, by 1840, this was literally the only food for almost half of Ireland's 8 million people.

Although there had been many outbreaks of famine in Ireland during the early part of the 19th century, forcing many of the country's eight million people to leave for England and Scotland, an almost nationwide blight completely ruined the potato crop in 1845, and then again in 1846. This caused dreadful suffering. The British Government haggled and bickered for so long that, when the Corn Laws were repealed, allowing the importation of cheap corn from America and elsewhere, the legislation was far too late. The Great Irish Potato Famine killed 25% of the Irish population – almost 1 million Irish men, women, and children; whilst over a million more emigrated to America – most of these coming through Liverpool.

Those that could not afford to continue their journey to either the New World or other parts of Britain – and there were tens of thousands of them – were forced to remain in Liverpool. This put intolerable pressures on what was an already heavily overburdened town, and the existing infrastructure could not cope. Thousands of victims of the Irish Famine found themselves in conditions no better than those that they had left behind. This rapidly expanding, vulnerable, and dependant population, exponentially increased the spread of disease and poverty, and of the social degeneration that followed in their wake.

Although mainly a Protestant community before the vast influx of Catholic Irish into the Town, Liverpool already had a small number of Catholic churches, and perhaps the best known of these is **St. Anthony's**. Being located, as it is, in **Scotland Road** – which became the heartland of the immigrant Irish population – this was soon the principal church serving this new and very large community.

The mainly Catholic Irish immigrants – although significant numbers of them were also Protestant – brought with them to Liverpool, not only their religious beliefs but also their politics, and this prompted a backlash by the indigenous Protestant population. By 1886, the sectarian geography of Liverpool had been established, with whole streets of Protestants declaring themselves around Netherfield Road and Everton Village, as well as throughout other parts of Liverpool. Great Homer Street was generally regarded as the border between the Catholic and Protestant hinterlands in the northern sections of the Town. This Protestant reaction to the growth in the Catholic population led to a rapid expansion in the membership of the **Loyal Order of Orangemen**, and the 12th July became an annual day of Orange-Lodge street-decorations, parades, and rallies. Naturally, the Irish Catholics responded with their own marches and demonstrations. Frequently they clashed, and extreme violence, injury, and death often resulted. Outbreaks of street fighting and sectarian intimidation – many of these led by prominent rabble-rousers on both sides – continued to affect many inner-City areas of Liverpool well into the mid-20th century.

Eventually however, a collapse of local, militant, religious extremism began in the 1960s, and this can be largely attributed to Liverpool's religious leaders at the time – the **Roman Catholic Archbishop Andrew Beck**, and the **Anglican Bishop Stuart Blanch**. These men began to work closely together, to facilitate a greater understanding and communication between the Catholic and Protestant communities of the City. Sadly, because of residual suspicions, their work had to take place largely behind closed doors.

However, their successors, **Archbishop Derek Worlock** and **Bishop David Sheppard** continued this work, and succeeded in building meaningful bridges between the denominations, which has left a permanent and positive legacy. Also, these men were now able to do so in a much more public and open way, to great effect.

The 1970s and 1980s were decades of extreme poverty and social unrest in many parts of the City, and both men sought to provide a united front in the battle against Liverpool's economic collapse, social decline, and inadequate political leadership. Consequently, as part of this process, they fostered a new spirit of religious harmony and ecumenicism between themselves, between their denominations, and also with other, non-Christian faiths. This new understanding was perhaps best demonstrated when Pope John Paul II visited Liverpool in 1982, and attended services at both the Roman Catholic and the Anglican Cathedrals.

By the beginning of the 1980s, the religious divisions were becoming a thing of the past. Today, the relationships between local communities, of all faiths, are something about which Liverpool people can feel justly proud. We celebrate diversity in culture, community, and Faith in our City, and this can be demonstrated by the very existence of the Merseyside Council of Faith.

But what of the Liverpool Irish? All that currently remains of Clarence Dock are the dock wall and its massive gateposts and, in 2000, an inappropriately small plaque was unveiled on the dock wall here. In Gaelic and English, this reads

"Through these gates passed most of the 1,300,000 Liverpool migrants who fled from the Great Famine and 'took the ship' to Liverpool in the years 1845-52 – Remember the Great Famine"

The story of the Irish in Liverpool is one of tragedy becoming triumph, of hostility transforming into harmony, of failure growing into success, and of alienation evolving into acceptance. The Irish have made a significant contribution to the character of Liverpool, to our dialect, to our diet, to our zest for life, and to our sense of community.

To Find Out More:
The Great Irish Famine
http://www.nde.state.ne.us/ss/irish/irish_pf.html
Irish Family History in Liverpool
http://freepages.genealogy.rootsweb.com/~hibernia/
St Anthony's Parish Church – Scotland Road
Phone: 0151 207 0177
http://www.scottiepress.org/gallery/anthonys.htm

Continuing along from Clarence Dock, you will see the massive brick warehouse of Stanley Dock looming over the roadway on the right. You will also see the wonderful bascule bridge, spanning the road ahead.

Drive across the bridge and park as soon as is safe and convenient, anywhere on the left:
From here you can walk back to view Stanley Dock; Stanley Dock Basin; and the Victoria Tower, across Collingwood and Salisbury Docks.

Stanley Dock and the Leeds Liverpool Canal

Stanley Dock

We now come to the final part of my Chapter on the Liverpool Waterfront: Stanley Dock. Just past Clarence Dock, and still on Waterloo Road with its wonderful Dock Perimeter Wall, we approach a rolling-bascule lifting bridge that was built in the 1930s.

Over this, on the inland side, the road runs in front of Stanley Dock, with its colossal **tobacco warehouse** and the entrance to the flight of four locks that lead to the Leeds-Liverpool Canal. On the opposite side of the road we can see Collingwood and Salisbury Docks, at the heart of the Central Docks.

The first shipment of tobacco from Virginia in America arrived in Liverpool in 1648. Once this trade took off, huge warehouses were needed to supply Liverpool's facilitation of an increasing national demand for the addictive plant.

Tobacco is a seasonal crop and, to keep markets stable, ports like Liverpool needed to store enough to last all year. By the mid-19th Century, Jesse Hartley built two warehouses on either side of the Stanley Dock basin, as an extension to the facilities already available at the Albert Dock.

The work took from 1852 to 1856 to complete, and the 14-storey buildings are very similar to those at Wapping, and are equally impressive.

The larger of the two buildings is the Tobacco Warehouse and, with 1.3 million square feet of capacity, it was capable of holding 60,000 hogsheads of tobacco.

Built of 27 million bricks, it was a powerful guardian over its precious stock – with as few exists as possible to prevent theft. It was also, at the time of its construction, the largest bonded warehouse in the world, and it remains the largest brick-built building in the world.

If you face the Dock Basin from the road bridge, on the left behind the warehouse wall, you will see a small brick outbuilding with a tall, narrow chimney-stack.

Built around 1900, this is where surplus tobacco was burned, so as not to lose duty by it being smuggled onto the market. Consequently, this chimney was known as the **King's Pipe**.

The tobacco warehouse was state-of-the-art when built but it fell out of use in the 1980s. Although frequently used as a location for film and television productions, the warehouse building, which is Grade II Listed, was under threat of demolition. However, the current owners of the dockside buildings complex, Kitgrove, plan to redevelop the site, by 2015, and at a cost of £100 million. Their proposals include the conversion of the warehouses intoo apartments, restaurants, bars, shops, and water-based leisure activities.

If you look to the river, towards Collingwood Dock, you can really see how Stanley Dock, and the rest of this vast network of basins and waterways, all links together and with the river. It is clear what the potential really is, which is why the Peel Ports proposals for Liverpool Waters are also so exciting.

On the quayside, overlooking the river and standing on an island between the dock river gates, you can also see the **Victoria Tower**. Designed by Jesse Hartley, principally as a home for the Pier Master, this unusual and attractive castellated granite building was built in 1878, and it also houses a bell tower and a clock with five faces.

This tower not only gave the time to the surrounding docks, and to departing and arriving ships, but it would also ring out high tide and warning notes. It is also worth having a good look at the bridge that allows the Dock Road to pass over the Leeds-Liverpool Canal, as it connects with the Central Docks and the river.

> "This is still a remarkable piece of engineering, even though it is currently in an appallingly neglected condition"

If you stand on the bridge and look into Stanley Dock, you can see where the Leeds-Liverpool Canal comes into the basin, and it is easy to travel back in time and imagine what the scene must have been like in the Dock's heyday, when the whole area would have been loud and hectic with barges and Dockers, busy at work.

The Leeds-Liverpool Canal

The Leeds-Liverpool Canal once terminated here at Stanley Dock Basin, and it remains one of the most significant waterways in Britain.

In the 18th century, businessmen and entrepreneurs of Liverpool recognised the importance of canals at an early stage. Their exploitation of this revolutionary method of transportation began with the opening of the Sankey Brook Navigation, in 1757, and which was constructed to carry barges of coal from the St. Helens coalfields, to connect with the River Mersey and then on to Liverpool.

This was the first man-made canal in England and the first commercial canal in the world. It was made possible by a partnership between the Liverpool Dock Trustees; Liverpool Corporation; and various Liverpool merchants, who invested their own capital in the project. Next came the Bridgewater Canal, built between 1761 and 1773; followed by the Grand Trunk Canal, built between 1766 and 1777.

These canals, and all the subsequent ones that were soon being dug across the rapidly developing industrial landscape of Britain, were excavated using only manpower. And the moving of tons of earth using only spades, picks, shovels, and brute-force, demanded a new breed of manual worker. Because of their jobs on what were referred to as 'navigations', these burly men became known as **'Navvies'**.

The Leeds-Liverpool Canal system formed a major link across the Pennines, carrying goods from Liverpool across Lancashire and into Yorkshire, on what is the longest canal in Britain, at 1271/4 miles long (204km). Construction began in 1770, with the first section – from Liverpool to Wigan, being opened in 1774.

The full length of the canal was finally completed in 1816, and the link between the town-centre of Leeds with that of Liverpool, and with many other towns along the canal's length, was established. The waterway originally ended in Liverpool at Pall

The Leeds-Liverpool Canal at the Stanley Lock

Mall, giving Leeds Street its name. This section of the canal was closed many years ago and so the system then terminated at Stanley Dock. Here, in 1848, a direct link via locks was made between the Liverpool Docks System and the main canal. These locks were designed and built by Jesse Hartley, and are another magnificent example of his skill and artistry.

> "These are the only all-granite canal locks in the country, and are Listed as Grade II."

As the 19th century progressed, the canal faced increasing competition from the railways. Also, the effects of World War One further damaged the canal's viability. By 1960, the Tate and Lyle sugar refinery and North Liverpool Gas Works were the only major clients using the canal. When these closed down, and after the severe winter of 1963 when the canal froze over – in many places for weeks, almost all commercial canal traffic ceased on the Leeds-Liverpool. However, with the modern increase in leisure pursuits, and following major investment in repair, restoration, and maintenance by the British Waterways Authority, many stretches of the canal are busy again.

With the extension of the canal into Liverpool's Central and South Docks, the regeneration and revitalisation of the canal has already begun. In fact, this is the only waterway in the world to pass through two World Heritage Sites – Liverpool, and Saltaire near Bradford in Yorkshire.

The canal link at the Pier Head

To Find Out More:
British Waterways
Phone: 01925 847700
www.britishwaterways.co.uk/home/index

Leeds-Liverpool Canal
www.penninewaterways.co.uk/ll

Leeds and Liverpool Canal Society
Phone: 01282 850430
http://townsleyb.members.beeb.net/llcs/

Sandon Dock Waste Water Treatment Centre

Just a little further along the Dock Road from Stanley Dock, is the Sandon Dock Waste Water Treatment Centre. One of the problems that Liverpool has had to overcome was the extensive pollution of the River Mersey.

The 19th century explosion of population, in and around Liverpool and the Wirral, meant that industrial waste and raw domestic sewage were discharged directly into the Mersey, in staggering quantities.

This was with absolutely no treatment at all for either liquid or solid waste, until the river was foul, evil-smelling, and poisonous to wildlife and to humans.

In the 20th century, increasingly massive amounts of chemical and industrial process waste were being pumped into the Mersey along its length, and the river was dying.

The waterway, which was once the home of salmon and trout, and to all forms of birds and wildlife, was a contaminated, muddy slick. It was always said that if one was unfortunate enough to fall into the Mersey, then the first treatment one received was to have one's stomach pumped!

"Enough was enough and, in 1980, a massive clean-up campaign began, and over £550 million has been spent to achieve this."

The process began with new legislation to criminalise industrial pollution, and this was followed by the construction of a 27 mile-long interceptor sewer. Owned and operated by United Utilities, this runs the length of the river and now collects the entire City's sewage, carrying it into the new Water Treatment Centre at Sandon Dock. Here it is fully treated, and only clean water is returned to the river.

The Mersey is the cleanest it has been for a century with record numbers of salmon and trout back in the river. There is even a movement to try to reintroduce otters to Otterspool, although this is unlikely to become a reality.

Guided tours around the state-of-the-art sewage works at Sandon Dock are available by appointment, and this is a sophisticated and fascinating facility.

To Find Out More:
Sandon Dock Wastewater Treatment Works
Phone: 01925 233 233
www.nww.co.uk
United Utilities
Phone: 01925 237 000

If you wish to do so, you can continue along the remainder of the Dock Road to take a look at the North Docks. However, this is now the end of my Tour, and so you will need to turn around and re-trace the route back towards the City Centre, and beyond.

Stanley Dock and the Tobacco Warehouse

The Liverpool Waterfront: Conclusion

In this Chapter we have travelled from the South Docks; through the City-centre; and we have passed the Central Docks of Trafalgar, Victoria, Clarence, Stanley, Collingwood, and Salisbury. To continue further north would bring us to mainly heavy industrial dockland with supporting infrastructure. This includes Nelson Dock, Bramley-Moore, Wellington, and the Sandon Half-Tide Dock; the names of which are inscribed on plaques, set into the Dock Perimeter Wall. At the end of the Dock road we would come to the Liverpool Freeport at Seaforth.

In its heyday, the full length of the docklands was in use, but the South Docks – where Festival Gardens are – fell into decline first. The Central and North Docks survived into the late 1960s and early 1970s, when many of these too began to close. Nevertheless, many are still in operation today, for ferries to Ireland, the shipping of goods, and for the processing and handling of foodstuffs and other commodities.

Our route has taken us on quite a journey through Liverpool's history and heritage. Indeed, there can be few cities in the world where a waterfront has had such a profound social and economic impact on its own local community, on its country, or on the world; but this is certainly true of Liverpool. Our City, through its waterfront, traded, communicated with, and shaped the world; and the people of Liverpool have been shaped in return. The world came here, and we also went out to meet and engage with the world. Today, through the circle of life and time, this is happening all over again, but now in a new form and on different terms.

As a World Heritage City, and Port, once again we look outwards beyond the confines of our shores, to extend a friendly, Scouse welcome to the peoples of the world.

The Liverpool Waterfront

Including:

The Church of St Francis Xavier

The Spectacular Views from Everton Ridge

Everton Village – The Toffee Shop and Lock-Up

Everton Football Club

Liverpool Football Club

The Hillsborough Memorial

Stanley Park and Anfield

Walton-on-the-Hill and The Tudor School

Anfield Cemetery

Ancient Tuebrook House

St John the Baptist Church, Tuebrook

Newsham Park

Everton's Goodison Park and Liverpool's Anfield; the current homes of the City's football clubs, are separated by Stanley Park

Fortunes, Fables and Football: The Tour

Important note: For obvious reasons, DON'T undertake this Tour on a weekend afternoon in the middle of the football season! The total distance covered by this Tour is 13 miles, and the suggested time for its completion is 5 hours.
Allow extra time if you have pre-booked Football Stadium Tours, and pre-arranged to visit SFX, St George's, Walton-on-the-Hill, and St John the Baptist churches; and of course, for meal and refreshment breaks.
This is a circular tour, so you can pick it up at any point on the route, however do always travel in the recommended direction, in this case CLOCKWISE, as the route has been designed to get you efficiently around Liverpool's sometimes confusing one-way systems.

NB Please remember to check all opening times and admission charges before setting off, to avoid disappointment should any venues be closed.

Contents

Route Map

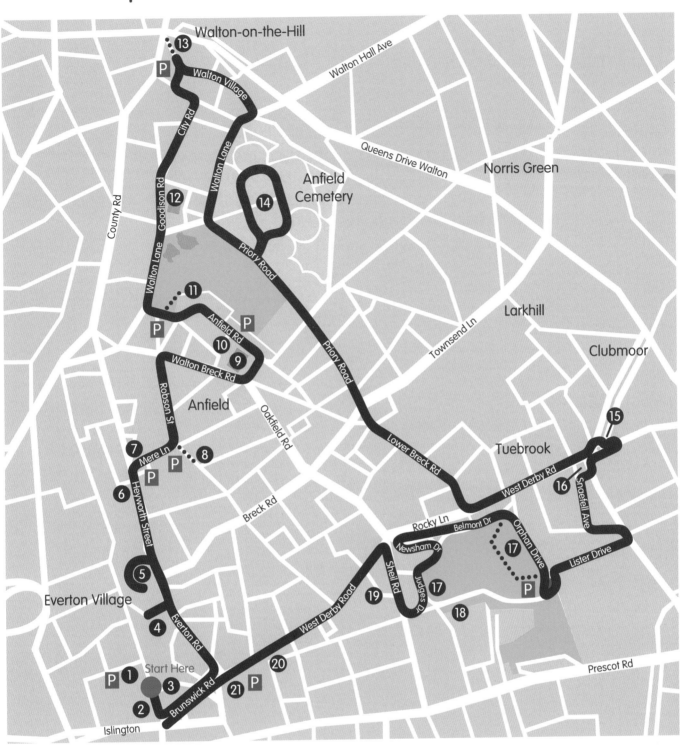

Walton-on-the-Hill

13

P

Walton Village

Walton Hall Ave

Walton Lane

Queens Drive Walton

Norris Green

City Rd

County Rd

Goodison Rd

Walton Lane

12

Anfield Cemetery

14

Priory Road

Larkhill

Townsend Ln

Clubmoor

11

P

Anfield Rd

P

10

9

Priory Road

Walton Breck Rd

Robson St

Anfield

Oakfield Rd

15

Tuebrook

Lower Breck Rd

7

Mere Ln

P

8

P

West Derby Rd

16

Snaefell Ave

6

Breck Rd

Heyworth Street

Lister Drive

5

Rocky Ln

Belmont Dr

17

Orphan Drive

Newsham Dr

P

Everton Village

4

Everton Rd

West Derby Road

Sheil Rd

19

Judges Dr

17

18

20

Start Here

P

1

3

21

P

2

Brunswick Rd

Islington

Prescot Rd

Key

Start Here   Starting Point

Walking Route

1   Map Reference

P   Parking Points

Driving Route

Railway

Fortunes, Fables and Football

Fortunes, Fables and Football
Introduction

The fortunes of Liverpool have risen and fallen over the centuries, and our continuing story is still an adventure. It was clearly our discovery by King John, in the 13th century, that began to make our fortune. He started a series of events that enabled Liverpool to become one of the greatest maritime and trading ports in the world.

Liverpool's rise to great wealth and international renown was spectacular, as was our eventual collapse. However, the indefatigability of Scousers means that whatever hurdles fortune places in our path, we always re-assert ourselves. And, throughout the 1990s, we began to fight back against fickle fortune.

A change in the political landscape of the City, together with an increasing determination in the people to positively re-shape our future, has changed our fortunes once more.

Our history and our heritage are important to us, and so are our legends, tales of local mystery, and stories about our eccentric characters; past and present. Liverpool abounds with such anecdotes, and the area that I have selected for this Chapter is no exception.

For example, not far from where we begin this Chapter, at the City end of Kensington, is Low Hill. This was once a pretty little hamlet with a lovely view across the Town and the river. However, a gentleman named Harrison once lived at Low Hill, in a large house that the locals referred to as **Rats' Castle**. This eccentric individual experimented with food, and he cooked and ate some nauseating meals of spiders, beetles, cats, rats, mice and other creatures. Even worse, he entertained and fed unsuspecting visitors with these gastronomic delicacies!

There are many things about Liverpudlians that set us apart from other communities, not the least of these being our very dry sense of humour. Also of great importance to us is a sense of community, neighbourhood, and family-life. Indeed, Liverpool families can often be more like mini-tribes, in our loyalty and sense of belonging. This is both macro and micro-cosmic, in that our tribal-sense at family level is replicated at community level.

Over the centuries, the fortunes of the City and its people have been mixed. We have known great failure and great success,

grinding poverty and great wealth, times of war and times of peace, times of sadness and times of joy. But our indomitable spirit, combined with our sense of community and our sense of humour, have always seen us through the lows of life; and the same spirit ensures that we enjoy the highs of life with real passion. And one of those passions, of course, is football.

For almost 150 years, soccer has been one of the core elements of social life in Liverpool, and doubly so, because we have two football teams!

"Indeed, mention Liverpool to anyone outside the City and our Football Clubs are one of the first things that they associate with us"

And this is appropriate, as the 'beautiful game' exemplifies how we share emotion and entertainment together, as a community.

The rivalry between Liverpool and Everton Football Clubs notwithstanding (and this is not as divisive as it might appear), we are united by the significance that we ascribe to this sport.

Both Clubs, as shall be seen in this Chapter, had their foundations in the terraced streets of working-class Liverpool and, because they grew out of their neighbourhoods, they were always part of that community.

The teams, and their individual players and managers, became part of the cultural life and the psyche of the people of the City. We still follow their successes and failures closely and take them all very personally, and the relationship between the City's football clubs and their supporters remains a personal one.

And so, let us begin to discover more about the fortunes, fables, and football teams of Liverpool.

To begin this Tour, turn into Shaw Street from Islington and Islington Square, in Everton. As you do so, on the right is an Office Suppliers Store, and on the left, some Georgian Houses.
You will then immediately see, also on the right, the magnificent buildings that are the Particular Baptist Chapel, and the former Liverpool Collegiate School. Take the first road on the left off Shaw Street, which is Langsdale Street, and this leads you to SFX Church; this is just past the Liverpool Hope University at Everton Campus.

Park anywhere that is safe and convenient to do so.

If you have made arrangements to visit the church (which may or may not be open anyway – but don't leave this to chance), then I suggest that you visit this first.
Then you can view the exterior of the Cornerstone Building at Hope University, The Collegiate Building, and the Baptist Chapel.
I suggest a 15-minute stop here; longer if you have pre-arranged a visit inside the church.

The Church of St Francis Xavier

Roman Catholics of the Jesuit Order had been working in the Liverpool area since the 17th century and, in 1712, they built the Town's first Roman Catholic Chapel since the Reformation. (This complete re-shaping of the religious face of Europe began, in October 1517, when Martin Luther nailed his 95 Theses on the practice of indulgences, to the door of the Castle Church in Wittenberg.)

A second, larger, chapel was built in Liverpool in 1736, only to be demolished by a mob in 1738. This was rebuilt the following year but it had to be disguised as a warehouse. This illustrates the difficulties that Catholics experienced in Liverpool, and elsewhere, since the time that King Henry VIII used the doctrines of European Protestantism to justify the anulment of his marriage to Queen Catherine of Aragon. This was so he could then marry his mistress, Anne Boleyn, whom he beheaded anyway a couple of years later, once she failed to give him a male heir. England and the English were then forced to become Protestants, and this process became known as the Reformation.

Before then, England had been a reasonably contented Catholic country. After this, Roman Catholics, and any other religious dissenters and non-conformists from the 'Established Church', became the victims of intolerance and discrimination at best, and of torture and execution at worst. Whilst there was some of the latter in Liverpool, there was much of the former, and Catholics did not begin to regain their basic rights, until the Relief Act of 1793 gave them the right to vote in elections, but not to sit in Parliament. Final complete emancipation only came with the enactment of the Roman Catholic Relief Act in 1829. The residue of this intolerance and discrimination, in fact, lasted in Liverpool well into the 1960s and 70s (see Chapter: 'The Liverpool Waterfront').

It was after this change in the Law that, in 1840, the idea was proposed for building a new Roman Catholic Church in the Town and, typically of Scousers, this happened in a pub! In that year, eight prominent Roman Catholic Liverpool businessmen met in the **Rose & Crown pub**, in Cheapside off Dale Street.

Two weeks later, they had 'secured a plot of land in Salisbury Street, in a respectable part of the Town and where a church would be desirable'. The church was designed by John Joseph Scholes, and its tall, elegant spire, which was added in 1883, remains a prominent local landmark.

And so, a small Jesuit College was opened in Everton, in 1843, followed five years later by the Church, which was dedicated to Saint Francis Xavier (SFX). The establishment of this major Catholic church – run by Jesuits – was a major social advance in the

The Church of St Francis Xavier has some beautiful stained glass windows

conservative, Protestant, Victorian Liverpool of that time; and its significance should not be underestimated.

Nevertheless, between the planning of the new church and its opening, the Great Irish Potato Famine had taken place, killing 25% of the Irish population – almost 1 million Irish men, women, and children; whilst 2 million more emigrated to America – most of these coming through Liverpool.

"The Town became swamped with tens of thousands of Catholic refugees. As a result, SFX church, which had been designed to hold 1,000 people, was now too small"

To provide extra space for services, in 1888 the beautiful **Sodality Chapel** – designed by Edmund Kirkby – was opened. This chapel is now used for most of the weekday services, because the population of the local parish has fallen dramatically in recent decades.

However, during the latter half of the 19th, and early half of the 20th centuries, the parish flourished and, by the outbreak of the Second World War, SFX was the largest Catholic Parish in England, and had over 13,000 Catholics living within its boundaries. It soon built a variety of schools, including SFX College, which was opened in 1843 as the first Catholic Secondary Grammar Day School in the country. Schools for the

Catholic poor of the parish were also established, in 1853. SFX Everton remained a large parish until the 1960s, at which time the Grammar School moved to Woolton, in the southern suburbs of the City.

At the same time, the City Council began to clear away the slums and re-house parishioners in other parts of the City, and beyond.

Everton went into a sharp decline and, by the early 1980s, there were plans to demolish the nave of SFX church. However, a massive, nationwide campaign was successfully fought to save the building; and it was certainly worth the battle. Inside, the church is a magnificent, mid-19th century, Roman, neo-gothic confection of iconography, sculpture, colour, and atmosphere. The predominant colour is in fact white, but this is brightly broken by the wonderful stained-glass windows, and by the rich ornamentation of the interior.

The church of Saint Francis Xavier is well worth visiting, and an even better place to sit, think, and perhaps pray, whatever your faith or philosophy.

Slowly, new houses have been built, and the community has now begun to regain some of its former self-confidence.

Over a decade ago, Liverpool Hope University, which is the only ecumenical university in Europe, moved part of its campus into the then disused SFX School buildings. Their subsequent redevelopment and regeneration of these included, as we shall see, accommodation for 200 students, and homes for their music, fine arts, community education, and drama departments. Hope University had also acquired the church when they bought the site from the Jesuits, but they have since returned it to the parish. Indeed, in 2001, two local parishes, St Joseph's and St Mary of the Angels, joined with SFX to form one new parish and, on December the 8th of that year, the Archbishop of Liverpool, Patrick Kelly, renamed the Sodality Chapel **The Chapel of St Mary of the Angels and St Joseph**. This amalgamation has given a new vitality to the church, to the parish, and to its people, and a new phase has begun in the story of Saint Francis Xavier's at Everton.

To Find Out More:
The Church of St Francis Xavier
Phone: 0151 298 1911/0151 207 2271
http://www.sfxchurchliverpool.com/

Liverpool Hope University at Everton

2

The Angel Field at Liverpool Hope University's Creative Campus

Liverpool Hope University has been present in Liverpool and the Northwest since 1844, but in the form of pre-existing Roman Catholic and Anglican Teacher Training Colleges.

The University was previously Hope University College and its origins were in the 19th century inner-City, at the Roman Catholic College of Notre Dame, in Mount Pleasant. By 1930, its Anglican roots were established at St. Katherine's Teacher Training College in Childwall, in the City's leafy suburbs.

Another college, also destined eventually to become part of Hope College, was Christ's Teacher Training College. This was built, in the 1960s, directly over the road from St. Katherine's College, on Taggart Avenue. In due course, all of these establishments amalgamated to become Liverpool Hope University College; now re-established as Liverpool Hope University. This is now the third of Liverpool's remarkable Higher Education establishments.

In 1995, the decision was made to re-affirm the Christian Mission of the College, and this included a renewed commitment to providing access to Higher Education for those traditionally denied it. In order to achieve this, an inner-city development site was purchased, on Shaw Street in West

Everton. As we have seen, this site was originally the neo-Gothic, 19th century, Jesuit church and college buildings, of Saint Francis Xavier.

When Hope University College first decided to buy and renovate the church and school, the buildings – together with much of the surrounding residential area – had been derelict for many years. They had remained so even after a number of abortive regeneration proposals for this part of Everton. This was one of the centres of urban decay that blighted so many parts of Liverpool, from the 1960s right through to the early 1990s. We shall discover more about this later in this Tour.

In the 1997-8 academic year, the site was bought from the church authorities and the initial funding, of £500,000, was secured from the local Neighbourhood Renewal Partnership. Building and restoration work began in October 1998, using local labour, and the whole complex was completely renovated and redesigned. Even so, many of the original features were retained, and demolition and remodelling were kept to a necessary minimum.

And so, the original Great Hall of the College and its unusual Singing Gallery, which had fallen into dreadful and dangerous

decay, as had the roof of the building threatening to collapse at any time, have now been completely restored. The Hall currently provides a marvellous meeting, entertainment, and celebration space, at the heart of the Hope at Everton campus.

The next stage of the renovation of the site was that of the church itself, which was closed for a year while a new slate roof was laid. Many other repairs and restorations were carried out on the spectacular building, especially to the bell tower and organ loft. As well as this, a new heating system was installed; the organ itself and the magnificent peal of bells were renovated; much crumbling stonework was restored; and the whole building was redecorated.

With beautiful gardens and an outstanding theatre, arts and studio complex in the **Capstone Building**, the University is not only investing in higher education but in the Everton community and neighbourhood.

To Find Out More:
Liverpool Hope University
– Hope at Everton
Phone: 0151 291 3457
www.hope.ac.uk

The Little Tramp

It has recently been discovered that, on 29th October 1900, a particular boy, who had been born in London, in 1889, and who was living temporarily in nearby Salisbury Street, was registered as a pupil at Saint Francis Xavier's Jesuit Secondary and Elementary Schools.

The young boy had an unhappy childhood, and his parents, Charles and Hannah, were touring vaudeville entertainers. But Charles was an alcoholic and Hannah began to suffer from severe headaches, resulting in her being committed to an asylum. The boy's father reluctantly took charge of the child and, from the age of five, the boy joined his father as a touring entertainer.

In 1898, he auditioned for a place in a dancing troupe, 'The Eight Lancashire Lads', run by actor-manager William Jackson. It was whilst performing as a clog-dancer with these troupers that the young lad came to Liverpool to appear at Hengler's Circus – later the Hippodrome Theatre, at the end of Everton Road on West Derby Road. At that time, the Law required that, whilst residing in the Town, he should register locally to receive some education. He attended SFX school, as it was in the same street where he was staying, except that he was Jewish. Nevertheless, a fellow pupil at the time reported that 'the Christian teachers were very kind and understanding, as were his fellow scholars, and he could sit at the side during religious lessons and services'.

When the boy was 11 years old, his father died of alcoholism and, four years later, his mother died, incarcerated in the asylum. The lad knew only theatre and music halls as a way of life and a source of income, so he stayed as a roving entertainer. Although only officially registered as a pupil at SFX School for two weeks, it is likely that he attended at other times too, because it is known that he returned to Liverpool on numerous occasions to appear at many venues in the Town.

By the time that he reached his mid-teenage years, the boy had entertained in London and Paris, and this ultimately led to his being invited, at the age of only 17, to join the internationally famous comedy company of Fred Karno. This took him to America, where he eventually joined Mack Sennett and the Keystone Company in Hollywood.

This talented young man then went on to become the greatest ever star of silent film comedies and, the little boy who once attended SFX School in Everton, grew up to be one of the world's greatest clowns, and to be known the world over as Charlie Chaplin, 'The Little Tramp'.

> **To Find Out More:**
> **Biography of Charlie Chaplin**
> www.clown-ministry.com
> /History/Charlie-Chaplin

Charlie Chaplin, who as a boy, attended SFX School (below)

Spring-Heeled Jack

Liverpool is full of fable, fantasy, and legend, and especially of tales about mysterious and curious personalities. The story of one such local individual is worth telling, and it is the tale of 'Spring-Heeled Jack'!

Between 1837 and 1920 – a total of 83 years, sightings of this bizarre character were reported, mainly in London, but also all over Britain, including Liverpool – in the districts of Toxteth, Aigburth, Childwall, and twice in Everton.

"Described as a tall, thin, powerful man wearing a black cloak, 'Spring-Heeled Jack', as he became known, had large pointy ears and an equally sharp nose. He had red glowing eyes, and was capable of spitting white and blue flames from his mouth"

Most remarkable of all, was that he was able to jump 20 to 30 feet vertically, and 'leap tall buildings at a single bound': Perhaps a not so benign predecessor of Superman?

This was because Jack made a habit of terrorising people, especially women, by appearing suddenly and then noisily spouting his flames at them. He would then spring away again, just as quickly.

There are many accurate reports of incidents involving Jack, some given by Vicars, Policemen, and other such pillars of the community. The first definite evidence of his existence comes from London, where complaints became so numerous about the amazing 'Jumping Man' that, in 1837, the Lord Mayor of the Capital instructed the Police to investigate a series of mysterious appearances and attacks, apparently all perpetrated by Jack. Then, throughout the 1850s and 1860s, Spring-Heeled Jack stories sprung up (rather like him) all over the country, before he finally 'appeared' in Liverpool.

Here, he was first seen in High Park Street in Toxteth, in the early 1880s, then, a few years later he was found jumping over garden walls in St Michaels-in-the-Hamlet, near Aigburth. Next, he appeared leaping around All Saints Church and the Childwall Abbey Inn, in Childwall, and then in 1888, here in Shaw Street.

In the same location, this time in 1904, he was spotted hanging from the steeple of St. Francis Xavier's Church on Salisbury Street. Hundreds of onlookers claimed that he suddenly dropped from the steeple and fell to the ground. Thinking that he had committed suicide, they rushed to the point where he had landed – behind some houses – only to find a helmeted man, clothed in white, standing there waiting for them. As soon as the crowd appeared he scuttled towards them, raised his arms, but abruptly he took to the air over William Henry Street, leaping in gigantic bounds, up and down from roadway to rooftop, and back to the ground again.

This extraordinary bouncing spectacle continued for about ten or twelve minutes before Jack simply disappeared. Many people were subsequently willing to confirm publicly what they had seen, including Police Officers and Priests. However, from that day to this, all sightings of Spring-Heeled Jack ceased and he was never seen again, at least not in Liverpool (that anyone is prepared to admit to!)

Several theories have been proposed to attempt to explain this phenomenon, everything from his simply being a normal man with some sort of spring apparatus on his feet; to his being an insane fire-eater; a costumed acrobat; a malicious phantom; or even the Devil Himself!

Indeed, it was reported that cloven footprints had been found at the site of one of the incidents. However, nothing conclusive has ever explained what or who, was Spring-Heeled Jack.

> **To Find Out More:**
> **Spring-Heeled Jack**
> www.unexplained-mysteries.com/articlejack
> www.geocities.com/Area51/Meteor/3602/springy

Opposite the Hope at Everton campus, across Shaw Street, stands the outstanding, old Liverpool Collegiate Boys' School.

This was built in 1840, and was one of the first public schools in the country, preceding such eminent educational establishments as Marlborough, Cheltenham, and Wellington. It was designed and built by Harvey Lonsdale Elmes, who was aged only 26 at the time, and who was also the original architect of St. George's Hall, in the City-centre. (See Chapter: 'Pool of Life & Culture'.) The main entrance porch is an imposing Tudor-style arch, above which is carved the coat of arms of the school. This is flanked by two statues in niches; on the left is the figure of the 13th Earl of Derby and, on the right, is the figure of Francis Egerton, the Earl of Ellesmere. These men were both patrons of the school.

The Education Acts, which ensured free state-education of all children, did not come into force until the end of the 19th century. So, until then, the poor people of the Town had to depend on local voluntary provision for the schooling of their children; if they bothered with education at all that is. This was usually provided free, and more often than not by the church.

The wealthy of Liverpool however, paid for the education of their younger children in small, privately-run establishments, or they employed individual, private tutors. Some of them extended their children's education, if they thought this to be of any value (and not all did), by then sending them to existing public schools.

Those families who were not so wealthy, paid what they could afford towards education, in such places as Dame Schools or other village schools, of varying standards of quality and effectiveness. There were two such schools at this time in Liverpool, one at Woolton in the south, and another at Walton in the north, and both had been established since Tudor times.

Alternatively, parents might send their older children to the Mechanics' Institute or to the Royal Institution School – both located in the centre of Liverpool, and where scholarships and other charitably-subsidised places were available. However, there was a local need for a large grammar school, of high standards but affordable fees, to meet the aspirations of the rising upper and middle classes of Victorian Liverpool.

Although the school began by running at a loss, pupil numbers soon rose to 400 in the early months and, whilst salaries were lower than average, the Headmaster attracted a young and promising staff, and the school began to develop a reputation for excellence.

The Collegiate never conformed to many of the stereotypes of other 19th century public schools, principally because few similar establishments were sited in such urban areas, and its only boarding pupils lived locally, in the homes of approved schoolmasters.

"Another significant difference between this and other public schools, was that it was known for its supportive and kindly, if strict and formal regime, and for its happy scholars"

Consequently, its reputation and status grew, as did its pupil numbers and income.

In the 20th century, the school ceased operating as a fee-paying establishment and it was taken over by the Local Authority, soon becoming a respected state grammar school. Sadly however, from 1970 the final years of the school's life were a period of steady decline, as the local area fell into ever increasing decay and because the Collegiate could not compete with other City schools.

It changed into a comprehensive school but the end was clearly inevitable. In 1985, a fire caused by vandals severely damaged the school, and completely gutted the assembly hall. Unfortunately, the damage was so extensive that it was not worth the cost of restoration and repair, and the school closed a few months later. Left to decay and further vandalism, the building was once again deliberately fired by arsonists in 1992, leaving the building an empty shell. The Collegiate was fortunately saved from the demolition that once appeared to be its fate by Urban Splash, the redevelopment company who have been responsible for much of the regeneration of Liverpool over the last 15 years or so. They converted the school into a private apartment complex, retaining the building's magnificent façade. The original octagonal assembly hall, in which I had given many talks to the Collegiate boys over the years, and which once was the first home of the Liverpool Philharmonic Orchestra, is now a delightful enclosed garden.

This is one of five refurbished buildings in the North West to have received special acknowledgment because, in 2002 the Collegiate Apartment Building, and Urban Splash, were honoured by the Royal Institute of British Architects. This was in recognition of the Company's contribution to the local environment, and of their high architectural standards. Elmes would be delighted.

The second interesting building in this area is across the road alongside the Collegiate Apartments. This is the Particular Baptist Chapel, another 19th century gem that was once the place of worship for a congregation of dissenting Protestants. It too was saved from the wrecking-ball and converted into apartments, whilst preserving the charm and architectural integrity of the original structure.

The Collegiate Apartments

Leave Langsdale Street and turn right, back into Shaw Street. At the traffic lights, turn left into Brunswick Street. At the top of the hill, filter left at the traffic lights into Everton Road. Continue along for about 500 yards, passing a row of Georgian houses on the left. Just before the road bends to the right, there is a pub on the right, called The Clarence. Immediately after this pub, on the left, is Village Street. This leads onto Brow Side – the heart of the 'lost village' of Everton.

Halfway along this road, as it begins to bend slightly to the right, you will see a pathway coming down from the right; park anywhere here. On the left of the road, behind the railings, is Everton Lock-up.

To the right of the Lock-Up, set into the hillside, are a set of steps. These follow the line of the pathway, and in fact are the site of the original Brow Side, which was the main street in ancient Everton Village. This was where Molly Bushell had her Toffee Shop, and Prince Rupert had his Cottage.

I suggest a 10-15 minute stop here to look at the Lock-Up and the site of the Shop and Cottage.

Everton Village and Everton Toffee

As you approach Village Street, on the right in the middle distance you will see a magnificent, Victorian, sandstone water tower. Connected to a large reservoir at its base, this was erected in 1857, and it still services the large local community.

Travelling along the top of Everton Ridge, we are now at the heart of what was once the ancient village of Everton. This is another of the many 'lost villages' that now make up the conurbation of Liverpool, and it was recorded in the Domesday Book of 1086.

Standing on the highest point in Liverpool, the village was known as 'Evreton' in 1094; as 'Euerton' in 1201; and as 'Everton' since the end of the 13th century. The name Everton derives from the Celtic-Roman 'evoracum', meaning 'wild boar', and the village has a fascinating history.

From the Middle Ages, Everton was a township in its own right, because the villagers held their lands in payment of a yearly rent and service directly to the King. This meant that they were not part of the greater manor of West Derby, which encompassed most of the surrounding area at that time and, consequently, the 'Evertonians' had a certain independence. This was much valued by the villagers, and this self-determination

Everton Lock-up

still characterises Everton people. Like any typical, small, rural community, the population of Everton remained static for centuries, and this was a settled and relatively isolated village. Even in 1801, the population was recorded as being only 499 people, and the Village grew up around an area that had previously been known as 'Sandstone Hill'.

However, during the English Civil War, in the mid 17th century (1642-46), the tranquillity and isolation of the village came to an abrupt end, and Everton suddenly took on a strategic importance. It was from Everton Heights, with its unobstructed overview of the Township of Liverpool, that **Prince Rupert of the Rhine** (1619-1682), who was the nephew of King Charles I (1600-1649), stood against the forces of Oliver Cromwell (1599-1658) and organised the siege of the Town. He established his headquarters in a cottage on Browside, the short lane that ran right through the heart of the old village. Modern Rupert Row and Rupert Lane are amongst the local places that are named after him. After the Civil War ended, **Prince Rupert's Cottage** became an ordinary home once more and, for many years, it was occupied as a family home.

This is not the only fable associated with Everton, because a local story tells that, on his march south from Scotland during his attempt to reclaim the English throne for the Stuarts, in 1745, **Bonnie Prince Charlie** (1720-88) once stayed at Prince Rupert's Cottage. Whilst there, he liked to use on an old oak chair that was believed to be the one used by his ancestral royal relative. Prince Charles had also come to Everton to take advantage of its strategic location of the village, and to plan an assault Liverpool. Indeed, the townspeople had erected some defences around the Town in the event of an attack. However, there is no evidence whatsoever that the Young Pretender ever came to Liverpool, let alone to Everton. However, that did not stop early Evertonians claiming that he did!

Around 1690, another larger cottage was built next to Prince Rupert's old cottage, and it was here, in 1753, that **Molly Bushel** (1746-1818) began to make the boiled sweets that she called **Everton Toffee**.

"This toffee was much prized, not just by local people, but also by the wealthier classes"

And so, in 1783, Molly converted her house into a shop and began to expand her range of confectionery. Later, Everton Toffee, which continued to be made by Molly's descendants, became a great favourite with Queen Victoria and her family, who had batches of it regularly shipped to Windsor Castle. Charles Dickens also ordered regular supplies of the sweet. The recipe was not Molly's own though. It had been given to her by its inventor, Doctor James Gerrard, who was a local physician and Town Council member.

During the time that Molly lived next door to Prince Rupert's Cottage, its current occupiers decided to sell off some of the furniture. At the sale, Molly bought the chair that was claimed to have supported the regal bottoms of Rupert and Charlie. Now, as well as bolstering her own buttocks, Molly used the chair to provide her with a profitable sideline to her toffee sales. She would charge visitors to her shop, a few pennies to see and perhaps to sit in the significant seat.

As Everton began to expand, the centre of life in the village was around the village green and Molly's Toffee Shop, and there was a significant rise in the numbers of visitors to the village. These people came to take the air, to buy the famous toffee, and to see Prince Rupert's old Cottage. Indeed, this was regularly the target of souvenir-hunters, who used to pull out chunks from the walls. Eventually, there were so many day-trippers that, in 1787, it was considered necessary to build a local lock-up 'to house drunks and unruly revellers overnight'. This became a well-known landmark, sometimes called **The Stone Jug**, and it is one of only two surviving village gaols in Liverpool, the other being located in the middle of Wavertree Village, to the south of the City. (See Chapter: 'Liverpool Lost and Found'.)

When Molly Bushell died, in 1818, her recipe, and her goods and chattels – including Prince Rupert's chair, passed to her family, who continued to make and sell the renowned and popular Everton Toffee. However, the depredations of the tourists continued to weaken the structure of Rupert's Cottage and it had to be pulled down in 1845. The previous year, and for similar reasons, Molly Bushell's Toffee Shop and cottage had already been demolished and, very soon after, so was the rest of Browside.

However, the Bushell family had by this time acquired another property and shop, at No 1 Netherfield Road, which was still in the heart of Everton Village. Everton Toffee continued to be sold by the family from this address until 1913, when, in that year, the last of the toffee making dynasty, Clara Bannister, retired. The shop and the toffee recipe were subsequently bought by the confectionary firm, Nobletts, who used the trademark 'Mother Noblett' – based on an image of Molly Bushell – to sell their version of Everton Toffee. Nobletts were eventually sold to Barker & Dobson, who continue to sell Everton Toffee. Nevertheless, this company do not claim that their recipe for it is authentic. So don't assume that what you taste when you eat modern Everton Toffee is the same as Molly Bushell's customers would have tasted!

The Netherfield Road shop was eventually pulled down to make way for new housing, but the Everton lock-up still stands, and is now a listed building. It is in excellent condition and is well-maintained by the City Council. Everton Football Club took the image of the lock-up as the central device on its club emblem, and the Club's nickname remains 'The Toffees', after Molly Bushell's famous sweets. Interestingly, there are descendants of Molly Bushell living on Merseyside, and they still own Molly's copper toffee-making pan, and Prince Rupert's wooden chair.

Liverpool's wealth grew during the late 18th century, with vast fortunes being made in the West Indies, America, and beyond, from the transport and sale of slaves and other 'commodities', such as cotton, tobacco, molasses, and sugar. (See Chapter: 'The Liverpool Waterfront'.) From the 1790's onwards, the more well-to-do merchants erected fine villas and mansions – surrounded by large gardens – 'out in the country' on 'the 'Everton Heights'. They knocked down cottages that had been standing for two or three hundred years to do so, and made the long ridge an enclave of wealth and privilege. Here, they established miniature stately-homes for themselves, and for their wives, children, and servants, and the quality of life for these people was very good indeed.

Fine views of the river, the Wirral, and North Wales, together with the pure sea air, made this a very healthy place to live. During this period, the district was the 'genteel' retreat from the crowded and increasing squalor of Liverpool. In 1800, Everton was described as 'a pretty village with a view, which embraces town, village, plain, pasture, river, and ocean.' Thirty years later, a visitor to the district noted that: 'Everton now abounds with handsome walled pleasure grounds and well-enclosed fields'.

New roads were built connecting Everton with the Town and, in the summer of 1812, over 70,000 people came to Everton to watch the ascent of the renowned balloonist, James Sadler. However, the idyllic life of Everton was soon to be shattered, following the Irish Potato Famine in 1845 and 1846, and because of the vast numbers of refugees who came to Liverpool as a result. Everton became one of the places that these desperate people came to settle, and a totally new and much more blighted form of family-life was to overtake the district.

To Find Out More:
Domesday Book
www.nationalarchives.gov.uk/domesday

The view over the city and Wirral from Everton Ridge

Village Street/Brow Side is a cul-de-sac, so turn around and reverse your route back up to Everton Road again. Turn left. At this point you get a good view of the nearby Victorian Water Tower.
Cross the traffic lights at Breck Road, and then take your next left, through the park gates, onto Everton Ridge. Take the driveway, and park anywhere on the look-out point above the City of Liverpool.
From here, not only can you see Liverpool laid out before you, but you can see the Mersey Estuary; right out onto the Irish Sea; the whole of the Wirral Peninsular; and, on a clear day, the hills of North Wales. I suggest a 10-15 minute stop here, to drink in the views.
The driveway on the Ridge is a cul-de-sac, with a mini-roundabout at the end, so it is easy to turn around.
Return back onto the main road once more, and turn left into what is now Heyworth Street; passing May Duncan's Pub on the left.
Follow the road as it snakes around, passing the Old Campfield Pub on the right: This is where Prince Rupert of the Rhine based his troops and cavalry, whilst he was besieging Liverpool during the English Civil War.
A further 500 yards along on the right, you will then see the extremely ornate Mere Bank Pub, standing on the corner of Mere Lane; turn right here and park alongside the pub. From this point you can visit the pub, the Library, and St George's Church – the site of Everton Beacon.
I suggest a 15-20 minute stop to visit these buildings. Longer if you have pre-arranged a visit to the church, or if you intend to take a break at the Mere Bank Pub.

His cannon were arrayed from where the Wellington Column now dominates William Brown Street, to a point now occupied by the Adelphi Hotel, and he besieged the Town, subjecting the people to a constant barrage of artillery. Nevertheless, the arrogant Prince was soon to discover to his cost, that the resistance mounted by the townspeople was considerable and determined. After a continuous cannonade against the Town, which the people of Liverpool returned in kind, he had been forced to use over 100 barrels of powder in numerous attacks, and had lost 1,500 of his men.

However, this only stiffened Rupert's resolve and, on the 11th June 1644, he ordered a secret, night-time attack that was aided by a 'fifth column' of Royalist sympathisers who lived in the Town, led by Caryll Molyneux (later to become 3rd Viscount Molyneux). Molyneux's men treacherously breached the Town's defensive walls in a number of places, and Rupert's troops poured into Liverpool. The assault was swift and exceptionally brutal and, in a bloody massacre, the Prince's men put to the sword everyone they encountered.

Caryll Molyneux himself personally killed a number of the Town's Burgesses, and the memory of this cruelty lived long in the hearts of the townspeople. During the siege and the subsequent sacking of the Town over 360 townsfolk lost their lives and, the Town records relate that of these were "some that had never borne arms... yea, even one poor blind man". It took the surviving men and the returning women six months to finish burying their dead.

Once the battle was over and all resistance quashed, Rupert ordered the complete sacking and firing of the town, which was plundered of all its money, gold, and treasures and left in smoking ruins. Liverpool Castle was one of the few buildings that survived the assault largely intact, and Rupert stayed there for nine nights before moving on to York, on the orders of King Charles I.

Rupert needed to move quickly and, legend has it that, as the loot of Liverpool – mostly gold bullion – amounted to a sizeable prize, and was difficult to transport across what was still war-torn countryside, the Prince needed a safe place to hide it. He decided that it should be buried in a tunnel that still runs from under the site of his Cottage, beneath Netherfield Road, down to the Dock Road at The Goree.

However, before it could be recovered by the Royalists, the War took a turn against them and on the 1st November 1644, the Town was recaptured by the Parliamentarians. Liverpool was then permanently held by the troops of Oliver Cromwell and their local supporters, until the end of the War, in 1646.

In fact, the Town's Governor, Colonel John Moore, became one of the Regicides, and Lord Derby was captured, and beheaded by the Puritans in 1651. He went to his death with great dignity and heroism, which began to soften the attitude of the townsfolk to his family, and the Stanleys soon won their way back into favour in the Town, whilst the Molyneuxs remained unpopular for centuries.

During the confusion following the end of the Civil War, the precise location of the missing treasure and the loot of Liverpool were lost. The tunnel under Everton was well known, even at that time, and has been explored by many treasure hunters in the subsequent centuries, but without success.

Liverpool, the English Civil War, and the Town's Lost Treasure

Early in the Civil War, in 1642, and when the population stood at around 1,000 people, the Royalists seized Liverpool Town and its Castle. Then, in April 1643, the Town was taken by the Parliamentarians. This was at the cost of 80 Royalist dead and 300 being taken prisoner; as against only seven Parliamentarians losing their lives.

The most prominent Baronial families in Liverpool at the time were the Stanleys (the Earls of Derby), and the Molyneuxs (later to become the Earls of Sefton; see Chapter: 'A Lordly Heritage'). As we have seen, Prince Rupert of the Rhine, then aged only 24, brought his troops here in May 1644, to recapture the Town for the King, and at the urging of Lord Derby.

The German Prince chose to plan his attack from Everton, not only because it afforded a magnificent overview of the Town, but also because the village was a Royalist stronghold, and was home to Catholic Priests who had been expelled from the Town by the dominant Puritans. And so, Rupert set up his headquarters and home in the cottage on Browside, in the heart of rural Everton Village. It was from this vantage-point that the Prince made his famous comment about taking Liverpool, by saying that the Town "was but a crow's nest that a parcel of boys could take".

Rupert had brought a large army of 10,000 men to attack the Town, and his men camped, with their horses, munitions, and supplies, on land now to the right of Heyworth Street, opposite Everton Ridge. The modern Campfield Pub, with its portrait of Prince Rupert as its signboard, commemorates this. A new Academy School now stands on the site of Prince Rupert's encampment. Realising the strength of the imminent attack, all the women and children were evacuated to safety on the Wirral. This left around 450 men defending the town.

Beginning his seige on the 6th June, Prince Rupert must have initially regretted his brashness, because his guns could not reach the Town from Everton, and he had to reposition his batteries in trenches much nearer to his target, on the edge of what was then 'The Great Heath', along the line of what is now Lime Street.

"Liverpool is a warren of subterranean passages, caverns, and tunnels; mostly natural but very many are man-made, whilst some are a combination of both, as in the case of the Everton tunnel"

However, there is a twist in this tale because, in the early 19th century, another such tunnel was discovered running from Ranelagh Street to what is now Beetham Plaza on Brunswick Street.

Not only were skeletons found, dating from the English Civil War, but also written records that actually referred to Rupert's Treasure and the Everton Tunnel. But these gave no clue to the whereabouts of the horde, and so the lost gold of Liverpool still lies somewhere under the City's busy modern streets; perhaps waiting to be discovered by a latter-day, Scouse, Indiana Jones!

Everton Beacon and St George's Church

6

The highest building in the ancient village of Everton was once the **Fire Beacon**. This stood on the highest point of the ridge, where St. George's Church now stands, and roughly in the position of the east corner of the present building.

It was six yards square and about 25 feet high, and was constructed in plain stone. There was a viewing platform on the roof with a guardroom below, and a kitchen area at ground level. Opinions vary as to when it was erected; with some historians suggesting that it was built in the 1220's, whilst others believe that it was built around 1580, specifically to warn against the Spanish Armada. The Beacon fire was indeed lit when the Spanish Fleet was sighted off the coast of England, as were all the other beacons around 'this blessed plot set in a silver sea'. However, most authorities believe that Everton Beacon was actually constructed in 1230, during the reign of King Henry III (1207-1272), by Ranulf the Earl of Chester (1172-1232), who was the first Baron of Liverpool.

For centuries, the Beacon was quite a feature of both the local geography and of community life as, on fine days, hundreds of people would gather on the grassy slopes below the tower to picnic and relax. Indeed, early in the reign of King Charles I and during the proscription of the Clergy, people would climb up to the top of the Beacon to get married. Throughout the period of the Napoleonic Wars when, in 1760 an attack on Liverpool by the French fleet was expected, local soldiers were stationed on the Beacon and instructed to light the warning fire if the foreign ships were sighted. Barrels of turpentine and pitch were kept in the guardroom for the purpose but, fortunately, the enemy fleet never came and this time the Beacon fire remained unlit.

The ancient fire-beacon that once stood on the site of St George's Church

Towards the end of the 18th century, the Beacon was becoming unsafe and by this time it was certainly at least 200 years old, if not very much older, and in a very bad state of repair. Discussions were underway about rebuilding it, but the local authorities were spared the trouble when, on a very stormy night in 1803, it blew down anyway. Nevertheless, the war with the French continued in full force and a warning system was still needed.

And so, it was agreed to adopt the very latest technology, and a mechanical **Semaphore Station** was built to replace the Beacon. However, this was abandoned after the Battle of Waterloo and the final defeat of the French, in 1815.

It was decided that a new church should now be built on the site, to represent peace after such a long period of war, and so a public subscription was organised that raised £11,500. By this time, a local man named **James Atherton** (1770-1838), who owned the site of the Beacon, donated the land for the new church. James was a wealthy property developer and speculator, who not only built many of the luxurious mansion houses in the area, but he was also responsible for the creation of the 'investment opportunity', which was to become the speculative resort Town of New Brighton on the Wirral.

And so, the site of the old Beacon and Semaphore Station was cleared, and construction on the new church began in 1815. As the excavations were underway, the bodies of two soldiers were unearthed, and these were believed to be members of Prince Rupert's troops from the Civil War, although no indication was found to explain how they died, or why they were buried on the top of the hill. The architect of the new church was Thomas Rickman (1776-1841), who was quite innovative for the time, and used much cast iron in the construction of the building. He was a master of working in iron, and a pioneer in building using methods of prefabrication. He also built the cast-iron church of St. Michael's-in-the-Hamlet near Aigburth, around the same time as he built St. George's.

St. George's church has served the parish and local community well for almost 200 years, and it was restored in 1937. It is a magnificent building, and it has certainly stood the test of time, to become what is now the oldest building in the district.

> **To Find Out More:**
> St George's Church Everton
> Phone: 0151 263 1943
> http://www.neighbourhoodservices .com/stgeorgeschurch/
> www.lookingatbuildings.org.uk/ default.asp?Document=3.H.2.6

Mere Brow Pub and Everton Library

Across St. Domingo Road, directly opposite the church on the corner of Mere Lane, stands the Mere Pub. This attractive and highly ornate hostelry was built in 1881.

It is decorated all over in flowers, which are set in white plaster panels and in the red terracotta walls. Statues of a medieval King and Queen dominate the front façade, and there is also a magnificent terracotta coat of arms surrounded by the Prince of Wales' feathers, shamrocks, Scottish thistles, Lancashire roses, English lions, and a Welsh harp.

To the left of the pub, on the corner of Beacon Lane, stands Everton Public Library.

This was once home to a Technical College as well as a public library.

The building was designed by Thomas Shelmerdine (1845-1921), who was the City Surveyor, and was built a few years later than the Mere Pub.

Costing the huge sum – for the time – of £11,300, it opened in 1896, in what was then one of the most densely populated parts of the City, and it was a much used local amenity.

There were originally separate reading rooms for ladies, boys, and the public, and over 25,000 books were available. Sadly, at the time of writing, this building is closed, but it remains a remarkable example of late-Victorian, public urban architecture.

Everton Library and the Mere Brow Pub

To visit the site of where both of Liverpool's Football Clubs were born, continue all the way along Mere Lane; passing the Derry Social Club on the left:
You are now in the protestant hinterland of Liverpool, and the territory of the Orange Lodge.
At the end of Mere Lane, at its junction with Breckfield Road North, you will see one of, if not the only surviving Victorian, double gas-lamps in the City. There is also a small lay-by on the left, so park here to visit the site of where Association Football in Liverpool had its roots. Cross over the road and walk along to the right. You will pass Salisbury Road and then come to St Domingo Grove. Between here and St Domingo Vale stands Liberton Court.
This is the site of St Domingo Methodist Church – where it all began.
But, be warned – there is nothing to see here except this rather nondescript, modern apartment block – so don't be disappointed!
This is a 5-minute stroll.

The Birth of 'The Blues' and 'The Reds'

Reds fans on The Kop at Anfield, home of Liverpool FC

The continuation of Heyworth Street is St. Domingo Road, and this name has much significance in this part of our story.

However, it became important in the mid-18th century, when it was the name of a very grand mansion set in an equally grand estate. The house once stood where Everton Library now stands on the corner of Beacon Lane, and it was called **St. Domingo House**.

This was built by George Campbell, who was a wealthy merchant with interests in the West Indies. He named his new home – which apparently looked like a miniature gothic cathedral – after a French ship that he had captured off the coast of San Domingo in the Caribbean. The house was demolished after Campbell's death, in 1773, but then a John Sparling built another mansion in its place, and he lived there until his own death, in 1800. The estate's grounds stretched as far as Walton Breck Road, St Domingo Vale, and St Domingo Grove, which also take their names from the original house.

Liverpool has not always had two footballs teams. In fact, its first Club was Everton FC, which was originally attached to the local English Methodist congregation, called New Connexion who, in 1868, wished to build a chapel in the Liverpool area. The church bought some land on Breckfield Road North, between St. Domingo Vale and St. Domingo Grove. Taking the name of **St. Domingo Methodist Church**, their new chapel was opened in 1871 and, six years later, they appointed Rev B.S. Chambers as the first Minister.

Concerned that the young men of his parish had little to occupy their free time productively, he established a cricket team. However, this is only a summer sport, and so he needed a pastime for other seasons as well. And so, a football club called **St. Domingo FC** was formed, in 1878. This generated a lot of interest from people outside the parish and so a public meeting was held, in November 1879. This took place in the Queen's Head Hotel in Village Street, close to the old Everton Toffee Shop. The meeting agreed to change the team name to **Everton Football Club**, after the surrounding district, but the newly constituted club soon adopted the nickname 'The Toffees', because of Molly Bushell's famous toffee.

From 1879, the Club played on open land on the southeast corner of Stanley Park and then, in 1882, a man named J. Cruitt donated land at Priory Road, which became the Club's ground for a couple of years. Then they moved again, in 1884, onto the site of the present Anfield Stadium. This land was owned by Joseph Orrell, who gave the club permission to use his field, on the basis that they kept the existing walls in good repair and did not cause a nuisance. A small sum was paid in rent.

The Everton FC president **John Houlding** (1833-1902), a local brewer and landlord of the nearby Sandon Hotel (which still stands), would soon become the Club's Anfield landlord, which meant he had split interests. He decided to put up the rent, and repeated the increase twice more. There was a serious boardroom row that reached fever pitch at the start of 1892. This resulted in a split within the Board, the team, and the supporters. George Mahon, a respected local figure and who was the organist at St. Domingo's Church (Everton's spiritual home), led the battle against Houlding and, in the summer of 1892, he took Everton to an ambitious new home on the north side of Stanley Park, called the Mere Green Field. This would soon be re-named **Goodison Park**.

The land was bought for £8,090 – a wasteland that would become one of the sporting wonders of Victorian England. The club retained the name Everton, despite a failed appeal to the Football Association by Houlding to retain the name at Anfield, where his breakaway football team eventually took the name **Liverpool Football Club**.

Nothing now remains of the site of St Domingo Methodist Church, where the remarkable story of football in Liverpool began. Long since demolished, the location is now a rather plain sheltered housing unit for the elderly, called **Liberton Court**.

However, inside the main entrance to the building is a memorial plaque dedicated to Everton FC's most illustrious player, the remarkable William Ralph 'Dixie' Dean, and which also marks the site of the old church.

Returning to your car, and from the end of Mere Lane turn left into Robson Street, and drive up to the traffic lights. On the left at the junction stands the Stanley Pub. This has a pair of large, grotesque, and fabulous dragon gargoyles on the high pediment over the main entrance.
Turn right at this junction into Walton Breck Road, and ahead you will immediately see the Liverpool Football Club Stadium, Anfield. At the end of the stadium, turn left into the car park.

Liverpool star, Steven Gerrard, celebrates at Anfield

Liverpool Football Club

Liverpool FC and Everton FC both have illustrious histories, and they are a major factor in the economic and social life of the City.

Arguably, the most famous manager of LFC was **Bill Shankly** (1913-1981), who was with the Club from 1959 to 1974. He once said: "We have the two best teams on Merseyside, Liverpool, and Liverpool Reserves"!

He also said: "Some people believe football is a matter of life and death. I'm very disappointed with that attitude. I can assure you, it is much, much more important than that"!

John Houlding was the chairman of the new Liverpool Football Club from 1892, and his pub, the Sandon, continued as the team's headquarters, having previously been Everton's base. Indeed, the first team photos were taken on the bowling green that once stood behind this pub, and which is now the car park. Before dressing rooms were built at their new playing field, the players would change into their kit at the pub, and then walk down Oakfield Road to play their matches on the team pitch.

Houlding was a brewer, an Alderman, a Justice of the Peace, and a former Lord Mayor of Liverpool, so he was certainly a force to be reckoned with! Indeed, he had played an active role in Everton becoming an original member of the Football League. He was also a member of the Masonic Order, which did not endear him to the older church-members of the board of Everton, and neither did his trade in 'the demon drink'! In fact, the Sandon is adorned with many Masonic signs and symbols. These differences, together with Houlding's dominant personality – as well as his increases in the rent for the football ground, led to the rancorous dispute that saw a new football club being created.

The Board members, players, and supporters who had split from the original club, formed themselves into this club, with Houlding as Chairman of the Board. They stayed at the Anfield Ground, which became their permanent home and, ever since those events, a fierce rivalry has existed between Everton FC and Liverpool FC, although one with much less rancour than sometimes occurs in other cities with two football teams!

Houlding tried to register his new team as the 'Everton Football Club and Athletic Grounds Company Limited', but the Football Association would not allow a second club to use the name of 'Everton'. Refusing to be defeated, in 1892, he registered his club under the name of 'Liverpool Football Club' instead. Now, as Chairman of the Liverpool FC Board, Houlding ran the Club with skill and real business-acumen, until he died 10 years later. In the meantime, he had made Liverpool FC a very serious rival to Everton FC, now located on the opposite side of Stanley Park.

9

This was the Afrikaans name, meaning 'spy hill' or 'look-out', of a hill near Ladysmith in South Africa. In 1900, this was the scene of a battle in the Boer War. The particular association with Anfield and LFC, stems from the fact that Liverpool is (or was) a Lancashire Club, and that the futile British assault on Spion Kop had been led by the 2nd Royal Lancaster Regiment and the 2nd Royal Lancashire Fusiliers, and many Scousers died in the engagement. Similar terraces at some other football grounds are also known as 'kops'.

The club was now well established, with a very large and loyal supporter network. The memory of the split with Everton was now a thing of the past, as the Club forged its own identity and playing style. By this time too, they had changed their strip, which had always been blue and white quarters, to the red shirts that are now so special to Liverpool FC fans.

In 1929, the Anfield ground was improved and the Kop was completely rebuilt: Now it consisted of 100 concrete steps, standing 50 feet high, 135 feet deep, and nearly 400 feet long. The team continued to be one of the most successful in British football – until the 1950s that is, when they were relegated to the Second Division once more. Nothing seemed to be able to turn round the club's fortunes; something dramatic had to be done. And so, the Club Chairman, Tom Williams, approached a former Preston North End player – the no-nonsense Bill Shankly – who became Liverpool FC's Manager, in December 1959.

"The Scotsman's passion, determination, and fierce loyalty to the club, his players, and especially to the fans, saw the Club develop into one of the greatest in the world"

Following Shankly's retirement in 1974, amid many tears and tributes, the management of the Club was taken over by **Bob Paisley** who, in terms of trophies, became the club's most successful manager. Perhaps the greatest night in the Club's history, up to that time, was on the 25th May 1977. Having retained the League title and unluckily lost an FA Cup Final, Liverpool beat the crack German side, Borussia Moenchengladbach 3-1, to win the European Cup in Rome.

However, during Paisley's time as manager, Bill Shankly died, in 1981. The Shankly Memorial Gates were erected at Anfield and dedicated by his widow, Nessie, on 26th August 1982. Bob Paisley retired in 1983 with gates also built in his name at the Kop end. The Club's subsequent Managers have followed in the illustrious footsteps of their predecessors and so, the 'breakaway club' has gone from strength to strength.

Liverpool FC remain one of the most successful and popular football clubs on the national and international sports scene. Indeed, the list of the Club's honours is so long that it would take up too much space in this article so, for more information, just have a look at the Club website and be prepared to be very impressed!

Whether a Liverpool FC supporter or not, to stand in any other part of the crowd during a match, and to hear the 'Kop Choir', is awe-inspiring, particularly when the whole stadium sings **'You'll Never Walk Alone'**. This finale song from the Rogers' and Hammerstein musical 'Carousel', tells of overcoming adversity through the support of others, and of fighting together against the odds. It became the Liverpool FC and Kop Anthem in 1963, after local pop group 'Gerry and the Pacemakers' gained a No 1 hit with the song. When Liverpool supporters sing this in unison, it is a powerful, moving, and poignant experience, especially since the tragedy of the Hillsborough Disaster.

Liverpool Football Club intend to move away from the Anfield ground, to a new, 80,000-seat, state-of-the-art stadium, being built on the car-park side of Stanley Park. This is actually just across the road from the existing Anfield ground. The new stadium will retain the name of Anfield, and the current position of the Hillsborough Memorial (which I shall mention shortly) would be taken into consideration when the final plans are confirmed. At the same time that the new football ground is built, Stanley Park and nearby Anfield Cemetery will be refurbished and re-landscaped.

When Liverpool Football Club does move to their new location, the current ground at Anfield will become 'Anfield Plaza'. The Plaza will be a major tourist attraction, which could include a small park and community buildings, shops, apartments and offices, and a hotel, bars and restaurants. It will cover an area of around 17,000 square metres and should create over a thousand jobs.

It is also hoped that a museum-cum-heritage feature will form part of the new complex, as a tribute to Liverpool Football Club, its managers, players, and supporters. But, at the time of writing, we wait to see how the next chapter in the story of Liverpool Football Club will be written.

Liverpool's first competitive match was played against Higher Walton, in the Lancashire League, with a thumping 8-0 victory. They went on to win the title, and also claimed the Liverpool Cup, but there was a sting in the tale. Both trophies were stolen and the board of directors had to pay £130 to replace them. After the club's first year, they applied to be admitted as members of the Football League. They were accepted and, in the 1893-94 season, Liverpool were admitted to the Second Division, ironically, at the expense of Mersey rivals Bootle FC. The team went on to win 26 of their next 28 League games, gaining promotion to the First Division.

However, Everton FC was undoubtedly the better team at this point, and at the end of their first League season, Liverpool FC were relegated back down to the Second Division.

But this was a temporary situation. The team returned to the top flight and, in 1901, won their first League Championship. From that time, their reputation, success, and income were assured. Also, Liverpool's performance consolidated to such an extent that, by 1904, they had won their second Championship title. To celebrate this, the directors of the Club decided to build a new supporters' terrace, of embanked brick and cinders, which they opened in 1906. The Liverpool Echo sports editor of the day, Ernest Edwards, described it as being like a **Spion Kop**.

To Find Out More:
Liverpool Football Club
Phone: 0151 263 2361
Tour Bookings: 0151 260 6677
http://www.liverpoolfc.tv/

Liverpool FC – Independent Fans
Website: www.redandwhitekop.com/

Club Honours
http://www.anfield-online.co.uk/
stats/honours.htm

New Anfield Football Stadium
www.newanfield.co.uk

From the Liverpool FC car park, turn left back into Walton Breck Road. At this point the road divides into Oakfield Road, bending to the right, and the continuation of Walton Breck Road, which forks left.

Take this left fork, and then the next left into Wylva Road. At the T-junction, turn left into Anfield Road. Pass the football ground on the left, and you will come to the Shankly Gates and the Hillsborough Memorial.

The Hillsborough Memorial

10

As we travel along Anfield Road, directly opposite the rear of the football stadium, stands Stanley House.

This was the home of John Houlding, who could well afford to build such a palatial home. He also constructed the platform-like balcony that still exists at the end of the house, so that he could watch his team playing from this excellent vantage point. Initially, he could watch the games being played on the St. Domingo's pitch in Stanley Park, and then, after moving to the present site at Anfield, he could face the other way and watch his new team playing there.

Liverpudlians are emotional people. We are caring and warm, and are known for our wit and our sense of humour. We are passionate, and are not afraid to share our feelings and our opinions with anyone and everyone; whether invited to or not! There is a unifying sense of community in the City, which crosses the boundaries of religion, politics, and income. This is seen at its best when the City is in genuine crisis: and the depression; the War; the 1960s industrial decline; the Toxteth Riots; the recession; and particularly the Hillsborough Disaster, have all brought us closer together.

The Hillsborough memorial

The memorial to this catastrophe is sited by the Bill Shankly Memorial Gates on Anfield Road, and it commemorates the deaths of 96 football supporters, many of them young people and children. They were crushed to death at a football match in Sheffield, on 15th April 1989, and the youngest victim was a boy of only 10 years-of-age.

Here, an eternal flame burns alongside a poignant list of the names and ages of the victims, but sadly, many of the victims' families are still fighting for the justice that they feel they have never received, from either the courts or the establishment.

As well as those killed, 766 people were injured, many of them being permanently disabled, and so, on many levels the suffering from Hillsborough continues. This tragedy is still significant in the hearts of many people in the City, as anyone will tell you who watched the horror unfold on television, or who laid flowers on the Anfield pitch in the days after the deaths. Football and family-life are so deeply rooted in our city culture, that the collective grief expressed continues to colour local attitudes. Liverpudlians are sensitive about how they are regarded by the rest of the world, and the way in which the Sun newspaper reported the Hillsborough Disaster still affects us.

It falsely accused Liverpool supporters of gross acts during the tragedy, and caused massive local resentment. Consequently, the tabloid still has its lowest sales of anywhere in the country, here on Merseyside.

To Find Out More:
The Hillsborough Memorial
www.liverpoolfc.tv/lfc_story/memorial/

From the memorial, continue along Anfield Road past the King Harry Pub, which has a heavily carved relief panel in the wall, stating that the pub was built in 1885. Just beyond the pub, park anywhere on the left that it is safe to do so. The entrance to Stanley Park is on the right-hand side of this road, through the railings, and to the left of the sandstone lodge house.
As you enter you will see the long-neglected palm house but, just beyond this is a remarkable sandstone gazebo, plus the delightful gardens and boating lake. I suggest 30-40 minutes to explore the park.

Stanley Park and Anfield

11

Anfield is the district behind Everton's high ridge, and it lies between Everton and the districts of Walton, West Derby, and Tuebrook.

Anfield takes its name from 'hanging field', which has nothing to do with executions; it simply means a sloping field. This is a reference to the long expanse of farmland that once existed adjacent to the village of Everton. Although Anfield is now a largely run-down, mid-Victorian suburb, the layout of many of its principal roads has remained unchanged for more than 200 years, and the district still has many interesting buildings and areas.

Anfield is a spacious neighbourhood, with tree-lined roads, and small recreation grounds and playing fields. However, its greatest asset, disregarding the Football Clubs, is Stanley Park.

This separates Liverpool FC's Anfield ground from Everton FC's ground at Goodison Park, and it was laid out in the late 1860s. During that decade it was decided that north Liverpool needed a large area of public space, and the concept of Stanley Park was that of Edward Robson, the Corporation Architect. Consequently, 95 acres of land in Anfield was bought from Lord Derby, at an original cost of £115,556,

and the Corporation also bought a number of small estates on what were then the fringes of Liverpool. These included Walton Lodge, the Woodlands Estate, and 'a small row of houses fronting Priory Lane', which were cleared for the new park.

This large area was then landscaped with trees, shrubberies, lakes, rambling pathways, and a dramatic terrace adorned with

The gardens in Stanley Park

sandstone shelters and gazebos. There were also aviaries and a large boating lake. This work was part-funded from the sales of large, detached houses, built around the park perimeter, and many of which survive. Stanley Park was named after Lord Derby, and landscaped by Edward Kemp (1817-1891), who was a protégé of Joseph Paxton. Kemp trained under Paxton, during work he carried out at Chatsworth House in Derbyshire and at Birkenhead Park on the Wirral. Frederick Law Olmstead, a landscape gardener and designer from America, who visited Liverpool and Birkenhead at the time, was very impressed by what he saw and learned. He returned home and later modelled New York's Central Park on Birkenhead Park.

Stanley Park opened to the public in May 1870 and, when it did so, it soon became celebrated for its views of the 'Cumberland, Westmoreland, and Yorkshire hills', especially when 'the state of the atmosphere and the time of the day are favourable'.

"Like its counterpart Sefton Park in the south, Stanley Park has a large, glazed, cast-iron Palm House"

Both of these structures were donated to the Town by Henry Yates Thompson (1838-1928), the great nephew of the founder of Princes Park, also in south Liverpool. The Stanley Park Palm House was known as **The Gladstone Conservatory**, in honour of the four-time Prime Minister, born in Rodney Street in the Town, in 1809. The building was badly damaged by a bomb blast in the Second World War, and was not reopened until September 15th 1958.

After being a hot house for plants, in the 1980s the Palm House became a restaurant, and then a nightclub of dubious reputation. Once empty, neglected, and badly vandalised, it has now been gloriously restored and reopened as the Isla Gladstone Conservatory; a great place for dining, functions and events.

Stanley Park retains a number of its other original features, including the lake, the landscaped gardens, bridges, walkways, playing fields, and a magnificent sandstone gazebo that was designed by Edward Robson.

At a cost of £19 million, the park and its features are about to be restored and improved, as part of the wider regeneration of the Anfield and Breckfield area. But, even before this work begins, this delightful and attractive park is well worth a visit.

To Find Out More:
Stanley Park Anfield
http://www.liverpool.gov.uk/Leisure_and_culture/Parks_and_recreation/Parks_and_gardens/

From Stanley Park, continue driving down Anfield Road and turn right at the T-Junction into Walton Lane. Continue along here to the traffic lights, and go straight across into Goodison Road, which runs along the left-hand side of Everton Football Stadium. As soon as you enter Goodison Road, the Club car-park entrance will be on your right; pull in here and park.

Everton FC players celebrate

Everton Football Club

Bill 'Dixie' Dean

In the introduction, and in the previous articles about football in this Chapter, I have already discussed the early history of both of the City's football clubs.

I have also talked about the history of local football generally, and about its role in community. So, to give you a sense of the development of Everton Football Club, I have chosen to do so simply by talking about their greatest player, **William Ralph 'Dixie' Dean**.

Bill Dean – as he always preferred to be known, never liking his nickname – was born in Birkenhead, on the Wirral, in 1907. Always an enthusiastic and skilled amateur footballer, Bill first signed as a professional player with Tranmere Rovers, his home team. However, by the early 1920s, his reputation across Merseyside was already well known and, in 1925, Everton Football Club made him an offer he could not refuse. He signed with the Liverpool-based club for a fee of £3,000, a huge amount at that time. And Everton's investment paid off because, in his first full season, Dean scored 32 goals. Then, in 1926, he was involved in a motorcycle accident, fracturing his skull and his jaw. He was hospitalised, and was out of the game for months. Even so, he returned to match fitness in time for the full 1927-28 season, albeit now with a tin plate in his head. And, by the end of that season, he had scored 60 goals in 39 matches (still a League record), and Everton had won the First Division title. But then the fortunes of the Club took a temporary dip and, in 1930, they were relegated to the Second Division.

Nevertheless, the skill and commitment of Dean, and of his team-mates, soon revived their fortunes once more and, in 1931, Everton won the Second Division title. This earned them promotion back to the First Division again where, in 1932, they won the title once again and, in 1933, Everton then won the FA Cup. Dean, now Team Captain, led Everton FC until 1937, when his failing fitness meant that the Club, reluctantly, had to drop him from the First Team. Going on to play for Notts County, and then Sligo Rovers in Ireland, Bill 'Dixie' Dean eventually retired to run a pub in Chester.

Always a life-long Everton supporter, in 1980 Bill Dean died of a heart attack at Goodison Park, whilst watching Everton lose 2-1 to Liverpool in a local Derby match, and just a few minutes after the final whistle. There are many remarkable facts about 'Dixie' Dean's football career, but some of the more notable are:

- He scored 383 goals for Everton, in 433 appearances
- He played 16 times for England, scoring 18 goals
- He was never sent off or even booked in his entire career
- 40,000 people attended his testimonial match, held 25 years after he had retired

In 2001, a full-scale bronze statue of the first, great Everton striker was erected in front of the Goodison Park perimeter wall. Now, facing towards Spellow Lane and Walton Lane, he can be seen ready to take yet another goal-scoring shot.

One of Britain's greatest sportsmen, Bill 'Dixie' Dean will always be remembered with honour, pride, and respect, by all football supporters in Liverpool, whether Blue or Red.

Everton FC – known as 'The Peoples' Club' – have had their fair share of city glory, winning nine League Championships and five FA Cups, as well as conquering Europe in 1985, when they won the now defunct Cup Winners Cup. The Eighties was the most successful period in the history of the club, under Howard Kendall, with two Championships, the FA Cup, and that Cup Winners Cup all on display in the trophy room.

> **To Find Out More:**
> Everton Football Club – Official Website
> Phone: 0870 442 1878
> www.evertonfc.com
>
> Toffee Web – Independent Website
> www.toffeeweb.com

Leaving Everton Football Club car park, turn right into City Road, and drive down to where the road forks. Take the right-hand fork – this is still City Road. Follow this, as it passes through ranks of narrow roads with their well-kept terraced houses.

At the T-junction, turn left into Church Road West. As you do so, note the house on the right, at the corner of the alleyway. This could well be the narrowest house in Liverpool! Its very short, wrought-iron balcony and exceptionally thin balcony door are particularly curious. About 200 yards further along on the right is Heathcote Road, turn down here, past the NCH Community Centre on the left. At the T-junction, turn left into Walton Village and, at the wall of the church grounds facing you, is a small pull-in on the left. Park here, in front of Church Flags. Before walking into the church grounds, just follow the wall around to the right. Here you will see, set into the wall, the original entrance to the church grounds, and the remains of the old hearse house.

Taking the pathway alongside Church Flags will lead you past the church and the tranquil yet mysterious burial ground – both securely locked behind railings. This path will also bring you to the gates by the old Tudor School House. At the end of the path, on the left, is the Black Horse Pub – another fine place for a drink and a meal, either inside the pub or in its large bowling green at the rear.

Walton Village, Walton-on-the-Hill and The Tudor School ⑬

St Mary's Walton-on-the Hill

We are now at the summit of another of the seven hills upon which Liverpool is built, and this district is known as Walton-on-the-Hill. This was an Anglo-Saxon settlement, and the name Walton derives from 'weald' and 'tun', or 'walled settlement', and it is mentioned in the Domesday Book of 1086. Walton is another of Liverpool's 'lost villages'.

It is believed that an ancient stone-circle once stood on the hill, but this was destroyed by the militant monks from Lindisfarne, who brought Christianity to the local community during the Dark Ages.

As part of the **Hundred of West Derby**, Walton was under the Stewardship of Henry de Walton from 1199, and the de Walton family then held considerable tracts of land on the east side of Liverpool. It is believed that a 'Hundred' was an area that could raise an army of 100 fighting men and, as the population was so thinly spread, this meant that the Hundred of West Derby covered a very large area. It spread from West Derby itself, as far as Meols to the north of Southport, across through Ormskirk, and on to Wigan. It also covered the area south of Liverpool, and east to include Warrington.

The site of the church is old enough to have also been specifically recorded in the Domesday Book, and the original building was noted as being made of wattle and daub. This was also on the site of an abbey that was founded by later a monastic order, the Benedictines, who came here just after the Norman Conquest. The first stone church on the hill was not erected until 1362, but little of the original building now remains, as it has been rebuilt and restored many times over the centuries. Even so, the parish church of St. Mary's Walton-on-the-Hill is probably the oldest church site within the area of the old Hundred of West Derby, and it was once the parish church of not only the Hundred, but of the Town of Liverpool itself, right up to the banks of the River Mersey.

Then, in the Middle-Ages, came a series of devastating plagues – the Black Death, which particularly ravaged Merseyside intermittently between 1348 and 1369, and the people of Walton were very badly stricken. A plague pit was dug near the church, but this was very soon filled with the dread disease's victims. There were so many bodies that the village could not cope with the burials, and so the Bishop of Lichfield – under whose authority the West Derby Hundred fell – gave permission for further bodies to be buried in the grounds of the old Liverpool chapel of **Our Lady and St. Nicholas**, on the shores of the River Mersey. Incidentally, this was not the only incidence of plague in Liverpool: It is known that the Town also suffered periodically throughout the Middle Ages and, as records improve, there are specific details of reoccurrences in 1558 – when between 240 and 250 people died, and also in 1610, 1648, 1651, and 1656.

The ancient parish of St. Mary's Walton-on-the-Hill was itself extensive, and included Formby, the Royal Park of Simonswood, Kirkby, Fazakerley, Bootle, Kirkdale, Everton, West Derby, Liverpool, and the Royal Hunting reserve of Toxteth Park.

"For centuries, people from the small township of Liverpool, walked the considerable distance to worship at St. Mary's Walton"

This remained the case until 1699, when **St. Peter's Church** was built in the centre of Liverpool – where the arcade entrance to Liverpool ONE now stands, on Church Street. A brass cross in the pavement, in front of this, now marks its site. (See Chapter: 'The Heart of the City'.)

By the middle of the 19th century, Walton had been a small rural community for over 1000 years, but commerce began to change the face of the local district forever. The principal coach road from Liverpool to Preston ran through the village and this brought an increase in trade and opportunity. From this time, Walton village was steadily transformed into a suburb. Between the years of 1801 and 1881, census figures show that the population rose from 700 to almost 19,000. In 1895, Walton – a place that had once been the most significant township in the whole area, was subsumed by Liverpool. However, the principal parts of the existing church are now no older than the 19th century, because much of the original building was destroyed by incendiary bombs, during the May Blitz of 1941. However, the tower, which still contains the original, 1000 year-old Saxon font, miraculously survived this wartime devastation.

There is an ancient burial ground alongside the church and, even though this is enclosed within high walls and Victorian railings, the tombstones are much vandalised. Also within the church grounds are a Victorian Mortuary, a Hearse House, and a 17th century sundial. There is also a hollowed-out sandstone base that once held a Saxon Cross. This too is 1000 years old.

In the corner of the churchyard, against the wall of the adjoining Black Horse pub, is an attractive building with mullioned windows. This was the old **Tudor Grammar School** for the poor boys of the district. Probably older that its date stone, which reads '1548', this remained a schoolhouse until the 1820s. From that time it became the parish rooms and Sunday school, and it now houses a day nursery and crèche facility, thus maintaining the educational traditions of the delightful building.

This is not the only ancient schoolhouse in the City; there is another in the village of Woolton (see Chapter: 'Liverpool Lost and Found').

Now return to your car, and drive back along Walton Village. Just as the road begins to bend to the left, on the left you will see the original and the modern buildings of The Alsop High School. On the right-hand side of the road you will pass a terrace of Arts & Crafts houses, which were erected in 1905. Walton Village snakes through what was once a farm track leading through the ancient village of Walton. At the end of the road, turn right at the T-junction into Walton Hall Avenue. At the traffic lights, turn left into Priory Road, passing the large and ornate main entrance into Anfield Cemetery on the corner. About 200 yards along on the left is the driveway into the Cemetery. Take this, and now you can drive around the burial ground. I suggest a 15-20 minute drive around – longer if you wish to go for a walk to investigate some of the fascinating tombs and memorials.

Anfield Cemetery

As Liverpool grew and expanded throughout the mid 19th century, and in common with other large British cities, the problem of what to do with the dead became a major issue.

Previously, and before the Industrial Revolution, most people were born, lived, died, and were buried in the same villages and communities. However, now that people were coming from the countryside into towns like Liverpool to find work, population figures were rocketing and the existing infrastructures could not cope. Part of this infrastructure was the existing small graveyards alongside the equally small parish churches. These were filling up and becoming overcrowded, which also meant that there were basic hygiene issues to be addressed. Consequently, the problem came before parliament and, in 1857, the Burial Act was passed. This obliged towns like Liverpool to set aside large acreages of land, outside the population centres, in which to create large public cemeteries. Anfield was one of a number of such extensive burial grounds established by the Corporation, and it was opened in 1863. This was planned, not just to be a large graveyard but, and with typical Victorian overstatement, it was designed as a Necropolis – a 'City of the Dead'. Indeed, soon after it opened it was described as Liverpool's equivalent of the Père-Lachaise Cemetery in Paris – and this was even before it began to fill up with bodies! This great Parisian cemetery was constructed on the site of a religious settlement founded by the Jesuits in 1626, and later enlarged by Louis XIV's confessor, Père Lachaise. After the French Revolution, the grounds were laid out as a cemetery and were first used in 1804.

Nevertheless, before long it was realised that even the new cemeteries would not be able to cope with continuing burials, and so Liverpool's first crematorium was opened, in 1896, although this in fact was only the fourth oldest crematorium in Britain.

Anfield Cemetery is an extensive complex of avenues and drives, which now wind their way through thousands of graves, tombs, ornate sepulchres, monuments, and memorials – many of them amazing architectural and artistic constructions in their own right. However, and perhaps as one might expect, not everything in the cemetery happens on the surface. In fact, during the construction of the burial ground, it was necessary to raise the level of a vast tract of the land. This gave the architects of the complex the opportunity to create four blocks of broad catacombs, which now lie 25 feet or so beneath the rest of the burial ground, with entrances on either side of the central driveway.

These underground 'streets of the dead' are lined on each side with deep stone tombs, ready to receive coffins.

Many well-known and significant Liverpudlians are buried at Anfield, including **William G. Herdman** (1805-1882), the great 19th century Liverpool artist. His contemporary illustrations of old Liverpool continue to provide historians with valuable information about what the Town looked like, before it became a City in 1880.

Jem Mace lies here. He died in 1910, and was described as the 'father of British boxing' and the 'last of the bare-knuckle fighters'. And so too is 'the first and greatest glove fighter of them all', the bantamweight Ike Bradley, who was buried here in 1951. Colonel Ellison, the architect of the Adelphi Hotel lies here, as does **T.J. Hughes**, whose London Road store still thrives. Canon Thomas Major Lester is also buried at Anfield. This kindly and caring 19th century Anglican cleric worked closely with the Roman Catholic priest, Father Nugent, to provide care and opportunity for poor and destitute Liverpool children and young people. Statues to both men stand in St. John's Gardens, behind St. George's Hall, in Liverpool City-centre.

Perhaps one of the saddest memorials in the cemetery is the commemorative monument and garden, laid out in memory of the 3,966 citizens of Liverpool who died in the German Bombing Raids over the City, during World War Two. This memorial was unveiled in 1951 and, behind it in a communal grave, lie the bodies of 554 men, women, and children who were killed in a single air raid in Liverpool, during the May Blitz of 1941. Of these bodies, 373 remain unidentified. This memorial was unveiled on May 8th 1951, the year in which I was born, and ten years after the May Blitz.

Anfield Cemetery is a well-maintained, attractive, curious, significant, and moving place to visit. I urge you take out some time to do so.

Some of the Victorian monuments in Anfield Cemetery

Leaving the Cemetery, turn left, back into Priory Road. On the left you will pass Anfield Community Comprehensive School and, opposite this, a large car park. This is where the new Liverpool FC Stadium is being built. You can see the existing Anfield Stadium beyond the car park. Cross over the traffic lights at Utting Avenue and Arkles Lane, and continue along Priory Road. Cross over the next set of traffic lights, at Breck Road and Townsend Lane. You will pass the Cockwell Inn and the Liverpool FC Supporters Club on the left as you enter Lower Breck Road. You will soon pass a children's playground and recreation ground on the left. A little further along on the right, you will pass St Margaret's C of E Primary School. This stands on what was, until the 1960s, the site of Liverpool's only Greyhound Racing Track – The White City. At the end of Lower Breck Road, turn left at the traffic lights, into West Derby Road. Continue along this dual-carriageway, under the railway bridge, and over the pedestrian crossing. Cross over the next set of traffic lights, at Green Lane, and then get in the right-hand lane as you approach the roundabout. Take the third exit up West Derby Road.

About 200 yards further along on the left, you will see the double-fronted, ancient Tuebrook House, with its date-stone reading '1615' over the front door.

Park on the side of the road, as soon as it is safe and convenient to do so, and take 5-minutes or so to look at this remarkable building.

Tuebrook House

Haunted Tuebrook House

The district of Tuebrook is named after a local stream called the Tew Brook which, after rising near the present Edge Lane, at a place appropriately named 'Springfield', once ran through a series of ponds and pools that covered the district.

However, the brook now runs completely underground, through culverts. Passing under Green Lane near St. John's Church, which we shall see shortly, Tew Brook now passes beneath Tuebrook House and, from there, it then flows out under the district of Clubmoor, into Walton Hall Park – where it feeds in and out of the boating lake. It then continues through Aintree to Croxteth, where it emerges to join the River Alt. This then wends its way towards the Lancashire coast. The Tew Brook was named after the Norse God 'Tiu', indicating that the district was once sacred to Norsemen, who probably settled in this part of Liverpool during the Viking invasions of Britain. The Goddess Tiu also gave her name to 'Tuesday'.

Modern Tuebrook is a residential area, made up of streets of terraced houses that are criss-crossed by the modern, broad, dual-carriageways of West Derby Road, Muirhead Avenue, Queens Drive, and by Green Lane. However, this was once a completely rural community, which sat on the edge of three great, 18th and 19th century rural estates. These were Club Moor, Norris Green, and

Larkhill, which are all now densely-packed residential areas. These were created in the early 20th century to accommodate the rapidly-expanding population.

The second oldest occupied house in Liverpool, after **Stanlawe Grange** in Aigburth, is the listed Tuebrook House. This is a farmhouse built in 1615 by John Mercer, a yeoman farmer, and the house is in excellent condition with the date stone over the front door also bearing Mercer's initials. The stone-floored, oak-beamed house has two floors, and is quite broad with two projecting wings. Inside the house, and between two chimneys, is a tiny secret room, probably a priest-hole. The entrance to this was bricked up years ago so there is no access, but footsteps and sometimes voices can often be heard coming from it.

The local legend is that a Catholic fugitive, hiding in the secret room from Oliver Cromwell's soldiers, died of a heart attack as the Roundheads were searching the building for him. His ghost now appears as a shimmering, grey image, flitting about the house when the clock strikes midnight.

Sometimes, door latches rattle and floorboards pop to portend his appearance and, occasionally, the sound of a horse galloping up to the front door accompanies the materialisation.

Tuebrook House is privately occupied and so is not available to visit, but you can park briefly on the road outside if you wish to have a closer look at the exterior of this fascinating building.

Modern Tuebrook is a largely Victorian creation: Miles of continuous, good quality, terraced houses were constructed here to accommodate City workers.

Continue up West Derby Road from Tuebrook House, and take the right-hand lane. About 100 metres up from Tuebrook House there is a break in the central reservation to allow cars to turn right. Take this, and double back along West Derby Road once more. Immediately, get into the left-hand lane and filter left, at the traffic lights, into Green Lane. Now take the first right, into Santon Avenue, alongside St John the Baptist Church. Park anywhere here that is safe and convenient, if you are visiting the church.

St. John the Baptist Church

This wonderful church was built between 1868 and 1870, and was designed by George Frederick Bodley (1827-1907), who was also the designer of the Lady Chapel of Liverpool's Anglican Cathedral.

Indeed, St. John's is a miniature cathedral in its own right, and is a perfect example of late-Victorian church architecture that was designed to reproduce an old-English church. The exterior style is Decorated Gothic – popular during the 14th century, and the church was built in locally quarried sandstone, and constructed in bands of cream and pink. The spire is 150 feet high and houses a peal of eight bells, and it dominates the surrounding houses and the main roads of West Derby Road and Green Lane.

The interior design and décor are outstanding, and put one in mind of the work of the eccentric Augustus Welby Pugin (1812-1852), who ornamented the Houses of Parliament at Westminster. Bodley may not have been as eccentric, but his use of colour, and the ornate nature of his interior design would rival anything of Pugin's. From the Byzantine frescos to the glorious stained-glass windows; from the Stations of the Cross to the gilded wooden statues; the whole is a glorious confection of colour and complexity. The Choir Screen is made of oak that has been stained black, but this has been overlaid in gold, greens, and reds, and is decorated with singing angels who hover between baskets of fruit and flowers. The highly-decorated hexagonal pulpit, the large and decorated sandstone font, the Minton tiled floor in the Choir, plus the other fixtures, all add to the overall effect. However, it is the oil paintings and murals that overwhelm the visitor with their glorious, neo-medieval imagery.

Restored in 1910, and again in 1971, the church contains detailed and delightful paintings by C E Kempe and other renowned artists and craftsmen, which reflect the Arts and Crafts style of the time. Those whose talents also contributed to the building were William Morris, Edward Burne-Jones, Anton Dapre, and Ninian Comper. Still serving the 'High Church' Anglican community of Tuebrook, the Grade I Listed church of St. John the Baptist is a magnificent work of art, as well as an active centre of Christian faith and worship, and it is well worth a visit.

As we leave the church, we drive down Snaefell Avenue. This connects with Brainerd Street, which we then take to continue into Newsham Park. However, this long, plain, apparently non-descript road, was once the location for large public air-raid shelters during the Second World War. It is fascinating now to imagine, the drama that must have once surrounded this location and its community.

Inside St. John The Baptist Church

To Find Out More:
St. John the Baptist Church, Tuebrook
Phone: 0151 228 2023

Fortunes, Fables and Football

From the church, you will continue along Santon Avenue, turning left into Snaefell Avenue.
At the T-junction turn left into Brainerd Street, and then right into Green Lane.
Immediately, take the next road on the right, which is Lister Drive, and follow this up the hill to the railway bridge. The road bends sharply to the left and then continues to the right down a steep embankment. This leads you onto Orphan Drive and into Newsham Park.
Turn right into Orphan Drive, and park anywhere that it is safe and convenient to do so. From here you can explore the park, particularly the lake perimeter, and I suggest a stop of around 20-30 minutes to do so.

Newsham Park

Newsham Park, on the edge of Tuebrook, is another one of the City's magnificent public open spaces.

When they laid it out, the Corporation did so on the site of an Anglo-Saxon settlement, once named 'Niweshum', meaning 'new houses', but no trace of this settlement now remains. The area that currently comprises the park was once a very small part of a sizeable and significant manor. Early records show that this manor, although in the township of Walton, also extended well into the region that later became the Township of West Derby. The same records reveal that, in 1199, the Norman nobleman Henry de Walton was given land at 'Newsam' by his grandfather, who was the Earl of Boulogne. This stayed in the hands of his family and their descendents for centuries but, in due course, the Manor of Newsham passed to other families. One of these, the Chorley family, were prominent in the Jacobite Rebellion of 1715, and Richard Chorley and his son Charles had to surrender to government troops at Preston. They were tried at Liverpool Assizes, where Richard was convicted of high treason, and was executed in 1716. His son was sentenced to imprisonment in one of the dungeons of **Liverpool Tower**, where he died of 'jail-fever' the following year. Consequently, their estates were confiscated and sold.

Part of Newsham had earlier passed into the ownership of Birkenhead Priory, and, after the Dissolution of the Monasteries, was seized by the Crown, and sold in 1557/58 to the Bolton family, by whom it continued to be owned until the 18th century, when it passed to Thomas Molyneux through his father's marriage with a Bolton. Thomas was a wealthy merchant and Mayor of Liverpool in 1806, and his family claim descent from an uncle of the first Baronet Molyneux.

After that date, or a little earlier, on the site of a much older house, Thomas Molyneux built the large, red-brick **Newsham House** mansion that now stands in the park, behind a security fence and high hedges. In 1846, Liverpool Corporation bought the house, together with the surrounding land, from Thomas Blayds Molyneux (grandson of Thomas) for £80,000, intending to open it for public use.

However, money was short and so it remained closed up for ten years. Then, in 1856, the grand mansion was converted into a **Judges Lodgings**. This was used to provide accommodation for Circuit Judges when they were presiding at Liverpool Assizes, and for VIPs who were visiting the City. Indeed, Queen Victoria stayed here for three days, during her visit to Liverpool, in 1886.

Newsham House is still the Judges' Lodgings today, and continues to accommodate visiting minor royalty and distinguished civic guests. However, the Queen and senior royals usually stay with Lord Derby at Knowsley Park when visiting Merseyside.

It was only after the conversion of Newsham House that the rest of the estate was developed as a public park, and it is now one of the most popular and picturesque in the City.

> To Find Out More:
> Newsham Park
> http://www.liverpool.gov.uk/Leisure_and_culture/Parks_and_recreation

Leaving the lake, and continuing along Orphan Drive, you will pass the Seaman's Orphanage on the right. Take the next left into Newsham Drive, opposite Park Lodge Nursing Home, and then turn first right into Park View. At the end of this very short road, turn left into Belmont Drive – this is the service road for all the mansion houses around the park perimeter. At the end of this road it bends to the left. Follow this around, passing the end of Denman Road on the right. The next road on the right is the narrow Judges Way; just past this is the entrance gate to The Judges Lodging at Newsham House. The road follows the perimeter of this stately home (which is not open to the public) and the splendour of Newsham Park is laid out before you, on the left.

The Seamen's Orphanage

On the appropriately named Orphan Drive in the park, adjacent to the large, kidney-shaped lake, stands **Newsham Park Hospital**. The renowned Liverpool architect, Alfred Waterhouse (1830-1905), originally built this as the **Seamen's Orphanage** in 1874. Waterhouse was the leader of the Gothic Revival in British architecture, and he designed many of Liverpool's, and Britain's, most significant buildings.

In Liverpool, these included the Prudential Assurance Building on Dale Street, the North Western Hotel on Lime Street, and the Liverpool University Victoria Tower.

He also designed many buildings in other parts of the country, including Manchester Town Hall, and the Natural History Museum in London.

The Seaman's Orphanage certainly is a huge edifice, with its spired central roof, its gabled windows, and great square tower.

And inside the huge neo-gothic building, the original long dormitories, sizeable refectory, a large chapel, and spacious classrooms still exist.

The building was constructed to feed, clothe and educate the children of those Liverpool seafarers who had been lost at sea, and whose surviving relatives could not afford to care for them.

However, it soon became used to accommodate other orphans as well as those of sailors, but the children of Liverpool seamen were always given preference.

The Ministry of Health acquired the building in 1954, and converted it into Park Hospital. Nevertheless, the building eventually proved to be surplus to requirements, and has now been standing empty for some years.

Currently a target for vandals, it is to be hoped that an imaginative scheme can be devised to make good use of this architectural, if somewhat monolithic gem, whilst preserving its architectural integrity.

A poster for Buffalo Bill's Wild West Show

(18)

Wild West Liverpool

The **Academy of St. Francis of Assisi** stands on the edge of what is now the neighbourhood of Elm Park.

Between here and Prescot Road, and flanked by Sheil Road and Balmoral Road, once stood the exceptionally large Fairfield Arena. It was to this spectacular entertainment venue that, in 1891, **Colonel William F. Cody** (1847-1917), made his first visit to Liverpool. Better known as 'Buffalo Bill', Cody brought with him his, by then, world famous 'Wild West Show'. Travelling with him as part of his troupe of entertainers were some of modern history's most charismatic characters, including the young, female sharp-shooter, **Annie Oakley** (1860-1926); and authentic Native American Indians.

The legendary Sioux Chief, Sitting Bull toured with the show, until his death in 1890 although it is sad that he should have ended his life touring around Europe, as an attraction in a public spectacle.

Indeed, Cody and his show formed a major element in the later Hollywood film musical about the life of Annie Oakley, 'Annie Get Your Gun'. Even though he was, quite literally, a legend in his own lifetime, to modern eyes Buffalo Bill was a brutal, mindless killer of animals and men – in vast numbers.

But what can one say? He was of his time and of his place. Cody made his name between 1876 and 1878, whilst working for the Kansas-Pacific Railway Company, which was building the great iron-road across the western plains of North America. His job was to feed the army of engineers, labourers, and track-layers, and he did so by slaughtering 4,280 bison, in 18 months!

In fact, he so decimated the breed that they almost became extinct.

It has taken decades of careful breeding programmes, and protective legislation, to

bring the species back to anything like a self-sustaining level.

Added to this was the fact that this slaughter brought the Plains Indian tribes to the brink of starvation.

At a stroke, he broke a centuries old symbiotic relationship between man and animal, and destroyed a culture. Still, he was a 'great American hero' after all!

"Buffalo Bill Cody, with his long-flowing hair, waxed moustache, and neatly-trimmed goatee beard, was undoubtedly a crack shot"

He is reputed to have played a major role in the Indian Wars in North America, being involved in more battles and skirmishes than any other man. It was Cody who killed the Cheyenne Chief, Yellow Knife, in a hand-to-hand encounter at the Battle of Indian Creek.

In his show, Cody, and his large troupe of Rough Riders, Wagon-Masters, Bronco-Busters, Sharp-Shooters, and Cowboys, re-enacted shoot-outs, and cattle round-ups, and Indian attacks on wagon trains and burning log-cabins.

In fact, there were over 400 people, of all ages, performing in the company, and these included authentic Sioux, Arapahoe, Cheyenne, and Brule Indians, as well as former US Cavalry Troopers.

There were also displays of particular Wild West skills, which is where Annie Oakley came into her own.

Although she was 31 years-old when she came to Liverpool, she really could shoot the centre out of an Ace of Spades playing card, with a rifle, at a distance of over 100 yards.

Added to this were displays of lassoing and trick riding, and so this all explains why every performance was sold out during its two-week run, in an Arena that could hold 4,000 people.

It also explains why the Corporation had to lay on 50 extra trams and buses for every performance, to carry people from all parts of the City to the Newsham Park showground.

Buffalo Bill Cody had been travelling around Europe with his Wild West Show since 1887, and he had received such a welcome in Liverpool, that he returned to the City in 1903. This time however, the venue was the great Exhibition Hall in Wavertree Park (Botanic Gardens) off Edge Lane Drive, and the run lasted three weeks.

As a boy, I remember my Nan telling me that, as a teenager, she actually met Buffalo Bill, whilst she was shopping on nearby Kensington. The great showman, in his fringed buckskin outfit, and wearing his six-guns, was strolling down the road acknowledging the greetings of amazed Scousers.

What especially impressed Nan though, was Bill's taciturn companion. He was a famous star of the show, the Native American Lakota Chief named **Charging Thunder**. This tall, imposing man was wearing a long buffalo-hide robe and leggings; plain moccasins; he had feathers sticking out at the back of his jet-black, plaited hair; and he was carrying a deep shopping bag stuffed full of cabbages!

At the traffic light, at the Park Gates, turn right into Sheil Road. Follow this all the way along to the next main cross-roads at West Derby Road, and turn left here at the traffic lights.

Continue around what is now Judges Drive, until it joins Gardners Drive, and turn right at this junction.
The new and environmentally friendly, mixed faith school of St Francis of Assisi Academy will be on your left.
Note the earth, grass, and wildflowers that cover part of the roof and walls of this remarkable building.

Fortunes, Fables and Football

Sheil Park

As we leave Newsham Park at Gardners Drive, and as we turn into Sheil Road, directly ahead of us is Boaler Street.

This runs through what was once **Plumpton's Hollow**, and it was this location that provides a link between Liverpool and Niagara Falls.

Jean Francois Blondin, the world famous tightrope-walker, crossed the great waterfall on a rope stretched between the American and Canadian sides of the torrent, in 1859. However, perhaps he took a greater risk as he crossed a high wire which, in 1861, had been stretched over the upturned heads and open mouths of astounded Scousers. They looked on aghast as he pushed a live lion, strapped into a wheelbarrow, across a tightrope, in what were then the **Liverpool Zoological Gardens** in 'the Hollow'.

This very popular zoo and pleasure grounds had been opened, in 1833, by a man named Atkins who was reputed to own the largest travelling animal-show in the country.

However, he had come to Liverpool to settle, with his animals, and he created the gardens as a major public attraction. Liverpool sea-captains would sell him exotic creatures that they had brought back from their voyages, so Atkins' zoo was always well-stocked. He also booked the best acts of the day to entertain the paying public, hence Blondin. Records show that Atkins left Liverpool in the 1850s. However, in 1859 the zoo then became a share-holding company under the name of the Liverpool Zoological Gardens Co. Ltd. To boost public interest, drinking booths were installed in the zoo but these attracted an undesirable clientele, and the paying public stayed away. In 1863, the zoo went bankrupt.

The land was bought by Liverpool Corporation who cleared away the old gardens and pleasure-ground buildings, and landscaped the area to create Sheil Park. This was named after an Alderman in the Town, Richard Sheil, who had originally suggested that the land be transformed into a more appropriate public amenity. In 1863, he also gave his name to Sheil Road, which was cut through the area to connect West Derby Road with Prescot Road.

With the creation of Newsham Park, in 1868, Sheil Park was no longer needed. The population of Liverpool was rapidly expanding during this period, as were the Town's boundaries, and so most of Sheil Park disappeared and the present ranks of terraced, artisans' dwellings took its place. However, some of the park did survive into the 1990s, until a further period of redevelopment took place. It is in this area that one can now find George Harrison Close, Paul McCartney Way, Ringo Starr Drive, and John Lennon Drive.

Continue along West Derby Road, passing St Michael's Primary School on the left, and then the former Imperial Tobacco Factory on the right. As the road now bends to the right, the Grafton Ballrooms stand on the left. Right next to this building is the Olympia.

Continue past these buildings up to the lights at the pedestrian crossing. The terrace of buildings that now appear on the left is Brougham Terrace; the site of Britain's first Mosque is at No 8, and this is identified with a circular plaque.

NB: At the time of writing, this has not as yet been refurbished and re-opened as The Abdullah Quilliam Heritage Centre but, if you wanted to take a look at this building; and at the Grafton and Olympia buildings, then turn left after the pedestrian crossing and park in Baker Street. Or, opposite Brougham Terrace and across West Derby Road, is the entrance to a tarmaced car park that you can also use.

The Grafton Rooms and The Olympia

Slightly more tangible forms of fable and fantasy than Spring-Heeled Jack, Prince Rupert's Treasure, and the Ghost of Tuebrook House, are those that have been enjoyed by generations of Liverpudlians in our theatres, music halls, and places of public entertainment. These are best exemplified by the two buildings that we now come to.

The Grafton Rooms

For almost four generations, this dance hall has seen, and still sees, lots of courting, dancing, and drinking, because it was in 1924 that the 'Liverpool legend' that is The Grafton Ballroom first opened its doors.

Built on the site of an old fairground, next to the Olympia, the Grafton was instantly popular with the young people of the inter-War years. They flocked to the new, sophisticated, and high-class venue in their hundreds, here to practise their technique at dances such as the Charleston, the Shimmy, the Cakewalk, and the Black Bottom. Because The Grafton was a purpose-built dance hall, its facilities and décor were the very latest, and of the best quality. This meant that these young dancers could disport themselves on a sprung, oak, dance floor, made extra buoyant with 200 springs that could support 1200 dancers.

Grafton Rooms staff discuss a function in 1977

The decor was lavish, with a marble stairway, an arched roof, brilliant lighting, the ostentatious Chinese Café, and a canopied bandstand. Refreshments were served in the Café but, in those days, only tea and coffee or soft drinks were available; certainly no alcohol! Throughout the 1930s, the Grafton was already established as one of the City's prime venues for dancing and dating. The Big Bands were providing the music and song, with renowned band leaders such as Roy Fox, Harry Roy, Wilf Hamer, Bert Ambrose, and Henry Hall regularly leading the entertainment.

It was during the years of the Second World War that the Grafton reached its peak of popularity. And, when the sound of air-raid sirens was heard, the choice was either to carry on dancing or to head down to the bomb-shelters. Of course, the music and dancing nearly always won out, especially as the War drew on, and the need for immediate fun and pleasure, in an increasingly uncertain world, became ever more urgent. Because Liverpool was one of the main British ports for the embarkation of troops, the 1940s also brought hundreds of soldiers, sailors, and airmen (and their female counterparts) into the City-centre, in search of entertainment and perhaps a brief-encounter or two. They usually found these at the Grafton, and overseas service personnel would return to their home countries, with lurid yet sentimental tales of the delights of the Grafton Rooms, and of the warm welcome offered by Liverpudlian lads and lasses. After the War, the Grafton remained popular, and big bands still played here, including Joe Loss, Victor Sylvester, Ted Heath, and Duke Ellington.

Then, in the 1950s and 60s, Rock and Roll came to Liverpool. All the local bands played the Grafton, as well as some well-known national pop-stars, but one of the most popular groups to play here, did so early in 1963. performing in front of an audience of only 200 people, they were paid the grand sum of £45 for the gig. A month after this appearance, the four lads – known as The Beatles – burst onto the world music scene.

Only a few months later, the group gave their last-ever public appearance on Merseyside, at the Grafton, on 2nd August 1963.

In the 1960s and 1970s, The Grafton was always particularly renowned for its 'Grab-a-Granny Nights', because the venue seemed to attract enthusiastic and available women of 'a certain age'. As a result, it was generally acknowledged that if you could not 'cop-off' at the Grafton, then you were a real no-hoper! Most recently owned by the same people as its next-door-neighbour, The Olympia, The Grafton is, at the time of writing, up for sale.

The Olympia

Next to the Grafton Rooms stands The Olympia Theatre. This was modelled on the Kirov Ballet in Moscow by its designer, Frank Matcham, the renowned Edwardian theatre-designer.

It opened on Easter Monday in April 1905, with a spectacular equestrian revue called 'Tally Ho!', which starred George Formby Senior. It was, at the time, Britain's largest variety theatre, and the vast auditorium could seat 3,750 people in what was then an extensively equipped, and thoroughly modern venue.

The Olympia could mount any type of production, from Music Hall to Pantomime, and from boxing bouts to fencing tournaments. Feature films could be shown, and classical concerts, ballet, and grand opera were all staged here. Indeed, it was at the Olympia that Liverpudlians first heard Wagner's, 'The Ring', and Puccini's, 'Girl of the Golden West'. The great dramatic actress, Sarah Bernhardt, gave her last performance in the City at the Olympia.

The theatre was also equipped to stage spectacular theatrical extravaganzas using the latest technology. This included a revolutionary hydraulic mechanism, which enabled the 42ft wide arena to collapse in on itself, in sections, and to disappear in 20 seconds.

Then, and in less than a minute, a lake containing 80,000 gallons of water would replace the arena, ready for aquatic displays and water pageants. Circuses were also presented here, and the first dozen rows of seats could be removed to make way for a sawdust circus ring. Consequently, in the basement there were areas of animal cages - a number of which may still exist. There were also special elevators, to raise the horses, elephants, lions, and other

The interior of the modern Olympia Theatre, following its last major refurbishment

creatures, up to the arena level. Nevertheless, the Olympia could not survive as a theatre and, on 7th March 1925, its last performances were of 'Faust' and 'Tannhauser', given by the British National Opera Company. This magnificent building was then converted to begin a new life as a 'super cinema', re-opening as such in only three weeks time, on 30th March 1925. Its first film presentation was 'The Thief of Baghdad', starring Douglas Fairbanks Senior, and its last presentation was on 29th March 1939, with a showing of 'Stablemates', with Mickey Rooney.

The story of the Olympia then takes many twists and turns. Throughout World War Two the building was used as a Naval Depot, and then, in 1948, it was bought by Mecca Ltd. This company refurbished and re-opened it as **The Locarno Ballroom** in 1949. In 1964, it began yet another life as a luxury bingo casino, which saved the old theatre from demolition.

However, by the mid-1970s, the population rapidly declined and the theatre, even as a Bingo Hall, became uneconomic to operate. In 1982, 'the Locarno' was closed and put up for sale and, whilst it was on the market, it was occasionally used as a film location.

In fact, the overtly sexual video for the hit record 'Relax', by the Liverpool group Frankie Goes to Hollywood, was filmed at the Locarno, in 1983. No buyers were found

for the old theatre and so, in 1987, the owners re-opened again, but only until 1993. In that year it was bought by Silver Leisure Ltd, who also owned the Grafton Rooms next door. This wonderful theatre then lay largely unused for 7 years, although still being used as an occasional film location.

Then, on Easter Monday in April 2000, with its original name restored, and 95 years to the day after it first opened, the Olympia re-opened as a cabaret showbar and nightclub.

And so, the City's only surviving Edwardian theatre reinvented itself as **Liverpool Olympia** and, following a further major refurbishment, it staged sporting events and a wide range of concert and cabaret performances, including spectacular Christmas pantomimes and theatrical productions.

But, as with The Grafton, the future for the Olympia is currently uncertain.

Fortunes, Fables and Football

The Abdullah Quilliam Heritage Centre

Brougham Terrace was the venue for many Liverpool marriages until the summer of 2000, and it was named after lawyer Henry Peter Brougham (1778-1868).

He was elected to Parliament in 1810, where he promoted many liberal causes, including popular education. He later served as Lord Chancellor, from 1830 to 1834, but, for most of the 20th century, Brougham Terrace was the principal location for the Registrars of Births, Marriages, and Deaths. However, the Terrace also has a different significance for many Liverpudlians, in that it was the location for Britain's first Mosque.

"In fact, the history of the now thriving Muslim community in Britain has quite an unorthodox beginning, being founded as it was, by a Scouser!"

William Henry Quilliam was born on 10th April 1856, at 22 Elliot Street in Liverpool City-centre. He was the son of a watchmaker and a descendant of Captain John Quilliam RN, who was First Lieutenant aboard HMS Victory, serving under Admiral Horatio Nelson. Known as Henry by his family, Quilliam was educated at Liverpool Institute (now Liverpool Institute for Performing Arts; the 'Fame' School), after which he qualified as a solicitor.

In 1882, he went to Morocco, where he developed an interest in the Islamic faith and culture and, in 1887 and at the age of 31, he proclaimed himself a Muslim convert. He took the name of Abdullah and, after returning to Liverpool, he gave a lecture on Islam at the Temperance League Hall in Mount Vernon Street. He began to hold regular meetings there, and soon he had his first convert in Mrs Elisabeth Cates, who took the Islamic name of Fatima. It was then that the Liverpool Muslim Institute was founded, by Quilliam, Cates, and their supporters. In 1889, the expanding group moved to their own premises at number 8 Brougham Terrace, where they established a small Mosque in the building; the first Mosque in Britain. In 1893, they began to publish a weekly newspaper, 'The Crescent', and later the monthly journal, 'The Islamic World'. This latter publication was distributed to more that 20 countries around the world, and was produced using their own printing press, which was operated from the basement in Brougham Terrace.

By the turn of the 20th century, the Liverpool Muslim Institute had 150 members – men, women, and children, and from all walks of life. Soon, they purchased the rest of Brougham Terrace and established a boarding school for boys, a day school for girls, a library, a reading room, a museum, and a scientific laboratory. Classes were held in the evenings in a variety of subjects, and these were available to all, whether Muslim or not.

The achievements of Abdullah, and his renown, soon spread throughout the Muslim world and, on a visit to Liverpool, the Sultan of Turkey conferred on Quilliam the title of 'Sheikh-ul-Islam of the British Isles'. This title was subsequently confirmed by the Amir of Afghanistan. By 1907, Islam had begun to spread so widely across Britain that the Liverpool Muslim Institute became the British Muslim Institute and, in 1908, Sheikh Abdullah Quilliam left England on an extended visit to Turkey.

Quilliam was such a dynamic personality that, soon after his departure, the Institute went into a decline, the buildings at Brougham Terrace were vacated, and the group dispersed. It seems that Abdullah never returned to Liverpool, but died in 1932, in London, and was buried in Brookwood Cemetery near Woking. It was to this town that many of the members of the original Liverpool group had moved, and it was also in Woking that a new Muslim community and Mosque were established. Quilliam is buried alongside other prominent British Muslims, including Abdullah Yousif Ali and Muhammad Marmaduke Pickthall, who first translated the Koran from Arabic into English.

Dr Mohammed Akbar Ali outside the Abdullah Quilliam Heritage Centre

In 1998, a small group of Liverpool Muslims formed the Abdullah Quilliam Society. Their first significant act was to place a plaque on the front wall of number 8 Brougham Terrace, commemorating the life and works of Sheikh Abdullah. An additional plaque was unveiled outside the prayer room in the building, by Mrs Patricia Gordon, Quilliam's granddaughter. The history of the terrace was the subject of a BBC documentary, in 2004 when, for the first time and after a lapse of 100 years, formal prayers (Salat) were said in the original mosque by Dr M Akbar Ali, the Chairman of **Abdullah Quilliam Society**.

The present owners of the properties at Brougham Terrace are the Liverpool City Council, who operated the Registry of Births, Marriages, and Deaths from the premises. The Council moved out and, recognising the historical importance and the cultural aspect of the buildings, they offered Brougham Terrace to Abdullah Quilliam Society at a peppercorn rent. This enabled the Society to establish the 'Abdullah Quilliam Heritage Centre'. Thus the Terrace, once again, will come into the stewardship of the local Muslim Community.

Currently, the Abdullah Quilliam Society is raising funds to repair and refurbish the buildings, and they intend to restore and re-open the original Mosque, which still exists at the rear of No. 8. They also plan to establish educational, research, and community facilities, and to promote greater understanding of the Muslim faith and of its relationship with other faiths and cultures. If successful in their aims, the Society will also provide a place for exhibitions, lectures, and seminars; for courses in the Arabic language; study workshops; Islamic classes for children and converts; and counselling services. The Muslim community, right across Merseyside, is now a large and thriving one and numbers approximately 30,000 people.

Most Merseyside Muslims now regularly worship at the **Al-Rahma Mosque** in Hatherley Street, in Toxteth, and the smaller mosques near Penny Lane and in Birkenhead. And now, it is to be hoped that soon we shall see Brougham Terrace take its place as a centre of excellence in the faith communities of Liverpool, and that the re-opened original British Mosque will provide interested visitors with an opportunity to gain a closer understanding of the Muslim faith, culture and people.

To Find Out More:
Islam In Liverpool
www.mersey-gateway.org/server.php?show=
ConWebDoc.1382
Muslims in Britain – Past and Present
www.islamfortoday.com/britain
Abdullah Quilliam Heritage Centre
www.bbc.co.uk/legacies/heritage/england/
liverpool/article_1

From Brougham Terrace, continue along West Derby Road, passing through the traffic lights at Everton Road. Follow the road as it bends to the left, passing the now derelict Gregson's Well pub on the left-hand corner. Get into the right-hand lane, and follow the road round to the right, into Brunswick Road. This now returns you to the end of Shaw Street, and to where we began this Tour.

Fortunes, Fables and Football: Conclusion

As we have seen throughout this Chapter, Liverpool is a City of contrasts – socially, economically, and environmentally. We have seen all shades of this, as we have explored what is one of the oldest parts of the City.

This Chapter, perhaps more than any of the others in the book, has revealed the true community roots of the people of Liverpool; through our shared community activities – particularly football; in our love of entertainment; our delight in fables, tales, and legends; and in our capacity to simply enjoy life. I chose Everton as the hub of the Chapter because it is the embodiment of all of these things, and of how Liverpudlians have coped with sometimes devastating changes in our fortunes. Whatever happens to us, and we have known great suffering as well as great triumph, we always come out on top – stronger, wiser, and more united than before.

Everton take on Liverpool on derby day

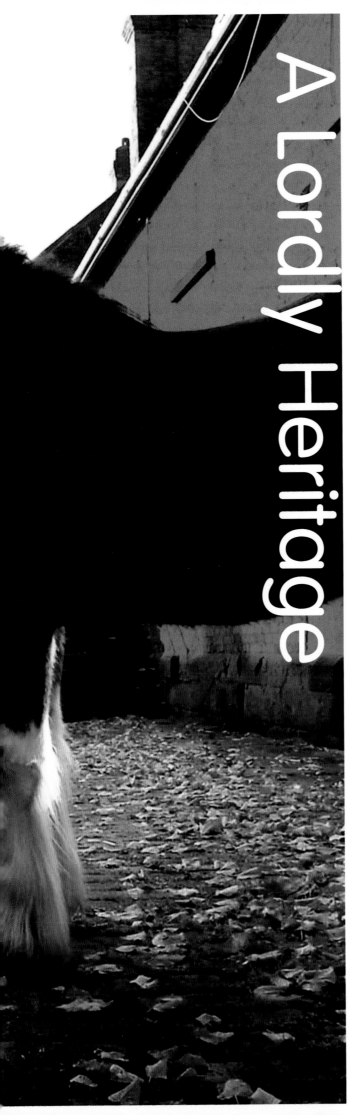

A Lordly Heritage

Including:

The Derby Family and Knowsley Park

Knowsley Village

The Molyneux Family, and Croxteth Hall and Country Park

West Derby Village

Castle Green

The Old Courthouse and Village Stocks

Little Bongs

Knotty Ash Village and Ken Dodd's Home

The National Wildflower Centre

Roby and Huyton Villages

Knowsley Safari Park

Equine encounters at Croxteth Hall

A Lordly Heritage : The Tour

The total distance covered by this Tour is 25 miles, and the suggested time for its completion is 6 hours.

This includes the time necessary to visit Croxteth Hall and Country Park, and the other suggested stops; but do add on an additional 2 hours if you also wish to visit Knowsley Safari Park. Also, add extra time if you have made prior-arrangements to visit any of the churches featured in the Tour.

This is a circular tour, so you can pick it up at any point on the route, however do always travel ANTI-CLOCKWISE. This is because the route has been designed to get you efficiently around Liverpool's sometimes confusing one-way systems.

NB Please remember to check all opening times and admission charges before setting off, to avoid disappointment should any venues be closed

Contents

Route Map

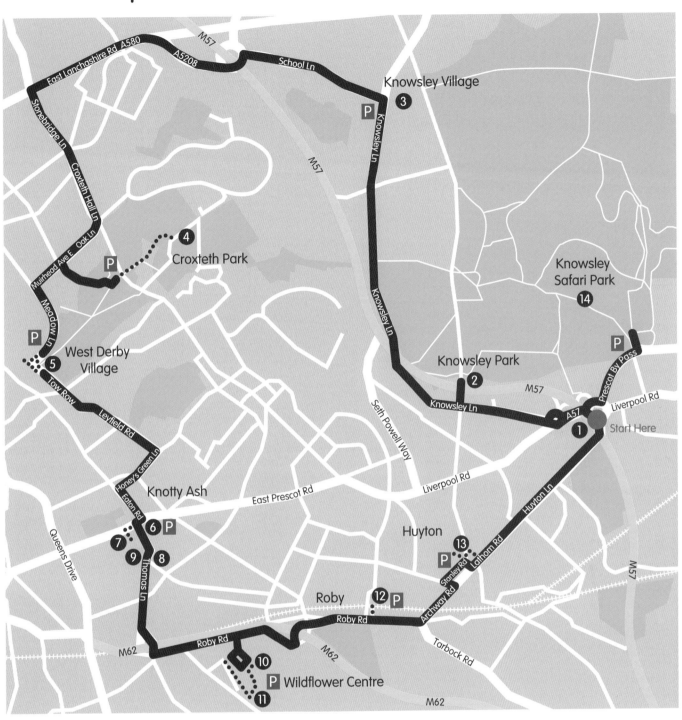

Key

● Start Here **Starting Point**	⁙ **Walking Route**
① **Map Reference**	🅿 **Parking Points**
▬ **Driving Route**	▨ **Railway**

A Lordly Heritage
Introduction

As we have seen in previous Chapters, Medieval Liverpool
was a largely insignificant little fishing hamlet,
bounded by the River Mersey to the south west,
by open heathland to the north,
and by the wide pool and a broad creek to the east.

After the Norman Conquest in 1066, all land in England fell nominally into the ownership of the King, William of Normandy – The Conqueror (c1028-1087). However, as was common practice throughout the Europe of that time, whilst retaining ownership of vast estates for himself, the Monarch sold parcels of land to raise income. He also gave large areas of territory as rewards or bribes, to his aristocratic peers; to relatives; to other people of rank or royal blood; to friends; to significant leading families; and to political supporters. As mentioned previously, when King John granted Liverpool its 'Letters Patent' or 'Charter' as a Borough and Town, the area became even more attractive, as there was now more money to be made from expanding commerce, and in supplying the King and his Court when they came north to hunt in the King's forests of Toxteth, West Derby, and Simonswood.

In and around the new Borough of 'Leverpul' at this time, were a number of large estates and manors, some dating from the time of the Norse invaders, and even some dating from the Anglo-Saxon Period. These estates included the Manors of Garston, Allerton, Speke, Fazakerley, Much Woolton, Little Woolton, Smithdown (or Esmedune), Childwall, Wavertree, Everton, Toxteth, Walton, Everton and the manor of West Derby.

"After King John died, in 1216, his ownership of the Borough of Liverpool, of the hunting forests, and of the Lordship of the Town, were inherited by his son, Henry III, who reigned until 1272"

It was this King who granted Liverpool, and its surrounding estates and Manors to Baronial families; the first 'Lords of Liverpool'.

A number of such families established themselves successively in the Town, with authority from the Monarch to govern and take an income from the people and the land. They each exercised great power, and the first of these was Ranulf, Earl of Chester (1172-1232), to whom Henry granted the Manor of Liverpool in return for political support.

Ranulf was succeeded by his brother-in-law, William de Ferrers (1193-1254) – one of the earlier holders of the title of Earl of Derby – who completed the building of Liverpool Castle around 1235. Then, from 1266 to 1399 – except for short periods – Liverpool, its Castle, and its surrounding lands were controlled by the Earls and Dukes of Lancaster, including John of Gaunt (1340-1399), who became Lord of Liverpool in 1393. They were followed by other aristocrats, who acquired estates all over South Lancashire, and of which modern Merseyside was then a part. These included the Molyneux family, later the Earls of Sefton, who were specifically awarded the Constableship of Liverpool Castle; and also the Stanley family, who held the fortified Tower of Liverpool and the Lordship of the Isle of Man.

This family, as we shall see, was to eventually assume the title of Earls of Derby. The rank of Earl, though certainly a powerful position to hold in the British Aristocratic pecking order, is third in order after the Monarch; with Duke being the first rank, and Marquess being the second.

Although these great Baronial families did not have large territorial holdings within the early Town of Liverpool, they were all 'Burgesses' of Liverpool in their own right, which, as we have seen, gave them significant political and economic privileges as landowners, and licences to trade in a variety of commodities and services.

However, their main sources of income came from the large estates that they held outside the Town. Nevertheless, they also derived much of their wealth from their ownership of buildings in Liverpool, such as the Castle and the Tower; from the vast surrounding forests; and from fees from the operation of farms, mills, markets, fairs, and ferries.

Throughout the later centuries of the Middle Ages, as the Town began to grow beyond the small, residential area of the original seven streets, prominent families from all over Lancashire and elsewhere saw opportunities and they moved in to exploit them.

These families were now leasing (and occasionally buying) land, estates, Manors, and income-rights from the Baronial families, and were becoming a new breed of lesser 'landed-gentry' in their own right. These were families, such as the Lathoms, Norrises, Moores, and Crosses, who all became Burgesses.

And so, throughout the 14th, 15th, and 16th centuries, real wealth began to be created on the shores of the River Mersey (see Chapter: 'The Heart of the City').

Throughout the Middle Ages, the Moore and the Crosse families, and the De Liverpool and Norris families, amongst others, were significant locally, and some great landowners were to remain influential right through to the 20th century. They ruled many of the smaller estates and Manors of what are now Merseyside, Lancashire, Cheshire, and parts of Greater Manchester. However, it was the Stanley and Molyneux families who became the most powerful local aristocrats, and for centuries these families co-existed, if not always amicably, with their great estates located side by side, to the east of the Town.

As Constables of Liverpool Castle, the Molyneuxs also held the Lordship of Liverpool, and hence the true political and economic power. Nevertheless, in 1672, and in return for permission to bridge the broad creek to the south of the Town, Lord Molyneux leased the Lordship to the Corporation of Liverpool. This was for a period of 1000 years, and at an annual rent of £30.

However, in 1777, and in dire need of cash, the then Lord Molyneux sold the Lordship outright to the Corporation, for the sum of £2,250. Now, and for the first time since the founding of the Town and Borough, the Corporation and the people were their own 'Lords of Liverpool'.

In this Chapter, we shall discover more about the Earls of Derby and Sefton, and we shall explore what remains of their legacy in and around this part of Liverpool and the Borough of Knowsley. By doing so, we shall gain a real sense of just how ancient our heritage is, and just how much it is intertwined with the histories of these aristocrats.

The suggested starting point for this Tour is at Junction 2 on the M57 Motorway; taking the B5194, along Knowsley Lane. This is marked as point No. 1 on the map.

The double roundabout at this junction can be complicated, so do make sure that you follow the road signs for Knowsley Hall – NOT Knowsley Safari Park. On the left corner of Knowsley Lane, as you enter it, are two large, four-storey blocks of neo-Georgian town houses. On the opposite corner are open fields and farmland, belonging to Lord Derby.

Continue along Knowsley Lane for approximately ¼ mile, and then turn right into George Hale Avenue. This is a dead-end, but it brings you to the main gates of Lord Derby's private estate at Knowsley Park. This is not open to the public, but the entrance to one of Britain's grandest private estates is worth a look.

The Stanley Family and Knowsley Park

The first great, local landowning family that we shall learn more about in this Chapter was, and remains, the Stanley family of Knowsley. They have figured significantly in English history for over 1,000 years, but the original owners of the Knowsley Estates, here to the east of Liverpool, were the Lathom family. They held lands across South Lancashire, and were an extremely influential and wealthy family during the 14th and 15th centuries.

In 1385, Isabella de Lathom (1364-1414) married Sir John de Stanley (1340-1414). He came from a family of Cheshire gentry, who had earlier fought alongside The Black Prince at the Battle of Poitiers; gaining for himself the reputation of being one of the most noted champions of single combat in Europe. The marriage united two great local families and made Sir John the lord of a great part of the Hundred of West Derby.

As we have already seen, this was a vast tract of land that included all of modern-day Liverpool, and much of Kirkby, Knowsley, and South Lancashire. The marriage of Sir John to Isabella also brought him vast estates throughout other parts of Lancashire and, although Isabella's family seat was originally at Lathom – 15 miles outside Liverpool, near Ormskirk – Sir John wanted to establish his own family estates. And so, he and his new wife moved to his Knowsley holdings, where they founded the Stanley dynasty. Adopting the family motto of 'Sans Changer', which translates as 'Without Change', the Stanleys were set to

become a major power in Liverpool and throughout the Kingdom.

In 1400, King Henry IV (1367-1413) appointed Sir John to be the Lieutenant of Ireland. Sir John acquitted himself so well in this post, and with such ruthless efficiency, that the King was delighted. However, the people of Ireland were far from pleased with the way in which he exploited them and their country, and he was a much-hated man. Nonetheless, in 1406, and as a reward for his achievements, King Henry awarded Sir John the title of King of Mann, directly representing the Monarch.

The Isle of Mann (now 'Man') is the small island that lies in the Irish Sea about halfway between Liverpool and Belfast, and this additional position now gave Stanley considerable power in the North of England, and significant influence at Court. When Sir John Stanley died, in 1414, the Stanleys continued to hold the title of King of Mann until the mid 18th century, when the 10th Earl of Derby, saying 'It is better to be a great lord than a petty King', changed the title to the Lord of Mann.

"It was in the 15th century that the Stanley family also took ownership of a large mansion house, which stood on the riverfront of the small town of Liverpool"

Knowsley Hall

The King gave them permission to fortify this, and so they created the **Tower of Liverpool** (see Chapter: 'The Heart of the City'). This gave the Stanleys a base from which to rule their 'Kingdom of Mann', and it also meant that they began to exert considerable influence over the Town and the people of Liverpool, and of the surrounding districts.

Whilst the Stanleys were consolidating their wealth and power in and around Liverpool and Lancashire, another family were also doing so. These were the Molyneux family who were descended from Norman Knights, and their family seat became Croxteth Hall and Park, not far from Knowsley. During the Middle Ages these families were rivals, and both had large private armies of well-armed men to reinforce their respective points of view!

However the fortunes of the Stanley family took a significant upward turn in 1485, during the Wars of the Roses. This happened when the Lancastrian Henry Tudor, who was then the Duke of Richmond, was facing the Yorkist army at **Bosworth Field**. He was challenging the ruling monarch, **King Richard III** (1452-1485), for the Crown of England and the King's position was extremely vulnerable. The battle could have gone either way, and the Stanley family were deeply involved in the conflict, but they were watching from the sidelines and had not yet committed their troops to the fight.

Richard knew that **Thomas Stanley** (1435-1504), whom he had made Constable of England, held the balance of power with his army of over 5,000 men. Richard was convinced that Thomas would support him, particularly as he was holding Stanley's son hostage. However, Thomas was married to the widowed mother of Henry Tudor, so his loyalty actually lay with his wife's family and therefore with Henry, who was his stepson.

Nevertheless, he did not want to side with the losers, whoever they might be, so Thomas Stanley bided his time.

"He watched and waited, with his troops, until he could assess which way the battle was going"

Then, at a decisive moment he saw an opportunity to turn the tide of battle against the King, and so he launched an attack on Richard's weary and wounded troops. History shows that Thomas made a shrewd decision, because Henry Tudor was victorious, whilst King Richard III was routed. Unhorsed after a skirmish, the King was desperately looking for a means of escape from the 'field of bloody conflict', when he was set upon by Stanley's men and slaughtered. William Shakespeare has the defeated Monarch crying out in desperation, "A horse, a horse; my kingdom for a horse!" as the bloodthirsty soldiers slowly approached him, swords drawn. There is a story, which tells of Thomas Stanley finding the crown of England lying in a thorn bush after the battle, and dramatically placing it on Henry Tudor's head. This may only be a legend but, from this time, Thomas Stanley was known as the 'Kingmaker'. (Not to be confused with the Earl of Warwick who, a generation before and perhaps more famously, is also known to posterity as 'The Kingmaker'.)

In the same year as the Battle of Bosworth and upon his accession to the throne, the new King Henry VII (1457-1509) bestowed the title of Earl of Derby on Thomas, whose descendants still hold the title (the title had first been granted to the De Ferrers family in 1139, until they forfeited this. It was then held by the family of Henry III, but the title lapsed when King Edward III succeeded to the throne in 1327). This new honour began the Stanley family's rise to increasing regional power and national significance and, although often challenged by that of the Molyneux family at Croxteth, this influence was ultimately to outlast the Molyneuxs, as we shall see.

In 1495, King Henry VII decided to pay his stepfather a visit at the Earl's Knowsley estate. To make his home an appropriate venue for the visit, Thomas partially rebuilt the original Knowsley Hall. This increased its magnificence, and began a trend that succeeding generations of Stanleys were to follow; continually adding to the building and eventually making Knowsley Hall one of the grandest

Lord Derby's Tower of Liverpool, in 1792

stately homes in Britain. The Stanley estates were once said to be the largest in England, standing at about 30,000 acres. This was before the confiscation of a very large part of them at the end of the Civil War when, in 1651, the 7th Earl was beheaded for his loyalty to King Charles I.

In 1660, following the Restoration of King Charles II, the Stanleys – like the Molyneuxs at Croxteth – recovered their estates and holdings. Also, further strategic marriages – something the Stanleys were particularly adept at – continued to consolidate the family's wealth and influence, and whilst, over the years, later members of the family sold off various parts of the remaining estate, the surviving land that surrounds Knowsley Hall today still covers an extensive area. The Stanleys also hold much other land and property in the UK.

Between 1722 and 1732, the 10th Earl built most of the present house and, up to 1953, it was still one of the largest private residences in the country. However, it was in this year that work began on demolishing almost half of Knowsley Hall. This involved the destruction of about 67 rooms, so that the building could be restored to its original, early 18th century appearance.

However, whilst the fortunes of the Stanleys were improving during the Middle Ages, so were those of the Molyneux family. Indeed, in 1445 Richard Molyneux was granted the hereditary title of Constable of Liverpool Castle, directly representing the Monarch. This gave the family increased power and influence, and with the Stanleys holding the fortified Tower of Liverpool, over the centuries a rivalry continued between these two, great South Lancashire families. However, after many ups and downs, and despite political and religious differences (the Molyneuxs had always been a Catholic family), by the end of the 19th century they had become much more friendly towards each other.

The Stanleys and the Molyneuxs were both inveterate gambling families, dedicated to card games, cock fighting, and to horse racing. In fact, the 12th Earl of Derby was very keen indeed on 'The Sport of Kings', founding two famous horse races in 1778; **The Oaks** (named after his house in Epsom), and also, what is arguably the world's most famous horse race, **The Derby**. Also, Sir William Philip Molyneux (1772-1838), the 2nd Earl of Sefton, helped to establish the **Grand National** horse race, at Aintree.

During the 19th century, Liverpool Tower was demolished. This meant that the influence of the Stanley family in the Town was to take a less political and more cultural form. The 13th Earl of Derby (1775-1851), who had assembled at Knowsley one of the finest natural history collections in the world, and a large, private zoo, was President of the Zoological Society. On a visit to Regent's Park Zoo in London he happened to notice a young **Edward Lear** (1838-1903) sketching the animals. The Earl was so impressed by the young man's skill that, for five years, he employed him to paint the animals in his own menagerie at Knowsley Park. Whilst there, Lear became very friendly with Lord Derby's young children and he was often found in the nursery, playing with and entertaining them. To amuse these youngsters, Lear began to compose the nonsense verse for which he was to become most famous and, in particular,

Knowsley Hall

his famous rhyme, **'The Owl and The Pussycat'**. This was specifically written for the Stanley children at Knowsley Hall, and a stuffed owl owned by the family provided the inspiration for the poem. In his will, the 13th Earl bequeathed his private museum and natural history collection, including the owl, to the City of Liverpool. This formed the basis of what was to become the Liverpool Museum.

"As we have seen, the Earls of Derby have always figured greatly in British political life, and Edward, the 14th Earl, was Prime Minister three times"

The present Earl of Derby, Edward Stanley (born 1962), is the 19th inheritor of the title and estates, and he succeeded his uncle in 1994. At this time, Knowsley Hall was no longer the Stanley family home, as it was occupied as offices of Merseyside Police on a long lease. The family lived, and continue to live, in a more modern house elsewhere on the estate. However, in 1997 the lease on the Hall expired, the Police moved out, and Lord and Lady Derby took over his old family seat once more, embarking upon a major refurbishment and restoration of the building.

Knowsley Hall is now available for hire as a conference venue, and it is a remarkable and unique place in which to hold weddings, functions, conferences, and exhibitions. Indeed, I frequently use it myself, for personal and professional events and functions.

The Stanley family continues to live at Knowsley Park; during the winter in the Hall, and during the rest of the year in their separate home on the estate. A thriving

community lives and works on the Knowsley Estate, maintaining and farming the land and its livestock, as well as serving the domestic, social, and commercial needs of the Earl and his family. Following the traditions of his forebears, Lord Derby involves himself deeply in national, military, community, business, and – naturally – in the sporting life of the country. He is particularly involved in the local Liverpool and Merseyside community, encouraging the development of local business and industry. He is also a great supporter of many local charities and community organisations, particularly those associated with children and young people.

To Find Out More:
Derby Family Website
www.knowsley.com/

Turn right out of George Hale Avenue, back onto Knowsley Lane, which skirts the western perimeter of the Knowsley Park Estate.

Follow the road as it bends to the right and goes over the M57 Motorway; notice just how many Lodge Houses there are along this route, providing private access to the estate.

You will soon pass three roads on the right; Home Farm Road, Sugar Lane, and Syders Grove. These are all roads leading into modern Knowsley village, but there are still many original, 19th century cottages and farm buildings in this area, which once housed Lord Derby's estate workers.

You will now see the spire of Knowsley Parish Church appearing above the trees on the right, slow down, and you will soon see Knowsley Village Green, with the large War Memorial Cross in the centre. Turn left here into School Lane, and immediately park as soon as it is safe and convenient to do so.

From here, you can walk around the Village Green and explore the heart of the village around the Church.

The Eagle and Child cre
at Knowsley Ha

Known by the name of 'Knouselegh', in 1258; 'Knouleslee', in 1261; 'Knusele', in 1262; and 'Knouslegh', in 1346, the modern village of Knowsley clearly has an ancient heritage. But, in the Domesday Book of 1086, Knowsley is listed as 'Chenulveslei', so it has had a lot of names! Earlier records show that the Anglo-Saxon Chieftain, Kenulf, whose name means 'Bold Wolf', was once the ruler of this community, and the owner of all the surrounding land – much of which was mainly meadow. This is clear from the fact that 'Kenulf' derives from the name 'Kenulf's Ley', by which the district was known for generations: The word 'ley' means meadowland. Even though the surrounding areas were heavily forested, ancient Knowsley remained open and arable land right up until after the Second World War, when urban redevelopment of this whole area began to re-shape the land.

The Lathom family had held Knowsley since the 12th century and, as we have

The parish church of St Mary the Virgin

seen, the marriage of Sir John de Stanley to Isabella de Lathom, in 1385, created a very wealthy and powerful dynasty. In fact, as well as this area, the manors of Roby, Huyton, and Tarbock had all been held by the Lathoms since well before 1200, but the core of this community was Knowsley Park.

The Stanleys soon became owners of huge tracts of land outside this part of ancient Lancashire and, throughout succeeding centuries, they increased their wealth. Indeed, the 17th Earl of Derby, in 1908, inherited nearly 70,000 acres of land in other parts of Britain. But things change; despite the Stanley's family motto and, during the 20th century, various Lords of Derby have sold off parts of their Knowsley estates to raise income, and to make their local holdings more manageable. This began in 1932, with the sale to the City of Liverpool of about 1,700 acres of the estate, for £185,000.

"This was the biggest land deal that the Corporation had undertaken since they acquired the Speke estates some time earlier"

However, this immediately increased the City boundaries, and opened up much needed land for building new housing estates for the rapidly expanding population of Liverpool.

Until the 1950s, Knowsley Village was still a secluded community, very much in the heart of the Knowsley Park estate and occupied by estate workers and their families. However, and much to their concern, in March 1950 the 18th Earl announced to his tenants that he would have to sell the Village, because of heavy taxation and death duties. Soon afterwards, part of Knowsley Village was sold to the then Whiston Rural District Council but, by 1974, the whole of the village had become part of the newly created Metropolitan Borough of Knowsley.

At the centre of Knowsley Village is the **parish church of St. Mary the Virgin**, which stands at the corner of the road at its junction with Knowsley Lane. This was built between 1841 and 1844, at a cost of £20,000, and it was paid for by the 13th Earl of Derby.

The inside of the Village Church has a number of interesting features: In 1871, a Memorial Chapel was erected, dedicated to the memory of the 14th Earl and paid for by the local community. This contains an effigy of the Earl, who was born at Knowsley Park in 1799, and who was buried in the church in 1869. St Mary's also contains an attractive mosaic on the Chancel and Sanctuary wall.

This was placed here in 1923 by the 17th Earl, in memory of his father. Indeed, the interior of the church is a fine example of 19th century Gothic Revival church architecture, with some fine stained-glass windows and a number of interesting memorials.

Three Earls of Derby are buried in vaults within the church; however, the water table here is particularly high, which means that the land is subject to flooding. This has badly affected the Stanley family tombs, and so more recent family burials have taken place outside the church, in a separate plot within the main churchyard. The last Earl of Derby to be interred in the church grounds was Edward John Stanley, the 18th Earl, who died in 1994, and who was the uncle of the present Lord Derby.

In the centre of the Village is the **village green**, on which stands the **First World War Memorial**. This part of the Village is known as the Knowsley Triangle, and around it stands the **Village Hall**; the old **Village School**, which is now a restaurant named Millbrook Manor; and a number of interesting farms and houses. It is worth strolling around the small Village centre, especially Tithebarn Road and the end of School Lane, and also around the Village Hall. Knowsley is made up of mostly 19th century buildings, which give the place a real charm, but there are one or two older farmhouses, almshouses, and other buildings that are worth seeking out. See if you can locate **Highfield Cottage**, which was built in 1759; **the vicarage** on Tithebarn Road; and **Maypole Farm** and **Village Hall Farms**, which stand on opposite sides of School Lane.

Beyond the Village, along School Lane, is a much more modern part of Knowsley, although this was once all farmland that was part of the Knowsley estate. This area is now the well-designed and economically successful Knowsley Industrial Park.

Not only does this small business and enterprise park provide much employment and economic growth to the local area, but it is attractively laid out and landscaped, making it quite exceptional amongst industrial estates.

To Find Out More:
Domesday Book
www.nationalarchives.gov.uk/domesday
St Mary's Parish Church, Knowsley
Phone: 0151 546 4266
http://www.stmary.knowsley.btinternet.co.uk

To leave Knowsley Village continue along School Lane. You will immediately see the delightful Knowsley Village Farm on the left and then, crossing straight over the roundabout, you will drive through Knowsley Business Park.

At the main roundabout at the end of the Lane, take your 2nd exit; signposted Liverpool and Bootle. Continue along this slip-road until it merges with the A580 (East Lancashire Road), which comes in from the right.

Cross the traffic lights at the Car Craft Showroom, and also the next set of lights; continue along here.

At the next set of traffic lights turn left, signposted Dovecot and West Derby: This is Stonebridge Lane.

This road now takes you through land that once formed part of Lord Sefton's Croxteth Park Estate.

Cross the traffic lights at Storrington Avenue – the road now becomes Croxteth Hall Lane. Turn right at the next set of traffic lights into Oak Lane. Continue along here for about 400 metres, to the roundabout. Take the first exit, which leads you through a set of imposing, wrought-iron gates into the drive through Croxteth Country Park. Take it slowly over the speed bumps, and follow the drive all the way to the end where you can park free of charge. From here it is only a short walk to Croxteth Hall.

I suggest a visit of 1 hour, to tour the Hall and stroll around the grounds.

Croxteth Hall

The second great, local, aristocratic family was the Molyneux family. Their motto, 'Vivere Sat Vincere' translates as, 'to live is enough to conquer' and, from Medieval times through to the 20th century, they were significant in politics and power, not just on Merseyside but throughout Britain. They were also close friends of many English monarchs.

The Molyneuxs were one of the oldest families in Britain, claiming descent from Guilliam Desmolines, who was a Knight who had come to England with William the Conqueror, in 1066. Soon after the Norman Conquest, they were first granted the vast Manor of Litherland, to the north of Liverpool, which included the village of Sefton from which they were eventually to take their title. They were also granted lands at Thornton, Little Crosby, and at Warbreck Moor, which was near modern Aintree.

The Molyneuxs established their family seat in the village of Sefton, where they lived in Sefton Old Hall. It is possible that this house already existed when they acquired the estate, but the family soon made it their own, and kept their surrounding and extensive grounds well stocked with deer. The Hall stood near the village church of Sefton, where family members were buried over the centuries, but the ancient house was pulled down in the 18th century, well after the family had moved to a house on their Croxteth Park estate.

The Molyneuxs were also soldiers who fought in the Crusades and, because of the patronage of successive monarchs, they became powerful and influential nobles.

"The reigns of Henry IV, V, and VI marked the high point in the development of Molyneux power and, after the Battle of Agincourt in 1446, Sir Richard Molyneux was granted the park of Croxteth"

The name 'Croxteth' is thought to derive from 'Crocker's Staithe', or 'the landing place of Crocker'. This was probably a Viking chieftain who would have landed here from the River Alt, which still passes through the Croxteth estate, although this is now little more than a brook.

At Croxteth Park the family moved into a large manor house that had been standing on the estate for some years. From here, they began to establish themselves in power and authority, in and around the developing town of Liverpool. As we have seen, and also in 1446, the family gained the hereditary office of Constable of Liverpool Castle, but they were also granted the hereditary offices of Steward of the Wapentake of West Derby; and the Master Foresterships of West Derby, Toxteth, and of Simonswood. This latter forest was itself a huge deer forest stretching from West Derby to St. Helens, and part of this now sits within the Knowsley Park estate of the present Lord Derby.

The Molyneuxs also held the tithes of Walton Parish; a very powerful position. Liverpool was at that time part of the Parish of Walton-on-the-Hill (see Chapter: 'Fortunes, Fables, and Football' and 'The Heart of the City'), and the Burgesses were required by Law to contribute a percentage of their earnings and produce to the Church.

Because the Molyneux family managed this process, and took their cut of the income, this gave them particular power in the Town. This authority, and their control of mills and tolls, also meant that they were independent from the other Burgesses, and not answerable – as everyone else was – to local jurisdictions and laws. This made the Burgesses resentful of the Molyneuxs' power and influence.

Despite the fact that the Stanleys were undoubtedly the most powerful family in South Lancashire during this period, from Norman times through to the 16th century, the Molyneuxs had also gained much territory and wealth by conquest and royal gift. Befitting their developing status, in 1575, Sir Richard Molyneux demolished the original Croxteth Hall, and replaced it with a much grander mansion. However, they retained ownership of Sefton

A Lordly Heritage

The stables and coachyard at Croxteth Hall

Old Hall, and they divided their time between their two residences and estates.

Since the time of King John, the Lordship of Liverpool had usually been held by the reigning monarch but, in 1628, Charles I was short of cash, and he broke this link by selling the Town to some merchants from London. In the same year, a later Richard Molyneux (1594-1636) was created the 1st Viscount Molyneux of Maryborough, in the Irish Peerage. Shortly after this, the family bought the Lordship of Liverpool from the London merchants, for £450, which made them even less popular in the Town than they had previously been.

Their reputation had already suffered major blows because, as Constables of the Castle and the owners of much arable land – which they charged local people to farm – the Molyneuxs had never been liked. Also, the rivalries between The Tower and The Castle impinged upon the lives of the townspeople, creating anxiety and insecurity. Indeed, the Molyneuxs' reputation was only to suffer further when, during the English Civil War (1642-1651), they supported the Royalists whilst much of the Town supported the Parliamentary cause. Richard's Molyneux's sons, Richard (1620-1654) and Caryll (1622-1699) – who were to become 2nd and 3rd Viscounts respectively – also fought on the side of the Royalists; seeing Liverpool Town and the Castle changing hands between the opposing factions a number of times.

In fact, it was Caryll who enabled the Royalist Troops to breach Liverpool's defences, thus recapturing the Town from the Parliamentarians. This was following Prince Rupert's brutal siege of the Liverpool, and his bombardment of the trapped people with heavy cannon. Hundreds of townspeople were brutally massacred as a result, and the memory of the Molyneux part in this bloodbath lived long with the people of Liverpool (see Chapter: 'Fortunes, Fables, and Football').

After the Civil War, much of the Molyneux lands and property were confiscated by Oliver Cromwell (1599-1658). However,

these were returned to them at the Restoration of the Monarchy, in 1660, when Charles II ascended the throne. During this period, the family had divided their time between Sefton Old Hall and Croxteth Hall, but they moved finally to Croxteth around 1710, leaving their original family seat forever. From this time the Molyneuxs consolidated their power and influence, not just across the North of England, but also throughout Britain. They became one of the country's leading families, both politically and socially, and they had a great impact on the legislative and cultural life of the Country, particularly during the 18th and 19th centuries.

This was despite, during the Jacobite Rebellions between 1688 and 1746, whilst the people of the Town – and Lord Derby – supported the Protestant succession, the Roman Catholic Molyneuxs supported the exiled Catholic Stuart dynasty.

"By 1720, the family had added an imposing new wing onto their existing Elizabethan Hall at Croxteth, and they began to lay out the park and gardens, and to make other improvements to the estate"

However, parts of the Tudor house can still be seen in the central courtyard of the current house – as can some finger marks of the peasant children who hand-made all the bricks. Also, a number of the outbuildings are from the Tudor and Stuart eras, and these include the estate workers' cottages, opposite the dairy. These carry a date stone, which is inscribed 'CM 1687', and which were the initials of Caryll, 3rd Viscount Molyneux.

In 1769, Isabella Stanhope (1748-1819), who was a renowned society beauty of the day, married Sir Charles William, the 8th Viscount Molyneux (1748-1794). Shortly afterwards, she sat for the painter Gainsborough at Bath, and this portrait is considered to be

one the artist's finest works. Throughout their ancestry, the Molyneux family had remained Roman Catholic but, in 1768, Isabella persuaded her husband, at least outwardly, to conform to the Church of England. In 1771, as a reward for this from the Protestant Monarch, he was created the first Earl of Sefton in the Irish Peerage. In 1831, Sir William Philip Molyneux (1772-1838), the 2nd Earl, was also created Baron Sefton in the English Peerage, and this title now gave him even greater credibility. He was quite a character; becoming known as 'Lord Dashalong', because of his fondness for driving a carriage and four 'at breakneck speed'.

Sir William was also a great horse racing enthusiast and regularly attended the Aintree Flat Races. These were replaced, in 1837, by a steeple-chase which, in 1847, was named 'The Grand National'. The name of this form of horse race derives from earlier times, before specialised race-tracks were devised, when the horses would be raced across open country from church steeple to church steeple.

The story of the Molyneuxs is one of highs and lows and, by the start of the 19th century, their fortunes turned and their wealth began to decline. Parts of the Croxteth estate were sold off, possibly to redeem gambling debts, and other land at Great Crosby, Melling, Maghull, Lydiate, and Aughton was also disposed of. Throughout the late 19th and early 20th centuries, more of Croxteth Park was sold to generate income, and to accommodate the expanding City of Liverpool.

Nevertheless, as far as the Molyneuxs were concerned, it seemed that their dynasty would continue forever, and Sir William Philip Molyneux, the 4th Earl (1835-1897), constructed a purpose-built nursery wing at Croxteth Hall. Sadly however, illness and misfortune blighted the succeeding generations, none of whom ever again had large families. Indeed, Charles William Hylton Molyneux, the 5th Earl (1867-1901), had a racing accident whilst riding in the Grand National, and never recovered from

Guides at Croxteth Hall in period costume

The estate workers' cottages, near the dairy, with the 'CM1687' date stone

his injuries. The estate then passed to his brother, Osbert Cecil Molyneux, the 6th Earl (1871-1930). Tragically, two of Osbert's three children died as teenagers, leaving only Hugh William Osbert Molyneux (born in 1898) to inherit the title of 7th Earl.

In 1952, a major fire completely destroyed the best rooms in the Queen Anne Wing of this once-great house. It ruined several rooms on the ground floor and most of the second and third floors, and every fire engine in Liverpool came out to contain the blaze. The Earl decided not to restore the damaged rooms and most of them remain empty, fire-damaged, and stripped back to the original brick walls; making them a very eerie place to visit.

The 7th Earl of Sefton died childless in 1972, followed by the last Countess of Sefton – the American model Josephine Armstrong Gwynne – in 1980.

"There being no apparent heirs to the title or inheritance, the estate and Hall were bequeathed to the people of Liverpool"

However, there is some question as to the legal ownership of the title and estates, and this is the cause of much speculation and research but, so far, no current claimants to the Earldom have been identified.

In the meantime, the Hall and Country Park were opened to the public, in 1986 by the City Council, which now maintains them. The house provides a fascinating glimpse of life in a stately home, and guided tours are available around the building.

There are 500 acres of attractive, spacious grounds and gardens to explore, and the Walled Garden is of particular interest. Built around 1850 and covering two acres, its purpose was to provide an all-year-round supply of fresh fruit, vegetables, and flowers for the Hall, and this continued until the death of the last Earl. There is a 'flue wall', with heated brick cavities that acted as huge radiators, and which kept frost from the flowers and fruit trees. Other attractions are the beehives; fruit trees; greenhouses; the mushroom house; the vegetable, herb, and rose gardens; and the fuchsia collection. The Home Farm, which was also established in the mid-19th century, is very well-maintained, and has a large collection of rare breeds of farm animals and poultry, making it an exciting added attraction.

To Find Out More:
Croxteth Hall & Country Park
www.croxteth.co.uk

From the car park at Croxteth Hall and Country Park re-join the main road, and turn left at the roundabout into Muirhead Avenue East. Take the 2nd road on the left, past the erby Mills pub, into Meadow Lane. This road takes you directly into the heart of West Derby Village.

As you drive along this road, the wall on the left marks where the boundary to Lord Sefton's estate used to be, and you will soon see the magnificent tower of St Mary's Church, dominating the view ahead of you.

As you draw alongside the church grounds you will see, on the right, a rectangular area of public open space. This is Castle Green; park anywhere around the perimeter road of the Green that is safe and convenient.

From here we shall be walking up Meadow Lane and around the village of West Derby, and I suggest a stop of around 20-30 minutes for this; plus any extra time if you want a drink or a snack.

However, before we explore the Village, let's have a look at Castle Green.

The Molyneux family crest

Castle Green, the ancient site of West Derby Castle

West Derby was an important township in its own right well before anyone had even heard of Liverpool. It was significant because of the large area of forest that covered the district, and the hunting that this made available to the local inhabitants. In fact, the name 'Derby' derives from Anglo-Saxon 'deor' meaning 'deer', implying 'good hunting', and 'by' indicating a township.

Where we are now, at **Castle Green**, which is a very important site because this dates back to the time when the Vikings came to West Derby, in the 9th century. They put their own stamp on the local bureaucracy, and increased the importance of the settlement, which warranted its own fortification to defend the community. This stood on what was much later named Castle Green and, in all likelihood, this was a wooden structure surrounded by a ditch.

However, in the 11th century and as the township became more important, the Norman invaders replaced this with a larger 'motte and bailey' construction, reflecting the district's continuing strategic significance. This was probably built by Roger de Poitou (1058-?) , who came over with William the Conqueror. In fact, the Norman monarch awarded Roger all the lands that later became the County of Lancashire, sometime around 1070.

Nevertheless, after nearby Liverpool became a Town and Borough, the economic significance of West Derby slowly declined, and **West Derby Castle** was allowed to decay. Indeed, as early as 1297, the village was described as being 'the site of an old castle'. But, West Derby remained politically and judicially important, up to the 17th century. The castle site was eventually cleared in 1826, and it was subsequently landscaped as a park but, from the air, the remnants of some of the lower castle walls may still be distinguished under the turf.

From Castle Green, we shall now explore the Village by leaving your car parked where it is, and continuing up Meadow Lane on foot. You will pass the church grounds on the left, and the delightful old **Village School** with its modern additions, standing on the right.

As you come to the end of Meadow Lane you will see, on the right, the **Yeoman's Cottage**. This dates from 1586, and is partially restored; however, it is in private hands and is not open to the public. Nevertheless, the house can be clearly seen from both the front and rear, and its architectural charm adds to the many delights to be found in West Derby Village. On the corner, at the side of the cottage, is what remains of the original pinfold for the villager's livestock. Inside this are the village stocks, but these are replicas that were placed here in 1887, to celebrate Queen Victoria's Jubilee. The original stocks were wooden and stood at the western end of the Courthouse.

"Records show that the stocks were in regular use, from late in the 15th century, as punishment for crimes such as drunkenness, nagging, or failing to attend Mass"

Cross over the pedestrian crossing to the other side of the main road, in front of the **Hare and Hounds Pub**. To the left of these is a small shopping area known locally as **Church View Shops**, which has some nice cafés. Any of these places can offer a pleasant opportunity for a bite to eat and a drink.

Just beyond the row of shops, by the bus stop, is the **Old Courthouse**. This was built in 1586, like the Yeoman's Cottage, and was commissioned by Queen Elizabeth I (1533-1603) to replace a much older courthouse. This was because, in the Middle Ages, West Derby had regained a particular importance because it was then the site of the local Manor Court, and so many legal cases were heard here. The present Medieval building was also the repository for the village records, and many of these still survive; some dating back as far as 1453. These records were kept in the old Town Chest, which for security reasons had many different locks and a number of different keyholes. Because of the significance of West Derby in Medieval times, the role of the Courthouse was even more important that of the court in Liverpool Town.

"Indeed, the number of offences tried here was much greater, with defendants being summonsed to attend from a very wide area"

The records of the cases make fascinating reading; such as those of Henry de Wavertree, who was fined 2d for non-payment of a debt; and of Edmund de Childwall, who was fined 4d for the same offence. William the Physician, and a certain Alan, were each find the significant sum of 2s 6d for brewing and selling ale, contrary to local byelaws.

The Courthouse was still in use once a year – to settle land disputes, as late as the 1900s, but it fell into disrepair and, by 1921, it was in danger of demolition. A group of local trustees rented the building from the local landowner, Lord Salisbury, for a peppercorn rent of two shillings and six pence per annum. In recent years the Courthouse has suffered much damage caused by mason bees. These particularly industrious insects burrow into the soft sandstone to build their hives. However, thanks to a grant from English Heritage, the bees have been removed and the building is now fully restored.

Volunteers are currently being trained as guides, and the West Derby Society plans to hold re-enactments of historic courts in the Village.

From the Courthouse, continue along the road and cross over the end of Mill Lane, to take you past the **Sefton Arms Pub**. If you have not already stopped somewhere for a rest and a snack, then you could do worse than visit this pub, which is a large and inviting place with an extensive beer garden and bowling green at the rear.

Now walk past the pub, to just at the end of its car park, and then cross over Town Row. In front of you on the other side of the road you will see the **Village Hall**. This beautiful Edwardian building was once the heart of Village social life, (the three pubs notwithstanding). It was built in 1912, 'in memory of Hugh McCubbin', but has now been converted into attractive private apartments. From here, walk back towards the centre of the Village once more, and you will come to the **War Memorial**. Adjacent to this is the drive leading to the Croxteth Hall estate of the Earls of Sefton.

Known as the **West Derby Gate**, this is generally open to allow pedestrians to walk down the carriage-drive, all the way to Croxteth Hall and Country Park (vehicles are not allowed to use this route). To the right of the gates is **The Lodge House**, which was designed by Victorian architect **William Eden Nesfield** (1835-1888), and on the front wall of which can be seen the Sefton 'S', as well as the family coat of arms. The lions that flank the gates each carry flags that are cut through with the Sefton Cross. This insignia is said to represent the vanes of a windmill, or 'moulin'. This is believed to be the source of the Norman name of Molyneuxs.

In front of the Lodge and West Derby Gate is the **Richard Meade-King Drinking Fountain**. This was erected as a 'contribution to public health', at the height of the Temperance Movement, by Liverpool City Council in 1894.

"Across the front is written the inscription, 'Water is best'!"

Next to the West Derby Gate stands the church but, before we visit this, walk past the entrance to the church grounds to have a look at the row of delightful **cottages** that face onto the main road. These were also designed by Nesfield and were built around 1867.

Next to these is the **West Derby Pub** and, in front of this stands the **Village Cross**. This was also built by Nesfield, in 1870, to mark the site of the altar of the West Derby Chapel. This old place of worship had stood here for over 500 years but was demolished when the new parish church was built. The Cross comprises a group of columns, containing a carved figure of a seated Christ, surrounded by small carvings and features. On the pediment, below the seated figure, are the figures of the four Evangelists.

Now double back and visit the **Parish Church of St. Mary the Virgin**, which is Grade II* Listed. The original church, known as the Ancient Chapel of St Mary the Virgin, is first mentioned in 1360 and appears in old prints as a plain, long building with short spires.

Its magnificent replacement was commissioned by the Earl of Sefton to be the church for his estate, and it was built by **Sir George Gilbert Scott** (1811-1878) between the years 1853 and 1856 (his grandson Giles, went on to design and build the Anglican Cathedral in the City). The entire cost of the building was provided by public subscription, which gives some idea of just how prosperous the area was in the 19th century.

The old township of West Derby was originally in the Diocese of Lichfield until 1542, when it then became part of the Diocese of Chester. In due course, St Mary's became part of the newly formed Diocese of Liverpool, in 1880. The oldest feature of the church is the sundial on the outside wall, which dates from 1793, and this was taken from the original chapel. Inside the church are some excellent stained glass windows, featuring Bible Stories, and these are set in the cloister-like walls of the building, facing neo-Gothic arches and columns. The white-painted walls set against the warm sandstone of the main structure, give the large building a warmth and calmness that is quite appealing.

Once you have visited the church, if you leave the grounds by the side entrance, facing onto Meadow Lane, this will bring you back to Castle Green and to where you parked your car.

West Derby Village Cross

From Castle Green, drive onto Meadow Lane and continue up into the Village. At the crossroads turn left into Town Row, and follow this twisting lane as it becomes Leyfield Road.
At the end of this road, there is a T-Junction with a triangular traffic island. Turn right here into Honeysgreen Lane. You will pass Cardinal Heenan RC High School on your left.
At the end of this road, and at another T-Junction, turn left into Eaton Road.
Alder Hey Children's Hospital will be on your right, after you turn, and continue along here up to the traffic lights at the road junction at East Prescot Road. Cross over the dual-carriageway and turn right. The former Knotty Ash Pub is immediately on your left, on the corner of Thomas Lane: Park in the pub car park.
I suggest a stop of 15-20 minutes to have a look at this end of the Village and to visit Little Bongs.

A Lordly Heritage

To Find Out More:
The West Derby Society
http://www.angelfire.com/al4/westderbysoc/index.html
St Mary's Parish Church, West Derby
http://www.stmarywestderby.org
Merseyside Campaign for Real Ale
www.merseycamra.org.uk

The former Knotty Ash Pub, standing on the site of the original 'knotty' ash tree

Knotty Ash is not just the imaginative creation of Liverpool comedian **Ken Dodd**, who still lives in the village; it is in fact, named after a large tree that once grew in the forecourt of the **Knotty Ash pub**. The tree was there long before the pub was, but nothing of the ash remains, except its name. The pub was originally built in the 19th century, but has now closed. At the time of writing it is a furniture showroom.

Across the road from the Knotty Ash pub is the **Village Hall**, with its bowling green. This was erected in the middle of the original village green, in the mid-19th century, when the grounds and bowling green were also laid. At that time, the Village Hall was not becalmed between two rivers of fast-flowing traffic, as it is now; in fact, the much narrower Prescot Road ran between the Knotty Ash pub and the Village Green. Indeed, the Hall was on the edge of the private Springfield Estate, and next to a delightful public garden, standing on what was then the corner of Eaton Road. The Hall is still the centre of local life in the village and, set in the wall that surrounds it – and no doubt deliberately facing the former Knotty Ash pub – is a **water fountain**. This was placed there in 1887, probably by the Temperance Society, and the inscription reads 'Water is Best'; the same text as appears on the fountain in West Derby Village.

During the 17th century, Knotty Ash was only a small collection of farmhouses and individual cottages, located near a spring, but this 'lost village' of Liverpool nevertheless had its own inn – well before the Knotty Ash pub was built. It also had its own church, a village green, a water pump, a manor house – with a squire, and a simple pack-horse track running through it. This bridleway connected Liverpool with the village of Prescot to the east. However, like the nearby district of Old Swan through which the track also passed, from the mid-18th century Knotty Ash grew in importance, because of the coach road that developed from the horse-track. East Prescot Road now runs over the route of this track and, in the 17th and early 18th centuries, Liverpool's coal was brought from Prescot along this route by packhorses and the occasional wagon.

However, in wet weather the track became waterlogged and impassable for wheeled vehicles, and so something had to be done to guarantee fuel supplies to the growing Town. Consequently, in 1725, Parliament granted Liverpool permission to widen and improve the surface of the road.

In 1759, the Prescot road from Liverpool, which also ran via Broad Green moor and Roby Village, was extended to Warrington. It was also **'turnpiked'**, which meant that barrier gates and toll-houses were placed at various points along its length, to raise income to pay for the continual maintenance of these principal routes. The gates would pivot at one end, on a vertical rod or 'pike', hence the name 'turnpike' road.

The toll-keepers were called 'Pikemen', and they wore a uniform that consisted of a tall, black hat; black stockings and knee britches; and short aprons with deep pockets to hold the money. One of these toll-bars was established in Knotty Ash village, and there was a place set aside by the toll where itinerant players and singers would earn a living by entertaining waiting travellers.

By 1761, the new 'highway' was extended further to then connect with other major routes; to carry the mails, goods, and news to and from Liverpool and Manchester, and also between the Town and the Midlands and London.

With the development of this delivery service, soon, people also began to travel on the coaches between Liverpool and all the local towns. In fact, it was in 1761 that the first combined passenger and mail stage-coach service to London began, from Liverpool Town via Warrington. The first coach was called 'The Flying Machine' and, for a fare of 2 shillings and 6 pence, it completed a one-way journey in 2 or 3 days, depending on the weather conditions.

The wealthy travellers of that period – those that lived in the great houses that the stage-coaches passed en route – were picked up at their gates. They were forewarned of the arrival of the coach – carrying post and people – by the driver, who blew through a long horn to herald their approach; hence, a 'post horn'. This route became very important, and lucrative, and one of the most important coaching inns in Liverpool was the 'Saracen's Head'.

This stood, between 1810 and 1853, on the site currently occupied by the City Council Headquarters at Municipal Buildings, in Dale Street. Coaches would leave this inn, travel down Dale Street, past Townsend Mill, up what is now William Brown Street, and onto 'the London road'. This traffic increased the fortunes of the districts and communities through which it passed, and encouraged the establishment of coaching inns, taverns, and travellers' suppliers, at significant points all along its length. (See Chapter: 'The Heart of the City'.)

As passenger-numbers grew, Liverpool's first horse-drawn omnibus service, which terminated at Knotty Ash, was started on May 12th 1830, by Mr. Bell. This was later taken over and operated by a Mr. Bullen. These buses ran regularly from Liverpool Town Hall, to travel through Edge Hill and across the Great Heath – also known as the Great Waste, and then via Old Swan, to arrive at the Turk's Head Inn in the Village. As the population and the importance of the towns on the outskirts of Liverpool grew, so did the volume of traffic on this important route.

Modern technology was then required to keep pace with demand and, on May 18th 1903, a through-route electric tramcar service was established, between Liverpool Pier Head and St. Helens, via Knotty Ash. This ran continuously, until the service was discontinued and replaced by motor-buses.

Electric trams first operated in Liverpool in November 1898 and, at the height of the tram operation in 1945, there were 744 trams running in Liverpool along 63 routes. Trams at this time outnumbered buses three-to-one. However, following the Second World War, Liverpool Corporation took the decision to move away from trams in favour of buses. From 1948 onwards the network was wound down, with the last trams running in 1957.

Like the other villages that were once outside Liverpool, Knotty Ash was absorbed by the expanding City in the early years of the 20th century, and the district has been subsequently built up, mostly with houses for City workers. However, the charms and romance of the original village, which was awarded conservation status in 2004, have not been entirely obliterated.

> Leaving your car in the Knotty Ash pub car-park, walk across the end of Thomas Lane, along East Prescot Road. As you do so you can see the village hall and the water fountain.
> About 100 metres or so along the road you will see, in the middle of the row of small cottages and shops, a quite unprepossessing archway. Turn into this, and follow it all the way to the end. This takes you into Little Bongs.

Some of the village's 18th century cottages, facing onto East Prescot Road

Little Bongs

As you walk down the broad pathway leading from the arch, ignore the very tacky cladding on the surrounding walls, and the fact that this looks like a mini-industrial wasteland (!) – keep the faith – it will be worth it! At the end of the passage turn right, and walk all the way along what now becomes a narrow, cobbled pathway.

Here, along the path, you will find a dozen or so delightful old cottages with very attractive individual front gardens, all nestling in a secret little area known as Little Bongs. Their cobbled surroundings and pretty gardens show what this tiny and secluded hamlet must once have looked like, before the area became built up.

The cottages of Little Bongs, as well as those facing East Prescot Road, were all built 200 years ago by Joseph Jones, a local brewer, who also erected and operated the former Knotty Ash Brewery. This was situated further along the cottage row, just past the arched entrance to Little Bongs. The name of this petite community might come from either the bungs used in casks of ale, or from an old field name, deriving from 'bong' meaning 'grassy bank'. In the same terrace as his cottages and brewery, Jones also built the Lord Nelson Pub, from which to sell his ales. The beer from this old brewery, which survived until 1927 when the much larger Higson's Brewery took it over, was renowned as 'Jones's famous Knotty Ash ales', and the company used the ash-tree symbol as its trademark.

> From East Prescot Road and Little Bongs, return to your car and leave the Knotty Ash Pub – turning down Thomas Lane opposite the Knotty Ash Village Hall, and drive all the way to the end. On the left, at the end of the Lane, stands St John's Church: Park anywhere here that it is safe to do so.

Little Bongs

St. John the Evangelist Church

At the end of Thomas Lane, on the left-hand corner, stands the Grade II Listed church of St. John the Evangelist, which was built in 1835. The building is imposing and, although now surrounded by trees and houses, it still dominates the hill around which the Village developed.

Inside, the stained-glass windows are particularly fine and were donated by various local benefactors, including members of the Masonic Order. Some of the windows were designed by the Pre-Raphaelite artist, Sir Edward Burne-Jones; and others by C E Kempe. There are many other interesting features in the church, not least of all being the fine carved, oak woodwork; and the examples of Della Robbia pottery.

Amongst the memorial tablets is a spectacular monument dedicated to the father of wealthy 19th century businessman Henry Yates Thompson. He donated the Palm Houses in Sefton and Stanley Parks to the City, and had his father's tablet made of porphyry. The only other equally fine example of British work in this rare and costly mineral,is on the tomb of King Henry VII, in Westminster Abbey.

Outside the church, the cemetery is said to house the bones of more former Mayors of Liverpool than any other burial ground in the City, and it also houses many bodies that were removed from Liverpool Parish Church of Our Lady and St Nicholas, when the Dock Road was widened. (See Chapter: 'The Heart of the City'.) Also, there are graves and tombs here, containing the bodies of members of the illustrious Gladstone

The Lych Gate at St John's Church

Family, of whom we'll hear more when we visit Court Hey Park, later in this Chapter. There is also a fine War Memorial in the churchyard, which is made from alabaster.

The particularly impressive Lych Gate, leading into the churchyard from Thomas Lane, is another fine example of mid-Victorian oak carving. The word 'lych' derives from the old Anglo-Saxon word 'lic', which means 'corpse'. It was under the lych gates that coffins would temporarily rest, on their way into the church, and as the priest performed the first part of the burial rites. Most of the wood used in the gate was taken from the furniture and beams belonging to a grand house in the district, named 'Boltons', and

which dated back to 1400. These timbers were themselves said to have come from a famous tree called 'The Croxteth Oak', which was said to be already 600 years old when it was felled. This came from the dense forest that once surrounded the former estate of the Earls of Sefton, which we have already visited in this Tour. 'Boltons' was demolished some years after St John's church was built.

To Find Out More:
St John the Evangelist, Knotty Ash
Phone: 0151 228 2396
www.stjohns-knottyash.org.uk

The Squire of Knotty Ash

9

The most famous choirboy who ever sang at St John's Church in Knotty Ash, and the Village's most well-known resident, is Ken Dodd. He was born on 8th November 1927, in **Oak House**, the house in which he still lives and which is the oldest house in the village. Built in 1782 as a manor and farmhouse, it is now a Listed Georgian building. Naturally, as his private residence, the house is not open to the public and, reasonably enough, Ken does not welcome uninvited visitors!

Ken claims the title of 'The Squire of Knotty Ash' and, with his 'Tickling-Stick' rampant, Ken presides over the area's famous 'jam-butty mines', 'snuff quarries', 'treacle mines', 'black-pudding plantation', 'moggie-ranch', and 'broken biscuit repair-works'.

The comedian's Great Uncle Jack (John Leech), who was a small man – known locally and affectionately as the Diddy-Man – inspired Doddy's well-known Diddy-Men. 'Diddy Jack' wore a long coat and a bowler hat, and he drove around the village in his two-wheeled, pony-drawn float, hardly being seen above the reins. As he drove along he could be heard singing all the latest music-hall songs, and he was a much-loved character in Knotty Ash.

Like his uncle, Ken himself is much-loved. After leaving the local village primary school, Ken attended Holt High Grammar School, (which was my own school) now called Childwall Comprehensive School. After leaving the Holt, he became a coal-man and then a door-to-door salesman. Ken says that these jobs allowed him to

learn the skills of banter, amusing gossip, and quick-fire humour. This gave Ken the idea of going into showbusiness, so he gave up being a tradesman and became a performer, making his professional debut at the Nottingham Empire, in 1954.

Ken Dodd

"Ken learnt his craft well, and began to gain a reputation around the theatres and variety clubs of the north of England"

However, he began his career as a ventriloquist, and he still incorporates this in his act today, with his dummy 'Dicky Mint'. He only really developed as a comedian with the advent of television, which also brought lots of radio work and, by the beginning of the 1960s, Ken Dodd was a household name right across Britain.

Ken is renowned for many things, including the extreme length of his performances, and he is known to be a passionate supporter of

Liverpool FC. His contribution to national comedy and entertainment was recognised when he was inducted into the All-Time Comedy Hall Of Fame. What may be less well known outside Liverpool, is the considerable amount of work that he does, and has always done, for charity. Ken remains popular in Liverpool, not just because of his talent, but because of his loyalty. Unlike many celebrities who 'make it big', he has chosen to continue to live in the City and this endears him to the public.

To Find Out More:
Ken Dodd
www.nostalgiacentral.com/music/
kendodd.htm

Resuming our driving Tour, at the end of Thomas Lane turn right into what is still Thomas Lane.
Continuing along here, cross over the traffic lights at Thingwall Hall Drive and follow the road as it bends to the left, under the M62 Motorway, and up to the traffic lights at Bowring Park Road.
Turn left at the lights, along what is the A5080, and continue through the next set of traffic lights at the road junction, and through another set at the pedestrian crossing.
You will then see a sign indicating a right turn into Court Hey Park and the National Wildflower Centre. Turn right here.

I suggest a visit of about 45 minutes or so, to visit the Centre and to stroll around the park.

Old railway sleepers line the driveway at the park

Cricketers at Court Hey Park

This small, suburban park is a truly delightful oasis, accessed from the main road that runs between Liverpool and Huyton alongside the busy M62 motorway.

Originally part of the arable lands of Lord Derby's estate of nearby Knowsley Park, this 60-acre property was bought in the mid-19th century by Robertson Gladstone (1805-1875). He was the elder brother of William Ewart Gladstone (1809-1898), who was born in Rodney Street in Liverpool, and who was British Prime Minister four times. (See Chapter: Pool of Life & Culture'.)

"The Gladstone family had been successful merchants for many years, and they played a significant role in the economic, political, and religious life of Liverpool, as well as of Britain."

Indeed, the family still own the Living of Liverpool Parish Church of Our Lady and St Nicholas, on the City waterfront (see Chapter: 'Heart of the City'), which means that they appoint the Rector of Liverpool – one of the most important ecclesiastical appointments in the City and the Diocese.

Robertson Gladstone built Court Hey Hall on his new estate in 1836, which was walled, and had lawns, woodlands, a rose garden, and sizeable stables. The Hall was a large, imposing, sandstone mansion house, which became a significant social centre for the 'great and the good' of the whole area. Gladstone was a Director of the Liverpool and Manchester Railway Company and, when the railway tracks were being replaced and upgraded, in 1842, he used the original sandstone railway sleepers, over which George Stephenson's famous 'Rocket' steam locomotive had once ridden, to line the main carriageway leading up to Court Hey Hall. These still perform this function, and they can be clearly seen as one drives into the modern park, towards the car park: Note the original track bolt-holes drilled into these large stones.

The last member of the Gladstone family to live on the Court Hey Estate was Walter Gladstone, who died in 1919. It was then that the family sold the lands, Hall, and outbuildings to the long-established Liverpool cattle-feed company of J Bibby and Sons.

After having been commandeered by the Ministry of Agriculture, Fisheries and Food, during World War Two, by the early 1950s Court Hey Hall had fallen into neglect and disrepair and, in 1956, it had to be demolished. Part of the grounds became a housing estate, whilst the remainder became the popular public park that we have today.

Superbly landscaped and maintained by Knowsley Borough Council, the park is still the scene of football and of cricket matches, it is also a tranquil place to stroll; to sit under the trees and read, contemplate, or snooze; or to picnic with family or friends. However, one of the most important features of Court Hey Park is that it is the home of The National Wildflower Centre.

A Lordly Heritage

Opened in 2000, and set in the 35 acres of parkland of Court Hey Park, the award-winning National Wildflower Centre is an innovative and fascinating place to visit. Established in the former walled garden of the Gladstone Estate and in and around the surviving – but much modernised – stable block and Victorian outbuildings, this was a Millennium Commission supported attraction, costing over £4 million to create.

This has now become not only a tourism centre, but a place for genuine education, research, and study into the natural fauna of Britain. Set around ponds, the gardens and growing areas are left to develop as naturally as possible, and with the minimum of intervention by the staff. The Centre encourages visitors to create their own wildflower gardens at home, and shows how to establish appropriate habitats. It also encourages people to welcome insects into their wild gardens, especially butterflies, but also those essential gardeners' friends – the worms.

Covering a surprisingly large area, though very easy to stroll round in a relatively short space of time, the walkways lead visitors through a range of environments and displays, which are unusual, interesting, and attractive. Seeds and plants can be bought in the shop, and there is a truly excellent café.

"The Wildflower Centre and Court Hey Park are also the setting for the annual Knowsley Flower Show, which is one of the largest free horticultural shows in the North West, and which regularly attracts attendances of over 10,000 people."

To Find Out More:
National Wildflower Centre
Phone: 0151 738 1913
E-Mail: info@nwc.org.uk
www.nwc.org.uk

Leaving the Wildflower Centre, turn right into what is now Roby Road. Continue to the roundabout at the junction with the M62 Motorway.
Take the 2nd exit, following the signs for Huyton, still on the A5080.
As you make this turn, take the right-hand lane towards Huyton and continue past the entrance to Bowring Park Golf Course on the right. About ¼ mile further along, you will come to the Derby Lodge Hotel on the right. This was built by Lord Derby, on whose land it once stood, as a home for his Estate Manager.

As you pass the hotel, the road bends to the right, passing Bridge Road on the left. Immediately after this road – with its small sweets and newspapers kiosk on the corner – take the next left into the narrow cul-de-sac; this is Station Road.

Park as soon as it is safe and convenient to do so, in front of the row of delightful and ornate cottages.

The National Wildflower Centre

Cottages in Roby village

We have now arrived at the modern districts of Roby and Huyton, which were originally ancient communities that became part of aristocratic estates. Although these modern 'villages' are in the Borough of Knowsley, they were originally – like Liverpool – part of Lancashire; and they have always retained close links with their nearby neighbour.

The village of Roby was, like adjoining Huyton, an ancient Norse settlement, and Roby is mentioned in the Domesday Book of 1086, and listed as 'Rabil'. This is an Anglo-Saxon name meaning 'boundary farm', and it was one of six large manors in Lancashire that were owned by Uctred. As mentioned in the Chapter: 'Liverpool Ancient & Modern', Uctred also held the ancient manor of Speke, and was a 'Thane'. This title signifies that he was the Anglo-Saxon equivalent of a Knight, who held the titles to his estates in return for service to the Monarch.

In later years, the manors of Roby, Huyton, and Knowsley were part of the holdings of the Lathom family and, through them and by marriage, they became part of the vast estates of the Stanley Family. As we saw earlier in this Chapter, in 1485 this important family became the Earls of Derby. However, the manor of Huyton then passed to another family.

"During the Middle Ages, Roby was a market village, which meant that it was a centre of local trade and commerce for the surrounding communities"

As such, it also generated a lot of income for the Lords of the Manor. However, and as with much of South Lancashire in the mid-14th century, the Black Death came to Roby and to Huyton, and the small communities must have been devastated by this. It was from this time that Roby's significance as a market centre began to decline. Nevertheless, the Roby estate was large enough in the 16th century to warrant the building of a grand mansion. This stood on the present site of Bowring Park Golf Course, and it was originally called Bury Hall after the family who lived there, only later becoming known as Roby Hall. Nothing of this great hall survives.

Where we are now parked, at the junction of Station Road and Roby Road, was once the main crossroads of the original village, and Carr Lane – which is now a cul-de-sac across the road – was once a track leading out towards Gateacre and Childwall. In fact, a public footpath, which is signposted to 'Netherley', still runs from the end of modern Carr Lane.

Station Road itself was originally part of

Twig Lane, which passed where the church of St Bartholomew's now stands. This was until the railway line and station were built, in the mid 19th century, and these then turned Station Road into a cul-de-sac. Indeed, the church itself was not built until 1850, and before this the people of Roby worshipped at the parish church of St Michael's, in nearby Huyton Village.

In the centre of Roby stands the **Village Cross**, also known as the Boundary Stone, although it is not clear why it was given this latter name, and the village stocks were sited next to it. The stone, which is Grade II Listed, did not originally stand in its present location, in front of the old **Turnpike Toll-Cottage**. It was moved here from the other side of the road when, in the 1960s, the road had to be widened and the cottages that originally stood there were demolished. The stocks have long-since vanished.

Roby remained a very quiet and largely isolated community until, in 1726, the turnpike road from Liverpool to Prescot was created and this ran through the village centre. It was then that the Toll-Cottage was built, and the amount of traffic passing through brought trade and a slight population growth. A hundred years later, George Stephenson was building the new Liverpool to Manchester Railway (see Chapter: 'Pool of Life & Culture'). He had planned a direct route across the Croxteth and Knowsley estates of Lord Sefton and Lord Derby but, predictably perhaps, they objected. The great engineer then had to re-route the line and this now passed through Broadgreen – where the M62 ends at 'The Rocket; named after his famous locomotive – and through Roby and Huyton: Stations were built at all three places, and this prompted the gradual urbanisation of all the communities through which the railway passed. Soon, new houses were being built, including grand mansions such as Edenhurst, which is now the Derby Lodge Hotel.

However, by the end of the 19th century, the district was becoming so built-up that the estates upon which Roby, Huyton, and nearby Tarbock stood, began to be broken up and sold off. Indeed, by 1894 the urban district of Huyton-with-Roby had been

created, then coming under the control of the Liverpool Corporation.

In 1974, with the re-drawing of many electoral boundaries in Britain, the Metropolitan Borough of Knowsley was created, and it was then that Roby – and Huyton – became part of this new Local Authority. All that now remains of the cottages and farms, and of the winding lanes and roads of Roby, is what we see here at Station Road. Apart from St Bartholomew's Church, which stands the other side of Roby Station at the bottom of the close, the ancient village has been completely absorbed into the suburbs of Liverpool. However, the delightful old cottages on Station Road, with their brightly decorated frontages; and the ones facing Roby Road, with their attractive wrought iron porches, make the tiny village-centre of Roby a worthwhile stop.

From Station Road, rejoin Roby Road towards Huyton.

You will pass the Stanley Arms pub on the left – with its 'eagle and child' emblem, and the Huyton Leisure Centre on the right. At the roundabout at the end of the road, take your first exit into Archway Road, under the railway bridge.

Continue along here and pass through the first set of traffic lights. At the next set of lights, just a short way further along, turn left into Rupert Road – opposite the petrol station. Take the first road on the right, which is Stanley Road. At the end of this road, park anywhere that it is safe and convenient to do so. This is the old Village Green of Huyton.

I suggest a 10-15 minute stop here, but longer if you have pre-arranged to visit the church.

A Lordly Heritage

As we drove from Roby towards Huyton, we passed the **Stanley Arms Pub**, which is obviously named after the Earls of Derby. The 'arms' to which the name refers are the ancient crest of the Stanley Family; a very large and colourful reproduction of which is mounted on the wall above the pub's entrance.

Another emblem of the Stanleys is the **Eagle and Child**, which appears on top of the pub sign itself, and there are a number of legends associated with this image.

However, the most commonly quoted is that it illustrates the story of a member of the Lathom family, who was walking across the Knowsley estate with his wife, when they found a baby lying on the ground, wrapped in a shawl and being guarded by a large eagle.

However, the bird flew away, and so the otherwise childless couple adopted the baby as their own. Another legend tells that an eagle simply flew off with one of the Lathom babies: I prefer the first story – it has a happier ending!

Like Roby, Huyton has a particularly interesting history and the Village has developed quite a character for itself over the centuries. The name 'Huyton' appears to derive from the Anglo-Saxon words 'heah' and 'tun', or from 'Hitune', both of which mean 'a high farmstead' or 'high compound', and the modern spelling of the name 'Huyton' seems to date from the mid-13th century.

That the Vikings settled here was confirmed when the prow of a Norse sailing vessel was found during the 19th century, as the foundations were being dug for the railway bridge under which we drove at Archway Road. The ship was buried well below the topsoil and in a deep layer of sand. This indicates that the River Alt, which rises near modern Huyton, was once a much wider and more important waterway than it is today.

"Also, this district was once famous for the manufacture of fishing nets, no doubt for use on the River Mersey when Liverpool was a fishing community"

Huyton, with neighbouring Tarbock, was part of a manor that was recorded in the Domesday Book as being owned by a thane called 'Dot' but, in the 14th century, the manor of Huyton passed to the Harrington family, who were a prominent local family of Catholics, and who remained true to their faith throughout the Reformation. However, by the late 17th century the estate had passed to the Molyneux family,

This delightful row of Victorian, neo-Tudor cottages continue to add charm to the Village

and then to a branch of that family – the Molyneux-Seels. There are very few remnants of the township's ancient heritage that still exist now, and those that do are scattered over a wide area.

Also, as with Roby, when the plague ravaged South Lancashire in the 14th century, Huyton lost most of its small population and the village took a long time to overcome this disaster. Nevertheless, recover it did and, with the coming of the coach road and then the railways, the community soon began to grow and expand.

In the centre of what is left of the ancient village green of Huyton, which is now a Conservation Area, stands the **Village Cross**.

This was built in 1897, to replace an earlier cross that was erected in 1819, and which originally stood in front of the nearby church. This was moved to its present location in the 19th century – alongside the Victorian houses of **Derby Terrace**.

However, the most significant building in the old village of Huyton is the one that dominates the surrounding community, and this is the **Parish Church of St Michael's**.

Records show that a church has stood on this site at least since the 12th century, but the present building dates from 1663 and is now Grade II* Listed.

Although much altered over the centuries, there are many signs of its ancient history in and around the building. Indeed, inside can be found two fonts; one which many archaeologists believe may date from the 8th or 9th centuries, and another from the 1600s.

As work was being carried out on the building, in 1872, the older font was discovered buried under the church tower, along with a capital from a Saxon stone column that is decorated with four helmeted heads. The church also contains an effigy of a local Medieval worthy, John de Winwick, who died in 1349, and the chancel

screen dates from 1460. This was once part of a private chapel in the church, used by the Harrington family, and the screen carries the Harrington Coat of Arms.

The graveyard of the church has some interesting tombs but, because of its elevated position and limited area of available land, additional space had to be found. Since the 19th century, an area adjacent to the village green has been used for burials, and access to this large graveyard is at the end of Derby Terrace, in the corner of the Village Green.

"A number of famous people have been associated with Huyton, as well as former Prime Minister Harold Wilson, and the nonsense poet and artist, Edward Lear"

These include Sir Rex Harrison, Freddie Starr, and Alan Bleasdale, who were all born in the district; and also 'lost Beatle' Stu Sutcliffe, who is buried in the graveyard of St Michael's.

To Find Out More
Huyton Parish Church of St Michael
Phone: 0151 449 3900

Following the Industrial Revolution, as well as road and rail transport changing the nature of Huyton, the township became a centre for many trades, including quarrying and coal mining. There were also a pottery, a gas works, an electric lamp factory, and an iron foundry. These industries needed workers, and so streets of terraced houses were built to accommodate people who, throughout the 19th century, were moving into the districts around Huyton to find work.

Also, in the 1930s, much of the land around Huyton was sold to Liverpool Corporation by Lord Derby, and this began to change dramatically the nature and character of the district. Indeed, the Huyton that we see now bears no resemblance whatsoever to the original village, as virtually all of the old houses, cottages, and surrounding farmlands have been pulled down and built over, especially during the 1960s. Beyond the Village Green, Huyton now largely consists of a large shopping centre, a new supermarket, and vast, sprawling housing estates. However, just across the road from St Michael's Church, is a delightful row of 19th century, **mock-Tudor Cottages** adding further charm to the old village.

From Stanley Road, turn left at the traffic lights into Huyton Lane.

Continue through the traffic lights at Lathom Road, and towards the small roundabout.

As you do so, you will pass two small roads on the left, these are Capper Grove and The Garth. On the right-hand side of the road, directly opposite the end of The Garth, you will see, between two buildings, a broad passageway. This is Corpse Way.

The passage opposite **The Garth** is all that now remains of a long track that once connected the village of Tarbock with the village of Huyton. Records, dating from 1520, show that it was along this old pathway that the Medieval inhabitants of Tarbock used to carry the bodies of their dead loved ones, for burial at St Michael's Church in Huyton Village: Hence the name of the passage - **Corpse Way**!

St Michael's Church

From Corpse Way, continue along Huyton Lane, crossing over the roundabout at the entrance to the ASDA Supermarket.

Pass through some traffic lights at a pedestrian crossing, and then continue through the next 2 sets of traffic lights – at Longview Lane and then at Longview Drive – and you will pass the King George V Playing Fields on the left. At the top of the hill, and as the road bends to the right, you will pass Huyton and Prescot Golf Club on the right. Through the trees you might catch a glimpse of their Clubhouse. This was formerly 'The Hurst', which is one of the last remaining grand mansions to be found in Huyton.

At the mini-roundabout take the first exit, and this will return you to the staring point of this Tour – at the junction with the M57 and the A57.

If however, you intend to visit Knowsley Safari Park, take the first roundabout and follow the signs for the Safari Park. Take your 2nd exit off the roundabout onto the dual-carriageway, and the entrance to the Safari Park is clearly signposted, on the left.

I suggest a minimum of 2 hours to visit the Safari Park – 1 hour to complete the drive, and another hour to take a break, and to visit the other attractions.

Huyton Village Cross

A Lordly Heritage

It was the 18th Earl of Derby (1918-1994); the uncle of the present Earl, who opened Knowsley Safari Park in July 1971. It had been his innovative idea to create a natural and safe setting for wild animals, in an environment in which they could be easily and safely encountered by the public. The concept of enabling cars to be driven around open compounds, based on the drive-through game reserves of East Africa was inspired and, assisted by the expertise and experience of members of the Chipperfield circus dynasty, the Earl produced one of the Northwest's most successful and popular visitor attractions.

When the idea was first proposed there were some concerns voiced by members of the local community. The Knowsley Estate is only 8 miles from Liverpool City-centre, and the villages of Knowsley, Huyton, and Prescot are nearer than that.

"Knowsley was the first Safari Park to be built close to a large conurbation, and some residents feared that they would come in from work one day to find lions and tigers making themselves at home in their front rooms, or working their way through their fridges!"

Nevertheless, the local authority approved the project, and it proved to be an immediate hit with the public. Indeed, at the time the park opened I was working in a children's home as a housefather, and I remember bringing coach loads of excited and thrilled children for trips around the animal reserves.

They were delighted by the lions, giraffes, zebra, elephants, and antelopes, as these animals wandered around in as natural a setting as was possible, on the outskirts of Liverpool. But the children were especially entertained by the monkeys who clambered all over our vehicles.

The Safari Park was such a success, that the original 3½ mile long drive was increased to 5 miles, in 1973. This meant that more breeds could be added to the park, and these included some tigers, and herds of camels, buffalo, and rhino.

Do make time to visit the park if you can, you won't be disappointed and, with all the other attractions and facilities that are available, you can make your visit last either a couple of hours, or a full day.

To Find Out More:
Knowsley Safari Park
Phone: 0151 430 9009
E-mail: safari.park@knowsley.com
www.knowsley.com/safari/
Opening Times: (Please call to check before visiting)
Summer : 1st Mar – 31st Oct / 10am – (Last entry) 4pm
Winter: 1st Nov – 28th Feb / 10.30am – (Last entry) 3pm

On leaving the Safari Park a left turn is compulsory. Follow the dual-carriageway to the end and, at the roundabout, make a U-turn and come back on yourself, to the M57/A57 junction once more.

One of the residents at Knowsley Safari Park

A lioness takes a stroll in the autumn mist

A Lordly Heritage: Conclusion

The Victorian hymn, 'All Things Bright and Beautiful', was written in 1848, and its little-known final verse runs,

The rich man in his castle,
The poor man at his gate,
God made them high or lowly
And ordered their estate

However, this has now been dropped from most hymn books, because it reflects and endorses the class structure that then prevailed across Britain, and which some would say still exists – to a greater or lesser extent. However, we no longer live in a feudal society and so can be a little more pragmatic, and romantic, as we review our history.

Nevertheless, whilst it is the ordinary people who have created and who sustain our community, it has often been the rich and powerful who have shaped our history and our destiny – for good or ill. This has certainly been the case in and around Liverpool, where monarchs and nobles have always taken an interest, and where many have made and maintained their fortunes.

The districts that I chose for this Chapter have only been a corner of our City, but what a corner this is: The impact and influence of the rich and powerful on the lives of the developing town of Liverpool and its people, is clearer to see here than perhaps in any other district of Liverpool.

The political and cultural structure of our society has altered radically over the centuries, but the legacy of the 'Lords of Liverpool' has added to the character of the City and its surrounding towns and villages, in both our culture and our built environment. I hope that this Chapter has given you a greater understanding of some of the main aristocratic characters that have shaped our history, and of how much of their legacy adds colour and richness to our modern communities and lifestyle.

A 'Hands On History' day at Croxteth Hall

Ancient and Modern

Including:

Hale Village

Hale Park

The Childe of Hale's Cottage

Hale Manor House

Within Way and the Old Ford

Hale Parish Church and The Childe's Grave

Hale Head and The Lighthouse

Pickering's Pasture and The Mersey Basin

The Hale Duck Decoy

Liverpool John Lennon Airport

Speke Hall and Grounds

The Art Deco Crowne Plaza Hotel

Artists at Speke Hall

Ancient and Modern : The Tour

This is a combined driving and walking Tour, with extra options for walking along sections of the Mersey Way Coastal Path. It begins at the village of Hale, just outside Speke at the southern end of Liverpool.

Here, and largely on foot, we shall explore this charming Medieval Township with its manor house and thatched cottages.

We shall then drive into Speke itself, where we visit ancient Speke Hall and also see examples of modern Liverpool's reconstruction and resurgence.

The total distance covered by this Tour is 11 miles, from the centre of Hale Village to the Crowne Plaza Hotel in Speke, and its suggested completion time is 4 Hours; plus additional time for a full tour of Speke Hall and its grounds.

NB Please remember to check all opening times and admission charges before setting off, to avoid disappointment should any venues be closed

Contents

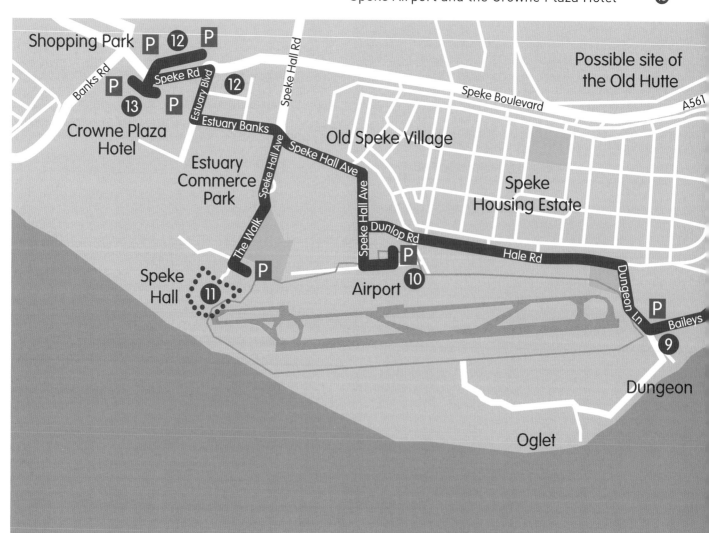

Getting to Hale

Finding Hale Village is not difficult, even though it is isolated on the banks of the River Mersey.

If you are travelling from the M56, or from Warrington, Runcorn, or Widnes, you need to come into Liverpool along the A562 – Speke Road. You will pass the junction with the A5300, which is the Knowsley Expressway with the M62 and the M57 if you are coming to Hale from these motorways.

Just after the A5300 junction, a slip-road branches off on the left, signposted 'A562 to Halewood and Woolton'; take this road. Then, take the first road on the left, which is Higher Road, and then the next road on the right, which is Ramsbrook Lane. After about a mile this meets Hale Road coming in from the right; continue straight across onto High Street, which takes you right into the Village.

If you are coming to Hale from Liverpool, you need to do so along the A561 Speke Road, as far as Speke Hall Road. Turn right down this dual carriageway, following signs for Liverpool John Lennon Airport. Take the second exit off the roundabout following the main dual carriageway, which is still Speke Hall Avenue, and follow this as it bends to the right.

Take the next road on the left, which is Dunlop Road, and this soon becomes Hale Road. Follow this for 2 miles or so, past some 19th and 20th century thatched houses. Then, after the road bends to the right, you will enter Hale village. You will see a triangle of land in front of you, on which stands a flagpole, the War Memorial, and a 20th century cannon. The Childe of Hale Pub is just on the right; park here.

Key

- **Start Here** Starting Point
- **1** Map Reference
- Driving Route
- Walking Route
- **P** Parking Points
- Railway

Route Map

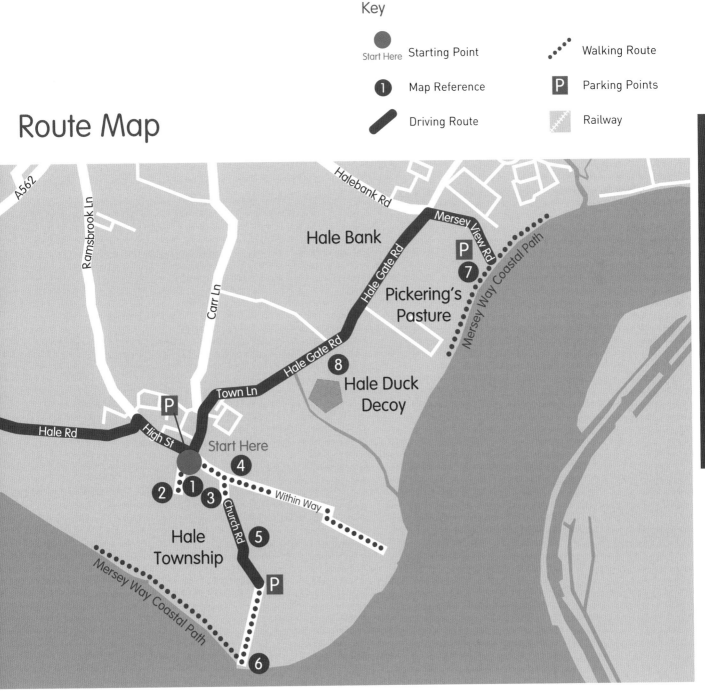

Ancient and Modern Introduction

As we have seen throughout this book, most of the ancient villages and communities that surrounded the original town of Liverpool were absorbed as the City grew, during the 19th and early 20th centuries.
All that is, except one: The Township of Hale.

We shall take some time to have a stroll around truly delightful Hale, which stands directly on the border with its large and powerful neighbour.

Just across that border I shall then take you to the district of Speke. Here, we shall see an area of Liverpool that was once exactly like Hale, but which has been exposed to over 75 years of urbanisation, and which now exemplifies the City's current economic and environmental regeneration.

The juxtaposition of a really attractive, countryside community, with a thriving, urban, industrial and retail centre is quite stark. Nevertheless, the two communities show how the charm and interest of our living heritage can genuinely co-exist, side-by-side, with everything that is modern and dynamic about our City.

So, I shall begin by describing the ancient heritage of both Hale and Speke, and then we shall set about discovering the modern legacies of both places.

The Township of Hale

The name of this village is believed to be of Anglo-Saxon origin, and it derives from 'healh', which means a corner or promontory of land, and this exactly describes Hale's location; sticking out as it does into the basin of the River Mersey.

The area developed as a farming community because the soil is so rich and fertile but, when the earliest people began to settle here, the land was also heavily forested and large acreages had to be cleared to create fields on which to grow crops and breed livestock.

It was not just the rich soil and forests that attracted the pre-Norman settlers to Hale, but also its close proximity to the freshwater streams that fed into the Mersey. They were also drawn to the river itself because of its plentiful quantities of fish and wildfowl.

"Hale was also the only place where, when the tide was out, the river could be forded on foot or on horseback. However, this was a treacherous crossing"

There are also large areas of salt-marsh between Hale and the river, which can flood when the tides are high or during storms, but around these were extensive osier willow beds.

These provided stems for use as a building material, and particularly for basket-making, which was an important trade.

In the Domesday Book of 1086, Hale is listed a being one of four estates that made up the large manor of Childwall and, in recognition for his loyalty and support, William the Conqueror granted a vast area of land to Roger de Poitou. This covered the whole area between the River Mersey and the River Ribble, and included the Hale estate. Roger was a Knight who had supported the King during his invasion of England, however, the loyalty of William's courtier was short-lived – at least as far as the King's son, the new King Henry I (1068-1135), was concerned.

This was because Roger was a member of an unsuccessful rebellion against Henry, and so the rebel's lands were confiscated. Hale then remained a Royal possession until 1203, when King John granted the Manor to Richard de Walton, who was a priest and the Chief Sergeant of the Hundred of West Derby.

At that time, the area that constituted the Manor of Hale covered not only the current Township but also nearby Halewood, and also parts of what is now Woolton. However, what makes Hale particularly significant locally is that, also in 1203, the Village received its charter as a Royal Borough from King John, and this was four years before nearby Liverpool received its own charter: This is a fact of which the people of Hale are fiercely proud.

As a 'Borough', people were allowed to become 'Burgesses', which meant that they could buy or lease land to farm, and on which they could erect a home. This status also brought with it certain tax advantages and the right to trade in a variety of goods and services.

King John liked hunting, as we have seen, and not only did he create the Royal Hunting Forest of Toxteth in Liverpool, but also at Simonswood and West Derby. He also claimed a private hunting reserve in the forests just north of Hale, at 'Hale's Wood', which became 'Halewood'.

By the 16th century however, much of this forest had been cleared, also for farming, and people had begun to settle in isolated communities throughout the district. In 1233, Richard de Walton granted the Hale estates to Cecilia de Columbers, and from her they eventually passed into the hands of the Ireland family.

Although generally referred to as a 'village', Hale is actually a Township. They gained this status in the 14th century, and it gave the people the right to elect 'Freemen', who had a role in the administration and governance of their community.

A Freeman was a Burgess or free tenant of the Township, who was under no obligation to work for the Lord of the Manor. These men were also exempt from the payment of various tolls and fees, unlike the rest of the people.

It was also in the 14th century, that the King granted the community the right to hold weekly markets and annual fairs, thus making Hale a centre for local trade and also strengthening the local economy.

The Hale estate remained in the ownership of the Ireland family until the death of Sir Gilbert Ireland, in 1675. Although childless, Gilbert was to have a nine-feet-tall 'childe' in his service, as you shall see later. Nevertheless, without direct descendants this left

Gilbert's siblings in line for the Manor and the Ireland estate.

He had three sisters and one brother, but inheriting the estates proved emotionally difficult and legally complicated for his surviving relatives, and it was 30 years later before the heirs of Gilbert's sister, Eleanor, finally took possession of the Manor of Hale. From her descendants the estates passed, in 1752, into the ownership of the Blackburne Family, and the subsequent fate of the Manor of Hale is described later in this Chapter.

Incidentally, the Blackburnes were very significant and wealthy traders in Liverpool and Hale, making their money from the Slave Trade and from salt refining. They also built Blackburne House in Hope Street in Liverpool. (See Chapter: 'Pool of Life & Culture.)

"From the 18th century, the Freemen of Hale were allowed to elect their own Lord Mayor – a very special privilege indeed – and this tradition continues"

Today however, the Freemen of Hale are local people who have a record of service to the community. Likewise, the Mayor – who serves a three year term – is elected on the basis of civic and community involvement. At Mayoral election time, the investitures take place in the Village, and sometimes in the Childe of Hale Pub or the Wellington Pub.

The independence of Hale and its community, as well as their somewhat 'backwater' location, saved Hale from the encroachments of Liverpool, and enabled the Township to preserve and strengthen its own identity.

Nevertheless, administratively, modern Hale is not part of the City of Liverpool, nor is it officially in Merseyside. Nominally, the Township falls under the jurisdiction of the Metropolitan Borough of Halton, which is in the County of Cheshire. However, Hale has always been a Manorial possession, and the entire Township and most of its lands are still in private hands; although the rights and privileges of the Lord of the Manor have long since been eroded.

Ancient Speke

Not much more than a mile away from the centre of Hale Township, and just across the border with Liverpool, stands the district of Speke. Although a place with a chequered history during the 20th century, and an area of challenges and opportunity in the 21st, Speke has a heritage just as venerable as that of its quaint neighbour.

The original name for the district was 'Spic', meaning 'bacon', as there were swine fields all over this area. At the time of the Norman Conquest, Uctred originally owned Speke: he was a 'Thane', which was the Anglo-Saxon equivalent of a Knight, and he held six large manors throughout Lancashire in return for service to the Crown. One of these, as we saw in a previous Chapter, was the Manor of Roby.

From Uctred, the Manor of Speke eventually passed to Adam de Molyneux, an ancestor of the future Earls of Sefton, and then, in the 13th century, to the wealthy and influential Norris family. This family then began to build Speke Hall as their family seat, and their magnificent Manor House still exists. Today this remains a wonderful, half-timbered manor house that stands in its own grounds, near the river.

The Manor of Speke was important because, like Hale, the land was rich and fertile. This made it profitable for the landowners and a source of work and trade for the common people: indeed, most of the local folk would have farmed land owned by the Lords of the Manor, or would have been employed by them in other ways.

Even the Freemen and Burgesses would have operated trades and professions that would have been used by the landowners and their families, thus ensuring that the Manors of Hale and Speke remained at the hub of the local economy.

Before and during the time that the Medieval aristocrats and other wealthy landowners owned the estates, Monks from religious communities across the river on the Wirral had settlements here, and at nearby Garston and Aigburth (see Chapter: 'Green and Pleasant Liverpool'). Here they had arable land, livestock, fisheries, and storage barns for their produce.

Also as in Hale, because the surrounding land was so heavily forested, there was plenty of timber for building of homes, barns, and stables. In fact, for some time this area was the location for a ship-building industry: Because of the close proximity to the river of so many oak trees, this was perfect for the building of warships for Medieval navies.

Hale cottages

There were also lots of reeds from the marshes that were used for thatching and, as well as the osier willow beds, coppices of hazel were maintained to provide long, flexible twigs – known as 'wattle' – which would be woven into wall panels for buildings. Clay – often mixed with horse-manure or horse-hair, and known as 'daub' – was then pressed into these and smoothed over, to provide finished walls for homes, barns, and chapels etc. There would be plenty of clay available because of the marshes, in which there were clay or 'marl' pits. This meant that the whole district was full of natural resources, making it ideal for human habitation and commerce.

For centuries though, Speke remained completely rural, and consisted of no more than a number of isolated cottages and hamlets, connected by tracks and pathways, and surrounding the Manor House and farms: Even its parish church and small school house were not built until the 19th century. Its population was never more than about 400 people, and this remained largely the case until Speke became the location for major urban, industrial, and housing redevelopment in the inter-War years. I shall talk about this later in this Chapter also.

And so, let us now take a look at parts of the Township of Hale, and enjoy seeing how much of this beautiful and ancient community has survived into modern times. Along the way we shall see some fascinating sights and meet some curious characters.

We shall then visit Speke, to see the only remaining evidence of that ancient Manor's past – the magnificent Mansion House of Speke Hall.

We shall also take a look at aspects of modern Speke, and discover why its new industrial, enterprise, and retail parks are emblematic of Liverpool's modern, 21st century regeneration.

The Childe of Hale Pub, the starting point for this Tour

To Find Out More
The Childe of Hale Pub
Phone: 0151 425 2954
12.00noon till 11.00pm (10.30pm Sunday)
www.pub-explorer.com/merseyside/pub/
childeofhalehale.htm

The starting point for this Tour is the Childe of Hale pub, which is Map Reference 1 on the Route Map. Indeed, this charming old pub is a fine place to have a meal or a snack, and to park you car whilst you explore the first part of Hale Village on foot.
NB: The pub only opens each day from noon, and there are no other tea shops, cafés, or restaurants in the Village. However, the Wellington Pub, on the way out of Hale towards Hale Bank, also serves food, but this too only opens late.

From the car park, walk left into Church End and, after about 50 metres, you will come to the entrance to Hale Park. The driveway here leads into the woods at the rear, which overlook the river. This woodland was once the site of Hale Hall, but now only a few outbuildings remain, plus some private houses on private land.

Hale Hall and Hale Park

(2)

As we have seen, Hale has always had its own Lord of the Manor, and it still does, although this role has much altered over the centuries. When the Ireland family inherited the estate their original home was at the Hutte, which was a huge, baronial, moated mansion at Halewood, situated in woodland and adjacent to three fishponds. This house appears to have been built some time in the 12th century, and records show that the Ireland family were already established in the Hutte from around 1291. There were a number of buildings and farms grouped around the mansion, and access to it was across a stone bridge and causeway, which are believed to have replaced an original drawbridge.

However, and as we shall see, the Ireland family found the Hutte not grand enough for their rising status in the local community, so they moved out in the 17th century. Nevertheless, the descendants of the Irelands, and later the Blackburnes, continued to own the Hutte as part of the Hale estate, and the old manor remained an important focal point for the local community. In fact, a broad track called Old Hutte Lane once led directly from the Manor through to Hale, and down to the small hamlet of Dungeon. This lies between Hale Head and the equally tiny community of Oglet.

It is known that the Hutte, its gatehouse, farms, stables, and a group of estate worker's cottages, certainly survived into the 17th century, but after this time there are no detailed records. However, by the early years of the 20th century, all that remained of the Old

Hutte and its buildings were a large gothic archway (which had stood across the drive to the Manor House, the gatehouse to the estate), Old Hutte farm, and six small cottages: the Old Hutte itself has long disappeared.

The gatehouse was a large, Elizabethan house that had been occupied, since 1935, by a local family named Lyons. They worked the farm as tenants of Major Blackburne who was the last private owner of this Halewood estate. He sold the entire property to Liverpool Corporation in the 1950s, who considered completely restoring the gatehouse and the other surviving buildings, and converting them into a folk museum. However, when inspectors were sent in to assess the potential for restoration, they discovered that the gatehouse was riddled with dry rot, and was far too costly to repair. It was then that the Ford Motor Company offered to buy the complete estate, as part of the land that they needed for a new car factory. And so, in 1960, the Old Hutte gatehouse, the farm and the cottages were sold to the American car manufacturers. The Lyons family then moved to Hunts Cross, and the Ford Factory opened in 1963, leaving nothing behind of the Old Hutte Manor except in the name of a local school and a very short stretch of Old Hutte Lane.

In the early 17th century the Ireland family, who then held the Manor of Hale and who needed a grander family seat than the Old Hutte, decided to move nearer to the centre of the Township. And so, in 1617, the foundations were laid for what was to become,

Hale Park

in 1626, Hale Hall. This house originally stood beyond the woods in Hale Park and here, in what is now public open space, were once the grounds and gardens of the Hall. This was truly a grand manor house. It had a gabled frontage, mullioned windows, and a tower with a turret.

The interior was spacious and very well appointed, complete with a magnificent oak-panelled great hall; suites of rooms; and extensive kitchens and household areas. It was altered and extended over the years and, in the mid-17th century, twelve beautiful stained glass windows were added to the building, depicting scenes of Roman Emperors.

"By the 19th century there was also a family museum, which contained collections of coins, stuffed birds, and a range of curiosities"

Following the traditions of 18th century landed-gentry, the original estate was landscaped, and clumps of woodlands were planted across acres of grasslands. Also, and in keeping with common practice at that time, parts of the village were demolished and villagers forcibly moved out as the Park estate was developed, 'to improve the landscape'. Indeed, the gardens and grounds at Hale Hall were renowned, not just for their beauty, but for their conservatories and collections of exotic plants. These included a banana plant, a tea tree, and a cork tree.

There was also a great Palm Tree that was presented to the family in 1737, and which was brought to Hale Hall in 1817. It was a mammoth tree, measuring 5ft in circumference and 34ft in height. When it died, in 1859, its trunk was donated to the museum at Kew Gardens.

Hale Hall was the centre of Township life, but it also was home to its own extensive community of family, servants, stable staff, groundsmen, and gamekeepers.

There was a home farm, and extensive produce gardens, the walls of which – like those at Croxteth Hall (see Chapter: 'A Lordly Heritage') – were honeycombed with flues, through which hot air was piped to keep frost from the plants and fruit trees. Also, and as we saw at Calderstones Park (see Chapter: 'Green and Pleasant Liverpool'), there were a number of Ha-Ha barriers constructed, to keep the grazing sheep and cattle from approaching too close to the house and gardens.

In 1876, John Ireland-Blackburne built a lodge house, which still stands at the entrance to the modern park. However, after the First World War parts of the Hall were demolished, and the landscaped grounds largely converted into arable farmland. In the 1930s, Gilbert Ireland-Blackburne left the Village and put the entire Hale Estate on the market.

This attractive and profitable holding was bought, in 1937, by a branch of the Ireland-Blackburne family, the Fleetwood-Heskeths, who also held estates in North Meols near Southport, and this is where the family still live today. Indeed, they still own the entire Hale Estate today, although they are no

longer 'Lords of the Manor' in the traditional sense, and have little or no influence on the lives of the community, except as landlords.

The new owners did not take up residence in Hale until 1947 but, by the outbreak of World War Two, Hale Hall had become almost uninhabitable through disrepair and age, and so Peter Fleetwood-Hesketh moved into the 18th Century Parsonage, which then became known as Hale Manor House.

Meanwhile, Hale Hall was abandoned and neglected and, during the 1950s, the grand old building was partially destroyed by fire and subsequently had to be demolished.

Now, only the parkland, a playground, and Hale Cricket Club exist on what was once the Hale Hall grounds, together with some remaining outbuildings that have now been converted to private residences.

To Find Out More:
Hale Township – Mike Royden
www.btinternet.com/~m.royden/
mrlhp/local/hale/hale.htm

From Hale Park, walk back along Church End, past the Childe of Hale Pub and, as the road bends slightly to the left you will see a low, white-walled, thatched cottage standing on the right. This was John Middleton's Cottage.

Ancient and Modern

John Middleton, otherwise known as 'The Childe of Hale', was born in the Village in 1578, in the cottage that he occupied all his life, and which survives today.

By the age of 20, John had grown to a height of 9ft 3ins, and at the time he was renowned as the 'tallest man in the world'. He was called the 'Childe', not as an ironic reference to his height, but because of his simple nature and gentle personality. John's thatched cottage, with its whitewashed walls, still has his hat pegs positioned 10ft from the floor, and no ceiling except the cruck-beam roof, which allowed him to stand upright; although, when viewed today the entrance door seems quite low, considering John's height.

A small plaque in the wall facing the road identifies his home, which, structurally at least, has altered little over the subsequent centuries.

Sir Gilbert Ireland, who was Lord of the Manor of Hale at the time, took John to be his personal bodyguard in 1604 – 'to walk with him, to stand behind his chair at meals, and to perform feats of strength for his friends'.

In 1617, on a return journey from Scotland, King James I was staying at Lathom, which was an estate to the north of Liverpool. It was here that he knighted Gilbert Ireland, and it is entirely possible that he heard about John from Gilbert at this time.

> "The King invited the newly enobled Sir Gilbert and his gigantic manservant to come to London to fight his own champion, who was described at the time as 'a huge wrestler of prodigious proportions'!"

John accepted the challenge and, dressed in a brand new suit bought for the purpose, he and Sir Gilbert made their way to London. The wrestling match was 'no-contest', with John Middleton winning the bout by a throw; gaining a 20-guinea purse; and snapping the thumb of the King's Champion into the bargain.

John and Sir Gilbert were then 'encouraged' to leave the capital, and so they made their way home, but by way of Brasenose College in Oxford. It was here that Sir Gilbert had been a student until 1578, and he and his magnificent servant were warmly welcomed by students and faculty alike.

In fact, John became such a celebrity and so popular with the students here, many of whom were from John's home county of Lancashire (the boundaries of which included Hale at that time), that his portrait was painted, and this is believed to be the painting that now hangs at Speke Hall.

John Middleton's cottage

Sir Gilbert stayed on for a little while longer at his old college, whilst John made his own way home separately, accompanied by some new-found travelling companions.

However, at an isolated spot on the long trek home, these people set upon John and, outnumbered and overpowered, they severely beat him and robbed him of his prize money.

John, 'the gentle giant', arrived back at Hale a much poorer man than when he originally set off, and with what had effectively been his pension stolen from him. In fact, local records state that John 'was oblig'd to follow the plow to his dying day'.

Nevertheless, John was loved and cherished by his fellow villagers at Hale, especially the children, and his simple manner and childlike ways ensured that he was never lonely or short of friendship; even though he never married or had children of his own.

John Middleton continued to work for Sir Gilbert and eventually died, in 1623, at the age of 45. He lies buried in the graveyard of Hale Parish Church of St Mary.

To Find Out More:
The Childe of Hale
www.forteantimes.com/articles/
187_childe1.shtml

The architecture of Hale Village is very mixed, reflecting all periods and all styles. Indeed, opposite the Childe of Hale's Cottage stand two Georgian-style houses. The more 'farmhouse-like' building on the left is period, but the ornate one on the right, with the date stone of 1858, is clearly Victorian neo-Georgian.

As we come to the centre of the Village, and to what remains of the Village Green, we shall see more architectural juxtapositions – many separated by centuries, rather than by just decades.

On the same side of the road as John Middleton's old home is a delightful terrace of cottages that date from the same period. The lowness of the roofs and the tiny dimensions of each home give us some idea of the lifestyle of people in medieval Hale. Continue past the cottages and, opposite these across the road, stands Hale Manor House.

It is the buildings in the heart of the Village that make Hale unique in Liverpool. Although – of course – it is not actually part of the City at all.

The very mixture of architectural styles and the centuries that separate them, as well as the sense of being peacefully miles away from urban life, make Hale such a pleasant and interesting place to stroll through. The Village has won the prestigious 'Best Kept Village' award on a number of occasions and it is easy to understand why. All this is best seen in and around the Village Green and, after the old cottages on Church End, the next building of real interest is the Manor House.

Hale Manor

When the Fleetwood-Hesketh family moved from Meols to take up residence in Hale, they were unable to do so in Hale Hall as the old mansion had been neglected for so long that it was almost derelict, so they needed to find an alternative 'stately home'.

They chose the old Parsonage House, which had been built in the mid-17th century, and after they moved in it became known as 'The Manor House'. This attractive building had been altered over the years and, in fact, it had originally been quite a small building until the early 18th century, when the grand façade was added. Indeed, from the side, it can be clearly seen that the front is simply that – a front; whilst the original parsonage building sticks out at the rear. The combined effect of the 'shy' parsonage, tucked behind the imposing grandeur of the front of the Manor, is both curious and charming.

The building at the rear is the equivalent of a modern large family home in capacity, whilst in the front section of the Manor can be found a beautiful panelled hall, with adjoining side rooms, and a curving stairway leading to rooms on the upper floor.

By the beginning of the 19th century, the building was no longer used as a parsonage and had become a farmhouse, and so it remained until the outbreak of the Second World War. It was then that the local 'Dad's Army' moved in, because the house became the district headquarters of the Home Guard. When the late Peter Fleetwood-Hesketh moved in after the War, he did much to refurbish the house and the farm, and he restored the Manor to its 18th century splendour: Indeed, in 1958 the building was Grade II* Listed.

The Fleetwood-Heskeths moved back to Meols in 1984, although the family still own the Hale Estate, and the Manor was left empty for three years. In 1987, a new family bought the old building, which by then needed another major restoration, and which its new occupants undertook with

Hale Manor House

love and care. Now, the Manor House once more makes a bold statement, as it dominates the Village Green and overlooks the row of ancient thatched cottages.

Within Way and the Old Ford

Immediately to the right of the Manor House is a road named Within Way, and this narrow lane leads south, after a mile or so, down to the banks of the River Mersey.

This once led travellers to the only place where, in ancient times, the River Mersey could be crossed on foot or on horseback.

Of course, this could only be accomplished at very low tide, but even then it was a treacherous journey; before industrialisation the river was much wider than it is now.

During the time of King John a ferry was operating from Hale to Runcorn, with the tolls going to the Crown.

"If a traveller could not afford the boat ride, then he could take his life into his hands and cross the river on foot, although he still had to pay a much smaller toll to the Lord of the Manor for the privilege!"

Over the centuries dozens of people, and even more animals, have met their deaths crossing the notorious Hale Ford, and a number of gravestones in the burial ground of Hale Parish Church tell tales of people drowning in the Mersey; some of their bodies being recovered, whilst others were lost forever.

During the English Civil War, many soldiers on both sides of the conflict used the ford to both escape from, and to mount attacks on, enemy forces.

Crossings of the river on foot continued right up to the end of the 19th century, until work began on the construction of the Manchester Ship Canal in November 1882, which effectively cut off all access to the other side of the river. Even so, there are records of horses and carts being driven across as late as 1880. Indeed, the last time that it appears to have been crossed was just before excavation work began on the new canal, when an intrepid (or foolhardy) man decided to cross it on foot in both directions, 'just to see if this could still be accomplished'! He made it from Hale to what is now Weston Point, with the river sloshing about his ankles. However, on the return trip the water was clearly beginning to rise, but he remained undaunted. Indeed, he removed all of his clothes and completed the hazardous crossing with them held above his head to keep them dry, and with the River Mersey lapping about his neck and shoulders!

If you wish to retrace the travellers' route down Within Way, at least as far as the riverbank – I would not recommend that you go any further! – then do walk, do not drive! The track is narrow, unsurfaced, and full of potholes.

Beyond the Manor House and the end of Within Way the road now becomes Church Road, and this takes you to St Mary's Parish Church.

Records show that, in 1081, a small chapel constructed of wattle and daub, stood on the site of the present Church of St Mary. This was then only a Chapel of Ease, because the tiny community of Hale was then in the parish of much larger Childwall, in south Liverpool. (See Chapter: 'Liverpool Lost and Found'.)

The chapel was built by John of Ireland, who was buried there when he died in 1088, and his remains were subsequently transferred to the later church, which completely replaced the chapel sometime in the early 14th century: Parish records refer to this as having been dedicated to St Mary by 1308, and the tower of the modern church dates from that period. There is a spiral stairway that leads up to the roof of the tower and, as one climbs the worn steps, the original stonemason's marks of the men who built the church can still be seen, etched in some of the sandstone blocks. The rest of the building was altered, rebuilt, and renovated a number of times during subsequent centuries, and indeed, the walls of the present nave date from 1758. These replaced the old wattle and daub walls of the 14th century building.

Hale Church had a ring of five bells, which were replaced in 1814 by a new ring of six bells, and the sound of these was renowned throughout Lancashire. Indeed, people would travel from miles around, simply to hear 'Hale's sweet bells'. Inside the church were some delightful, and ancient, memorials and hatchments, representing the many family names who had held title to the Manor of Hale over the years, and there was also a wonderful organ, and a carved, wooden, Georgian gallery and choir stalls.

You may wonder why I describe these things in the past tense: This is because, on the night of October 19th 1977, vandals deliberately set fire to the church, which was completely gutted. Everything inside the building was destroyed, and only the tower and the church walls remained standing. The people of Hale were devastated by the senseless arson attack, which removed the heart from the centre of their community. However, the spirit of the villagers made them determined to see their church rise from its own ashes. But, this was not to be straightforward, because the insurance money did not completely cover the costs of replacement and refitting, and the church lay derelict for a year, whilst legal battles were fought. At the same time the people of Hale, of all denominations, established a campaign to raise funds to rebuild the church. Eventually, work began, but then the Government of the day insisted in applying VAT to the rebuilding costs. During the reconstruction also, the rate of VAT was raised from 8% to 15%, almost crippling the project.

Nevertheless, the courage and strength of this close community won through, and St Mary's did indeed rise phoenix-like and, on the 28th May 1980, the new church was re-consecrated by the then Bishop of Liverpool, Rev. David Sheppard.

As part of the rebuilding, the roof level was lowered a few feet; the oak panelled gallery was replaced; and the Medieval hatchments and memorials were replaced by modern replicas, reproduced using photographs of the originals. During the restoration of the church, several gravestones of members of the Ireland-Blackburne family were discovered beneath the chancel floor, and these still rest there. undisturbed.

Everything else that now furnishes the church came from other churches around Britain; either from redundant buildings or as gifts from other parishes. This includes the 16th century pulpit, which came from York Minster, and a new peal of eight bells. Consequently, modern St Mary's is much plainer inside than the original. Even so, the replacement ceiling is made of chestnut, was created by a single carpenter, and is a fine piece of work.

St Mary's Church Hale is a welcoming building once more, which has resumed its place at the heart of Township life.

Surrounding the church building, and entered through two Lych Gates in the surrounding old sandstone wall, is the church graveyard.

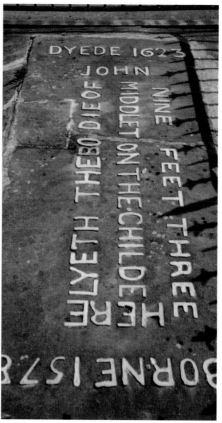

The Childe of Hale's Grave can be found at the Parish Church of St Mary

This too dates back to the founding of the original chapel but, to cope with the passage of time, the graveyard has had to be extended into a nearby field to accommodate more recent burials.

In the old burial ground there are many fascinating graves, including empty ones to mark loved ones from the Village who were lost at sea, and whose bodies were never recovered. Whilst there are one or two 17th century tombstones, most graves only date back to the 18th century.

This is because at Hale, and in common with churches throughout Britain until that time, once a graveyard was full it was simply ploughed over and re-used. Sometimes a new layer of topsoil was used – as we saw at Childwall Parish church in a previous Chapter – and sometimes not.

However, undoubtedly the most fascinating grave in St Mary's churchyard belongs to John Middleton, the Childe of Hale, and this can be seen surrounded by railings. But what strikes most people as odd is that, considering how tall John was supposed to be, why is his grave no longer than that of a more ordinary-sized person?

This is because he was originally buried doubled up; still lengthways, but with his fingers touching his toes.

Why this would have been the case I have no idea, but what we do know is that, in 1768, his bones were removed from his burial place and taken to Hale Hall, allegedly for preservation. However, the opportunity was taken to measure them to satisfy arguments about John's actual dimensions.

His thighbones alone were found to be as long as half the height of an average man; and his hands measured 17 inches from the base of the wrist to the tip of the middle finger, and 8½ inches across the palm. In fact, the measurements revealed that John was probably between 4 and 6 inches taller than people had originally thought him to be!

Whatever, his bones were later re-interred in the graveyard, where the Childe of Hale now lies at rest.

A curious custom seems to persist in Hale; because every time that I visit John's grave I see copper coins placed carefully on his tombstone. Why this should be the case I have not been able to establish; perhaps it is some sort of folk memory of 'paying the ferryman' for the journey across the River Styx in the Underworld:

There are many long walks to be taken from the centre of Hale Village, as well as the one along Within Way to the old ford: One takes you from the Church to Hale Head and the Lighthouse. However, it might be as well at this point to return to your car, and then to drive back to the Church and on towards the Lighthouse along Church Road.
At the end of the tarmaced roadway are a small turning area and a parking space for two cars. From here, through a gate and along a $^1/_3$ mile track, you can walk to the Lighthouse and the Red Rocks, on the Mersey foreshore.

Hale Head and The Lighthouse

The present lighthouse that stands on Hale Head was built in 1906, to replace a previous light set on top of a shorter stack, which had been erected in 1838. The current stack is 45ft tall and, when its lamp was lit, its static white beam shone across the Mersey Basin at a height of 70 feet above sea-level. The light was lit by oil, and yet it was said that the beam could be seen over forty miles away. This was very important, as this is the widest point of the River Mersey and the light served a very useful purpose for vessels on the crowded waterway, warning them of the dangers of Hale Head, and of its surrounding shallow shoals and treacherous rocks.

The light was kept lit throughout the Second World War, although this did attract an enemy aircraft on one occasion, and bombs were dropped nearby. However, the lighthouse escaped damage, although the keeper's wife was machine-gunned by a passing Nazi plane as she opened the shutters on the windows of the adjoining cottage. Fortunately, she was not hit.

In 1958, the decision was taken to finally turn off the light. There was no longer any shipping at this end of the river so the lighthouse had become redundant. All the building's equipment was removed, but the lenses for the light can now be seen in the Merseyside Maritime Museum. The lighthouse, and its cottage and surrounding land, were then sold as a private residence and it has remained so ever since. As such, it is not open to the public, but the footpath passes alongside the structure, giving visitors an excellent view of the old building.

Apart from the vessels that one can see sailing along the Manchester Ship Canal on the opposite bank, this stretch of the river is now largely deserted; a far cry from what it was like 100 years ago. Because it is so tranquil here now, this part of the Mersey Basin, as we shall see when we visit Pickering's Pasture, is a haven for wildfowl. It is also a good point to view the hills at Frodsham and Helsby across the river, and to perhaps take a stroll along part of the Mersey Way, which is the coastal path that runs from Widnes, along in front of Hale and Speke, to Garston.

rather like the old custom of putting pennies on they eyes of corpses. Or, perhaps it is just some form of tribute, or gift, to the Childe of Hale. But, whatever it signifies, I always now leave a penny on his grave – as my own tribute to his memory.

To Find Out More:
Hale Parish Church
Phone: 0151 425 3195
www.welcome.to/hale-church

Hale History Tree

Opposite the church stands the **Hale History Tree**, carved in the likeness of John Middleton, and decorated with symbols of local significance.

Unveiled in 1996, it was sculpted from the stump of a beech tree that had stood in the Village for 130 years. The artist, Philip Bews, who carved the figure assisted by Geoff Wilson, organised community workshops so that local people – especially children and young people – could carve part of their local history into the figure. A list of everyone who took part in the work is kept in the records of the Parish Council.

On the figure can be seen a lighthouse, a ship, animals and birds, and many more images reflecting the life and history of Hale. However, and sadly, it has not completely escaped the attentions of vandals.

The figure of John stands 4 metres high, which is 13 feet, so it is about a metre higher than the Childe was in real life but, nevertheless, it helps give us some idea of just how tall he actually was.

After visiting Hale Head and the lighthouse, return to your car and drive back along Church Road. Once you are back in the Village return to the War Memorial triangle, by the Childe of Hale Pub, and turn right into Town Lane.
Follow this as it bends right and leads you out of Hale; you will pass Pepper Street, a row of modern shop fronts, and then the Wellington Pub on the left hand side. Continue along as the road now becomes Hale Gate Road.

Hale lighthouse overlooking the broad Mersey Basin

As you leave Hale you can see how rural the surrounding area remains, even though its farmlands, woods, and marshes are surrounded on all sides by industrialisation and conurbation: Hale really is an oasis on the border between Merseyside and Cheshire.

Just beyond the village the road straightens and begins to rise slightly, crossing over Ram's Brook. On the left of the road, across the fields, can be seen three stands of woodland; the furthest away is known as Clamley Wood

Plantation; in front of this you can see Big Boar's Wood; and the nearest wood is Little Boar's Wood – with Boar's Wood Cottage standing on the edge of the trees.

If you look to the right of the road you will see, standing in the middle of the salt marshes, a large clump of mixed woodland with some obviously dead trees poking up through the tree-line. This is the Hale Duck Decoy, about which I shall talk shortly.

Ahead of you, at the brow of the hill and on the right, stands Hale Gate Farm.

> Continue past Hale Gate Farm, and follow the road into Hale Bank. You come to a crossroads, with signs to Runcorn and Widnes, and to Speke and Liverpool. Turn right into Mersey View Road; the Mersey View Pub will be on the right-hand corner. At the very end of this road is the entrance to Pickering's Pasture Nature Reserve.

Pickering's Pasture and the Mersey Basin

Pickering's Pasture is a broad area of open pasture alongside the banks of the River Mersey, through which the **Mersey Way Coastal Path** runs along the shore.

From the Pasture there are remarkable views of the industrialisation on the edges of the river, including the chemical plant at Weston Point, the oil refinery at Stanlow, and the Manchester Ship Canal. The Silver Jubilee and Stephenson railway bridges are also part of the scene, and yet they do not dominate the view. In fact, behind all of these processing and factory sites, rise natural embankments and hills, covered by a combination of homes, farms, fields, heath, and woodland.

The hills of Frodsham and Helsby, are almost directly ahead of us and to the right from this viewpoint, and these, together with the views of the river snaking left around the bend, towards Warrington, and also broadening out on the right, towards Speke, Liverpool, and Liverpool Bay, make the perspective rich and varied: a reflection of the mixed and modern world that we all inhabit.

Yet nature still has her way here, despite the surrounding industry and commerce.

> "The pasture and the surrounding open land support a wealth of wildflowers and insect life, whilst the Mersey Basin attracts birds and waterfowl of all descriptions"

One can clearly imagine what these upper reaches of the Mersey must have been like when man was fewer in numbers; when his habitation was in small cottages and shelters; and when his only industry was fishing, farming, and husbandry. In fact, I find that if you stand quietly on the edge of Pickering's Pasture and detach yourself from the sounds of the 21st century, then with only a little imagination, you can be transported back to our simpler ancestry.

It was in early Medieval times, and where Stanlow Oil Refinery now stands, that Stanlawe Abbey was once home to the Monks who had their fisheries and granaries at Speke, Garston, and Aigburth. And there are tales of a four-mile long tunnel, running under the river from their Abbey to Speke, which was used by these Medieval clerics. It is said that they cut it to extend existing natural caves and tunnels.

For century upon century, life in, on, and around the river remained tranquil and unchanging, until that is, the Industrial Revolution came to this part of England. Nevertheless, for over a hundred years from that time, this side of the river remained fields, marshes and heathland. This was until the 1940s, when the land upon which we are now standing became a huge dumping ground for industrial and household waste. Until the 1960s, this process destroyed this stretch of the riverbank; driving away the birds and the animals, and blighting the soil. Then the dumping ceased, but the land lay waste for another 20 years.

The waters of the Mersey by this time had become our shame. Indeed, when Michael Heseltine was made Minister for Merseyside in 1981, he declared our river to be the most polluted in Europe.

Its waters were grey and sluggish; saturated with vast amounts of industrial waste; and a sluice for raw effluent and sewage. In hot weather the stink could be appalling and, in heavy weather and storms, the waters would leave tide marks of waste and filth on the riverbanks. This was despite regular, continuing water-quality monitoring systems already having been established in 1963 and, from 1972, also despite the setting up of a variety of committees to investigate the problems. But Heseltine's comments provoked real action, from regional and national government, and from all the local authorities in and around the Mersey Basin. Also, in the 1990s, United Utilities began the construction of the Interceptor Sewer along both banks of the Mersey, to clean it up. (See Chapter: 'The Liverpool Waterfront'.) Legislation was introduced to make it possible to reconstruct and repair our river, and to prosecute polluters. Business, industry, and the public, began to be re-educated about our environment, and the healing of one of the world's greatest rivers slowly, but inexorably, began to take place.

One of the most recent developments to affect the river and its waterfront, on both sides of the Mersey, was the setting up of the Mersey Waterfront Regional Park in 2003. This was the first agency specifically dedicated to the particular investments of time, money, imagination, expertise. and sustainability into the riverfront of the Mersey. and into its life and its communities – plant, animal. and human. However, another agency has been in existence for around 20 years, often working against great odds to sustain the environmental regeneration of the entire Mersey Basin, and this is The Mersey Basin Campaign. But what of Pickering's Pasture?

In 1982, Halton Borough Council and Cheshire County Council determined to wipe clean the land here, and to restore it to as natural a state as possible. Their plan was to create a publicly accessible, but carefully managed and maintained nature reserve, giving people from South Liverpool, Hale, and Halton, an opportunity to rediscover the natural beauty of their landscape and the wildlife that inhabits it – given the opportunity to do so!

The wildflower meadows that we now see here, and the animals and insects that have returned to re-establish themselves, provide a rich diversity of life and environment for us to stroll through, picnic on, or relax and ponder in. The site was opened to the public in 1986, and it officially became a Local Nature Reserve in 1991. Pickering's Pasture then achieved Green Flag status in 1999.

Depending on how much time you have, why not take a short stroll along the Coastal Path, either east towards Widnes, or west towards Hale? Also, and depending on the season in which you visit, look out for Ox Eye Daisies, Bellflower, Orchids, and Cornflower: Chase the dragon flies with their scintillating colours and tantalising zig-zag flight paths: Watch the Golden Plover, the Waders, the Mallards, and the Teal as they swim or dive on the waters: And keep your eyes open for the falcons hovering overhead, as they wait for just the right moment to swoop on their prey.

George Stephenson's railway bridge and The Silver Jubilee road bridge over the Mersey, as seen from Pickering's Pasture

To Find Out More:
Pickering's Pasture
Phone: 0151 425 4706

Mersey Waterfront Regional Park
http://www.merseywaterfront.com/

The Mersey Basin Campaign
http://www.merseybasin.org.uk/

From Pickering's Pasture it is possible to take part in organised walks to visit the remarkable ancient site that is the Hale Duck Decoy. However, this is only possible at certain times of the year, so you will need to check beforehand and pre-book. Information on how to arrange visits is given at the end of the following article.

PLEASE NOTE: Do not attempt to make your own way to the Duck Decoy: The ground is treacherous because the Decoy sits in the middle of the marshes. Also, when you get to the site it is surrounded by a moat, which is only accessed by a swinging footbridge that has to be unlocked by a Ranger. These security arrangements are essential to preserve and protect what is now a sensitive and ancient wildlife habitat.

Next, I will tell you something of the purpose and history of this unusual feature, which sits in the marsh just outside the Township of Hale.

The Hale Duck Decoy

One of the ancient pipes in the Hale Duck Decoy

The story of the 'Childe' is not the only magnificent curiosity to be found at Hale, there is also the Duck Decoy, which in fact, is an important Scheduled Ancient Monument.

Lowland coastal areas of England, such as Hale and its environs, were not only suitable for pasture in Medieval and later times, but the seasonal flooding that takes place in them created marshes and pools that attracted wildfowl to the area. For centuries, these birds provided an additional source of food that was important to the local community; and such was the case at Hale. Throughout England during the 16th and 17th centuries, and possibly inspired by the Dutch, an ingenious method of trapping ducks for food and feathers began to become established, and the Hale Duck Decoy is one of the finest surviving examples of such a system.

There were 215 duck decoys recorded in 1868, mostly on the east coast of England, but only 44 of these were working at that time. Now, only five such decoys survive – all in nature reserves. However, there were only ever three in the North West, of which Hale is the only survivor.

Built in either 1613 or 1631 (historians are unclear), and standing on Decoy Marsh adjacent to Halegate Farm, the Hale Duck Decoy is a specially constructed, irregular, pentagonal pond, surrounded by a wooded copse and a moat that is 16 feet wide. This is crossed by a swing bridge.

The Decoy was designed to resemble other, natural coverts that were dotted around the surrounding landscape, and which attracted hundreds of waterfowl that annually came to the Hale Marshes, to nest and breed. The ducks were attracted to the Decoy because it was secluded and sheltered, and they found the artificially created environment ideal for nesting; believing it to be no different from other nesting sites.

The layout of the Duck Decoy is particularly clever, and it comprises five channels that radiate out from the central pond; each one is brick-lined; is caged over with hoops and a net, known as a 'pipe'; and which curves and tapers from a wide opening facing onto the pond, into a narrow point in the bank. The mouth of the pipe is a semicircle of about 10 to 15 feet in circumference; so large that it remains unnoticeable from a duck's point of view. This means that they swim from the pond into the channels, unaware that they are entering the fat end of a watery wedge. Each pipe is 150 feet long and bends out of sight into the woodland, so that the birds do not realise that these lead nowhere, except into suddenly narrowing points with trap-nets at the end.

Between each pipe are small areas of additional woodland and, when the Decoy was working, the channels were fenced on both sides, in a zigzag pattern, by slatted screens or closely woven osier fences, 11 feet high. These had small holes cut in them, at intervals, so that a duck hunter could stand concealed behind them, at the broad end of the trap, and upwind from the nesting birds. Ducks always fly into the wind when taking off so, having five pipes positioned around the pond gave flexibility to the hunter to set his trap, always against the wind.

The birds would unwittingly swim into the mouths of the pipes, as the hunter watched and waited behind the wooden boards, with his special breed of dog. These dynamic little canines were trained to run between the zigzag boards, to draw in the ducks deeper into the trap, and the birds were usually further encouraged to continue down the pipe by the hunter's assistants beating on the fences. The ducks would fly deep into the pipe until they reached the

The Hale Duck Decoy

hunter's nets at the end, where they would be easily bagged. Interestingly, it seems that far from flying away from the dogs, the ducks would fly or swim towards them because they regarded the barking creatures as small predators, and so they wanted to drive them away from their nests in the pond. The dogs used by the hunters were a specific breed, known as 'Duck Toller', and these were chosen particularly for their colour, which resembled that of a fox, and so this would appropriately panic the ducks. Consequently, the dogs acted as lures as opposed to terriers, and between 750 and 1500 ducks were caught each season, making the Hale Duck Decoy a very effective and sophisticated hunting system.

Today the Decoy is still a haven for ducks and, in the autumn, it can attract an average of 800 Teal and 400 Mallard. In the spring, around 100 Sheldrake can be found at any given time in the Decoy. When the Decoy was in use however, a Teal was only classed as $^1/_2$ the value of a Mallard, so the hunter had to double his 'bag' to get paid an appropriate amount. There are also lots of fish in the pond, mostly roach, which are managed but not fished; so adding to the life of the Duck Decoy.

Although one or two of the pipes, channels, and nets have also been restored, the birds are perfectly safe, as never again will the Decoy be used for its original purpose! The surrounding moat has also been cleaned up and de-silted, and its banks renewed and strengthened. Also, the original hunters' cottage, which had the date '1633' over the door, has been re-built, and its fireplace, benches, and storage cupboards have been recreated. Money is also being used to build effective defences against encroachment by an often wild River Mersey.

The Hale Decoy is now open to the public.

However, the site is so environmentally sensitive that this can only be accessed on ranger-guided walks and tours, which set off from Pickering's Pasture. These only take place at certain times of year, to limit the impact that visitors have on the Decoy: although additional special visits can be arranged for specific research purposes, or for special-interest groups and for educational tours. Even so, all such visiting groups are limited to about 20 people at a time.

It is very important to point out that the area surrounding the Decoy – Hale Marsh – is treacherous. As mentioned previously, do not attempt to access the Decoy unguided or without permission: You would not be able to cross the moat anyway, as the swing bridge is locked up on the landward side of the Decoy. You can contact the Ranger Station at Pickering's Pasture Nature Reserve to find out when public guided tours are taking place.

To Find Out More:
Hale Duck Decoy
Tours Info: 0151 425 4706
E-mail: Rob.Smith@halton.gov.uk
http://www.halton.gov.uk/nature/content/localnature
reserves/haleduckdecoy/?a=5441

From Pickering's Pasture, retrace your route back along Mersey View Road, turning left at the crossroads into Hale Gate Road, and return to Hale Village. At the War Memorial, follow the road as it takes you around to the right and out of the Village towards Liverpool, along Hale Road.

After about half a mile, and just beyond the large, thatched houses that you will pass on the left, you will come to a left fork, take this into Bailey's Lane. The road now takes you beneath the flightpath approach to Liverpool John Lennon Airport, and it ends at a T-Junction with Dungeon Lane. Park anywhere you can here, where it is safe to do so.

Dungeon and Oglet

At this point in this Chapter, where Bailey's Lane meets Dungeon Lane, it is worth mentioning that a major industry once flourished on the banks of the Mersey, here at Hale. Indeed, Dungeon Lane used to continue from the end of Bailey's Lane to the river, and on to the hamlets of Dungeon and Oglet.

However, the name 'Dungeon' has nothing to do with prisons or incarceration of any form! In fact, it is probably derived from the Anglo-Saxon words 'dunge' or 'denge', meaning 'marshland' or 'land that adjoins marsh'. Where there are now only an isolated farm house, some outbuildings, and an area of heathland and coastline, was once an important local centre of the salt-refining and shipping industries.

The salt-refining trade really developed following the discovery of rock salt in Cheshire in the 17th century, and it was to Dungeon that flatboats and barges brought rock salt to be refined, and then shipped onwards.

By the late 1840s, and for reasons that are unclear, the salt works closed at Dungeon, and the quays were then used by a firm of ship-breakers. However, as the river channels began to silt up, the shipyard closed in 1912. All industry then ceased at Dungeon, and it reverted once more to being an isolated backwater, with only a few cottages and a post-industrial riverfront. Nothing now remains at Dungeon, except for part of the sandstone

quay and some rubble and broken rocks, left behind from the foundations of the salt refinery that once dominated this now almost desolate stretch of the Mersey foreshore.

From Dungeon, and just a little way further along the shore towards Liverpool, is Oglet. Before the developments at Speke Airport that transformed it into Liverpool John Lennon Airport, a long, narrow lane led to what was once a small, isolated hamlet of fishermen's cottages, and to sandy Oglet Bay. This had always been a pretty and secluded piece of coastline, where local folk fished the river for shrimps. Indeed, before World War Two, women from Oglet would carry their freshly caught wares to sell at the local markets at Speke and Garston.

Also, people from these local districts, and further afield, would come to picnic, play, and swim in this bay off the River Mersey.

I have happy memories of coming here with my parents, as a child in the late 1950s, to do just that; skipping around the concrete pyramids on the beach, which had been laid as tank-traps during the War, to deter invading Nazi hordes from landing at Oglet!

I also have even happier memories of times spent on the sands of Oglet Shore, as an older teenager in the 1960s, necking and suchlike with my intimate companions: Either in splendid isolation, or perhaps sometimes with my mates and their girlfriends, who were similarly engaged in physical friendship!

"I do have joyful recollections of frolicsome, night-time, skinny-dipping parties on Oglet Shore – Ah, the heady days of free love and youthful abandon!"

Actually, this was quite a daring thing to do; not because of any fear of getting caught prancing about naked, but because we were swimming in the river before it was cleaned up, and before the days of the Interceptor Sewer. (See Chapter: 'The Liverpool Waterfront'.) Actually, upon reflection, it is a surprise that my friends and I didn't end up with dysentery!

We do not visit Dungeon or Oglet on this Tour, simply because they are very difficult to get to and, with the extending of the Airport's runway, there is little left to see.

From the end of Bailey's Lane turn right into Dungeon Lane. Continue up to the T-Junction at Hale Road and turn left here. You will drive past the perimeter fence for the car parks and terminal at Liverpool John Lennon Airport, on the left.

Youngsters have fun at Oglet during the early 60s

Ancient and Modern

Modern Speke

As we leave Hale and pass the outskirts of Liverpool John Lennon Airport, we are forcefully reminded how the ancient and modern in Liverpool sit closely side-by-side.

The differences between the two communities are dramatic, and it is clear that we have left the rural surroundings of Hale behind as, on the left side of the road we see industry and commerce in all its glory. On the right side of the road, we see the densely packed houses and streets, and urban challenges, of the Speke Housing Estate.

Before I talk about the Airport, I will now set the scene for the next stage of our exploration, by explaining a little about how and why modern Speke came into existence.

In the early decades of the 20th century, and to help cope with the housing shortage for the rapidly expanding population of the City, Liverpool Corporation needed to build a new housing estate to re-house workers from other parts of Liverpool, and to serve a developing industrial estate at Speke.

A purpose-built community was planned and, in 1929, Liverpool Corporation bought parts of the Speke estate and other parcels of privately-owned land, and construction work began in 1937.

The new houses were filled with families from all over Liverpool, but particularly from the inner-City areas, where some slum-clearance work had begun. During the 1930s, businesses were encouraged to set up at Speke, on newly created industrial estates, to provide employment for the new population. Many companies did so, including the Distillers Company; Evans Medical; Whitley, Lang & Neil Engineers; Dunlop's; Standard-Triumph car manufacturers; Brough's Oil Drums; the Metal Box Company – where I served my own apprenticeship as an engineer; and later, in the 1960s, other companies such as the Ford Motor Company. On paper this all seemed bold, visionary, and well-planned. Indeed, it was hailed as a 'model town for the rest of the country'. But then, things began to go wrong.

First came the Second World War and, after this, the Speke Housing Estate was rapidly extended to accommodate hundreds families who had been bombed out of their homes by the Nazis, plus more people from slum clearance areas. Even though, in most cases, these new homes were much better than the ones that these new residents of Speke had left behind, the communities and neighbourhoods to which these people had originally belonged had been split up and scattered around the City. This caused the break-up of some families and much social disorientation.

Also, concept and design flaws began to reveal themselves in the new suburb that

Ancient and modern Speke

the planners had created. They had failed to provide sufficient or adequate social and community facilities and services, to meet the needs of such a large and growing population.

> "Bus services were limited and, as few people owned or could afford cars in the district, Speke became isolated from the rest of the conurbation"

This was also because it sits like an island, between the river; the airport and the industrial estates; the fields and marshes; and a four-lane, high-speed trunk road, with only one crossing point.

Added to this was the fact that the success of the housing estate was tied to the success of the industrial estate and, during the 1950s and 1960s, as businesses failed in the post-War slump, strikes and industrial action further damaged the floundering local economy. Many companies simply closed down or moved away, and unemployment rose rapidly. As it did so, all the social problems that naturally accompany economic failure came to the fore, and the quality of life for the people of Speke began to degenerate. The final major blow to the community was the closure, in the 1970s, of Dunlop's and the Standard Triumph car plant.

Crime rates soared, and Speke - and adjacent Garston - became renowned for pockets of violence, drug-taking, poverty, and squalor. Money was either unavailable or just not being spent on maintaining the infrastructure of the community, so housing stock and civic amenity degenerated, thus adding to the environment of neglect and desperation.

However, despite the poor quality of their surroundings and, to a large extent the hopelessness of their outlook, the people of Speke had a pride in themselves and in

their community, which helped to sustain them through difficult times. There is also a warmth and a generosity in the people of this community, so typical of Liverpudlians, which binds them together and strengthens their bonds of family and friendship.

And then, together with the rest of Merseyside and Liverpool in particular, Speke was destined to receive major injections of funding from the European Union, throughout the latter half of the 1990s and currently. This money, and the agencies established to spend it, which were the Speke-Garston Development Corporation, South Liverpool Housing, and the Liverpool Land Development Company, have fuelled improvements in the housing stock and infrastructure, and the regeneration of Speke and the surrounding areas. This is obvious, as people drive along Speke Boulevard, past the Estuary Commerce Park, the Crowne Plaza Hotel, and the Shopping Park, and on into Liverpool City: or, as they make their way to Liverpool John Lennon Airport.

As you approach the end of Hale Road this becomes Dunlop Road. At the T-Junction, turn left into Speke Hall Avenue and continue up to the roundabout. Take the 1st exit, which will lead you into the Airport Terminal.
Follow the signs for the 'Short Stay Car Park' where you can park free of charge for 10 minutes. This will allow you to have a brief look at the Yellow Submarine.
However, if you wish to have a longer look at the terminal building you will need to pay for a longer stay but, be warned, this could be expensive!

Liverpool John Lennon Airport

What was always locally known as **Speke Airport**, was originally sited in and around the building that is now the Marriott Hotel on Speke Boulevard, but Liverpool's airport and its surrounding support facilities moved to this present location in 1986.

Liverpool's airport had always been under Local Authority control, but Liverpool City Council sold it to Peel Holdings in 1997, who then invested seriously in the facility.

"Over the following four or five years, the terminal buildings and facilities increased in size and improved in quality at a phenomenal rate"

The airport is now a major source of revenue and prestige, not only for Liverpool, but for Merseyside and the North West.

As part of a major re-branding process, and as a tribute to John Lennon (1940-1980), it was re-named 'Liverpool John Lennon Airport' in March 2002, by John's widow Yoko Ono. What was by then a completely new terminal complex was then officially opened, in July 2002 by Her Majesty the Queen, who also unveiled the motto of the Airport, which is taken from the lyrics of John Lennon's song 'Imagine', and quotes: '....above us only sky....'

The modern terminal has recently been increased by three times its previous size, and the speed and extent of expanding business demands mean that Peel Holdings are planning to further increase the facilities at the airport.

The new terminal building cost £32.5 million, and its ultra modern design and services mean that it can now cope with the ever-increasing number of passengers that fly to and from Liverpool each year. During 2002, a record 2.84 million passengers travelled through Liverpool John Lennon Airport, which was an increase of 26% over the previous year. In 2005, 4.4 million people passed through the terminal, and well over 5 million passengers flew in or out of Liverpool by the beginning of 2007. This is an overall growth of 547% since 1997, making Liverpool John Lennon Airport the fastest growing airport in Europe.

Although Liverpool John Lennon Airport is not a tourist site as such – unless you are passing through on your holidays – tours of the terminal are available, but only for organised groups. These consist of a 40-minute presentation on the 'Past, Present, and Future' of the airport, followed by a guided visit to all the airport facilities on the landward side. For obvious security reasons tours do not go airside.

If however, you simply wish to drive in and have a quick look at the terminal building, and perhaps at the John Lennon memorial statue inside, then park in the short-stay car park, where the first 10 minutes are free. From here you can also see the Yellow Submarine. This large re-creation of the vessel, which appeared in the Beatles cartoon of the same name, was built by apprentices of the former Cammell Laird shipyards in Birkenhead, for the International Garden Festival that was held in Liverpool in May 1984. It is worth a look.

Yoko Ono meets Queen Elizabeth II at the opening of John Lennon Airport

The Yellow Submarine in front of the terminal building

To Find Out More:
Liverpool John Lennon Airport
Phone: 0870 129 8484
www.liverpooljohnlennonairport.com
Airport Tours Information
Phone: 0151 907 1640
Peel Holdings
Phone: 0161 629 8200
www.peeladmin.co.uk/peelholdings
Speke Airport in the past www.bwpics.co.uk/gallery/airport

From Liverpool John Lennon Airport, return via the airport roundabout to Speke Hall Avenue. Follow this past the Industrial Estate on the left and, as the road bends to the left, you will catch a glimpse of the spire of Speke Parish Church on the right – consecrated in 1876 – and of the nearby old Schoolhouse. Apart from a small terrace of cottages, these buildings are all that remains of the lost village of Speke.
Follow the dual carriageway up to the main roundabout, and take the first exit. This takes you past the entrance to Speke Hall Industrial Estate and to the driveway to Speke Hall. You get a wonderful view of this remarkable mansion house from the head of the drive. Continue all the way along the drive to the car park. This is a National Trust Property, so members of the Trust can gain free admission to the House and Grounds.

Ancient and Modern

In the 14th century, the Norris family acquired the Manor of Speke. They were an important local family of Saxon origins, who may well have been established in the Speke area since well before the time of the Norman Conquest. However, local records only show them residing in Speke from around 1314.

It was Sir William Norris who, in 1467, began the Tudor rebuilding of Speke Hall, on the site of a much older mansion. He had made his fortune as a soldier, who had won much prize money and taken much loot during his battles. He demolished much of the original sandstone manor house that had certainly stood there since 1314, but left some of the original foundations below where the Great Hall now stands, to support his much grander family seat. Also, the sandstone mullioned window in the kitchen is a remnant of the older house.

Speke Hall is timber-framed, and was constructed in four separate parts, at different times. The rear of the present building, incorporating the Great Hall, was the first part to be erected. The two wings on either side of the central, cobbled courtyard were next, and finally, the front was added.

In the courtyard are two ancient yew trees, which have been named Adam and Eve. These are believed to have been planted by Sir William Norris, which would make them at least 500 years old. The house is surrounded on three sides by a moat, which is now dry, and the front entrance is approached across an attractive and ornate stone bridge. Above the entrance to the house is an inscription in the lintel, which reads: 'This worke 25 yds long was wholly built by Edw: N: Esq: ano 1589'. This refers only to the front and final block of the building.

When Sir William died in 1506, he was succeeded by Henry Norris, and then by Henry's son, another William, who died in 1568. The next in line was Edward Norris, and it was he and his father who added to and altered the Hall, which was complete by the time that Edward Norris himself died, in 1606: And the work that these successive Norrises carried out on their home was of the highest quality, employing the best craftsmen of the day. The Hall has many fine rooms and hallways, with finely carved panelling, and much of the original furniture and fittings survive.

Like many old Lancashire families, the Norrises were staunch Roman Catholics until, in 1651, Thomas Norris became the first head of the family to convert to Protestantism; albeit reluctantly. There are many secret passages and priest holes throughout the building, created to hide visiting priests who had come to celebrate Mass with the family. These were later also used during the Civil War, to keep Royalist sympathisers out of the clutches of searching Parliamentarian soldiers.

As you tour the house, ask a guide to point out the spy-hole to you, in one of the bedroom walls. This gives an unobtrusive view of the long drive up to the Hall from the north lodge, so that any approaching troops could be seen, and advance warning given to the household.

Things got worse for the Norrises at the end of the Civil War, because their estates were finally confiscated by Parliament. These were not regained until 1662, after the Restoration of King Charles II, but by then the steady financial and social decline of this once extremely wealthy and powerful family had begun. However, they remained influential in Liverpool politics for some years.

By the early 1700s, the Norris family could no longer afford the upkeep of the large Speke Estates, which by this time amounted to around 2,400 acres of land, and the family left the house and moved to live in London. In 1731, the line of direct Norris descendants ended with the death of Richard Norris, who had been both an MP for Liverpool and Mayor of the Town. Charles Beauclerk then inherited the house, which was almost derelict in parts, and he repaired and restored much of it. However, in 1795 he sold the Hall and estate to Richard Watt. Richard's descendant,

Speke Hall and its beautiful grounds with Adam and Eve, the ancient yews, in the cour

Adelaide Watt, was Speke Hall's last private resident owner, but she never married, and died in 1921, aged 64. She left the hall and the surrounding estate lands and properties to trustees who were, in fact, descendants of branches of the original Norris family, but they never lived at Speke Hall, and the house remained unoccupied for a number of years.

During this period of trusteeship, the entire estate was sold to the Corporation of Liverpool, and it was from this point that the nature of the district began to change forever.

"The once large estate was carved up; some of it becoming the new housing estates, some the industrial estates, and some the City's greatest local achievement – Speke Airport"

This means that the large Jacobean mansion now stands in grounds which, although still extensive, are only a fraction of the size of the original Speke Manor lands. In the meantime, the Corporation did some basic maintenance work on the Hall, and kept it weatherproof, but they did no restoration work on the ancient and vulnerable building.

However, in 1942, and because of a specific clause in Adelaide Watt's will, Speke Hall passed to the ownership of The National Trust, from whom the City Council leased it for 99 years. It was then that the Hall was partially renovated and restored, and was first opened to the public. Between 1976, and for ten years, the lease passed to Merseyside County Council who embarked on a massive restoration of the Hall and Gardens, including a major repair of the entire roof. However, with the dissolution of the County Council in 1986, the National Trust took over the management of the property again, with funding support from the National Museums Liverpool.

Legends tell that the ghosts of a woman and her baby haunt Speke Hall: She was supposedly the wife of an early Norris who, when she found that her husband had lost the family fortune, threw her baby through the window into the moat, and then hanged herself in the Great Hall. Her dejected moans and the tragic crying of the infant are said to be heard throughout the corridors, and the bedroom has a distinct cold spot.

In recent years, a massive injection of funds into the estate has seen the creation of extensive new family-friendly visitor facilities, without diminishing the character of the Hall and estate. The house and grounds, of what is now recognised as being one of the best preserved half-timbered houses in Britain, are open to the public throughout the year. The gardens are lovely, and the mansion is a fascinating glimpse into many periods of English history. There is a restaurant and a gift shop, play areas, and tranquil walks through the woods and grounds. One of these takes you along the top of the semi-circular, protective barrier-mound that separates the estate from the airport runway and the river. Strolling along here affords wonderful views across the Mersey Basin and of the surrounding area. You can also see the aircraft as they taxi behind the Hall, on the massive runway running parallel to the Mersey. I certainly recommend a visit to Speke Hall, but allow at least a couple of hours to do justice to this one, surviving, ancient piece of Speke, surrounded as it is by everything that is modern.

To Find Out More:
National Trust – Speke Hall
Phone: 0151 427 7231/ 08457 585702 (Info line)/
0151 728 5847 (Learning)
E-Mail: spekehall@nationaltrust.org.uk
www.nationaltrust.org.uk/main/w-vh/w-visits/
w-findaplace/w-spekehall

From Speke Hall, drive back up to the roundabout at Speke Hall Avenue.

If the gates are open, you can now take the first exit into Estuary Commerce Park, and follow this road all the way to the roundabout in the centre of the estate. Turn right here, to leave the Park through another set of gates. Turn left out of the Park, at the roundabout, onto Speke Road.

NB. If the gates are closed to the Commerce Park, continue along Speke Hall Avenue up to the traffic lights. Turn left here into Speke Road, and continue across the roundabout at the other gates to the Commerce Park.

At the next set of traffic lights you will have a choice; either to turn right and park in the New Mersey Shopping Park; or to turn left and park in front of the Crowne Plaza Hotel: This occupies what was once the old Speke Airport terminal building.

The Shopping Park is free, whereas the hotel car park is accessed through a barrier. However, an exit code is available from reception, and parking is free if you eat or drink at the hotel.

Alternatively, you can park in the free car park of Damon's, an American-themed diner on the same site as the hotel. You can either find somewhere for a meal or a snack in the Shopping Park, and then walk to visit the hotel: Or you can eat at the Art Deco Hotel, or at Damon's, and then explore the shops across the road.

Speke Boulevard is the main arterial road into the City from the M56 Motorway, and from Widnes and Runcorn.

This was once a truly depressing thoroughfare, but no longer: landscaping and the planting of a large numbers of trees and shrubs, which are overlooked by the new industrial and commercial developments, give a feeling of success and optimism as one drives past. Indeed, on the corner of Speke Hall Avenue and Speke Road, outside the Bank of Scotland's modern building in the Business Park, is a tall and striking sculpture entitled, **'Coming Together'**. Constructed in polished aluminium, this 60ft high work shows three streamlined figures in a triangular formation, reaching into the centre to touch each other. Artist Stephen Broadbent deliberately created an aeronautical feel to the work, in recognition of Speke's relationship with aircraft. He also designed it to show the coming together, not only of the Bank's enterprises, but of the Speke and Garston communities.

Another fine example of modern public art is on Speke Boulevard, near the Jaguar factory. Here, one drivers past the vanes of an equally powerful piece of colossal artwork called **'The Mersey Wave'**. Comprising two sets of five, erect, wave-shaped fins, standing on either side of the dual carriageway and fanning out like pointed fingers, this dominating sculpture was erected in 2003, and it presents a dramatic gateway to the southern entrance to the City. Costing £700,000, the work is built in aluminium, with each 'hand' measuring 236ft long, and each fin reaching to a height of 98ft above ground. The Wave towers over the dual carriageway, and the fins, which are illuminated at night by internal lighting, make a spectacular sight.

We saw earlier how 20th century Speke began, and then how it developed, then declined, and how it has now re-asserted itself.

Since 1996, Speke has benefited from a major public sector-led regeneration programme to revitalise the economy of the area.

Considerable professional, technical and financial investment was made in the urban and industrial infrastructure of the Speke and Garston area, throughout the later years of the 1990s and into the beginning of the 21st century. The award-winning Speke Garston Development Company was responsible for leading the physical and economic regeneration of the area, which resulted in new inward investment from companies such as Marriott Hotels, Halifax Bank of Scotland, and Vertex.

Estuary Commerce Park

However, the transition from ruin into regeneration came when the Ford Motor Factory, at the Halewood site on Speke Boulevard, became Jaguar Cars. The factory where the Ford Anglia, Corsair, Cortina, Zodiac, Zephyr, and Escort cars were built, had a troubled industrial-relations history throughout the 1960s and 1970s, and at times the parent company nearly closed the site down.

However, it survived and, by 1993, in a joint venture, Jaguar body panels were being produced at Speke. The last Ford car left the Halewood factory in 2000, and the site then officially became Jaguar Cars. This was a real sign of the rebirth of the industrial and commercial life of Speke.

Estuary Commerce Park

The whole Speke/Garston/Halewood area is now one of the key economic growth areas of Liverpool, and this is best exemplified by the new industrial estates and retail parks.

One of these is the Estuary Commerce Park, which was originally managed by the Liverpool Land Development Company.

Redeveloped from large areas of disused airport runway and maintenance sites, and from arid brownfield ex-industrial areas, the site has now been extended to create the International Business Park. Both land areas have been beautifully redesigned and landscaped, and the park are home to The National Blood Service, the National Bio-Manufacturing Centre, DHL, The Riverside Group, Classic Couverture, and other major companies.

It is worth driving through the Parks to look at the state-of-the-art business premisess and to watch the herons and other waterfowl that frequent the reed beds and waterways that criss-cross the estate.

New Mersey Shopping Park

A little further along Speke Road, past the second gates to the Estuary Park, we come to the Crowne Plaza Hotel. Directly opposite this is the New Mersey Shopping Park.

This site of once largely run-down furniture and carpet retail outlets was sold, in 1997, to a development company called British Land, for £4m.

Subsequent to their own investment of £40m in the site, this company then sold the site on, in 2001, for £60m. Sold again, in 2003, this time for £160m, this out-of-town shopping centre (after further investment by the current owners and a complete redevelopment of the site) is now considered to be one of the fastest growing, most financially successful retail parks in Britain.

There are some places to eat here, of the fast-food variety, and the range of shops is considerable, making this always a busy and popular shopping venue. That people are returning to Speke to spend their money is a remarkable turn of events, as is the large number of local jobs that have been generated on this site, and on the new commercial and industrial parks.

To Find Out More:
Speke-Garston Partnership
www.sgp.org.uk/sgp.htm
Liverpool Land Development Company
Phone: 0151 494 2555
www.liverpooldev.co.uk/speke
_halewood/introduction.asp?open=6
New Mersey Retail Park
www.britishland.com/newmersey.htm
South Liverpool Housing
www.slhgroup.co.uk

Speke Airport was officially opened in 1933, and the first flight from a regional airport to Europe took place from here in 1934. In 1950, the first scheduled passenger helicopter service in Britain also began from Speke, with flights to Cardiff.

Then, in 1952, Britain's first package air holidays left from Liverpool, so this is indeed a significant airport. In fact, Speke Airport was established 3 years before Gatwick and 13 years before Heathrow airports!

The idea of an airport for Liverpool was first proposed in 1927, by 'The Liverpool Organisation', which was one of the earliest examples in the City of a public-private partnership. They first considered Hooton near Ellesmere Port on the Wirral, which was already the home of the Liverpool and District Aero Club, but they chose Speke. This was because it was located outside the City-centre but not too far away to be difficult to get to, and the proposed airport site was in an area of prime development land, for which the Council, as we have seen, had great plans. Also, there was a clear approach to the airport for aircraft descending down the line of the River Mersey and over the Mersey Basin, and Speke was known to be generally clear of fog, so this seemed to be a safe location for the new airport.

The Corporation had already acquired the Speke Manor Estate, as well as some other privately owned farms in the area and so, by 1930, they began work on the runway and the terminal buildings. When the airport was opened by the Marquis of Londonderry, who was Secretary of State for Air at the time, the terminal complex was considered to be a triumph of contemporary architecture.

After the terminal building, the hangars were constructed, with the one on the left of the complex being the first. This was in fact, designed and built by Fokker, the German engineering firm. They went on of course, to design the German fighter planes bearing their name, and which were used during World War Two against Britain and her Allies. The hangar was completed just before the outbreak of the War and, when Fokker submitted their bill, the City refused to pay it!

Even though the City suffered dreadful bombing during World War Two, especially during the May Blitz of 1941, the airport – which was a major target – stayed open and fully functional throughout the conflict. On what was to become the Post-War Dunlop factory, adjacent to the airfield, warplanes were built and then simply wheeled out onto the runway ready for action. From Speke, not only British pilots, but Polish, Czech, and American airmen flew from Liverpool, to take on the Nazis.

After the War, businesses were drawn to the airport and it was quite busy. However, as the rest of Liverpool, especially the docks, declined throughout the 1950s and 1960s, so did Speke Airport. Nevertheless, I can recall, as a child in the late 50s, taking buses out to Speke to watch the aircraft taking off and landing. In later years, as a young man, I would dine out with friends in the lavish airport restaurant and bar, below the control tower in the main building. When, in 1986, the new Liverpool Airport terminal was opened to meet the needs for a much more modern facility,

the original terminal buildings and hangars were closed down, and they fell into neglect and decay. Fortunately, as part of the regeneration of Speke and Garston, the complex became a flagship redevelopment site for the area. The old aircraft hangars have now been redeveloped; one as the headquarters of the Littlewoods organisation, and the other as a state-of-the-art David Lloyd Sports and Leisure Centre. The original terminal building has also been refurbished, and is now a luxury hotel, originally a Marriott, this is now part of the Crowne Plaza Group.

The City's original airport buildings once famously thronged with fans of The Beatles, in the 1960s, welcoming home the Fab Four from their spectacular tour of America. Now, the hotel chain has set up home in Liverpool, at what is one of the finest and most exciting buildings in the North West. All the classic, thirties, Art-Deco architectural style and features of the original airport terminal have been incorporated into the now Grade II Listed Building, paying homage to the significance of what was the first provincial airport outside London.

I recommend the food and wine at the hotel, either in the more formal Starways Restaurant, or in the Club Central lounge and bar. Also, Damon's American style diner on the same site as the Crowne Plaza offers something for all the family.

The old Speke Airport, pictured in 1968

To Find Out More:
Crowne Plaza Hotel Liverpool Airport, Speke
Phone: 0151 494 5000
www.ichotelsgroup.com

Damon's American Restaurant
Phone: 0151 4943322
www.damons.co.uk/restaurant/index.htm

History of Speke Airport
www.south-lancs-aviation.co.uk/history_of_speke_airport

Ancient and Modern: Conclusion

The Crowne Plaza Hotel at Speke is, it seems to me, an ideal place to end this Chapter, as this building represents the (not so) ancient providing a home for the modern.

Also, the close proximity of the modern Commerce and Shopping Parks, and the Airport, to the ancient Speke Hall, shows how such places can sit side-by-side, and how we can preserve the best of the old whilst embracing the new.

The phrase 'those who fail to learn from the past are condemned to repeat it', is an apt one, but so is 'those who fail to preserve and value the past, condemn themselves to an empty present and a hollow future'. And, as we now come to the end of this book, I do hope that you have truly discovered Liverpool;
the glories of its past; the wonders and pleasures of its present;
and the optimism and bold vision of its future.

Author's Note and Acknowledgements

All opinions expressed in 'Discover Liverpool' are those of the author alone, and not of any other individual or organisation. Extensive research, using a wide range of sources, plus regular and repeated drives and walks around the City and its suburbs, have gone into the production of this book and the Tours. Whilst every effort has been made to ensure the accuracy of dates and the historical data, I apologise for any errors.

My sincere thanks are extended to the many people of Liverpool and Merseyside, professionals and otherwise, whose recollections, anecdotes, and knowledge – so willingly given – have provided much information and many stories for inclusion in my book. And, for their specific contributions, I would like to express my particular gratitude to:

The Rt. Hon. The Earl of Derby DL

His Grace the Rt. Reverend James Jones,
the Bishop of Liverpool

Rt Rev Tom Williams,
Auxiliary Bishop of Liverpool,
Liverpool Roman Catholic Archdiocese

Sir Alan Waterworth KCVO JP,
former Lord-Lieutenant of Merseyside

Mr John Hinchliffe,
World Heritage Officer, Liverpool City Council

Canon Nicholas Frayling,
former Rector of Liverpool

Paul Oldfield,
Nature Conservation Officer, Halton Borough Council

Dr Cecil Moss,
Princes Road Synagogue

Graham Boxer,
former Director, St. George's Hall

Amy de Joia,
Director of Development & Communications, NML

Lynn Saunders,
Head of Inward Investment, North West Vision

Colin McKeown,
Producer, Liverpool Academy Productions Ltd

Sean Marley, Managing Director, Lime Pictures

Neil Pakey, Chief Executive, Peel Airports

Roger Phillips, Broadcaster, BBC Radio Merseyside

Jim Gill, Chief Executive, Liverpool Vision

Bernard Cliffe,
Information Officer, The Ancient Chapel of Toxteth

Alec Ellis,
Parish Historian, All Hallows Church, Allerton

Vincent O'Brien,
Public Relations Assistant, Liverpool Football Club

Michael Kelly
Author and Historian

Tom Clay,
Director of Arena Regeneration,
Arena Housing Association

Brother Ken Vance SJ,
Honorary Chaplain & Parish Administrator,
St Francis Xavier's Church

Dave Bridson,
Centre Manager,
The Williamson Tunnels Heritage Centre

Nigel Sharp,
Parks and Open Spaces Development Officer,
Liverpool City Council

Rosemary Kay,
Former Operations Director, Blackburne House Group

Mark Featherstone-Witty,
Founding Principal and Chief Executive,
Liverpool Institute for Performing Arts

Brian Kerr,
Business Development Manager, Mersey Ferries

Commodore John Madgwick RN, OBE,
Former Naval Regional Officer Northern England

Jim Jenkins,
Previously, Mersey Docks and Harbour Company

Tracey McGeagh,
Head of Marketing and Communications,
National Museums Liverpool

Fr Paul Nener,
Vicar, St John the Baptist Church, Tuebrook

Mumin Khan,
Chief Executive, The Abdullah Quilliam Heritage Centre

Guy Butler,
Development Manager, Grosvenor Liverpool

Simon Ryder, Former Chairman, Bluecoat Arts Centre

Thomas and Katy Bushell

Steve Lambert, Former House Manager,
Liverpool Town Hall

David Armstrong, Former Visitor Services Manager,
Speke Hall

and also to the staff of **The Liverpool Record Office at the Liverpool Central Library**, William Brown Street, and the officers and staff of many departments of Liverpool City Council.

I would also like to acknowledge the research facilities provided to me by **The Athenaeum**, Church Alley, Liverpool, and also the support and contributions of **John Tiernan**, Former Chairman of the Athenaeum Library Sub-Committee and of the Liverpool History Society.

About The Author

Until the end of 2009, and for 10 years, Ken Pye was Senior Programme Director with the international, leadership development organisation, Common Purpose. In this position Ken had national responsibilities, but principally constructed and delivered highly-specialised leadership programmes; becoming a recognised and respected leader in his own right. Ken's then accepted a position as the University Director of Professional Education and Enterprise Fellow at Liverpool Hope University; in parallel with his role as Joint Director of the 3-Thinking Programme. Underscoring all of this, Ken also facilitates an independent, non-aligned, informal business network of over 3,500 senior professionals, from all walks of life. This is known as The Intelligence Network, and its associates share the same ethical business standards, and seek to make their own organisations and companies more successful, but to the benefit of society and not at its expense.

Ken is in great demand as a business-development mentor; programme and conference facilitator; and as a respected speaker at events and training courses - delivering on business leadership and development. Indeed, he features in Dan Kenyon's collection of photographic portraits of Liverpool leaders and luminaries; 'Sung and Unsung'.

Ken began his working life in 1967, as a Mechanical Engineering Apprentice for The Metal Box Co. Ltd, in Speke, Liverpool - a job he hated with a passion. Consequently, upon completing his apprenticeship, in 1971, and with a desire for a more fulfilling and productive career, Ken obtained a post as a Residential Assistant-Housefather in a unit for severely emotionally disturbed children, at a large children's village run by a national charity. Following this, he worked as a Residential Housefather in a Reception and Assessment Centre, with children who had come into care largely through the courts.

After 3 years of this work, Ken wanted to work with families and communities under stress, and became a Community Projects Manager for International Voluntary Service in inner-city Liverpool; establishing care projects and support facilities for individuals and families at risk.

In 1976, he was invited to become the Community Development Officer for Toxteth, then known simply as 'Liverpool 8'. In 1982, Ken then joined Barnardos as the Merseyside Area Appeals Organiser, going on a year later to become their Regional Appeals, Education & Projects Officer - a post he held until 1990, when he decided to establish and run his own company:

'Ken Pye Associates' operated successfully throughout the 1990s, providing Organisational Empowerment and Facilitation advice and intervention, by assisting organisations to access and utilise European funding regimes to deliver Objective 1 and Pathways initiatives. Ken only gave this up when, in 1997, he was 'made an offer he could not refuse', to become the National Partnership Director for the Business Environment Association.

In this post, it was his responsibility to generate new partnerships between educational service-delivery organisations, and networks of SME's - tapping into ESF and ERDF funding, to promote economic development and regeneration across the U.K. It was in 1999 that Ken joined Common Purpose.

In addition to his many professional roles, and under his own branding 'Discover-Liverpool', Ken is a frequent contributor to journals, magazines, and newspapers, and is a popular local historian and after-dinner speaker. He is also a regular broadcaster for both radio and television.

Ken is also widely known for his writing on local history. As well as the 'Discover Liverpool' book and series of DVD documentaries, he was also a principal contributor to the book, 'Scousers'. Ken's most recent work is, 'A Brighter Hope' - about the founding and history of Liverpool Hope University, published by Liverpool Hope University Press. He is currently writing two books for The Earl of Derby and another for The History Press.

Amongst his many voluntary community activities, Ken has established a local Scouting network and founded his neighbourhood community association, 'The Avenues Neighbourhood Network' - which he went on to chair for six years. He is also the Chair of the Governors of a Primary School; the Patron of a national charity; a board member and trustee of a number of voluntary and community agencies; a life-member of a number of local history societies and organisations; a Proprietor of the Liverpool Athenaeum; and a Fellow of the Royal Society of Arts.

On a personal basis and if pressed (better still, if taken out for dinner) Ken will regale you with tales about his experiences during the Toxteth Riots; as a Bingo Caller; as the Lead Singer of a Pop Group; and as a Mortuary Attendant. He might also tell you of his early encounters with John Lennon and Billy Fury; and with Sir Alec Guinness and Nicholas Monsarrat – amongst others. He might also tell of his early relationship with Cilla Black.

Ken is married to Jackie, and they live in Sefton Park in Liverpool, with their three children; Ben aged 25, Samantha aged 21, and Danny aged 15.

© Ken Pye 2011 www.discover-liverpool.com

The Special Years: A Liverpool Timeline

432 St Patrick sailed from Liverpool down the River Mersey on his mission to Ireland

1125 First Mersey Ferry established by Benedictine Monks at Birkenhead Priory

1207 On 28th August, King John granted Liverpool its Royal Charter

1296 The Stanley and Molyneux families were granted land by the King, eventually becoming the Earls of Derby and Sefton, respectively

1351 First (recorded) Mayor, William son of Adam was elected

1580 Self-elected Town Council formed

1596 The Earl of Derby partially disafforests Toxteth Park

1647 Liverpool is declared a free port, no longer subject to Chester

1648 First recorded cargo from America landed in the Town

1700 POPULATION: 5,715

1700 First Liverpool slave ship sold 220 slaves in Barbados

1708 First recorded reference to the dish 'Scouse'

1709 First cargo of cotton traded

1715 World's first commercial wet dock (controlled by floodgates) built

1770 Work begins on the Leeds-Liverpool Canal

1776 First use of ether as an anaesthetic occurs in Liverpool

1786 Europe's first purpose-built prison erected in Liverpool

1790 World's first American Consul established

1791 First school for blind people built

1793 Liverpool given the right to print its own money

1800 POPULATION: 77,708

1820 Present Town Hall completed

1825 World's first school for deaf people built

1829 Rainhill Railway Trials won by the 'Rocket'

1830 World's first passenger railway opened, between Liverpool and Manchester

1835 World's first railway timetable published in Liverpool

1840 World's first scheduled transatlantic passenger service begins

Britain's first Borough Engineer appointed

1841 The forerunner of the RSPCA is founded

1842 First ever municipal baths and wash-houses built

1845 Liverpool was the destination of world's first package tour (Thomas Cook Company)

1847 Dr William Henry Duncan appointed as world's first Medical Officer of Health

1848 First British Trades Council established in Liverpool

1851 POPULATION: 376, 065

1857 World's first Rugby Club and Britain's first Chess Club founded

1860 First purpose-built public library

1864 First slum-clearance programme

1867 Britain's first Cycling Club established

1869 Britain's first Council houses built

1877 Britain's first public Art Gallery, the Walker, is opened

1880 Liverpool granted a Royal Charter to become a City

1883 Liverpool SPCC founded (now the NSPCC)

1884 Britain's first female doctor opens a practice in Liverpool

1886 World's first under-river railway tunnel opened

1887 Establishment of Britain's first Mosque

1892 John Brodie invents first football goal-nets

1893 World's first overhead electric railway opened

Royal Charter granted to confer the title of Lord Mayor on the City's Chief Magistrate

1901 POPULATION: 685,000

1909 Eleanor Rathbone becomes the first woman councillor

1912 Britain's first telephone exchange opens

1927 Margaret Beavan elected as Britain's first woman Lord Mayor

1934 First Mersey Road Tunnel opened

1936 First purpose-built municipal industrial estate built at Speke

1937 POPULATION: 867,000

1956 Overhead Railway demolished

1962-1970 The Beatles take the world by storm

1971 POPULATION: 610,000

1972 Merseyside Metropolitan County Council established

1981 Toxteth Riots

1981 POPULATION: 519,000

1984 Liverpool Freeport opened International Garden Festival held

1986 Merseyside Metropolitan County Council abolished

1989 The Hillsborough Disaster

1991 POPULATION: 481,000

1997 Roy Castle Foundation for Lung Cancer Research opens as the only such research centre in the world

2001 Liverpool is named world Capital of Pop with 53 No 1 recordings since 1953

Liverpool FC is the first football club to win the FA Cup, League Cup, and UEFA Cup in one season

2002 Liverpool airport re-named by Yoko Ono as 'Liverpool John Lennon Airport'

Liverpool shortlisted to become the European Capital of Culture in 2008

2003 Liverpool wins the coveted title of European capital of Culture for 2008 and begins working on plans to instigate a major programme of investment, regeneration and celebration, which will culminate in the celebration year.

2004 Liverpool is awarded World Heritage Site status, to join places such as Venice, the Taj Mahal and the Grand Canyon

2007 Liverpool has a year-long 800th Birthday Party

2008 Liverpool begins an ongoing period of celebrations and special events, marking its status as a European Capital of Culture and a 'World Class' City

CURRENT POPULATION: 485,000